Third Edition

THE COLOU
DEMOCRACY
Racism in Canadian Society

W9-BNH-121

Frances Henry

Carol Tator

with

Winston Mattis

and Tim Rees

THOMSON

NELSON

Australia   Canada   Mexico   Singapore   Spain   United Kingdom   United States

THOMSON

NELSON

The Colour of Democracy: Racism in Canadian Society
Third Edition

by Frances Henry and Carol Tator

Associate Vice-President, Editorial Director:
Evelyn Veitch

Publisher, Social Sciences & Humanities:
Joanna Cotton

Acquisitions Editor:
Cara Yarzab

Marketing Manager:
Lenore Taylor

Developmental Editor:
Glen Herbert

Permissions Coordinator:
Nicola Winstanley

Production Editor:
Lara Caplan

Copy Editor and Proofreader:
Rodney Rawlings

Indexer:
Belle Wong

Production Coordinator:
Hedy Sellers

Creative Director:
Angela Cluer

Interior Design:
Sarah Battersby

Cover Design:
Andrew Adams

Cover Image:
Stuart McClymont/
Stone/Getty Images

Compositors:
Pamela Clayton
Carol Magee

Printer:
Transcontinental

Library and Archives Canada Cataloguing in Publication

Henry, Frances, 1931–
The colour of democracy : racism in Canadian society / Frances Henry, Carol Tator.—3rd ed.

Includes index.
Previous eds. written by Frances Henry ... [et al.].
ISBN 0-17-622486-6

1. Racism—Canada—Textbooks.
2. Canada—Race relations—Textbooks.
3. Canada—Social conditions—Textbooks. I. Tator, Carol

FC104.H45 2005   305.8'00971
C2004-906195-X

The memory of a history of division and hate, injustice and suffering, inhumanity of

person against person should inspire us to celebrate our own demonstration of the

capacity of human beings to progress, to go forward, to improve, to do better.

——Nelson Mandela, May 10, 2004, in an
address during a joint sitting of Parliament to
mark 10 years of democracy in South Africa

ABOUT THE AUTHORS

Frances Henry, a professor emerita of social anthropology and pioneering scholar in the field of racism and anti-racist research, was the first academic in Canada to carry out studies on the dynamics of racism. One of her earliest studies on racist attitudes found that 51 percent of Canadians had somewhat or very racist beliefs (Henry, 1978). Her groundbreaking field study of racial discrimination in employment provided dramatic evidence of the extensive barriers that affect Black job seekers (Henry and Ginzberg, 1984). She is also the author of a major ethnographic study (1994) of the Caribbean-Canadian community in Toronto. As a former professor at York University, she taught courses on racism for more than two decades and published many articles and books on the subject.

Carol Tator worked on the front lines of the anti-racism movement in one of the first voluntary race relations organizations in Canada. She has participated in many coalitions formed by people of colour and other equality seekers and has been involved in many organizations working to dismantle racist structures and systems. Ms. Tator has contributed to a number of government inquiries and task forces on racism and has worked in the areas of anti-racist research, policy development, program implementation and evaluation, strategic planning, and training. She is a co-author, with Frances Henry and Winston Mattis, of a text on racism and the arts (1998) and co-author with Frances Henry of a text on racial bias in Canada's print media (2002). Currently, Carol Tator is completing a book with Frances Henry on racial profiling in Canada. She has been a course director in the Department of Anthropology at York University for over a decade.

In this third edition, Winston Mattis and Tim Rees are contributing authors. Winston Mattis has experience in community development, employment equity, organizational change, and public administration. He has a particular understanding of racism as it affects the Black community in Canada and has worked on the frontlines of both the voluntary and the private sector. His particular interest is in policing, justice, and the law. Winston Mattis is a lawyer specializing in employment law.

Tim Rees has worked in the field of racism and anti-racism as a researcher and policy and program manager with the Ontario government, City of Toronto, and the Greater Toronto Authority. He was also the editor of the first journal in Canada focused on racism. He currently works in the United Kingdom as a policy adviser on anti-racism with the Metropolitan Police Authority in London.

The authors have worked extensively with public-sector institutions to address racism in the institutions' policies, programs, and practices. Their work with large and complex organizations has focused on assisting agencies to analyze barriers to access, participation, and equity in the major arenas of Canadian society. They have also done research and provided consultation to municipal, provincial, and federal government agencies, boards of education, colleges and universities, human-service delivery organizations, media corporations, and law enforcement and justice agencies.

References

Henry, F. (1978). *Dynamics of Racism in Toronto*. North York: York University.

———. (1994). *The Caribbean Diaspora in Toronto: Learning to Live with Racism*. Toronto: University of Toronto Press.

Henry, F., and C. Tator. (2002). *Discourses of Domination: Racial Bias in the Canadian-English Language Press*. Toronto: University of Toronto Press.

Henry, F., and E. Ginzberg. (1984). *Who Gets the Work? A Test of Racial Discrimination in Employment*. Toronto: Urban Alliance on Race Relations.

Tator, C., F. Henry, and W. Mattis. (1998). *Challenging Racism in the Arts: Case Studies of Controversy and Conflict*. Toronto: University of Toronto Press.

PREFACE

This book's approach to the subject of racism in Canada attempts to link theory to practice, thought to experience, the personal to the political, the community to the state, and advocacy to social change. Its authors reflect both academic and practical perspectives.

This book presents a multidimensional analysis of racism by discussing, first, how dominant or majority group values, norms, and conflicting ideologies affect the development and maintenance of inequitable social, economic, and cultural systems and structures in Canada. Second, racism is analyzed by looking at how it is manifested in government, education, media, human services, employment, justice, and law enforcement. Third, the concept of democratic racism is applied to explain why racism continues to flourish in the policies and practices of media and cultural organizations, schools and universities, social and health care agencies, police forces, and justice agencies. Fourth, the book examines the ways in which Canadian society has responded to racism. It documents the struggle and the obstacles that face people of colour and Aboriginal people in their quest for racial justice and equity.

Finally, a word about the authors' purpose in writing this book. The objective of writing a book on racism in Canada was to link the growing theoretical and empirical knowledge produced by the academic community with the first-hand experience of those involved in the struggle against racism. The challenge of writing this book was to make it accessible to students of various disciplines who wish to deepen their understanding of racism as both ideology and practice. It was also written to enhance the knowledge and skills of those who work in fields related to the practice of anti-racism. The authors hope that *The Colour of Democracy: Racism in Canadian Society* will challenge racialized beliefs and ideologies, behaviours, and practices and lead to the development, implementation, and institutionalization of new strategies, models, and mechanisms for the development of a more just and equitable society.

ACKNOWLEDGMENTS

This book documents the nature and dynamics of racism as it affects the everyday life of people of colour in Canada and as it is manifested in Canadian culture and institutions. Across Canada, there are individuals who have been steadfast in their efforts to challenge racial prejudice and discrimination in all its insidious forms. They come from various walks of life and include community activists, writers and artists, educators, bureaucrats, advocates and consultants, and academics and practitioners. They are people of colour, Aboriginal people, and "mainstream" Canadians. They are Muslims, Jews, Christians, Hindus, and members of other faiths.

We are deeply indebted to the contribution of our many friends and colleagues who share our vision of making Canada a more just and equitable society for all Canadians. We owe our sincere thanks to all those who shared suggestions for the development of this book.

Statistics Canada information is used with the permission of the Minister of Industry, as the minister responsible for Statistics Canada. Information on the availability of the wide range of data from Statistics Canada can be obtained from Statistics Canada's regional offices, its website at http://www.statscan.ca, and its toll-free access number, 1-800-263-1136.

We wish to thank the following reviewers for their contributions to this text:

Chandra Budhu, George Brown College/St. James

Cecil Foster, University of Guelph

Cynthia Levine-Rasky, Queen's University

David Ryniker, University of British Columbia

Tracy Nielsen, Mount Royal College

BRIEF CONTENTS

CONTENTS

CHAPTER 3 • Racism in Canadian History   67

PART FOUR THE IMPACT OF DEMOCRATIC RACISM ON CANADIAN INSTITUTIONS AND CULTURE 279

INTRODUCTION

I am not a racist.

She/he is not a racist.

This is not a racist institution.

Canada is not a racist society.

In spite of the historical and contemporary evidence of racism as a pervasive and intractable reality in Canada, the above statements have become mantras, which, when repeated, cast an illusory spell that has allowed Canadians to ignore the harsh reality of a society divided by colour and ethnicity. Canada suffers from historical amnesia. Its citizens and institutions function in a state of collective denial. Canadians have obliterated from their collective memory the racist laws, policies, and practices that have shaped their major social, cultural, political, and economic institutions for three hundred years.

Racist beliefs and practices, although widespread and persistent, are frequently invisible to everyone but those who suffer from them. White Canadians tend to dismiss evidence of their racial prejudice and their differential treatment of minorities. Victims' testimonies are unheard and their experiences unacknowledged. Public-sector agencies conduct extensive consultations and then fail to translate their knowledge into substantive initiatives. Government bodies establish task forces and commissions of inquiry on racism to demonstrate their grave concern; their findings and recommendations are ignored. Academics produce empirical studies documenting the ways **people of colour** are denied power, equity, and rights, and the studies are then buried. Politicians and the power elite rationalize the racial barriers that prevent people of colour from fully participating in the political process, education, employment, media, justice, human services, and the arts.

In recent years, racism has received increased attention. Racial unrest in Vancouver, Toronto, Montreal, and Halifax, and the demands of **racial-minority** communities for greater participation in Canadian society, have become difficult to ignore. As a result, various levels of government and public-sector organizations such as boards of education, police forces, and human-services and cultural organizations have developed policies and programs and modified some of their traditional practices to respond to demands for equity. Money has been allocated, racial-minority communities have been consulted, and people of colour have been hired and appointed to serve in previously all-White organizations and institutions.

However, fundamental racial inequality continues to affect the lives of people of colour and Aboriginal peoples in Canada. Racial prejudice and discrimination exist in the workplace and the classroom. The racist assumptions and practices of the print and electronic media marginalize racial minorities by portraying them as invisible and by depicting them as outsiders. Arts and cultural organizations ignore and exclude the creative images, words, and voices of people of colour. Patterns of policing and the attitudes and behaviour of police officers are marked by prejudice and the differential treatment of people of colour, particularly Blacks and Aboriginal peoples. The school and university are sites of struggle and inequity for ethno-racial minority students and staff. The justice system fails to give fair and equal treatment to Aboriginal peoples and people of colour. Eurocentric barriers impair the delivery of accessible and appropriate services by social and health care agencies. The state, through its legislation and public policies, further reinforces racist ideology and practices.

In each of these sectors, resistance to **anti-racism** policies and programs and the backlash against equity initiatives is found among individuals, organizations, and systems. Widespread opposition to any change in the status quo dramatically reduces the effectiveness of any efforts to promote equity.

At the federal level of government, there is no policy to deal with racism. Some argue that **multiculturalism**, as a public policy enshrined in legislation, provides a framework for legitimizing cultural and racial diversity and for ensuring the rights of all Canadians. Yet, despite the Multiculturalism Act's affirmation of the pluralistic nature of Canadian society, Canadians appear deeply ambivalent about the public recognition of other cultures, the freedom of non-White racial and non-European cultural groups to maintain their unique identities, and the right of minorities to function in a society free of racism.

Canada's racist heritage has bequeathed to both earlier and present generations of Canadians a powerful set of perceptions and behavioural patterns regarding people of colour. A deeply entrenched system of White dominance perpetuates inequity and oppression against the socially and economically disadvantaged.

However, racism as a commanding force in this country is constantly challenged and denied by applying the arguments of democratic liberalism. In a society that espouses equality, tolerance, social harmony, and respect for individual rights, the existence of racial prejudice, discrimination, and disadvantage is difficult to acknowledge and therefore remedy. Canadians have a deep attachment to the assumptions that in a democratic society individuals are rewarded solely on the basis of their individual merit and that no one group is singled out for discrimination. Consistent with these liberal, democratic values is the assumption that physical differences such as **skin colour** are irrelevant in determining one's status. Therefore, those who experience racial bias or differential treatment are considered somehow responsible for their state, resulting in a "blame it on the victim" syndrome.

This conflict between democratic liberalism and the collective racism of the dominant culture creates a dissonance in Canadian society. There is a constant and fundamental moral tension between the everyday experiences of people of colour and Aboriginal peoples and the perceptions of those who have the power to redefine that reality—politicians, bureaucrats, educators, judges, journalists, and the corporate elite. While lip service is paid to the need to ensure equality in a pluralistic society, most Canadian individuals, organizations, and institutions are far more committed to maintaining or increasing their own power.

The multiplicity of ways these values conflict is the subject of this book. It examines this phenomenon and analyzes the impact of "democratic racism" on Canadian society and its institutions.

The third edition of this book continues to explore the changing face of racism and the dynamics of democratic racism. We continue our focus on the construct of **racist** or **racialized discourse**, that is, an exploration of the link between the collective values, beliefs, and practices of the dominant White culture and the discourse of racism buried in our language, national narratives and myths, public accounts, and everyday common-sense interpretations, explanations, and rationalizations. Discourse is not just a symptom of the problem of racism (Smitherman-Donaldson and van Dijk, 1988). It essentially reinforces and reproduces the racist beliefs and actions of the dominant culture. In the chapters dealing with institutions such as policing, justice, human services, education, arts and culture, media, and the state, the authors explore how liberal principles such as individualism, universalism, equal opportunity, and tolerance become the language and conceptual framework through which inferiorization and exclusion are defined and defended (Mackey, 2002; Goldberg, 1993).

In this third edition, certain themes that were woven throughout the text of the first and second editions have been strengthened. We look more closely at how each of our institutions are discursive spaces that intersect with one another and with broader societal discourses, and that function to categorize, inferiorize, marginalize, and exclude racialized populations. Using new case studies in the history chapter and each of the institutional chapters and other analytical tools, the interconnectedness of institutions such as media, arts, education, policing, justice, human services, and systems of governance are examined. This web of institutionalized interactions serves a central function in a society divided by colour, ethnicity, gender, class, and other forms of oppression. These interlocking institutions, structures, and systems, wittingly or unwittingly, support and reinforce racism, sexism, classicism, and other forms of oppression, in the cohesiveness of their ideologies, discourses, and written and unwritten policies and practices. Each dominant White sector depends on another to give it authority and power. This approach highlights the fact that racialized individuals and communities experience **systemic racism** both simultaneously and separately. Therefore, to analyze what is happening "out there" the interrelationships between our social, cultural, political, and economic institutions in terms of the everyday beliefs, values, and norms that support racial inequality need to be examined and deconstructed.

This edition continues to emphasize the saliency of racism as a social marker of difference and oppression, but more examples of the intersection of racism with other forms of oppression such as gender and class are presented. The evidence of such intersectionality is seen throughout the text.

The book also provides more narrative analysis that draws upon the lived experiences of people of colour and incorporates their individual experiences and collective stories and voices. These narratives are more than anecdotal evidence because narrative inquiry is a powerful tool in analyzing human experience, and particularly the experience of racism. While the stories are often contextualized in personal and individual experience, they communicate broader cultural assumptions, beliefs, and experiences (Bourdieu, 1999). The telling and analysis of narratives can serve not only as primary data in academic research, but also as a powerful educational and organizing tool for social change (Bell, 1987; Williams, 1991; Delgado, 1995).

On the other hand, dominant narratives, the stories told by White elite authorities, provide a "public transcript" (Scott, 1990) of the beliefs, assumptions, and values that are incorporated into the every talk and text of the White elite and public authorities that includes journalists, educators, politicians, bureaucrats, social workers, police, judges, the corporate elite, and many others. Narrative analysis helps to explore and reflect the dialectical tension between the dominant discourses of the White power elite and the counter-narratives of opposition and resistance articulated by ethno-racial minorities. These stories serve to give voice and document racial oppression within institutional, administrative, and discursive spaces. The plurality of counter-hegemonic narratives highlights the meaning and significance of race and racism in the everyday lives of people of colour in relation to the construction of Canada as a democratic racist society. In this regard, the important work of many more researchers of colour, particularly women, have been added. Their scholarship, their stories, and their voices enrich our approach and deepen the analysis in this edition.

Another new dimension to this examination of racism in Canadian society is the way in which racism has affected Muslim, Arab, and other Canadians of Middle-East backgrounds since September 11. These communities across Canada have experienced racial bias and discrimination in their neighbourhoods, workplaces, and schools. They have witnessed the destruction of their properties and been subjected to the discourses of the media, politicians, and other public authorities that have served to reinforce the message of their "otherness." Public policies such as the Anti-Terrorism Act are a demonstration of a new tension that has emerged in North America since 9/11 that challenges democratic liberal values. The debate over this legislation and other recent policies are symptomatic of a conflict between preserving public rights to security and securing the fundamental rights and freedoms of all Canadians.

Finally, this edition more fully explores the central role of **Whiteness** as ideology, discourse, and social practice in a democratic racialized society. Throughout the book, drawing upon a burgeoning body of scholarship, the authors analyze how Whiteness functions as a racial signifier in the preservation of systems of domination and as a vehicle to reinforce structural inequality. Whiteness is examined as a process, "a constantly shifting location upon complex maps of social, economic and political power" (Ellsworth, 1997:264). It is important to emphasize that when we speak of Whiteness, we are not critiquing White people as individuals, but rather see Whiteness as an invisible social process by which power and privilege is exercised in a society divided by colour, as well as other social markers.

Terminology

One of the first challenges that confronts anyone analyzing racism is identifying an appropriate terminology. One must search for words that themselves are not racialized and, at the same time, clearly and accurately communicate what racism means. As the phenomenon of racism continues to show diverse manifestations, so too does the language evolve. Not only do new words emerge, but also the historical context of "old" words affects the ways they are used.

The sometimes-radical changes that language undergoes suggest there is no fixed or correct meaning for any term (Williams, 1983). Apple expresses the challenge of language in this way: "Concepts do not remain still very long. They have wings so to speak, and can be induced to fly from place to place" (1993:25). One therefore needs to look for the meanings of particular terms in their specific contextual use. Concepts such as culture, race, history, truth, freedom of expression, and universalism, for example, are not neutral; rather, they exist as part of many different social and interpretative frameworks. There are powerful currents that alter interpretations, depending on the situation, location, and social context (Lentricchia and McLaughlin, 1990; Fiske, 1994).

Although colour remains the nucleus of the race classification system, paradoxically it bears little relation to the actual skin tones of human beings. No White person is truly white, nor is any Black individual truly black. Whites do not consider themselves part of the colour spectrum but rather identify their group as constituting the universal norm. However, the gradations of colour from white to black associated with various racial groups have economic, social, and cultural consequences. The ideology that defines Whites as superior renders people of different colours inferior.

As is demonstrated in every chapter of this book, skin colour has an important relationship to status and position in Canadian society. Razack argues that the language of colour delineates the politics of domination and subordination, observing that "White ... is the colour of domination" (1998:11). Making this point in terms of her personal experience as a person of colour, St. Lewis observes: "In conversations about race, all of my being is telescoped to my skin. The colour of my skin drives the engine of my public life.

It defines relationships and sets out possibilities. Attitudes and beliefs make it real" (1996:28).

It is for these reasons that references to colour in this text are used in their political sense, and the terms "Black" and "White" are capitalized to reflect this context. The reader will note that references citing British literature or experiences tend to use the term "Black" inclusively, to refer to people of colour generally. However, in all other discussions, the term refers specifically to people of African descent.

The terms "**mainstream**," "Anglo," and "the **dominant/majority group/culture**" are used interchangeably throughout this book to refer to the group in Canadian society that maintains the power to define itself and its culture as the norm.

Although the phrases "racial minorities" and "people of colour" appear frequently in this book, they are used cautiously. Referring to groups of people who represent four-fifths of the world's population as "minorities" is, at the very least, inaccurate. Furthermore, huge distinctions exist among racial minorities or people of colour. There are, for example, in each of the groups examined in this book, significant differences that relate to class and gender. The experiences of recent affluent immigrants from Hong Kong, who come to Canada with significant resources and business skills, bear little similarity to those of the unskilled worker who is a third-generation Canadian or the Chinese refugee fleeing from political persecution.

In using the phrases "racial minorities" and "people of colour," we refer to groups of people who because of their physical characteristics are subjected to differential and unequal treatment in Canada. Their minority status is the result of a lack of access to power, privilege, and prestige in relation to the White majority group. Although there are significant differences among "racial minorities" or "people of colour," as there are within any ethno-racial group, members of these diverse communities share a history of exposure to racial bias and discriminatory barriers based on the colour of their skin. So, for the purposes of this book, they are grouped together. The term "visible minority" is a phrase coined by the federal government when employment equity was enacted in 1984. It is now also commonly used in statistical analyses by public agencies. The term "Aboriginal peoples" is used most commonly in this book, although there are also references to "First Nations" and "indigenous peoples." Again, these terms refer to an extremely heterogeneous population.

Finally, what is meant by "race" and "racism"? The theoretical perspective is that race is a socially constructed phenomenon (see Chapters 1 and 2 for more detailed definitions) based on the erroneous assumption that physical differences such as skin colour, hair colour and texture, and facial features are related to intellectual, moral, or cultural superiority. The concept of race has no basis in biological reality and, as such, has no meaning independent of its social definitions. But, as a social construction, race significantly affects the lives of people of colour.

Racism (more correctly, "social racism") refers to the assumptions, attitudes, beliefs, and behaviours of individuals as well as to the institutional policies, processes, and practices that flow from those understandings. Racism as racialized language or discourse is manifested in the articulation of ideologies and policies through euphemisms, metaphors, omissions, and passive language. It is reflected in the collective belief systems of the dominant culture, and it is woven into the laws, language, rules, and norms of Canadian society.

Another term frequently used in this book, **racialization**, often appears in studies on racism produced in the United Kingdom, particularly those that use a political economy perspective. The terms "racialized" and "racist" are sometimes used interchangeably in this book in reference to discourse (as both language and social practice). "Racialized," less familiar to North American readers, has been defined as "processes by which meanings are attributed to particular objects, features and processes, in such a way that the latter are given special significance and carry or are embodied with a set of additional meanings" (Miles, 1989:70). Racialization is part of a broader process whereby categories of the population are constructed, differentiated, inferiorized, and excluded (Anthias, 1998:7). However, as Sherene Razack (1998) points out, these processes depend on the local and historical contexts within which they exist.

Skin colour as a feature of race therefore carries with it more than the signification of "colour"; it also includes a set of meanings attached to the cultural traits of those who are a certain colour, and these meanings are incorporated into everyday language and the discursive practices of politicians, bureaucrats, institutional authorities, the media, and other opinion shapers (Stam, 1993). The assertion that "Blacks are prone to commit crimes," and the phrase "Yellow Peril," in reference to Japanese and Chinese Canadians, therefore signify that members of a racial group, identified by their skin colour, have a propensity for certain behaviour. Ideological racialization refers to the ways discourse concerning a set of principles becomes imbued with racial dimensions.

For example, in Canada, the debate about immigration has become racialized because substantial numbers of immigrants are now people of colour. Restricting immigration therefore becomes a means of excluding these groups. The racialization of crime results in the stigmatization of certain groups. For example, racialization in the media results in news stories and editorials in which Blacks figure prominently in crimes that are also committed by members of other groups. Thus, it can be argued that the processes of racialization and criminalization of ethno-racial communities move across sectors from policing and justice to the courts and lawmakers, from the vehicles of popular culture (e.g., film, newsmaking and television programming) to immigration. Each dominant White system depends on another to give it its power.

Perspective

Before embarking on an analysis of racism in Canadian society, some of the book's limitations should be noted. The authors have tried to provide a national perspective on racism in Canada and, wherever possible, to draw on the experiences and expertise of theoreticians and practitioners across the country. However, for the past three decades, Ontario has been one of the primary sites of the anti-racism struggle in Canada. It has the greatest number of people of colour in its population, and its minority communities, especially in Toronto, have perhaps been more politicized and more insistent on ensuring that racism and anti-racism become part of the public agenda. Many of the examples and case studies presented in this book are about the day-to-day experiences of people of colour as they go about the routine business of living. Since the authors live in Ontario, it is not surprising that many examples are drawn from events which have taken place in that province and specifically in Toronto. On the other hand, however, the work of scholars from around the country is cited and referenced throughout the book.

The authors' work as anti-racism and equity educators, scholars, and practitioners has provided them with direct knowledge of the organizational and institutional processes occurring in each of the arenas described in Part Two. Although they document the events, issues, and activities in other Canadian jurisdictions as well as in the United States and the United Kingdom, they believe that the sometimes-strong emphasis on Ontario will be of interest and educational value to readers everywhere.

Throughout this book, there are frequent references to the literature of other jurisdictions, including the United States. However, the British experience with racism and anti-racism is of particular interest. Although important differences exist between Canada and the United Kingdom, many similarities exist with respect to the patterns of bias and discrimination against people of colour. Moreover, an extensive body of literature documents racism in British society, its effects on the victims, and various strategies for dismantling racist ideologies, structures, and practices (Hall, 1991, 1997; Benyon and Solomos, 1987; Gilroy, 1987). The British evidence, therefore, is both timely and relevant to the discussion of racism and anti-racism in Canadian society. The United Kingdom is, in many ways, a paradigm for Canadian society. It has had a similar pattern of immigration from the Commonwealth of Nations. Immigrants of colour from the Caribbean and Asia began arriving in large numbers in Britain more than twenty years before they did so in Canada. Thinking that they would be well received as members of the Commonwealth, immigrants of colour in Britain were shocked at the racism they faced in employment, housing, social services, policing, and the justice system (Gilroy, 1982; Hall et al., 1978).

Framework of the Book

Part One establishes a framework for understanding the nature of democratic racism. Chapter 1 introduces the reader to the concept of democratic racism by examining a central ideological struggle in Canadian society: the conflict between the image of a country with a strong and cherished tradition of democratic liberalism and the reality of persistent and pervasive inequality based on colour. While individuals, organizations, institutions, and the state vigorously deny the presence of racism, it flourishes in this liberal democratic country, deeply affecting the daily lives of people of colour. This chapter looks at how democratic racism functions in terms of individual and collective belief systems and behaviour. It challenges the many myths articulated in a multiplicity of racialized discourses that prevent Canadians from confronting and responding to racism. The discourses of democratic racism are identified.

Chapter 2 provides a brief overview of theories of racism developed in the United States, the United Kingdom, and Canada. A new section in this edition examines the role of social science research in relation to theory development and methodologies that have failed to address the question of race and racism in relation to structural inequalities of power. The theoretical framework of discursive formation is introduced and linked to a new discussion of the ways the invisible social processes of Whiteness as ideology, discourse, and social practice function to reinforce racial hierarchies in society. The chapter also provides definitions of terms used in the study of racism. It then turns to the problems of assessing and measuring racism.

Chapter 3 provides both an historical scan and contemporary evidence of racism in Canada by looking at the experiences of specific groups in the history of this country. It draws on the findings of research studies, task forces, government inquiries, and polls and surveys conducted over the past two decades. One of the main thrusts of this chapter, however, is to demonstrate the extent of individual and everyday racism in Canada. The documented experiences of people of colour provide commanding evidence of racism in Canada. Analyses of some of the contemporary immigration discourses in recent literature reflect the continuing dominant ideology and discourse of "otherness." This is also reflected in the growing levels of poverty among people of colour and Aboriginal people. A case study of employment discrimination at Health Canada and recent statistical data on racial inequality in employment provide compelling evidence that racism continues to be deeply embedded in the fabric of Canadian society. In its most overt form, racial bias is manifested in hate-group activity and the proliferation of White-supremacist groups on the Internet.

Chapter 4 examines democratic racism and its impact on Aboriginal communities of Canada. It is important to point out that the relationship between Aboriginal peoples and the state is significantly different from the relationship between racial minorities and the state. Treaties and legislation govern the position of Aboriginal peoples. Their role and status is determined by formal mechanisms, and the solutions to their systemic racial oppression lie in a unique set of strategies (e.g., self-government) that are unavailable to other people of colour. The chapter documents how Aboriginal peoples were inferiorized, pathologized, and oppressed in every aspect of their existence. Residential schools and child welfare practices are analyzed as two examples of how deep and pervasive racism was in the daily lives of Aboriginal peoples and its catastrophic legacy. Despite the distinct and unique position and status of the First Nations, there are also some common elements in the politics of race, racism, and cultural hegemony in the context of both the democratic liberalism and the hierarchical social relations that characterize Canadian society.

Part Two analyzes a number of key institutions in Canadian society—particularly service providers in the public sector—within which racism continues to be a significant source of tension, conflict, and oppression. The chapters in this part—on policing, the justice system, and the human services—demonstrate how the policies, programs, procedures, and delivery systems of the major institutions in Canada discriminate against people of colour. The analysis of these key institutions illuminates both the processes of Whiteness and the dynamics of racism it is manifested in both overt and covert organizational and discursive practices.

Chapter 5 examines the justice system from the perspective of the differential treatment of racial minorities in the granting of administrate tribunals, courtroom practices such as jury selection, bail and sentencing disparities, attitudes and perceptions of judges, Crown attorneys, defence counsel, etc. and the lack of minority representation in the system. The analysis of the justice system draws upon new case studies to highlight the racialized attitudes and discursive practices that characterize inequality in the justice system. The case study of Rocky Jones and Ann Derrick and the case study of racial bias in administrative tribunals illustrate one of the major themes in this text: the intersection of racism between sectors and systems.

Chapter 6 analyzes racism in Canadian law enforcement agencies. It explores the culture of policing, the racialization of crime, and the overpolicing and underpolicing of minority communities. The construct of racial profiling is examined through a new section, based on an analysis of the racial profiling of Black men in Toronto conducted by the *Toronto Star*. It incorporates the findings of a number of new studies that document the reality of differential treatment toward African Canadians and its impact. This is followed by a powerful example of racial profiling of Aboriginal men in the provinces of Saskatchewan and British Columbia, in which several men have died under mysterious circumstances. The chapter critically examines the responses of police forces across Canada in areas such as training, policy development, employment equity, civilian review mechanisms, community relations, and the use of force.

Chapter 7 examines the models and delivery of human services. It shows how racism is reflected in the professional values, assumptions, and practices of social workers and other human-service practitioners. It emphasizes the role, position, and status of "minority" workers as an example of how the processes of Whiteness and racialization function in mainstream organizations. In this edition, there is a new emphasis on the barriers to access of both mental and health care services experienced by people of colour and Aboriginal peoples, and the significant impact that these barriers pose for minority and Aboriginal women. A case study on SARS demonstrates how a health care crisis becomes racialized in terms of the Asian community in Toronto.

In continuing to examine the institutional arenas in Canadian social structure, Part Three analyzes racism in education (schools, colleges, and universities), the media, and the arts. These powerful social institutions develop, protect, and support a society's values, beliefs, and systems. The chapters in this Part focus on the ways the ideology of racism is supported and sustained in these institutional defenders of Canada's collective belief system. They also show how the myths and assumptions of democratic racism are employed as discursive strategies to avoid the necessity of acknowledging that the ideology of racism is central to the definition of Canada. Each chapter in this section explores how Whiteness functions as a form of cultural hegemony, while at the same time, remaining invisible to those who possess its power.

Chapter 8 looks at one of the most powerful socializing agents in society, the educational system, and at the ways racism pervades the teaching process and learning environment and forms an intrinsic part of the organizational structure of schools and classrooms. It explores the ways Eurocentric and assimilationist values and ideologies continue to influence curriculum and teaching practices. Examples are presented of the ways racial bias and differential treatment affect the educational opportunities of students of colour, particularly Black students. The case study of the killing of a South-Asian Canadian student, Reena Virk, in British Columbia demonstrates how the processes of categorization, inferiorization, and marginalization can lead, in some circumstances, to death. The analysis related to postsecondary institutions challenges the widespread notion that colleges and universities are inclusive and neutral environments free of racism. Manifestations of racial bias and differential treatment in the education system include: the lack of minority representation in hiring, promotion, and tenure decisions; the prevalence of Eurocentric curriculum and pedagogy; racial tensions and harassment in the schools; and the impact of the policy of "Zero Tolerance" on the marginalization and exclusion of Black students. The "chilly climate" among students and between students and faculty in colleges and universities is examined. A new case study illuminates the processes of racialization experienced by women of colour and Aboriginal women in the academy.

Chapter 9 analyzes **cultural racism** by looking at the Eurocentric values and assumptions of arts and cultural organizations in Canada. An important dimension of cultural racism is reflected in the power of White culture to define the standards of excellence and professionalism in the arts and to determine what images and voices are outside the boundaries of mainstream culture. This chapter analyzes the **appropriation** of minority cultural experiences and symbols by people outside those cultures as another manifestation of racism. It examines the barriers to participation in the arts in the context of the underrepresentation of racial-minority artists and writers in art galleries, museums, publishing houses, art councils, unions, and associations. Two case studies illustrate how people of colour do not have control over cultural systems constructed by the dominant culture, which promotes, supports, and affirms forms of marginalization and exclusion. A new case study explores the contested issue of "colour-blind" casting in theatre. On a more positive note, the chapter points to indicators of positive change, particularly in the recognition of many writers of colour who have received positive affirmation of their work as reflected in a number of literary awards.

Chapter 10 focuses on the mass media and explores how the print and electronic media use their enormous influence to marginalize racial minorities in Canada. It shows how the media, contrary to public myth, are linked to political, social, and corporate elites and legitimate White power structures. The chapter traces the role of influential White power brokers in print and electronic media organizations as they shape agendas, provide information, and create images that then become part of the collective racialized ideology and national discourse. The case study of the racialization of the Muslim Canadian community provides a vehicle for understanding how negative images and ideas are circulated by mass media. The process of "othering" by the media is also examined in the context of the racialization and criminalization of Black/Jamaican Canadians in news coverage. The new case study on programming reflects the discursive theme of the "rightness of Whiteness" in media production.

Part Four provides an analysis of the impact of democratic racism on the state and society by focusing on the ways organizational authorities, politicians, bureaucrats, the legal system, and public policies maintain, reinforce, and reproduce racist ideologies and discursive practices. By examining the change process used by many of these agencies, it is possible to identify some of the powerful and widespread forms of resistance to organizational and institutional change, despite these agencies' stated commitment to the liberal principles of fairness, tolerance, and equality.

Chapter 11 examines the rhetorical strategies underlying the development of central state policies, doctrines, and legislative frameworks. Through this analysis, it is possible to identify the powerful but invisible ambivalence that characterizes democratic racism at the level of the state. This chapter poses the question concerning the role that the state plays in perpetuating and reproducing racism. It looks at the laws, policies, and practices of various levels of government that affect the lives of people of colour in Canadian society. Multiculturalism in its many forms is examined as ideology, legislative act, and discursive practice. The Canadian Charter of Rights and Freedoms and provincial human rights codes and commissions are briefly analyzed. Critical questions are raised about the new Anti-Terrorism Act and its consequences for Muslim and other Canadians of colour post-9/11. The examination of state responses includes an analysis of employment equity legislation and of the resistance to it as a prime example of the politics of resistance engaged in by the dominant White culture.

Chapter 12 analyzes the weaknesses of the approaches and strategies identified in the preceding chapters in dealing with racism in Canadian society and institutions. Despite a proliferation of public policies that articulate support for diversity and equity, anti-racism continues to be resisted at various levels within the organizational core values and normative practices. In exploring resistance to change, the analysis reveals again how democratic racism works in terms of discursive practices and organizational structures, policies, values, and norms. Individuals and organizations continue to assert their commitment to fairness and equality for all, while at the same time opposing measures that would ensure racial equity.

Chapter 13 concludes the book by summarizing the ways democratic racism and the ideology of Whiteness is manifested in individual ideologies, public discourses, and organizational and institutional practices. Democratic racism is offered as an explanation for the failure of many policies and programs that ostensibly have been developed to alleviate the oppression of people of colour. Analyzing the weaknesses of many of the current approaches also allows for some reflection on strategies for change. The authors argue that one of the tools of social change is the power of the counter-narrative. The public documenting and sharing of stories and experiences of people of colour and First Nations Peoples not only are important as a research tool, but also, and more importantly, provide a powerful mechanism for mobilization and empowerment.

A number of other measures are examined as possible future directions. We emphasize the importance the socialization process in preparing Canadians for creating more just and equitable institutions and systems. We emphasize the development of critical self-awareness, reflective skills, and practices for educators, media practitioners, human-service workers, cultural workers, police, judges, employers, decision-makers in public and private institutions, and others. We point to the many examples of community empowerment. We consider some of mechanisms for responding to institutional resistance, and the development of organizational and administrative measures and accountability systems based on recognition of the pervasiveness of racism in the central institutions of Canadian society. In our final argument, we suggest that dealing with racism in a transformative way requires society to deal with the dissonance in the core values that underlie our current understanding of democracy.

References

Anthias, F. (1998). "Limits of Ethnic Diversity." *Patterns of Prejudice* 32(4):6–19.

Apple, M. (1993). "Constructing the 'Other': Rightist Reconstructions of Common Sense." In C. McCarthy and W. Crichlow (eds.), *Race, Identity and Representation in Education*. New York and London: Routledge. 24–39.

Bell, D. (1987). *And We Are Not Saved: The Elusive Quest for Racial Justice*. New York: Basic Books.

Benyon, J., and J. Solomos (eds.). (1987). *The Roots of Urban Unrest*. Oxford: Pergamon Press.

Bourdieu, P. (1999). "Language and Symbolic Power." In A. Jaworski and N. Coupland (eds.), *The Discourse Reader*. London: Routledge. 502–513.

Crenshaw, K., and G. Peller. (1993). *Reading Rodney King: Reading Urban Uprising*. New York, London: Routledge: 1993.

Delgado, R. (1995). "Legal Storytelling: Storytelling for Oppositionists and Others: A Plea for Narrative. In R. Delgado (ed.), *Critical Race Theory: The Cutting Edge*. Philadelphia: Temple University Press. 64–74.

Ellsworth, E. (1997). "Double Binds of Whiteness" In M. Fine, L. Weis, L. Powell, L. Mun Wong, *Of White Readings of Race, Power and Society*. New York, London: 259–269.

Fiske, J. (1994). *Media Matters: Everyday Culture and Political Change*. Minneapolis: University of Minnesota Press.

Gilroy, P. (1982). "Preface." In Centre for Contemporary Cultural Studies (ed.), *The Empire Strikes Back: Race and Racism in 70's Britain*. London: Hutchinson. 7–8.

———. (1987). *There Ain't No Black in the Union Jack: The Cultural Politics of Race and Nation*. London: Hutchinson.

Goldberg, D.S. (1993). *Racist Culture: Philosophy and Politics of Meaning*. Oxford, UK, and Cambridge, MA: Blackwell.

Hall, S. (ed.). (1997). *Representation: Cultural Representations and Signifying Practices*. London: Sage.

Hall, S. (1991). "Old and New Identities: Old and New Ethnicities." In A. King (ed.), *Culture, Globalization, and the World System*. Binghamton: Department of Art History, State University of New York.

———, et al. (1978). *Policing the Crisis*. London: Macmillan.

Lentricchia, F., and T. McLaughlin (eds.). (1990). *Critical Terms for Literary Study*. 2nd ed. Chicago: University of Chicago Press.

Mackey, E. (2002). *The House of Difference: Cultural Politics and National Identity in Canada*. Toronto: University of Toronto Press.

Miles, R. (1989). *Racism*. London: Routledge.

Razack, S. (1998). *Looking White People in the Eye: Gender, Race and Culture in Courtrooms and Classrooms*. Toronto: University of Toronto Press.

Rex, J. (1988). *The Ghetto and the Underclass*. Aldershot, UK, and Brookfield, VT: Avebury.

Scott, J. (1990). *Domination and the Arts of Resistance: Hidden Transcripts*. New Haven, CT: Yale University Press.

Smitherman-Donaldson, G., and T. van Dijk. (1988). *Discourse and Discrimination*. Detroit: Wayne State University.

Stam, R. (1993). "From Stereotype to Discourse." *Cine-Action* (23)(Fall):12–29.

St. Lewis, J. (1996). "Identity and Black Consciousness in North America." In J. Littleton (ed.), *Clash of Identities: Essays on Media, Manipulation and Politics of Self*. Englewood Cliffs, NJ: Prentice Hall. 21–30.

Williams, P. (1991). *The Alchemy of Race and Rights*. Cambridge, MA: Harvard University Press.

Williams, R. (1983). *Keywords: A Vocabulary of Culture and Society*. 2nd ed. London: Fontana.

PART ONE

Perspectives
on Racism

*This Part introduces the concept of democratic racism and
provides a general perspective on racism. A discussion of the theoretical
explanations of racism, as documented by social science literature,
is presented in Chapter 2. Chapter 3 reviews the evidence of racism
in Canadian society, drawing on historical examples
as well as current studies, polls, and surveys.
Chapter 4 reviews the history of racism in relation to
Canada's Aboriginal peoples.*

CHAPTER 1

THE IDEOLOGY OF RACISM

We are at one of those critical junctures where two ideals are in conflict. There's the principle of the legal equality of all. There's the fact that there are serious inequalities in our society, many of which can only be remedied by treating people unequally. Which puts liberals like myself at war with ourselves.

—*Gwyn (1993)*

This chapter examines the **ideology** of **racism** in Canada today. It begins with a brief examination of the function of ideology as the basis of social behaviour and then explores the nature of **racist ideology**. This ideology provides the foundation for understanding the racist **attitudes** and behaviours of individuals, the maintenance of racist policies and practices in Canadian **institutions**, and the promulgation of racist doctrines and laws by the state. The chapter analyzes the role and functions of racist ideology and introduces the concept of **democratic racism**. The last section of this chapter examines the discourse of democratic racism and some of the myths that support and reinforce racism as ideology and praxis.

Democratic racism is an ideology that permits and sustains people's ability to maintain two apparently conflicting sets of values. One set consists of a commitment to a liberal, democratic society motivated by the egalitarian values of fairness, justice, and equality. Conflicting with these values are attitudes and behaviours that include negative feelings about people of colour and that result in differential treatment of them, or **discrimination** against them. Democratic racism, in its simplest form, is an ideology that reduces the conflict between maintaining a commitment to both egalitarian and non-egalitarian values.

Introduction

What Is Ideology?

Ideology is a set of beliefs, perceptions, assumptions, and values that provide members of a group with an understanding and an explanation of their world. At another level, ideology provides a framework for "organizing, maintaining and transforming relations of power and dominance in society" (Fleras and Elliott, 1992:54).

Ideology influences the ways in which people interpret social, cultural, political, and economic systems and structures, and it is linked to their perceived needs, hopes, and fears. Ideological formations are not static but organic and constantly evolving, often as a result of contradictory experiences (Hall, 1983).

People are often unaware of their ideologies:

> It is indeed a peculiarity of ideology that it imposes (without appearing to do so) obviousness as obviousness which we cannot fail to recognize and before which we have the inevitable and natural reaction of crying out (aloud or in the still small voice of conscience): "That's obvious! That's right! That's true!" (Althusser, 1971:127)

Within these everyday ideological constructs, ideas about **race**, gender, and class are produced, preserved, and promoted. These ideas form the basis for social behaviour. Therefore, understanding ideology is crucial to an understanding of the marginalization, **exclusion**, and domination of people of colour in Canadian society.

The Definition and Function of Racist Ideology

Racist ideology provides the conceptual framework for the political, social, and cultural structures of inequality and systems of dominance based on race, as well as the processes of exclusion and marginalization of people of colour that characterize Canadian society.

The cognitive dimensions of racism are located in collective patterns of thought, knowledge, and beliefs as well as individual attitudes, perceptions, and behaviours. "Racism as ideology includes the whole range of concepts, ideas, images and institutions that provide the framework of interpretation and meaning for racial thought in society" (Essed, 1990:44). Racist ideology therefore organizes, preserves, and perpetuates the power structures in a society. It creates and preserves a system of dominance based on race and is communicated and reproduced through agencies of socialization and cultural transmission, such as the mass media, schools and universities, religious doctrines, symbols and images, art, music, and literature. It is reflected and regenerated in the very language we read, write, and speak.

The Elusive Nature of Racism

One of the most complex aspects of racism is its elusive and changing nature. The most commonly accepted concept of racism in Canada is one that refers to the individual expression of overt feelings or actions. Racism is generally understood to refer to physical assaults that have been perpetrated by bigoted individuals, racial slurs and **harassment** in schools or in the workplace, defacing property with racial graffiti, and similar overt acts. There seems to be an extremely limited understanding of racism in public discourse. Racism manifests itself not only within individuals, but also in groups, organizations, and

Figure 1.1

IDEOLOGY AND ITS EFFECTS

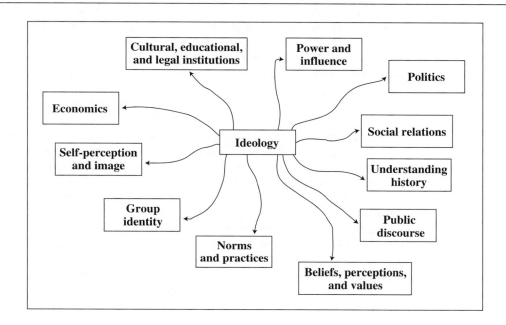

institutions, at the state level, and in the value system of society. In each arena, racism assumes a different form. This will be discussed in more detail in Chapter 2. It has "a geographic, social and historical specificity. In any country, at any point of time, the realization of racist practice will be of a specific nature" (Brandt, 1986:67–68).

Racism is not a natural element in society, just waiting for a series of events to trigger its manifestations:

> It has no natural and universal law of development. It does not always assume the same shape. There have been many significantly different *racisms*—each historically specific and articulated in a different way. Racism is always historically specific in this way, whatever common features it may appear to share with other similar social phenomena. It always assumes specific forms which arise out of the *present*—not the past—conditions and organization of society. (Hall, 1978:26)

Thus, the ways in which racism manifests itself at any particular time are fluid, dynamic, and ever-changing. They are affected by the social contexts in which racism develops.

In a similar vein, the study of racism provides "a picture … of historically variant racism both continuously and discontinuously transformed from one period to another. Subject, objects, and modes alter. Developments and changes in racist discourse are demonstrated to be functions of dominant interests, aims, and purposes" (Goldberg, 1990:xiii).

Another important dimension of racism is its ability to be so subtly expressed or indirectly implied that its targets are not even aware of it. Conversely, racism is sometimes visible only to its victims. It remains indiscernible to others, who therefore deny its existence.

The subtle and ever-changing nature of racism helps to explain both its persistence over time and the difficulties of defining and measuring it. However, although many are confused by the term, racism rests on this mystification of social relations—the necessary illusions that secure the order of public authority (Gilroy, 1987).

Racist ideology forms part of "common sense." Racist thinking, according to this view, is natural and forms part of the ways in which ordinary people view the world—they do not need to have specialized knowledge about **minority groups** to be racist. "Commonsense" racism is not based on theory, nor does it have a unified body of knowledge to support it; it contains a "storehouse of knowledge" that guides the thinking of "the practical struggle of everyday life of the popular masses" (Lawrence, 1982:49).

The construction of and belief in a racist ideology helps people to understand the increasingly complex societies in which they live. Thus, recently unemployed people can easily blame the new immigrants who have taken their jobs away. People who are fearful in their homes and on the streets can now blame all those Black or Asian people who commit crimes. Teachers whose Black students are underachieving can believe that it has nothing to do with their racial attitudes or classroom practices. The corporate manager is able to justify a refusal to hire those who are racially "different" on the basis of not wanting to disrupt the harmony of the workforce.

Racist assumptions and beliefs provide a ready explanation for the stress experienced by people who live in a country undergoing rapid social and cultural change:

> Racism is not a set of false pleas which swim around in the head. They're not a set of mistaken perceptions. They have their basis in real material conditions of existence. They arise because of concrete problems of different classes and groups in society. Racism represents the attempt ideologically to construct those conditions, contradictions, and problems in such a way that they can be dealt with and deflected in the same moment. (Hall, 1978:35)

Ideology may go far beyond individual beliefs and attitudes; it carries with it a predisposition to behave in negative, derogatory, or discriminary ways toward members of the targeted group. An ideology of racism therefore is more powerful than mere attitudes or beliefs (Hall et al., 1978). Ideology denotes a set of ideas and values that legitimate particular economic and social conditions. It penetrates and saturates everyday discourses in the form of common sense and provides codes of meaning (Hebridge, 1993:363).

Whiteness plays a crucial role in the social construction of racism. Whiteness is more than a description of **identity**; it also functions as a symbol, experience, and ideology (see Frankenberg, 1993; Roman, 1993; Fine et al., 1997). Whiteness is a collective set of beliefs and discursive and social practices that demands and creates hierarchy, inferiorization, and marginalization. However, it is invisible to those who possess it. Most White people perceive themselves as colourless and therefore without subjectivities, interests, or privileges. White culture is the hidden norm against which the "differences" of all other groups are evaluated. For those who have inherited its mantle, Whiteness is associated with a repertoire of superior cultural values including: normality, civility, truth, knowledge, merit, and achievement (Roman, 1993). However, Whiteness is not limited to a physical White identity as reflected in the light colour of one's skin, but rather should be understood as a process or continuously shifting location that delineates social, economic, and political power (Ellsworth, 1997). Frankenberg views Whiteness as a "practice rather than object, in relation to racial formation and historical process …" (1993:20). See Chapter 2 for more discussion on Whiteness.

The Concept of Democratic Racism

The primary characteristic of democratic racism—the most appropriate model for understanding how and why racism continues in Canada—is the justification of the inherent conflict between the egalitarian values of liberalism, justice and fairness, and the racist ideologies reflected in the collective mass belief system as well as the racist attitudes, perceptions, and assumptions of individuals.

Racist beliefs and practices continue to pervade Canadian society. Attitude surveys have found that many Canadians hold racist views. In the first such survey carried out in Canada, about 16 percent of Canadian adults were found to be confirmed bigots, while a further 35 percent held somewhat intolerant views. Another 30 percent leaned toward tolerance, and the remaining 20 percent were extremely tolerant (Henry, 1978). Later surveys and polls support these findings (see Chapter 3). Most Canadians therefore hold some degree of racist attitudes. But, living in a society that believes in democracy, most Canadians also recognize that these attitudes are socially unacceptable. In order to maintain their racist beliefs while championing democratic values, Canadians have developed the ideology of democratic racism—a set of justificatory arguments and mechanisms that permit these contradictory ideologies to coexist.

Democratic racism, therefore, results from the retention of racist beliefs and behaviours in a "democratic" society. The obfuscation and justificatory arguments of democratic racism are deployed to demonstrate continuing faith in the principles of an egalitarian society while at the same time undermining and sabotaging those ideals.

Before discussing this ideology as it pertains to Canada, it is useful to analyze it in the context of the United Kingdom and the United States. In the former the concept of "new racism" has been elaborated, while in the latter "aversive racism" has appeared in the literature. These aspects of racism, identified by critical theorists in the United Kingdom, are also relevant to Canada and are included in democratic racism.

New Racism in the United Kingdom

Distancing themselves from the crude ideas of biological inferiority and superiority, "new racists" have defined a national British **culture** that is homogeneously White. It is concerned with

> mechanisms of inclusion and exclusion. It specifies who may legitimately belong to the national community and simultaneously advances reasons for the segregation or banishment of those whose "origin" ... assigns them elsewhere. [West Indians, and for different reasons Asians] are judged to be incompatible with authentic forms of Englishness. Alien cultures come to embody a threat which, in turn, invites the conclusion that national decline and weakness have been precipitated by the arrival of Blacks. (Gilroy, 1987:45–46)

Scholars in the United Kingdom have analyzed the trend toward the increasing racialization of state policies "in all areas of social life" (CCCS, 1982:19). For at least the past two decades, observers have noted the central government's lack of sympathy and support for racial-equality initiatives (Ball and Solomos, 1990). The policy interventions of the central government have tended to affirm a deep-seated commitment to the rights of the White majority rather than those of minority communities. Herman Ouseley notes that the failure "to implement radical race equality policies was the result of inadequate attempts by national and local politicians" (Ball and Solomos, 1990). Such state policies reinforce the racist thinking of much of the population.

Lawrence (1982) identified a number of racial ideologies characteristic of the Conservative-run state in Great Britain. At their heart is a definition of "British" that clearly excludes people of colour who come from former (and present) Commonwealth countries. This definition affirms the "naturalness" of British values, British culture, and especially British family life. Within the politics of nationalism, sovereignty, and cultural identity, it defines the nation as a unified *cultural* community (Gilroy, 1987). Thus, White anti-racists are regarded as having been influenced by "alien" ideas.

Although new racism no longer espouses doctrines of racial superiority (there are exceptions, particularly in academia and the extreme right), it nevertheless denigrates people of colour. The myths that fuel new racism often derive from a negative evaluation of other cultures rather than from a focus on race. This ideology, for example, expresses itself in a negative evaluation of Black culture, particularly the "deviant" Black family and the "aberrant" behaviour of Black youth. Thus, although police officials do not consider themselves racist, they believe that Blacks are culturally disposed to criminal behaviour. Further, the media, while not admitting racism, publish report after report in which derogatory cultural characteristics are highlighted.

New racism cites pathological cultural patterns as major reasons for criminal behaviour, poverty, poor achievement in school, and an assortment of other social problems. Blacks show their inferiority by having a propensity for loud music and raucous conversation. New racists therefore cloak their negative attitudes toward other groups by claiming that while they do not believe in racial superiority, not all cultures are equally valid. The cultural behaviour of the "others," such as Blacks, demonstrates that they are not the same as Whites and cannot be part of the national culture.

When race is identified with identity and culture, careful language enables people to "speak about race without mentioning the word" (Gilroy, 1987:53). The crude and overtly racist labels of the far right are avoided, but the new racism can be articulated by the choice of carefully coded language: "'They,' despite the good qualities of some of 'them,' are held to be different from 'us' and would, on the whole, be better off back in 'their' countries" (Billig et al., 1988:107).

Another form of discourse in which overt racism is avoided occurs in the "two-handedness of the 'on the one hand, on the other hand' formulation. Having stated an opposition to racism or to **prejudice**, the way is then opened for an expression of racist or prejudiced views" (Billig et al., 1988:109). These formulations appear in an ideology in which traditional racism is eschewed but a newer, masked, and more subtle form is allowed expression. Modern racism is expressed in a rhetorical context, demonstrated in comments such as "I'm not a racist, but … ," which are followed by an overtly racist statement.

Aversive Racism in the United States

In the United States, a new form of democratic racism has been explored by social psychologists, who analyze the individual's attitudes. Gaertner and Dovidio (1986) present the results of studies of racism among the "well intentioned":

> Our work has focused on those White Americans, who, in terms of racism and public policy, seem "well intentioned." That is, they genuinely profess egalitarianism, as well as the desire to ameliorate the consequences of racism and poverty. However, we believe that the racial attitudes of many of these well-intentioned

people may be characterized by a special type of ambivalence: aversiveness. (Gaertner and Dovidio, 1981:208)

Their analysis builds on what was earlier identified as "aversive racism" (Kovel, 1970). In this pioneering work, Kovel distinguished "dominative" racists—strong hard-core bigots who are prepared to act on their attitudes—from "aversive" racists. The latter also believe in White supremacy, but do nothing about it. Aversive racists are prejudiced but do not act in discriminatory ways. Some avoid contact with Blacks and other minorities, but when contact is unavoidable, they are polite.

Other aversive racists, however, "are impelled by a strong social conscience, consider themselves liberals and, despite their sense of aversion (which may not be admitted inwardly) do their best within the given structure of society to ameliorate the conditions of the Negro" (Kovel, 1970:55). They believe in fairness and equality for all and pride themselves on their strong social conscience. They may not be aware of their aversion to Blacks (or other minorities) and appear to have a positive racial attitude. Gaertner and Dovidio note that this attitude is superficial, ambiguous, and complex. Their studies have identified a number of characteristics of aversive racists, including the following (from Gaertner, 1976:208):

- Aversive racists consider themselves prejudice-free but attempt to avoid contact with the minority group to which they are averse.
- Aversive racists think of themselves as politically liberal and non-discriminatory. In a situation in which clearly prescribed norms call for tolerant behaviour, they will behave appropriately. However, in situations in which there are no clear prescriptive norms, they may indulge in discriminatory behaviour because it would not be obvious.
- Aversive racists' positive actions toward minority groups relate less to a genuine effort to help minorities or to implement egalitarian values than to reaffirm their own lack of prejudice. This attitude may result in tokenism: aversive racists affirm that they are prejudice-free by making trivial gestures that preclude the necessity for extensive, costly action.

Aversive racism therefore "represents a particular type of ambivalence in which the conflict is between feelings and beliefs associated with a sincerely egalitarian value system and unacknowledged negative feelings and beliefs about Blacks" (Gaertner and Dovidio, 1986:62). Moreover, this type of racism does not necessarily include feelings of hate or hostility, nor will it usually express itself in hostile or discriminatory behaviour. Aversive racism involves "discomfort, uneasiness, disgust, and sometimes fear, which tend to motivate avoidance rather than intentionally destructive behaviours" (Gaertner and Dovidio, 1986:63).

Aversive racism stems from socialization and is reinforced by social and cultural factors. In the United States, for example, the denigration of Black culture, Black **stereotypes**, and the constant association of Black people with poverty, crime, and delinquency reinforces negative racial attitudes. Moreover, the differential distribution of social, economic, and political power between Blacks and Whites further reinforces these attitudes.

Symbolic Racism

Closely aligned to the aversive form, symbolic racism is an attitude in which "abstract moral assertions are made about Blacks' behaviour as a group, concerning what Blacks deserve, how they ought to act, whether or not they are treated equitably, and so on" (Sears and McConahay, 1973:138). Symbolic racism manifests itself in "acts that are rationalized on a non-racial basis but that actually maintain the racial status quo by continuing discrimination against Blacks" (Sears and McConahay, 1973:24). In the United States, these acts include voting for White rather than Black candidates, opposing affirmative action programs, and opposing desegregation in housing and education. In Canada, opposing **affirmative action** and **employment equity** is an act of symbolic racism.

Other aspects of symbolic racism have relevance for Canada. For example, unlike the older "redneck" bigotry, which denied equal rights and opportunities for people of colour, symbolic racism allows a person to uphold these values but still believe that Blacks are "too pushy" because they are making too many demands for equality too quickly. Moreover, Whites who hold these views may not feel personally threatened by Black claims to equality but feel that their values are endangered: Black assertiveness may be regarded as a threat to the very fabric of society. Another important component of symbolic racism is that, as its name implies, it operates through symbols rather than overt discrimination. Thus, there is opposition to welfare, Black politicians, and fair housing laws because they symbolize the unreasonable demands being made by Blacks. In sum, then, symbolic racism is the expression in terms of abstract ideological symbols and symbolic behaviours of the feeling that Blacks are violating cherished values and making illegitimate demands for changes in the racial status quo (McConahay and Hough, 1976:38).

Democratic Racism

Although democratic racism pertains largely to ideology and stresses the role of value differences as these are reflected in systems and institutions, individuals are largely responsible for the development of policies and the implementation of procedures that regulate systems and institutions. Thus democratic racism is related to new racism, aversive racism, and symbolic racism. It differs from them by positing a value conflict.

Democratic racism is an ideology in which two conflicting sets of values are made congruent to each other. Commitments to democratic principles such as justice, equality, and fairness conflict but coexist with attitudes and behaviours that include negative feelings about minority groups, differential treatment, and discrimination against them.

One of the consequences of the conflict is a lack of support for policies and practices that might ameliorate the low status of people of colour. These policies and practices tend to require changes in the existing social, economic, and political order, usually by state intervention. The intervention, however, is perceived to be in conflict with and a threat to liberal democracy. Thus democratic racism holds that the spread of racism should only be dealt with—if at all—by leaving basic economic structures and societal relations essentially unchanged (Gilroy, 1987). Efforts to combat racism that require intervention to change the cultural, social, economic, and political order will lack political support. More importantly, they will lack legitimacy, according to the egalitarian principles of liberal democracy.

The Discourses of Democratic Racism

How is democratic racism manifested in the daily lives, opinions, and feelings of people? What are the values, assumptions, and arguments of democratic racism? As Wellman (1977) noted, the maintenance of a wide array of myths and misconceptions about racism has permitted a pattern of denial that has led to a wholly inadequate response to racism.

Democratic racism in its ideological and discursive form is deeply embedded in popular culture and popular discourse. It is located within what has been called society's frames of reference (Hebridge, 1993). These frames of reference are a largely unacknowledged set of beliefs, assumptions, feelings, stories, and quasi memories that underlie, sustain, and inform perceptions, thoughts, and actions. Democratic racism as racist discourse begins in the families that nurture us, the communities that socialize us, the schools and universities that educate us, the media that communicate ideas and images to us, and the popular culture that entertains us.

Goldberg (1993) contends that racist discourse covers a wide spectrum of expressions and representations, including a nation's recorded history; scientific forms of racist explanations (such as Rushton's theory of racial differences); economic, legal, and bureaucratic forms of doctrine; cultural representations in the form of national narratives, images, and symbols; and so on. Social power is reflected in racist discourse.

The conflict between the ideology of democratic liberalism and the racist ideology present in the collective belief system of the dominant culture is reflected in the racist discourse that operates in the schools, the media, the courts, law enforcement agencies, arts organizations and cultural institutions, human services, government bureaucracies, and political authorities. The school, the university, the newspaper and the television station, the courtroom, police headquarters, the hospital, and the government office are discursive spaces. Within these spaces, controlled mainly by a dominant White culture, there exists a constant moral tension: the everyday experiences of people of colour, juxtaposed with the perceptions and responses of those who have the power to redefine that reality.

Many people resist anti-racism and **equity** initiatives because they are unwilling to question *their* own belief and value systems and discursive practices, *their* organizational and professional norms, *their* positions of power and privilege within the workplace and society. Thus, they are unable to examine the relation between cultural and racial differences and the power dynamics constructed around ideas about those differences. Acknowledging that ethno-racial differences make a difference in the lives of people is to concede that Euro-Canadian hegemony continues to function and organize the structures within which the delivery of mainstream programs and services operates (Dei, 1996). In each of these discursive spaces we see tension and resistance in relation to how multicultural and anti-racism ideologies and policies are "imagined, internalized and acted upon" (Yon, 1995:315).

Resistance may manifest itself as active opposition, expressed openly, but it is more commonly articulated in more subtle forms of discourse. Discourses on race and racism converge with concerns about Canadian identity, national unity, ethnicity, multiculturalism, and so on. Discourse provides the conceptual models for mapping the world around us and incorporates both social relationships and power relations (Goldberg, 1993), but as Yon (2000) demonstrates in his ethnographic study of students and teachers in a Toronto high school, discourse about identity and nation that never mentions the word "race" can also be considered racist discourse.

Increasingly, the discourse of liberalism is juxtaposed with popular conservative ideology, and individuals slide ambivalently between the two. As Yon (1995) points out: "Resistance and accommodation can be present in the same moment. Discourse often reveals ambivalence, contradiction and subtleties in relation to the issues of difference. For example, discussions about culture are often framed in the context of being 'tolerant,' 'sensitive' and sufficiently enlightened to appreciate and respect the diverse cultures of the 'others.'" Cultural discourse tends to cover up the "unpleasantness" of domination and inequity (Wetherell and Potter, 1992).

The following section outlines a framework for examining the discourse of dominance, which includes myths, explanations, codes of meaning, and rationalizations that have the effect of establishing, sustaining, and reinforcing democratic racism. In this analysis and throughout the book, note how this discourse is contextualized within liberal democratic, humanistic values. As the following chapters show, the central values of liberal ideologies carry different meanings and connotations, depending on the context. Goldberg (1993) contends that tolerance, equality, and liberty, central concepts in liberal discourse, have immensely flexible meanings.

The paradox of a postmodern liberal society is that as modernity commits itself to these liberal ideals and to the moral irrelevance of race, there is a proliferation of racial identities and an assortment of exclusions they support and sustain. Making a similar point, Mackey contends that "liberal principles are the very language and conceptual framework through which **intolerance** and exclusion are enabled, reinforced, defined and defended" (Mackey, 1996:305).

The elusive nature of the dominant discourse allows it to mask its racialized ideas (Fiske, 1994). Within it are unchallenged assumptions, or myths. These myths attempt to explain, rationalize, and resolve unsupportable contradictions and problems in society. Myths arise at particular historical moments in response to a perceived need within society. They function as a guideline for new ideas and behaviours. The final section of this chapter explores some of the prevailing myths that underpin democratic racism.

The Discourse of Denial

The discourse of denial is a dominant discursive theme within mainstream culture and is reflected in the everyday discourses of individuals and institutions. It is the central and controlling rhetorical strategy and is therefore implicitly contained within all the discourses listed below. Within this discourse the principle assumption is that racism simply does not exist in a democratic society. There is a refusal to accept the reality of racism, despite the evidence of racial prejudice and discrimination in, and the effects of racism on, the lives of people of colour. The assumption here is that because Canada is a society that upholds the ideals of a liberal democracy, it could not possibly be racist. When racism is shown to exist, it tends to be identified as an isolated phenomenon relating to a limited number of social deviants, economic instability, or the consequence of "undemocratic" traditions that are disappearing from the Canadian scene. This discourse resists the notion that racism is systemic and inherently embedded in Canada's cultural values and democratic institutions.

The Discourse of Political Correctness

"Politically correct" is defined by *Merriam-Webster's Collegiate Dictionary* as "conforming to a belief that language and practices which could offend political sensibilities (as in matters of sex or race) should be eliminated." Political correctness is, however, an elusive concept, and, as Fleras and Elliott (1996) point out, difficult to define because of its lack of tangible reference points. It is neither an ideology nor a coherent social movement.

Political correctness is a phrase that in recent years has become a central part of the public discourse across political and ideological spectrums. It is a commonplace response by neoconservatives and neoliberals. It represents an expression of their resistance to forms of social change. The demands of marginalized minorities for inclusive language and proactive policies (such as employment equity) and practices are discredited as an "overdose of political correctness." Those opposed to proactive measures that would ensure the inclusion of non-dominant voices, stories, and perspectives dismiss these concerns as the wailing and whining of radicals whose polemics (and actions) threaten the cornerstones of democratic liberalism. The phrase is commonly used by culturally conservative academics, journalists, politicians, writers, and cultural critics, and also without hesitation by many so-called "liberals" to deride the aspirations of minorities.

The discourse of political correctness is part of a larger and ongoing debate about very different visions of society and diverse paradigms of social change. It is a rhetoric that has intensified and polarized positions with respect to issues of **inclusion**, **representation** (language and images), multiculturalism, equity, racism, and sexism in universities, schools, and human-service and government agencies (Srivastava, 1996).

Toni Morrison suggests that political correctness is a "weighty phrase with a pseudo-intellectual cast" designed to make people desist from having certain kinds of discussion. It serves to stifle dissent. "The political correctness debate is really about … the power to be able to redefine. The definers want the power to name. And the defined are now taking the power away from them" (Miller, Swift, and Maggio, 1997:54).

The Discourse of Colour-Blindness

Colour-blindness or colour evasiveness is a powerful and appealing liberal discourse in which White people insist that they do not notice the skin colour of a racial-minority person. But, as Gotanda (1991) suggests, this technique of observing but not considering "race" is a "technical fiction. It is impossible not to think about a subject without having first thought about it a little" (101). The refusal to recognize that race is part of the "baggage" that people of colour carry with them, and the refusal to recognize racism as part of everyday values, policies, programs, and practices, is part of the psychological and cultural power of racial constructions (James, 1994). Colour-blindness or colour evasion leads to power evasion (Frankenberg, 1993). Dei and Calliste (2000) contend "that none of us can afford to be blind to the colour of racism" (162).

The Discourse of Equal Opportunity

This discourse suggests that all we need to do is treat everyone the same, and fairness will be ensured. This notion is based on a historical premise as follows: We all begin from the same starting point and that everyone competes on a level playing field. Society merely provides the conditions within which individuals differentially endowed can make their mark. All have an equal opportunity to succeed and the same rights. Thus, individual merit determines who will succeed in the workplace, school, politics, the arts.

This view ignores the social construction of race, in which power and privilege belongs to those who are White (among other social markers of privilege, including gender, class, sexual orientation, and able-bodiedness). Equal opportunity represents a passive approach and does not require the dismantling of White institutional power or the redistribution of White social capital (Crenshaw, 1997). This paradigm demands no form of proactive institutional or state intervention such as employment equity or anti-racism policies.

The Discourse of Blaming the Victim

If equal opportunity and racial equality are assumed to exist, then a minority population's lack of success must be attributed to some other set of conditions. One explanation used by the dominant culture is the notion that certain minority communities themselves are culturally deficient—they may be lacking intellectual prowess or be more prone to aggressive behaviour or other forms of "deviant behaviour." In this form of dominant discourse, it is assumed that certain communities (such as African Canadians) lack the motivation, education, or skills to participate fully in the workplace, educational system, and other arenas of Canadian society.

Alternatively, it is argued that the failure of certain groups to succeed and integrate into the mainstream dominant culture is largely due to recalcitrant members of these groups refusing to adapt their "traditional," "different" cultural values and norms to fit into Canadian society and making unreasonable demands on the "host" society.

The Discourse of White Victimization

In this discourse it is argued that White European immigrants also experience prejudice and discrimination in Canada. According to this view, the social system is open but all immigrant groups must expect to start at the bottom of the social and economic ladder. It is only through their own initiative that they can achieve upward mobility and thereby receive full and equal treatment. Therefore there is no need for preferential policies or programs.

This assumption is based on the traditional view that race, ethnicity, and the immigrant experience are one and the same phenomenon. It does not recognize that genetic racial features such as skin colour do not simply disappear over time. It ignores the fact that second- and third-generation Canadian people of colour continue to experience the same prejudiced attitudes and discriminatory behaviour as their parents and grandparents. They continue to be severely impeded in their opportunities for upward mobility. Equating racial **disadvantage** and discrimination with the experiences of White European immigrants ignores the importance of the history of colonization, subjugation, and **oppression** of people of colour by Canadians of European origin.

The Discourse of Reverse Racism

In a semantic reversal, those associated with the dominant culture contend that they are *now* the victims of a new form of oppression and exclusion. Anti-racism and equity policies are discredited by suggesting in strong, emotive language that they are nothing more than "apartheid in reverse," a "new inquisition," or "McCarthyite witch hunts."

Positive and proactive policies and programs are thus aligned with creeping totalitarianism and accused of incorporating the antidemocratic, authoritarian methods of the extreme right. "These are fertile times for hate-mongers and reactionaries. The defenders of the status quo have discovered a wonderful refuge in their opposition to the excesses of political correctness" (DiManno, 1993).

Those concerned with addressing racial inequalities have frequently been accused of belonging to radical, extremist groups. The implication of these reproaches is that the issue of race is being used as a cover for promoting conflict in pursuit of other, questionable political ends. Those concerned with racial injustice have been labelled radicals who are using an anti-racism platform to subvert Canada's fundamental institutions, values, and beliefs.

The Discourse of Binary Polarization

The fragmentation into "we" and "they" groups is usually framed in the context of an examination of the relative values and norms of the majority versus minority populations. "We" are the White dominant culture or the culture of the organization (police, school, workplace); "they" are the communities who are the "other," possessing "different" (undesirable) values, beliefs, and norms. "We" are law-abiding, hardworking, decent, and homogeneous. "We" are the "Canadian-Canadians" (Mackey, 1996), the "birthright Canadians" (Dabydeen, 1994). The "theys" are very different and therefore undeserving (Apple, 1993). Those marked as "other" are positioned outside of the "imagined" community (Anderson, 1983) of Canada and national identity of Canadians.

The discourse of "otherness" is supported by stereotypical images embedded in the fabric of the dominant culture. Although these stereotypes have little basis in reality, they nevertheless have a significant social impact. When minorities have no power to produce or disseminate other real and more positive images in the public domain, these stereotypes increase their vulnerability in terms of cultural, social, economic, and political participation in the mainstream of Canadian society (Pieterse, 1992).

The Discourse of Moral Panic

The economic and political destabilization and social dislocations experienced by societies such as Canada, the United States, the United Kingdom, and Germany have created a climate of uncertainty, fear, and threat. Some scholars have identified this phenomenon as "moral panic" (Husband, 1994; Hall, 1978; Cohen, 1972), in which those identified with the mainstream population or the dominant culture experience a loss of control, authority, and equilibrium. The country is described as being in crisis or under siege: "We are not who we used to be" (McFarlane, 1995:20).

This siege mentality is most evident in the public sphere, among groups such as the police, government, academia, and the media. The anti-racism initiatives of the late 1980s and early 1990s have been either significantly weakened or eliminated. Equality is being redefined—and is less and less considered the responsibility of the state. It is no longer linked to group oppression and systemic disadvantage and discrimination (Apple, 1993).

These new "moral panics" are based mainly on fears about cultural and racial differences that imperil the national culture and identity. They take the form of "propaganda" campaigns in which a group is perceived, represented, and constructed as an imminent threat to "normal, civilized" society. The subtext in the discourse of "moral panic" is almost invariably ethnic or racial exclusionism.

The Discourse of Multiculturalism: Tolerance, Accommodation, Harmony, and Diversity

The concepts of tolerance, accommodation, sensitivity, harmony, and diversity lie at the core of multicultural ideology and are firmly embedded in multicultural policy and discourse (see Chapter 11 on the state). The emphasis on tolerance and sensitivity suggests that while one must accept the idiosyncrasies of the "others," the underlying premise is that the dominant way is superior.

Within this minimal form of recognition of difference, the dominant culture creates a ceiling on tolerance, that is, it stipulates what differences are tolerable. This ceiling is reflected in responses in public opinion polls and in surveys dealing with multiculturalism (Mirchandani and Tastsoglou, 1998), in which a significant number of respondents take a position that "we" cannot tolerate too much difference because it generates dissent, disruption, and conflict. According to this view, paying unnecessary attention to "differences" leads to division, disharmony, and disorder in society. Where possible, the dominant culture attempts to accommodate "their" idiosyncratic cultural differences.

Declarations of the need for tolerance and harmony tend to conceal the messy business of structural and systemic inequality and the unequal relations of power that continue to exist in a democratic liberal society. Mohanty contends that "differences defined as asymmetrical and incommensurate cultural spheres situated within hierarchies of domination and resistance cannot be accommodated with a discourse of 'harmony in diversity'" (1993:72).

The Discourse of Liberal Values: Individualism, Truth, Tradition, Universalism, and Freedom of Expression

Democratic liberalism is distinguished by a set of beliefs that includes, among many other ideals: the primacy of individual rights over collective or group rights; the power of (one) truth, tradition, and history; an appeal to universalism; the sacredness of the principle of freedom of expression; and a commitment to human rights and equality. But as many scholars observe, liberalism is full of paradoxes and contradictions and assumes different meanings, depending on one's social location and angle of vision (Hall, 1986; Goldberg, 1993; Apple, 1993; Winant, 1997). As Parekh argues, "Liberalism is both egalitarian and inegalitarian." It simultaneously supports the unity of humankind and the hierarchy of cultures. It is both tolerant and intolerant (1986:82)." Ignatieff claims, "We live by liberal fictions"; despite the fact that human beings are "incorrigibly different ... equality is a moral story which governs our hypotheses" (1998:19).

From the perspective of the marginalized and excluded, traditional liberal values have been found wanting. In the interests of expanding liberal democratic principles and extending the promises of liberalism to those who have not enjoyed its benefits, minority communities are demanding an "affirmative" correction of historical injustices (Stam, 1993).

However, those individuals and groups who invoke the validity of alternative voices, experiences, traditions, perspectives, and histories are seen to be violating a sacred body of principles, values, and beliefs. There is only one truth, a single "authentic" history, a noble Euro-American tradition, a universal form of human understanding and expression that includes and transcends all cultural and racial boundaries.

The Discourse of National Identity

The discourse of national identity is marked by erasures, omissions, and silences. Ethnoracial minorities have been placed outside the "national project" of Canada and excluded from the "imagined community" (Anderson, 1983) of Canadian society. From Canada's earliest history, the idea of "hyphenated" Canadians has been a fundamental part of the national discourse, but it has been limited to two identities: English Canada and French Canada. The Fathers of Confederation ignored the cultural plurality that existed even at that time. Aboriginal and other cultures were omitted from the national discourse and thereby rendered invisible. Later, a category of "others" was added—but only two of these had constitutional rights.

National discourse constructs meanings and influences "our actions and our conceptions of ourselves" (Hall, 1992:292). National culture defines identity by "producing meanings about the nation with which we can identify; these are contained in the stories which are told about it, memories which connect it with its past, and the images which are constructed of it" (Hall, 1992:282).

The debate over national identity is fundamental to Canadian discourse. Canada's search for national unity is really a search for cultural stability. The question of cultural identity is influenced by the politics of difference, a politics shaped by the interplay of history, culture, race, and power. In the struggle over national identity, the dominant culture is reluctant to include identities of "others" that it has constructed, perpetuated, and used to its advantage. To discard "otherness" would in a sense be to abandon the vehicles through which inequalities and imbalances are legitimized.

Many Canadians see themselves as egalitarian and have little difficulty in rejecting the more overt expressions of racism. They may make symbolic gestures of inclusivity. However, beyond these token efforts, the struggles of people of colour are met with the arbitrary use of political, economic, and cultural institutional power in the interests of "maintaining democracy."

This book explores this fundamental tension in Canadian discourse, policies, and practices as an expression of democratic racism. Anti-racism, ethno-racial access, and equity are a necessary part of the legitimization of a new ideology requiring a commitment to a different set of values, discourses, and practices.

References

Althusser, L. (1971). "Ideology and Ideological State. *Philos Apparatuses.*" In *Lenin and Philosophy and Other Essays.* London: Monthly Review.

Anderson, B. (1983). *Imagined Communities.* London: Verso.

Apple, M. (1993). "Constructing the 'Other': Rightist Reconstructions of Common Sense." In C. McCarthy and W. Crichlow (eds.), *Race, Identity and Representation in Education.* New York and London: Routledge.

Ball, W., and J. Solomos. (1990). *Race and Local Politics.* London: Macmillan.

Billig, M., et al. (1988). *Ideological Dilemmas: A Social Psychology of Everyday Thinking.* London: Sage.

Brandt, G. (1986). *The Realization of Anti-Racist Education.* London: Falmer Press.

CCCS (Centre for Contemporary Cultural Studies). (1982). "The Organic Crisis of British Capitalism and Race." In CCCS, *The Empire Strikes Back: Race and Racism in 70's Britain.* London: Hutchinson.

Cohen, S. (1972). *Folk Devils and Moral Panics: The Creation of the Mods and Rockers.* London: MacKibbon and Kee.

Crenshaw, K. (1997). "Color-Blind Dreams and Racial Nightmares: Reconfiguring Racism in the Post-Civil Rights Era." In T. Morrison and C. Brodsky Lacour (eds.), *Birth of a Nation'Hood: Gaze, Script, and Spectacle in the O.J. Simpson Case.* New York: Pantheon Books. 97–168.

Dabydeen, Cyril. (1994). "Citizenship Is More Than a Birthright." *Toronto Star,* September 20:A23.

Dei, G. (1996). *Anti-Racism Education: Theory and Practice.* Halifax: Fernwood.

Dei, G., and A. Calliste. (eds.). (2000). "Resisting Academic Closure: Rethinking Anti-Racism Education for the New Millennium. In *Power, Knowledge and Anti-Racism Education: A Critical Reader.* Halifax: Fernwood. 162–164.

DiManno, R. (1993). *Toronto Star,* September 6.

Ellsworth, E. (1997). "Double Binds of Whiteness. In M. Fine, L. Weiss, L. Powell, and L. Mung Wong, *Off White: Readings on Race, Power and Society.* New York: Routledge. 259–269.

Essed, P. (1990). *Everyday Racism: Reports from Women of Two Cultures.* Alameda, CA: Hunter House.

Fine, M., L. Weiss, L. Powell, and L. Mung Wong. (1997). *Off White: Readings on Race, Power and Society.* New York: Routledge.

Fiske, J. (1994). *Media Matters: Everyday Culture and Political Change.* Minneapolis: University of Minnesota Press.

Fleras, A., and J. Elliott. (1992). *Multiculturalism in Canada.* Scarborough, ON: Nelson.

———. (1996). *Unequal Relations: An Introduction to Race, Ethnic and Aboriginal Dynamics in Canada.* 2nd ed. Scarborough, ON: Prentice Hall.

Frankenberg, R. (1993). *White Women, Race Matters: The Social Construction of Whiteness.* Minneapolis: University of Minnesota Press.

Gaertner, S.L. (1976). "Nonreactive Measures in Racial Attitude Research: A Focus on Liberals." In P. Katz (ed.), *Towards the Elimination of Racism.* New York: Pergamon Press.

Gaertner, S.L., and J.F. Dovidio. (1981). "Racism Among the Well Intentioned." In E.G. Clausen and J. Bermingham (eds.), *Pluralism, Racism and Public Policy.* Boston: G.K. Hall.

———. (1986). "The Aversive Forms of Racism." In S.L. Gaertner and J.F. Dovidio (eds.), *Prejudice, Discrimination and Racism.* New York: Academic Press.

Gilroy, P. (1987). *There Ain't No Black in the Union Jack.* Chicago: University of Chicago Press.

Goldberg, D.S. (ed.). (1990). *The Anatomy of Racism.* Minneapolis: University of Minnesota Press.

————. (1993). *Racist Culture: Philosophy and the Politics of Meaning*. Oxford: Blackwell.

Gotanda, N. (1991). "A Critique of 'Our Constitution Is Color-Blind.'" *Stanford Law Review* 44(1):1–73.

Gwyn, Richard. (1993). *Toronto Star*, July 18.

Hall, S. (1978). "Racism and Reaction." In *Five Views of Multi-Racial Britain*. London: Commission for Racial Equality.

———— et al. (1978). *Policing the Crisis*. London: Macmillan.

————. (1983). "The Great Moving Show." In S. Hall and M. Jacques (eds.), *The Politics of Thatcherism*. London: Lawrence and Wishart.

————. (1986). "Variants of Liberalism." In J. Donald and S. Hall (eds.), *Politics and Ideology*. Milton Keynes: Open University Press.

————. (1992). "The Question of Cultural Identity." In S. Hall, D. Held, and T. McGrew (eds.), *Modernity and Its Future*. Cambridge, UK: Polity Press in association with Open University. 273–326.

Hebridge, D. (1993). "From Culture to Hegemony." In S. During (ed.), *The Cultural Studies Reader*. London: Routledge.

Henry, F. (1978). *Dynamics of Racism in Toronto*. North York, ON: York University.

Husband, C. (1994). "Crisis of National Identity as the 'New Moral Panics': Political Agenda-Setting About Definitions of Nationhood." *New Community* (Warwick) 20(2)(January):191–206.

Ignatieff, M. (1998). "Identity Parades." *Prospect* (April):19–23.

James, C. (1994). "The Paradox of Power and Privilege: Race, Gender and Occupational Position." *Canadian Woman Studies: Race and Gender* 14(2):47–51.

Kovel, J. (1970). *White Racism: A Psychohistory*. New York: Pantheon.

Lawrence, E. (1982). "Just Plain Common Sense: The 'Roots' of Racism." In CCCS, *The Empire Strikes Back: Race and Racism in 70's Britain*. London: Hutchinson.

Mackey, E. (1996). "Managing and Imagining Diversity: Multiculturalism and the Construction of National Identity in Canada." Ph.D. thesis, Department of Social Anthropology, University of Sussex.

McConahay, J.B., and J.C. Hough, Jr. (1976). "Symbolic Racism." *Journal of Social Issues* 32(2):23–45.

McFarlane, S. (1995). "The Haunt of Race: Canada's Multiculturalism Act, the Politics of Incorporation and Writing Thru Race." *Fuse* 18(3)(Spring):18–31.

Miller, C., K. Swift, and R. Maggio. (1997). "Liberating Language." *Ms.*, September–October:51–54.

Mirchandani, K., and E. Tastsoglou. (1998). "Toward a Diversity Beyond Tolerance." Manuscript submitted to the *Journal of Status in Political Economy*.

Mohanty, T.C. (1993). *Beyond a Dream: Deferred Multicultural Education and the Politics of Excellence*. Minneapolis: University of Minnesota Press.

Parekh, B. (1986). "The 'New Right' and the Politics of Nationhood." In *The New Right: Image and Reality*. London: Runnymede Trust.

Pieterse, N.J. (1992). *White on Black: Images of Africa and Blacks in Western Popular Culture*. New Haven and London: Yale University Press.

Roman, L. (1993). "White Is a Colour!: White Defensiveness, Postmodernism, and Anti-Racist Pedagogy." In C. McCarthy and W. Crichlow (eds.), *Race, Identity, and Representation in Education*. New York: Routledge.

Sears, D., and J. McConahay, Jr. (1973). *The Politics of Violence: The New Urban Blacks and the Watts Riot*. Boston: Houghton Mifflin.

Srivastava, S. (1996). "Song and Dance? The Performance of Antiracist Workshops." *CRSA/RCSA* 33(3):291–315.

Stam, R. (1993). "From Stereotype to Discourse." *Cine-Action* 23(Fall):12–29.

Wellman, D. (1977). *Portraits of White Racism*. Cambridge: Cambridge University Press.

Wetherell, M., and J. Potter (1992). *Mapping the Language of Racism*. New York: Columbia University Press.

Winant, H. (1997). "Behind Blue Eyes: Whiteness and Contemporary U.S. Racial Politics." In M. Fine et al. (eds.), *Off White: Readings on Race, Power and Society*. New York and London: Routledge. 40–56.

Yon, D. (1995). "Unstable Terrain: Explorations in Identity, Race and Culture in a Toronto High School." Ph.D. thesis, Department of Anthropology, York University.

————. (2000). *Elusive Culture: Schooling, Race, and Identity in Global Times*. Albany: State University Press of New York.

CHAPTER 2

THEORETICAL PERSPECTIVES

Theory is always a (necessary) detour on the way to something more important.

—*Hall (1991)*

Today, the theory of race has been utterly transformed. The socially constructed
status of the concept of race ... is widely recognized, so much so that it is now often
conservatives who argue that race is an illusion. ... Our central work is to focus
attention on the continuing significance and changing meaning of race.

—*Omi and Winant (1993)*

This chapter reviews the substantial theoretical literature on the subject of race and racism. It begins with theories of biological and cultural superiority and ends with sophisticated societal paradigms. Before beginning a brief review of some of the critical developments in the history of racial theory, however, we raise the critical question of how social science theory has dealt with the subjects of race and racism. The theories are then presented and—to expedite the review—the theories are presented chronologically and identify the major trends in the United Kingdom, the United States, and Canada. In addition to conventional theories, the newer approaches of *critical race theory*, cultural studies, discourse analysis, and Whiteness studies are briefly presented. The various forms of racism—individual, systemic, and ideological—are defined. The chapter concludes by examining some of the methodological and measurement problems in the study of racism.

Introduction

Before discussing theories used by the social science disciplines to analyze issues of race and racism, a comment on the general perspective taken by these disciplines to this subject is required. For the most part, and until very recently, social science research on race and racism has reinforced the marginality and exclusion of people of colour especially in modern industrialized societies. While not being directly or overtly racist—with some exceptions to be discussed below—social science theory and methodology has, for the most part, developed theories and explanation about the dynamics of society that uncritically accept the status quo. Until the rise of critical theory in the late 1970s and 1980s—

theories that directly challenged, questioned, and problematized the status quo—the positions of ethnic, but especially racial, minorities were uncritically accepted into static spaces.

This discussion begins with some of the most important theoretical developments in the social sciences and, especially, in sociology and anthropology that were dominant in the early and mid-twentieth century. One of the main theories was functionalism, dominant in the early to mid-twentieth century. It is based on a consensus model of society—one that envisions the smooth, orderly, and stable nature of societies. The starting point of functionalist theory is that all societies have certain basic needs or "functional" requirements—which must be met if a society is to survive. It looks at whole societies and examines the ways in which its parts contribute to the successful or unsuccessful functioning of the entire social order. A common value system holds the parts in dynamic equilibrium to the whole; these values include **equality of opportunity**, Christian morality, materialism, democracy, and productivity.

Against this theoretical background, assimilationism developed in response to the particular historical events in the United States which experienced, beginning in the nineteenth century and continuing onward, a huge rise in immigration. The need to absorb, integrate, or assimilate these newly arrived people, primarily from Europe, demanded that the framework provided by functionalist theory provide answers to what rapidly became a practical problem for policy-makers at all levels of society. Assimilationism therefore posited the notion that assimilation into mainstream society was the final stage for ethnic and racial groups. The theory was largely based on the study of the adaptation of ethnic groups of European origin, but it was also applied to racial groups, primarily (in the terminology of the time) "American Negroes." The dominance of these conservative consensus models of society led to an uncritical acceptance of things as they were. While liberal lip service was paid to equality of opportunity and the need to ameliorate the poor conditions under which American Blacks lived, research and policy did not critically challenge their position. For much of the life of the nineteenth and the twentieth centuries, conservative status quo–oriented theories strongly influenced the construction of knowledge produced in the social sciences. Race and racism was understood according to the following propositions: (1) race and racial differences were still accepted as biological factors that separated the human species and (2) most of the research on social relations in society, while attempting to understand the dynamics of stratification that led to the disadvantaged positioning of people of colour and primarily Blacks, did very little to challenge that position. Functionalism led to separate and disparate case studies of Black life, especially in the United States, while its later sister, assimilationism, merely assumed that they too would be integrated in the natural order of social change. Even in the United Kingdom, a "race relations" model rather than one that emphasized the unequal distribution of power relations influenced much of the early work on race and racism. This essentially conservative theoretical tradition remained undisputed until the late 1960s, with the emergence of critical theory informed by a neo-Marxian approach.

Today, despite the strong influence of critical theory and its many important theoretical and empirical outcomes, there is still a considerable body of theory and research in the social sciences that is strongly influenced by what has been called the "new racism." This "school" includes not only academics such as the University of Western Ontario's psychology professor Philippe Rushton (1995) and other academic racists, but also scholars who now focus on, as the African-American sociologist Melvin Thomas names it, "anything but race" theories (2000). These theories provide an explanation of the continued marginalized and disadvantaged status of people of colour in modern industrialized societies. These "anything but race" perspectives focus on social class, essentialized notions of cultural deficiencies (e.g., cognitive ability, lack of work ethic, and lack of morality), human capital, spatial mismatch, and family structure, while ignoring or paying lip service only to structural inequalities and the role of racism.

Social class rather than **racial discrimination** has resurfaced as a major variable in attempting to explain the continued marginality of African Americans. William Wilson's influential book *The Declining Significance of Race* (1980), first published in the late seventies, emphasized the importance of race over class by suggesting that the Blacks are overrepresented in the lower classes because past discrimination has denied them the opportunity for skill enhancement and education necessary for social class mobility today. But, Wilson goes on to contend, because a growing number of Blacks have become mobile and created a substantial middle class, discrimination can no longer be blamed for the continued economic and social stagnation of the Black lower classes. While this argument has currency in some academic circles, it is contradicted by a large number of empirical studies and indices demonstrating that race is still the primary determinant of the quality of life for Blacks in the United States. Wilson's book and the theory upon which it is based were very popular especially among Whites because they deemphasized their racism.

Cultural deprivation is one of the most frequently cited factors used in recent times to explain away the marginalized status of people of colour in North America, the United Kingdom, and parts of Europe. Thus, cultural patterns that include laziness, lack of motivation, lax morals leading to promiscuity, and other such factors are blamed for the low position of Caribbean peoples in the United Kingdom and of African Americans. These same cultural explanations have surfaced in the popular discourse in Canada. A central theme in this discourse is that Blacks have a weak and dysfunctional family structure that influences the development of an "underclass" composed of uneducated, unskilled individuals who have a propensity for criminal activity.

Much social science research puts the blame for marginalization on the victim.

The Influence of Physical Science on the Social Sciences: Academic Racism

The physical sciences also played a key role, especially in the nineteenth century, and that strongly influenced theoretical and methodological developments in the social sciences. For example, the development of Social Darwinism—especially physical anthropology's focus on classifying human beings according to racial genetic characteristics and their use of measurement, especially brain measurements, to define human intelligence—had great influence. Much of social science came to believe that social evolution followed similar patterns and that some "races" were naturally less intelligent than others. In the early twentieth century, this culminated in the powerful role of the eugenics movement with its emphasis on the need to breed intelligence. While eugenics-inspired beliefs have largely disappeared from the social and physical science disciplines, remnants of such ideology have resurfaced today in the form of academic racism. Respected scholars in their disciplines, such as Jensen (1997), Eysenck (1971), and others have maintained that Blacks are less intelligent than other "races." More recently, Herrnstein and Murray's *The Bell Curve*, published in 1994, claims to use scientific data to prove that Blacks are inferior to Whites. In Canada, psychologist J. Philippe Rushton (1995) follows the same ideological path, arguing that there exists a hierarchical racial classification system that accounts for significant differences in intelligence and other behavioural traits.

Another major movement that originated in the physical sciences but influenced social science, at least to some extent, is that of sociobiology. *Sociobiology*, essentially founded by Edward Wilson who published a book by that title in 1975, is based on the notion that all human behaviour is genetically determined. Aside from the many criticisms levelled against the sociobiological approach to human behaviour, it is evident that any genetically based theory will provide greater impetus to scientific racism, because the critical factors such as poverty, inequality, and racial discrimination—all social variables—to explain disadvantage are deemphasized. Sociobiologists contend that such social factors are present in societies because of genetic or biological conditioning, so the argument becomes circular; but in any event the end result of biological explanations reinforces the ideology and practice of racism in modern societies.

The use of biological, genetic, or morphological models is also related to the history of social science methodologies. For example, Galton's (cited in Zuberi, 2001) statistical methodology was based on isolating human differences and especially those related to race. He was a strong and early defender of eugenics, committed to the idea that human evolution might be improved by selective mating practices. Other founding statisticians such as Karl Pearson and Ronald Fisher held similar views, and in fact it has been argued that eugenics ideas were at the centre of the development of statistical methods (cited in Zuberi, 2001). Eighteenth- and nineteenth-century natural science was also committed to positivism, which maintains that the natural world is governed by objective laws that can also be applied to the social world. The influence of positivism, with its emphasis on probability, has been maintained in much of the social sciences even today. These principles served to reify the concept of race. Race was understood as a "material reality" that lent itself to scientific observation. Race was not even studied as a biological or genetic "fact" but only as a morphological element. In other words, it was studied or classified in terms of obvious observable features such as skin colour and hair texture. Racial classifications could therefore be easily developed because one merely had to look at an individual for proper classification.

All these influences have played a role in academic racism. More importantly, however, the very concept of racial classification must be challenged, because it is based on a simplistic, reified, and not necessarily accurate understanding of human variation. While racial classifications such as those used in South Africa and parts of the United States for political purposes are no longer imposed on the population, the concept of classification is still routinely used to divide statistical samples in the course of much of social science research.[1]

Even today, the old theory of assimilationism is being revived, especially in the United States. Theories put forward by Portes and Rumbaut (2001) in their influential books deal with the subject of the social dangers faced by second-generation immigrant youth. Their many other publications are now shaping or determining public perception of African Americans, Haitian Americans, Puerto Ricans, Nicaraguans, and other immigrant groups. Developing a theory called the "segmented assimilation model," these authors and their many colleagues maintain that, for example, Cubans in the United States have become economically and socially mobile largely by using networking to maximize the social capital available to them, whereas African Americans, without a pool of social capital, have been unable to assimilate. While the social capital argument has much merit, the lack of it in Black communities is not the result of their poor work habits or lack of ethics but rather the racial discrimination that has not allowed a pool of social capital to develop. Thus, this more sophisticated version of the older assimilation theory falls prey to the same problem: the inability to understand that it is inequality and racism that is behind the disadvantaged social positioning of African Americans. Portes and Rumbaut (ibid.) extend their argument to other groups newly arrived in the United States, such as Haitians and Nicaraguans, who are in danger of becoming an underclass and whose children "show alarming signs of dissonant acculturation ... [because] they embrace rather than shun the culture of the ghetto" (quoted in Alonso-Donate, 2002). Many of these children live in close proximity to African Americans and "tough" Latino neighbourhoods whose culture they respect and want to emulate, and as a result "second-generation" Nicaraguans "show symptoms of decline—a social darkening of sorts" (ibid.). The racist connotations of such a conclusion are obvious. In terms of policy applications, Portes and Rumbaut call on social scientists, community activists, and government at all levels to develop a political agenda that protects their children from the evils associated with "dissonant acculturation"—read "Black culture." More specifically, they advocate private bilingual schools for second-generation immigrant children, because this is a primary vehicle for the "institutional promotion of selective acculturation." Their "segmented assimilation model" has been generally well received and may even influence both theoretical and policy orientations in Canada.

This brief overview highlights some theoretical developments in the social sciences—both at earlier points in time and in the contemporary period—to show that theory and methodology in these fields, however inadvertently, promote and reinforce some aspects of racism. It once again makes the point that these disciplines, despite the position still taken by some hardliners, are not value-free and their perspectives and even methods are influenced by the societal climate in which they live and work.

From the Nineteenth Century to the Mid-Twentieth Century: Race and Racial Classification

Race as a biological classification has a long history, but in the nineteenth century the biological classification of human beings into "races" became prominent. When social theorists such as Herbert Spencer began to apply the concept of race to social categories, a new school, Social Darwinism, was created. Although Social Darwinists did not intend their work to be racist, others such as Joseph-Arthur de Gobineau and Houston Stewart Chamberlain applied the theory to construct a school of social racism in which the supremacy of the White race and European civilization was dramatically featured (Banton, 1983).

Throughout the nineteenth century and most of the twentieth, the term "race" was used not only to distinguish between groups but also to establish a hierarchical division of races. Physical appearances were thought to correlate with social, psychological, intellectual, moral, and cultural differences. Characteristics such as skin colour were used to establish a racial classification system. This racial order and discourse was then used to rationalize and legitimize the exploitation and oppression of racial minorities.

Not until the mid-twentieth century was the concept of the inferiority of people of colour fundamentally altered. In the 1950s and 1960s, many biologists and social scientists met to produce new theoretical models to explain "race." In addition, a number of conferences were organized by the United Nations Educational, Scientific and Cultural Organization to address the issue (UNESCO, 1950). Clear messages and definitive statements emerged from these forums to challenge popular myths about race. There was a consensus among scientists that all humans belonged to a single species, that is, one race.

The concepts of race and racial classification can be rejected as unnecessary and unscientific, because they add nothing to the understanding of the human species. Humanity cannot be divided into discrete portions distinguished by biological properties (Rex, 1983). All races are mixtures of populations, and "the term 'pure' race is an absurdity" (Mayr, 1963). In fact, some social scientists have suggested that "race" should be removed from the vocabulary of the field (Banton, 1977). It has been called "man's most dangerous myth" (Montagu, 1964).

However, the consequences of the discourse on race and the social relations within which it has been embedded for the past two centuries cannot be ignored. Human societies continue to function as if races do exist. Racial differentiation continues to affect all areas of social interaction. For all practical purposes, then, race is not so much a biological phenomenon as a social myth that has had devastating consequences as one of the most important causes of human inequality.

The 1950s and 1960s: Assimilation and Integration

Race relations have a long history in the United States. Park (1950) and his associates at the University of Chicago developed the concept of a race relations "cycle" in which **assimilation** into mainstream society was the final stage for ethnic and racial groups. The theory was largely based on the study of the adaptation of **ethnic groups** of European origin. It was also applied to racial groups, primarily "American Negroes."

The assimilationist perspective, which conceptualized the **integration** of all groups into mainstream society, was popular for many years. An earlier important work in the assimilationist tradition was *An American Dilemma*, by the Swedish scholar Gunnar Myrdal (1944), which propounded the view that prejudice and racial conflict were a "White problem" that could only be resolved by changing the attitudes and behaviours of Whites toward Blacks. The "dilemma" had occurred, according to this pioneering work, because America had allowed a series of racial discriminatory practices and policies to develop that were in direct conflict with the "American Creed," which emphasized freedom, equality, and justice. Myrdal was the first to call attention to this fundamental value conflict.

In another important theoretical development stemming from the discipline of social psychology, the distinction between prejudice—the attitudes held by individuals—and discrimination—the behaviour prompted by these prejudices—was examined by Gordon Allport's seminal work *The Nature of Prejudice* (1954).

The psychological nature of prejudice as defined by Allport was reviewed by Black scholars such as Jones, who in *Prejudice and Racism* (1972) took the view that attitudes are less important than unequal power relations and institutional practices. However, other social psychologists, such as Gaertner and Dovidio, and McConahay and Hough, moved beyond the study of prejudice and began to develop theories of racism (see Chapter 1).

Another earlier development of some theoretical importance was the work of Frantz Fanon, who, influenced by Marxian, Freudian, and existential philosophy, published *Black Skin, White Masks* (Fanon, 1967). In this work, he called attention to the symbolic analysis of racism and dealt with the duality between Blacks and Whites as expressed in real and symbolic terms. As well, Fanon called attention to the oppressive role of colonization in structuring relations between racial groups.

The Late 1960s and 1970s: From Race Relations to Racism

In the 1960s, Black scholars in the United States were instrumental in changing the focus from "race relations," with its assimilationist, value-conflict approach in which attitudinal prejudice was stressed, to "racism." This shift in perspective resulted in a focus on power relations in which social, economic, and political inequalities between groups become the centre of attention. It examined in greater depth the role of institutions in both the public and the private sector.

A landmark in the understanding of structural racism was the publication in 1967 of *Black Power*, by Stokely Carmichael and Charles Hamilton. The authors defined racism as "the predication of decisions and policies on considerations of race for purposes of subordinating a racial group" (Drake, 1991:33). They also drew an important distinction between individual and institutional racism. Whereas the former related to individual attitudes and behaviours, the latter drew attention to the importance of institutions in creating and maintaining policies and practices that, even inadvertently, may exclude a group and result in unequal distributions of economic, social, and political power. Later, the term "systemic" racism came to mean any form of discriminatory policy or practice in a system, whether advertent or inadvertent.

The impetus for the development of institutional or systematic racism came from the mercantilist expansion of European countries into Asia, Africa, and the Americas.

> The empirical evidence … supports the view that prejudice and discrimination based upon skin colour existed [before European expansion] but were not accompanied by any systematic doctrines of racial inferiority or superiority, that is, "racism." … Nor were colour prejudice and discrimination institutionalized as structural principles defining systems of slavery, caste, or class. Slavery is a phenomenon that has existed in many times and places without any connection with either skin colour prejudice or racism. (Drake, 1991:7)

Marxist Orientations: The Growth of Critical Race Theory

During the 1950s, writings on racism, especially in the United Kingdom, tended to focus on race relations. Assimilationists were, however, increasingly challenged by a number of theorists who applied Marxian perspectives to their analysis of race relations. Since neither Karl Marx nor Friedrich Engels wrote about race (or gender, for that matter), most neo-Marxists subsumed issues of race and racism into the more traditional class analysis. A prominent Marxist writing in the 1950s argued that modern racism was a product of capitalism and provided European countries with a rationale for exploiting "native people" and their resources (Cox, 1976).

More recently, however, several important theoretical developments in the United Kingdom have inspired considerable controversy. Partially in reaction to the traditional functionalist,[2] assimilationist "race relations" approach, there is a strong neo-Marxist thrust apparent in the writings of Miles and Phizacklea (1984) and others. Neo-Marxists in the United Kingdom, the United States, and Canada have explored the links between immigrant workers and racism by highlighting the exploitation of wage labour, capital accumulation, and resultant class division. Rex (1983), one of the pioneers in the field in Britain, has attempted to bridge functionalism with a neo-Marxist approach, and Marxist-inspired writers such as Hall et al. (1978) have gained prominence. There is a continuing controversy in the U.K. literature with respect to the primacy of class versus the autonomy of race in the analysis of racism.

Another important perspective, largely stimulated by the work of Solomos (1987, 1993) and Black scholars associated with the Centre for Contemporary Cultural Studies (CCCS, 1982) in Birmingham, emphasizes the role of the state in developing a "politics of racism."

Whereas traditional Marxists give primacy to class and the means of production, neo-Marxists focus on the process of racialization that occurs in capitalist systems. Thus Canadian scholars such as Bolaria and Li (1988:7) note that "race problems begin as labour problems." Racism as an ideology therefore emerged particularly in earlier periods of history in colonial societies. This analysis of racism argues that because capitalist employers needed large pools of labour to maximize their profits, racism served as a rationale for labour exploitation.

Satzewich (1989), writing about racism in Canadian immigration practices, argues that racism is "an ideology imposed from above by those who own the means of production on those who do not: racism acts to mystify social reality, justifies the exploitation of certain groups of peoples' labour power, and contributes to the maintenance of the status quo." He stresses the relationship between racism and immigrant labour in industrial societies, including Canada. According to this view, racist ideology is preserved in order to maintain a cheap labour supply. Racism is something imposed from above, from the privileged members of society, and is received by the lower orders.

There are a number of weaknesses in this approach; the main one is that it does not apply to all situations. For example, racism can work to the disadvantage of employers, particularly with respect to workforce disruptions and workforce harassment based on race. It says little, if anything, about racism and other divisions in the working class.

Neo-Marxist approaches are also popular in the United States. The debate about race and class, in particular, is still an important issue. For example, Franklin (1991:xiii) poses the question: Is the subordinate position of the Black population ultimately derived from the stigma of colour, or is it due to the Black population's inferior class or economic position?

Franklin argues that the choice of emphasis influences Blacks' status as well as the nature of discrimination in the United States. Moreover, choosing one or the other of the race–class dichotomy influences the policies and strategies for overcoming racial inequity. Franklin believes that only by creating equality in income and job allocations will the "dominant–subordinate" patterns that maintain racism be eliminated. He looks to the revitalization of American cities, where most African Americans live, to bring this about.

In the United Kingdom, Miles and Phizacklea (1984) attempted to refine some of these earlier notions while maintaining that race and race relations emerge from class—as an epiphenomenon of class and its relation to the means of production. They note that a high demand for labour characterized the British economy during the 1970s and 1980s. People of colour from the Commonwealth provided the necessary labour, but they were relegated to lower-level semiskilled and unskilled jobs. Thus, part of the working class became racialized. Race, in this model, is an ideological construction rather than an analytical category. The primary focus should be on the capitalist relations of production, which become more important than race (Ben-Tovin and Gabriel, 1986).

A more recent Marxist-influenced approach considers racism and other forms of oppression as part of the hegemonic order. This approach has been particularly well received in the United Kingdom, most notably by Stuart Hall (1991). Although Hall considers race a construct, he argues that it cannot be reduced to classicism or any other phenomenon but must be understood as part of the broad socioeconomic and political context within which it flourishes: race and class have an interactive relationship.

In attempting to bridge several neo-Marxian approaches, Rex focused on "race relations situations," which he defined as situations in which two or more groups with distinct identities and recognisable characteristics are forced by economic and political circumstances to live together in society. … There is a high degree of conflict between the groups and ascriptive criteria are used to mark out the members of each group in order that one group may pursue one of a number of hostile policies against the other. … [T]he ascriptive allocation of roles and rights referred to are [sic] justified in terms of some kind of deterministic theory … scientific, religious, historical, ideological or sociological. (1983:159–60)

Rex and his colleagues attempted to analyze racism by specifying the situations in which it occurs, including those in which race is not a factor. For example, the conflict in Ireland, which is largely based on ethnicity rather than race, would nevertheless qualify as a "race-relations situation" according to this view. Rex's primary aim was to call attention to the unequal access of Black migrants in the United Kingdom to goods and services as well as to examine the consequences of inequality among both the White and Black working classes (Rex and Moore, 1967; Rex and Tomlinson, 1979).

Critical race theory (CRT) emerged as a theory and movement led by legal scholars in the mid-1970s. It was developed to apply to the legal system and provided a counter-legal discourse of civil rights. CRT is based on a critique of liberalism and argues that critical legal theory fails to address the racism embedded in the fabric of American society. It distinguishes itself from mainstream legal scholarship in a number of ways but, perhaps most significantly, it is founded on the concept that racism is "normal," not aberrant (Delgado, 1995:xiv). Later, the theory was expanded to challenge conceptions of antidiscrimination policies that do not take fully into account the complex linkages between race, class, and gender in structuring the everyday racialized experiences of African Americans in other sectors and systems such as education and the media (Ladson-Billings, 1998). Another important contribution of critical race theorists is their emphasis on the role of narrative/storytelling to analyze the nature, dynamics, and impact of racism. CRT theorists argue that (victims') stories offer the necessary context for understanding feelings and experiences, interpreting myths and misconceptions, deconstructing beliefs and commonsense understandings regarding race, and unpacking the ahistorical and acontextual nature of law and other "science" that renders the voices of the marginalized group members mute. The role of "voice" therefore is central to a critical race approach (Williams, 1991; Bell, 1992).

In summary, a basic change in perspective occurred in the late 1960s and 1970s—from the assimilationist race relations approach in both the United States and the United Kingdom to an emphasis on racism.[3] Analysts concluded that "it was not black people who should be examined but white society; it was not a question of educating blacks and whites for integration, but of fighting institutional racism; it was not race relations that was the field of study, but racism" (Bourne and Sivanandan, 1974:339).

The 1980s: Critical Race Theory Continued and the Anti-Racism Movement

Another important shift in the study of race relations occurred in the 1980s. Although many still use the term "racism" to describe the social construction of the biological concept of race, the designation "anti-racism" has taken on some currency.

The word "race"—however positively used (e.g., in "multiracial education")—validates the basic ideas upon which racism is built (Brandt, 1986). Its use negatively influences the development of both policy and practices. Therefore, a more appropriate vocabulary would include "anti-racism," which counters the notion of "races."

The development of a theoretical framework underlying anti-racism focuses on an integrative and critical approach to the examination of the discourses of race and racism and an analysis of the systems of differential and unequal treatment (Calliste, 1996). It is also "an educational political action-oriented strategy for institutional and systemic change to address racism and the interlocking systems of social oppression" (Dei, 1996:25).

"Anti-racism" suggests, in the first instance, that racist institutional policies and practices are the locus of the problem of racism in contemporary society. Thus, in a general sense, anti-racism refers to measures and mechanisms designed—by the state, institutions, organizations, groups, and individuals—to counteract racism. Some social scientists point out that the aims of anti-racism are, by definition, oppositional: its intention is to oppose any organizational or institutional policy or practice that oppresses, represses, or disenfranchises members of a racial group (Brandt, 1986). An anti-racism praxis is oppositional to White hegemony and the attending social, economic, and political interests of the dominant culture (Dei, 1996). At the same time, anti-racism examines the meaning of Whiteness and the power and privilege of White skin, which is largely invisible to those who possess it (McIntosh, 1990; Fine et al., 1997).

A further important dimension of anti-racism theory and practice is a critique of liberalism. Relying on traditional liberal principles, concepts, and approaches (such as "individualism," "equal opportunity," "colour-blindness," or "education") is flawed because it focuses on incremental change rather than on the more radical notion of transforming social action (Crenshaw, 1997).

Anti-racism is a strong trend in both the United Kingdom and the United States, and more recently in Canada. Anti-racism education in these jurisdictions is aimed primarily at dismantling structures and systems that have generated and perpetuated racial barriers and inequities in the policies, programs, and practices of the educational system. Anti-racism also targets administrative procedures that exclude racial-minority educators from full and equal participation in educational institutions. It assumes that a system of inequality exists and that legislation, policy-making, program implementation, and monitoring are required to dismantle it.

Anti-racism theory provides a vehicle for critically examining the role of both the state and societal institutions (such as legislative and bureaucratic agencies, the workplace, schools, justice, and the media) in reproducing racial, gender, and class-based inequalities. It recognizes the need to address the social construction of difference and the interlocking systems of oppression that result from these beliefs. Anti-racism situates power relations at the centre of the analysis of race and social difference. It focuses on the urgent need for a social system that is more representative, equitable, inclusive, and capable of responding to the concerns and aspirations of marginalized communities (Calliste and Dei, 2000).

Social Research in Canada: Ethnicity, Multiculturalism, and Racism

The field of race relations and its recent emphasis on racism and anti-racist approaches are often combined with studies of ethnicity and multiculturalism (Frideres, 1989). In North American universities, for example, "Race and Ethnic Relations" has been a popular course in sociology. This approach assumes that race and ethnicity are closely related and that a racial group is simply another kind of ethnic group.

Thus a textbook in this field may include the study of Greeks, Italians, Scots, Germans, Blacks, and Chinese. Its assimilationist perspective suggests that the experiences of all groups are similar. In Canada, the experiences of European immigrants who arrived here after 1945 and who suffered discrimination are often cited. It is implied that they overcame discrimination because they were industrious and worked hard, and that this eased their eventual adaptation to Canadian society. This view suggests that, in the long run, race and colour will become unimportant in much the same way that ethnic origins become less important as time goes on and generations change.

The study of race and ethnic relations gradually began to give way to the study of ethnicity. American scholars in particular noticed that people whose ancestors had migrated to the United States in the last part of the nineteenth century and in the early twentieth century were reclaiming their origins. Ethnicity, it was discovered, is not totally lost as generations change. Third- and fourth-generation immigrants who had successfully integrated experienced a renewed interest in their origins (Reitz, 1980). Moreover, some ethnic cultural patterns, particularly food habits, had carried over to successive generations. Meanwhile, the United States was receiving migrants from countries such as Mexico, Puerto Rico, and other Hispanic countries. These groups continued to value their ethnic origins and culture in the face of racism directed against them and their relative exclusion from American institutions.

An important work establishing the credibility of the study of ethnicity was Glazer and Moynihan's *Ethnicity: Theory and Experience* (1975), which defined the field of study as "all the groups of a society characterized by a distinctive sense of difference owing to culture and descent." Ethnicity was a central concept in understanding the many subgroups in society and was as important as social class as a segmenting variable. In this formulation, race and colour were not considered important factors in maintaining ethnicity. It essentially ignored the differential treatment that racial minorities would continue to experience. In response, Black scholars took the view that emphasizing ethnicity was simply another way of not dealing with the central issue of racism.

Race and ethnicity are often considered to be closely related because both variables differentiate groups in plural or heterogeneous societies. However, considering the two concepts as equal partners, or tagging race onto ethnicity, subsumes race under ethnicity. Ethnicity involves a notion of blood, kinship, a common sense of belonging, and often a common geographic or national origin. It refers to the social origins of groups, whereas race refers to the biological status of groups and the social construction of racism, which often follows.

Race and ethnicity do overlap at times, particularly in areas in which Blacks and Whites are members of the same ethnic group. The most obvious example occurs in the United States, where both racial groups are ethnically American yet do not share equally in the distribution of wealth, power, and privilege. It is not surprising, therefore, that those who have a strong commitment to the elimination of racism perceive ethnicity studies as drawing attention away from racism. This belief has affected Black studies programs at American universities:

> There was pressure on some campuses to transform [Black Studies programs] into Ethnic Studies programs. In some instances, Black Studies publications were reconceived as Ethnic Studies publications. ... One response to the Black Consciousness and Black Power movements in the United States was to try to deracialize them, to argue that the Black Experience was similar to that of European ethnic groups and that the passage of time would make race and colour increasingly irrelevant. (Drake, 1991:59)

In the United Kingdom, a similar movement toward multiculturalism has taken place, particularly in the schools, where multicultural education consists of learning about the heritage and cultures of people rather than dealing with structural racism. One of the most powerful critics of that movement notes that

> anti-racism in the seventies was only fought and resisted in the community, in the localities, behind the slogan of a Black politics and the Black experience. In that moment, the enemy was ethnicity. The enemy had to be what we called "multiculturalism." Because multiculturalism was precisely what I called the exotic. The exotica of difference. Nobody would talk about racism but they were prepared to have "international evenings" when we would all come and cook our native dishes, sing our own native songs and appear in our own native costumes. (Hall, 1991:56)

In describing the situation in the United Kingdom, Hall equates the concepts of ethnicity and multiculturalism. In Canadian studies, however, multiculturalism has a more applied meaning because its main impetus comes from the state, in the form of federal legislation. There has been some work on ethnicity in Canada (e.g., Breton, 1989; Isajiw, 1997; Bibby, 1990; Anderson and Frideres, 1981), but more attention has been paid to multiculturalism (e.g., Fleras and Elliott, 1992, 1996; Kymlicka, 1998).

The 1990s: Cultural Studies and Discourse Analysis

One of the most intriguing theoretical developments in the social sciences in recent years has been the growth of a field of inquiry called **cultural studies**. Strongly influenced by postmodern perspectives, it is an approach to the study of culture that began in the United Kingdom more than twenty years ago because it was recognized that the traditional disciplines that study culture—anthropology, sociology, history, literature, and so on—had become so fragmented and formalized into separate disciplines that culture came to be studied in disparate pieces (During, 1994). Moreover, traditional academic disciplines and their practitioners were isolated from the public sphere, where popular culture, one of the distinguishing characteristics of postmodern society, has its nexus.

The field of cultural studies encourages a critical examination of dominant culture and an effective resistance to its hegemonic control. It is inherently oppositional in its approach to dominance. Although it has been difficult to define the boundaries of this field because of its overwhelming subject matter, a useful approach emphasizes the function of cultural studies

> largely as a term of convenience for a fairly dispersed array of theoretical and political positions which, however widely divergent they might be in other respects, share a commitment to examining cultural practices from the point of view of their interaction with, and within, relations of power. (Bennett, 1992:23)

Of major concern to the field of cultural studies are questions relating to race, national identity, and ethnicity as these operate in a transnational, new world order. The increasing movement of people and ideas between nations has not only created conditions of multiculturalism and diversity in countries that had earlier enjoyed a monocultural existence; it has also created concerns about race, ethnicity, and the politics of diversity. This new field breaks with the conventions of traditional social science in many ways.

In its emphasis on subjectivity, it studies culture in relation to the way it affects the daily experiences of people rather than as an abstraction divorced from the reality of everyday experience. Culture is not a social construct, nor is it meant to be defined by high culture and its forms. Cultural studies analyze the impact of societal inequality on the lives of those most affected, such as women and racial minorities. It is very much concerned with diversity's effects on mainstream traditional institutions and organizations and with how ethno-racial and women's groups are maintaining and elaborating their autonomous values, identities, and cultural products. Thus, cultural studies affirm otherness and difference in what has been called the "politics of survival" (During, 1994) and the "politics of difference" (West, 1990). This approach is part of a theory of society in which difference and otherness are central and in which the dynamic of pluralism and heterogeneity are emphasized. Theoretical explanation in the field of cultural studies does not necessarily depend upon the forces of capitalism or a free-market economy as central causes of structural inequality but works toward creating conditions of autonomy for all "othered" groups. In this view, society does not need a total revolution in its mode of production, but it does need to create conditions of equality and equity. Cultural studies focuses on a critical view of multiculturalism in denying the singular or privileged position of the traditional Eurocentric state and its culture, and it values alternative forms of culture and their expression.

The Centre for Contemporary Cultural Studies at the University of Birmingham, which emerged after World War II, was the locus for this new interdisciplinary framework that initially drew on sociology, literary criticism, and history for its disciplinary grounding. One of its most important contributions was to conceptualize the area of "popular culture" as the location or site of resistance for marginalized and powerless groups such as women, racial minorities, gays and lesbians, and others on the margins of society. The Centre was grounded in British New Left politics, which emerged in postwar Britain, and its founders, Richard Hoggart among others, were influential figures in the New Left movement. As a result, its intellectual tradition is strongly Marxist-influenced, and class relations were the guiding framework for their studies of popular culture, which were seen as the focus of class expression and agency. The Centre's intellectual perspectives can be described as "cultural Marxism," in that culture is the site in which inequality and hierarchy are produced and contested. Divisions in modern societies are manifested along lines of class, gender, ethnicity, and race; and it is in the area of culture that classes, and especially underclasses, may begin to show resistance.

In the late 1960s, Stuart Hall became director of the Centre and its focus, while retaining its Marxist nexus, added the deconstructionalist approach of Jacques Derrida to their work. Thus, the study, examination, and unpacking of the rhetoric and assumptions within "text"—including media, literary, film, and other popular cultural texts—occupied their research. Hall's classic *Policing the Crisis* (1978) in which he demonstrated that the media produced a stereotypic image of the black "mugger" criminal exemplified this approach.

Cultural studies migrated to the United States and somewhat later to Canadian universities, where it has been a useful discipline to bring together ethnic studies, women's studies, research on race and racism, and les/bi/gay/queer studies. All of these disciplines are positioned within the framework of poststructuralism. The analysis of text is combined with more traditional ethnographic methodologies, but there is also, as in the United Kingdom, an emphasis on subjectivity and qualitative methods of analysis.

Another significant feature of the cultural studies approach both in Canada and in the United Kingdom is its opposition to the values of the "New Right" and its moral agenda, which emphasizes the preservation of traditional values and the maintenance of existing power relations. A cultural studies approach criticizes the homogeneous image of the national culture and its images of a monocultural society. It supports a competing set of insurgent values with an emphasis on collective rights and freedoms. Cultural studies also underscore the important role of popular culture in the transmission and reproduction of values. The traditional difference between "high" and popular culture, so characteristic of Eurocentric discourses of the past, is deemphasized. There is also a strong emphasis on identifying those ideologies operating in a specific **cultural artifact** or project that make inequalities appear natural and just, thus marking the ways in which power and domination are encoded in cultural **texts**, images, and narratives (Kellner, 1995).

Cultural studies provide a framework for critically examining the artifacts of contemporary culture, including cultural institutional policies, practices, norms, and values that affect cultural production. Systems of representation such as film, theatre, publishing, the visual arts, music, media, and academia are the subject of public scrutiny and cultural criticism by those who have been marginalized, excluded, and silenced by Eurocentric cultural traditions and practices (Hutcheon, 1988, 1991). Indeed, a critique of the discursive practices buried within these cultural institutions provides an illuminating and powerful form of analysis. The discursive approach incorporates an analysis of how forms of discourse create, reinforce, and reproduce systems of inequality.

Discourse and Discourse Analysis

Central to a cultural studies perspective is the notion of **discourse**, which stems from Foucault's seminal work (1980). "Discourse" is, however, elusive and difficult to define. There are at least two basic meanings of the term. It is most closely associated with language and the written or oral text, and it emphasizes the relationship between the speaker and those being addressed, or between the writer and the reader. Sometimes, discourse refers more narrowly to the differences between spoken dialogue and written text. Or it may refer to the style of language used in a particular situation ("e.g., newspaper discourse, classroom discourse," Fairclough, 1992:3). Fiske (1994) defines the notion of discourse as language in social use and observes that it is a language marked by its history of domination, subordination, and resistance and shaped by the social conditions of those who use it.

Discourse analysis goes beyond the social origins of linguistic forms, however, since it also includes those sets of social relations ordered by a particular discourse. Thus, in addition to texts, there are values, norms, attitudes, and behavioural practices associated with a specific discourse.

In its second basic meaning, "discourse" is used in social theory and analysis following the pioneering theorizing of Foucault to refer to "different ways of structuring knowledge and social practice" (Fiske, 1994). Thus, for example, the dominant discourse of immigration in Canadian society today differs markedly from earlier discourses. Moreover, there are also alternative discourses on this topic espoused by immigrants, people of colour, and other non-dominant groups in Canadian society.

Discourses do more than represent social beings and social relations, since they actually construct or define systems of beliefs and ideologies and position the players within it (as, for example, the difference in positioning between the immigration officer and the would-be immigrant). Thus, discourse contains within it power that usually reflect the interests of the dominant elite. Elite opinion leaders in society such as politicians, bureaucrats, judges, editors and journalists, academic experts, and others play an important role in defining issues and developing the boundaries of what is considered legitimate discourse. Thus, those who oppose the elite structure of society can easily be relegated to **marginal** positions by defining their issues and concerns as those of "radicals" or "special interest groups."

Discourse analysis is often used as a tool to identify and define social, economic, and historical power relations between dominant and subordinate groups. The field of discourse involves, as D. Goldberg (1993:295) notes, "discursive formation," which is the totality of ordered relations and correlations of subjects to each other and to objects; of economic production and reproduction; of cultural symbols and signification; of laws and moral rules; and of social, political, economic, or legal inclusion or exclusion.

Discourses in a modern transglobal and multicultural world are always dynamic, shifting, and ever-changing. The main function of discourse is to make sense of the reality of experience.

Racist Discourse

Racist discourse, racialized discourse, or the discourse of racism, advances the interests of Whites. It has an identifiable repertoire of words, images, and practices through which racial power is directed against minorities. D. Goldberg (1993:47) contends that racialized discourse includes far more than a set of overt descriptive representations about minority people (e.g., describing African Canadians as "criminals," refugees as "gate-crashers and welfare abusers," and Chinese Canadians as the builders of "monster houses"). These representations, more fully described in Chapter 10, are merely the tip of the iceberg of a series of racist assumptions and ideas that form the foundation of a racialized discourse.

Racist discourse includes the idea that human beings can be hierarchically classified according to their intellectual and physical abilities; that people can exclude, disrespect, and dominate those whom they consider inferior to themselves; and that institutional regulations and practices can restrict equal access to education, employment, and other benefits of society. Racialized discourse is expressed in many ways, but all serve to support patterns of domination, exclusion, and marginalization.

Smitherman-Donaldson and van Dijk (1988) argue that the links between language and discourse and between discrimination and racism are complex and varied, forming part of an intricate network of social relationships in which power plays a pivotal role. Discourse is vital in the reproduction of the racial oppression and control of people of colour and other minorities. Racist discourse as part of culture may be understood as the fundamental form of racism because it includes ideas that are deeply embedded in the value system of society. It is part of the invisible network of beliefs, attitudes, and assumptions that define the cultural value system of society (Wetherell and Potter, 1992; Kellner, 1995; Tator et al., 1998).

Central to racialized discourse is **Eurocentrism**, or the belief in the dominance of everything European in origin. It is a form of racism in which certain cultures are perceived to be superior while others are and will always be inferior (Shohat and Stam, 1994). This is an important element in the racist discourse that characterizes Western societies. Because this discourse is so central to thought and behaviour, its effects are deep-rooted and pervasive. The belief in European superiority pervades Western society and exerts a strong influence on the behaviour of the people who work in institutions and organizations, and also on the everyday behaviour of the citizenry. As will be demonstrated throughout this book, discourses on minorities, race, and racism converge with questions about national and cultural identity and raise provocative questions about the meaning of such cherished liberal democratic values as individualism, freedom of expression, and tolerance.

The New Millennium: Whiteness Studies

In recent years, a major new area of study has emerged, a field called "Whiteness Studies." It is the result of the growing recognition among scholars that so called race studies have focused only on people of colour, while excluding the Whites who have traditionally held hegemonic positions of power over all other racialized groups. This new field of inquiry recognizes that although race is a social construct with little or no genetic viability, it is still used to categorize people, particularly in the United States. The role of Whites in constructing hierarchical structures of exclusion and marginality became an important part of this analytical framework. In Whiteness studies scholars contend that Whites must accept a race category for themselves, but one that does not include the assumption that they are biologically superior to other "races." Thus, Whiteness is viewed as another, but very powerful socially constructed identity. Its focus is on a critical problematization of Whiteness as a vehicle for perpetuating social inequity. This field of study owes much to literary figures such Toni Morrison (1992), popular culture scholar Richard Dyer (1997), and others including Ruth Frankenberg, whose seminal "White Women, Race Matters" succinctly defined the field. Whiteness in her view consists of three interlinked dimensions: it is "a location of structural advantage; … it is a 'standpoint' or place from which White people look at ourselves, at others and at society[;] … and it refers to a set of cultural practices that are usually unmarked and unnamed" (Frankenberg, 1997:447). Toni Morrison further extends the field by putting the onus of responsibility on the "racial subject," namely White people: "My project is an effort to avert the critical gaze from the racial object to the racial subject; from the described and imagined to the describers and imaginers; from the serving to the served" (Morrison, 1992:90).

This shifts the onus in studies of institutionalized racism, racism in popular culture, and racism in society from the disadvantaged groups of colour to those who perpetuate systems of dominance; that is, to those who are White and privileged and whose views are considered natural, normative, and basically raceless. Whiteness studies racialize this group for the purpose of critically examining its role in fostering inferiorization, marginalization, and exclusion. One of its aims is the possibility of destabilizing Whiteness as an identity and an ideology to acquire a different conceptualization of society.

Whiteness studies are scholarly examinations of the role White privilege has played for generations. Having White skin automatically assigns a superior role of privilege in most societies including those that have been subjected to European **colonialism**. White privilege confers benefits in almost all sectors of society, whereas people of colour are often disadvantaged, excluded, and marginalized because of their skin colour and its associated stereotypic constructs. It is important to add, however, that Whiteness does not confer on all White people the same access to privilege. The White mother on welfare, the homeless White male do not form a homogeneous community with White journalists, judges, educators, and CEOs, and clearly do not enjoy equal access to White privilege (Ying Yee and Dumbrill, 2003; Gabriel, 1998).

Whiteness contests the often-held view of colour-blindness—the notion that one does not see skin colour—as untrue and inaccurate. Whites see the "colour" in others in the same manner as they are seen as White. Most White people do not, however, recognize themselves as a racial category, and their self-identification rarely includes the descriptor "White." Such people are often not even aware of being White, and without that essential self-recognition they find difficulty in recognizing and accepting their role as perpetrators of racial discrimination and exclusion.

It is important to remember that "Whiteness," like "colour" or "Blackness," are essentially social constructs applied to human beings rather than veritable truths that have universal validity. The power of Whiteness, however, is manifested by the ways in which racialized Whiteness becomes transformed into social, political, economic, and cultural behaviour. White culture, norms, and values in all these areas become normative and natural. They become the standard against which all other cultures, groups, and individuals are measured and usually found to be inferior. Whiteness comes to mean truth, objectivity, and merit. "As an ideology … whiteness universalizes identities and common sense notions of rightness" (Visano, 2002:210) and thereby all cultural systems are defined in its terms. This also includes the law, as Visano (ibid.) argues, even though it is often considered universalistic and transcendent.

It is against this background that critical race scholars of Whiteness are now attempting to gain insight and perspective into these dynamics with the ultimate aim of exposing the power of Whiteness, in order to dismantle some of its overwhelming hegemony over those who are "non-White." "White people must learn to share space rather than control it" (Simpson: 2003:130).

Postcolonial Studies

In a general sense, the field of postcolonial studies examines the interactions between European nations and the societies they colonized in the last few centuries. The field deals with the impact of colonization on postcolonial history, economy, science, culture, the cultural productions of colonized societies, and feminism. Although Canada was not a colonizing power—with the exception of its role relative to its **Aboriginal peoples**—and was itself colonized, postcolonial studies has something to offer to Canadians. According to the most recent census, 17 percent of Canadians are recent immigrants or children of immigrants coming from over 100 countries and bringing with them their often colonized or hybrid culture, values, and practices. The multicultural nature of Canadian society therefore obliges us to include this field of study. It is especially useful because of its emphasis on identity and the processes of changing identity. Begun by Said's seminal book *Orientalism* (1978) and followed by many notable scholars including today's most expressive postcolonial voice, Homi Bhabha (1990), the field points our attention to the ways in which the values of colonized people became over-laden with European norms and values. In extreme cases, the culture of the oppressor was preferred to the indigenous one, resulting in complex and multifaceted mechanisms of identity formation. Bhabha coined the term "hybrid" to describe persons who are in a liminal state, between two cultures, and whose culture and behaviour is neither one nor the other. Such persons occupy "interstitial" spaces and their personal identifications are often mixed or hybrid.

Postcolonial studies is closely related to the aforementioned Whiteness studies, because, as Shome (1999:108) notes, Whiteness travels and has historically travelled to other worlds—whether it was the physical travel of White imperial bodies colonizing other worlds or today's neocolonial travel of White cultural products, media, music, television, products, academic texts, and Anglo fashions to other worlds. Taken together, Whiteness and postcolonial studies result in a body of knowledge that informs:

> Whiteness, thus, is not merely a discourse that is contained in societies inhabited by white people; it is not a phenomenon that is enacted only where white bodies exist. Whiteness is not just about bodies and skin color, but rather more about the discursive practices that, because of colonialism and neocolonialism, privilege and sustain the global dominance of white imperial subjects and Eurocentric world-views. (Shome: 1999, 108)

These postcolonial concepts are extremely useful in describing the dynamics of people and their movement in a globalizing, transnational world, and Canada has been the recipient of many such hybridized groups.

Race, Gender, and Class Paradigms in Canada

In Canada, as in other complex societies with heterogeneous populations, social relations are influenced by such factors as class, gender, and race. The totality of social life can best be explained in terms of the interactions of these and other distinguishing characteristics.

Although race is an important segmenter of Canadian (and other) societies, class and gender also create significant inequities. Many modern paradigms of society include the "interlocking nature of relevant systems of domination and the varieties of consciousness that flow from them, with a view to understanding how they affect collective action" (Morris, 1992:361).

The interrelationships of class, race, ethnicity, and gender have especially been reexamined from the perspective of feminist neo-Marxism (Smith, 1987). Feminist neo-Marxists have criticized the ethnicity and class perspectives of sociology, in which the issues of gender and race are usually ignored. While Ng (1993) maintains that race and ethnicity can be taken together because of their constructed character, she concludes: "gender, race/ethnicity, and class are not fixed entities. They are socially constructed in and through the productive and reproductive relations in which we all participate. Thus, what constitutes sexism, racism, as well as class oppression, changes over time as productive relations change" (195).

Making a similar point, Khayatt (1994) argues: "Unless the boundaries of race, gender, class and sexuality intersect to make visible the various nuances of each category, the usefulness of each becomes lost in a hierarchicalization of oppressions." In other words, these various categories of identity must be considered together, determining the way they intersect, the way they differ and, at the same time, taking into account the distinctiveness of individual experience.

Another Canadian approach to this area is represented by Calliste (1989, 1992), whose studies of Caribbean immigrant women show that historically they have been used as cheap domestic labour. The exclusion of black women from nursing in Canada before the late 1940s (Calliste, 1996) was rationalized by an ideological construction of racially specific femininity and sexuality, representing the opposite models of White, middle-class womanhood. A further example of the interrelationship between race and gender is manifested in the racism that continues to be experienced by Black nurses in Canadian hospitals (Calliste, 1996) in the 1990s.

Razack (1998) and Shakir (1995) point to the impact of gendered racism in the treatment of Aboriginal women and immigrant women of colour in the justice system. Both these theorists emphasize that gender can be culturalized and can replace race as the key interactive relationship (e.g., consider the erroneous assumption that the passivity of South Asian women and their position of submission to the patriarchy of their cultures accounts for spousal abuse).

Razack (1998), in analyzing the interlocking systems of race, gender, and class, identifies the complex ways in which systems of oppression support one another. She cites the example of domestic workers and the largely White professional women they work for as a symbiotic but hierarchical relationship.

Similarly, Bakan and Stasiulis (1995) demonstrate how the increasing demand for home child care in developed capitalist states and the controlled supply of Third World immigrant women work together to structure differences in citizenship rights across national boundaries.

These approaches in Canadian research, as elsewhere, have been greatly influenced by the research and writings of Black feminists. Although there is still some dissension around the issue of how to define "Black feminism" without reifying the notion of Blackness, this approach involves the recognition that Black women's experiences with racial and gender oppression brings about needs, issues, and problems that are distinct from those of White women and Black men. The struggle involves therefore the struggle for equality as women and as African Americans (Collins, 2000:27). bell hooks is generally credited with distinguishing Black feminists from White feminists because she recognizes that White feminists are still contaminated by racism. Inevitably this led to a separation between the two groups that is also evident in Canada. In addition to separating themselves from White feminists, Black writers on this subject note that their relation to patriarchy is different from that of White women, since racism against Black men insures that they do not have the same relationship to hierarchical capitalist structures of society as do White men. The relationships between gender and class are therefore different for Black women, and their theorizing must consequently reflect these differences (Carby, 2000). One of the main areas of research concentration among Black feminists is the role of women's work and their general participation in the workforce both in metropolitan countries and in the peripheral—that is, colonized and formerly colonized—areas of the world.

The Debate over Multiculturalism

Over the last three decades, discourse about Canadian national identity has been framed within the debate concerning multiculturalism (see Chapter 11) and its promise to recognize, respect, and value cultural and racial differences.[4] There is a multiplicity of responses to multiculturalism, both as ideology and as public policy (a policy on multiculturalism was introduced in the House of Commons by Prime Minister Trudeau in 1971, and the Canadian Multiculturalism Act was passed in 1988). For many Canadians, contemporary multiculturalism poses a threat to the way that they have imagined and constructed Canadian identity. They hold on to an image of Canada as distinguished from other countries, and particularly the United States, by its French–English duality. Canadians want to resolve the French–English tensions without having to address the multicultural aspect of identity. Those who oppose multiculturalism hold that it is a fundamentally flawed approach to Canada's cultural and racial diversity. They perceive that support for the expression of ethnic and racial differences represents a serious threat to Euro-Canadian values and individual rights and freedoms, and ultimately leads to a society torn by division and cultural separation (Bissoondath, 1994; Gwyn, 1995).

On the other hand, others such as Kymlicka (1998) argue that multiculturalism is consistent with liberal democratic values and that it has been a positive force in the integration of ethno-racial communities. Moreover, Kymlicka asserts that because of its policy of multiculturalism, both at the federal level and as it has filtered down into public institutions such as the schools, Canada protects both individual and group rights more effectively than does any country that has not adopted multiculturalism.

Yet another view of multiculturalism is that the policy and practice of multiculturalism continues to position certain ethno-racial groups at the margins, rather than in the mainstream of public culture and national identity. While "tolerating," "accommodating," "appreciating," and "celebrating" differences, it allows for the preservation of the cultural hegemony of the dominant cultural group. Many writers and theorists (Mackey, 2002; Bannerji, 2000; Goldberg, 1994) have identified as a major weakness of multiculturalism its failure to deal with the problems of systemic racism in Canada. This race-based analysis documents the ways that multiculturalism as ideology has provided a veneer for liberal-pluralist discourse, in which democratic values such as individualism, tolerance, and equality are espoused and supported, without altering the core of the common culture or ensuring the rights of people of colour. This critique of multiculturalism points to its inability to dismantle systems of inequality and diminish White power and privilege.

The race-based analysis of multiculturalism has led to a new form of discourse labelled **radical** or **critical multiculturalism** (Shohat and Stam, 1994; Goldberg, 1994), or "insurgent multiculturalism" (quoted in St. Lewis, 1996:28). Critical multiculturalism moves away from a paradigm of pluralism premised on a hierarchical order of cultures that under certain conditions "allows" non-dominant cultures to participate in the dominant culture. This more proactive, radical model of multiculturalism focuses on *empowerment* and *resistance* to forms of subjugation; the *politicization* and *mobilization* of marginalized groups; the *transformation* of social, cultural, and economic institutions; and the *dismantling* of dominant cultural hierarchies, structures, and systems of representation.

Racism as a Field of Inquiry

The academic establishment, particularly in the social sciences, has been singularly remiss in undertaking research on racism. It is true that some work on discrimination against Aboriginal peoples has been undertaken; social anthropologists in particular have been in the forefront of research concerning Aboriginal rights to resources and land. But the general situation has been one of neglect.

There are many reasons for this, but one important factor is that studies concentrating solely on racism did not appear until the late 1970s.[5] Growth in the field was slow, and the literature on race and racism in Canada remains limited. Another important factor is that race as a variable of differentiation is still considered a subset of ethnicity and ethnic relations. Thus, courses, books, and studies on "race and ethnic relations" remain popular. Race and ethnicity are not distinguished for the purposes of applied policy-oriented research.

One of the first research undertakings in the study of race and social racism in Canada was the demonstration of the existence of racism in Canadian society. Examples include Henry and Ginzberg's (1984) study of employment discrimination; studies of racism in education, such as those of Ramcharan (1974) and Adair and Rosenstock (1976); and studies of racial discrimination, such as Jain's and the beginning work of Li.[6] Much of the work published in the 1970s was undertaken by academics using traditional scholarly perspectives and methods to influence public policy.

Another trend was to consider race in studies of ethnic groups, particularly those of colour. Important work on the Chinese in British Columbia, Haitians in Montreal, and South Asians in Canada was done in the 1970s and continues to the present. These works reveal that it is not only culture and ethnicity that influence integration into a new host society, but also the forces of racism.[7]

More recently, scholarly research on racism has increased. For example, Reitz and Breton (1996) undertook a comparative analysis of racism and racial discrimination in Canada and the United States. Another reason is that more racial-minority scholars have been hired by universities and government agencies that have a research function.[8] An example of important work resulting from this is the Pendakur and Pendakur (1995) study of income differentials.

Three discernible trends can be identified in the current literature. The first is the use of a neo-Marxian political economy model in which the role of labour migration and labour exploitation is highlighted. Strongly influenced by the theoretical work of Miles

(1989), this approach is best exemplified in Satzewich (1993), which brings together the results of a conference held on the subject of immigration, racism, and multiculturalism that was sponsored by the Social Research Unit of the University of Saskatchewan.

The second trend, also neo-Marxian, is research that uses a race, gender, or class paradigm to highlight the many factors involved in unequal power relations in societies such as Canada. Feminist scholars, especially feminist scholars of colour, are in the forefront of this approach.[9] In Canada as elsewhere, they have disputed the dynamics of the relationships of class, ethnicity, and race, and all three as they relate to gender (Ng, 1993). Lastly, studies that use a cultural-studies approach and focus on questions of cultural, racial, and national identity are enjoying a modest success (Yon, 1991, 1995; Amit-Talai and Knowles, 1996).

One of the major reasons for the preponderance of attention to ethnicity and multiculturalism is Canada's immigration policies and demographic patterns. The aftermath of World War II resulted in considerable numbers of Europeans migrating to Canada. Not until the liberalization of immigration legislation in 1967 did substantial numbers of people of colour arrive in Canada. Thus, late-twentieth-century Canadian society was first diversified by the arrival of Europeans who were neither British nor French. A focus on ethnicity and the beginnings of multiculturalism became evident. Even today, "ethnic revitalization" is occurring in Canada (Herberg, 1989; Driedger, 1989; Breton et al., 1990). In addition to creating a substantial literature on ethnicity, Canadian scholarship has paid considerable attention to multiculturalism (e.g., Fleras and Elliott, 1992, 1996).

The policy of the present federal government is to consider the dynamics of racism in the context of multiculturalism. Multiculturalism, however, must be distinguished from racism and strategies to promote anti-racism. The essential question is, if federal legislation and policies recognize and legitimize cultural diversity, should

> multicultural initiatives focus on the perpetuation of culture or the enhancement of ethnoracial equality? If the latter, multiculturalism must accentuate the needs and aspirations of *racial* minorities. ... However, does this mean that folkloric multiculturalism is obsolete and in danger of being replaced by an "instrumental" multiculturalism, with its commitment to race relations, social equality, and institutional accommodation? (Fleras and Elliott, 1992:6)

An emphasis on the needs of racial minorities in Canada is viewed with caution because of the government's fear that it would be perceived negatively by White mainstream and ethnic communities. It is unlikely, therefore, that the present government will ignore the celebration of cultural diversity in Canada.[10]

A considerable amount of good work has been done under the rubric of multiculturalism, and a legitimate case can be made for its benefits (Fleras and Elliott, 1992). However, racial inequalities and the social construction of racism should have pride of place at the level of the state, in public- and private-sector institutions, in teaching curricula and educational institutions, and in scholarly research. Multiculturalism can readily be understood but racism is a difficult and multifaceted area of human experience which takes many forms.

The Forms of Racism

Racism is an exceedingly complex aspect of human behaviour. The context within which it occurs largely determines the form it takes. In its simplest form, racism has three components: individual, systemic, and cultural or ideological. In **individual racism**, a further distinction must be made between an individual's attitudes and her or his behaviour. An individual might hold a set of attitudes about Black people—for example, that they are lazy, unmotivated, or slow. These attitudes may remain at the level of thought, or they may result in a certain form of behaviour, such as "everyday racism," which includes small acts like not shaking a Black person's hand or not sitting next to a person of colour on a bus.

Another form of racism occurs in collectivities or organizations that have developed policies and practices that are, intentionally or unintentionally, discriminatory. Within police organizations, for example, the former policy requiring officers to be of a certain height and weight was discriminatory toward certain groups of people.

The overarching form of racism resides in cultural symbols and is expressed through language, religion, and art. "Cultural racism" refers to collective and mass beliefs about race that are woven into the fabric of the dominant culture. The use of the word "black" to denote something negative or evil (as in "blackmail") is an example of cultural racism.

At each of these three levels, the racism may be overtly expressed or take on a covert, subtle, or hidden form.

Individual Racism

Individual racism involves both the attitudes held by an individual and the overt behaviour prompted by those attitudes. The attitudes are often obvious: extremely intolerant, bigoted individuals tend to be proud of their attitudes and articulate them overtly and publicly. In a society such as Canada's, however, most people are uncomfortable about expressing their attitudes openly because these attitudes run counter to the prevailing norms. They may show their attitudes by practising racial discrimination.

Individual racism has been defined as the attitude, belief, or opinion that one's own racial group has superior values, customs, and norms and, conversely, that other racial groups possess inferior traits and attributes. Individual racist beliefs provide a lens through which one sees, interprets, and interacts with the world. Because it is rooted in the individual's belief system, racism is a form of prejudice, "an emotionally rigid attitude … toward a group of people. It involves not only prejudgment but … misjudgment as well. It is categorical thinking that systematically misinterprets the facts" (Wellman, 1977:24).

Prejudiced attitudes are largely unconscious and, as such, are unnoticed by most people. They are strongly connected to the ways in which social relations are structured:

> Racist attitudes are largely derivative in nature. … They do not spring up or survive in a vacuum … but grow out of and are continually sustained by the structure of social relations of which they are largely a psychological reflection. (Parekh, 1987:viii)

Implicit in this notion is a rejection of earlier social psychology theories that suggest that racist thinking, intolerance, or prejudiced beliefs are rooted in certain deviant personality types (e.g., the authoritarian personality) or related to low socioeconomic status. Wellman (1977) and others argue that middle-class Whites are trained to subscribe to "liberal" ideas of equality and therefore tend to verbalize tolerance, while holding ambivalent and sometimes conflicting attitudes.

In this view, prejudice needs to be placed in a broader sociological context because attitudinal manifestations of racial inequality are related to social, political, and economic stratifications that form social structures and arrangements. This approach shifts the focus on misconceptions that White people might have about "others" to an emphasis on mea-

Table 2.1

THE FORMS OF RACISM

Type	Manifestations
Individual	Attitudes; everyday behaviour
Institutional/systemic	Policies and practices of an organization; rules woven into a social system
Cultural/ideological	Values embedded in dominant culture

suring interpersonal, interracial animosity. It views the basis of racism as being the dominant position of White people in Western society and the benefits that result from this position. This analysis concludes that "personal prejudice is really a disguised way to defend privilege" (Wellman, 1977:39).

A central question about individual racism is: Do racist beliefs necessarily result in discriminatory behaviour and, if so, under what conditions? While there is some debate in the literature regarding the causal relationship between prejudice and discrimination, a body of research demonstrates a clear link (Howitt and McCabe, 1978). Researchers found that in circumstances in which behaviour has no observable victim, there was a clear correspondence between attitudes and behaviour. However, Howitt and Owusu-Bempah (1990) draw an important distinction: racism is not only something done by racists; it is a sociocultural system that achieves specific objectives. It is therefore important to move the conception of racism beyond a focus on interpersonal animosity.

Using a similar analysis, it can be argued that the racist ideology of individuals, like sexist attitudes, is only a symptom of the more serious malaise in the relationships between racial groups. Social and psychological considerations should be examined within the sociocultural context that produces and reproduces inequality and injustice (Howitt and Owusu-Bempah, 1990).

> Personal attitudes far from exhaust the catalogue of discriminatory behaviour. … Discrimination remains so pervasive and entrenched because it is not solely personal…. It permeates both power and private relationships. … The racist, sexist or homophobe is not an aberrational figure in our culture. … It is the collective culture as much as individual citizens. (Hutchinson and Carpenter, 1992)

Racist beliefs and attitudes can also be considered as a continuum of weak to strong. A weak attitude merely uses and identifies racial classifications without necessarily prescribing any action. Reeves (1983) identifies *weak* racism to include beliefs

- that races of human beings exist;
- that these races differ from one another;
- that the differences are deeply rooted and enduring;
- that the differences are significant, possibly because they appear in themselves to be explanatory, or because explanations of other social features may be inferred from them; and
- that the differences have social consequences, for example, for social policy.

There is no moral evaluation of differences, nor does any form of prescriptive action flow from them.

A *medium* racist attitude accords more favourable treatment to the alleged superior race while denying goods and services to the alleged inferior races. Medium racist belief systems may include

- precise details of how and in what way the races differ;
- an explanation for the continuing existence of races and racial differences;
- reasons for the assumptions being thought significant in terms of social consequences that result or have resulted from racial differences; and
- the belief that differences between races make certain races superior or inferior and that races can be placed in some sort of rank order.

Finally, *strong* racist beliefs include a prescription for action that follows from all of the above beliefs: that the superior race is entitled to more favourable treatment than the inferior race.

Everyday Racism

Everyday racism involves the many and sometimes small ways in which racism is experienced by people of colour in their interactions with the dominant White group. It expresses itself in glances, gestures, forms of speech, and physical movements. Sometimes it is not even consciously experienced by its perpetrators, but it is immediately and painfully felt by its victims—the empty seat next to a person of colour, which is the last to be occupied in a crowded bus; the slight movement away from a person of colour in an elevator; the over-attention to the Black customer in the shop; the inability to make direct eye contact with a person of colour; the racist joke told at a meeting; and the ubiquitous question "Where did you come from?"

From a research perspective, these incidents are difficult to quantify because they are only revealed in the thoughts, feelings, and articulations of victims:

> It is very difficult to determine "objectively" the nature of everyday interaction between Whites and Blacks. ... a variety of studies have shown that those who are discriminated against appear to have more insight into discrimination mechanisms than those who discriminate. ... Blacks have a certain amount of expertise about racism through extensive experience with Whites. The latter, conversely, are often hardly aware of the racism in their own attitudes and behaviour. (Essed, 1990)

And, although people of colour are often sensitive to everyday racism, it may be so subtle that they are unaware of it. Research on racism has therefore tended to focus on what is more immediately visible and measurable. Thus racial discrimination in employment, in the media, and other more visible manifestations of racism have been studied.

In analyzing everyday racism, a further important distinction can be made between active and passive racism. Active racism includes

> all acts that—consciously or unconsciously—emerge directly from the motivation to exclude or to inferiorize Blacks because they are Black. Passive racism is complicity with someone else's racism. Laughing at a humiliating joke ... and "not hearing" others' racist comments are passively racist acts. (Essed, 1990)

Institutional and Systemic Racism

Institutional racism is manifested in the policies, practices, and procedures of various institutions, which may, directly or indirectly, consciously or unwittingly, promote, sustain, or entrench differential advantage or privilege for people of certain races. An example of institutional racism is the common practice of "word-of-mouth recruitment," which generally excludes racial minorities from the process.

Institutional racism generally encompasses overt individual acts of racism to which there is no serious organizational response, such as discriminatory hiring decisions based on the employer's **bias**. It also includes organizational policies and practices that, regardless of intent, are directly or indirectly disadvantageous to racial minorities, such as the lack of recognition of foreign credentials or the imposition of inflated educational requirements for a position.

> Institutional racism can be defined as those established laws, customs and practices which systematically reflect and produce racial inequalities in American society. If racist consequences accrue to institutional laws, customs or practices the institution is racist whether or not the individuals maintaining those practices have racist intentions. (Williams, 1985:131)

Systemic racism, although similar to institutional racism, refers more broadly to the laws, rules, and norms woven into the social system that result in an unequal distribution of economic, political, and social resources and rewards among various racial groups. It is the denial of access, participation, and equity to racial minorities for services such as education, employment, and housing. Systemic racism is manifested in the media by, for example, the negative representation of people of colour, the erasure of their voices and experiences, and the repetition of racist images and discourse.

Cultural and Ideological Racism

Cultural racism is sometimes difficult to isolate because it is deeply embedded in the society's value system. It consists of the tacit network of beliefs and values that encourage and justify discriminatory practices. Writers such as Lawrence (1982) are very specific in their connotation of cultural racism and cite the misunderstanding of the cultural patterns of some groups as a basis for it. Lawrence writes specifically about the perception of the Black, particularly Caribbean, family, which differs from the type of family considered "normal" by the dominant culture. If the family does not include a male breadwinner, a financially dependent wife, and their offspring, it is thought to be pathological or deviant. British politicians, for example, routinely display cultural racism when they claim that the "race problem" is caused by pathological cultural patterns (Lawrence, 1982). Some writers prefer the use of the term "ideological racism" (Reeves, 1983), but both terms refer to racism formulated as a set of values and ideas.

Essed (1990) argues that cultural racism precedes other forms of racism in society. It is reflected in everyday language—"whiteness" is associated with overwhelmingly positive connotations, while "blackness," in *Roget's Thesaurus*, has no fewer than sixty distinctively negative synonyms, twenty of which are related to race. It is reflected in the images generated by the mass media (racial minorities are often portrayed as problems) and by the arts (literature, poetry, and visual art). It is also manifested in religious doctrines, ideologies, and practices.

Figure 2.1

THE DIMENSIONS OF RACISM

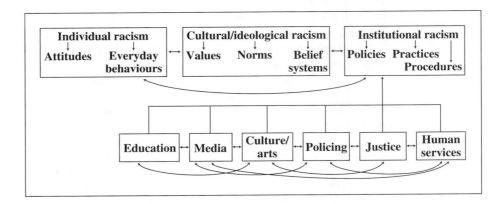

Cultural racism creates a "we and they" mentality in which one's own racial group is considered to be better than other groups. This ubiquitous tendency to view all peoples and cultures in terms of one's own cultural standards and values is known as **ethnocentrism** and plays a central role in racism.

Cultural racism is maintained through the socialization of the new generation. Children learn the cultural beliefs and values of their society at an early age. Ideas and beliefs about races and racism are included in this early learning (Ijaz and Ijaz, 1981; Milner, 1983).

Finally, an important component of ideological racism identified as the "new or modern racism" (Gilroy, 1987) provides the conceptual framework of this book. "Democratic racism" provides an important insight into why, in a democratic society, many forms of racism exist. As the title of this book indicates, the paradox is that both a liberal democratic value system *and* racist beliefs and behaviours—belief systems that should be in conflict with each other—nevertheless coexist.

Although the various forms of racism can be isolated for discussion purposes, in reality they form a complex dynamic of interrelated attitudes, feelings, and behaviours that are linked to the collective belief system and are expressed in institutional policies and practices. While institutional racism is for many theorists the focus of attention—because the very real discrimination that people of colour face often emanates from institutions—these institutions consist of individuals who make the policies and implement the actions. Institutional and systemic racism is therefore the result of a series of interactions between the individuals who function within the system and the forces of the system itself.

This approach is strongly influenced by Hall (1991) and others in viewing racism as a social construction of difference. It is based on the idea that minor physical and genetic differences between people can be used as a basis of social differentiation. Thus, social, cultural, and intellectual values are ascribed to these minute differences. These ascriptions lead to racial discrimination and inequality. Racism functions in society to maintain the power and privilege of certain groups at the expense of others. People of colour living as minorities in White-dominated societies are often treated as less than full citizens so that the balance of power relations will not be upset.

Racism takes many forms. At the individual level, prejudiced attitudes may be expressed in the many slights characteristic of everyday racism. It is demonstrated at the cultural and ideological level by the myths and stereotypes that circulate about the inferiority of certain kinds of people. And it is embedded in the policies and practices that regulate social, economic, political, and cultural institutions.

The Measurement of Racism

One of the most problematic aspects of racism is measuring its many manifestations. What is acceptable as evidence that racism has occurred, and how can this evidence be quantified?

Little research has been conducted in Canada on the issue of measurement. Much evidence of racism must be culled from other indicators. As Weinfeld (1990) notes, data of adequate reliability and validity, transformed into recognized indicators and disseminated appropriately, are not available. Thus, most attempts to answer questions such as "To what extent is Canada a racist society?" are based on partial snapshots, hunches, or the predispositions of the analyst.

Since racism and its many manifestations are now issues of central concern to contemporary social policy and practice, the question of measurement is a critical issue. Moreover, the media spend a great deal of time reporting, analyzing, and editorializing about racism. This attention leads people at all levels to pontificate on it, often with little knowledge of the subject, and increases or decreases in racism are frequently alleged. These public comments may be motivated by the political agendas of the speakers and writers who have a stake in this field.

Public spokespersons use different criteria to measure racism. Some cite poll results that show changes in attitudes; others cite economic criteria such as differences in income or employment, examples of discrimination in employment, or the number of cases brought to human rights commissions. Using different criteria to document racism leads to confusion about the meaning of the term and the ways in which it can be measured.

Clearly, a multidimensional approach to the measurement of racism is required, but even researchers in the field have relied on various approaches (Weinfeld, 1990). Neither the various spokespersons nor the academic researchers necessarily project an accurate picture. But what is an "accurate" picture?

How do we know, first, what racism is? Second, how can it be quantified not only for research purposes but for the development and implementation of anti-racist policies and practices? A review of the Ontario Human Rights Commission's disposition of complaints involving racism has shown that racial inequality is difficult to prove because of its hidden nature (Frideres and Reeves, 1989). If it is hard to demonstrate, how can it be measured?

In the first instance, it is again necessary to distinguish between overt individual forms of racism, such as the articulation of prejudicial attitudes, and the commonplace events and incidents that racial minorities confront daily. Attitudes can be studied and measured in a variety of ways. For example, a number of attitude studies undertaken in Canada show that from 12 to 16 percent of the population hold bigoted and intolerant attitudes (Henry, 1978). But how accurate are attitude surveys and polls as a measurement of racism?

In Canada, as elsewhere, studies of racism first focused on prejudicial attitudes on the assumption that racism was caused solely by individuals acting on their negative feelings. More recently, a number of polls and surveys have considered the issues of racism and ethnicity. Polls have also been taken on matters relating to immigration. However, Gallup and similar polls are crude indicators, and their interpretation is often open to question. Questions asking for a perception of the increase in racism can be interpreted in many ways: a positive response can mean that the respondents have seen a greater number of racist incidents; it can also mean that a larger number of incidents are considered racist today, whereas formerly the respondents considered the incidents related to factors other than racism.

The first interpretation may mean that racism is on the rise, but the second may mean that a concern about racism and its negative effects is on the rise. Similarly, questions about the numbers of people who should be admitted to Canada give rise to various interpretations. People who respond negatively may simply be reflecting the view that Canada has more people than its economy can handle, which is not the same as the view that racial-minority immigration should be controlled.

Conversely, many Canadians pride themselves on their tolerance and respect for diversity and profess belief in the traditional democratic values of fairness and equality. Thus, their answers to pollsters' questions are unconsciously skewed to correspond to what they think a "liberal" response should be. Their ambivalent views are filtered out of the answers. The result is that a more positive response is projected. This is an example of ambivalent or aversive racism, in which people hold two opposing and contradictory attitudes—one friendly, the other hostile (Gaertner and Dovidio, 1986).

A further problem in measuring racism exists in relation to the results of polls and surveys. Since racial attitudes are frequently unconscious, unarticulated, and non-deliberate (Wellman, 1977; Barrett, 1987; Essed, 1990), "self-reports" of racial attitudes do not necessarily conform to behaviour (Phillips, 1971). A gap exists between attitude and behaviour, belief and action, prejudice and discrimination. But the extent of this divergence is not very clear (Barrett, 1987).

Several critical dimensions of the measurement conundrum, particularly with respect to polls and surveys, were revealed in an analysis of **anti-Semitism** in the United States (J.J. Goldberg, 1993). When representatives of major Jewish organizations met to draft a statement about anti-Semitism, a number of facts and figures were presented that seemed to indicate that anti-Semitism was greatly on the increase. One in five Americans, according to one poll, held strong anti-Semitic views; the number of bias crimes against Jews, ranging from graffiti to murder, seemed to have increased; and a number of constitutional challenges against hate-crime laws had been introduced in several states. The American Jewish Committee released a poll showing that 47 percent of New Yorkers, including 63 percent of Blacks, believed that "Jews have too much influence." A national poll revealed that 20 percent of Americans and 37 percent of Black Americans were anti-Semitic.

Although these poll results showed alarming numbers, other indicators of anti-Semitism presented a different picture. For example, overt discrimination against Jews in housing, jobs, and education had all but disappeared in the United States. Moreover, poll questions about Jews having too much influence are not necessarily indicators of anti-Semitism. Is perceived influence a measure of anti-Semitism or anti-Black prejudice? Increasingly, poll questions that allegedly test for negative stereotypes, such as the notion that "Jews stick together," are considered positive rather than negative traits.

In addition to challenging poll questions, this analysis also revealed that little attention is paid to longitudinal comparisons with earlier polling results. For example, the figure of 20 percent of Americans being anti-Semitic represents a drop of nearly one-third from a 1964 result of 29 percent. The only indicator of anti-Semitism that does show an increase is the number of actual incidents—a total of 1879 in 1991, which consisted primarily of epithets and swastika daubings. This still amounts to five incidents per day in a total population of 250 million.

Although most poll and survey results do not appear to indicate any massive increase in prejudice, the vast majority of U.S. Jews (85 percent, in contrast with 45 percent in 1983) believe that "anti-Semitism is a serious problem in America today." This disparity is blamed by some on Jewish agencies who use anxiety about anti-Semitism as a means of fundraising. ("People don't give if you tell them everything's okay.") J.J. Goldberg (1993) concludes by noting that "the masses are driving the leadership. ... Maybe it's time for the leadership to start leading, and tell their public the truth."

Although polls and attitude surveys present considerable obstacles to understanding the manifestations of racism, it is even more difficult to study everyday racism. Everyday racism must be studied from the perspective of the victims who experience it in looks, gestures, and forms of speech. Part of the problem may be that most researchers are White and have not themselves experienced these daily slights. However, the problem of measuring the hidden, innermost feelings and experiences of victims also plays a significant role in limiting research (Silvera, 1989).[11]

An additional, important factor is that evidence based on the everyday experiences of victims—"victim testimony"—is not the kind of evidence that authorities and decision-makers trust. Victims are believed to have "chips on their shoulders" and therefore not to be objective. Victim testimony has been collected by some task forces and commissions investigating aspects of racism in Canadian society. Although their reports have used public consultation to elicit data, they are not considered reliable studies of overt racism.

Some racial-minority leaders maintain that the denial of victim testimony is in itself a form of subtle racism. On the other hand, some minority leaders in responsible positions argue against research of any kind and for a reliance on victim testimony as the only acceptable documentation of racism. Clearly, there is a danger here of "throwing out the baby with the bathwater," and a balanced perspective that includes both testimonials and research on measurement must be established.

Measuring Institutional and Systemic Racism

It is difficult to study and measure covert racism in its institutional or systemic form. What is usually considered evidence is the consequences of alleged discrimination, rather than the intent to discriminate. One of the main problems with the concept of institutional racism is that it does not differentiate the structural features of institutions in society from the actions of groups of individuals. To what extent is racism embodied in institutions, and how can its institutional manifestation be measured?

Weinfeld (1990) has listed a large number of indicators of racism in all its forms. With respect to institutional racism, his list includes socioeconomic measures such as

- *education*: level of attainment and areas of specialization;
- *occupation:* income; mobility; measures of unemployment, underemployment, labour-force participation, and poverty; workplace measures such as racial harassment;
- *representation rates:* in upper and middle levels of firms and organizations; degree of racial segregation in work settings and sectors; job **ghettoization**;
- *housing data:* residential segregation and quality of housing; incidents of discrimination by landlords and realtors.

It is almost impossible to answer the question "Is racism on the increase?" because the answer largely depends on which of its many facets is being considered and by what method it is being measured. When public figures discuss the alarming increase in racism, they usually rely on snapshots of attitudes—polls or surveys. Such studies are often enough only crude indicators at best, and "remarkably uninformative; for the most part, they tell us about the relative readiness of sections of the population to subscribe to one set of verbal formula rather than another" (Zubaida, 1972).

Institutional, cultural, and individual racism figure in many of the incidents that occur in institutional contexts. The confluence of individual attitudes and cultural ideologies in institutional contexts results in innumerable examples of both intended and unintended racism. Although the three major forms of racism outlined in this chapter can be isolated for historical analyses, it is often difficult to identify the forms of racism that occur in everyday life. The ways in which racism is manifested are "so much a part of each other that they are often inseparable. ... To see how white people do racism ... we cannot compartmentalize their thoughts and actions; to see the full picture, the three distinct concepts need to be combined" (Wellman, 1977:39).

Summary

This chapter has reviewed the main theoretical formulations devised by social scientists in the United States, the United Kingdom, and Canada to explain the phenomenon of racism in modern society. It has also discussed the role of social science theory and methodology in maintaining structural inequality. There are essentially four main themes in the theoretical literature:

- *assimilation models,* developed earlier in this century, in which race is assumed to be part of ethnicity, and members of racial groups are therefore expected to assimilate into mainstream society with the same ease as did members of White ethnic groups;
- *race relations models,* in which race and racism are considered variables that segment or fractionalize groups in society;
- *anti-racist approaches,* in which society in general and institutions in particular are expected to challenge racism, which includes critical race theory;
- *cultural studies perspectives,* in which race and racism are placed within the context of globalization and the increasing ethno-racial heterogeneity of complex societies.

Assimilation approaches generally assume consensus and homogeneity in society, whereas the later theories, especially those that are Marxian-derived, generally consider racism as a manifestation of class-derived conflict. The most recent theoretical themes in the literature stress the manner in which racism is embedded in the language, text, and cultural symbols of increasingly complex modern societies.

This chapter also defined three major forms of racism: *individual racism,* which can be considered in its attitudinal and behavioural dimensions; *institutional or systemic racism*; and *cultural or ideological racism.* The chapter concluded with a discussion of the difficulties and complexities of measuring racism.

Notes

1. Many studies conducted by social scientists use an inferential statistical model that includes an outcome or effect variable and a predictor variable to determine relationship between two or more variables. And, according to Zuberi (2001), this often leads to the confusion between cause and effect. When "race" is a predictor variable on an outcome such as intelligence, for example, the interpretation of results of such studies are not necessarily accurate, because what is being measured is a morphological characteristic such as skin colour with another trait of an individual. The relationship between race and intelligence cannot be understood by merely correlating the two variables. Intervening variables that determine intelligence such as poverty, lack of access to education, and other social factors play a major role. Limiting studies only to the

relationship of two variables as is done in many studies cannot establish an accurate causal relationship.

2. "Functionalist" in this context refers to the idea that society is composed of institutions, beliefs, and values, all of which function together to form a whole. Theories that emphasize the assimilation of ethnic and racial groups assume that these groups will ultimately fit into and become part of the larger society.

3. Until very recently Canadian scholars have written relatively little on racism, compared with their counterparts in the United States and United Kingdom. The dominant concern in Canadian scholarship had been ethnicity and multicultural studies. Notable exceptions were the publication of Bolaria and Li (1988) and Ramcharan (1982). In the last decade however, Canadian scholars, and more specifically scholars of colour, have created a significant body of scholarship.

4. Multiculturalism as both policy and ideology is contested in many countries in the ever-increasing globalization of the world. See, for example, Isajiw (1997).

5. Henry (1978) was one of the first attitude surveys published on this subject. Other factors responsible for the neglect in this field include the fact that racial-minority communities in the first instance expressed their concerns about racism to government; the absence of racial-minority researchers and faculty members; and the inability to obtain research funds for studies on racism in Canada because racism was considered an American problem.

6. Others include Henry and Ginzberg (1984), Ramcharan (1983), Adair and Rosenstock (1976), Anderson and Grant (1975), Jain (1981), and Hughes and Kallen (1974).

7. Labelle, LaRose, and Piche (1983), LaFerrière (1983), Ujimoto and Hirabayashi (1980), Warburton (1992), Anderson (1991), Buchignani and Indra (1986), James (1990), and Adachi (1976).

8. An even more recent trend in Canadian scholarship is the acceptance of a social construct model of racism, such as that taken in this book. This perspective is demonstrated in the recent work of Peter Li, whose study of housing and the racialization of the Chinese community in Vancouver is an important example of this approach. Another significant example is Audrey Kobayashi's (1990) work on the racialization of the law.

9. Ng (1993); Ng and Ramirez (1981); and Calliste (1989, 1992).

10. Irshad Manji, writing in the *Toronto Star*, July 5, 1992, noted that in the previous year "the federal Department of Multiculturalism spent nearly as much on promoting heritage cultures as it did on fighting racism. Yet pursuing both goals at the same time, and with almost equal amounts of money is stupid: racism makes the benefits of promoting heritage cultures null and void. Racism reduces culture to bright outfits, cute accents and tongue-burning foods. It also limits the audiences of ethnic celebrations to those who'd come out and see Ukrainians dancing anyway. *Racism makes multiculturalism premature*."

11. In the Canadian literature, Silvera (1989), which describes the experiences of Black domestics, comes closest to this kind of study.

References

Adachi, K. (1976). *The Enemy That Never Was: A History of the Japanese Canadians*. Toronto: McClelland & Stewart.

Adair, J., and D. Rosenstock. (1976). *Multiracialism in the Classroom: A Survey of Interracial Attitudes in the Schools*. Ottawa: Secretary of State.

Allport, G. (1954). *The Nature of Prejudice*. New York: Doubleday.

Alonso-Donate, G. (2002). "Nuestra America in Global Miami: Comparative Immigrant Incorporation in the Shadow of the State." Conference paper given at Transnational Migration and Social Justice in the Global City, Marquette University, November 14–16. Milwaukee, WI.

Amit-Talai, V., and C. Knowles. (1996). *Resituating Identities: The Politics of Race, Ethnicity and Culture*. Peterborough, ON: Broadview Press.

Anderson, A., and J. Frideres. (1981). *Ethnicity in Canada: Theoretical Perspectives*. Toronto: Butterworths.

Anderson, K. (1991). *Vancouver's Chinatown: Racial Discourse in Canada, 1875–1980*. Montreal and Kingston: McGill-Queen's University Press.

Anderson, W., and R. Grant. (1975). *The Newcomers: Problems of Adjustment of West Indian Immigrant Children in Metro Toronto Schools.* North York, ON: York University.

Bakan, A., and D. Stasiulis. (1995). "Making the Match: Domestic Placement Agencies and the Racialization of Women's Household Work." *Signs: Journal of Women in Culture and Society* 20(2):303–35.

Bannerji, H. (2000). *The Dark Side of the Nation: Essays on Multiculturalism, Nationalism and Gender.* Toronto: Canadian Scholars' Press.

Banton, M. (1977). *The Idea of Race.* London: Tavistock.

———. (1983). *Racial and Ethnic Competition.* Cambridge and New York: Cambridge University Press.

Barrett, S. (1987). *Is God a Racist? The Right Wing in Canada.* Toronto: University of Toronto Press.

Bell, D. (1992). 3rd ed. *Race, Racism and American.* Boston; Toronto: Little Brown.

Ben-Tovin, G., and G. Gabriel. (1986). *The Local Politics of Race.* London: Macmillan.

Bennett, T. (1992). "Putting Policy into Cultural Studies." In L. Grossberg, C. Nelson, and P. Treichler (eds.), *Cultural Studies.* New York and London: Routledge. 23–34.

Bhabha, H. (ed.). (1990). *Nation and Narration.* London and New York: Routledge.

Bibby, R.W. (1990). *Mosaic Madness.* Toronto: Stoddart.

Bissoondath, N. (1994). *Selling Illusions: The Cult of Multiculturalism.* Toronto: Penguin.

Bolaria, B.S., and P. Li (eds.). (1988). *Racial Oppression in Canada.* 2nd ed. Toronto: Garamond.

Bourne, J., and A. Sivanandan. (1974). "Cheerleaders and Ombudsmen: The Sociology of Race Relations in Britain." *Race and Class* 21(4):331–52.

Brandt, G. (1986). *The Realization of Anti-Racist Teaching.* London: Falmer Press.

Breton, R. (1989). "Canadian Ethnicity in the Year 2000." In J. Frideres (ed.), *Multiculturalism and Intergroup Relations.* New York: Greenwood Press. 149–52.

Breton, R., W. Isajiw, W. Kalbach, and J. Reitz. (1990). *Ethnic Identity and Equality: Varieties of Experience in a Canadian City.* Toronto: University of Toronto Press.

Buchignani, N., and D. Indra. (1986). *Continuous Journey: A Social History of South Asians in Canada.* Toronto: McClelland & Stewart.

Calliste, A. (1989). "Canada's Immigration Policy and Domestics from the Caribbean: The Second Domestic Scheme." *Race, Class, Gender: Bonds and Barriers: Socialist Studies* 5:133–65.

———. (1992). "Women of Exceptional Merit: Immigration of Caribbean Nurses to Canada." *Canadian Journal of Women and the Law* 6:85–102.

———. (1996). "Anti-Racism Organizing and Resistance in Nursing." *CRSA/RCSA* 33(3):361–90.

Calliste, A., and G. Dei (eds.). (2000). *Anti-racist Feminism: Critical Race and Gender Studies.* Halifax: Fernwood.

Carby, H.V. (2000). "White Woman Listen!" In L. Back and J. Solomos (eds.), *Theories of Race and Racism: A Reader.* London: Routledge. 389–403.

Carmichael, S., and C. Hamilton. (1967). *Black Power: The Politics of Liberation in America.* New York: Random House.

CCCS (Centre for Contemporary Cultural Studies). (1982). *The Empire Strikes Back: Race and Racism in 70's Britain.* London: Hutchinson.

Collins, P.H. (2000). "Black Feminist Thought." In L. Back and J. Solomos (eds.), *Theories of Race and Racism: A Reader.* London: Routledge.

Cox, O. (1976). *Race Relations: Elements and Social Dynamics.* Detroit: Wayne State University Press.

Crenshaw, K. (1997). "Colour-Blind Dreams and Racial Nightmares: Reconfiguring Racism in the Post–Civil Rights Era." In T. Morrison and C. Brodsky Lacour (eds.), *Birth of a Nation'hood: Gaze, Script, and Spectacle in the O.J. Simpson Case.* New York: Pantheon Books. 97–168.

Dei, G. (1996). "Critical Perspectives in Antiracism: An Introduction." *CRSA/RCSA* 33(3):247–67.

Delgado, R. (1995). *Critical Race Theory: The Cutting Edge.* Philadelphia: Temple University Press.

Drake, S.C. (1991). *Black Folk Here and There.* 2 vols. Los Angeles: Centre for Afro-American Studies and University of California Press.

Driedger, L. (ed.). (1989). *The Ethnic Factor: Identity in Diversity.* Toronto: McGraw-Hill Ryerson.

During, S. (ed.). (1994). *The Cultural Studies Reader.* London: Routledge.

Dyer, Richard. (1997). *White.* London: Routledge.

Essed, P. (1990). *Everyday Racism: Reports from Women of Two Cultures.* Claremont, CA: Hunter House.

Eysenck, H. (1971). *The IQ Argument: Race, Intelligence and Education.* New York: Library Press.

Fairclough, N. (1992). *Discourse and Social Change.* Cambridge: Polity Press.

Fanon, F. (1967). *Black Skin, White Masks.* New York: Grove Press.

Fine, M., L. Weiss, L. Powell, and L. Mun Wong. (1997). *Off White: Readings on Race, Power and Society.* London: Routledge.

Fiske, J. (1994). *Media Matters: Everyday Culture and Political Change.* London: Routledge.

Fleras, A., and J. Elliott. (1992). *Multiculturalism.* Scarborough, ON: Nelson.

———. (1996). *Unequal Relations: An Introduction to Race, Ethnic and Aboriginal Dynamics in Canada.* 2nd ed. Scarborough, ON: Prentice Hall.

Foucault, M. (1980). In C. Gordon (ed.), *Power/Knowledge: Selected Interviews and Other Writings, 1972–1977.* New York: Pantheon.

Frankenberg, R. (1997). "White Women, Race Matters." In L. Back and J. Solomos (eds.), *Theories of Race and Racism: A Reader.* London: Routledge: 447–461.

Franklin, R.S. (1991). *Shadows of Race and Class.* Minneapolis: University of Minnesota Press.

Frideres, J. (ed.). (1989). *Multiculturalism and Intergroup Relations.* New York: Greenwood Press.

————, and W.J. Reeves. (1989). "The Ability to Implement Human Rights Legislation in Canada: A Research Note." *Canadian Review of Sociology and Anthropology* 26(May):311–32.

Gabriel, J. (1998). *Whitewash: Racialized Politics and the Media.* London: Routledge.

Gaertner, S.L., and J.F. Dovidio. (1986). "The Aversive Forms of Racism." In S.L. Gaertner and J.F. Dovidio (eds.), *Prejudice, Discrimination and Racism.* New York: Academic Press.

Gilroy, P. (1987). *There Ain't No Black in the Union Jack.* Chicago: University of Chicago Press.

Glazer, N., and D. Moynihan. (1975). *Ethnicity: Theory and Experience.* Cambridge, MA: Harvard University Press.

Goldberg, D. (1993). *Racist Culture: Philosophy and the Politics of Meaning.* Oxford: Blackwell.

————. (ed.). (1994). *Multiculturalism: A Critical Reader.* Oxford: Blackwell.

Goldberg, J.J. (1993). "Overanxious About Anti-Semitism." *Globe and Mail* (May 24).

Gwyn, R. (1995). *Nationalism Without Walls.* Toronto: McClelland & Stewart.

Hall, S. (1991). "Old and New Identities: Old and New Ethnicities." In A. King (ed.), *Culture, Globalization and the World System.* Binghamton, NY: Department of Art History, State University of New York.

————, et al. (1978). *Policing the Crisis.* London: Macmillan.

Henry, F. (1978). *The Dynamics of Racism in Toronto.* North York, ON: York University.

————, and E. Ginzberg. (1984). *Who Gets the Work? A Test of Racial Discrimination in Employment.* Toronto: Urban Alliance on Race Relations.

Herberg, E. (1989). *Ethnic Groups in Canada: Adaptations and Transitions.* Scarborough, ON: Nelson.

Herrnstein, R. and C. Murray. (1994). *The Bell Curve: Intelligence and Class Structure in American Life.* New York: Free Press.

Howitt, D., and J. McCabe. (1978). "Attitudes to Predict Behaviour in Males." *British Journal of Social and Clinical Psychology* 17:285–86.

————, and J. Owusu-Bempah. (1990). "The Pragmatics of Institutional Racism: Beyond Words." *Human Relations* 43(9):885–99.

Hughes, D., and E. Kallen. (1974). *The Anatomy of Racism: Canadian Dimensions.* Montreal: Harvest House.

Hutcheon, L. (1988). *A Poetics of Postmodernism: History, Theory, Fiction.* New York: Routledge.

————. (1991). *Splitting Images: Contemporary Canadian Ironies.* Toronto: Oxford University Press.

Hutchinson, A., and P. Carpenter. (1992). "Can Women Be Misogynous or Gays Homophobic?" *Toronto Star* (March 5):A23.

Ijaz, A., and H. Ijaz. (1981). "Ethnic Prejudice in Children." *Guidance and Counselling* 2(1)(September):28–39.

Isajiw, W.W. (ed.). (1997). *Multiculturalism in North America and Europe: Comparative Perspectives on Interethnic Relations and Social Incorporation.* Toronto: Canadian Scholars' Press.

Jain, H. (1981). *Race and Sex Discrimination in the Workplace in Canada: An Analysis of Theory and Research and Public Policy in Canada.* Ottawa: Employment and Immigration.

James, C. (1990). *Making It: Black Youth, Racism and Career Aspirations in a Big City.* Mosaic Press.

Jensen, A. (1997). "The Psychometrics of Intelligence." In M. Nyborg (ed.), *The Study of Human Nature.* NY: Elsevier

Jones, J.J. (1972). *Prejudice and Racism.* Reading, MA: Addison-Wesley.

Kellner, D. (1995). "Cultural Studies, Multiculturalism and Media Culture." In G. Dines and J. Humez (eds.), *Cultural Studies, Multiculturalism and Media Culture.* Thousand Oaks, CA: Sage.

Khayatt, D. (1994). "The Boundaries of Identity at the Intersection of Race, Class and Gender." *Canadian Women Studies* 14(2):6–12.

Kobayashi, A. (1990). "Racism and the Law." *Urban Geography* 11(5):447–73.

Kymlicka, W. (1998). *Finding Our Way: Rethinking Ethnocultural Relations in Canada.* Toronto: Oxford University Press.

Labelle, M., S. LaRose, and V. Piche. (1983). "Emigration et Immigration: Les Haitians au Québec." *Sociologie et Société* 15:73–88.

Ladson-Billings, G. (1998). "Just What Is Critical Race Theory and What's It Doing in a Nice Field Like Education?" *Qualitative Studies in Education* 2(1): 7–24.

LaFerrière, M. (1983). "Blacks in Quebec: Minorities Among Minorities." In C. Marrett and C. Leggon (eds.), *Research in Race and Ethnic Relations.* JAI Press.

Lawrence, E. (1982). "Just Plain Common Sense: The Roots of Racism." In CCCS, *The Empire Strikes Back: Race and Racism in 70's Britain.* London: Hutchinson.

Li, P. (1988). *The Chinese in Canada.* Toronto: Oxford University Press.

————. (ed.). (1990). *Race and Ethnic Relations in Canada.* Toronto: Oxford University Press.

Mackey, E. (2002). *House of Difference: Cultural Politics and National Identity in Canada.* Toronto: University of Toronto Press.

Mayr, E. (1963). *Animal Species and Evolution.* Cambridge, MA: Harvard University Press.

McIntosh, P. (1990). "White Privilege: Unpacking the Invisible Knapsack." *Independent School* 49(2):31–36.

Miles, R. (1989). *Racism.* London: Routledge.

———, and A. Phizacklea. (1984). *White Man's Country: Racism in British Politics.* London: Pluto Press.

Milner, D. (1983). *Children and Race: Ten Years Later.* London: Alan Sutton.

Montagu, A. (1964). *Man's Most Dangerous Myth: The Fallacy of Race.* Cleveland: World Publishing.

Morris, A. (1992). "Political Consciousness and Collective Action." In A. Morris and C. Mueller (eds.), *Frontiers in Social Movement Theory.* New Haven, CT: Yale University Press.

Morrison, T. (1992). *Playing in the Dark: Whiteness and the Literary Imagination.* Toronto and New York: Vintage (Random House).

Myrdal, G. (1944). *An American Dilemma.* New York: McGraw-Hill.

Ng, R. (1993). "Sexism, Racism, Canadian Nationalism." In H. Bannerji (ed.), *Returning the Gaze: Essays on Racism, Feminism and Politics.* Toronto: Sister Vision Press.

———, and J. Ramirez. (1981). *Immigrant Housewives in Canada.* Toronto: Immigrant Women's Centre.

Omi, M., and H. Winant. (1993). "On the Theoretical Concept of Race." In C. McCarthy and W. Crichlow (eds.), *Race, Identity and Representation in Education.* New York: Routledge.

Parekh, B. (1987). "Preface." In J. Shaw et al. (eds.), *Strategies for Improving Race Relations: The Anglo-American Experience.* Manchester: Manchester University Press.

Park, R.E. (1950). *Race and Culture.* New York: Free Press.

Pendakur, K., and R. Pendakur. (1995). *The Colour of Money: Earnings Differentials Among Ethnic Groups in Canada—Strategic Research and Analysis.* Ottawa: Department of Canadian Heritage.

Phillips, D. (1971). *Knowledge from What? Theories and Methods in Social Research.* Chicago: Rand McNally.

Portes, A., and R. Rumbaut. (2001). *Legacies: The Story of the Immigrant Second Generation.* Berkley: University of California Press.

Ramcharan, S. (1974). "Adaptation of West Indians in Canada." Ph.D. thesis. Department of Sociology, York University.

———. (1982). *Racism: Nonwhites in Canada.* Toronto: Butterworths.

———. (1983). *Racism in Canada.* Toronto: Butterworths.

Razack, S. (1998). *Looking White People in the Eye: Gender, Race and Culture in Courtrooms and Classrooms.* Toronto: University of Toronto Press.

Reeves, F. (1983). *British Racial Discourse.* Cambridge: Cambridge University Press.

Reitz, J. (1980). *The Survival of Ethnic Groups.* Toronto: McGraw-Hill Ryerson.

———, and R. Breton (1996). *The Illusion of Difference: Realities of Ethnicity in Canada and the United States.* Ottawa: C.D. Howe Institute.

Rex, J. (1983). *Race Relations in Sociological Theory.* London: Routledge and Kegan Paul.

———, and R. Moore. (1967). *Race, Community and Conflict.* London: Oxford University Press.

———, and S. Tomlinson. (1979). *Colonial Immigrants in a British City: A Class Analysis.* London: Routledge and Kegan Paul.

Rushton, P. (1995). *Race, Evolution and Behaviour: Life History Perspectives.* New Brunswick, NJ: Transaction Publishers.

Said, E. (1978). *Orientalism.* New York: Pantheon.

St. Lewis, J. (1996). "Identity and Black Consciousness in North America." In J. Littleton (ed.), *Clash of Identities: Essays on Media, Manipulation, and Politics of the Self.* Toronto: Prentice Hall. 21–30.

Satzewich, V. (1989). "Racism and Canadian Immigration Policy: The Government's View of Caribbean Migration, 1962–66." *Canadian Ethnic Studies* 30(1):77–97.

———. (1993). *Deconstructing a Nation: Immigration, Multiculturalism and Racism in 90's Canada.* Halifax: Fernwood.

Shakir, U. (1995). *Presencing at the Boundary: Wife Assault in the South Asian Community.* Toronto: Multicultural Coalition for Access to Family Services.

Shohat, E., and R. Stam. (1994). *Unthinking Eurocentrism: Multiculturalism and the Media.* London: Routledge.

Shome, R. (1999). "Whiteness and the Politics of Location." In Nakayama and Martin (eds.), *Whiteness: The Communication Of Social Identity.* Sage: London.

Silvera, M. (1989). *Silenced.* Toronto: Sister Vision Press.

Simpson, J.S. 2003. *I Have Been Waiting: Race and U.S. Higher Education.* Toronto. University of Toronto.

Smith, D. (1987). *The Everyday World as Problematic: A Feminist Sociology.* Toronto: University of Toronto Press.

Smitherman-Donaldson, G., and T. van Dijk. (1988). *Discourse and Discrimination.* Detroit: Wayne State University.

Solomos, J. (1987). *The Roots of Urban Unrest.* Oxford: Pergamon Press.

———. (1993). *Race and Racism in Britain.* London: Macmillan.

Tator, C., F. Henry, and W. Mattis. (1998). *Challenging Racism in the Arts: Case Studies of Controversy and Conflict.* Toronto: University of Toronto Press.

Thomas, Melvin. (2000). "Anything but Race: The Social Science Retreat from Racism." *African American Research Perspectives* 6(1):79–96. Available <http://rcgd.isr.umich.edu/prba/perspectives/winter2000/mthomas.pdf>, accessed October 29, 2004.

Ujimoto, V., and G. Hirabayashi. (1980). *Visible Minorities and Multiculturalism: Asians in Canada.* Toronto: Butterworths.

UNESCO. (1950). "Statement on Race." In Ashley Montagu (ed.), *Statement on Race.* New York: Oxford University Press, 1972).

Visano, L. (2002). "The Impact of Whiteness on the Culture of Law: From Theory to Practice." In C. Levine-Rasky (ed.), *Working Through Whiteness: International Perspectives.* Albany: State University Press. 209–237.

Warburton, R. (1992). "Neglected Aspects of Political Economy of Asian Racialization in British Columbia." In V. Satzewich (ed.), *Deconstructing a Nation: Immigration, Multiculturalism and Racism in 90's Canada.* Halifax: Fernwood.

Weinfeld, M. (1990). "Racism in Canada: A Multi-dimensional Approach to Measurement." Paper prepared for Conference on Race Relations in the United Kingdom and Canada (June). North York, ON: York University.

Wellman, D. (1977). *Portraits of White Racism.* Cambridge: Cambridge University Press.

West, C. (1990). "The New Cultural Politics of Difference." In R. Ferguson (ed.), *Out There: Marginalization and Contemporary Culture.* New York: New Museum of Contemporary Art.

Wetherell, M., and J. Potter (1992). *Mapping the Language of Racism.* New York: Columbia University Press.

Williams. J. (1985). "Redefining Institutional Racism." *Ethnic and Racial Studies* 8(3)(July):323–47.

Williams, P. (1991). *Seeing a Colour-Blind Future: The Paradox of Race.* NY: Noonday Press

Wilson, W. (1980). 2nd ed. *The Declining Significance of Race: Blacks and Changing American Institutions.* Chicago: University of Chicago Press.

Ying Yee, J. and G. Dumbrill. (2003). "Whiteout: Looking for Race in Canadian Social Work Practice." In Al-Krenawi and J. Graham (eds.), *Multicultural Social Work in Canada: Working with Diverse Ethno-racial Communities.* Don Mills, ON: Oxford University Press.

Yon, D. (1991). "Schooling and the Politics of Identity: A Study of Caribbean Students in a Toronto High School." In H. Diaz (ed.), *Forging Identities and Patterns of Development.* Toronto: Canadian Scholars' Press.

———. (1995). "Unstable Terrain: Explorations in Identity, Race and Culture in a Toronto High School." Ph.D. thesis, Department of Anthropology, York University.

Zubaida, S. (1972). "Sociologists and Race Relations." In *Proceedings of a Seminar: Problems and Prospects of Socio-legal Research.* Oxford: Nuffield College.

Zuberi, T. (2001). *Thicker Than Blood: How Racial Statistics Lie.* Minneapolis. University of Minnesota Press.

CHAPTER 3

RACISM IN CANADIAN HISTORY

It always amazes me when people express surprise that there might be a
"race problem" in Canada, or when they attribute the "problem" to a
minority of prejudiced individuals. Racism is, and always has been,
one of the bedrock institutions of Canadian society, embedded in
the very fabric of our thinking, our personality.

—Shadd (1989)

The historical overview in this chapter focuses on the relationship between the dominant White majority group and people of colour. It examines four racial-minority groups—African Canadians (Blacks), Chinese Canadians, Japanese Canadians, and South-Asian Canadians—that are the primary targets of racial bias and discrimination in Canada. (Aboriginal peoples are considered in the following chapter.) This chapter goes on to identify racism in Canada's immigration policies and practices during the past one hundred years. It then explores the evidence of racism in contemporary society, drawing on some of the studies and surveys conducted over the past fifteen years and identifying evidence of overt racism, which is manifested in racist attitudes, assumptions, and practices. The more extreme expressions of beliefs and actions of right-wing "hate groups" are also discussed. Finally, the chapter focuses on discrimination in employment and housing, strong indices of racial discrimination in Canadian society.

Introduction

Racism in Canada is generally considered a contemporary phenomenon linked to the recent arrival of people of colour. However, the legacy of racial prejudice, discrimination, and disadvantage has its origins in the earliest period of Canadian history. Since more detailed historical accounts of racism exist in other sources, this chapter examines only some of the most telling examples and evidence.

Manifestations of Racism

African (Black) Canadians

The enslavement of Africans and the racial segregation of and discrimination against "free" Black people is also part of the history of Canada (Alexander and Glaze, 1996). Black slavery was introduced into Canada by the French as early as 1608, and the first slave brought directly into New France from Africa came from Madagascar in 1629. In the St. Lawrence and Niagara regions of Upper Canada, slaves were brought by United Empire Loyalists during and after the American Revolution, and at least six of the sixteen legislators in the first Parliament of Upper Canada owned slaves (Hill, 1981; Lampert and Curtis, 1989). Although slavery did not reach major proportions in Upper Canada, primarily because the land did not lend itself to monocrop agriculture, it was nevertheless actively practised (Walker, 1980).

Contrary to popular belief, until the early nineteenth century—throughout the founding of the present Quebec, New Brunswick, Nova Scotia, and Ontario—there was never a time when Blacks were not held as slaves in Canada (Walker, 1980).

There was blatant discrimination even for the three thousand Black Loyalists who had been emancipated in the American colonies in exchange for supporting the British and who entered Canada in 1783 as "free" persons. Although they had been promised treatment equal to the White Loyalists in the granting of land contracts, they were bitterly disappointed. While the British promised all Black and White Loyalists settling in Canada hundred-acre (40.5 hectare) lots, Blacks received either no land at all or were given barren one-acre lots on the fringes of White Loyalist townships.

Deprived of the rights of British subjects, Black Loyalists found themselves desperate and destitute. Many were compelled to work as hired or indentured servants to White settlers. Because they were paid about one-quarter the wages of White workers, they were deeply resented by unemployed Whites (Winks, 1971). The hostility led to Canada's first race riot in Shelbourne and Birchtown, Nova Scotia, in 1784. A mob destroyed Black property and drove Blacks out of the townships (Shepard, 1991).

The precariousness and vulnerability of their lives in Canada convinced about 1200 disillusioned Nova Scotian Blacks to accept an offer by the Sierra Leone Company to sail for West Africa in 1792. The loss to the Black community was significant; many of those who chose to leave were teachers, preachers, and community leaders (Walker, 1980).

After the passage of the U.S. Abolition Act in 1793, which classified any runaway slaves as free, many fugitives from the United States entered Upper Canada. Several thousand Black slaves escaping slavery found their way into Canada via the "Underground Railroad." Many of these early fugitives settled close to the border in the southwestern part of Ontario. Some chose to go to New Brunswick, and smaller numbers went to Montreal.

The passage of the second Fugitive Slave Act in the United States in 1850 brought a significant increase in the Black population of Canada. There may have been sixty thousand Blacks in Canada by 1860 (Bolaria and Li, 1988). Their life in Canada was marked by overt prejudice and discrimination. In the 1850s, they were restricted in their ownership of property and were unable to secure education for their children because many White people were opposed to Black children in their schools. Blacks were exposed to ridicule and derision in the local newspapers. Throughout British North America, Blacks were thought, by some, to be responsible for "all the outrageous crimes, and two thirds of the minor ones" (Winks, 1971:248).

With the outbreak of the U.S. Civil War and the Emancipation Proclamation of 1863, many Canadian Blacks chose to return to the United States, recognizing that the value attributed to the colour of one's skin would continue to marginalize them in Canada. The discrimination and exploitation they experienced in almost every aspect of their lives led them to feel that Canada was an inhospitable environment for people of colour (Henry, 1974).

In the early 1900s, the Canadian government sought ways of denying access to Black Americans without directly antagonizing American officials. Although the government had undertaken an extensive advertising campaign to attract farmers from the United States, the Immigration Branch of the federal Department of the Interior informed its American agents that "the Canadian Government is not particularly desirous of encouraging the immigration of negroes" (Shepard, 1991:17). So, instead of placing an explicit ban on immigration, officials engaged in a campaign to discourage Black American applicants from settling on the Canadian prairies, and rejected them on medical or other grounds rather than race. A 1910 editorial in the *Edmonton Capitol* summarizes the attitude of the White community toward Black immigration:

> The Board of Trade has done well to call attention to the amount of negro immigration which is taking place into this district. It has already attained such proportions as to discourage White settlers from going into certain sections. The immigration department has no excuse for encouraging it at all. … We prefer to have the southern race problem left behind. The task of assimilating all the White people who enter our borders is quite a heavy enough one without the colour proposition being added. (Shepard, 1991:19)

J.S. Woodsworth, superintendent of the People's Mission in Winnipeg and later one of the founders of the Co-operative Commonwealth Federation (CCF), had the same general attitude toward people of colour in 1903: the "very qualities of intelligence and manliness which are the essentials for citizens in a democracy were systematically expunged from the Negro race." He argued that the American Black was still "cursed with the burden of his African ancestry. … All travellers speak of their impulsiveness, strong sexual passion and lack of willpower. … Hardly a desirable settler" (Troper, 1972:121).

Blacks who remained in Canada lived in largely segregated communities in Nova Scotia, New Brunswick, and Ontario (Winks, 1971). Racial disparity continued to be evident in the schools, government, the workplace, residential housing, and elsewhere. The Ontario legislature established segregated schools; legal challenges to this segregation failed, and separate schools continued. The legislation remained on the statute books until 1964, after Professor Harry Arthurs drew attention to it in a note in the *Canadian Bar Review* (Arthurs, 1963). Segregated schools were also a part of Black education in Nova Scotia, and to a lesser extent (because of a smaller population of Blacks) in New Brunswick. Segregated schools continued in Nova Scotia until the 1960s (Winks, 1978).

Residential segregation was widespread and legally enforced through the use of racially restrictive covenants attached to deeds and leases. Separation and refusal of service was commonplace in restaurants, theatres, and recreational facilities. Several court challenges were launched against these practices by Black Canadians; in one challenge, in 1919, a Quebec court ruled that racial discrimination was not contrary to public order or morality in Canada. The most celebrated case began with a refusal to serve a Black customer in a Montreal tavern in 1931. It ended in the Supreme Court of Canada in 1939, when the nation's highest tribunal concluded that racial discrimination was legally enforceable (Walker, 1985).

The racist attitudes of Whites in Canada were probably reinforced by the pseudoscientific concept of race popular in Western Europe, Britain, and the United States in the late nineteenth century. The concept of White cultural, intellectual, and moral superiority over the Black race was widely held then and continued to flourish well into the twentieth century.

As the study of race was "scientifically" organized, as stereotypes of the "Negro" became more widely known in Canada, and as the forces gathered under the rubrics of nationalism and racism began to have their effect, "Negroes" in Canada found themselves sliding down an inclined plane from mere neglect to active dislike (Winks, 1971:292).

Chinese Canadians

The first wave of Chinese to settle in Canada arrived in British Columbia in the 1850s in search of gold. By 1860, however, most of the mines were depleted, and the Chinese who did not return to China turned to other forms of labour. Chinese Canadians were hired for various projects in British Columbia, including the building of railways, bridges, and roads, and work in coal mines and mills (Baureiss, 1985).

In the 1880s, over 1500 labourers were recruited to help lay the track for the Canadian Pacific Railway (CPR) in British Columbia. The emigration was in the form of "Coolie-trade," in which companies advanced the passage ticket and a small sum of money to the Chinese, who, before leaving their country, would give bonds, contracting to work for a period of five to ten years. The companies would hold all the Chinese workers' earnings, and were obligated only to provide the workers with the bare essentials (Creese, 1991).

The work assigned to the Chinese contract workers was brutally hard and dangerous. Accidents were frequent, with far more Chinese than Whites as victims. Many workers died from exhaustion and rock explosions and were buried in collapsed tunnels. Their living conditions were appalling. Food and shelter were in insufficient supply, and malnutrition was widespread. There was almost no medical attention, contributing to a high fatality rate from diseases such as scurvy and smallpox. It is estimated that there were six hundred deaths in British Columbia of Chinese labourers working on the construction of the railway (Lampkin, 1985).

After the CPR was completed, new industries, such as mining, fishing, and sawmills, required additional labourers. As the supply of manual labour from Europe and the United States began to dwindle, the Canadian government reluctantly permitted Chinese Canadian labourers to fill the demand for largely contract labour required by these industries. From 1881 to 1883, 13 245 Chinese male labourers were recruited to compensate for the shortage of White workers (Bolaria and Li, 1988). These immigrants were not permitted to bring their wives and children with them or to have sexual relations with White women, for fear of spreading the "yellow menace" (Chan, 1983).

Chinese workers were paid one-quarter to one-half less than their White counterparts. The living conditions were appalling, and from 1881 to 1885 hundreds of Chinese died from disease, malnutrition, and exhaustion (Lampkin, 1985). Bolaria and Li (1988) argue that the Chinese immigration during this period was encouraged solely for the purpose of labour exploitation. Immigrants were "welcomed" only so long as there was a shortage of White workers. As soon as there was a labour surplus, the Chinese immigrants were considered a threat to Canadian society and were subjected to intense racial bias and discrimination.

By the mid-1880s, governments were feeling pressure from the White population to limit further Chinese immigration. The federal government passed the first anti-Chinese bill in 1885. In addition, British Columbia passed several anti-Chinese bills to curtail the political and civil rights of the Chinese in the province. The Coal Mines Act of 1890, for example, prevented Chinese from working underground and from performing skilled jobs in coal mines.

Other provincial legislation, introduced as early as 1875, disenfranchised the Chinese so that they were prohibited from voting in provincial and municipal elections (S.B.C. 1875, c. 2). Disenfranchisement was applied to *citizens* as well (Tarnopolsky, 1991). The Chinese were further subjected to a number of discriminatory acts that made it difficult for them to acquire Crown lands, work in skilled jobs in the mines, and obtain liquor licences. They could not serve in public office; they could not serve on juries or work in the public service; they were barred from the professions of law and pharmacy and excluded from White labour unions (Li, 1988).

Differential wage rates were entrenched in union agreements that allowed lower minimum wages for "Orientals" than for "Occidental" workers. Differential Asian and White rates were legitimized by assumptions that different wages reflected the inherently different "value" of the labour. In a perverse form of contract compliance, private contractors working with the British Columbia government on federal projects were required by the government not to hire "Orientals" (Creese, 1991).

As anti-Chinese sentiment and discrimination grew, Chinese Canadians found that almost the only areas of the labour market open to them were certain sectors of the service industry. Thus, throughout the early twentieth century, Chinese Canadians were forced to give up their position in the core labour market and to move into domestic service, laundries, and restaurants, where there was less likely to be competition from White workers and employers (Bolaria and Li, 1988). Even so, their presence sufficiently threatened the White community that, in 1907, the latent hostility erupted into brutal violence when large numbers of Whites in Vancouver invaded Chinatown and the Japanese quarter, smashing and destroying property.

One of the most bizarre discriminatory labour policies in Canada was a series of provincial laws preventing "oriental" males from hiring White females. The intent of the Saskatchewan Female Employment Act of 1912, for example, was to "protect" White women from the alleged danger of working for "orientals" (Tarnopolsky, 1991).

The refusal to accept the Chinese Canadians, as well as other racial groups, as full citizens manifested itself in yet another way. For the first two years of World War I, racial minorities and Aboriginal people were rejected for military service. Although the militia headquarters did not actually establish a colour bar, local commanders were encouraged to turn away volunteers on the grounds of the inferiority of their race. Only as the war progressed and shortages began to impede Canada's war effort were racial-minority recruits admitted. Again, in World War II, Black volunteers, along with Canadians of Chinese, Japanese, and East Indian ancestry, were at first not accepted. These barriers were also removed in face of military requirements for more soldiers (Creese, 1991).

A further manifestation of racist ideology translated into racist practice was the concerted effort of British Columbia school boards to keep "Asians" (Chinese Canadian and Japanese Canadian children) out of the public schools. As Li notes:

> Institutional racism disrupted the life of the Chinese in Canada in many ways. ... Over time, the social stigma attached to the Chinese as undesirable citizens and unwelcome workers became their defining characteristic. In this way, belonging to the Chinese race in itself became sufficient grounds for discrimination and mistreatment. (Li, 1988:47)

It should also be noted that the Chinese Canadians did not receive the right to vote in federal elections until 1947. (Japanese Canadians were able to vote one year later.)

Japanese Canadians

Japanese Canadians experienced similar discriminatory treatment from the time they first settled in British Columbia in the 1870s. They were subjected to economic exploitation, paid lower wages than White labourers, barred from both the federal and provincial franchise, subjected to discriminatory housing covenants, and segregated in schools and public places (Lampkin, 1985).

In 1907, largely as a result of a significant increase in the number of Japanese entering Canada, and as a reaction to existing populations of Chinese and East Indians in Vancouver, an organization known as the Asiatic Exclusion League was formed. Its goal was to restrict Asian admission into Canada. The league was a forerunner to the right-wing extremist organizations that would become widespread in Canada in the 1920s and 1930s. Following the arrival of over a thousand Japanese and a few hundred Sikhs, the Asiatic Exclusion League carried out a major demonstration, which culminated in the worst race riot in British Columbia history (Adachi, 1976; Bolaria and Li, 1988).

After the riot, the Canadian government entered into negotiations with the Japanese government, ending with the "Gentlemen's Agreement" of 1908. Under this agreement, the Japanese government agreed to permit entry to only certain categories of persons. These included returning immigrants, their wives and children, immigrants engaged for personal or domestic service, and labourers under specific Canadian government contracts or contracts with Japanese-Canadian farmers. A quota was fixed for all but the first group (Adachi, 1976).

Another example of racial discrimination targeting Japanese Canadians was the efforts of the British Columbia legislature to press the federal government to restrict fishing licences to Japanese Canadians in the 1920s. The ultimate intention of this pressure was to drive these people out of the fisheries (Adachi, 1976).

In the late 1930s, anti-Asian sentiment, which had been dormant for about a decade, was inflamed by Japan's invasion of China. Anti-Japanese feelings swept across North America and became virulent once again in British Columbia. The bombing of Pearl Harbor by Japan in 1941 brought it into war against the Allies, and the Canadian government took an unprecedented action (Adachi, 1976). Rejecting the counsel of Canada's senior police and military officers, the Cabinet amended the Defence of Canada Regulations (Order in Council, P.C. 1486, February 24, 1942) to give the minister of justice the authority to remove "any and all persons" from any "protected" area in Canada and to detain such persons without trial (Sunahara, 1981).

Canadians of Japanese origin, including Canadian-born and naturalized citizens—men, women, and children—were expelled from the west coast of British Columbia and their civil rights were suspended. Twenty-three thousand people of Japanese ancestry, 13 300 of them Canadian-born, were sent to relocation and detention camps in isolated areas in the interior of British Columbia, southern Alberta, and Manitoba.

They were relieved of their property, and 1200 fishing boats owned by Japanese Canadians and naturalized citizens were impounded. Japanese-language schools were closed. Houses, automobiles, and businesses were sold, and savings were impounded. For example, a disabled Japanese Canadian veteran of World War I was given $39.32 for 19 acres of fertile land in the Fraser Valley, a two-storey house, four chicken houses, an electric incubator, and 2500 hens and roosters. He later received an additional $2209.70, after an appeal to the 1947 royal commission established to deal with Japanese-Canadian claims for compensation. The settlement clearly did not approach the value of the confiscated property (Lampkin, 1985).

Men were incarcerated in jails and internment camps and were sent to work on road construction projects or sugar-beet farms in British Columbia, Alberta, Manitoba, and

Ontario. Abandoned mining towns were reopened to house the evacuees, who were forced to live in abysmal living conditions (Adachi, 1976).

For several years, conditions of virtual apartheid existed for Japanese Canadians (Adachi, 1976; Sunahara, 1981; Kobayashi, 1987). The reason given for this mass denial of rights was wartime security, but no Japanese Canadian was ever charged with sabotage or any other kind of disloyalty before, during, or after the war. The Canadian government did not release the Japanese Canadians until 1947, and it took another two years before they were able to resettle on the west coast. It is now agreed that the prime factor in their internment was the latent racist feelings harboured by Canadian officials against Japanese Canadians (Ujimoto, 1988).

Sunahara (1981) summarizes the major factors leading to this unprecedented act of racism, including the powerful anti-Asian lobby in British Columbia and a federal cabinet and civil service predisposed to basing its policy on the views of that lobby. However, underlying these considerations were the racist attitudes prevalent among politicians, bureaucrats, and the public: the manifest superiority of the Caucasian race and its "natural" obligation to rule "inferior," less endowed, non-White peoples (Sunahara, 1981). Not until 1988 was "justice" finally achieved for those Japanese Canadians who were still living, when 12 000 Japanese Canadians were paid $20 000 each as compensation for their internment. As well, they were given a formal apology by Parliament (Ujimoto, 1988).

South-Asian Canadians

South Asians are people who were born or whose ancestors were born in the Indian subcontinent, and include people from India, Pakistan, Sri Lanka, Bhutan, and Bangladesh. It also includes people with roots in South Asia who have immigrated from Kenya, Tanzania, Uganda, the Caribbean nations, and other countries.

The first South Asians to enter Canada were Sikhs, who came to British Columbia in the late nineteenth century. By the early twentieth century, the small numbers of South Asians (approximately five thousand in 1908) were viewed with the same racial bias, hostility, and resentment as was directed at other minority racial groups (Buchignani and Indra, 1985).

As was the case with Chinese and Japanese immigrants, Whites reacted antagonistically to any sign that the non-White population was increasing. The South Asian presence in British Columbia was viewed as a "Hindu invasion." Articles and editorials appearing in British Columbia newspapers emphasized the importance of maintaining Anglo-Saxon superiority (Raj, 1980). The Victoria *Daily Colonist* issued the call:

> To prepare ourselves for the irrepressible conflict, Canada must remain a White Man's country. On this western frontier of the Empire will be the forefront of the coming struggle. ... Therefore we ought to maintain this country for the Anglo-Saxon and those races which are able to assimilate themselves to them. If this is done, we believe that history will repeat itself and the supremacy of our race will continue. (Cited in Ward, 1978:259–60)

To ensure Anglo-Saxon supremacy, legislation was enacted to control the economic and social mobility of South Asians and to prevent more from coming. Even though citizens of India were British subjects, British Columbia in 1907 disenfranchised them. The government feared that the South Asians might participate in the provincial elections that year. Again, the message communicated by the press was designed to engender fear and emphasize that the White population needed to be protected against "Hindus." The effect of this paranoia was an amendment to the B.C. Election Act that added "Hindus" to other "Asian undesirables" (Raj, 1980).

The denial of the franchise had serious economic consequences for the South Asian community in British Columbia. Since the voters' list was the basis for both provincial and municipal contracts, South Asians were prevented from bidding on them. Also, as it was with the Chinese and Japanese, the denial of political rights meant that South Asians were unable to enter professions such as education, law, and pharmacy, and they could not engage in the sale of Crown timber.

They also experienced overt prejudice in the form of racial stereotyping and physical abuse. They were called "ragheads." They could not go to a movie in their native dress. People refused to sit next to them on trains. They could not own property in some sections of Vancouver. Discrimination in housing resulted in many South Asians living in very poor conditions (Bolaria and Li, 1988).

While it was estimated that only a small community of South Asians remained in British Columbia, they continued to press for a repeal of the discriminatory clause in the Elections Act. In 1947, they finally won the right to vote in federal and provincial elections. In 1948, the right was extended to municipal elections (Lampkin, 1985).

South Asians who are also Muslims are today experiencing more marginalization and even racism as a result of the events of 9/11 in the United States. As well, persons of Middle Eastern origin or persons who look as though they come from these areas of the world are increasingly under suspicion.

In each of these brief summaries of prejudice and discrimination—against Canadian Blacks, Chinese Canadians, Japanese Canadians, and South-Asian Canadians—there is a common thread. Racism in Canada is, in large measure, related to the dominant group's need for cheap labour. It can be attributed to the division of labour under capitalism (Ng, 1992; Bolaria and Li, 1988); it is a function of social organization and power differences (Creese, 1993). Racism is deeply rooted in the legacy and ideology of "White settler" colonialism, which reinforces patterns of power and privilege based on racial distinctions (Creese, 1993).

Immigration Policies and Practices

From the 1880s to the 1960s

Immigration first became a major issue in Canada in the late 1880s. By the late nineteenth century the labour needs of the country required large numbers of workers from abroad, so the federal government actively encouraged *White* immigrants to settle and farm the vast areas of the country recently brought under Canadian control. As a result, most immigrants came from Britain and the United States, but thousands of Italians, Finns, Ukrainians, and other Europeans also arrived. More workers, however, were still required, and many thousands of Chinese workers were recruited in the 1880s.

The White population was openly antagonistic toward the newcomers. As soon as the completion of the CPR was in sight, the federal government passed a highly discriminatory piece of legislation, entrenching racism for the first time in the laws of the land. The first anti-Chinese law, the Chinese Immigration Act, was passed in 1885.

A head tax was established on all Chinese males arriving in Canada (women and children were excluded from admission), partly in response to the demands of White workers, who wanted to eliminate job competition. The tax was set at $50 in 1888, and by 1903 it was $500. Under increasing pressure to "stem the flood" of Chinese immigration, the Canadian government passed the Chinese Exclusion Act (S.C. 1923, c. 38), which banned Chinese immigration from 1923 to 1947 (Bolaria and Li, 1988).

Additional restrictive immigration policies were imposed on other racial minorities. In 1907, British Columbia disenfranchised South Asians and the federal government passed an order-in-council requiring South Asians to have $200 in their possession upon arrival in Canada. Canada pressed the British and Indian governments to pass regulations and legislation to stop Indian immigration to Canada. These efforts failed, and as a result Canada passed an order-in-council restricting Indian immigration.

In 1908 the federal government passed the Continuous Passage Act, which stipulated that all immigrants must arrive by an uninterrupted journey, on through tickets, from their country of origin. As citizens of the British Empire, Indians should have had access to Canada, but immigration was made almost impossible by the Act (Buchignani and Indra, 1985). Mackenzie King, in presenting a defence of the policy to British authorities, argued that "Canada should desire to restrict immigration from the orient is natural; that Canada should remain a White man's country is believed to be not only desirable for economic and social reasons, but highly necessary on political and national grounds" (King, 1908).

The government was careful not to explicitly bar a particular group from landing, for this might have jeopardized Canada's relations with the rest of the British Empire. Instead, the Continuous Passage Act amended the Immigration Act to allow the government to control East Indian immigration without having the appearance of doing so (Cohen, 1987). In addition, the policy also effectively barred Japanese and other "undesirables" from entry into Canada (Sampat-Mehta, 1984). The Chinese Exclusion Act, the Continuous Passage Act, and various regulations to restrict immigration were effective mechanisms for ensuring that almost no Asians or East Indians emigrated to Canada until after World War II.

The 1910 Immigration Act enshrined the government's discriminatory policies in law by creating an excluded class of immigrants deemed undesirable because of Canada's climate or its social, educational, labour, or other requirements—or because their customs or habits were deemed to result in a probable inability to become readily assimilated (Malarek, 1987). The legislation did not specify the countries that had sufficiently different customs or habits to be excluded. Thus it gave immigration officials wide discretion to exclude almost any prospective immigrant on the basis of race, national or ethnic origin, and creed.

Differential treatment based on race and ethnicity was firmly established as government policy. A list of preferred and non-preferred countries was established, and selection was carried out on the basis of whether applicants were from those countries on the "preferred" list: those with affinities to the United Kingdom and United States. Next in preference came immigrants from northern and western Europe, followed by those from central and eastern Europe, and then those from southern Europe. A special permit class included immigrants from Greece, Syria, and Turkey, and European Jews (Bolaria and Li, 1988).

When, in 1914, a shipload of four hundred would-be immigrants from India sailed directly from Calcutta and arrived in the Vancouver harbour aboard the Japanese freighter the *Komagata Maru*, they were denied entry. The passengers were held aboard the ship for nearly three months before the *Komagata Maru* was forced to return to India (Buchignani and Indra, 1985).

Throughout the history of Canadian immigration, overt and covert policies have excluded racial-minority women immigrants in the hope that excluding women would keep the total number of minority-group immigrants down. A 1927 report on "Oriental immigration activities" in British Columbia showed that between 1906 and 1925, 45 women and 41 children had entered Canada, in contrast with 4909 men (Lampkin, 1985).

The Great Depression, beginning in 1929, prompted the government to invoke a series of restrictive measures to further limit new immigrants to those from the preferred groups. Canadian immigration policy continued to be racist in the 1930s. The dominant and pervasive mindset underlying the policy and the administrative and political framework was "Whites only." White immigrants from Britain were given preferential treatment; next in preference were White immigrants from the United States and France. Only if these traditional sources of immigration proved insufficient would the government consider admitting White Europeans from countries other than France and Britain.

In 1942, when Adolf Hitler activated his "Final Solution" to eliminate the Jewish people, Canada closed its doors to refugees fleeing Europe. The ship *St. Louis*, carrying Jewish refugees from Europe, attempted to land in Halifax as well as many other ports in North and South America and was denied entrance to all ports. Of all Western countries, Canada admitted the fewest Jewish refugees (Abella and Troper, 1982).

In 1947, in a House of Commons debate, Mackenzie King affirmed Canada's need for a larger population and a "proactive" immigration policy. However, he cautioned his colleagues about the importance of selecting "desirable" immigrants, stating that the people of Canada

> do not wish, as a result of mass immigration, to make any fundamental alteration in the character of our population. Large-scale immigration from the Orient would change the fundamental composition of the Canadian population. Any considerable Oriental immigration would, moreover, be certain to give rise to social and economic problems of a character that might lead to serious difficulties in the field of international relations. (Malarek, 1987:15)

In 1952, s. 61 of the new Immigration Act gave the government the power to limit or prohibit the entry of immigrants for reasons of "nationality, citizenship, ethnic group, class or geographic area of origin, peculiar customs, habits, modes of life ... or probable inability to become readily assimilated." The Act gave clear preferential status to all White immigrants.

In summarizing Canada's immigration policy until 1967, it can be said that the policy divided the world's population into two parts: preferred immigrants, who were of British and European ancestry and White; and the rest of the world, largely composed of people of colour. The Canadian government's discriminatory policy of immigration was based on the premise that Asians and other people of colour were "inassimilable," that is, they had genetic, cultural, and social traits that made them both inferior and inadaptable (Bolaria and Li, 1988).

The year 1967 marked the beginning of a series of radical reforms in immigration policy, largely as a result of changing demographics and economic pressure to replenish the labour supply. The traditional sources of labour were no longer producing sufficient numbers of immigrants as postwar Europe began to prosper. New labour needs were emerging in Canada; rapid industrialization and expanding new technologies required workers with high levels of skills and education. In response, Canada dropped its racially discriminatory immigration policies. Yet, despite reforms, in a 1975 brief to Parliament the Canadian Civil Liberties Association stated that during a 26-month period, approximately two thousand persons were allowed to enter Canada subject to the posting of cash bonds. All of them were non-Europeans, mostly Asians, South Americans, and West Indians. In no instance were such requirements made of Europeans (Mattis, 1990).

During the 1960s, a new Immigration Act introduced a point system whereby immigrants, regardless of origin or colour, were given points based on job training, experience, skills, level of education, knowledge of English or French, degree of demand for the applicant's occupation, and job offers. The new act opened the doors to immigration from previously excluded countries. While the Act allowed for a more open immigration process, some argue that it maintained some of the racist administrative practices of earlier immigration policies (Cohen, 1987; Bolaria and Li, 1988).

From the 1970s to the 1990s

New immigration policies opened the door to immigrants from areas that for the past two hundred years had been largely excluded—Asia, the Caribbean, Latin America, and Africa. The "point system" uses nine criteria to assess an applicant's chances of successful integration: age, occupational demand, vocational preparation, arranged employment, location, education, relatives in Canada, official-language competence, and personal suitability. Prospective immigrants are placed in three broad categories: economic, social, and humanitarian. From these categories, they are classified as independent immigrants, family-class immigrants, or convention refugees.

The changes incorporated into the 1978 Immigration Act are a result of a number of factors. First was internal pressure, in the form of a multicultural policy that recognized racial and cultural diversity as a fact of life in Canada. The policy affirmed the contributions of racial and ethnic minorities to the economic, social, and cultural development of Canada. Second, the increasing politicization and mobilization of minority groups led to new demands for a more accessible, non-discriminatory immigration policy. Third, pressure was exerted by human rights activists and lawyers representing organizations such as the Canadian Civil Liberties Association.

A fourth factor was pressure from the international community to eradicate overt racism. Canada's international reputation was badly tarnished by its treatment of Japanese Canadians and Jewish refugees during World War II. Both the formal and informal methods of exclusion that had shaped Canada's immigration policy for over a hundred years were viewed as a contravention of international conventions.

Finally, and probably the most significant force for change, was the economic factor. Immigration from traditional source countries had declined in the 1960s. The postwar recovery of Europe and the establishment of the European Economic Community (EEC) gave Europeans freer access to economic opportunities in Europe and a sense of greater optimism: there was no longer a need to emigrate in order to find work. Also, the labour needs of Canada in the 1960s changed from a dependence on unskilled, manual labour toward the need for a more highly educated and skilled workforce. This fundamental alteration benefited people from developing countries because Europe was unable to supply these workers in sufficient numbers. The result of all the above factors was a dramatic change in the characteristics of immigrants to Canada in the past two decades.

Superficially, the change in immigration policy to a point system suggests that Canada's policy is motivated by equal access and tolerance. However, there may still be inequity, especially in the ways in which the policy is implemented. Richmond, for example, succinctly makes the point that

> Immigration policies need not completely exclude certain nationalities in order to warrant description as "racist." If the intended or unintended consequence of particular regulations is to put certain ethnic groups at a disadvantage while making it easier for others to gain admission, then such policies may be designated "quasi-

racist" or systemic forms of discrimination, even though the admissions criteria make no reference to "race" as such. Thus, visa requirements, literacy tests, health regulations and medical examinations, quotas, preference for close relatives, patrial clauses, the location of immigration officers abroad, and even exclusions based on environmental considerations can have a differential impact on particular ethnic groups. (Richmond, 1994:155)

In a similar vein, Cohen (1987) points out that discrimination did not disappear from Canada's immigration policy. Despite the more universal system and the commitment to non-discrimination in the Act's policy objectives, discrimination was still possible in the immigration process. Under the guise of a universal selection process, myriad seemingly neutral administrative procedures had an **adverse impact** on racial-minority immigrants and constituted differential treatment and racial discrimination.

In the first instance, visa offices were unevenly distributed in developing countries, and few resources were committed to them. Until 1990, there was only one visa office in India and one in China. Moreover, there were differences in processing time for assisted relatives (those sponsored by family members who are Canadian citizens) from developing regions, such as Pakistan, as compared with the United Kingdom. Although visitors from the United States were exempt from visa requirements, countries such as India and Jamaica, originally exempt, now required visas.

Immigration officers were given wide latitude and discretion, which allowed for individual prejudices and even overt racism in their decisions. For example, the point system's "personal suitability" category requires immigration officials to assess an immigrant's "adaptability, motivation, initiative, resourcefulness and other similar qualities" and entitles the officer to evaluate the applicant's cultural background and personal style. The officials, however, lacked an objective method to assess the qualifications that potential immigrants had acquired in other jurisdictions, especially developing countries (Malarek, 1987). One critical analysis of Canada's immigration laws and policies (Jakubowski, 1997) provides a detailed chapter on the relationship of race to immigration policy and concludes that while Canadian immigration law is alleged to be non-discriminatory, unfairness and inequity still characterize aspects of it.

2000 and Beyond

In response to many criticisms of immigration practices, the government of Canada implemented the Immigration and Refugee Protection Act (IRPA) in June 2002. It provided for three classes of immigrants: economic, family class, and refugees. The economic class of immigrants is the one most promoted, and in fact it accounted for 61 percent of all immigrants in the year preceding the new act. Family class accounted for 27 percent and refugees, 11 percent.

The IRPA focused on the Skilled Worker Class, whose selection criteria emphasized the human capital attributes and skills of potential immigrants including language skills, education, age, employment experience, and a category called "adaptability." Critics of the new act charge that it overemphasizes the economic and focuses on how well immigrants are able to contribute to the Canadian economy while ignoring some of the other purposes of immigration to this country. The emphasis on their utilitarian usefulness to the economy resulted in "two normative types: the more desirable 'selected' immigrants who meet the selection criteria of education ... as economic immigrants, and the less desirable 'unsolicited or self-selected' immigrants who are admitted as family members or refugees not screened for human capital" (Li, 2003b:25). Other critics, however, were more concerned with the numbers being admitted to the country in the past few years, questioning the official position that Canada's aging population and low birth rates make substantial immigration necessary. Critics such as Stoffman (2002), Collacott (2002), and journalist Diane Francis (2002) argue that 200 000 or more immigrants per year is excessive. Collacott is especially critical of Canada's policy of allowing extended family members into the country. Arguing that these immigrants are responsible for the decline in the economic performance of new immigrants, he says that the priority given to bringing in such family members who "do not have to meet the skills and language requirements" necessary for integration is ill advised (Collacott, cited in Francis, 2001). Francis is particularly aggressive in her anti-refugee and anti-immigrant stance and admits that she is on an anti-immigration "crusade."

From the perspective of the public, immigration policy is a highly charged issue and one that lends itself to considerable controversy. As the results of the many polls demonstrate (see below, "Polls and Surveys"), large segments of the population do not support an open policy. In fact, a racist discourse of fear of immigration is part of the public agenda. In this discourse, both the numbers and the racial identities of immigrant populations cause racism. The argument here is that if immigration is curbed (particularly from the "Third World"), racism will decrease. However, racism existed well before the large-scale immigration of people of colour into Canada, as evidenced by the exploitative relationship between White colonizers and Aboriginal peoples throughout the history of this country.

Since the 1980s the majority of immigrants to Canada have come from Asia, Africa, Latin America, and the Caribbean. Anti-immigration attitudes are reflected, not in obvious racial terms, but in a collection of myths such as:

- Immigrants take jobs away from Canadians.
- Immigrants are a drain on the economy.
- Immigrants are unskilled, uneducated, and live in poverty.
- Immigrants exploit the welfare system.
- Immigrants commit more crimes.

These statements are clearly fallacious. Numerous studies (e.g., Economic Council of Canada, 1991; Samuel, 1989, 1998) have concluded that immigrants make more jobs than they take. These studies have found that immigrants are more likely to be self-employed and that they bring a significant degree of skill, education, self-reliance, and innovative flair to the Canadian economy. Immigrants do not displace Canadian residents from jobs; they tend to take jobs that residents do not want. Since 1971, immigrants have paid more in taxes than they have used in services. Finally, immigrant rates of criminality are lower than those of the native-born population (Samuel, 1989).

Anti-immigration sentiment also views racism as the inevitable result of different cultures being brought into close proximity, prompting cultural jealousies and conflicts. Racism, however, is not made inevitable by cultural differences. There is no inescapable tension between people who are different. Racial conflict exists only when one group has power over another. The White majority in Canada has political, economic, and social control over most Canadian institutions. When racial discrimination is entrenched in a society's institutions and value systems, the social and economic exclusion of people of colour is to be expected.

Domestic Workers

Canada's domestic workers' program was established in 1955 to deal with the chronic shortage of workers prepared to accept low wages and undesirable working conditions.

Initially the program targeted Black women from the Caribbean region, and later it focused on women from the Philippines. Many of these women who entered Canada as "domestics" were in fact qualified teachers, nurses, and secretaries who were unable to immigrate to Canada because of racist immigration practices. Although they were able to seek other employment after a year's service, they generally faced significant discrimination in the labour market (Ng, 1992; Henry, 1968).

Over the years their status changed, and by 1981, 87.9 percent of domestic workers had temporary work permits, and many of them could expect at some point to be asked to return to their country of origin. Securing permanent resident status from within Canada was discretionary (Task Force on Immigration Practices and Procedures, 1981). The government's immigrant domestic program was structured to allow domestic workers who had worked in Canada continuously for at least two years to apply for landed-immigrant status. But, in order to qualify, workers must demonstrate "self-sufficiency" or the potential to achieve "self-sufficiency." These decisions appear to be based on subjective criteria (Cohen, 1987).

The conditions in which many of the domestic workers are compelled to work underline their marginal status in the Canadian workforce. Although unemployment-insurance premiums and Canada Pension Plan deductions are made from their paycheques, they are unlikely to secure benefits from their contributions (Silvera, 1993:204). They are denied the right to organize into a trade union and therefore lack the power to bargain collectively for better wages or working conditions. In Ontario, they are not covered by the province's health and safety legislation. The amended (1982) Employment Standards Act in Ontario provided greater protection for domestic workers by requiring domestic workers to be paid minimum wage and stipulated the work week. In 1992 Employment and Immigration established certain minimum requirements. The worker should receive $710 per month in Ontario with a deduction of $210 per month for room and board. However, as Silvera (1989) notes, these entitlements are seen as bureaucratic jargon. The reality remains the same: the domestics remain intimidated; complaints are rarely laid. Their tenuous legal status in Canada leads many women to fear reporting employers who fail to comply with the regulations.

The federal government in February 1992 implemented a requirement for prospective domestic workers (nannies) to have Grade 12 education and at least six months' professional child-care experience. While most European workers would be able to meet the new criteria, countries such as the Philippines, India, and Jamaica (where most domestic workers currently come from) have no such training programs; and those workers with Grade 12 equivalency would be unlikely to want to work for minimum wage (Hernandez, 1992; Ng, 1992).

Migrant Workers

In addition to domestic workers who are largely women of colour, Canada also has a migrant labour scheme in which workers from Mexico and the Caribbean come to plant and harvest fruit and vegetables, primarily in southern Ontario. They earn minimum wages and must contribute to the Employment Insurance Act. However, if they fall sick or are injured they are usually sent to their countries of origin and thus lose the benefits they have paid for under the insurance act. (A constitutional challenge was launched against this in 2003.) The agricultural workers are often housed in substandard accommodation, and some of them claim that they are not well treated by their employers. Despite their low earnings by Canadian standards, many return to this scheme because they earn valuable Canadian currency, which helps support their families at home.

Contemporary Racism

The Changing Nature of Canadian Society

Despite the continuing residue of racial discrimination in Canada's immigration policies, a significant shift has occurred in the composition of Canadian society. This changing demographic pattern is largely the result of the ending of the most overt forms of racism in immigration policies and the opening up of immigration to Third World countries.[1]

Canada's population has become increasingly racially diverse. From what was a country largely inhabited by Whites and Aboriginal peoples, the population has changed to include people from more than seventy countries. In 2001, the proportion of foreign-born was the highest it has been for nearly 70 years. As of May 15, 2001, 5.4 million people, or 18.4 percent of the total population, were born outside the country. This was the highest proportion since 1931, when the foreign-born population was 22.2 percent. In 1996, the proportion was 17.4 percent.

The population of Canada now contains more than 200 ethnic groups. The source countries from which Canada's immigrants come have, however, changed from European countries to primarily Asian ones. As a result, the numbers of people of colour or "visible minorities"[2]—the category used by the government of Canada—shows that 13.4 percent of the population, or almost 4 million persons, identified themselves as visible minorities in the most recent census of 2001. This indicates a marked increase, because in 1981 only 1.1 million, or 4.7 percent of the total population, were visible minorities. Moreover, this group is growing more rapidly than the total Canadian population; during the 1990s there was only a 5 percent increase in the total population but the visible minority population increased by 27 percent. The overall increase in the numbers of visible minorities in Canada was largely accounted for by the increased immigration levels of people of colour and the growing number of such persons born in this country. In fact, three out of every ten persons who identified as visible minority were born in Canada. Thus, there is a rapidly expanding second generation of people of colour in this country. Among Japanese, who have been in the country the longest, 65 percent are Canadian-born; while among Blacks, 45 percent are born here. This would probably include indigenous Blacks in the Maritimes and the small settlements in Alberta and Ontario.

There is a special significance in the increase in the numbers of Canadian-born people of colour, because of the continued racism directed against them although many are no longer immigrants. This highlights the difference between race and ethnicity as the second generation of White ethnic immigrants no longer face the discrimination of being immigrants but second-generation people of colour, despite their birth status, still do.

The census analysis of these trends maintains that "If recent immigration trends continue, the visible minority population will continue to grow rapidly over the next couple of decades. Projections show that by 2016, visible minorities will account for one-fifth of Canada's population" (Census of Canada, 2001).

Figure 3.1 shows the rise in levels of the visible minority population as a percentage of the total population over the last twenty years.

The Chinese are the largest visible minority group in Canada, now surpassing 1 million persons. They accounted for 3.5 percent of the total national population and 26 percent of the visible minority population. Chinese make up the largest proportion of the visible minority population in British Columbia (44 percent), Alberta (30 percent), and Saskatchewan (29 percent). Although Ontario had the highest number of Chinese

Figure 3.1

PROPORTION OF VISIBLE MINORITIES, CANADA, 1981–2001

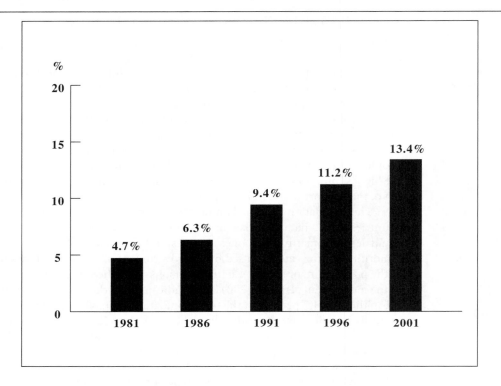

Source: "Proportion of Visible Minorities, Canada, 1981–2001," Statistics Canada website <http://www12.statcan.ca/english/census01/ products/ analytic/companion/etoimm/canada.cfm#threefold_increase>, accessed August 13, 2004.

(481 500), they made up the second-highest proportion (22 percent) of the visible minorities in that province, behind South Asians (26 percent).

The three largest visible minority groups in 2001—Chinese, South Asians and Blacks—accounted for two-thirds of the overall visible minority population. The second largest group is South Asians—917 100 were enumerated in the 2001 census. This figure is up from 670 600 in 1996. South Asians represented 3.1 percent of Canada's population and 23 percent of the total visible minority population. They accounted for at least one-quarter of the visible minority populations in Ontario, Newfoundland and Labrador, and British Columbia.

The census enumerated 662 200 Blacks in 2001, up 15 percent from 573 900 in 1996. This third largest visible minority group represented 2.2 percent of the country's total population and 17 percent of the visible minority population.

Canada's visible minority population also included Filipinos (8 percent), Arabs and West Asians (8 percent), Latin Americans (5 percent), Southeast Asians (5 percent), Koreans (3 percent), and Japanese (2 percent). Combined, their population of about 1.2 million represented one-third of the total visible minority population in 2001.

Figure 3.2

VISIBLE MINORITY GROUPS IN CANADA, 1981–2001

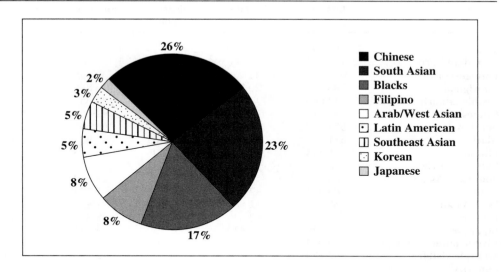

Source: "Proportion of Visible Minorities, Canada, Montreal, Toronto and Vancouver," Statistics Canada website <http://www12.statcan.ca/english/census01/products/analytic/companion/etoimm/canada.cfm#threefold_increase>, accessed August 13, 2004.

In the past twenty years or so, Canada has seen a significant rise in the number of minority communities, as Figure 3.2 shows. The majority of racial-minority groups are located in the three largest urban areas and it has grown over the years primarily through increased immigration. For example, the percentage of visible minorities in the entire country has increased from 4.7 percent in 1981 to 13.4 percent in 2001. In Toronto for the same time period, the shift is from 13.6 to 36.8 percent; in Vancouver the growth is significant, from 13.9 to 35.9 percent. In the city of Montreal, for the same time period, it is from 5.2 to 13.6 percent. Thus, all three of Canada's major cities have received substantial numbers of visible minority immigrants.

The disaggregated data for these three cities shows that Toronto has the largest numbers of foreign-born as compared to Montreal and Vancouver. Table 3.1 provides data on the proportion of visible minorities in both the three major cities and their provinces.

Ontario and Toronto continue to receive the highest number of immigrants in Canada. It is particularly interesting to note that the numbers of Canadian-born and foreign-born in the city of Toronto are quite close. Toronto has nearly twice the number of foreign-born of Vancouver and of Montreal. Ontario also has more Aboriginal people than either of the two other provinces.

In sum, the 2001 census data shows a substantial increase in the numbers of visible minority populations in Canada. The issue of immigration continues to be strongly contested, and many opposing discourses pervade the public agenda. Some of these are discussed in the following section.

Table 3.1

VISIBLE MINORITIES AND ABORIGINALS IN ONTARIO, BRITISH COLUMBIA, AND QUEBEC

	Ontario	Toronto	British Columbia	Vancouver	Quebec	Montreal
Total	11 285 545	4 647 960	3 868 875	1 967 475	7 125 575	3 380 640
Canadian-born	8 164 860	2 556 860	2 821 870	1 199 760	6 378 420	2 724 205
Foreign-born	3 030 075	2 032 960	1 009 815	738 555	706 965	621 890
Aboriginal	188 315	20 300	170 025	36 855	79 400	11 085
Visible minority	2 153 045	1 712 530	836 445	725 655	497 975	458 330
Chinese	481 510	409 535	365 490	342 665	56 830	52 110
South Asian	554 870	473 810	210 295	164 365	59 510	57 935
Black	411 090	310 500	25 465	18 405	152 195	139 305
Filipino	156 515	133 675	64 005	57 025	18 550	17 890
Latin American	106 835	75 915	23 885	18 715	59 520	53 155
Southeast Asian	86 410	53 565	34 970	28 460	44 115	39 570
Arab	88 545	42 830	6 605	5 905	73 345	67 830
West Asian	67 100	52 980	22 380	21 435	12 425	11 580
Korean	53 955	42 620	31 965	28 850	4 410	3 760
Japanese	24 925	17 420	32 730	24 025	2 830	2 295
Visible minority n.i.e.[a]	78 915	66 455	4 195	3 320	7 555	6 785
Multiple visible minority[b]	42 375	33 240	14 465	12 490	6 705	6 115

[a]Not included elsewhere; for example, those who cited ethnicity of Polynesian, Guyanese, Mauritian.
[b]For example, "Black and South Asian."

Source: Statistics Canada site <http://www.statcan.ca/english>.

Contemporary Immigration Discourses

Despite Canada's relatively open immigration laws, this issue remains hotly contested, especially among those on the right or conservative end of the political spectrum. Critics maintain that the country is taking in too many immigrants, that they are oversettling in the three major urban areas, and that they are beginning to be the focus of the urban poor. For most critics, the question of immigration levels remains a serious one, since it is believed that current levels of about 250 000 per year are too high. It is argued that immigration should be only one tool for meeting labour needs and replacing aging populations.

Current immigration practice divides into three streams. The first includes economic immigrants, who numbered 153 000 in 2001, but of these only 65 700 were workers and the rest were accompanying family members. There were also 27 800 refugees, and 66 600 persons who were classified as family members of immigrants already in the country, for a total of 250 346 for that year.

It is such figures that have provoked four books published in 2002–2003 on the subject. Three are written by those who might be described as holding more ideologically more conservative beliefs: Daniel Stoffman's *Who Gets In* (2002), Diane Francis' *Immigration: The Economic Case* (2002), and Martin Collacott's report published for the Fraser Institute (2002). The fourth book, written by Peter Li, is *Destination Canada: Immigration Debates and Issues* (2003); it presents a more balanced and scholarly discussion of the issue. (A discussion of how the media presents other representations and images of immigrants can be found in Henry and Tator, 2002.)

Stoffman takes a cynical outlook on immigration. He challenges the official view that immigration is necessary to sustain economic growth, but does not provide much evidence to support his claim. He believes that a "myth" of immigration has been foisted on the public, making them believe Canada needs immigration for growth despite evidence from the last census that the population grew only by 4 percent since the 1996 census. He calls the need for growth policy a "cancer-cell theory of economics" (97) but presents no evidence to support a contrary argument. In a chapter headed "The Illusion of Multiculturalism," Stoffman identifies a number of cultural practices that immigrants bring with them and that are not acceptable to Canadians, such as the eating of dog, chewing khat, and other supposedly offensive practices. He argues that since such practices are not acceptable to Canadians, the country does not have a truly multicultural policy. Such sophistic arguments pervade the book. Stoffman is especially critical of the Immigration and Refugee Board and its members whom he calls political hacks. He believes that politicians who work for immigration are essentially a "liberal dominated committee … acting as a lobby group for the immigration and refugee industry" (157) and that the system generally has been taken over by "Canadian lawyers and consultants whose livelihood depend on a steady flow of self-selected claimants and smuggling racketeers"(154). He cites at length a fact-finding hearing of the House of Commons Standing Committee on Citizenship and Immigration meeting in 2001 that he compares to "Canada's version of [Joe] McCarthy" (175). Throughout, Stoffman declares himself to be a middle-of-the-roader in favour of a more limited immigration system that he claims will be of more benefit to the country. Aside from a somewhat narrow understanding of immigration and refugee dynamics, Stoffman rarely cites evidence for his conclusions, and the work is seriously marred by this omission.

Martin Collacott, on the other hand, attempts to present a more balanced view, but he too seriously challenges the numbers admitted under the country's present determination system. He argues that the country neither wants nor needs a larger population and that it is facing a "massive skills shortage" is not supported by the facts (2). He contends that economic growth does not require larger populations. He believes that a significant number of newly arrived immigrants are living under the poverty line, but he does not recognize that one of the major obstacles to their economic integration is the inability of the public and private sectors to recognize immigrant credentials. He acknowledges that this lack of recognition exists but not that it helps in creating the pockets of immigrant poverty he cites. ("The poverty levels of those who arrived before 1986 was 19.7 per cent," says Collacott's 51-page study. "The poverty level of those who came after 1991 has reached a disturbing 52.1 per cent.")

Collacott argues that there are better ways of dealing with an aging population than bringing in immigrants, and he cites training more Canadians as an additional strategy. He contends that the government is at fault because its "principal reason for promoting high immigration levels is the belief that most newcomers will vote for the Liberal Party," and he notes that "A major part of the costs fall on provincial and municipal governments even though the programs are designed with the interests of the federal government in mind." While he rarely indulges in the diatribes or inflammatory language of the other two writers on this subject, Collacott nevertheless recommends decreasing immigration levels, and he calls for a better and more comprehensive government policy not motivated by politics.

One of the most vociferous of critics has been Diane Francis, who admits that she is on an anti-immigration "crusade." She has, over the years, written many columns on the dangers of our immigration system, and much of her work relates to the qualities of the immigrants and refugees let into the country. Her main thesis appears to be that there are many "bad apples" among them. She comments:

that nobody is committed to getting rid of them. The costs to society of this immigration are unknown, in both monetary terms as well as human terms. How many lives are ruined as a result of violence by outsiders? Pockets picked? Seniors shaken down? Teens hooked on heroin? Women raped? Children unsupported by deadbeat dads? Banks robbed and companies or governments defrauded? Most importantly why should we put up with anyone from elsewhere who commits a serious crime? (76)

Her plan for improving the system includes a reduction in immigration targets, and eligibility for citizenship based on having a clean criminal record after having lived 10 years within the country.

The fourth book published during this period, Li's, merely presents the issue under debate without engaging in polemical or vitriolic discourse. The intent of the book is to provide information on questions such as: Should Canada follow an expansionist policy in admitting immigrants? Is Canada benefited or harmed by immigrants? And above all: How can such costs and benefits be assessed objectively" (8)? Recognizing that immigration presents complex challenges to a country like Canada, Li notes that even an open debate on these contested issues can provide information to the public and clear up some of the misleading myths that surround the issue. After careful review of the evidence and despite the lack of conceptual clarity in terms used in the debate, Li concludes that if Canada does not maintain its current immigration levels, its position "is likely to erode in comparison to the United States, which has been expanding in population size and in the scale of the advanced economy" (177).

While critics challenge Canada's relatively open immigration policies, the government itself is committed to maintaining current levels at anywhere between 200 000 and 250 000 immigrants per year. Recent data compiled though Statistics Canada, however, reveals that immigrants are continuing to find barriers to employment especially among professional and managerially trained immigrants. Six out of ten immigrants have to change their fields of specialization in order to find work in Canada. For example, of 38.6 percent of immigrants trained in the natural and applied sciences, only 18.8 percent found employment in their fields. Barriers created by the non-recognition of foreign credentials, lack of contacts, and language problems were the primary issues (Statistics Canada, 2003).

Evidence of Racism

The demographics of the country are rapidly changing, as the census data indicates, but unfortunately racism and racial discrimination in all its many forms still impacts on the many communities and peoples of colour now resident in Canada. The evidence for their continued victimization is to be found in many different sources, one of which is the most important and reliable: people's direct experience. More evidence is in the numerous reports of task forces, commissions, and surveys often conducted by academics, public authorities, and ad hoc advisory committees, and in the oral histories of people of colour. A growing body of literature documents the experiences of racial minorities. Although these kinds of data are sometimes dismissed as too subjective, they are critical to the understanding of racism.

Another source is the polls and surveys that seek to measure racist attitudes among individuals or groups. In the past two decades, government agencies, politicians, the media, and academics have initiated many such surveys. Yet another is the research findings of academics and commissioned studies by universities and other public-sector agencies.

The next sections of this chapter examine the evidence of employment discrimination. Employment discrimination has been singled out for special attention because it is perhaps the single most important arena in which racism flourishes. Barriers to access and equity in the workplace ultimately affect all other areas of social functioning.

Victims' Manifestations

This form of evidence of racism in Canadian society has a long history. It can be found in a large number of government-sponsored inquiries, task forces, and commissions, which are usually established after a series of highly publicized events or incidents involving members of racial-minority communities. While both federal and provincial governments have, over the years, publicly stated their intentions to eliminate racism in Canadian society, the evidence indicates otherwise.

As far back as 1977, the Pittman report found sufficient evidence of racism in Toronto, including subway attacks and racial violence in public areas, to warrant action. In the same year, the annual report of the Ontario Human Rights Commission raised concerns about the dramatic increase in reported incidents of assaults and verbal abuse against racial minorities. Another report that year (Ubale, 1977), documenting a series of case histories of **racial incidents** as related by South-Asian victims, indicated that the individuals responsible belonged to all groups and socioeconomic categories and even included police and immigration officers. Like Pittman, Ubale identified racism as the root cause and suggested that it was linked to the racial bias and discrimination of Canadian institutions.

Head (1981) conducted a study on the adaptation of racial-minority immigrants in Canadian society by analyzing their perceptions of discriminatory treatment in the areas of housing, employment, and access to community services. He identified a number of barriers that prevented racial minorities from gaining suitable employment, such as the requirement for "Canadian experience." More than half of the respondents indicated that their present employment was not the type of work they were seeking or trained for. When respondents were asked about their perceptions of the extent of racial discrimination in Metropolitan Toronto, almost 90 percent of Blacks and 72.2 percent of South Asians felt "some" or a "great deal" of discrimination.

In 1981, following the killing of a South-Asian man in Vancouver, 1800 people demonstrated. The rally was a response to the growing incidence of violent attacks and the widespread racist activities of the Ku Klux Klan. During the rally, several people required hospitalization (Barrett, 1984). In 1982, the federal government investigation into racial tensions in 11 urban communities across the country found that the racial climate was "tense." The study catalogued expressions of racism that ranged from the subtle acts of "polite racists" to the "sometimes violent" acts of zealots in each of these communities (Secretary of State, 1982).

In the same year, the Quebec Human Rights Commission investigated violence between Haitian-born cabbies and Whites in the taxi industry that resulted from the firing of 20 Black taxi drivers from one company. The inquiry found that customers regularly asked for and were given White drivers only. Moreover, many taxi companies were refusing to hire Blacks. The widespread discrimination against Black taxi drivers was found to be only the latest in a series of racial incidents.

Continuing racial tension in Vancouver resulted in the publication of an important survey documenting racist incidents involving South-Asian Canadians in that city (Robson and Breems, 1985). It found that about half of Indo-Canadians (South Asians) had experienced at least one hostile incident in the two-year time frame of the study. The most frequently cited incidents involved name-calling, verbal threats, and physical gestures, which occurred in cars, on the streets, in shopping malls, and in other public places.

In the mid-1980s, the federal government established a parliamentary task force to examine the nature and extent of racism in Canadian society. The catalyst for the task force was the cumulative effect of "racist incidents" that could no longer be ignored by the government. The report, *Equality Now*, was published in 1984. Authors of the briefs and witnesses who appeared before the task force described the devastating experiences and debilitating effects of racial prejudice and discrimination on the then approximately two million people of colour living in Canada in 1984. The racial barriers identified included both the intentional discriminatory behaviour of racist individuals and the systematic and systemic barriers created by the major institutions in Canadian society, including schools, employers, media, justice, and law enforcement.

In the late 1980s, evidence of the growing intolerance and acts of discrimination were also documented in the annual reports of the Canadian Human Rights Commission. The 1989 report, for example, raised concerns about the nature of the controversy over whether Sikhs should be allowed to wear turbans in the Royal Canadian Mounted Police (RCMP). The issue resulted in petitions tabled in the Commons carrying the names of as many as 250 000 Canadians who supported the proposition "that a handful of Sikhs wearing turbans would 'crack up the RCMP'" (Camp, 1990). Racist pins and calendars depicting turban-clad Mounties appeared across Canada.

In 1991, two major incidents in Nova Scotia drew attention to the racism directed at its Black community. In Cole Harbour, a community east of Dartmouth, a fight between a Black and a White youth attending a high school led to a larger confrontation involving about fifty Black and White students and non-students. The RCMP were called in to investigate, and charges were laid against 18 people, 10 of whom were Black. The parents unanimously protested the arrest of the students from these communities and decided to unite to ease racial tensions. Eventually the charges were dropped, except those against five Black defendants. The *Report of the Nova Scotia Advisory Group on Race Relations* (1991) found that racism was rampant in the province and in all levels of the school system. The report also focused on the racial implications of unemployment among Blacks. In the same year, another incident in Nova Scotia escalated into a series of racial disturbances involving Black youths who were refused entrance to a downtown Halifax bar. It culminated in a demonstration involving more than a thousand people.

The *Report* provided the context for these incidents. It suggested that Blacks in the province had been excluded from all areas of mainstream life in the communities in which they, their parents, grandparents, and great-grandparents were born. Racist attitudes converged with racist policies and practices to deprive Blacks and other minorities from access to housing, education, employment, and other services that most White Canadians take for granted, such as access to bars and restaurants.

The responses of the White and Black communities to incidents of racial unrest underscore how the two groups (one with power and privilege, the other deprived of fundamental rights) understand racism. Many Blacks readily speak of the explosion of racial tension as inevitable in a racist society, whereas White individuals express shock and anger at the threat of increased racial violence.

In the summer of 1992, the premier of Ontario, Bob Rae, appointed a former Canadian ambassador to the United Nations, Stephen Lewis, to lead a special inquiry on race relations following a disturbance in Toronto a few weeks before. A night of violence and looting followed a peaceful protest by a mixed-race crowd of more than two thousand people decrying the acquittal of Los Angeles police officers whose beating of a Black man was caught on videotape. While the rioters were of all races, the provincial government saw it as a symptom of racial unrest and called for an investigation.

Lewis consulted widely with individuals and groups from racial minorities, particularly the Black community, across the province. He concluded in his report that the root of the problem was anti-Black racism. He argued that while every racial-minority community experienced the impact of systemic discrimination across Ontario, it is the Black community that is the most deeply impacted. He noted:

> It is Blacks who are being shot, it is Black youth that is unemployed in excessive numbers, it is Black students who are being inappropriately streamed in schools, it is Black kids who are disproportionately dropping out. … It is Black employees, professional and non-professional, on whom the doors of upward equity slam shut. (Lewis, 1992:2)

Concerns about racism and the justice system, including the police shootings of Black men and the overrepresentation of Blacks in the prisons, led the Ontario government to appoint a commission to inquire into racism in the justice system. (Its findings are discussed in Chapter 5 of this book.)

Moving to the present period, the Ontario Human Rights Commission undertook a major project in which it asked persons of colour who believed themselves to be victims of racial profiling by police or other sectors of society (e.g., education, media, employment, etc.) to share their experiences. This inquiry followed upon the publication of a series of highly publicized articles in the *Toronto Star* that showed the extent of police racial profiling of Blacks (*Toronto Star*, October–December 2002). The Commission received over 800 responses, some of which were cited in their recent report. The intent of the inquiry was to give voice to those individuals and communities who had experienced racial profiling, and to bridge the gap between those who continue to deny the existence of racism and the communities who feel targeted by racial bias and differential treatment (Ontario Human Rights Commission, 2003).

Another form of evidence can be found in the recently published books of racial-minority scholars, especially women of colour, who have been writing about racism in a general sense but specifically how they manage and maneuver themselves and their identity in ways that make them empowered rather than victims. Yvonne Bobb-Smith's *I Know Who I Am: A Caribbean Woman's Identity* (2003) is a case in point. She recorded the stories of 45 Caribbean women living in Canada and their experiences with racism and sexism in their everyday lives, including her own as a professional academic. The book celebrates the empowerment of these women whose identity has not been submerged by racism. In a similar vein, Vijay Agnew's *Where I Come From* (2003) relies on her personal journey as an academic in a Canadian university coping with painful experiences of racism and discrimination while attempting to retain aspects of her identity as a woman of South-Asian origin (see further examples in Chapter 8).

Although often dismissed as "anecdotal evidence," personal stories of those most impacted by racism provides a powerful counter-narrative to the dominant discourse of denial so pervasive in Canadian society.

Polls and Surveys

Despite criticism of polls and surveys about ethno-racial attitudes (Li, 2003:172–173), they are routinely used to monitor public opinion on this and many other issues. The most recent and probably the most important survey conducted on this subject was not devised as an opinion poll, but merely to inform public and governmental policy. The *Ethnic Diversity Survey* was developed by Statistics Canada in collaboration with the Department of Canadian Heritage. Telephone interviews of 42 500 persons aged 15 and over were conducted in April through August 2002 and initial results were released in September 2003. While it covered many topics related to ethnicity, of particular concern to this book are its findings on racism and discrimination.

While 80 percent of respondents never felt "uncomfortable or out of place," 20 percent did and, of these, visible minorities were more likely to feel uncomfortable. An overwhelming majority of over 80 percent of the respondents said they did not experience discrimination or unfair treatment but 20 percent of visible minorities did so. And of these, Blacks were far more likely to report such experiences—nearly one-third, 32 percent— while 21 percent of South Asians and 18 percent of Chinese did. The main reason for their unfair treatment and feelings of discomfort were because of skin colour (71 percent). Of particular interest is that a large majority of those who had experienced discrimination or unfair treatment did so when applying for a job or at their workplace. Stores, banks, and restaurants were also cited but less often.

This survey is extremely important not only for its results—which, however, are not especially surprising given the many studies cited throughout this book that clearly demonstrate racism and discrimination are pervasive in Canadian society[3]—but also for the care and attention the substantial resources of these government agencies were able to bring to methodology, sampling procedure, and other aspects of research design.

White Supremacist and Hate Groups

An ideology of White supremacy was long considered within the bounds of respectable, defensible opinion in Canada. In the colonial era, Aboriginal peoples were portrayed by church and state as "heathens" and "savages" and somehow less than human. These images provided justification for the extermination, segregation, and subjugation of Aboriginal peoples. The dehumanizing impact of such blatant propaganda is clearly evident today in the conditions of many Aboriginal communities (Frideres, 1983).

The 1920s and the 1930s saw the development of racist organizations such as the Ku Klux Klan (KKK), which openly promoted hatred against Catholics, Jews, Blacks, and other minorities. The original Klan was founded in Tennessee in 1866. It established bases in Alberta, Manitoba, Saskatchewan, British Columbia, and Ontario, feeding on Canadian anti-Semitism and the fear of Blacks and southern Europeans. While the KKK in Canada today appears to have only a handful of members, a network of other groups peddle hate propaganda, including the Heritage Front, the Liberty Lobby, the Church of the Creator, the Church of Jesus Christ–Aryan Nation, the Aryan Resistance Movement, and the Western Guard. All these groups share an ideology that supports the view that the Aryan—defined as the superior White race—is superior to all others morally, intellectually, and culturally and that it is Whites' manifest destiny to dominate society.

Barrett (1987) made a significant contribution to understanding the recent activities of the extreme right in Canada. He found 130 organizations but under 600 members, many of whom belonged to more than one organization. An important strategy used by these groups is to defend their activities by presenting themselves as defenders of free expression. Since they consider themselves to be promoting the principles of civil libertarianism, any attempts to curb their activities are portrayed as **censorship** and therefore anti-democratic.

Since the publication of Barrett's pioneering work, the numbers of right-wing groups have proliferated in Canada. KKK branches are active in all of Canada's major cities.

Offshoots such as the Heritage Front, the Church of the Creator, the Knights for White Rights, and the Aryan Nation are flourishing. Their presence is felt in the many telephone "hot lines" established throughout the country that spew hate messages, many directed at Aboriginal peoples and racial minorities. Multiculturalism and immigration policies are also frequently criticized. The messages hammer home the theme "Keep Canada White." Today the emphasis of these groups is less on organized meetings and more on the development of websites, including those organized by Tri-City Skins, Canadian Ethnic Cleansing Team, Canadian Heritage Alliance, the Freedom-Site, Canadian Hooligans, Resistance, and many others. There are thousands of sites today, and they are growing because there are no controls on what can be put on the Net.

In 1995, the Federal Department of Justice issued a report that indicates that the majority of hate crimes recorded by police across Canada were directed against racial minorities:

- Sixty-one percent of all hate crime incidents were directed against racial minorities.
- Twenty-three percent were against religious minorities.
- Eleven percent were against gays or lesbians.
- Five percent were against ethnic minorities. (Roberts, 1995)

In the early 1990s, the Canadian Human Rights Commission began launching actions to prohibit telephone hate lines. Several of these lines in Vancouver, Toronto, and Manitoba were ordered to cease airing hate messages. In addition the Commission has had several hearings and decisions against White supremacists on the Net, including Ernst Zundel, a prominent White supremacist and purveyor of hate messages.

Recent Research

Hate crime activity has risen dramatically in Canada as a result of the September 11, 2001 terrorist attacks in the United States. In Toronto, for example, the Hate Crime Unit of the Toronto Police Service reported that the number of such crimes rose to 338 incidents up from 204 the previous year (Mock, 2003). Many of the new incidents were directed against Muslims and Arabs living in Canada and their mosques and temples were specifically targeted. The incidents include:

- Sixteen bomb threats toward mosques in Canada, and three known acts of arson— in Montreal, in St. Catharines, and in Hamilton, Ontario.
- Muslim students at Laval University in Quebec were harassed and threatened; similar reports came in from campuses and schools across the country.
- A 15-year-old Arab boy in Ottawa was beaten by 12 teenagers and left unconscious.
- Female staff members of an Islamic school in London wearing the traditional hijab were taunted by passing motorists.
- There were 11 reported hate-based incidents in Toronto, and 7 in Montreal of harassment, vandalism, and bomb threats against Jewish individuals and institutions, and many additional hateful messages on the Internet.
- A Surrey, British Columbia Aboriginal man and his fiancée, mistaken for Sikhs, were viciously attacked by teens armed with a crowbar (cited in Mock, 2003).

The Canadian Race Relations Foundation noted that not only did incidents against Muslim, Arab, and South-Asian Canadians escalate during this period, but so did the continuing "scapegoating of Jews, immigrants and refugees. ... Hate crime is indeed a serious problem in Canada today confirmed by reports in Halifax, Montreal, Toronto, Calgary, Vancouver and affecting local communities from coast to coast."

In its most recent study, the Canadian Centre for Justice Statistics (2004) reported that most hate crime victims were targeted because of race or ethnicity. In the category of religious persecution, most victims were Jewish.

Research also indicates that actual acts of violence or hate crimes committed against racial and other minorities have increased. A study commissioned to determine the nature and extent of hate activity in Metro Toronto (Mock, 1996) offered the following definitions of hate activity:

- *hate/bias crime:* "criminal offense against a person or property that is based solely on the victim's race, religion, nationality, ethnic origin or sexual orientation";
- *hate/bias incidents:* "incidents of harassment and other biased activity that is not criminal, including name calling, taunting, slurs, graffiti, derogatory or offensive material, vandalism and threatening or offensive behaviour based on the victim's race, creed, ethnicity or sexual orientation" (Mock, 1996:14).

The study examined a wide variety of statistical indicators. These included the data from the only three agencies that keep such records, including the Metro Toronto Police Hate Crimes Unit. Qualitative measures such as interviews, focus-group discussions, and reviews of other available literature were also used. The findings reveal that

> as the population of Metropolitan Toronto continues to become more diverse, and as difficult economic times continue to fuel the backlash against immigrants and minority groups, the reported incidents of hate motivated activity have steadily increased. While these findings could be the result of increased awareness of reporting mechanisms … it is unlikely, since the anecdotal evidence of the perceptions of community workers and caseworkers corroborates the statistical findings. (Mock, 1996:57)

Moreover, the groups most singled out were Jews, Blacks, and homosexuals.

In a comprehensive statistical analysis of hate crimes in Canada, Roberts (1995) estimated that the total number of hate crimes committed in 1994 in nine major urban centres in Canada was approximately 60 000, including crimes motivated by race hatred as well as ethnicity and religion.

In sum, although the research evidence does not generally support an increase in negative attitudes, there has apparently been an increase in actual behaviour as measured by the escalation of hate-related criminal activity.

Employment Discrimination

One of the clearest demonstrations of racism in a society is the lack of access and equity experienced by people of colour in the workplace. A number of studies over the past two decades have documented the nature and extent of racial bias and discrimination in employment. One study, *Who Gets the Work?* (Henry and Ginzberg, 1984), examined access to employment. In this field research, evenly matched Black and White job seekers were sent to apply for entry positions advertised in a major newspaper. An analysis of the results of several hundred applications and interviews revealed that White applicants received job offers three times more often than Black applicants did. In addition, telephone callers with accents, particularly those from South Asia and the Caribbean, were more often screened out when they phoned to inquire about a job vacancy.

A follow-up study to *Who Gets the Work?* focused on the attitude, hiring, and management practices of large businesses and corporations in Toronto. This report, *No Discrimination Here*, documented the perceptions of employers and personnel managers in these organizations. In personnel interviews, recruitment, hiring, promotion, training, and termination practices, a high level of both racial prejudice and discrimination was demonstrated; 28 percent of the respondents felt that racial minorities did not have the ability to meet performance criteria as well as Whites did (Billingsley and Musynski, 1985).

Thus, racist behaviour stretches along a wide continuum. At one end are the overt and covert daily acts of discrimination involving a significant proportion of the mainstream community; at the other are far more explicit and extreme racist activity in the form of hate propaganda and racial violence perpetrated by a small minority of the population.

Discrimination in the Workplace

Employment discrimination is a form of systemic discrimination that operates in corporate public- and private-sector organizations. It results from the operation of established procedures of recruitment, hiring, and promotion, most of which is not necessarily designed to promote discrimination. The discrimination is then reinforced by the very exclusion of the disadvantaged group because the exclusion fosters the belief, both within and outside the group, that it is the result of natural or essentialized forces—as, for example, the common belief that women "just can't do the job."

It is often difficult to prove discrimination in its systemic forms, especially when it concerns race in jobs with more complex responsibilities such as high-level management— the so-called "glass ceiling" cases. "Cases involving race may more often have a basis in informal practices, which are more difficult to prove than cases involving violations of formalized institutional behaviour" (Beck, Reitz, and Weiner, 2002:377).

Discrimination in the workplace, directed primarily at immigrants, and immigrants of colour in particular, has not disappeared. In fact, if anything, areas of inequity are as startling today as they were in former times. In the mid-1980s, concern over employment discrimination against people of colour, women, persons with disabilities, and Aboriginal peoples led the federal government to establish a royal commission on equality in employment (Abella, 1984). Its task was to inquire into the employment practices of 11 designated Crown and government-owned corporations and to explore the most effective means of promoting equality in employment for four groups: women, Native peoples, disabled persons, and racial minorities. Its findings echoed the conclusions of the report *Equality Now* (1984) that racial bias and discrimination were a pervasive reality in the employment system. The commissioner, Judge Rosalie Abella, observed that "strong measures were needed to remedy the impact of discriminatory attitudes and behaviour." The remedy she recommended was employment equity legislation (Abella, 1984).

Federal employment equity legislation for the four target groups identified by the Abella Commission was first introduced in 1986, and strengthened in 1995 and again in 2001 with a proactive initiative called Embracing Change that set targets for the four groups. In 1995, the annual report of the president of the Treasury Board revealed that small progress had been made with respect to the hiring of members of equity-targeted groups. For example, the percentage of women in the public service increased from 42.9 percent in 1988 to 47.4 percent in 1995. The percentage of Aboriginal representation increased from 1.7 to 2.2 percent, while visible-minority representation increased from 2.9 to 4.1 percent. In all of these categories, the available labour pool is much higher.

In 2001, the Federal Human Rights Commission found that representation of visible minorities in the private sector increased from 4.9 percent in 1987 to 11.7 percent as of December 31, 2001, and that the percentage of hires increased from 12 percent in 2000 to 12.6 percent in 2001, which surpassed the 1996 census benchmark of 11.6 percent of

CASE STUDY 3.1

CASE STUDY OF EMPLOYMENT DISCRIMINATION: *NATIONAL CAPITAL ALLIANCE ON RACE RELATIONS (NCARR) V. HEALTH AND WELFARE CANADA*

Background

In 1997, a Canadian Human Rights Tribunal decision in *National Capital Alliance on Race Relations (NCARR) v. Health and Welfare Canada* was a milestone in the control of workplace racial discrimination. This was the first successful human rights case of systemic racial discrimination in Canada, and one that also included an effective employment equity remedy. NCARR, a nonprofit anti-racism advocacy group, filed its complaint with the Canadian Human Rights Commission (CHRC) in 1992. The resulting decision, focusing on barriers to promotion of visible minorities to top management positions—the so-called "glass ceiling" phenomenon—was particularly important because it underscored how systemic racial discrimination is sometimes hidden and obscure. The respondent in the case was not an obviously prejudiced rogue employer. It was the Government of Canada—more specifically the Federal Public Service (FPS), which regularly affirms its commitment to equal opportunity and multiculturalism. The Tribunal's decision resulted in strong public exposure of the employment discrimination in the public service of Canada. As part of the Tribunal's work, a survey of Health Canada employees was undertaken.

The survey was designed to provide a description of access to career development opportunities, and also the processes by which such access was gained for different racial groups. The federal public service union assisted in developing the survey questions, and it provided access to the addresses of its members for mailing questionnaires. The union also financed the survey, using its own staff to administer a mail-back questionnaire. It coded the data and retained a survey analyst to oversee technical issues, analyze the data, and write a report (Reitz, 1996).

The survey showed that visible minorities lacked equal access to management-relevant career development training (the Health Canada Management Development Program or some similar course) particularly among males, persons with a graduate degree, and supervisors. It also showed that visible minorities less often sat on selection boards (the ad hoc committees that interview and select candidates for promotion), particularly among those more senior in terms of educational qualifications, years of experience at Health Canada, and supervisory responsibility. Since service on selection boards is a managerial decision, it appeared that managers very strongly favoured White candidates over minorities. Additionally, the report provided telling results in two other areas. Career development training and holding acting positions boosted supervisory responsibilities more often for Whites than for non-Whites, so even where visible minorities managed to obtain the same type of experience as Whites they were not being given managerial responsibilities. With respect to encouragement, Whites more often reported that their managers had encouraged them to apply for management training and acting positions, while visible minorities were more often proactive in seeking these opportunities. This suggests that proactive efforts by minorities may have offset what could otherwise have been a somewhat larger racial disparity in training experiences and acting opportunities. The survey report concluded that the survey data indicated racial minorities experience significant disadvantages in exposure to career development opportunities at Health Canada, particularly in such discretionary areas as encouragement to seek training and acting opportunities and service on selection boards.

Source: Beck, Reitz, and Weiner, 2003.

visible minorities in the population. In the public sector, visible minorities held only 2.7 percent of all positions in the federal public service. By March 31, 2002, this had increased to 6.8 percent. Despite the improvement the Human Rights Commission is concerned that "at the current rate of progress, the government will fail to meet its target," which, as contained in the new Embracing Change initiative, was set at 20 percent hiring to be attained by March 2003. There is a specific need to apply new hiring goals to the executive category, where visible minorities held only 3.8 percent of positions, and of 73 new hires in this category in 2001–2002 only three went to visible minorities.

In its most recent report of 2003, the Commission again found that hiring and promotion had not reached the targets set earlier by the Treasury Board. Visible minority representation in the public service reached 7.4 percent—still less than the target—and their share of new hires, 9.5 percent, was less than half the target. In the executive category, only 7 out of 82 persons were visible minorities (Canadian Human Rights Commission, 2003).

In a report released in September 2002 and prepared by the Public Service Commission, it was found that federal hiring rules are widely ignored by managers and that favouritism is still very common. Managers continue to hire spouses, siblings, cousins, and people they know rather than conforming to the rules designed to ensure public service jobs are accessible to everyone. Hiring transactions often appear to be developed with the aim of appointing an already known person to the position. The report is based on more than 1000 hirings that took place in eight government departments (cited in *The Ottawa Citizen*, January 2, 2004). These practices have very serious implications for the employment of visible minorities because they substantially limit their access to public service positions.[4]

Although the federal government has attempted to increase its representation of minorities, downsizing as well as residual racist attitudes have led to smaller than required gains. In addition, minority-group employees complained in a survey that employment practices were unfair and racially biased. A number of complaints to the Canadian Human Rights Commission, including a class action representing more than one hundred employees of Health Canada, were made in the 1990s. Most involved professional employees who believed that they had not had equal access to promotional opportunities in the public service, particularly with respect to managerial positions. A tribunal of the commission found in favour of the complainants in the class action against Health Canada. In sum, there has been little real progress for minorities in the federal public service, due largely to the inability and unwillingness of this institution to respond to social and demographic imperatives.

Levels of Education and Income Differentials

Educational qualifications are extremely important in seeking employment as well as promotion. Members of racial-minority groups have higher levels of education than other Canadians. An early study by Reitz, Calzavara, and Dasko (1981) found, for example, that 23 percent had university degrees, in contrast with 14 percent of other Canadians. Moreover, racial minorities had consistently higher levels of education than other workers in the lower-paying occupations. Despite higher levels of education, members of racial-minority groups were paid lower salaries than other Canadians. The study also demonstrated that considerable income disparities existed among various ethno-racial groups. People of colour, such as those from the Caribbean and more recently arrived groups such as Portuguese, ranked lowest in incomes.

More recent studies continue to confirm income differentials despite higher levels of education. The average salary for all levels of education for a member of a racial minority in both the upper and middle levels and other management occupations was approximately 18 percent lower than that of the total population (Employment and Immigration Canada, 1992:57). Even in the "other manual workers" category, including all levels of education, members of racial minorities earned nearly 10 percent less than all other manual workers. Another study issued in 1995, and provocatively entitled "The Colour of Money," found that Aboriginal and visible-minority men earned significantly less income than native-born and White immigrant men in Canada. The earnings differentials were not explained by socioeconomic variables such as education, place of schooling, occupation, and others, which were controlled for in this study. Even visible-minority men born in Canada suffered about a 10 percent earnings penalty. These differences were, however, not found among visible-minority women as compared with Canadian-born or immigrant White women. The researchers also noted that while there were clear-cut earning differentials between Whites and visible minorities, there was also a considerable degree of heterogeneity within each of these categories (Pendakur and Pendakur, 1995).

More recently, a Statistics Canada report (Frenette and Morissette, 2003) on immigrant earnings and education revealed that the wage gap between recent immigrants, most of whom are immigrants of colour, and Canadian-born workers is growing. Men earned nearly 40 percent less than their Canadian-born counterparts for the same age and education levels in the year 2000. This is almost double the wage gap of twenty years earlier. Women fared even worse, earning 45 percent less than their similarly placed Canadian-born counterparts—virtually double the gap of the earlier period. The study also demonstrated that both men and women immigrants had higher education levels than Canadian-born. While some of these findings can be explained by lack of language proficiency and other settlement-related issues such as foreign accreditation of credentials, some undoubtedly relates to the basic issue of skin colour and racism.

Other studies using the most recent census data from 2001 also show that recently arrived immigrants are earning less than their Canadian-born counterparts; but, more significantly, those who have been here for 10 or more years still earn less than the Canadian-born. For example, the census provides data on 805 000 immigrants aged 25 to 54 who arrived in the last decade. Some 40 percent of this group had a university education—in contrast to 23 percent of their Canadian-born counterparts. Despite their high education credentials, immigrants were lower on almost every income measure. Male newcomers in 2000 could expect to earn 63.1 cents for every dollar of Canadian-born wages after one year in the country, down from 63.4 cents in 1990 and 71.6 cents in 1980. Women earned just 60.5 cents, compared to 70.5 cents in 1990. In regard to the Black population in Canada, the latest Statistics Canada report notes that although Canadian-born Blacks aged between 25 and 54 and Whites in the same age group were equal in regard to university education, the Blacks' annual income was substantially lower than for all Canadian-born. Blacks born outside of Canada earned less than all foreign-born persons in this same age group (Milan and Tran, 2004).

In 2000, male immigrants earned just 79.8 cents of the Canadian-born workers' dollar after 10 years of residence in Canada, in contrast to over 90 cents in 1990 and dollar-for-dollar in 1980. Women immigrants fared somewhat better with 87.3 cents in 2000, down from 93.3 cents in 1990 and $1.03 in 1980. "Even with knowledge of an official language, earnings did not rise much after three or four years in the country" (Statistics Canada, 2001). In 2000, immigrants who had been here for 10 years and were comfortable in one of the official languages were still earning about $10 000 less than the Canadian average.

One of the key barriers preventing immigrants of colour from access and equity in the labour market is credentialism. A series of recent community-based research projects on credentialism (Canadian Heritage, 2001) found these barriers still persist. Some of the common impediments identified in these reports included: a problem in the processes of accessing appropriate academic or professional institutions in order to obtain an assessment of equivalency of education, training, and work experience; gatekeepers at the professional level; perceived discrimination; retraining requirements; etc. One of the important findings was that problems encountered at the institutional level have a profound negative consequence at the individual level.

Discrimination in the workplace, directed primarily at immigrants, and immigrants of colour in particular, has not disappeared. In fact, if anything areas of inequity are as startling today as they were in former times. Because the point system of immigration favours education, and since there is an increasing emphasis on bringing in skilled immigrants, more recent arrivals are on average better educated and qualified than immigrants in past eras. However, the workforce marginalizes many skilled and credentialized immigrants for even longer periods than their predecessors. Reitz's study (2001) on employment discrimination and income differentials noted the ways immigrants are disadvantaged in the workforce:

- Their education, skills, and experience are thought not to be up to Canadian standards.
- Immigrants' skills are underutilized.
- Immigrants are not paid as much as the native-born; thus they end up earning less than they should. Earning differentials are found among both high-skilled and low-skilled immigrants.
- People of colour, "Blacks from Africa and the Caribbean, plus Chinese, South Asians, Filipinos, and other Asians[,] earn between 15 and 25 percent lower than most immigrants of European origins."

The differences do not disappear at the second-generational level. Even native-born Blacks earn less than their White counterparts. And although the differences are not as great as for Blacks, among Canadian-born Chinese and South Asians there are still disparities. Even more disturbing is the census finding that shows the poverty rate among immigrants who had arrived within the last five years was almost 36 percent in 2000, up from 24.6 percent some years earlier. The increase in poverty held for all education levels, age groupings, and language abilities.

"Now essentially we have two kinds of Canadians—those who were born here and those who weren't—and the gap between the two is getting worse" (John Anderson, director of research for the Canadian Council on Social Development, quoted in Carey, 2003). Most of the increase in poverty in Toronto, Vancouver, and Montreal was concentrated among immigrants.

A report released by the Canadian Labour Congress (Jackson, 2002) noted that racial status is responsible for the growing gaps in income. Racialized workers earned substantially less than Whites, often as much as 15 to 20 percent less than Whites in similar jobs. "[The] research points to racism as a major factor in the growing income and job security gap between workers of colour and other workers in this country. ... It's an ugly thing to say, but the facts speak for themselves. The time for denial is over." Noting that it is often believed that the disadvantaged workers are recent immigrants, the report condemns the so-called "catch-up" theory that maintains economic differences based on race will disappear as immigrants gain more Canadian job experience and move into the mainstream, just like previous White European immigrants. Such explanations rely on older and outmoded theories of immigrant absorption that applied to ethnic-origin migrants but not to racialized migrants for whom race and not ethnicity is the main factor leading to differential behaviour.

These data on income differentials among the immigrant population and especially the more recently arrived migrants paints a disappointing picture. Such figures lead many right-wing journalists and other conservative-thinking persons to repeatedly call for a decrease in the immigration levels (see above). What is not emphasized in their views, however, are the barriers that face migrants in the labour market. Reitz summarizes how immigrants are disadvantaged in their job searches:

- Their credentials are not recognized by official licensing agencies, especially in professional fields that require licensing.
- Their credentials are not recognized in nonlicensed jobs and professions.
- Their credentials are not recognized by employers.
- Their foreign experience that may not have led to a credential is not recognized even though it is relevant to the ability to do the job.
- Their educational credentials are not recognized.
- Other factors favour Canadians over immigrants in the job search, including networking, word-of-mouth recruitment, selective advertisement and the like.
- Racial bias persists.

All these barriers are forms of employment discrimination that face newly arrived immigrants and directly influence their level of earnings. Income differentials therefore must be examined from the perspective of what causes them rather than merely identifying the statistics. Harish Jain, who has done extensive research (Jain, Sloane, and Horwitz, 2003; Jain, 1988; Jain and Hackett, 1989) on employment discrimination in Canada, suggested that racial minorities, as well as women, Aboriginal peoples, and people with disabilities, encounter both entry-level and postemployment discrimination in the workplace. Jain (1985) argued that human-rights statutes across Canada were ineffective in ensuring equality of opportunity in the workplace. Jain identified numerous job barriers in the employment system, including narrow recruitment channels and procedures (such as word-of-mouth recruitment, inflated educational qualifications, biased testing, prejudice and stereotyping in the job interview process, poor performance evaluation, and lack of promotions, transfers, and/or salary increases). Unions are another potential source of both racism and sexism (Leah, 1989).

Other Factors Influencing Employment

Research on the Caribbean communities in Toronto (Henry, 1994) has yielded some interesting information on the continuing impact of racial discrimination on employment. More than one hundred in-depth interviews and many hundreds of hours of participant observation among persons of Caribbean origin in Toronto indicated that the community shows a fairly high level of institutional completeness, considering the recentness of Caribbean migration to Canada. Although there are no Caribbean-owned financial institutions within the community, most service and retail sectors have developed to the extent that goods and services of many kinds can be obtained from Caribbean-owned and -managed businesses.

One of the main reasons for private entrepreneurship among the community was the racial discrimination experienced by job seekers and workers employed in mainstream-owned and -managed firms. Difficulty in obtaining employment was often cited as a major reason for dissatisfaction with living in Canada. In addition, racial harassment on the job and the inability to advance in the company was cited as a contributory factor in private entrepreneurship. Restaurateurs, clothiers, and variety shop owners said they were "fed up" with racial harassment.

Torczyner, primarily using census data and focusing on diversity, mobility, and change among Black communities in Canada, made similar findings (1997). The study found that although Black people in Canada had levels of education similar to those of the total population, they had substantially lower incomes, were less likely to be self-employed, and were less likely to occupy senior management positions. Many more Blacks than Whites lived in poverty, and Black women had greater poverty rates than men.

A report on socioeconomic indicators of equality conducted among ethno-racial communities in Toronto in the early 1990s found that while the overall rate of unemployment in Metro Toronto was 9.6 percent, the unemployment rate of non-Europeans far exceeded this (Ornstein, 1997). For example, Africans had a 25.8 percent unemployment rate, followed by Mexicans and Central Americans at 24 percent and Tamils at 23.9 percent. Other groups with a higher than average unemployment rate included Arabs and West Asians, Sri Lankans, Vietnamese, and Aboriginal people. Jamaicans, especially youth between the ages of 15 and 24, had high rates of unemployment as compared with other youth in the same age category. The study also found a weak link between employment and education and concluded that groups with the most unemployment were not those with the least education; many non-European groups found it difficult to convert their educational qualifications into jobs. Ornstein (1997) concluded that many people in Toronto were affected by poverty and inequality. The report acknowledged that the groups most affected were those who found access to employment, housing, education, and other resources constrained due to a variety of economic and social factors. A recent report by the Centre for Social Justice argues persuasively that the various economic differentials between racialized minorities and others in Canada is already severe and shows signs of increasing. Accordingly, the author entitled the report *Canada's Creeping Economic Apartheid* (Galabuzi, 2001).

Summary

This chapter has provided an overview of the historical and contemporary evidence of racism in Canada. The examples cited demonstrate both the highly complex nature of racism and the diverse forms it takes. There is a brief examination of how racial bias and discrimination have affected specific minority communities, including Black Canadians, Chinese Canadians, Japanese Canadians, East-Indian Canadians, and Canadian Jews.

Racist ideology strongly influences the development of public policies and legislative enactments. The historical evidence demonstrates how racial bias and discriminatory practices have limited access to education, housing, and employment, and have resulted in the denial of the fundamental civil rights to racial minorities in Canada. The development of restrictive and racist immigration policies lasting over one hundred years is compelling evidence of racism in Canada.

The last section of this chapter has documented some of the extensive data on employment and housing discrimination, further illustrating the extent to which racial bias and discrimination function and flourish in Canadian society. The history of racism in Canada can be characterized by the development and maintenance of policies and practices based on the marginalization, exclusion, segregation, and domination of racial minorities.

Notes

1. This section is drawn from the projections of T.J. Samuel, *Visible Minorities in Canada: A Projection* (Toronto: Race Relations Advisory Council on Advertising, Canadian Advertising Foundation, 1992).
2. The term "visible minority" is used in the Census of Canada as well as in publications that use census or other government-generated data. It is used in this book when discussing such research.
3. Polling and survey data from other countries are similar to those of Canada. For example, a survey conducted in the European Union countries revealed that racism is rampant. The data showed that one-third of respondents are racist; some admitted that they were "very" racist, and others reported being "quite racist" (*North Africa Journal*, 1998). Surveys on racism and attitudes toward immigrants in Australia revealed similar figures to those of Canada (see Adelman et al., 1994).
4. Since the employment equity act in Ontario (1993) was rescinded by the incoming Progressive Conservative government in 1995, data on the Ontario Public Service and other public sector agencies has been difficult to access. To the best of our knowledge, the Eye Count Survey of the Ontario government public sector in 1995 was the last official document of its kind. Informal estimates suggest that not only has the entire public service been reduced especially at seasonal, temporary, and casual levels, but the hires and retentions of people with disability and Aboriginals is less today than ten years ago.

References

Abella, I., and H. Troper. (1982). *None Is Too Many*. Toronto: Lester & Orpen Dennys.

Abella, R. (1984). *Report of the Commission on Equality in Employment*. Ottawa: Supply and Services Canada.

Adachi, K. (1976). *The Enemy That Never Was: A History of the Japanese Canadians*. Toronto: McClelland & Stewart.

Adelman, H., A. Borowski, M. Burnstein, and L. Foster (eds.). (1994). *Immigration and Refugee Policy: Australia and Canada Compared*. Melbourne: Melbourne University Press.

Agnew, V. (2003). *Where I Come From*. Waterloo, ON: Wilfrid Laurier University Press.

Alexander, K., and A. Glaze. (1996). *Towards Freedom: The African Canadian Experience*. Toronto: Umbrella Press.

Arthurs, H. (1963). "Civil Liberties and Public Schools: Segregation of Negro Students." *Canadian Bar Review* 4:453–57.

Barrett, S. (1984). "White Supremists and Neo Fascists: Laboratories for the Analysis of Racism in Wider Society." In O. McKague (ed.), *Racism in Canada*. Saskatoon: Fifth House. 85–99.

———. (1987). *Is God a Racist? The Right Wing in Canada*. Toronto: University of Toronto Press.

Baureiss, G. (1985). "Discrimination and Response: The Chinese in Canada." In R. Bienvenue and J. Goldstein (eds.), *Ethnicity and Ethnic Relations in Canada*. 2nd ed. Toronto: Butterworths.

Beck, H., J. Reitz, and N. Weiner. (2002). "Addressing Systemic Racial Discrimination in Employment: The Health Canada Case and Implications of Legislative Change." *Canadian Public Policy* 28(3)(September):373–394. Available <http://www.utoronto.ca/ethnicstudies/Beck_Reitz_Wein.pdf>, accessed August 13, 2004.

Billingsley, B., and L. Musynski. (1985). *No Discrimination Here*. Toronto: Social Planning Council of Metro Toronto and the Urban Alliance on Race Relations.

Bobb-Smith, Y. (2003). *I Know Who I Am: A Caribbean Woman's Identity*. Women's Press, Toronto.

Bolaria, B.S., and P. Li. (1988). *Racial Oppression in Canada*. 2nd ed. Toronto: Garamond Press.

Buchignani, N., and D. Indra. (1985). *Continuous Journey: A Social History of South Asians in Canada*. Toronto: McClelland & Stewart.

Camp, D. (1990). "Diefenbaker Would Have Backed Turbans in the RCMP." *Toronto Star* (March 21):A25.

Canadian Centre for Justice Statistics. (2004). "Pilot Survey of Hate Crime." *Juristat: Hate Crime in Canada* 24(4). Catalogue No. 85-002-XIE.

Canadian Council of Christian and Jews. (1993). *Survey of Canadian Attitudes Towards Ethnic and Race Relations in Canada*. Toronto: Decima Research.

Canadian Heritage. (2001). *Recognition of Foreign Credentials: A Survey of Recent Community-Based and Research Projects*. Multiculturalism Programs,

Department of Canadian Heritage. Available <http://www.canadianheritage.gc.ca/progs/multi/pubs/sra-ras/contents_e.cfm>, accessed August 13, 2004.

Canadian Human Rights Commission (2003). "Annual Report." Ottawa.

Carey, E. (2003). "Income Gap Growing Between Immigrants, Native-Born." *Toronto Star* (June 20). Available <http://www.exateccanada.com/articulos/ Income_Gap.html>, accessed August 26, 2004.

Census of Canada. (2001).

Chan, A. (1983). *The Gold Mountain: The Chinese in the New World.* Vancouver: New Star.

Cohen, T. (1987). *Race Relations and the Law.* Toronto: Canadian Jewish Congress.

Collacott, M. (2002). *Canadian Immigration Policy: The Need for Major Reform.* Vancouver: Fraser Institute.

Creese, G. (1991). "Organizing Against Racism in the Workplace: Chinese Workers in Vancouver Before the Second World War." In O. McKague (ed.), *Racism in Canada.* Saskatoon: Fifth House.

———. (1993). "The Sociology of British Columbia." *BC Studies* 100(Winter 1993–94).

Economic Council of Canada. (1991). *Report.* Ottawa.

Employment and Immigration Canada. (1992). *Annual Report, Employment Equity.* Ottawa: Minister of Supply and Services.

Environics. (1988). *Focus Canada Survey.*

Equality Now! Report of the Special Committee on Participation of Visible Minorities in Canadian Society. (1984). Ottawa: Queen's Printer.

Francis, D. (2001). "Flooded with the Unqualified," *Financial Post* (May 8).

———. (2002). *Immigration: The Economic Case.* Toronto. Key Porter Books.

Frenette, M., and R. Morissette. (2003). "Earnings of Immigrant Workers and Canadian Born Workers, 1980–2000." Statistics Canada (October 8).

Frideres, J. (1983). *Native Peoples in Conflict.* Scarborough, ON: Prentice Hall.

Galabuzi, G.-E. (2001). *Canada's Creeping Economic Apartheid.* Toronto: Centre for Social Justice.

Gould, T. (1990). "Who Do You Hate." *Toronto Life* (October).

Head, W. (1981). *Adaptation of Immigrants: Perceptions of Ethnic and Racial Discrimination.* North York, ON: York University.

Henry, F. (1968). "The West Indian Domestic Scheme in Canada." In *Social and Economic Studies* 17(1):83–91. Mona, Jamaica: University of the West Indies.

———. (1974). *The Forgotten Canadians: The Blacks of Nova Scotia.* Don Mills, ON: Longmans.

———. (1994). *The Caribbean Diaspora in Toronto: Learning to Live with Racism.* Toronto: University of Toronto Press.

Henry, F., and E. Ginzberg. (1984). *Who Gets the Work? A Test of Racial Discrimination in Employment.* Toronto: Urban Alliance on Race Relations and the Social Planning Council of Toronto.

Henry, F., and C. Tator. (2002). *Discourses of Domination: Racial Bias in the Canadian English-Language Press.* Toronto: University of Toronto Press.

Hernandez, C. (1992). "Nanny Rule Will Have Racist Outcome." *Toronto Star* (February 15).

Hill, D. (1981). *The Freedom Seekers: Blacks in Early Canada.* Agincourt, ON: Book Society of Canada.

Jackson, J. (2002). *Is Work Working for People of Colour?* Toronto: Canadian Labour Congress.

Jain, H. (1985). *Anti-discrimination Staffing Policies: Implications of Human Rights Legislation for Employers and Trade Unions.* Ottawa: Secretary of State.

———. (1988). "Affirmative Action/Employment Equity Programmes and Visible Minorities in Canada." *Currents: Readings in Race Relations* 5(1)(4):3–7.

Jain, H., and R. Hackett. (1989). "Measuring Effectiveness of Employment Equity Programmes in Canada: Public Policy and a Survey." *Canadian Public Policy* 15(2):189–204.

Jain, H., P. Sloane, and F. Horwitz. (2003). *Employment Equity and Affirmative Action: An International Perspective.* Armonk, NY: M.E. Sharpe.

Jakubowski, L.M. (1997). *Immigration and the Legalization of Racism.* Halifax: Fernwood.

King, W.L.M. (1908). *Report of the Commissioner Appointed to Enquire into the Methods by Which Oriental Labourers Have Been Induced to Come to Canada.* Ottawa: King's Printer.

Kobayashi, A. (1987). "From Tyranny to Justice: The Uprooting of the Japanese Canadians in 1941." *Tribune Juive* 5:28–35.

Lampert, R., and J. Curtis. (1989). "The Racial Attitudes of Canadians." In L. Tepperman and J. Curtis (eds.), *Readings in Sociology.* Toronto: McGraw-Hill Ryerson.

Lampkin, L. (1985). "Visible Minorities in Canada." Research paper for the Abella Royal Commission. *Equality in Employment.* Ottawa: Minister of Supply and Services Canada.

Leah, R. (1989). "Linking the Struggles: Racism, Sexism and the Union Movement." In J. Vorst et al. (eds.), *Race, Class, Gender: Bonds and Barriers.* Toronto: Between the Lines.

Lewis, S. (1992). *Report on Race Relations to Premier Bob Rae.* Toronto: Queen's Printer. Excerpt reproduced with permission from the Queen's Printer for Ontario.

Li, P. (2003a). *Destination Canada: Immigration Debates and Issues.* Don Mills, ON: Oxford University Press.

———. (2003b). "Understanding Economic Performance of Immigrants." In *Metropolis, Canadian Issues: Immigration.* Association of Canadian Studies. April 2003.

————. (1988). *The Chinese in Canada*. Rev. ed. Toronto: Oxford University Press.

Malarek, V. (1987). *Heaven's Gate: Canada's Immigration Fiasco*. Toronto: Macmillan.

Mattis, W. (1990). "Canadian Immigration Policy 1867–1990: More of the Same." Unpublished manuscript. Toronto.

Milan, Anne, and Tran, Kelly. (2004). "Blacks in Canada: A Long History." *Canadian Social Trends* 72(Spring). Statistics Canada.

Mock, K. (2003). "Recognizing and Reacting to Hate Crime in Canada Today." Toronto: Canadian Race Relations Foundation. Available <http://www.crr.ca/en/Publications/ EducationalTools/RecognizingandReacting.htm>, accessed August 13, 2004.

————. (1996). *The Extent of Hate Activity and Racism in Metropolitan Toronto*. Toronto: Access and Equity Centre of the Municipality of Metropolitan Toronto. Excerpts reproduced with permission from Access and Equity Centre of the Municipality of Metropolitan Toronto and Dr. Karen Mock, League for Human Rights, B'nai B'rith, Canada.

Ng, R. (1992). "Managing Female Immigration: A Case of Institutional Sexism and Racism." *Canadian Woman Studies* 12(3)(Spring):20–23.

Ontario Human Rights Commission. (2003). *Paying the Price: The Human Cost of Racial Profiling*. Toronto: OHRC.

Ornstein, M. (1997). *Report on Ethno-Racial Inequality in Metropolitan Toronto: Analysis of the 1991 Census*. Access and Equity Centre of the (former) Municipality of Metropolitan Toronto.

Pendakur, K., and R. Pendakur. (1995). *The Colour of Money: Earnings Differentials Among Ethnic Groups in Canada*. Strategic Research and Analysis. Ottawa: Department of Canadian Heritage.

Quann, D. (1979). *Racial Discrimination in Housing*. Ottawa: Canadian Council on Social Development.

Raj, S. (1980). "Some Aspects of East Indian Struggle in Canada, 1905–1947." In K. Ujimoto and G. Hirabayashi (eds.), *Visible Minorities and Multiculturalism: Asians in Canada*. Toronto: Butterworths.

Reitz, J. (2001). "Immigrant Skill Utilization in the Canadian Labour Market: Implications of Human Capital Research." *Journal of International Migration and Integration* 2(3). Available http://www.utoronto.ca/ ethnicstudies/Reitz_Skill.pdf, accessed August 13, 2004.

Reitz, J., L. Calzavara, and D. Dasko. (1981). *Ethnic Inequality and Segregation in Jobs*. Toronto: Centre for Urban and Community Studies, University of Toronto.

Report of the Nova Scotia Advisory Group on Race Relations. (1991). Halifax.

Richmond, A.H. (1994). *Global Apartheid: Refugees, Racism and the New World Order*. Toronto: Oxford University Press.

Roberts, J.V. (1995). "Disproportionate Harm: Hate Crime in Canada: An Analysis of Recent Statistics." Ottawa: Department of Justice, Research, Statistics and Evaluation Directorate. Available <http://canada .justice.gc.ca/en/ps/rs/ rep/wd95-11a-e.html>, accessed August 13, 2004.

Robson, R., and B. Breems. (1985). *Ethnic Conflict in Vancouver*. Vancouver: B.C. Civil Liberties Association.

Sampat-Mehta, R. (1984). "The First Fifty Years of South Asian Immigration: A Historical Perspective." In R. Ranungo (ed.), *South Asians in the Canadian Mosaic*. Montreal: Kala Bharati.

Samuel, T.J. (1989). "Canada's Visible Minorities and the Labour Market: Vision 2000." In O.P. Dwivedi et al., *Canada 2000: Race Relations and Public Policy*. Guelph: University of Guelph.

————. (1998). "Debunking Myths of Immigrants." *Toronto Star* (June 17).

Secretary of State. (1982). *Study of Racial Tensions in 11 Major Cities in Canada*. Ottawa: Secretary of State.

Shadd, A.S. (1989). "Institutionalized Racism and Canadian History: Note of a Black Canadian." Appendix in C. James (ed.), *Seeing Ourselves: Exploring Race, Ethnicity and Culture*. Toronto: Sheridan College.

Shepard, B. (1991). "Plain Racism: The Reaction Against Oklahoma Black Immigration to the Canadian Plains." In O. McKague (ed.), *Racism in Canada*. Saskatoon: Fifth House.

Silvera, M. (1989). *Silenced*. 2nd ed. Toronto: Sister Vision Press.

————. (1993). "Speaking of Women's Lives and Imperialist Economics: Two Introductions from *Silenced*." In H. Bannerji (ed.), *The Gaze: Essays on Racism, Feminism and Politics*. Toronto: Sister Vision Press.

Statistics Canada. (2001). "Earnings of Canadians: Making a Living in the New Economy." Analysis Series. Available <http://www12.statcan.ca/english/census01/ Products/Analytic/companion/earn/canada.cfm>, accessed August 13, 2004.

————. (2003). *Longitudinal Survey of Immigrants to Canada* (September 4).

Stoffman, D. (2002). *Who Gets In: What's Wrong with Canada's Immigration and How to Fix It*. Toronto. Macfarlane, Walter & Ross.

Sunahara, A. (1981). *The Politics of Racism: The Uprooting of Japanese Canadians During the Second World War*. Toronto: James Lorimer.

Tarnopolsky, W. (1991). "Discrimination and the Law in Canada." In *Seminar on Race, Ethnic and Cultural Equity*. Vancouver: Western Judicial Centre.

Task Force on Immigration Practices and Procedures. (1981). *Domestic Workers on Employment Authorizations: A Report.* Ottawa.

Torczyner, J.L. (1997). *Diversity, Mobility and Change: The Dynamics of Black Communities in Canada.* Montreal: McGill School of Social Work.

Troper, A. (1972). *Only Farmers Need Apply.* Toronto: Griffin House.

Ubale, B. (1977). *Equal Opportunity and Public Policy: A Report on Concerns of the South Asian Community regarding their Place in the Canadian Mosaic.* Toronto: Ontario Ministry of the Attorney General.

Ujimoto, K. (1988). "Racial Discrimination and Internment: Japanese in Canada." In B.S. Bolaria and P. Li (eds.), *Racial Oppression in Canada.* 2nd ed. Toronto: Garamond Press.

Walker, J. (1980). *The History of Blacks in Canada: A Study Guide for Teachers and Students.* Ottawa: Minister of State for Multiculturalism.

———. (1985). *Race and the Historian: Some Lessons from Canadian Public Policy.* Waterloo: University of Waterloo.

Winks, R. (1971). *The Blacks in Canada: A History.* New Haven, CT: Yale University Press.

———. (1978). *The Blacks in Canada: A History.* New Haven, CT: Yale University Press.

CHAPTER 4

RACISM AND ABORIGINAL PEOPLES

*Let us have Christianity and civilization among the Indian tribes. … Let us have
a wise and paternal government … doing its utmost to help and elevate the Indian
population who have been cast upon our case. … And Canada will be enabled
to feel, in a truly patriotic spirit, our country has done its duty to the red man.*

—Alexander Morris, nineteenth-century treaty negotiator, as quoted in Cayo (1997)

*[T]he relationship that has developed over the last 400 years between Aboriginal
and non-Aboriginal people in Canada … has been … built on a foundation of false
promises—that Canada was for all intents and purposes an unoccupied land when the
newcomers arrived from Europe; that the inhabitants were a wild, untutored and
ignorant people given to strange customs and ungodly practices; that they would in
time, through precept and example, come to appreciate the superior wisdom of the
strangers and adopt their ways; or, alternatively, that they would be left behind in
the march of progress and survive only as an anthropological footnote.*

—Report of the Royal Commission on Aboriginal Peoples (1996)

This chapter examines the nature of Aboriginal-White relations in Canada from a historical perspective.[1] It examines the relationship from the perspective of differential values, assumptions, and beliefs and shows how the racist ideology of the dominant society continues to have a negative impact on Aboriginal peoples. We will look at how policies and practices that evolved between Aboriginal peoples and White society over the past four hundred years have been based on the assumption that Aboriginal people were inherently inferior and incapable of governing themselves and that, therefore, actions deemed to be for their benefit could be carried out without their consent or involvement in design or implementation. Treaties and other agreements were, by and large, not covenants of trust and obligation but devices of state—formally acknowledged but frequently ignored.

Before the 1960s, Aboriginal people were treated as objects of policy paternalism and wardship. An assumption that has evolved since then is that they constitute an interest group, one among many in a pluralistic society. They have not been considered to have legitimate political authority as nations entitled to treatment as such.

This history of Aboriginal-White relations can perhaps be understood as occurring in four discrete periods (Miller, 1991). Apart from sporadic and intermittent Norse, Basque, and other European contacts beginning in A.D. 1000, a sustained non-Aboriginal presence has existed in Canada since the end of the fifteenth century, when European involvement focused on developing the fisheries and the fur trade. Although there were exceptions, this early period was marked by many instances of mutual tolerance and respect.

The second period, which occurred during the eighteenth century, was dominated by trading and military alliances as France and England battled for imperial dominance over North America. This period was also marked by incidents of conflict, by increasing numbers of European immigrants, and by a steep decline in Aboriginal populations following the ravages of diseases to which they had little resistance.

The third period of displacement and assimilation began at various times throughout northern North America—in the Maritimes it had begun by the 1780s, in the interior of Quebec and Ontario after the end of the War of 1812, and on the west coast by 1870. This period was marked by a continuing saga of expropriation, exclusion, discrimination, coercion, subjugation, oppression, deceit, theft, appropriation, and extreme regulation.

The fourth period, still in progress, has been described by the 1996 Royal Commission on Aboriginal Peoples as a period of negotiation and renewal that began after World War II and accelerated after publication of the federal government's White Paper on Indian Policy in 1969.

Introduction

Before contact with Europeans, Aboriginal nations were fully independent and "organized in societies and occupying the land as their forefathers had done for centuries." These societies had varying degrees of sociocultural, economic, and political complexity. Many practised agricultural techniques and had established intricate systems of political and commercial alliances among themselves.

Most of these people had been in their locations for thousands of years; they spoke about fifty languages that have been classified into twelve families, of which six are exclusive to present-day British Columbia. The greater language diversity of the Pacific coast suggests much earlier settlement there than in the rest of the country (Dickason, 1992).

The ethnic diversity of the Aboriginal population was much greater than that of Europe. However, whether encountering the cultures of the Beothuk of Newfoundland, the Mi'kmaq of Nova Scotia, the Maliseet of New Brunswick, the Innu of northern Quebec, the Algonquin and Huron of Ontario, the Cree of Manitoba, the Chipewyan of Saskatchewan, the Sarsi or Blackfoot of Alberta, or the Haida, Nisga'a, or Tlingit of British Columbia, incoming Europeans found it difficult to recognize this diversity of economic and social organization, language, religion, and values, and labelled all Aboriginal peoples as "Indians" (Frideres, 1993). This inability to recognize the huge diversity among Aboriginal peoples had reverberations throughout the long history of Aboriginal-White relations.

"Discovery"

When the Europeans arrived in "the New World," they attempted to justify their assumption of political sovereignty and title to Aboriginal lands on the basis of a reinterpretation of the doctrine of discovery. This doctrine was based on the notion of *terra nullius*—a Latin term referring to empty, essentially barren, and uninhabited land. Under norms of international law at the time of contact, the European "discovery" of such land gave the discovering nation immediate sovereignty and all rights and title to the land. Over the course of time, however, the concept of *terra nullius* was extended to include lands that were not in possession of "civilized" peoples or that were not being put to proper, "civilized" use. Europeans were therefore legally justified in assuming full, sovereign ownership of the "discovered" lands, since Aboriginal peoples could not possibly have the civilized and Christian attributes that would enable them to assert sovereign ownership. Over time, these ethnocentric notions gained currency and were given further legitimacy by various court decisions, such as *St. Catharines Milling and Lumber Co. v. The Queen* (1887): "To maintain their position the appellants must assume that the Indians have a regular form of government, whereas nothing is more clear than that they have no government and no organization, and cannot be regarded as a nation capable of holding lands."

While European notions of property and government were used to justify appropriating Aboriginal lands, a further self-serving justification was presented that argued that Europeans would use the land more productively, produce a greater quantity of conveniences, and produce far greater opportunities to work by expanding the division of labour (Tully, 1995).

These kinds of arguments, which distorted the reality of the situation, converted cultural *differences* into *inferiorities* and continue to have impact on government policy and court proceedings up to the present day.

Aboriginal belief systems, cultures, and forms of social organization differ substantially from European patterns. These differences continue to be at the heart of the present struggle of Aboriginal peoples to reclaim possession not only of their traditional lands, but also of their traditional cultures and forms of political organization.

Contact and Cooperation

The Aboriginal peoples' initial contacts with Europeans were through participation and partnerships in the fisheries and the fur trade. Until the eighteenth century, the links between Aboriginal and non-Aboriginal societies were primarily commercial. They did not interfere in a major way with long-standing Aboriginal patterns of pursuing their livelihood and, in some ways, actually reinforced Aboriginal strengths in hunting, fishing, trapping, trading, and transporting. This commerce also appears to have strengthened Aboriginal social organization.

The social, cultural, and political differences between the two societies were respected, by and large. Each was regarded as distinct and autonomous, left to govern its own internal affairs but cooperating in areas of mutual interest. The relationship was characterized by considerable interdependence, a complementary of roles, and some mutual benefit. However, trade also had destructive consequences. The first and most serious were epidemics of European origin, which began to decimate the Aboriginal population.

Military Alliances and Commercial Cooperation in the Eighteenth Century

The second phase of Aboriginal-White relations, which occurred in the 1700s, was dominated by a combination of commercial partnerships and military alliances as the French and English struggled for imperial dominance over North America.

This period marked a process of change that reflected imperial ambitions tempered by cautious realism. Although the Europeans preferred some form of sovereign control over the Aboriginal peoples, they often had to settle for a mixture of trading agreements, alliances, or simple neutrality. Similarly, while Aboriginal nations might have wished to assert their total independence, in practice they often found themselves reliant on European trade and military protection. In 1763, the Treaty of Paris ended the Seven Years' War and New France was ceded to Britain. The policy of the new colonial government was based on the Royal Proclamation of 1763, in which King George III instructed his colonial governments to ensure that Aboriginal peoples should not be disturbed in their lands, "but that, if at any time, any of the said Indians should be inclined to dispose of said land, the same shall be purchased for Us, in our Name, at some public Meeting or Assembly of the said Indians, to be held for that purpose" (*Report of the Royal Commission on Aboriginal Peoples*, 1996: Vol. 1, App. D).

Aboriginal-English relations had stabilized to the point where they could be seen to be grounded in two fundamental principles (Glavin, 1998). Under the first principle, while Aboriginal peoples were regarded as British subjects, they also were generally recognized as autonomous political units capable of having treaty relations with the Crown. The second principle acknowledged that Aboriginal nations were entitled to the territories in their possession, unless or until they ceded them to others.

The Crown therefore guaranteed that any Aboriginal lands not previously ceded or purchased by the British Crown were reserved for Aboriginal peoples, and that these lands could not be purchased or settled without the special leave and licence of the Crown.

Paradoxically, however, the Royal Proclamation referred to Aboriginal lands as Crown lands, despite their prior occupation by Aboriginal nations. Thus, while setting out new rules for Aboriginal land cessions, the proclamation retained the colonial assumptions of the discovery doctrine.

Displacement and Assimilation

The third phase of Aboriginal-White relations began at various times throughout North America during the eighteenth century. The past relationship of mutually beneficial cooperation and practical accommodation changed to a pervasive and sustained attack on the respectful, egalitarian nation-to-nation principles. Confronted with a powerful and growing colonial society, the strength of the Aboriginal nations declined. Colonial governments appeared to have neither the will nor the means to counter the illegal occupation of the remaining lands of the indigenous population. Encroachment became more common as the colonial economic base changed to an emphasis on agriculture and a decline in the importance of the fur trade and the traditional harvesting economy. In addition, Britain's normalization of relations with the United States after the War of 1812 no longer required its cultivation of Aboriginal peoples as military allies.

Social Darwinism

Europeans' initial impressions of Aboriginal peoples as "savage" were reinforced by the scientific racism and Social Darwinism of the late nineteenth and early twentieth centuries. These views were reflected in many legal provisions concerning Aboriginal peoples, up to and including the 1951 federal Indian Act.

To justify their actions against Aboriginal peoples, the European settlers relied on a belief system that judged the original inhabitants to be inferior. Originally based on religious and philosophical grounds, this sense of moral and cultural superiority was further buttressed by pseudoscientific theories of Social Darwinism that rested ultimately on ethnocentric and racist premises.

The isolationist–assimilationist strategy toward Aboriginal peoples was justified by beliefs in "progress" and in the evolutionary development of human cultures from lesser to greater states of civilization. The long-standing Western belief in Europe's racial and cultural superiority were given a scientific veneer to justify existing assumptions. This was accompanied by a belief in the destiny of European cultures to expand across North America and take over the whole land base.

Western society was seen to be at the forefront of evolutionary development, and Aboriginal peoples lagged far behind. As a result, Aboriginal peoples needed to be guided— even directed—to catch up, in a process of accelerated evolution. Consequently, a whole philosophy and belief system justified the establishment of unilateral decision-making and a centralized administrative system to merge the Aboriginal peoples into Western society.

The belief in the superiority of European culture and the desire to "civilize" and Christianize other cultures went hand in hand with the political and economic expansion of European imperialism. The characterization of Aboriginal peoples as "savage" and biologically inferior enabled Europeans to remain blind to the complexity of Aboriginal cultures, customs, beliefs, and traditions. At the same time, it permitted the imposition of European values and the control of Aboriginal peoples by outsiders.

Christianization

The important role of the Christian church in supporting the systematic annihilation of Aboriginal values, norms, religions, and language has been well documented. The Jesuits and other missionaries, who believed that Aboriginal peoples should not be left in their "inferior" natural state, considered it their duty to replace Aboriginal cultures with Christian beliefs, values, rituals, and practices (Bolaria and Li, 1988).

There was general agreement that the propagation of Christianity entitled Europeans to intervene in the lives of the Aboriginal peoples and to exercise force, if necessary, to achieve this end. Combined with the legal doctrine of territorial rights of discovery, the notion of a Christian's duty to evangelize and civilize "Indians" provided a virtually open mandate for European colonization (Dyck, 1991).

The role of the churches was to "civilize and educate Native people," and the churches were given Aboriginal land to undertake this task (Powless, 1985). To the Jesuits, their mission was a war against satanic forces. A strong and enduring component of European conceptions of the inferiority of Aboriginal peoples was the conviction that they were heathen. As a result of this conviction, Europeans determined that it was their religious duty to convert Aboriginal peoples to Christianity.

Since most Whites viewed all aspects of Aboriginal life and organization as culturally and morally inferior, missionaries made efforts to change matrilineal kinship patterns in those societies that practised it and instead promoted the norms of the dominant

European patrilineal society (Ng, 1993; Bienvenue and Goldstein, 1985). The perceived differences between men and women were used by nineteenth-century missionaries to organize the Aboriginal peoples into European male and female roles. For example, a man's place was in the economic, food-production world, while a woman's was in the domestic, food-preparation world. This altered the prime economic unit from the tribe to the European version of the family—the nuclear family (Clubine, 1991:16)—which led to a deconstruction of traditional male-female relations among Aboriginal people and a reconstruction into male-female roles appropriate to and approved by colonial society (Ng, 1993:54).

Another powerful manifestation of racialized ideology has been the role of the mainstream child welfare system in its treatment of Aboriginal families. McKenzie and Morrissette (2003) contend that, like the residential school system, the child welfare system in the 1960s and 1970s was designed to ensure institutionalized assimilation. This widespread phenomenon was referred as the "Sixties Scoop." During this period high numbers of Aboriginal children were seized from their families, communities, and culture. Patrick Johnson coined the term "Sixties Scoop" and cites the shift from the mid-1950s when less than 1 percent of children in care in different provinces across the country were of Indian ancestry, to the mid-1960s when children of Aboriginal ancestry accounted for a third. Arbitrary decisions were often made to remove children without consent of parents, and without concern about the impact of denial of kinship care practices or the long-term impact of these separations on individuals or families. The majority of these children were placed in White foster and adoptive homes. This disastrous policy continues to have a powerful impact on the lives of Aboriginal peoples. Many adult adoptees have articulated their sense of loss, which include: a loss of cultural identity; lost contact with the birth families; barred access from medical histories; and, for status Indian children, loss of status.

Aboriginal peoples, deemed to be inferior, were schooled for inferiority, and as a result they indeed largely did end up at the bottom ranks of Canadian society. Outwardly espousing assimilation through education, the federal government provided neither the leadership nor the resources to achieve any other goal than the self-affirming prophecy inherent in racist rhetoric (Barman, 1996).

The doctrine of Euro-Canadian "superiority" and Aboriginal "inferiority" over several centuries has become "a created body of theory and practice" in which, for many generations, there has been a sustained social and material investment (Dyck, 1991).

Legislation

As British imperial power became firmly established in northern North America following the War of 1812, the drive to assimilation took on a new intensity. This was the beginning of the great land-cession treaties, by which the British sought to extinguish the limited land rights they had previously recognized.

The displacement and assimilation of Aboriginal peoples throughout the nineteenth and early twentieth centuries was motivated largely by economics and was the most significant factor in developing and maintaining the reserve system (Bolaria and Li, 1988). The commercial economy, based on the fur trade and other natural resources, was pushed from centre stage and replaced by the drive for expansionary settlement and for agricultural and, later, industrial production. Aboriginal peoples clearly stood in the settlers' way, for they inhabited and claimed title to vast stretches of land.

The fundamental differences in world views can be seen in the very different ways the treaty process was approached. Aboriginal conceptions of how relations in human

RESIDENTIAL SCHOOLS

One of the most powerful examples of racist ideology and practice in Canada was the treatment of Aboriginal children in residential schools in many provinces.

Education was considered the most effective means to achieve the transformation of Aboriginal children into European Canadians. Residential schools represent one of the starker examples of Canada's paternalism toward Aboriginal people, its civilizing strategy, and its stern assimilative determination. As a solution to the Indian "problem," education would, as Minister of Indian Affairs Frank Oliver predicted in 1908, "elevate the Indian from his condition of savagery" and "make him a self-supporting member of the state, and eventually a citizen in good standing."

The residential school system was an attempt by successive governments to appropriate and shape the future of Canada's Aboriginal peoples by removing thousands of children from their homes and community and placing them in the care of strangers.

The common wisdom of the day maintained that Aboriginal children had to be rescued from their "evil surroundings" and "prejudicial influences." They should, therefore, be isolated from parents, family, and community, and kept constantly within "the circle of civilized conditions." Residential schools were conceived as an all-encompassing environment of resocialization. The schools were seen as a bridge from the Aboriginal world into non-Aboriginal communities. That passage was marked out in clear stages: separation, socialization, and finally assimilation through enfranchisement.

Residential schools were operated by missionary societies under the aegis of the federal government. Through a process of coercive assimilation, supported by the government agencies and churches that ran the schools, Aboriginal children were forbidden to speak their language, to practise their traditions and customs, and to learn about their history.

The residential schools suffered from appalling mismanagement and inferior educational services. Christian missionaries were more concerned with saving souls than with literacy education. Few had the qualification to teach. The inadequate education ensured that Aboriginal children could not in fact assimilate or compete on any basis of equity with their non-Aboriginal counterparts. The focus was merely on the acquisition of practical skills in order to function at the very bottom levels of the economic mainstream.

Underfunding (which resulted in an inadequate diet), overwork in non-academic activities to sustain the "self-supporting activities" of the institution, and overcrowding contributed to rampant ill health and tuberculosis among the children. This situation caused such a high death rate that *Saturday Night* magazine concluded, "Even war seldom shows as large a percentage of fatalities as does the education system we have imposed upon our Indian wards" (November 23, 1907). At one point it was estimated that "fifty percent of the children who passed through these schools did not live to benefit from the education which they had received therein" (Scott, 1914).

The persistent and unrelieved neglect of the children—hungry, malnourished, ill clothed, dying of tuberculosis, and overworked—was compounded by harsh discipline, cruelty, and physical and sexual abuse. The system of transformation from "savage" to "civilized" was suffused with not just strict discipline and punishment but with a violent savagery. Children were frequently beaten severely with whips, rods, and fists; they were chained and shackled, bound hand and foot, and locked in closets, basements, and bathrooms, and they had their heads shaved or hair closely cropped.

In the 1960s, many residential schools were shut down; the last one closed in 1988. However, the abuses perpetrated in these schools continue to haunt the present.

The survivors of the Indian residential school system have, in many cases, continued to have their lives shaped by the experiences in these schools. Persons who attended these schools continue to struggle with their identity after years of being taught to hate themselves and the culture. The residential school led to disruption in the transference of parenting skills from one generation to the next. Without these skills, many survivors had had difficulty raising their own children. In residential schools, they learned that adults often exert power and control through abuse. The lessons learned in childhood are often repeated in adulthood, with the result that many survivors of the residential school system often inflict abuse on their own children. (Ing, 1991)

Haig-Brown (1988), who documented the experiences of several Aboriginal people who were forced to attend residential schools over a period of sixty years, suggested that the cultural oppression and ethnocentric indoctrination of the educational process were a microcosm of the domination of Euro-Canadian culture over all aspects of Aboriginal life. Cummins (1992:3) stated that it is not unreasonable to conclude that one of the central goals of these schools was to "prepare children of subordinated groups for their status in life by rekindling shame from one generation to the next."

Psychologist Roland Chrisjohn defined the residential school "as an institution formed to make war on First Nations languages, religions and societies." In extensive interviews conducted with Aboriginal students, he found that those who attended these schools felt that the experience had deeply affected their sexual relations, their ability as parents, and their feelings about their religion and culture and had contributed to alcohol abuse, high levels of suicide, and wife abuse (Wilson, 1991).

According to Stanley McKay, a Cree-Ojibwa from Manitoba who is the first Aboriginal moderator of the United Church of Canada, residential schools collaborated in the cultural **genocide** of Aboriginal peoples. He considers his experiences in residential school as a form of incarceration: "My spirit was not broken but my anger is there. It is something that should not have happened. Some people were desperately scarred and wounded" (Roberts, 1993:A1).

The Assembly of First Nations, in its study of the impact of residential schools (1994), described Aboriginal children's experiences in terms of their emotional, mental, physical, and spiritual impact. The process of cultural genocide toward Aboriginal children was carried out by having their feelings ridiculed, their creativity and independent thinking stifled, their bodily needs ignored or violated, and their ways of life denied (Barman, 1996).

The residential schools did incredible damage. They resulted in loss of life, the denigration of culture, the destruction of self-respect and self-esteem, and the torture of families. The impact of these traumas on succeeding generations is overwhelming, as is the enormity of the cultural triumphalism that lay behind the enterprise.

Not only were residential schools an abject failure in assimilation, but they further marginalized generations of men and women not only from the Canadian mainstream but also from their own home environments.

societies and with the natural world should be conducted assumed a relationship of equality among nations, in which each nation retained its autonomy and distinctiveness, each nation had a separate as well as a shared land base, and the natural world was respected (Dockstator, 1993).

The Aboriginal world view was of a universal sacred order made up of compacts and kinship relations among human beings, other living beings, and the creator. This concept of sharing with other forms of life is alien to Judeo-Christian thought. Aboriginal systems reflected an ideology of land use, not of individual land ownership. The Crown, to claim absolute title, would have to obtain surrender from past generations as well as those of the future. As far as Aboriginal peoples were concerned, when they signed treaties, they were not giving up their lands but sharing them (Dickason, 1992).

Aboriginal societies therefore operated on the assumption that they were maintaining a nation-to-nation relationship when they signed treaties. They expected that treaties would grow more valuable with time, as the parties came to know each other better, to trust one another, and to make the most of their treaty relationships.

Governments and courts in Canada, however, often considered treaties as instruments of surrender rather than as compacts of coexistence and mutual benefit. Property law, as created in liberal democracies such as Canada, severely restricts Aboriginal peoples' ability to institutionalize and render into legal form their unique relations with the land. The Canadian legal system has not been able to embrace Aboriginal ideas of tradition, of what has often been referred to as natural law. Canadian laws, based on the principle of adversarial relations, have not recognized Aboriginal customary laws, which are based on the principles of relations and consensus (Monture-Angus, 1995). These fundamentally different understandings have characterized all of the treaties.

The economic ambitions of the settlers became increasingly incompatible with the rights and ways of life of the Aboriginal peoples, on whose land this new development was to take place. Throughout the nineteenth century and into the twentieth, the British Crown and then the new Dominion of Canada entered into treaties in Ontario, the prairie provinces, and parts of the North, under which Indians agreed to the creation of reserves in exchange for sharing their lands and resources with the newcomers.

While the segregationist policy of creating reserves was being enacted, it was at the same time being supplemented by assimilationist policies, such as the 1857 Act to Encourage the Gradual Civilization of the Indian Tribes in This Province. It provided for the voluntary enfranchisement—the release from Indian status—of individuals of good character, as determined by a board of examiners. Upon enfranchisement, volunteers would no longer be considered "Indians" and would acquire instead the rights common to ordinary non-Aboriginal settlers. In addition, they would take a portion of tribal land with them.

This enfranchisement policy was a direct attack on the integrity and land base of Aboriginal communities. At the same time it was an assimilative strategy to move educated Indians away from the "backward" culture of the reserves. Aboriginal communities strongly opposed the Gradual Civilization Act and largely succeeded because only one man is known to have volunteered for enfranchisement in the two decades following passage of the Act.

The federal Enfranchisement Act of 1869 interfered with tribal self-government by establishing the supremacy of bureaucratic authority over traditional leaders and restricted the jurisdiction of band councils to that of municipal governments. The Act defined an "Indian" as possessing at least one-quarter Indian blood and expanded the differentiation between officially registered "status" Indians and nonregistered "non-status" Indians. Indian status could also be lost through obtaining a university degree. In addition, Indian women married to non-Indian men lost their Indian status, thus maintaining European assumptions about women taking on the identity of their husbands. This discriminatory section of the Indian Act remained in place until 1985, surviving several court challenges (McMillan, 1995).

The 1876 Indian Act further strengthened the 1869 act's provisions instituting elected rather than traditional band councils. This act also positioned Aboriginal people as "wards" of the federal Department of Indian Affairs. Although the Indian Act was amended many times and underwent a major revision in 1951, its fundamental purpose was assimilation.

Meanwhile, as the assimilative and relocation policies were in force, Aboriginal peoples were starving, the Métis were struggling for recognition, and land claims were being ignored. The notion of accommodation with "savages" was unthinkable, at least in the realm of practical politics (Dickason, 1992). The Canadian government could disregard the concerns of Aboriginal people because they were considered inferior—they were "others," strangers.

From the moment that the federal government assumed jurisdiction over Aboriginal peoples, Canada's relationship with them has been based on cultural, social, economic, and political oppression. It has been characterized by an endless struggle against cultural annihilation and poverty (Duclos, 1990). Aboriginal peoples were displaced from the land that formed the basis of their culture, their way of life, and their livelihood. They were placed on reserves to provide land for newly arrived European immigrants and settlers from the United States.

Although the reserves were located in areas that the various tribes had long occupied, they were much smaller than the groups' previous territories. Land on the reserves could not be disposed of without the permission of the federal government. Aboriginal people were expected to survive on the reserves and not to rely on the resources or services available in settler communities. Traditional Aboriginal governments were supplemented by band councils that had little power or influence (Bienvenue and Goldstein, 1985).

Negotiation and Renewal

After World War II, there was growing public and international concern about the racist treatment of Canada's Aboriginal peoples. Although the 1951 revisions to the Indian Act removed some of the more coercive instruments, the Act retained its assimilative intent: the end of Aboriginal culture. Civilization was to be encouraged but not so blatantly forced on Aboriginal peoples (Miller, 1991).

The 1969 White Paper on Indian Policy, introduced by Minister of Indian Affairs Jean Chrétien, argued that Canada's Indians were disadvantaged simply because they enjoyed a unique legal status. It therefore recommended the abolition of Indian status. Indians as Indians would therefore disappear and become just another element in a multicultural Canada (Miller, 1991). The controversy and opposition that the White Paper provoked also stimulated political mobilization and the reinforcement of a shared common history of "Indianness"—a history of being subjected to a form of tutelage that was intended to take Aboriginal people out of their existing social groups and to force them into mainstream Canadian society (Dyck, 1991).

Population

At the time of initial sustained contact with Europeans, the Aboriginal population of North America was estimated to be at least 500 000 (Dickason, 1992). The diseases brought to North America by Europeans from the late 1400s onward, such as smallpox, tuberculosis, influenza, scarlet fever, and measles, reduced the population drastically. Armed hostilities and starvation also claimed many lives, to the point that in 1871, the Aboriginal population was estimated to be about 100 000.

Since the 1940s, however, there has been a rapid growth in the Aboriginal population. Between 1981 and 1991, the on-reserve Indian population of Canada increased by one-third, the off-reserve Indian population more than doubled, and the Inuit population increased by one-third (Frideres, 1993). Aboriginal birth rates were much higher than

THE INDIAN ACT

The Indian Act, first passed in 1876, is the legislation that has intruded on the lives and cultures of status Indians more than any other law. Though amended repeatedly, the Act's fundamental provisions have scarcely changed. They give the state powers that range from defining how one is born or naturalized into "Indian" status to administering the estate of an Aboriginal person after death.

The 1876 Indian Act rested on the principle "that the aborigines are to be kept in a condition of tutelage and treated as wards or children of the State" (Department of the Interior, 1877:xiv). The Act gave Parliament control over Indian political structures, landholding patterns, and resource and economic development. It covered almost every important aspect of the daily lives of Aboriginal peoples on reserves. The overall effect was to subject Aboriginal people to the almost unfettered rule of federal bureaucrats. The Act imposed non-Aboriginal forms on traditional governance, landholding practices, and cultural practices.

The Indian Act provided a means of removing political sovereignty from indigenous people by introducing a system of indirect rule and segregation (Fleras and Elliott, 1992). The sweeping regulations under the Act included prohibitions against owning land. Early clauses, which have only in recent years been eliminated, controlled every aspect of the lives and lifestyles of Aboriginal peoples, from denying them the right to vote to prohibiting them from purchasing and consuming alcohol (Bienvenue and Goldstein, 1985).

For example, the Indian Act of 1876 and various amendments up to the 1930s decreed:

- The majority of Aboriginal people living on reserves could not vote in federal elections. (This was not changed until 1960.) Those who wished to have the franchise were forced to give up their status and lose all the benefits conferred by the Indian Act, including rights to land, homes, and community (Sharzer, 1985).

- Aboriginal people could not manage their own reserve lands or money and were under the supervision of federally appointed Indian Agents.
- All chiefs and band councillors were to be elected for three-year terms. Exclusionary and sexist, the Act also decreed that only men were to be allowed to vote in band elections. (Aboriginal women were not given the right to vote in band elections until the 1951 Indian Act.)
- Protected reserve lands were to be converted to provincial lands upon the enfranchisement of an Indian.
- Aboriginal peoples did not have power to decide whether non-Indians could reside on or use reserve lands.
- Public authorities were given the power (in 1911) to expropriate reserve land without a surrender, as long as the expropriation was for the purpose of public works.
- No Aboriginal peoples could develop land without the Agents' consent.
- For an Indian to be intoxicated on or off the reserve was an offence punishable by one month in jail.
- The sale of agricultural products was prohibited without official permission.

In 1885, a pass system was instituted by the federal government prohibiting Aboriginal people from leaving their reserve without the written authorization of their Agent. This move was designed to restrict parental visits to residential schools. The Indian Act was also amended to authorize the arrest of Indians found on reserves other than their home reserve. This amendment, supported by missionaries, had the effect of prohibiting communal sun dances, thirst dances, and ghost dances. This ban was extended to all forms of Aboriginal dances in 1906.

Another example of the concerted attack on Aboriginal cultural practices was the 1884 amendments to the Indian Act that banned the west coast potlatch and other ceremonies. Potlatch "giveaways" were deemed incompatible with Euro-Canadian economic practices and the concept of private property. Using ritual, ceremony, and celebration, the potlatch provided a central organizing framework in which new leaders were installed, wealth was distributed, names were given and recorded, political councils were held and decisions made, history instruction was provided, and spiritual guidance was given. The Aboriginal peoples were not only denied an opportunity to participate in an important ceremonial festival but also lost control over their political life (Ponting and Gibbons, 1980).

The Indian Act of 1927, in recognizing the failures and inadequacies of the coercive assimilationist strategy, tried to bolster it by providing even stronger measures to intervene in and control the affairs of Aboriginal societies. This included further efforts to develop an agricultural economy, in the expectation that social and cultural change would follow in its wake. In responding to Aboriginal political organizations pursuing land issues, especially in British Columbia, the Act also made "raising a fund or providing money for the prosecution of any claim" a crime unless permission was obtained.

By the beginning of the twentieth century, the administration of "Indian affairs" had assumed a format that continued with few changes until after World War II. The Indian Act provided the Department of Indian Affairs with exclusive jurisdiction over Aboriginal people and gave its officers the authority to supervise most facets of their lives.

In summary, the Canadian government, through the Indian Act, imposed a form of institutionalized racism in the relationship between Canada and its Aboriginal peoples (Frideres, 1993; Bolaria and Li, 1988). The Act was designed to promote coercive assimilation, in which Aboriginal peoples were expected to adopt the cultural attitudes and norms of the dominant culture and give up their own cultural

traditions, histories, values, customs, and language (Richardson, 1993; Bolaria and Li, 1988). Aboriginal social and political institutions were systematically dismantled.

The Indian Act also set out to define "who was an Indian." Yet, as Daniel Raunet pointed out, "to ask the question in legal terms is in itself discriminatory. ... People do not need legislation to know their origin or place on this earth" (in Ducharme, 1986). For the White lawgiver, the Indian was a person registered in an "Indian Register." Indian women who married non-status Indian men simply lost their status. These legal definitions relating to identity totally ignored the fact that Aboriginal peoples were not a monolithic group but represented extraordinarily diverse and distinct populations with different customs, traditions, histories, cultures, and languages (Ducharme, 1986).

The Indian Act persists as an essentially repressive instrument of containment (Fleras and Elliott, 1996). Founded on the ethnocentric certainties of the nineteenth century, it continues to interfere profoundly in the lives, cultures, and communities of First Nations peoples today.

In summary, throughout this period of displacement and assimilation, Aboriginal peoples were denied access to their traditional territories and often forced to move to new locations selected by colonial authorities. They were also displaced socially and culturally by being subjected to intense missionary activity and the establishment of schools that undermined Aboriginal parents' ability to pass on traditional values to their children. They had imposed upon them male-oriented Victorian values, while traditional activities such as significant dances and other ceremonies were attacked and made unlawful. They were also displaced politically, forced by colonial laws to abandon or at least disguise traditional governing structures and processes in favour of municipal-style institutions.

CASE STUDY 4.3

THE PHYSICAL DISPLACEMENT AND RELOCATION OF ABORIGINAL PEOPLES

The displacement of Aboriginal peoples often took the form of deliberate initiatives by governments to move particular Aboriginal communities. Governments saw relocation as an apparent solution to a number of problems. Aboriginal lands with valuable resources were often expropriated when provincial and federal government agencies required them for the building of railways, roads, and dams (Bienvenue and Goldstein, 1985). The Métis in Saskatchewan, the Cree along James Bay, and many other Aboriginal groups were uprooted and relocated at the convenience and for the economic gain of various Canadian governments (Ducharme, 1986). In Manitoba and Saskatchewan, band councils claim to have lost over a million acres as a result of the government expropriation and sale of reserve lands (Kellough, 1980).

If Aboriginal communities appeared to be undernourished, they might be moved to where game was more plentiful. If they were suffering severe health problems, they might be placed in new communities where health care services and other amenities were available. Addressing Aboriginal medical and welfare problems in this way also provided an opportunity for governments to achieve their social objective of assimilation. If Aboriginal people were thought to be indolent, the new communities would provide education and training facilities. If they were in the way of expanding agricultural frontiers or happened to occupy land needed for urban settlements, they could be moved "for their own protection." And, if their traditional lands held natural resources—minerals to be exploited, forests to be cut, rivers to be drained—they could be relocated "in the national interest" (*Report of the Royal Commission on Aboriginal Peoples*, 1996).

Justified by this attitude of paternalism and employing the discourse of democratic racism, the practice of relocation by the Canadian government was widespread. Decisions were made with little or no consultation, and Aboriginal communities were relocated on short notice. Relocation has been described as the "last major pre-liberal policy thrust through which a distinctly paternalistic inclination can be seen." Many relocations were carried out to ease the administration and costs of government services. Examples include the centralization of the Mi'kmaq of Nova Scotia in the 1940s, and the movement of the Gwa'Sala and 'Nakwaxda'xw of British Columbia in 1964, the Mushuau Innu of Labrador to Davis Inlet in 1967, the Inuit of Hebron in Labrador, the Sayisi Dene in northern Labrador, and the Yukon First Nations.

Addressing the perceived needs of Aboriginal peoples often involved moving them "back to the land" from a more or less settled existence. Administrators attempted to encourage Aboriginal peoples to resume or relearn what was considered the traditional way of life. This approach was directed particularly at the Inuit. For the government, this paternalism was linked to another political motivation: the need to assert Canadian sovereignty in the High Arctic, which would be enhanced by effective occupation. The "first official Eskimo relocation project" involved the dispersal of Baffin Island Inuit to Devon Island between 1934 and 1947.

In a research study for the Royal Commission on Aboriginal Peoples, it was noted, "The analogy of human pawns being moved on an Arctic chessboard is perhaps never more strikingly illustrated than in the instance of Devon Island, of relocation of a small group of Inuit to form new sites in succession, as it suited the experimental interests of the Hudson's Bay Company, and set against the background of the geopolitical interests of the State" (*Report of the Royal Commission on Aboriginal Peoples*, 1996). Other Inuit relocations motivated by the same rationale included Nueltin Lake (1949), Henik Lake (1957–58), Rankin Inlet and Whale Cove, Banks Island (1951–52), and Baffin Island throughout the 1950s and 1960s.

Development relocation was carried out in the "public interest" for the purposes of agricultural expansion, urban development, mineral exploitation, and hydroelectric power generation. Examples include

- the Saugeen Ojibwa on Ontario's Bruce Peninsula throughout the latter half of the nineteenth century; they were moved to the Cape Croker Reserve to make way for the agricultural needs of European settlers
- the Songhees, a Coast Salish people who were relocated to land near Esquimault to make way for the growth of Victoria, British Columbia, in 1910
- the Métis community of Ste. Madeleine, Manitoba, which was relocated in the late 1930s to make room for cattle
- the Ouje-Bougnoumou Cree of Quebec, who have been moved seven times since 1927, all to meet the needs of mining companies
- the Churchill Falls project in Labrador, Alcan's Kemano hydroelectric project on the Fraser River, the Grand Rapids hydroelectric project on the Saskatchewan River, the Talston River Hydroelectric System in the Northwest Territories, and the northern Manitoba hydroelectric system that resulted in the flooding of Aboriginal lands and forced relocation

The impact of these relocations was disastrous. Not only did they impose dramatic changes on the Aboriginal way of life, family, and community structure, but they also resulted in the loss of economic livelihood and the swift establishment of welfare dependency, increased family violence, and a variety of social and health problems.

Although the federal government backed down from the White Paper, its underlying philosophy continued to animate federal policy for years to come. The 1984 Nielson Task Force also provoked similar opposition when it recom-mended the dissolution of the Department of Indian Affairs and the devolution of the department's responsibilities to the provinces and band councils. The legacy of distrust was maintained as avenues of redress continued to be tightly controlled and regulated. Throughout the 1970s and 1980s, the federal government was generally not prepared to move beyond the limited strategies of administrative decentralization of programs and services and the granting of municipal-style governing powers to community-based Aboriginal governments.

There continue to the present day to be differing perspectives and objectives regarding self-government. On the one hand, Aboriginal leaders continue to push strongly for self-government as an inherent right, arguing that its roots lie in Aboriginal existence before contact. On the other hand, the notion of "existing Aboriginal and treaty rights" as recognized in Canada's constitution has, from a non-Aboriginal perspective, tended to be limited to those rights already recognized and defined by institutions such as the courts. The only requirement of government, therefore, is to enumerate and define them more precisely. From an Aboriginal perspective, however, the term includes many rights that have not yet been defined or recognized by non-Aboriginal society (Assembly of First Nations, 1994).

One of the more obvious criticisms of the present land-claims process is the federal government's conflict of interest in attempting to deal with these matters. On the one hand, the federal government has a fiduciary or trust-like responsibility toward Aboriginal people to act in their best interests, while on the other hand it seeks to act in its own best interests—to minimize its legal and financial obligations. It is in the position of being both judge and jury in dealing with claims against itself. It sets the criteria, decides what claims are acceptable, and controls the entire negotiating process, including funding support (Assembly of First Nations, 1994).

As a result of the criteria, processes, and costs, very few settlements have been reached. Aboriginal peoples are consequently questioning the viability of the claims mechanism as a means of obtaining their constitutionally protected Aboriginal and treaty rights. They see their political relationship with Canada as not much more than an extension of the racist and paternalistic attitude toward Aboriginal peoples that characterized Canada's colonial traditions.

With so few land claims being settled, the 1990s witnessed a number of acts of civil disobedience and conflict as a consequence of Aboriginal peoples' growing frustration with the process. Violent confrontations occurred in Akwesasne on the Quebec-Ontario border, Oka in Quebec, Gustafsen Lake in British Columbia, and Ipperwash in Ontario.

At the same time, however, there has been some movement toward a greater understanding and recognition of Aboriginal aspirations. It no longer seems so important that Aboriginal societies follow the evolutionary path toward assimilation within non-Aboriginal society.

Of particular significance is the establishment of the Tungavila Federation of Nunavut in 1999, after twenty-five years of negotiation. Covering over 350 000 square kilometres in the Eastern Arctic—a fifth of Canada's land mass—it comprises about 20 000 people, of whom 85 percent are Inuit. The territory will be self-governing, though not with the full powers of a province. The agreement provides financial compensation of $1.14 billion to be paid out over 14 years, $13 million for a training trust fund, and royalties from mineral development (Frideres, 1993).

A second significant example is the 1998 treaty with the Nisga'a people in northwestern British Columbia. The treaty, the first in British Columbia between an Aboriginal people and government in almost 140 years, allows a form of government elected only by the Nisga'a people, with authority to make laws on culture, language, employment, public works, land use, traffic, and marriage. It will provide for health, child welfare, and education services, a police force that meets provincial standards, and a court system with jurisdiction over Nisga'a laws on Nisga'a lands. Non-Nisga'a people will be subject to the Nisga'a law on the Nisga'a lands, but they will also have the option of using the provincial court system.

The treaty gives the Nisga'a government power to tax Nisga'a citizens on Nisga'a land and to impose property taxes on non-Nisga'a residents. Income and sales tax exemptions that now exist under the Indian Act will be eliminated. The Canadian Charter of Rights and Freedoms and the Criminal Code remain paramount, and all Nisga'a regulations dealing with wildlife, the environment, and all other areas must meet federal and provincial regulations. The treaty includes provisions that the deal is final and that future generations cannot demand more. The Nisga'a have agreed to give up historic rights granted them under the Indian Act (*Globe and Mail*, 1998). Unlike any other agreement, the treaty combines the Nisga'a land claims and recognition of a central Nisga'a Nation government with powers to tax, regulate land use, and administer a justice system.

those of the larger Canadian population, but even more important was the rapid decline of the infant mortality rate.

Defining and measuring Aboriginal ethnicity and the size and composition of Canada's Aboriginal population is not an easy task. Demographically, the Aboriginal population is quite different from the rest of the Canadian population: it is much younger and faster-growing, with fertility rates almost twice those of non-Aboriginal people and life expectancy rates averaging ten years less than those of the average Canadian (Norris, 1996).

Considerable discussion exists regarding the limitations and undercoverage of Canada's Aboriginal peoples in census data. Table 4.1 presents the most recently published data source of the current Aboriginal population by province. Today, Canada's Aboriginal population has been considered to consist of four major groups: status Indians, who are registered under the Indian Act; non-status Indians, who have lost or never had status under the Act; Métis, who are of mixed Aboriginal and non-Aboriginal ancestry; and Inuit. Table 4.2 shows the latest census data on ethnicity. The Royal Commission on Aboriginal Peoples projected that by the year 2016, Canada's Aboriginal population would reach 1.2 million.

Table 4.1

POPULATION REPORTING ABORIGINAL IDENTITY, CANADA, PROVINCES AND TERRITORIES, 2001

	Number	%
Canada	976 310	100.0
Newfoundland and Labrador	18 780	1.9
Prince Edward Island	1 345	0.1
Nova Scotia	17 015	1.7
New Brunswick	16 990	1.7
Quebec	79 400	8.1
Ontario	188 315	19.3
Manitoba	150 040	15.4
Saskatchewan	130 190	13.3
Alberta	156 220	16.0
British Columbia	170 025	17.4
Yukon Territory	6 540	0.7
Northwest Territories	18 725	1.9
Nunavut	22 720	2.3

Source: Statistics Canada, "Aboriginal Peoples of Canada," Census of Canada, 2001.

Table 4.2

SIZE AND GROWTH OF THE POPULATION REPORTING ABORIGINAL ANCESTRY AND ABORIGINAL IDENTITY, CANADA, 1996–2001

	2001	1996	Percentage Growth 1996–2001
Total: Aboriginal ancestry[a]	**1 319 890**	**1 101 960**	**19.8**
Total: Aboriginal identity	**976 305**	**799 010**	**22.2**
North American Indian[b]	608 850	529 040	15.1
Métis[b]	292 310	204 115	43.2
Inuit[b]	45 070	40 220	12.1
Multiple and other Aboriginal responses[c]	30 080	25 640	17.3

[a]Also known as *Aboriginal origin*.
[b]Includes persons who reported a North American Indian, Métis, or Inuit identity only.
[c]Includes persons who reported more than one Aboriginal identity group (North American Indian, Métis, or Inuit) and those who reported being a Registered Indian and/or band member without reporting an Aboriginal identity.

Source: Statistics Canada, "Aboriginal Peoples of Canada," Census of Canada, 2001.

The Abuse of the Rights of Aboriginal Women and Children

An example of racism against Aboriginal women and children is the relationship between child welfare agencies and Aboriginal families. Since the late 1970s, when provincial welfare programs were first extended to Aboriginal people living on reserves, the system has removed many Aboriginal children from their natural parents, their extended families, and their communities. These children were routinely placed in non-Aboriginal foster homes or given for adoption to non-Aboriginal families, with devastating emotional and psychological effects on the children, the parents, and the Aboriginal community (Kline, 1992). Social workers, using middle-class norms to assess Aboriginal families, took significant numbers of children into "care" and placed them for adoption, ignoring the child adoption practices of the Aboriginal extended family (Johnson, 1983).

A study conducted by the Canadian Bar Association (1988) revealed that Aboriginal children in British Columbia and Ontario were eight times more likely to be apprehended by the child welfare system than were non-Aboriginal children. Aboriginal children represented 30 percent of the children in care in Alberta, and over 60 percent in Manitoba; similar figures existed in other parts of Canada.

Aboriginal women have been, and continue to be, the most victimized group in Canadian society. From birth, the Aboriginal woman must confront all forms of discrimination—gender, race, and class. Her very identity has been determined by a law established by White men. She is frequently the victim of systematic emotional, sexual, and physical abuse, perpetrated since childhood by fathers, foster and adoptive parents, husbands, teachers, priests, social workers, and police (Elizabeth Fry Society of Saskatchewan, 1992).

Submissions to the Royal Commission on Aboriginal Peoples documented the endemic violence against Aboriginal women. Briefs documented the high levels of sexual, physical, and psychological abuse they endured and the lack of transition homes or services in most of the communities in which they lived (*Report of the Royal Commission on Aboriginal Peoples*, 1996). Economically, they are more vulnerable than both non-Aboriginal women and Aboriginal men in relation to levels of income and employment opportunities (Fleras and Elliott, 1992).

Conclusion

The struggles, injustices, prejudice, and discrimination that have plagued Aboriginal peoples for more than three centuries are still grim realities today. The failure of Canada's racist policies toward Aboriginal peoples is reflected in high levels of unemployment: the jobless rate averages nearly 70 percent, and 62 percent of Aboriginal people living on reserves receive social assistance. Aboriginal peoples' income averages little more than half that of non-Aboriginals.

Aboriginal infant mortality rates are more than double the Canadian rate. The functional illiteracy of the Aboriginal peoples is 45 percent, in contrast with the Canadian rate of 17 percent; only 20 percent of Aboriginal children complete their high school education, in contrast with a national rate of 75 percent. The Aboriginal suicide rate is three times the national rate; for young people aged 17–24, the rate is seven times as high (Canadian Labour Congress, 1992).

Numerous government task forces and reports have documented systemic racism against Aboriginal peoples in the justice system, including the reports of the Donald Marshall Inquiry in Nova Scotia (1989), the Task Force on the Criminal Justice System and Its Impact on the Indian and Métis People of Alberta (1991), the Aboriginal Justice Inquiry of Manitoba (1991), the Saskatchewan Métis Justice Review Committee (1991), and the Law Reform Commission of Canada on Aboriginal Peoples and Criminal Justice (1991).

The Aboriginal population of all provincial prisons in 1989 was 57 percent of all inmates (*Report of the Aboriginal Justice Inquiry of Manitoba*, 1991). In 1988, Aboriginal people represented 4 percent of the national population, yet they constituted 10 percent of the federal penitentiary population. They make up almost all of the inmates in certain women's prisons in Yukon and Labrador, and over 70 percent in the Northwest Territories, Manitoba, and Saskatchewan. Aboriginal people account for 52 percent of all prison admissions in Manitoba; in Saskatchewan, 61 percent; in Alberta, 25 percent; and in British Columbia, 17 percent (Canadian Bar Association, 1988).

Economic disadvantage, underemployment, substance abuse, and other factors that are used to explain Aboriginal over-involvement in crime are not the source of the problem but symptoms of the problems of a society structured on discriminatory values, beliefs, and practices (Monture-Angus, 1995). As the *Report of the Aboriginal Justice Inquiry of Manitoba* (1991) concluded, the causes of Aboriginal criminal behaviour are rooted in the long history of discrimination and social inequality that has impoverished Aboriginal people and consigned them to the margins of society.

What can be concluded from this brief overview is that the legacy of centuries of dispossession, oppression, and exploitation directed at the Aboriginal peoples of Canada is reflected today in Aboriginal peoples' high rates of physical and mental illness, suicide, homicide, incarceration, unemployment, and poverty—the direct result of pervasive and intractable racism.

This brief overview of the relations that have evolved between Aboriginal peoples and White society over the last four hundred years also highlights some of the discursive forms of democratic racism that have been, and continue to be, expressed to justify the experiences and continued ill treatment of Aboriginal peoples. They include:

- *The discourse of nationality:* The quotation of Alexander Morris, a nineteenth-century treaty negotiator, that begins this chapter eloquently and crudely captures the application of nationalism and the notion of patriotic duty as the underlying rationale for a policy of assimilation. The notion of the "other" could not be tolerated by a society in the pursuit of a unifying national identity grounded on Western values.

- *The discourse of paternalism:* Alexander Morris' remark also captures the sense of dominance, superiority, and munificent benevolence of a colonial government intent on "Christianizing" and "civilizing" the Aboriginal peoples to retrieve them from their assumed inferior, unchristian, uncivilized state. Reinforced by the scientific racism of Social Darwinism and by the Christian duty to evangelize and civilize, non-Aboriginals were provided with a discourse to justify plundering Aboriginal lands and destroying their cultures, languages, and traditions. Such a discourse also provided the framework for the Indian Act and the treatment of Aboriginal peoples as wards of the state.

- *The discourse of "blame the victim":* Notwithstanding four hundred years of policies and practices of displacement and oppression, with the result that Aboriginal peoples exist at the bottom ranks of Canadian society, the resolution of this state of affairs continues to focus on Aboriginal people themselves. In the words of Patricia Monture-Angus (1995): "When are those of you who inflict racism, who appropriate pain, who speak with no knowledge or respect when you ought to know to listen and accept, going to take hard looks at yourself instead of me? How can you continue to look to me to carry what is your responsibility?"

- *The discourse of multiculturalism:* In the context of Aboriginal peoples, this discourse began to be reflected in government policies of the 1970s and 1980s. These policies indicated a desire on the part of the federal government to decentralize and dismantle its obligations to Aboriginal peoples, and to deal with them as just another element in a multicultural Canada.

- *The discourse of a monolithic "other":* A constant theme in the history of Aboriginal-White relations is non-Aboriginals' inability to recognize the enormous complexity and sophistication of Aboriginal societies and the enormous ethnic, linguistic, cultural, and economic diversity of the Aboriginal population. Such a discourse imposed a common history of "Indianness" as determined and defined by mainstream Canadian society.

Notes

1. There is a considerable literature on Aboriginal peoples in Canada. In addition to the references cited in this chapter, the reader is encouraged to consult J. Rick Ponting (ed.), *First Nations in Canada: Perspectives on Opportunity, Empowerment, and Self-Determination* (Toronto: McGraw-Hill Ryerson, 1997); V. Satzewich and T. Wotherspoon, *First Nations: Race, Class and Gender Relations* (Scarborough, ON: Nelson, 1993); and Darrell Buffalo, *Socio-Economic Indicators in Indian Reserves and Comparable Communities, 1971–1991* (Ottawa: Department of Indian Affairs and Northern Development, 1997).

References

Assembly of First Nations. (1994). *Breaking the Silence.* Ottawa: Assembly of First Nations.

Barman, J. (1996). "Aboriginal Education at the Crossroads: The Legacy of Residential Schools and the Way Ahead." In D. Long and O. Dickason (eds.), *Visions of the Heart: Canadian Aboriginal Issues.* Toronto: Harcourt Brace.

Bienvenue, R., and J. Goldstein (eds.). (1985). *Ethnicity and Ethnic Relations in Canada.* Toronto: Butterworths.

Bolaria, B.S., and P. Li. (1988). *Racial Oppression in Canada.* 2nd ed. Toronto: Garamond Press.

Buffalo, D. (1997). *Socio-Economic Indicators in Indian Reserves and Comparable Communities, 1971–1991.* Ottawa: Department of Indian Affairs and Northern Development.

Canadian Bar Association. (1988). *Aboriginal Rights in Canada: An Agenda for Action.* Ottawa: Special Committee Report.

Canadian Labour Congress. (1992). *19th Constitutional Convention: Aboriginal Rights Policy Statement.* Ottawa: CLC.

Cayo, D. (1997). "The Seventh Direction." *The New Brunswick Reader* (July 12).

Clubine, C. (1991). "Racism, Assimilation and Indian Education in Upper Canada." Unpublished manuscript. Ontario Institute of Education, Department of Sociology, University of Toronto.

Cummins, J. (1992). "Lies We Live By: National Identity and Social Justice." *International Journal of the Sociology of Language* 110:145–155.

Department of the Interior. (1877). *Annual Report for the Year Ended 30th June 1876.* Parliament, Sessional Papers, No. 11.

Dickason, O. (1992). *Canada's First Nations: A History of the Founding Peoples from Earliest Times.* Toronto: McClelland & Stewart.

Dockstator, M. (1993). *Towards an Understanding of Aboriginal Self-Government.* Osgoode Hall Law School, York University.

Ducharme, M. (1986). "The Segregation of Native People in Canada: Voluntary or Compulsory?" *Current Readings in Race Relations* 3(4):3–4.

Duclos, N. (1990). "Lessons of Difference: Feminist Theory on Cultural Diversity." *Buffalo Law Review* 38:325.

Dyck, N. (1991). *What Is the Indian "Problem": Tutelage and Resistance in Canadian Indian Administration.* St. John's: Institute of Social and Economic Research, Memorial University.

Elizabeth Fry Society of Saskatchewan. (1992). "Aboriginal Women in the Criminal Justice System." In *Western Judicial Education Centre on Racial, Ethnic, and Cultural Equity.* Saskatoon: WJEC.

Fleras, A., and J. Elliott. (1992). *The Nations Within: Aboriginal-State Relations in Canada, United States and New Zealand.* Toronto: Oxford University Press.

————. (1996). *Unequal Relations: An Introduction to Race, Ethnic and Aboriginal Dynamics in Canada.* 2nd ed. Scarborough, ON: Prentice Hall.

Frideres, J. (1993). *Native People in Canada: Contemporary Conflicts.* 4th ed. Scarborough, ON: Prentice Hall.

Glavin, T. (1998). "Death of an Ideology." *Globe and Mail* (August 8).

Globe and Mail. (1998). "Landmark Treaty Raises Inequality Concerns." (July 17):A1.

Haig-Brown, C. (1988). *Resistance and Renewal: Surviving the Indian Residential School.* Vancouver: Tillicum Library.

Ing, N.R. (1991). "The Effects of Residential Schools on Native Child-Rearing Practices." *Canadian Journal of Native Education* 18(Supplement).

Johnson, P. (1983). *Native Children and the Child Welfare System.* Toronto: James Lorimer.

Kellough, G. (1980). "From Colonialism to Economic Imperialism: The Experience of the Canadian Indian." In J. Harp and J. Hoffley (eds.), *Structural Inequality in Canada.* Scarborough, ON: Prentice Hall.

Kline, M. (1992). "Best-Interests Ideology in First Nations Child Welfare Cases." *Osgoode Hall Law Journal* 30:375–425.

McKenzie, B., and V. Morrissette. (2003). "Social Work Practice with Canadians of Aboriginal Background: Guidelines for Respectful Social Work." In A. Al-Krenawi and J. Graham (eds.), *Multicultural Social Work in Canada: Working with Diverse Ethno-Racial*

Communities. Don Mills, ON: Oxford University Press. 251–282.

McMillan, A. (1995). *Native Peoples and Cultures of Canada: An Anthropological Overview.* Toronto: Douglas & McIntyre.

Miller, J. (1991). *Sweet Promises: A History of Indian-White Relations in Canada.* Toronto: University of Toronto Press.

Monture-Angus, P. (1995). *Thunder in My Soul: A Mohawk Woman Speaks.* Halifax: Fernwood.

Ng, R. (1993). "Racism, Sexism and Nation Building." In C. McCarthy and W. Crichlow (eds.), *Race, Identity and Representation in Education.* New York and London: Routledge.

Norris, M. (1996). "Contemporary Demography of Aboriginal Peoples in Canada." In D. Long and O. Dickason (eds.), *Visions of the Heart: Canadian Aboriginal Issues.* Toronto: Harcourt Brace.

Ponting, J.R. (ed.). (1997). *First Nations in Canada: Perspectives on Opportunity, Empowerment, and Self-Determination.* Toronto: McGraw-Hill Ryerson.

Ponting, R., and R. Gibbons. (1980). *Out of Irrelevance.* Toronto: Butterworths.

Powless, C. (1985). "Native People and Employment: A National Tragedy." In *Research Studies of the Commission on Equality in Empowerment.* Ottawa: Department of Supply and Services Canada.

Report of the Aboriginal Justice Inquiry of Manitoba. (1991). Winnipeg.

Report of the Donald Marshall Inquiry in Nova Scotia. (1989). Halifax.

Report of the Law Reform Commission of Canada on Aboriginal Peoples and Criminal Justice. (1991). Ottawa.

Report of the Royal Commission on Aboriginal Peoples. (1996). Ottawa.

Report of the Saskatchewan Métis Justice Review Committee. (1991). Regina.

Report of the Task Force on the Criminal Justice System and Its Impact on the Indian and Métis People of Alberta. (1991). Edmonton.

Richardson, B. (1993). *People of Terra Nullius: Betrayal and Rebirth in Aboriginal Canada.* Vancouver and Toronto: Douglas & McIntyre.

Roberts, D. (1993). "A Stranger in God's House." *Globe and Mail* (December 1):A1.

St. Catharines Milling and Lumber Co. v. The Queen. (1887). *Supreme Court Reports* 12:577 at 596–597.

Satzewich, V., and T. Wotherspoon. (1993). *First Nations: Race, Class and Gender Relations.* Scarborough, ON: Nelson.

Scott, D. (1914). "Indian Affairs, 1867–1912." In A. Shortt and A.G. Doughty (eds.), *Canada and Its Provinces: A History of the Canadian People and Their Institutions.* Toronto: Glasgow, Brook.

Sharzer, S. (1985). "Native People: Some Issues." In *Research Studies of the Commission on Equality in Employment.* Ottawa: Department of Supply and Services Canada.

Tully, J. (1995). "Aboriginal Property and Western Theory: Recovering a Middle Ground." In E.F. Paul, F.D. Miller, and G. Paul (eds.), *Property Rights.* Cambridge: Cambridge University Press.

Wilson, D. (1991). "Native Bands Demand Action on School's Abuse of Children." *Globe and Mail* (June 19):A4.

PART TWO

Racism in Canadian Public-Sector Organizations

*This Part examines a number of key institutions in
Canadian society, particularly those that represent systems of social control.
The analysis of racism in the justice system, policing, and human services
demonstrates how the ideology of Whiteness impacts on the policies, programs,
and everyday practices within these institutions. The discussions in these chapters
illuminate the processes of racialization that sustain and reinforce White power
and privilege and isolate, stigmatize, and marginalize people of colour.*

CHAPTER 5

RACISM AND THE JUSTICE SYSTEM

A Black youth faces a White-dominated system with White police,
White lawyers and White Judge, and a White Crown attorney.

—A Black youth at the Jamaican Canadian Association Conference (1990)

This chapter examines the justice system[1] from the perspective of differential treatment and racism. The evidence from studies and the various official inquiries into the justice system will be discussed. Specific issues of concern include differential treatment in the courts, such as in the granting of bail and sentencing disparities, and the attitudes of justice system officials. The lack of minority representation in the justice system will also be highlighted. The chapter includes case studies of two views of racism in the justice system.

Introduction

Canada's system of justice is complex. It consists of many actors, each playing a part in its various processes. Structurally, the system consists of courts of inherent jurisdiction as well as statutory courts and tribunals. Administrative tribunals now adjudicate an increasing number of disputes involving the rights of Canadians, residents, and others. Administrative employees often have little, if any, legal training but are sometimes called upon to make far-reaching decisions without any formal training in the technicalities of the law.

The system of justice includes prosecutors, Crown attorneys, defence counsel, decision-makers, police, court staff, sheriffs, court clerks, experts, witnesses, and a variety of technocrats each working to preserve a system aimed at proving versions of the truth. Results negotiated by the parties to a dispute form an integral part of the process of dispute resolution in the criminal, civil litigation, or administrative contexts.

Canada's justice system strives to provide an impartial adjudicative process that dispenses "justice" regardless of race, culture, creed, national, and ethnic origin. A system of justice that discriminates on any of the foregoing grounds brings the administration of justice into disrepute, contrary to constitutional principles and the stated values of our Charter of Rights and Freedoms. Despite these principles, the justice system does not deliver its promise of equality to people of colour.

For the most part, the issue is not whether racism in the justice system would bring the administration of justice into disrepute. Rather, the issue is whether racism is expressed in Canada's justice system. Although at least one appeal court noted that "our society has been infected with the evil of racism" (*Regina v. Parks*:369) many decision-makers continue to think of themselves, their values, thought processes, and "common sense" realities and understanding of issues such as fairness, equality, and tolerance as immune from the pervasiveness of racism.

Racism gets expressed in complex ways within the justice system. At the outset, it should be stated that many lawyers, judges, and other legal practitioners are unfamiliar with race issues. Many are ill equipped with the skills, knowledge, and understanding to identify when race is a significant issue in a case. Others may recognize race as an issue, but fear the repercussion of raising race issues in pleadings or at other stages of the litigation process. This despite the existence of rules of professional conduct across the country that require a solicitor to raise any and every issue fearlessly in the representation of clients (Pinto, 2000).

Common law doctrines, statutory principles, and provisions neutral on their face can easily be employed and interpreted to produce racially biased results. Racism continues unabated when decision-makers distrust minority lawyers, or fail to respect them in the course of hearing; when law societies fail to discipline members of the profession who either ignore race issues or perpetuate them in the justice system; when law societies across the country fail to include an understanding of race issues within the requirement for competence.

One of the main factors in the manifestation of racism is whether a court takes judicial notice of racism, or even permits issues of race to be adjudicated outside of human rights forums or the hate crimes provisions of the Criminal Code. Similarly, rules of procedure may be employed in ways that perpetuate racism. Appellate courts easily perpetuate racism by reinforcing the decisions of an inferior court or tribunal's decision that has already affirmed racial inequality either by design or by impact. The refusal of an appellate court to revive issues of race from its own review of the transcripts when a tribunal or inferior court erases race from its decision helps not only to perpetuate racial discrimination, but also to freeze the law from development. At the heart of the expression of racism in the justice system is the manner in which its incumbents exercise discretion and judgment when dealing with people of colour whether they be litigants, lawyers, court staff, or others.

While racial discrimination in Canada's justice system has not been extensively or systematically studied, data appears to be more prevalent with respect to the criminal process than within the civil litigation or administrative contexts. In addressing the topic of racism in the justice system, particularly in the courts, Pomerant outlined a consistent problem with respect to the identification and validation of racism:

> Minority persons and groups often allege that discrimination is regularly encountered by them in their contacts with the Canadian criminal process. Unfortunately, its incidence is difficult to objectively verify. ... A court can readily justify matters such as credibility findings, detention orders and harsh sentences by articulation of "legitimate factors." (1992:6)

Objective research evidence of differential treatment in the criminal courts is confined to a very small number of studies. Part of the problem stems from the fact that the study of racial discrimination in the justice system in Canada is beset by a wide range of methodological constraints.[2] The most problematic is the absence of systematic and comprehensive forms of data collection and analysis. For instance, how does one study systematically the intersection between race and the interpretive process so central to decision-making in the justice system? What unit of analysis would one use to determine the intersection between race and findings of credibility a judge is so often called upon to make in many cases with limited information and within the confines of rules of evidence? How does one systematically study the relationship between judicial discourse and findings of fact related to the intention of a party before the court?

In the civil litigation context these are important questions, because so much of the dispute in that forum is about money. Not much attention is usually paid to the intersection between race, gender, and class. For instance, how might a judge respond to a person of colour who raised issues of race in an application for security for costs? How might one approach such a study, and how would one attribute outcomes specifically to racism?

Only recently has there been any attempt to identify and document the effects of bias and discrimination in the institutional structures of Canadian society and in the justice system in particular.[3] Moreover, it is only in fairly recent times that theorizing about the meaning of discrimination as defined by the legal system has taken a different perspective. In the mid-1980s, human rights tribunals began to attach a more progressive meaning to the term, emphasizing its effects on victims rather than on the intent of the perpetrator, which, especially when it is seemingly motivated by attitudes or states of mind, is difficult to prove in a court. Some courts were, however, still clinging to the more traditional intent-based theory of discrimination.

Racial Minorities and the Justice System[4]

Several commissions have outlined the problems of Aboriginal people with the justice system and show that racism appears to be widespread in the administration of justice in regard to them (see Chapter 4). Racism in the system also applies to racial minorities. The issue has been examined from the perspective of the minority perceptions of the justice system. If the perceptions even moderately reflect the extent of the problem, it can be concluded that racism is a major problem in the system.[5]

In acknowledging the existence of racism in the justice system, the minister of state for multiculturalism and citizenship noted:

> Can we really be surprised that prosecutors and judges and Crown attorneys should discount eyewitness testimony and disbelieve evidence given under oath? Or that law enforcement officers should approach Native Canadians from the point of view of skepticism and conclude their investigation at the first convenient moment, whether or not all the ends are tied up neatly? ... But injustice before the court does exist and, perhaps no less important, confidence in the justice system to eliminate that injustice does not. (Wiener, 1990)

With respect to racial minorities in Ontario, Lewis described the relationship between the justice system and minorities as "two solitudes in life" (1992:3), and went on to recommend a comprehensive review of Ontario's criminal justice process with a broad mandate that included the judiciary. In Nova Scotia, it was noted that

> by some unspoken societal consensus, a generalized negativity towards Blackness persistently links Black skin to criminality. All too frequently Black skin colour becomes the initiating catalytic factor which jettisons Black people into the criminal justice system. It is also Black pigmentation that colours and preconditions and

plots the quality of our trajectory through a system seemingly inimical to our interests. (Thornhill, 1988:68)

The problem of racism in the justice system was also acknowledged by the Law Reform Commission of Canada (1992), when it noted that "racism in the justice system is a consistently expressed and central concern to Canada's minorities." It is exemplified in the lack of jobs and positions of power and influence in the justice institutions. It is also evident in the lack of access to police protection and legal aid, police harassment, and differential treatment in sentencing. The Commission went on to acknowledge that "the racism of which these groups speak mirrors attitudes and behaviour found in Canadian society as a whole" (Law Reform Commission of Canada, 1992:10).

Perhaps the most extensive research conducted on racism in the criminal dimension of the justice system was included in the *Report of the Commission on Systemic Racism in the Ontario Criminal Justice System* (1995). The Commission found that many people both within and outside of the criminal dimension of the justice system believe that differential treatment takes place. One-third of the White population, for example, believe that judges do not treat Blacks the same as Whites. Although the majority of judges and lawyers do not accept that differential treatment of Blacks takes place, at least one-third of the judges did believe so, as did nearly 40 percent of defence counsel. With respect to prison admissions, both Black men and Black women were overrepresented. White accused was more likely to be released by the police and less likely to be detained after a bail hearing. Blacks constituted not quite 3 percent of the population of Ontario, yet they accounted for 15 percent of the prison population. During the six-year period from 1986 to 1992, the Black imprisoned population increased by 204 percent! With regard to drug offences, the Commission found that White accused were twice as likely as Black accused to be released by the police. Moreover, Black accused were three times more likely to be refused bail. It also found strong differences with regard to sentencing. Generally speaking, Whites found guilty were less likely to be sentenced to prison, and Whites were sentenced more lightly than Blacks even when they had a criminal record and a more serious record of past criminal activity. Far more Blacks were sent to prison for drug offences than Whites. The Commission also found that racist behaviour, both systemic and individual, was directed primarily against Black prisoners and was rampant in the prisons.

The differential treatment of Aboriginal peoples and people of colour in Canada's criminal justice system has, therefore, been documented. It is evident in the perceptions of victims of discrimination in the justice system. The findings of the studies also indicate that minorities are treated differently at every stage of the process of dispensing justice or lack thereof in criminal law. Differential treatment is meted out by the police, in the courts, and in the correctional system. Growing evidence confirms that differential assessments of Aboriginal peoples and racial minorities, leading to differential decisions, start at the point of entry into the system and continue to the point of exit (Razack, 1998; St. Lewis, 1996).

It would be wrong to believe that racism and its manifestations are confined to criminal law. In civil litigation the issue is perhaps more widespread even though it has not been the subject of systematic study. Economic issues are also critical. For instance, there is presently no accepted legal framework that would assist a court in awarding punitive damages in an employment law case where racism is a factor similar to the hate-crimes provisions of the Criminal Code. In a personal injury case, would a court be receptive to an increase in an award where the injury was motivated by racism, such as, for example, in a swarming? At present, the attitude appears to be not to entertain submissions on race in cases other than in criminal law. Such a reserved approach helps to perpetuate and fails even to acknowledge issues specific to the civil litigation and administrative forum.

The Manifestations of Racism

It has been argued that the law that is the foundation of the practices and policies exercised by the courts is itself racist because the principles germane to its interpretation were developed during an era in which people of colour and other disadvantaged groups were barred from participating in society and the justice system. It is only in recent years that the central concept of discrimination has been redefined to include its effects as well as its intent.

Many people understand law as being neutral. The fallacy of this approach becomes obvious when it is understood that laws maintained slavery and made it illegal for Blacks to learn to read and write and participate in public life. Laws were also used to restrict the entry of racial minorities into Canada, to intern Japanese Canadians, and to rob Aboriginal peoples of their land, history, and culture. Constance Backhouse noted many examples of judicial support for racial segregation (1999:40). Every statute has its neutral-construct proponents and its opponents. The text of each statute simply represents codified political outcomes. Both the common law and codified law are inherently political. Law cannot, therefore, be understood as a neutral construct.

The lack of neutrality of the law was recognized by critical race theorists who began to apply critical concepts to the legal system. Critical race theory is both an offshoot of, and a distinct entity from, the earlier movement called *critical legal studies*. It first emerged in the United States as a counter-legal discourse to the positivist liberal legal discourse of civil rights. Legal scholars of colour led the movement, which is based on a critique of liberalism and argues that legal theory fails to address racism deeply embedded in the fabric of American culture. Critical race theory provided another, less traditional theoretical framework and offered an ideology focused on altering the bond between law and racial power, which later was applied to many other fields such as education, human services, and media (Billings, 1998).

The precursors to today's critical race theories were various Marxist-oriented critiques of the justice system. Reiman (1984), for example, argued that the justice system should be viewed as a functional institution that maintains the status quo in the interests of the dominant class. He argued that it is properly functioning for the dominant elite in society by maintaining their interests under the guise of legitimately controlling for law and order. Reiman asserted that the goal of the system is not to reduce crime or achieve justice, but to project to the public a visible image of the threat of crime, such as that of the activities of poor, Black youth. He suggested that society derives benefit from the existence of crime, and thus there is reason to believe that social institutions work to maintain rather than to eliminate crime.

Another theoretician, Staples (1975), used a colonial model to analyze race and the law. This type of historical analysis identified the origins of racism that permeate modern racial and economic stratification. Staples argued that Blacks are not protected by the law because they have no power to enforce the law. The power to define what constitutes a crime is in the hands of the dominant members of society, and this power is a mechanism of racial subordination. The colonial model assesses the Black community as an underdeveloped colony whose economics and politics are controlled by leaders of the racially dominant group. Staples contended that crime by Blacks and the treatment of Blacks by the legal system is a result of the neocolonialist structure of society. The central theme of

MANIFESTATIONS OF RACISM IN THE JUSTICE SYSTEM

Racially biased attitudes and practices of
judges, jurors, lawyers, and other court
officials
Biased jury-selection procedures
Sentencing disparities

Lack of representation
Perceived neutrality of law
Perceptions of guilt of minority accused
Discretion by Crown attorneys

the arguments put forth by these theorists was the importance of ideological control for the maintenance of inequality in society.

Thus, with few exceptions, law has at the very least ignored or omitted racism in its deliberations. However, it is not entirely innocent of the charge of active racism. Kobayashi (1990:449) argues that the culpability of the law can be examined in many ways: "the law has been used through direct action, interpretation, silence and complicity. The law has been wielded as an instrument to create a common sense justification of racial differences, to reinforce common sense notions already deeply embedded within a cultural system of values."

Later work in critical legal theory posited the need to establish a connection between law and culture, "situating legal theory within social, political, and economic conditions, and interpreting juridical procedures according to dominant ideologies" (Kobayashi, 1990:449). Such contexts were not evident in traditional legal discourse because law, like other disciplines, did not "address the meaning of law outside [its] own terms." The study of law in abstraction from the social relations and the social system that it purports to regulate will always be idealistic, artificial, and inherently biased. The legal system produces and reproduces the essential character of law as a means of rationalizing, normalizing, and legitimizing social control on behalf of those who hold power and the interests they represent (Razack, 1998; Williams, 1991).

The law that governs the Western world was largely developed in an era of enlightened liberalism. Liberalism emphasized the capacity of every individual to claim rights, which were to be exercised without interference from the state, providing that the exercise of those rights did not impair the rights of another. Canada's justice system falls within the traditional belief that justice is blind and that all people are equal before the law. It does not recognize collective or group rights based on race, gender, or class because of its focus on individuals.

To argue that an individual is disadvantaged because he or she is a member of a specific *group* goes against the liberal tradition. The concept of an "independent, decontextualized" individual, isolated from his or her various communities, leads to a view that dismisses the possibility that group membership alters and limits individual choices, opportunities, and rights (Razack, 1998:26). This becomes vitally important with respect to the law that governs the justice system, because of the stereotypical and racist beliefs held by many of its members. To present an individual as part of a community and to describe that community as disadvantaged, marginalized, and subject to racial discrimination is to pose a fundamental challenge to legal discourse.

The traditional liberal argument is that the law is objective. Those who support this view fear that a more relativistic approach that identifies such characteristics as race and sex will shift the focus from justice to social activism. According to a former British Columbia assistant deputy attorney general, "It allows groups to bring to the floor their own sense of injustice whether it has anything to do with the crime or not. ... The danger is that the law will become meaningless, and the subjective approach extended not just to minority groups but to any individual" (McDiarmid in Cunningham, 1997). Furthermore, it is difficult to prove empirically the claims of an individual that are based on his or her group membership, and courts almost always require this proof in making a determination. The personal experiences of individuals who are subjected to racism are often given little weight by court officials, who generally demand empirical proof of the allegation.

Initial Contact: The Police

For most individuals, the police are the first point of contact with the justice system.[6] This first contact often influences a case's future developments and the decisions with respect to it.

Racial minorities often complain of overpolicing. Squad cars often cruise through communities that are densely populated by racial minorities. Despite this oversurveillance, racial-minority persons complain that they do not receive equal protection under the law. For example, a frequent complaint is that the response time of police is greater in racial-minority communities than it is for the general population (Jamaican Canadian Association, 1990).

At the Jamaican Canadian Association's 1990 Toronto conference, the concerns of Black youth were specifically examined. The youth stated unequivocally that they felt alienated from the systems that administer justice in Ontario. Conference participants stated that they bore the brunt of police arbitrary stops, searches, charges of resisting arrest, and use of force. Black youth talked extensively about the negative stereotyping of members of their community. For example, they said that when a group of them congregated in a public place, they were more likely to gain the attention of police officers than were a group of White youths. They explained that this occurs because of a prevailing stereotype that Black youths are believed to be criminals. When Black youths get together, police are thought to assume that they are plotting a crime.

As a result, the relationship between police and racial-minority communities is extremely tense, especially in urban areas. In Toronto and Montreal, several highly publicized shootings of Black youth have added to the tension.

Representation

The lack of representation of racial minorities in the justice system contributes to the perpetuation of racial stereotypes in the system. It leads racial minorities accused of committing a crime to perceive that justice will not be done as the system itself does not understand them.

In recent years, the number of racial-minority and Aboriginal students in law schools has somewhat increased. As a result, there are now more minority lawyers in practice, especially in Ontario. The number of racial-minority judges in all provinces, however, is still small. In fact, their relative absence in higher courts such as provincial appeal courts and especially the Supreme Court of Canada has recently been worsened (Hamalengwa, 2004).

Attitudes and Perceptions of Judges and Lawyers

Many of the respondents interviewed in a study conducted as part of the Marshall inquiry (Head, 1991) voiced significant fears about racial discrimination in the courts. Several respondents felt that judges pose the problem, and there was criticism that Blacks are usually tried by White judges and White juries. A White legal aid lawyer expressed his concerns:

There is an unmistakable change in the atmosphere when I enter the courtroom with a Black client. The hostility of court personnel, including judges and others, is unmistakable and is recognized by all including the alleged lawbreaker. It is impossible, under these conditions, for a Black client to receive equal justice. (Head, 1991)

The study, based on a sample of more than five hundred individuals, also found that Blacks showed a high level of distrust and hostility toward the criminal justice system. They expressed the view that Blacks were treated more harshly than Whites in "some instances."

In a project undertaken in Toronto, racial minorities' perceptions of the justice system were studied (Equal Opportunity Consultants, 1989). This study found that racial minorities criticized the criminal justice system for being unrepresentative of the increasingly diverse population of Ontario. It was repeatedly stressed that the overwhelming majority of judges, Crown attorneys, and other legal professionals were White, male, and mainstream Canadians.

Judges were especially criticized for stereotypical attitudes, behaviours, and views of racial minorities. In particular, members of the Black community consistently said that most judges believe that Black people are more prone to criminal behaviour, because they see so many of them in their courtrooms.

Minority lawyers interviewed as part of the same project said that some judges make racist comments from the bench. In one case, a lawyer requested a conditional discharge for a youth whose case had all the elements for a compassionate hearing. The presiding judge said: "I am not accepting that. People like him need to be sent to prison." In another case, a judge, while sentencing a tall, heavily built Black man convicted of trafficking a small amount of cocaine, stated: "I am afraid of you. I'm going to give you a year in prison."

In addition, minority respondents felt that some judges do not believe that racial-minority accused are "innocent until proven guilty." Some racial minorities believe that they must prove their innocence to the court, not the reverse. Moreover, in instances in which defence counsel recommend bail at a preliminary hearing, the judge often refuses to grant it for racial-minority offenders. A standard rationalization for the refusal to grant bail is that most racial minorities "can't raise the money." This raises some questions about what is "reasonable bail." For example, a minority lawyer argued that although the bail may be granted, it appears to be disproportionately high for members of racial-minority groups (Westmoreland-Traoré, 1982:23).

In Manitoba, a series of complaints against a particularly contentious member of the judiciary has taken place over a period of twenty years. The judge made disparaging remarks about women and Aboriginal peoples. In one instance, he said that it would be a "joyful result if residents of the Long Plains Indian Reserve killed each other off." Although the judge was suspended when the transcript of these remarks was made public, a formal judicial hearing into his conduct has not taken place because such a hearing would stir up "too much publicity; plus it would make the entire profession and system look bad." This excuse was offered by a former chief provincial judge of the province to the Manitoba Judicial Council (*Globe and Mail*, 1993).

Judicial misconduct has been noted in a number of cases brought to the attention of the National Judicial Council. In one incident, a federal judge was accused of making inappropriate comments about Aboriginal society by describing it as being in an "adolescent" state of development when compared with "non-Indian adult societies." The judicial council merely asked that the judge refrain from allowing his personal opinions to influence his judgments. No further sanctions were imposed (Hutchinson, 1998).

The embarrassment caused by these and other offensive comments by judges has led to the creation of a set of guidelines that provides standards for behaviour of federally appointed judges. The guidelines state that judges should keep their political opinions to themselves, stop making sexist and offensive remarks to women, and not make racist comments to visible minorities. The *Toronto Star* obtained a copy of this confidential document and noted that its adoption by the National Judicial Council was uncertain: "A vocal minority of judges are opposed to behavioural guidelines, arguing they would interfere with 'judicial independence'" (1997:A1).

Justices of the peace have also been criticized for their role in perpetuating racism in the justice system. Respondents in the Toronto study described the racist attitudes of many justices of the peace appointed by the system. The issues of bail and assessing the financial credibility of sponsors were specifically cited. Other examples included the laying of charges. In one case, a justice of the peace refused to lay charges that had been brought by racial-minority persons. In one such case a young, Black, male lawyer was assaulted by a police officer in a legal clinic. He went to a justice of the peace to lay a charge against the police officer without revealing that he was a lawyer. The justice of the peace refused to lay the charge and asked: "Were any of your bones broken?" Eventually, the lawyer was assured that the officer would be charged. He returned to the justice of the peace some days later and found, to his surprise, that the charge had not been laid. When the young man revealed that he was a lawyer by showing his law society membership card, the charge was laid instantly.

Racist attitudes are said to be found among other court personnel such as Crown and defence counsel as well as duty counsel. A frequent complaint is that both the Crown and the defence counsel often have not adequately prepared their cases involving racial minorities. Sometimes, inexperienced Crown counsels are assigned to prosecute high-profile cases involving minorities. Moreover, many Crown and defence counsel are thought to harbour racially biased attitudes. These attitudes are expressed in many ways, including counsel's submissions to the court. A frequent complaint is that counsel often advise racial minorities to plead guilty either because "no one will believe your story" or to expedite a case. Many racial minorities are not aware that a guilty plea guarantees a conviction. They therefore agree with their defence counsel's advice and find themselves with a criminal record for a crime they did not commit.

The consistent omission of information about the racial overtones of a case applies also to Crown attorneys, who have a considerable amount of discretion.[7] Although Crown attorneys do not initiate prosecutions, they play a crucial role in advising the police with respect to whether a *prima facie* case can be made from the accumulated evidence and whether prosecution is justified. They also have the power to withhold evidence until the trial and, as well, to proceed summarily or by indictment. Abusing their power by not recognizing or accepting the racial overtones of a case often leads to situations in which victims of racially motivated crimes find themselves the accused party in the criminal justice system (Westmoreland-Traoré, 1982:18).

Although much criticism is directed toward Crown attorneys and judges, one area in which defence counsel have been sharply criticized is their refusal to believe in the existence of racially motivated attacks. As in any criminal case, defence counsel face the challenge of advising their clients to the best of their ability. However, this task is made more difficult by the nature of the defence and the prevalent skepticism about the existence of racially motivated attacks. In these cases, victims are often dissuaded by their own defence counsel from raising questions of racism by being told that to do so would only make matters worse for them. For the same reason, countercharges are very infrequent (Westmoreland-Traoré, 1982:27).

Victims of racially motivated incidents are therefore doubly jeopardized because of the systematic omission or suppression of vital information from the record of the court. Thus, the court is rarely forced to rule on the matter of racial motivation either as part of *mens rea*[8] or as a factor in sentencing. The victim therefore has little opportunity to obtain satisfaction from the court for racially motivated attacks.

Aspects of racism do not take place only in the criminal justice system. In civil litigation there have also been instances where people of colour and especially Blacks were subjected to differential treatment and differential decision-making. Case Study 5.2 reveals one such instance, in which a Black nurse was summarily dismissed from her employment despite the very ambiguous evidence against her.

As is demonstrated in many cases, the justice system interrelates with many other institutional sectors of society. In fact, as discussed in other sections of this book, there is to a significant degree a web of interrelationships and interactions among all the institutions of society, particularly in the context of racism, sexism, and classism, as well as other forms of oppression. In Case Study 5.3, the interweaving of law enforcement, the media, the education system, and the administration of justice are brought to bear on a situation that began with an alleged strip search of Black school girls and ended with a trial for libel.

Jury Selection Processes

Jury bias has been identified as a major contributor to the perpetuation of racism in the justice system (Pomerant, 1992; Petersen, 1993). Jury selection is critical to the process of providing justice, in both civil and criminal cases; in the Toronto study, many Black respondents singled out this issue as extremely important. Having a Black accused tried by a White jury did not, according to the perceptions of racial-minority people, fulfil the criterion of "trial by a jury of peers." The issue of the extent to which a jury is representative of the community raises questions about the appropriateness of the current practice of using voters' lists to select juries. Many minorities are not eligible to vote, so they are underrepresented on voters' lists.

The use of voters' lists to compose a pool has also been called into question because the lists quickly become inaccurate. They fail to include persons who move into or exclude those who move out of the community after each election. They are also not updated until a new election is called. Jurors are required to be Canadian citizens, a qualification that effectively eliminates members of immigrant communities who have not been in the country long enough to qualify for citizenship. It also disqualifies people who came to this country as children and whose parents neglected to make them citizens as well as those who, for whatever reason, have failed to apply for citizenship.

Pomerant (1992) and others have argued that for equality in jury trials to have meaning, jury selection should provide reasonable and equal opportunities and means for the parties to challenge the selection pool. It is also necessary to challenge the selection of jury panels and exclude from service unqualified, incompetent, or morally biased prospective jurors. In addition, it is argued that minority jurors should have the same opportunities as anyone else to be chosen for service. Their minority status should not prevent them from being chosen.

The use of the peremptory challenge by either the Crown or the defence counsel can further limit the diversity of a jury. In one case, a jury was being selected for the trial of a police officer accused of shooting a Black person. A Black woman, after answering questions with respect to her impartiality, was declared impartial and accepted by the prosecutor. The defence counsel for the police officer promptly rejected her as a juror. The final

THE SUPREME COURT JUDGE

Judge Corrine Sparks is the first Black woman to be appointed to the Bench in Nova Scotia. In December 1994, she presided over a case in which a Black youth, R.D.S., was charged with assaulting a White police officer during the arrest of his cousin. When R.D.S. arrived on the scene, he asked if he should call his cousin's mother. The arresting officer replied, "Shut up or you'll be under arrest too," at which point R.D.S. was placed in a choke hold and charged with striking the officer with his bike.

Judge Sparks found that a reasonable doubt existed and acquitted R.D.S. of all charges. After handing down the acquittal and while responding to the Crown's question as to why the police officer should lie, she made some comments about the relationship of Black youth and the police. She noted that strained relations exist between the police and the Black community and that police can sometimes overreact when dealing with Black youth. Claiming judicial bias, the Crown appealed her decision to the Nova Scotia Supreme Court, which held that these remarks could lead people to believe that the judge was biased. It reversed her acquittal decision. Its judgment noted that Judge Sparks' decision "flowed from a racially based bias against the police" (*Toronto Star*, September 27, 1997). The Nova Scotia Court of Appeal upheld the reversal. Thus, Judge Sparks was not only accused of judicial bias but had her decision reversed by two provincial courts. A defence team then appealed these decisions to the Supreme Court of Canada.

Up to this point, the case had created considerable reaction in the Black community as well as among segments of the legal establishment. It was also widely reported in the media. Judge Sparks' remarks, made after a decision was rendered, were not sufficient to claim judicial bias and were, in any case, true. Observers wondered, if a White judge had made these comments, would his or her decision have been appealed on grounds of bias? Accusing her of bias in a case involving a Black youth raised some doubt about the standard of judicial neutrality required of judges as well as their ability to refer to the common knowledge of racism. Moreover, there was a perception that this Black judge's behaviour was examined more than is usually necessary.

The case engendered further controversy when it reached the Supreme Court of Canada. Chief Justice Antonio Lamer made the following comments during the hearing on March 10, 1997 (these comments were taken from the video proceedings of the event):

> For many years when I was practising as a lawyer in Montreal, I had clients who were Chinese. Chinese were very much into gambling, they are tremendous gamblers. … If a Chinese is accused of illegal gambling, the casino in Terre des Hommes is constantly occupied by the Chinese community. Can I take that into account? Can I factor in that he is a Chinese and he says he wasn't gambling and the police who is non-Chinese—a non-Chinese police officer might have a bias against Chinese people? On the other hand, Chinese people have a propensity for gambling. I'm just concerned how far down the slope we are going to go if we do this.
>
> We will not classify people in a blanket way—all young Blacks are suspect of stealing cars. Why? Because they don't have money because they don't have jobs … no jobs because they are Black and being discriminated against. Conclude, its more likely that a young non-White, Black, or Afro Canadian or Afro-American is going to steal a car if the police officer says he caught him stealing a car. It works both ways.
>
> What if I take judicial notice of the fact that 95 percent—and I'm saying this and I

have no fact—I wouldn't want to offend that community—that 95 percent of Gypsies are pickpockets. And I'm dealing with a pickpocketer and assessing the police officer's credibility. I'm just pretending—and it's a hypothetical.

Every police officer … is not the same colour as [the] person being arrested. There is racism. To some people, I'm a hunky. To others I am a frog. We are all subjects to the intolerance of others but now talking of the credibility of a witness … am I to take into account that there are social tensions right now and factor them in every case because what applies here will be applicable in other areas? I'm wondering how far we're going.

The Supreme Court of Canada, in a 6–3 judgment, upheld the original acquittal granted by Judge Sparks. Dissenting judges, including the chief justice, said there should be a new trial for R.D.S. because the trial judge, Sparks, had stereotyped police as racists and liars.

The decision of the Supreme Court was hailed by many community and legal groups. Others, including a lead editorial in the *Ottawa Citizen*, were outraged, claiming that

the decision was disastrous. The defendant hadn't introduced any evidence of racism, or even alleged it, so Judge Sparks had effectively introduced evidence herself—to put it charitably, since the "evidence" was only her personal opinion—which the Crown wasn't given a chance to rebut. It flew in the face of our adversarial system of justice. … The justice system now allows judges to violate basic principles and introduce gross stereotypes only if those stereotypes sit well with the political left. (*Ottawa Citizen*, 1998)

Several themes emerge from this important case. In the first instance, there is the assumption made by many members of the legal system that this particular judge should not have used her personal knowledge and experience of racism. There is also concern about the oversurveillance

of a Black judge, particularly in a province in which people of colour are poorly represented in the legal establishment. These and many aspects of racism were then compounded by the inappropriate use of racial and ethnic stereotypes by the chief justice of the Supreme Court.

If the trial judge should not have used her personal experience of racism against Blacks in Nova Scotia, should the chief justice of the land have made such blatantly stereotypical comments about Chinese and Gypsies? Should he have trivialized the issues of racism by verbally playing with the relationship of colour to car theft? Should he have commented about his own experience in being called a "hunky" or a "frog" and compared that with racism against people of colour?

There are probably many people, especially in Quebec, who would agree that the ethnic factor should be taken into account in the example cited by the chief justice when an English Canadian police officer arrests a French Canadian.

After the publication of some of his remarks, the Chinese Canadian National Council lodged a complaint to the National Judicial Council against Chief Justice Lamer that said that he "racially stereotyped Chinese as 'tremendous gamblers.'" In his defence, Lamer said that he was using these examples as "hypothetical examples of stereotypes, not factual assertions, and that I did not mean any offence by them" (*Toronto Star*, November 5, 1997). Furthermore, he noted that "I find it outrageous to be accused of stereotyping when I was actually giving examples of how wrong stereotyping would be." Chief Justice Lamer included an apology to the Chinese Canadian community in his letter to them and maintained that he had not intended to offend any group.

This case brings the powerful and important role of judges into sharp relief. It also questions their alleged impartiality, particularly in cases involving racism, sexism, homophobia, and other arenas of behaviour that have only recently been brought to public attention.

CASE STUDY 5.2

RACIAL BIAS IN ADMINISTRATIVE TRIBUNALS

Background

On December 26, 2001 a panel—Marsha Taylor, Gabrielle Bridle, Kim Pittaway, Jayne Sanger, and Kay Whitherall of the Disciplinary Committee of the College of Nurses ("the Tribunal")—found Ms. Calpruner Reid, a Black, female practical nurse of 22 years with an unblemished health care record, guilty of misconduct allegedly for speaking harshly to and striking a patient of West Park Hospital, Ms. Proszycka. Ms. Reid left West Park Hospital where she had received accolades for the quality of her nursing care to pursue studies in Florida. She returned to work at West Park Hospital in or about Spring 1999.

On September 7, 1999, West Park Hospital admitted Ms. Irena Proszycka, a 70-year-old Polish woman whose English-language skills were restricted to communications through an interpreter, to a unit specializing in rehabilitating stroke victims. Ms. Proszycka suffered from a cardiovascular attack and left-side paralysis from a stroke, and was severely disabled.

Between September 7, 1999 and September 10, 1999, Ms. Proszycka occupied a hospital room with two other stroke victims, Anne Wolfe and Grace Way. On September 20, 1999, Ms. Proszycka alleged that Ms. Reid had physically abused and spoke harshly to her a few days earlier. West Park Hospital, as a result of the allegations, terminated Ms. Reid's employment, before substantiating the allegations. Ms. Reid's union represented her, but the matter was not taken to arbitration. Instead, Ms. Reid received a severance package.

Ms. Proszycka alleged that, despite her medical conditions, she got up from her hospital bed, positioned herself in a wheelchair, transported herself to Ms. Wolfe's bed, and started to comfort Ms. Wolfe, a stroke victim suffering from aphasia, because Ms. Wolfe's foot was sore. Ms. Proszycka claimed that while standing, holding onto the rail, Ms. Reid, without any provocation, conversation or other utterances, hit her in her left shoulder, turned around, and left the room.

Despite serious inconsistencies in the account of the alleged event given by Ms. Proszycka and Ms. Wolfe, the College of Nurses proceeded with a disciplinary hearing against Ms. Reid, and no representation was available through the union.

At the commencement of the hearing it was clear that Ms. Reid was having difficulties understanding the process, as she was unrepresented. The Tribunal discharged its own lawyer and the only lawyer present represented the College. At various points in the hearing Ms. Proszycka's mental incapacity became evident. Moreover, the tribunal permitted Ms. Wolfe to give inadmissible opinion evidence, and the Tribunal posed questions that were admitted by counsel for the College of Nurses to be inadmissible.

At the hearing, Ms. Reid maintained her innocence, as was her right. The case came down to credibility. The Tribunal disbelieved the Appellant's evidence that she did not strike the patient and as a result the five-White-woman Tribunal found Ms. Reid guilty of misconduct.

Ms. Reid hired counsel to represent her at the sentencing portion of the hearing. Counsel for Ms. Reid submitted that there were cultural issues and a cultural context into which the case falls that therefore must be interpreted. Defence counsel questioned the definition of "harsh" tone when dealing in a cross-cultural and multiracial society. In imposing the sentence, the Tribunal rejected that cultural issues were at work in the facts of the case. The Tribunal stated that there was no evidence of cultural issues before it, and implicitly held that Ms. Reid maintenance of her innocence equated with an absence of remorse that would justify a reduction in penalty. The Tribunal suspended Ms. Reid's licence for a period of three months, imposed conditions on her licence, and required that she attend for a reprimand. Ms. Reid's appeal to the Divisional Court was dismissed.

According to the Divisional Court the appropriate standard of review was not the correctness of the Tribunal's decision, but its reasonableness. Ms. Reid's application for leave to appeal to the court of appeal was dismissed with cost. Ms. Reid refused to attend the College for a Reprimand, as she continues to maintain her innocence.

Analysis

The subtle ways in which racism was expressed in a case before administrative tribunals is highlighted by this case. For instance, labelling Ms. Reid aggressive and having a threatening tone of voice plays on an age-old stereotype that was employed in this case—this despite the Supreme Court of Canada's clear direction in the Seaboyer case against stereotypical decision-making. For the Tribunal to consider Ms. Reid's maintenance of her innocence, as was her right, when assessing credibility demonstrates that Ms. Reid was guilty in the panel's eyes before any evidence was presented. Furthermore, the Tribunal stated that there was no evidence of cultural issues despite the role that language presented in this case suggested ignorance of the importance of culture. It also ignored the possibility that the patient could not have formed such a close bond with fellow patient Ms. Wolfe, who came from a non-Polish background.

What is clear from the Tribunal's decision is that it lacks the competence to assess cultural and racial issues. More fundamentally, for the Tribunal, wholly reliant on an interpreter to facilitate communication, to decide that there were no cultural issues before it was either an exercise in intellectually dishonest decision-making, or incompetence based on Tribunal ignorance of how these issues affected Black nurses.

The Tribunal found that Ms. Proszycka's failure to report her complaint in a timely manner did not mean the incident did not occur. It adopted a harsher standard when assessing Ms. Reid's failure to document Ms. Proszycka's alleged aggressive behaviour. Were the Tribunal competent to adjudicate issues of race, would it have understood why a Black nurse faced with everyday racism might choose not to insert a comment such as "immigrant" on a patient's chart?

A Tribunal must be taken to know that its decision must be seen to be fair. It is clear that the Tribunal did not think it required its own counsel's advice, because only the College counsel was present. Even though it knew that Ms. Reid was having difficulties understanding the process, it decided to discharge its own counsel from further attendance after the first day of hearing . The impact of that decision is that the College obtained an unfair advantage in the sense that the Tribunal members, not being lawyers, would tend to look to the College counsel, whomever that might be, as the legal expert. It should be noted that the Tribunal had its own counsel present at the sentencing portion of the hearing to advise it on the submissions of counsel for Ms. Reid.

To say that Ms. Proszycka's account of events was believable and reasonable is to engage in a kind of anti-commonsense decision-making that justifies a desired result. To come to the conclusion that Ms. Proszycka and Ms. Wolfe had nothing to gain from bringing the complaint is to ignore the dynamics of racism in the provision of health care services. First, no evidence was called on whether the patients had anything to gain or lose, it was just assumed by the Tribunal. Yet the Tribunal was not prepared to acknowledge the cultural or racial underpinnings to the case. It was quite possible that the patients simply did not want care from a Black nurse and wanted her gone, permanently.

What this case shows is how bizarre decisions can become when dealing with Black people as litigants. The institutional mindset is such that it could not even at the sentencing stage contemplate racism as a factor in the case, let alone in its own decision-making, unless the evidence for it was blatant. Moreover, the manner in which the Tribunal constructed the litigants, "the Black accused versus the frail elderly," helped it interpret facts and sustain racism by the inferences drawn from facts presented in evidence. The Tribunal simply wrote racism out of the picture. It then rationalized racism's nonexistence by using language and referring to factors that seemed objective; that is, it objectified the decision. One wonders whether the College of Nurses would have proceeded with this case had the nurse been a White woman.

CASE STUDY 5.3

DEFAMATION IN HALIFAX: THE POLICE ACTION AGAINST LAWYERS ROCKY JONES AND ANN DERRICK

Background

This case is about a libel or defamation action brought by a police officer against two lawyers in Halifax, which presents a very challenging example of how the processes of racialization operate across systems and sectors.

In March 1995, police constable Carol Campbell was called to an elementary school in the north end of Halifax located in a working-class neighbourhood in which many of the residents were Black. The school's vice-principal informed her that three hundred dollars had been stolen from a librarian. As well, a ten-dollar bill had also been stolen by one of three 12-year-old Black girls.

One group of White students identified as possibly being involved in the larger theft were taken to a classroom. The Black girls were sent to the guidance office.

After informing the officer of the situation, the vice-principal left the guidance office. The officer had been told that one of the girls had hidden the bill in her panties. At the trial the officer stated that she asked the three students to pull open the front of their pants and pull their panties away from their bodies. She also asked them to remove their sneakers and socks. The girls maintained that they had been totally strip-searched without the presence of their parents or guardians—who were not initially called to the school until after the alleged incident took place. The school later admitted that it had mishandled the situation and should have requested the presence and/or permission of the minor girls' parents. Moreover, Constable Campbell was reprimanded in an internal police review of the matter for failing to remind the girls of their right to a lawyer. The officer issued a formal apology for this failure in May 1997. Local media reported the incident several times.

The parents of the three girls were extremely angry at this situation. Two of them retained Burnley ("Rocky") Jones and the third Anne S. Derrick to represent them in their planned complaint to the police department. The two lawyers filed letters of complaint with the Halifax Police Chief and announced a press conference on the matter. About one month after the incident, Rocky Jones, who is Black, and Anne Derrick, who is White, held the press conference. They sent letters to the press and made public statements stating that the police officer had strip-searched the girls. In a television interview they also stated that the strip search would not have happened to White girls in an affluent (White) neighbourhood.

The police officer launched a libel suit and alleged that the lawyers had portrayed her as a racist who discriminated against the Black and poor girls. She also charged damage to her reputation. (The police officer also filed a defamation suit against various media who had, she alleged, damaged her reputation by articles that appeared to accept that a strip search had taken place.) During the trial, both Jones and Derrick maintained that their comments were not directed against any one individual police officer but toward the issue of systemic racism within the criminal justice system.

The subtle issue of racism was underplayed at the trial. The main issue for the defence was that of freedom of expression and the fact that the lawyers had a right to "qualified privilege" or communicating information to the public in the interests of social justice. The main charge of the complainant, the police officer, was defamation of character. Nevertheless, defence counsel deemed it necessary to provide the court with evidence about racism and its manifestations in Canadian society in general and in policing in particular. Accordingly, one of the authors of this book (Dr. Frances Henry) was retained as an expert witness who wrote a lengthy report demonstrating that racism against not only poor but also Black people was one of the reasons motivating the behaviour of the police officer. The only part of her report allowed into evidence by the trial judge was the first four pages in which definitions and manifestations of racism in a general sense were established, rather than her analysis of how these issues impacted upon this case. During her testimony, she was allowed to address only the general subject without applying them to the case. The trial ended with the libel charges laid by Constable Campbell against the lawyers being upheld, and the respondents were charged to pay damages of $240 000 to her.

Subsequently, in 2002, Jones and Derrick appealed the decision to the Nova Scotia Court of Appeal and won their case. The appeal decision again was not centred on racist issues as such, but noted that circumstances can create an occasion for "qualified privilege." It argued that public statements made in a press conference can be allowed because the circumstances in which they occurred must be taken into consideration (i.e., that racism may have played a role in the events). In attempting to appeal the appeal, the police officer submitted the case to the Supreme Court of Canada. In May 2003, the Supreme Court dismissed the application.

Analysis

This case involves the interaction across four institutional spaces: policing, justice, education, and the media. Its main focus was the action of the police officer in laying a charge of defamation against the lawyers. Such a charge signals the defensiveness of the police to allegations of racism. In this incident, the police saw an unusual opportunity to clear themselves of charges of racism against people of colour that frequently take place in a city such as Halifax, which has a substantial Black population. In laying the charge, the police turned officially to the justice system to render a decision. The matter involved a full jury trial and, in addition to a senior Crown attorney, high-profile, prestigious lawyers represented the two lawyers. The full panoply of the justice system was therefore brought to bear on this case, which took 22 days at trial.

The role of the media was crucial, because the event that sparked the police defamation charge took place at a *press conference*. During the trial, the local media were in regular attendance and reported often as important evidence

was cited. Generally speaking, the local media provided descriptive and balanced reportage of the trial and its subsequent appeals.

Jones and Derrick appealed the decision, again not involving the racial factor but basing their appeal on the fact that qualified privilege and qualified reporting privilege had been denied them, and on errors made by the trial judge in his instructions to the jury. Included in his summary, the trial judge admitted that

> No right thinking person could deny a duty to speak about a public interest in hearing about police misconduct involving the mistreatment of individuals because of their youth, poverty or Black heritage. Particularly in the latter in this province where, as everyone knows, the long history of African Nova Scotians involves the suffering of racism, overt and unconscious. ..." (Cited in Nova Scotia Court of Appeal, *Campbell v. Jones*, 2002, NSCA 128, Oct. 24, 2002)

He went on to say that he agrees with "public exposure" as an "effective tool for combating systemic racism. I base that upon the testimony of the experts in this case and upon common sense ..." (ibid).

Despite these assertions, the trial judge argued that because the police officer's complaint, which arose as a result of the press conference, had not yet been investigated, the lawyers' communication to the public was not warranted and was not protected by the idea of "qualified privilege." This suggests that while he agrees that the suffering of Black Nova Scotians as a result of racism is well known, it is not sufficient, in and of itself, to be reinforced by the lawyers stating that it was a factor in this case. Winning their appeal was not, however, sufficient for the police force that, still believing in the rightness of their case, applied for leave to the Supreme Court, which was denied.

The education system as represented by this school was also involved, because it appeared that its officials had made some serious errors in their handling of the Black girls. As minors, they should not have been subjected to any form of police intervention without the presence of parents or guardians. It is also unclear why the vice-principal did not stay in the room with the girls and Constable Campbell.

In sum, however, and despite only minimal attention to racism influencing this case, from a legal, justice, and anti-racist perspective this case had a satisfactory conclusion.

jury included six men and six women, one of whom was Asian. The racial designation of the jurors became an issue in this case. A pre-trial motion put forward by the Crown argued that the Canadian Charter of Rights and Freedoms, which bans racial discrimination, should apply to jury selection so that lawyers could not reject potential jurors because of their race. The defence argued against the motion, and it was rejected by the judge, who noted that this would open up the selection procedure to too many factors. He noted that a jury should reflect the racial composition of a community but urged lawyers to "be guided by their own conscience" (*Toronto Star*, 1993b).

In this instance, a peremptory challenge was used in the selection process to keep a racial-minority person off the jury because the accused was a police officer. The challenge is most frequently used, however, to determine whether jurors hold prejudices or opinions that would bias their objectivity. Bias or racist attitudes were not usually questioned in the *voir dire*.[9] In the late 1980s, Frances Henry began testifying as an expert witness on racism to help lawyers argue for this process. In the first few cases, judges accepted the challenge in only two cases out of six. Slowly, a few judges accepted the challenge both with and without expert-witness testimony. In 1993, the Ontario Court of Appeal, hearing the appeal of *Regina v. Parks* (appealed because the challenge for cause on racism was not allowed), found that the challenge of racism for the Black accused was legitimate because of the prevalence of racism in the system.

The challenge for cause based upon the landmark *Parks* decision has now been used hundreds of times in criminal trials involving Black accused. Anywhere from 10 to 40 percent of jury panels have been excused as a result. Because the *Parks* decision applied only to Metropolitan Toronto, there was resistance from some judges in areas such as Durham and Peel counties, who claimed that while racism against Blacks might exist in Toronto, it was not present in these bordering communities. These judges clung to the idea that racism stops outside of Toronto's borders. They failed to recognize that residents in these areas read the same Toronto-based media, from which most people derive their information and which helps to formulate and reinforce misconceptions and racial stereotypes.

While testifying as an expert witness in a case involving a Black accused, Henry and the lawyer who had retained her decided to mount a small-scale empirical study to prove to the judge who had stated that he would reject the challenge for cause on racism that racism was also prevalent in the Durham region. Using similar questions developed by an earlier Angus Reid poll on racial attitudes in Toronto, a sample of over two hundred people in Whitby, Ontario, were questioned. The study found, as did the Angus Reid poll, that nearly two-thirds of respondents believed a link existed between an individual's race and a propensity toward criminal activity. Most frequently cited as having this propensity were Jamaicans (and other Blacks), as well as Vietnamese (Henry, Hastings, and Freer, 1996).

The finding that many people link racial status and crime has helped the court in deciding that the challenge for cause on racism is a necessary precaution to ensure a fair trial for Black accused. A number of important decisions have followed *Parks*. In *Regina v. Wilson*, the Ontario Court of Appeal decided that the challenge for cause on racism could be used outside the borders of Metropolitan Toronto.

The *Parks* decision also does not apply to non-Black racial minorities. While, increasingly, Crown prosecutors and judges have accepted its application to Vietnamese, Chinese, and other minority groups, some still demand an evidentiary foundation for its use for non-Black accused. A later decision on this issue established another landmark. The Supreme Court of Canada in *Regina v. Williams* in June 1998 decided that the challenge for cause on racism could be used in all cases, regardless of the ethnic or racial status of the accused, if there is evidence of widespread bias against the group to which the accused belongs. The court held that either evidence of the bias should be presented by the party seeking the challenge or a judge may simply take judicial notice of it.[10] And finally on this same issue, in Quebec, the case of *Regina v. Mankwe* (October 2, 2001) involved a challenge to the jury on the basis of racial bias which was not allowed by the trial judge. This case was sent to the Supreme Court who ordered a new trial.

Tanovich, Paciocco, and Skurka (1997) critically examine the use of the challenge for cause to potential jurors. Analyzing judicial decisions on jury selection emphasizing the use of the challenge for cause procedure, their book argues for the use of the challenge and provides statistics showing that between 11 and 59 percent of jurors were discharged after being challenged in cases involving sexual assault. Although no systematic study of the success rate of the challenge on racism has been published, Henry, who has often appeared as an expert witness in such cases, believes that the success rate is anywhere from 10 to 30 percent.

The issue of jury selection and bias is important because the jury verdict all but binds a trial jury, at least in terms of establishing guilt or innocence. The Rodney King case in the United States showed that an impartial jury is a critical factor in ensuring the community's confidence in the justice system. Ensuring that the jury itself does not detract from a fair trial is an important part of the preservation of democracy.

Racial Profiling

The publication of a series of articles revealing the extent of racial profiling by the Toronto police in the fall of 2003 brought this issue back onto the public agenda. Although the studies conducted by the *Toronto Star* for this series focused on police procedures, there was some inevitable spillover into the justice system. One of the most important cases involving racial profiling was that of Dee Dee Brown (*Regina v. Brown*, April 16, 2003, Appeal Court of Ontario), a Black Toronto Raptors basketball player who was stopped and charged by a White police officer simply for driving a late-model expensive car. He was convicted at trial and the judge refused to consider the defence argument of racial profiling. The judge also made some comments indicating his displeasure at this sort of argument. The appellate judges decided there was sufficient evidence for the judge to have considered the role racial profiling might have played in this case. Accordingly, they decided on a new trial for Brown. As well, Crown Attorney James Stewart was commended for stating that racial profiling by police does take place.

Two other important cases involving racism can be cited to show that the justice system is slowly taking heed of racial profiling. The case *Regina v. Richards* (April 5, 1999, Ontario Court of Appeal) involved a stop by a White police officer of a Black driver and the subsequent altercation between them. The driver was convicted and the Ontario Court of Appeal upheld his appeal from that conviction. Although racial profiling did not become an issue, the appeal court decided that the trial judge made errors in his credibility assessment of the White officer. In effect, he chose to believe the White officer over the Black accused.

Although not about racial profiling as such, another fairly recent case relates to the issue. In *Regina v. Golden* (February 15, 2001), the Supreme Court heard a case from the Ontario Court of Appeal in which the issue was whether a Black man was illegally strip-searched after having been stopped for the alleged possession of crack cocaine. He was convicted and his appeal was denied. The Supreme Court, however, decided that his appeal should be allowed.

Responses to Racism

Lack of Political Will

How has the justice system responded to allegations of inequity and racial bias? One of its agencies, the Law Reform Commission of Canada, noted in a 1992 publication that politicians had, for the past twenty years, refused to deal with racism in the criminal justice system due to a lack of political will. Former Supreme Court Judge Bertha Wilson, after calling attention to the issue of gender bias, went on to head an investigation on this aspect of inequity in the system. It is hoped that the recognition of gender bias signals an equal concern with racial bias. Justice Beverly McLaughlin (now Chief Justice) later spoke out against racism and stereotyping in all the institutions of Canadian society. One form of response, therefore, has been the recognition of the issue by important agencies and high-profile members of the legal profession.

Denial

The above examples have been a few voices in the wilderness, however. There is still a persistent and considerable denial of racism in the courts. Judges and Crown counsel, on the rare occasions when they do address allegations of racism, invariably deny them. "Crown attorneys have no control over intake and arrest, we deal with everyone equally. … I have never noticed that one group is treated differently. I don't care whether someone is Black, White or green," said Stephen Leggett, head Crown counsel at a court in Toronto (*Toronto Star*, 1992). Others, such as defence counsel Peter Abrahams, believe that race makes a difference in the legal system:

> You find that Black youths are denied bail more often than their young White counterparts. The first question you're asked as a lawyer going into a hearing is whether your client is Black. Everybody knows that there is a racial element to a criminal trial. Police, Crown attorneys and judges are not immune to it. (*Toronto Star*, 1992)

The denial of racism in the justice system is not confined to the legal profession. There was considerable criticism of the then Attorney General of Ontario, Howard Hampton, for creating a task force to investigate the issue in the early 1990s. A Progressive Conservative MPP angrily stated in the legislature that members of the justice system had been "slandered":

> You stated publicly that it was your opinion that the justice system was rife with systemic racism. Statements such as these slander the reputation of every judge, Crown attorney, justice of the peace and police officer who makes up the justice system. (*Toronto Star*, 1992)

Faced with continuing pressure from minority communities, especially Blacks, the government of Ontario announced some new initiatives for the justice system. A new method of developing jury pools to increase minority-group representation on juries was announced by the attorney general. The announcement was greeted with allegations of reverse racism and fears about the imposition of jury quotas (*Toronto Star*, 1993a). One of Canada's most prominent lawyers, Edward Greenspan, said that "there is something fundamentally wrong with the notion that 12 people of one colour can't fairly try an accused of a different colour." Hutchinson countered this argument tellingly:

> In a society that still divides power and opportunity along racial, class and other lines, it is a profound error to imagine that one's race and background does not give one a certain perspective on social values, how society works and what others think. … It is the privilege of the White establishment to pretend that race is not important and that it does not contribute heavily to the kinds of lives that people live. (Hutchinson, 1992)

While recognizing that the views of individuals are as diverse as their backgrounds, Hutchinson argued that there was at least a chance of an accused receiving a fairer and more balanced decision when it reflected "the views of the whole community, not only part of it" (*Toronto Star*, 1993a).

These and other concerns led the government of Ontario to appoint a commission to study racism in the criminal justice system. Some of its findings have already been noted above. This commission provided a unique opportunity for changes to be made in the justice system. Although appointed in 1992, the commission did not release its findings and report until December 1995. A new government in the province, less favourable to the implementation of changes in its justice system, has neglected the report for eight years and its many excellent recommendations. In the context of growing pressure to address racial profiling across this country, it is hoped that many of the recommendations of various task force reports and commission studies will be given more serious attention and action.

Employment Equity

In Ontario, pending employment equity legislation forced a number of hiring and appointment measures to be taken. In the 1990s, a concerted effort was made to hire more minority lawyers in the public service and to appoint more to the judiciary. A Black Legal Aid Clinic was formed to provide services to the Black community; similar services were already available for the Chinese and Aboriginal communities. There was also a small increase in the number of racial-minority students being accepted into law schools, and the overall number of racial-minority lawyers in practice increased marginally. In addition, a "Black" legal firm was established in Toronto. The employment equity legislation in Ontario was, however, the first piece of legislation to be revoked by the new government in 1995. The legislation repealing the Employment Equity Act was inappropriately named: "The Job Quota Repeal Act." The very name of the legislation repealing the Employment Equity Act plays on myths disseminated by corporate elites, the media, and politicians about what employment equity was. It should be noted that a constitutional challenge of the repeal of the Employment Equity Act was launched and failed.

Training

Only a limited amount of anti-racist training has been undertaken in the justice system. The Judicial Education Committee in Ontario, which had earlier sponsored gender training, agreed in principle to offer anti-racist training to judges but was constrained by lack of money. Some training was undertaken by Ministry of the Attorney General for staff such as Crown counsel and offices that fell under its jurisdiction, such as the Public Complaints Commission. For the most part, however, practising judges, defence and Crown counsel, and other members of the justice system have not had any comprehensive training in matters relating to the manifestations of racism in public systems.

Herein lies a significant problem. Far too many of those who claim that racism is a fabrication do so without the skill set even to identify differential impact. So many decision-makers believe that accepting any such training would inevitably convert them into advocates of one position or the other. Without the critical content theory of anti-racism, many decision-makers remain oblivious to the impact of their decisions, particularly in the civil litigation context. Blindly awarding costs at the conclusion of a motion involving an unsuccessful minority or failing to award cost when a minority lawyer is successful on a motion when examined in isolation is not very instructive.

Summary

There is now sufficient evidence of racism in the justice system to suggest that it is of grave concern in Canada. Various public inquiries, task forces, and commissions have been conducted, and the evidence gathered in public consultations with individuals, organizations, and racial-minority communities reflects a growing sense of distrust and fear of the justice system in Canada. There is a fundamental absence of faith in the fairness of the system.

Racial unrest in the 1990s in Toronto, Montreal, Halifax, and other Canadian cities has been, in part, a response to the perception among Black people that they are the victims of racial bias and discrimination, which are widespread in law enforcement agencies as well as in the courts. Allegations of police brutality and harassment are widespread. Growing concerns have been expressed about the low numbers of racial minorities and Aboriginal peoples employed in the legal system as well as on juries.

The justice system in Canada is plagued by a systemic bias that results in the over-criminalization of particular groups in society. Blacks (and other racial minorities) face discriminatory practices and procedures at every stage of the administration of justice. Over-criminalization is reinforced by the media, which consistently report the alleged criminal activities of racial-minority people. As most people learn about people different from themselves from the media, it is not surprising that many members of the public now make the link between race and the propensity toward criminal activity.

This chapter demonstrates how democratic racism is manifested within the justice system. It examines the value conflict between the ideals and principles of democratic liberalism that are central to the provision of justice and the racism that is reflected in the everyday discursive practices of judges, lawyers, jurors, witnesses, and others in the justice system.

The examples and case studies illustrate the fact that despite the philosophical foundation of democratic liberalism underpinning the justice system, the law is neither impartial nor value-neutral. It reflects the political, cultural, and social biases of those who create the law and administer it. Judges, juries, and lawyers are frequently not impartial, but subscribe to the same stereotypes and hold the same biases as exist in the broader Canadian society. Therefore, a critique of the legal system cannot be accomplished without recognizing that the law and its institutions are in a dialectical relationship with the broader society.

Democratic racism is manifested in courtroom discursive practices. Racism is denied by some of the personnel who administer the legal and justice systems. They find it difficult to acknowledge cultural, institutional, and systemic forms of racism, even where they are manifested so clearly in the formal and informal practices of the legal system. The discourse of colour-blindness is very powerful in this system. However, justice is not colour-blind, despite the fact that 64 percent of provincial division judges and 72 percent of general division judges believed that the courts treated White and racial-minority people in the same way (*Report of the Commission on Systemic Racism*, 1995:30). As one judge sincerely noted: "My experience is that the court is colour blind. … I can honestly say that the minority parties have been treated no differently than any other by judges, juries, courts staff, lawyers, etc." (1995:31).

In the same way, the liberal discourse that fairness is best achieved by treating everyone equally (or in the same way) is shown by the many examples in this chapter to be a myth. A more relativistic perspective argues that an accused's gender and race must be considered in any determination. There is some consensus among scholars that racial disparities in the criminal justice system have developed because policies, practices, and procedures have been adopted without systematic efforts being made to find out whether they have a differential effect on members of racial-minority communities. While a fundamental principle and discourse in justice is that the accused is presumed innocent, in the case of racial minorities and Aboriginal peoples there is often an assumption of guilt.

Racial discrimination is not limited to the justice system; it exists in virtually every other social institution. However, the justice system has a special responsibility to function with fairness and to show that discrimination in any form is a denial of the justice it claims to uphold.

Notes

1. "Justice system" here refers to police institutions, the courts, and correctional facilities.
2. Racial or any other form of discrimination cannot be dealt with in civil law except in the province of Quebec. In all other provinces, discrimination is not considered to be a tort; that is, victims cannot claim costs for personal injury as a result of discriminatory actions. Discrimination falls under the exclusive jurisdiction of human rights tribunals.
3. See *Report of the Commission on Systemic Racism in the Ontario Criminal Justice System* (1995).
4. For an overview, see Wortley, 2003.
5. The Aboriginal Justice Strategy was introduced in 1996 and provides help in establishing community sentencing circles, mediation in civil matters, and dispute resolution mechanisms.
6. Although this book contains a separate chapter on policing, it is necessary here to briefly review some material on police, who are the first point of contact before individuals reach the courts.
7. For a systematic presentation of the powers of Crown attorneys see Morris Manning, "Abuse of Power by Crown Attorneys," *Special Lectures of the Law Society of Upper Canada* (Toronto: LSUC, 1979).
8. *Mens rea* refers to the conscious intention of a person to commit a crime.
9. *Voir dire*: "to speak the truth."
10. The challenge for cause based on racial discrimination was upheld by the Ontario Court of Appeal in *Regina v. Parks*. Justice Doherty accepted the fact that bias among jury members is possible in a society in which "wide spread anti-Black racism is a grim reality" (*Toronto Star*, December 15, 1993:25).

    Presumably the way has now been cleared for lawyers to use the challenge whenever appropriate. Although this judgment and that of the Provincial Court (Macdonald, 1993) have shown progress occurring in the justice system with respect to the issue of racism, it should also be noted that the Ontario attorney general appealed the Court of Appeal's decision to the Supreme Court of Canada and asked that court to condone trials in which people of colour are not allowed to question the jury on racism. The Supreme Court of Canada in April 1994 denied the province leave to appeal.

However, in June 1998, Frances Henry was involved in a challenge for cause on racism on behalf of a Vietnamese accused. Despite the Supreme Court decision in *Williams*, which stated that any minority had the right to challenge the jury on cause, the Crown attorney maintained that he required evidence to support the use of the challenge. Moreover, he hired another expert witness to counteract Henry's evidence. Furthermore, the judge did not intervene to reason with the Crown attorney in the light of the Supreme Court decision. This case reveals clearly that the system contains many members unwilling to accept that racism in its various guises not only exists in society but is played out within the justice system. The denial of racism is still evident despite major decisions, including those made by the Supreme Court of Canada.

References

Backhouse, C. (1999). *Colour-Coded: A Legal History of Racism in Canada 1900–1950.* Toronto: The Osgoode Society for Canadian Legal History by the University of Toronto Press.

Billings, G.L. (1998). "Just What Is Critical Race Theory and What's It Doing in a Nice Field Like Education?" *Qualitative Education* 11(1):7–24.

Cunningham, D. (1997). "We're Not Equal Before the Law After All: British Columbia's Judges Are Told to Treat Minorities and Women Differently." *Western Report* 12(46)(December 15):35.

Equal Opportunity Consultants. (1989). *Perceptions of Racial Minorities Related to the Services of the Ministry of the Attorney General.* Toronto: Ontario Ministry of the Attorney General.

Globe and Mail. (1993). (June 28).

Hamalengwa, M. (2004). "Supreme Injustice." *Toronto Star* (September 3).

Head, W. (1991). "The Donald Marshall Prosecution: A Case Study of Racism and the Criminal Justice System." *Currents: Readings in Race Relations* 7(1)(April).

Henry, F., P. Hastings, and B. Freer. (1996). "Perceptions of Race and Crime in Ontario: Empirical Evidence from Toronto and the Durham Region." *Canadian Journal of Criminology* (October):469–76.

Hutchinson, A.C. (1992). *Globe and Mail* (December 3).

———. (1998). "Rules About Court Bias Should Apply to Judges, Too." *Toronto Star* (June 22).

Jamaican Canadian Association. (1990). "Meeting the Challenge—Police–Black Relations." Conference, Toronto.

Kobayashi, A. (1990). "Racism and the Law." *Urban Geography* 11(5):447–73.

Law Reform Commission of Canada. (1992). "Consultation Document." Ottawa: The Commission.

Lewis, S. (1992). *Report to the Premier of Ontario.* (June 9). Toronto.

Macdonald, J.A. (1993). *Decision on Challenge for Cause in Regina v. Griffiths.* Toronto: Ontario Provincial Court. (August).

Manning, M. (1979). "Abuse of Power by Crown Attorneys." *Special Lectures of the Law Society of Upper Canada.* Toronto: LSUC.

Ottawa Citizen. (1998). "We Told You So." Editorial. (February 28).

Petersen, C. (1993). "Institutionalized Racism: The Need for Reform of the Criminal Jury Selection Process." *McGill University Law Journal* 38:147–79.

Pinto, A. (2000). *Race, Courts, and Tribunal.* Toronto: Law Society of Upper Canada. Tab 3C.

Pomerant, D. (1992). *Jury Selection and Multicultural Issues.* Ottawa: Law Reform Commission of Canada.

Razack, S. (1998). *Looking White People in the Eye: Gender, Race and Culture in the Courtrooms and Classroom.* Toronto: University of Toronto Press.

Reiman, J.H. (1984). *The Rich Get Richer and the Poor Get Prison: Ideology, Class, and Criminal Justice.* New York: Wiley.

Report of the Commission on Systemic Racism in the Ontario Criminal Justice System. (1995). Toronto: Queen's Printer.

St. Lewis, J. (1996). "Racism and the Justice System." In C. James (ed.), *Perspectives on Racism and the Human Services Sector.* Toronto: University of Toronto Press. 104–19.

Staples, R. (1975). "White Racism, Black Crime, and American Justice: An Application of the Colonial Model to Explain Crime and Race." *Phylon* 36(1)(Spring 1975):14–22.

Tanovich, D.M., D.M. Paciocco, and S. Skurka. (1997). *Jury Selection in Criminal Cases: Skills, Science and the Law.* Concord, ON: Irwin Law.

Thornhill, E. (1988). "Presentation to the Donald Marshall Inquiry." In *Proceedings of Consultative Conference on Discrimination Against Natives and Blacks in the Criminal Justice System and the Role of the Attorney General*. Halifax.

Toronto Star. (1992). (October 12):24.

———. (1993). "Should Juries Reflect a Society's Racial Mix?" (May 22):D4.

———. (1997). "Judges Face Conduct Crackdown." (September 21):A1.

Westmoreland-Traoré, J. (1982). "Race Relations and the Criminal Justice System." Paper presented at conference on Justice and Minorities. Vancouver (April).

Wiener, J. (1990). "Speech to the Western Judicial Education Centre, Vancouver." (May 13).

Williams, P. (1991). *The Alchemy of Race and Rights: Diary of a Law Professor*. Cambridge, MA: Harvard University Press.

Wortley, S. (2003). "Hidden Intersections: Research on Race, Crime and Criminal Justice in Canada." *Canadian Ethnic Studies* 35(3):99–118.

CHAPTER 6

RACISM AND POLICING

We don't believe it exists.

—*President, Ontario Association of Chiefs of Police (2002)*

This chapter explores racism in policing. In order to put this dynamic into context, the chapter begins with a brief exploration of the "culture of policing." It continues by examining attitudes and behaviours of policing and shows how police discretionary powers can lead to both the overpolicing and the underpolicing of minority communities. The chapter then discusses the issue of racial profiling, the racialization of crime, and the criminalization of minorities. Police accountability, response to pressure from minority groups, professional competence, and its relationship to the representation of people of colour on police forces are also discussed. A brief overview of some of the issues relating to police culture and the public-complaints process is presented.

The second part of the chapter examines the responses of police services across the country. It concludes with a discussion of the initiatives taken by the police in such areas as policies, training, employment equity, community relations, community-based policing, and use-of-force guidelines.

Introduction

No single area of Canadian life has perhaps caused more concern and more persistent tension and conflict than the relationship between the police and people of colour. For many years, people of colour and Aboriginal peoples have strongly indicated that policing in Canada was not carried out with an even hand, and that they are the objects of a constant systemic pattern of harassment and unnecessary violence and of insensitivity to their lifestyles and needs.

A public survey carried out for the Royal Commission on the Donald Marshall Jr. Prosecution (Province of Nova Scotia, 1989), found that about 60 percent of respondents agreed that police discriminated against Blacks. In a similar survey conducted in Montreal, 53 percent of respondents agreed that the police mistreated citizens from ethnic minorities (Davis, 1993). A 1998 survey undertaken in Toronto found that 38 percent of respondents believed that Toronto police did not treat all racial and economic groups fairly (Grayson, 1998). One of the studies sponsored by the Commission on Systemic Racism in the Ontario Criminal Justice System found that a majority of Toronto residents were not confident that the police treated all members of society equally, and the vast majority of Blacks (79 percent) believed they were treated worse than Whites. According to a poll conducted for the *Toronto Star*, Black Torontonians in general feel that they are more discriminated against than any other group in the city (July 3, 1999). In particular, nearly three-quarters of the Jamaican community feel that they are treated unfairly by police (ibid.). These findings represent a disturbingly low level of regard and trust for the police by members of the Black community.

The results of these public attitude surveys portray a consistent message—a serious crisis of confidence and a widespread loss of faith in the fairness and impartiality of policing systems that purportedly exist to protect the rights of all individuals equally. The relationship between the police and people of colour will always, it seems, be a sensitive matter. In many ways, relations between the police and racial-minority communities can be seen as the flashpoint, the means to gauge the general temper of race relations in Canada. Relations between the police and people of colour will always be extremely fragile because the police are the most visible embodiment of the dominant group's power.

Clearly, if one were to succeed in eliminating racism in the wider society, it would be much easier to attain a much more positive police–minority climate. The policing of Canada's racial-minority communities cannot be divorced from the way in which society at large views those communities. The attitudes of the police are a reflection not only of the current social perceptions of people of colour, but also of the historical attitudes of the White majority. The consequence of this is that the police are more likely to mistreat individuals who are stigmatized by the dominant society. These individuals are more likely to be subjected to small or gross indignities and mistreatment at the hands of the police. This police behaviour leads to accusations of both "overpolicing" and "underprotecting" of minorities. This complex interrelationship can, in part, be explained by the unique aspects of the culture of policing.

Culture of Policing

Racism in policing is a deeply complex phenomenon. It is based on a *shared* system of beliefs, assumptions, and attitudes that the dominant or White culture uses to make sense of, and render intelligible, the way a capitalistic, highly stratified society works (Hall et al., 1978). These belief systems or ideologies help to organize, maintain, and regulate particular forms of power and dominance. Racist ideology operates at a collective level, rather than simply as a function of individual racialized beliefs. It works at the level of cognition but it is acted out behaviourally through individual, organizational, or systemic discrimination. Racist ideology provides the processes for excluding and marginalizing people of colour within Canadian society in both law enforcement organizations and outside of these agencies. Racist ideology is embedded in the overall patterns of police culture.

Both the Canadian literature and research conducted in other jurisdictions provide some insights into the complex nature of the racialization processes that are embedded in policing culture. For example, in an audit of the Metropolitan Toronto Police Association, Andrews (1992) found that while police had done a reasonable job of ensuring that those recruited to the police do not *display* an overt racial bias, he observed

that a change occurs after joining the Force. There was significant evidence that many police officers who are constantly in contact with public develop strong feelings and beliefs as to attributes of individuals, based on factors such as appearance and racial background. These officers would no doubt be offended if their attitudes were described as potentially racist. Nevertheless, the same attitudes can and do produce a bias in behaviour which results in unequal treatment of individuals of different cultural or racial backgrounds.

What is involved here is not so much the personal beliefs of individual police officers, but evidence of a strongly developed culture and value system within the organization that produces, supports, and reinforces racial bias and discrimination. In the literature around police subculture theory there is considerable evidence that, to a significant extent, individuals learn values and beliefs and adopt norms as a result of their occupational experiences. Ungerleider (1992b) studied two Canadian municipal police forces. On the basis of a sample of 251 officers, he examined the judgments that police officers made about others, and found that 25 percent expressed views that could be categorized as reflecting "confusion" and as being "irrationally negative" towards visible minorities. He called the existence of large numbers of Canadian police officers that make irrational judgments about others "disquieting." What is evident here is not so much a symptom of individual negative attitudes toward others, but can be seen as evidence of a developed culture and value system within the organization. Within this model of socialization theory is the notion that the changes in the behaviour of police officers are related to their job experiences and interactions with fellow officers. Again, drawing from the audit of the Metropolitan Toronto Police Association (1992), the review found there was strong proof that police who were in regular contact with the public acquired deep-seated emotions and beliefs as to the attributes of individuals, based on factors such as appearance and racial background. Over time they came to hold perceptions and views of particular groups consonant with the prevailing notions of the majority of the force. These views tended to be more conservative and authoritarian.

The power and influence of organizational culture on the individuals who work within that culture is well documented. Waddington (1999) argues that "the racism of police culture is embedded in routine practices such as joking, banter and shared pastimes like off-duty drinking, that are not intrinsically racist, but which succeed in excluding ethnic minority officers and reinforcing stereotypes" (290). York (1994) identifies other elements in police culture, sometimes referred to as "canteen culture," such as isolation, conservatism, machismo, a sense of mission, a siege mentality, and what is referred to as the "thin blue line" mindset, which distinguishes between "us" and "them." It can be said that policing culture manifests the cultural pattern and orientation of closed institutions. York suggests that these closed social institutions had their origins in pre-modern social settings such as armies, religious orders, asylums, jails, and hospitals. A further characteristic of policing as a culture is the attempt to close themselves off from the broader community by deploying special behaviours, rituals, clothing, and semantic markers (specialized language and discourse) to maintain their separateness and their special sense of mission.

Another framework from which to examine the culture of policing suggests that certain aspects of the environment may be unique to the work of police officers (Skolnick, 1994). Among the many roles that the police officer performs, two of the principal variables are danger and authority. It can be argued that these variables contribute to the isolation of the police from the citizens of the community. Another norm that is commonly associated with police culture is the requirement of officers to always be suspicious of their surroundings. Because their work requires them to be occupied continually with potential violence, police officers develop a shorthand technique to identify certain kinds of people as symbolic assailants, that is, persons who are non-White, or who use verbal and body language that the police have come to associate as a prelude to violence (ibid.:44).

This dimension of policing culture linked to the element of danger that is part of police work reinforces a number of different professional norms. It allows for a high level of individual officers' discretion in decisions to stop, search, or arrest suspects. Such discretion is often influenced by stereotypes of what constitutes "normality" or "suspiciousness." Chan (1997) argues that occupational culture of policing "condones various forms of stereotyping, harassment or even violence against those who are seen to be 'rough' or 'disreputable'" (1997:44). The high level of danger that sometimes or often exists leads to a strong sense of solidarity with other officers. Roberg (1993) observes that the police share a general feeling that the public does not support them. They often feel alienated, isolated, and detached, and feel a need to maintain a code of secrecy. The code of silence commonly attributed to police culture may lead police to be very protective toward each other. At times, this means that when confronted with external threats police officers will defend and assist their colleagues and, when necessary, will maintain secrecy in the face of external investigations (Chan, 1997; Goldsmith, 1991). Cashmore (2001:264) expands on this point as it relates to racism in policing culture:

> It is imperative that colleagues, even those who are known to hold racist views, need to be trusted. You're going to need back up at some time and a delay of thirty seconds can mean the difference between life and death. … Tolerating or even countenancing racism may be an expedient decision on behalf of ethnic minority officers who may feel their safety is compromised if they report a racist colleague.

All of these dimensions of policing culture contribute to the culture's resistance to change. This point is particularly powerful in culturally pluralistic and racially diverse countries such as Canada, the United States, the United Kingdom, and Australia, where White police officers still represent the norm.

The Discourse of Democratic Racism and Policing

An underlying tenet of Canadian democracy is the obligation of its public institutions to explain and justify their activities in public. This accountability provides legitimacy to the democratic state. With regard to policing, it requires police forces to accept the notion of community control and participation either directly or through its elected community representatives in the decision-making processes of policing.

Another underlying tenet of our democratic system is that every member of society should have equal access both to the benefits of effective public services—in this case policing (an orderly society, peace, safety, security, etc.)—and to the processes through which this is achieved, without discrimination in the basis of race, creed, gender, class, etc. The Ontario Police Services Act (1990), for example, requires that policing be provided in accordance with "safeguarding the fundamental rights guaranteed by the Canadian Charter of Rights and Freedoms and the Ontario Human Rights Code." If the police feel that they are not directly accountable to the racially diverse communities they serve, they are less likely to reflect and respond to the needs and concerns of those communities.

Most Canadians know little about the operation of their police forces. Policing is still, in many ways and for many Canadians, a "closed" public institution, surrounded by mystery and secrecy. The isolation of the police from the racially diverse community they serve exists in part because relatively few members of the public have taken an active interest in the police.

It has also been suggested that the police have been disinclined to conform to this democratic obligation of accountability. It has been suggested that the notion of a democratically accountable police force is a contradiction in terms, particularly when the police are empowered to infringe on the liberties of citizens and are legally entitled to use force and violence to uphold law and order. The police deal in and with conflict and are empowered by the state to do so (Cashmore and McLaughlin, 1991:110).

Rather than having a democratic notion of accountability—to a political process and to the community—the police tend to view their accountability in different terms. Within this policing ideology, an obligation to the political process—which is portrayed as partisan—is seen in negative terms. The police are seen as preferring to derive their legitimacy and authority from a general acceptance of the laws and regulations they enforce and the values they stand for. It is toward this process of upholding legally defined standards that the police feel they are accountable. At the same time, it is within this broader framework that they feel they directly represent the "common good." This discourse of accountability to upholding the laws of the land rather than an accountability and responsiveness to the multiracial public they serve is a manifestation of democratic racism.

It has also been noted that policing institutions have a tendency to capitalize on societal tensions as a strategy for further mobilizing their legitimacy as society's crisis managers. The police, for example, in wanting greater authority and resources as the sole protectors of order, have at the same time been criticized for the release of self-serving crime statistics that tend to encourage a fear of crime and social disintegration.

The idea of chaos and crisis in every area of society, and the image of the police vainly trying to cope with the overwhelming demands of a society in turmoil, is an image that the police are unlikely to refute in their requests for more resources and greater autonomy.

The need for more democratic accountability on the part of the police in this "urban battlefield" scenario might therefore be seen as an unnecessary intrusion. The police would prefer to be released from these political, legislative, bureaucratic, and financial fetters so that they can better contain the explosion of violent crime. An example of this attitude is the comment by the Metropolitan Toronto Police Association that police were "probably the most regulated group of working people in Ontario" (Metropolitan Toronto Police Association, 1992). They saw a number of government initiatives as "additional controls." These "arbitrary" actions "engendered a growing sense of frustration and anger among the police, especially front-line officers confronting increasing crime."

A protest against the Ontario government by the Metropolitan Toronto and provincial police associations in the fall of 1992 was in large part symptomatic of this police outrage at "political intervention." Attempts to introduce some mechanisms for greater democratic accountability were viewed as something that should be discouraged and nullified. Such intervention was viewed by the police as either a socialist conspiracy or as a result of the unreasonable demands of vociferous special-interest groups. Notions of public accountability were consequently interpreted by the police as challenging the maintenance of law and order.

The demands for increasing police empowerment and greater professional autonomy are further promoted by the notion that policing is so specialized that nobody outside policing can be expected to comprehend its distinct and peculiar complexities. In this type of thinking, the police feel that any errant behaviour or irregularities by police officers should be handled internally. That is why one of the demands made by the police associations in Ontario to the provincial government (in their protest of 1992) was for a review of the need for the Special Investigations Unit, a semiautonomous unit under provincial jurisdiction that was established to investigate shootings by police.

If the policing ideology of accountability dictates police decision-making, it will clearly diminish the responsibility of the police to negotiate or justify their presence in neighbourhoods. Such notions lessen the requirement of the police to cultivate the

MANIFESTATIONS OF RACISM IN POLICING

Overpolicing and racial profiling
Underpolicing
Lack of representation
Use of force
Racialization of crime

Police culture
Poor police–community relations
Racist attitudes and behaviour
Lack of accountability
Lack of professional competence

consent of the community or to take into account its needs. The police will consequently have to be less responsive to changing expectations of policing and to the changing nature, needs, and concerns of the population.

The Manifestations of Racism

Police forces make many discretionary decisions about who they hire, what is to be done, the priorities assigned to activities, and how to carry out these activities. Some of the most important of these decisions are made in the course of enforcing the criminal law, such as decisions whether to stop and search, arrest, and detain suspects and whether to investigate citizens' complaints. Each of these decisions may present opportunities for discrimination. Various royal commissions and public inquiries have confirmed minority-group and Aboriginal concerns that these decisions have been biased in a manner that reflects selectivity based on race. These reports have highlighted many of the inherently unfair and racist practices of police forces across the country.

The Commission on Systemic Racism in the Ontario Criminal Justice System (Province of Ontario, 1995), for example, reviewed police discretionary decisions that produced a disproportionate number of people of colour in the court and prison system. How the police exercise their discretion to stop and question people contributes to a lack of confidence in equal treatment. The Commission's studies found that Black men were particularly vulnerable to being stopped by the police. About 43 percent of Black male residents, but only 25 percent of White and 19 percent of Chinese male residents, reported being stopped by the police in the previous two years.

Racist Attitudes and Behaviour

Although extensive racism among the police is often alleged and anecdotal evidence of significant incidents has been offered, documented research evidence for this assertion is relatively slim. Most studies relate to police "personality" traits such as authoritarianism, dogmatism, and conservatism. The first study in Canada on this subject was undertaken by Ungerleider, who sampled 251 uniformed officers in two major municipalities in Canada. His study examined the judgments that police officers made about others. It found that 25 percent of the officers were either confused in their judgments of others or irrationally negative, and it concluded "the existence of a large number of Canadian police officers who make irrational judgments about others is disquieting" (Ungerleider, 1992b).

Another perspective on this sensitive issue as to whether police officers are more likely to betray racist tendencies (above and beyond the occasional "bad apple" incident) has been put forward in a study of the Metropolitan Toronto Police Force that found no evidence of organized, intentional prejudice or bias against people of colour. (Andrews, 1992)

RACIAL PROFILING

The issue of disproportionality in stop-and-search rates by the police became a public issue when the *Toronto Star* published a series of articles on racial profiling of Black males in Toronto.

Background

On October 19, 2002, the *Toronto Star* began a series of stories on racial profiling. The articles were based on a two-year probe of race and crime statistics gathered from a Toronto police database that documents arrests and charges laid. The database details more than 480 000 incidents in which an individual was arrested or ticketed for an offence, and nearly 800 000 criminal and other charges laid by police from late 1996 to early 2002. The data was accessed through the Ontario Freedom of Information and Protection of Privacy Act after police denied the *Star* access to their own records. The analysis of the crime data revealed significant disparities in the ways in which Blacks and Whites are treated in law enforcement practices. More specifically, the data showed: (1) a disproportionate number of Black motorists are ticketed for violations that only surface following a traffic stop, (2) Black people, charged with simple drug possession, are taken to police stations more often than Whites facing the same charge, and (3) once at the station, accused Blacks are held overnight for a bail hearing at twice the rate of Whites.

The Response by White Public Authorities

A discourse of denial was evident in the reaction of those closely affiliated with policing structures. Police Chief Julian Fantino is quoted in that paper as saying:

> We do not do racial profiling. We do not deal with people on the basis of their ethnicity, their race or any other factor. We're not perfect people but you're barking up the wrong tree. There's no racism ... it seems that, according to some people, no

matter what honest efforts people make, there are always those who are intent on causing trouble. Obviously this [story] is going to do exactly that. ... (*Toronto Star*, October 19, 2002)

A few days later, the President of the Ontario Association of Chiefs of Police supported Fantino's position. He is quoted as saying:

> We don't see this as being a widespread issue across the province. ... It's certainly not something that we're that concerned about because we don't believe it exists. ... It's our position that [racial profiling] doesn't exist. We're not doing that. (*Toronto Star*, October 29, 2002)

The Toronto Police Association not only supported Chief Fantino's discourse of denial but also went several steps further. Craig Bromell, its President, is quoted as saying

> No racial profiling has ever been conducted by the Toronto Police Service and we question the *Toronto Star's* interpretation of its statistical information. ... (*Toronto Star*, October 22, 2002)

Bromell not only questioned the methodology and statistical analysis undertaken by the newspaper but also asked that citizens boycott the paper by cancelling their subscriptions.

The Toronto Police Services Board, the regulatory agency that supervises the police, was the next police-related agency to use the discourse of denial. Its chairperson Norm Gardner described the newspapers findings as

> Reckless ... some of the people involved, who are trying to keep on bringing this stuff up ... they make a good living out of social unrest. (*Toronto Star*, October 20, 2002)

Gardner is also cited as saying that he is confident the police don't use racial profiling, and the Board's vice-chair, Gloria Luby, agreed with Gardner adding that statistics can be used to prove anything and that "police discrimination has not been an issue."

As the discourse moves to the political level, then-mayor of Toronto Mel Lastman continued the discourse of denial by saying

> The police only arrest "bad guys." ... I don't believe the Toronto police engage in racial profiling in any way, shape or form. Quite the opposite, they're very sensitive to our different communities. (*Toronto Star*, October 20, 2002)

Following this study, the Ontario Human Rights Commission conducted an inquiry (2003) in which they called for submissions of accounts of personal experiences with racial profiling.[1] The Report looked at the human cost of racial profiling on those who have experienced it, their families, their communities, and the detrimental impact on society.

In March 2004, two additional reports on racial profiling commissioned by the African Canadian Community Coalition on Racial Profiling (ACCCRP) were released. *In Their Own Voices* by Maureen Brown was based on interviews with Black youth and adults across the Greater Toronto Area. The interviews detailed encounters with police in which respondents communicated that they were targeted, harassed, and disrespected by police in their everyday life. The second report, *Crisis, Conflict and Accountability* by Charles Smith, examines the history of relations between the African-Canadian community and the police in Canada and compares it with the findings of a huge body of research done in the United States and the United Kingdom. The report bases its Canadian content on studies, task force reports and inquiries, public forums, community consultations, and media reports over the past thirty years. Both Brown and Smith argue that we need to move past the debate over whether profiling happens and begin to address the effects of profiling on the community's perception of the police.

CASE STUDY 6.2

RACIAL PROFILING OF ABORIGINAL MEN

Background

Racial profiling by police also characterizes the relationship between the Aboriginal communities of Canada and the police. In recent years there have been several cases of Aboriginal men who have found frozen to death in Saskatoon. In 1990, an Aboriginal teenager Neil Stonechild's frozen body was found in a field just outside the city. A friend reported that he last saw Stonechild in a police car, screaming that the police were going to kill him. In January 2000, the body of Lloyd Dusthorn was found frozen to death outside his locked apartment after having been seen in police custody. Also, in January 2000, the frozen body of Rodney Naistus was found on the outskirts of Saskatoon, near the Queen Elizabeth II Power Station. Five days later, Lawrence Wegner, a social work student, was last seen alive banging on the doors of family members in Saskatoon. It is testified that he ran away when police were called. His frozen body was later found near the power plant. After Wegner's body was found, another man, Darrell Night, came forward. Night reported that he had been dropped off by police south of the city on a bitterly cold night but had managed to get to a nearby power station for help. Two Saskatoon police officers were found guilty of unlawful confinement in the Night case and were sentenced to eight months in jail (Canadian Press, 2004).

Saskatchewan's Commission on First Nations and Métis Peoples and Justice Reform was established in 2001 to conduct an investigation into Saskatchewan's justice system, which released its findings in June 2004. It found that anti-native racism exists in the police system. Among its 122 recommendations were that an agency be established to handle complaints against police and that police stations have Aboriginal liaison officers. The Commissioner, Wilton Littlechild, said that interviewed police officers expressed frustration at the number of false accusations. However, on the basis of the evidence presented to the Commission, he believed such racism to be widespread. Among the report's 122 recommendations were that an independent agency be established to handle allegations of police abuse and excessive force (Commission on First Nations and Métis Peoples and Justice Reform, 2004).

Discussion

In a democratic and liberal society where racism is seen as the aberrant belief and behaviour of isolated and dysfunctional extremists, denials of racism are pervasive in public discourse. These denials are often articulated in the context of doubt about acts of discrimination. Denial is often followed by the claim that people of colour and other minority groups are hypersensitive about prejudice and discrimination and often see bias where there is none. The assumption here is that because Canada is a society that upholds the values and ideals of a liberal democracy, it cannot be racist, nor are its major institutions racist. Central to this discourse is the need for positive self-presentation ("I am not a racist"; "This is not a racist organization"; "This is not a racist society"). These denials are based on a very limited understanding of how racism is manifested in contemporary society. For the most part, racism is still understood by most people in its overt and "redneck" expressions of racial hatred. Racists are those who use strongly pejorative words and labels, physically attack people of colour and their property, or are aligned with extremist political movements. The denial of racism is part of a defensive strategy that actually

enhances in-group preservation through positive self-representation (van Dijk, 1991).

Police discretionary actions may contribute significantly to racial inequality in imprisonment before trial. The police make the critical decision about whether to arrest an accused person, and in most circumstances they also decide to release or detain pending a bail hearing. In addition, the police prepare "show cause" reports that summarize information about the accused and the alleged offences. Crown attorneys generally use these reports when deciding if the state should seek the imprisonment of an accused and when making submissions to a justice at a bail hearing. This aspect of the police function, no less than the arrest and release powers, may be influenced by social constructions of Black people as more likely than White people to warrant detention before trial.

Exercise of the arrest power is highly discretionary and, except when the police obtain prior authorization in the form of a warrant, it is difficult to scrutinize. As the Law Reform Commission of Canada (1991) noted, this discretion and low visibility make the arrest power open to many types of abuse, including discriminatory treatment.

Wortley (2001), in an examination of court records involving 1800 criminal cases in two Toronto bail courts, found Blacks were 1.5 times more likely to be detained than Whites. In addition Wortley found that "officers write much more powerful character assassinations of black defendants than white defendants" (*Toronto Star,* October 19, 2003:A13).

What is evident here is not so much a symptom of personal belief but of a developed culture and value system within the organization referred to above as the "culture of policing." As a result of work experience whereby police officers are exposed to an extremely selective cross-section of the population, an attitudinal bias toward people of colour may creep in.

Discussing a concern that biased behaviour exists among police officers is not the same as saying that every police officer does so. Or that it is an intentional activity if those that do engage in it. While it certainly can be intentional, it can also be inadvertent. And saying that racially biased policing occurs should not necessarily be interpreted as an accusation that those who engage in it are racist.

What is of concern here is a strongly developed set of institutional practices and cultural behaviours that produces, supports, and strengthens racially different outcomes.

These aggregated and collective patterns of police attitude and behaviour are often more sophisticated, elusive, and coded. They tend to operate invisibly beneath the radar that is presently employed to detect discriminatory practice (Crank, 1998; Chan, 1997).

Minority ethnic officers interviewed by Cashmore (2001) reported being advised to stop "Black kids with baseball caps, wearing jewellery," in order to boost their recordable activities and enhance their performance. Other officers were said to "subscribe to the philosophy that, if you see four black youths in a car, it's worth giving them a pull, at least one of them is going to be guilty of something or other."

This type of thinking is consistent with patterns of selective enforcement by police officers, based on stereotyping and their heightened suspicion of ethnic minorities. Their heightened suspiciousness of Black people may significantly increase the chances of Black people coming to the attention of the police relative to other groups.

The many commissions of inquiry on relations between the police and Aboriginal people all identified a state of hostility and distrust, which increased the likelihood of conflict and high arrest rates (Sukahara, 1992). In its investigation into the circumstances surrounding the shooting death of J.J. Harper by a Winnipeg police officer and the subsequent mishandling of the investigation, the Manitoba Aboriginal Justice Inquiry concluded that "racism played a part in the shooting of J.J. Harper and the events that followed" (Province of Manitoba, 1991).

There is little disagreement that policing activities and resources ought to be focused on areas of high risk, those having a high probability of criminal activity or requiring high levels of service. But what constitutes "high risk" or a "higher level of service"? For example, fraud and white-collar crimes are on the increase. These cases have overloaded the system to the point where the police have advised that many of these crimes will go uninvestigated and that an affected private company should do the preliminary investigation itself before going to the police. In other words, the actions or functions of the police suggest that white-collar crimes can go unchecked, relative to other crimes. Most such crimes are committed by White people who occupy positions of power, rank, and confidence in an organization (Russell, 1998; Reiman, 1984). Thus, by choosing not to make these crimes a priority, the police simultaneously remove a large segment of the community from potential criminal liability. The segment of the community largely responsible for white-collar crime might therefore be described as being underpoliced.

Defining what is "high risk" or a "higher level of service," however, is not an objective exercise. As already noted, police race relations are influenced by the structural features of a society in which opportunities, rewards, and constraints are unequally and unfairly distributed.

Canadian society is hierarchically stratified along a number of dimensions, including ascribed attributes such as skin colour, ethnicity, sex, and religion, as well as along such lines as economic and political power. As Ungerleider argues,

> The categorization of people in this way can provide a shared sense of identity as well as distinctive perceptual, normative and behavioural patterns. These differences are injected into society's policing process including affecting criminal justice—creating disputes about what behaviours are to be considered criminal and how seriously particular criminal violations are to be regarded. (1992a)

The criminal justice system reflects and promotes the interests of the more powerful members of society. These members, in turn, exert influence to diminish the priority and resources given by the police to those criminal activities in which they themselves are more likely to engage (e.g., white-collar crime) and to increase the priority given to "street" crimes, which are committed by less advantaged people.

The long-held perceptions and experiences of Black people have led them to believe that one of the main reasons for the large number of accused Black people—totally out of proportion to their numbers in the population—is the insidious nature of these kinds of informal police priorities and actions.

Evidence therefore has suggested that it is the intersection of social and racial stratification with police planning, priority setting, and practice that creates the conditions for unfair treatment. In any encounter—but especially encounters between the police and the public—a person's behaviour is influenced by his or her perceived location in the society's system of social satisfaction. If police officers are unable to separate their office from their own self-concepts, they may perceive challenges to their office as challenges to themselves. Using colour, age, appearance, language, and other behaviours, the officer may have stereotyped the main actor in a street encounter as someone unrepresentative of the "community" and the values it represents. And the officer may consequently feel that the actor is more deserving of suspicion, of being stopped and searched for an alleged transgression of community standards.

Relations between the police and people of colour and Aboriginal peoples are thus influenced by the structural features of a society in which opportunity, rewards, and constraints are unequally and unfairly distributed. Within the context of the criminal justice system, which reflects the interests and values of the dominant society, the police contribute to the criminalization of marginalized individuals by selectively perceiving and responding to deviance. A contributing factor, then, to overpolicing or racial profiling is the influence of this wider sociopolitical context in which the police operate.

So while it may be rare today for individuals to be targeted by the police solely because of racial prejudice, the colour of one's skin can often be the decisive factor in guiding a police officer's decision about who to stop, search, or question. Such selective enforcement, based in part on race, is no less pernicious or offensive to the principle of equal justice than enforcement based solely on race. Because it is more subtle, more prevalent, more invisible than explicit racism, it may in fact be that much more damaging to the image and credibility of the police.

Overpolicing

"Overpolicing" refers to the extent to which police use discretion in the surveillance of a community and the apprehension of people within that community. Are police cruisers seen more frequently, for example, in communities that are densely populated by people of colour? Is the police presence more clearly noticeable at any event involving people of colour? Are business establishments such as restaurants and clubs that are owned, managed, or patronized by Black people under more frequent police surveillance? Sometimes such police presence may be obvious and visible; at other times, unmarked cars and plain clothes hide their surveillance.

One notable result of overpolicing is that charges tend to be more frequently laid against Blacks. For example, the report of the Commission on Systemic Racism in the Ontario Criminal Justice System (Province of Ontario, 1995) noted the discretionary changes in policing policies and strategies from the mid-1980s to more intensive policing of low-income areas with high proportions of Blacks, as well as greater use of law enforcement as a primary strategy to control drug abuse. One of the consequences of these policing priorities has been a dramatic increase in prison admissions of Black people. Between 1986 and 1993 there was a 204 percent increase in the incarceration of Blacks in

Ontario, in contrast with a 23 percent increase for Whites. The 1992–93 statistics showed that Black people accounted for 15 percent of Ontario's prison population while forming only 3.1 percent of the province's general population.

Perhaps one of the most significant aspects of the Commission's work was the study undertaken by the Canadian Centre for Justice Statistics to investigate the use of discretion in the remand process. Using Toronto for the study sample, the study examined imprisonment decisions for a sample of Black and White adult males charged with any of five offence types: drug charges, sexual assaults, bail violations, serious nonsexual assaults, and robbery. The sample, 821 adult males described by the police as Black and 832 adult males described as White, included equal numbers of Black and White accused for each of the five offences.

The study found that the overrepresentation of Black adults was much higher among those imprisoned before trial than among sentenced admissions. Although White men were imprisoned before trial at about the same rate as after sentencing (approximately 329 per 100 000 persons in the population before trial, and 334 after sentencing), the pre-trial admission rate of Black men was twice their sentenced admission rate (approximately 2136 per 100 000 before trial, and 1051 after sentencing).

The data from the study revealed no evidence of differential treatment for some types of charges laid against White and Black accused, but substantial differences for other charges. Differential treatment was most pronounced for accused charged with drug offences. Within this subsample, White accused (60 percent) were twice as likely as Black accused (30 percent) to be released by the police. Black accused (31 percent) were three times more likely than White accused (10 percent) to be refused bail and ordered detained.

Further analysis of the drug-charge sample indicates separate patterns of discrimination at the police and court stages of pre-trial detention. Across the sample as a whole, the results of differential treatment evident at the police stage were subsequently transmitted into the court process. Police decisions to detain Black accused at a higher rate than White accused meant that the bail courts saw a significantly higher proportion of Black accused. Thus, even similar rates of denying bail at court resulted in larger proportions of Black accused being jailed before trial.

The Commission's research confirmed the perception held by many members of racial-minority communities in Toronto that one of the reasons for the number of accused Blacks being totally out of proportion to their numbers in the total population is informal police priorities and actions.

The overpolicing of racial minorities can be understood, therefore, within the larger sociopolitical context, in which the police contribute to the criminalization of marginalized individuals and groups by selecting what is "high risk" criminal behaviour. It can also be seen in the methods chosen to address that deviant behaviour. Several scholars (Smith, 2004; Jiwani, 2002; Stenning, 1998) suggest that racial profiling has created a disproportionately large class of racialized offenders. It has also criminalized numerous predominantly Black neighbourhoods in Toronto that are commonly viewed by the police as "high crime areas." This perception has led to the perpetuation of the belief that there that there is a link between race and crime.

This experience of overpolicing clearly contributes to the notion that certain racial groups, particularly Blacks, are more disposed to commit crimes than are Whites. The evidence presented by the Commission on Systemic Racism in the Ontario Criminal Justice System suggests that the discretionary actions of the police are not only racializing crime, but also contributing to the public perception that Blacks are a high-crime group and the related notion that their criminality is an expression of their distinctive culture. This further reinforces the need for "overpolicing" and helps to further legitimize the differential treatment by the police toward members of the Black community.

Overpolicing can be seen, as well, in the discretionary decisions and behaviour of individual police officers. For example, the Race Relations and Policing Task Force (C. Lewis, 1992) heard numerous examples of the active harassment of racial minorities by police. The task force quoted one presenter: "Harassment is being released from prison, finding a job, to have a police officer come to your job and ask your employer, 'Why have you hired him, don't you know he's a criminal?'" This presenter went on to tell of racial-minority young people constantly being stopped by police on the street, especially after dark. She told the task force: "The questions are always being asked [by police]: 'Where are you going?' 'Where are you coming from?'"

The task force found that Black youth in particular tended to view police with distrust and fear, feelings said to be rooted in confrontations involving physical and verbal abuse by some police officers. The task force was told by several Black youths of police using racial slurs and exercising their right to use force in excessive or humiliating ways:

> We will talk about jay-walking. There are situations in Windsor where five people will walk across a street on a red light, which is jay-walking. If one or two of them are Black, they are the ones that will get the jay-walking ticket. If a Black is out going to work in the wee hours of the morning ... and most people working in the Big Three are out there at 5:30, 6:00 o'clock in the morning waiting for a bus ... he is apt to be harassed there. [The police] will go so far as to look in your lunch bag, and things of this nature. (C. Lewis, 1992)

Those who have not experienced a stop-and-search may be inclined to view it as nothing more than a mere inconvenience. However, from the evidence of witnesses to the Ontario Human Rights Commission (OHRC, 2003), and the community consultations conducted by Brown (2004), repeated stop-and-searches upon innocent citizens is more than a hassle or annoyance; it has real and direct consequences. Those large numbers of innocent citizens who experience it often pay the price emotionally, mentally, and in some cases even financially and physically. To argue that the widespread and disproportionate use of stop-and-search for certain communities as a police practice is harmless, that it only hurts those who break the law, is to totally ignore the psychological and social costs that can result from always being considered one of the usual suspects.

As one witness said:

> Some may find this practice is justified because there are a lot of bad people out there and it is relatively easy to group certain clusters together based on statistics and probability factors, etc. but each person wants to be viewed and thought of as an individual. Think about the harm that is being done to those who find themselves in a cluster they do not belong in. Who can begin to appreciate the level of frustration within these individuals and the future cost to society that disenfranchises these innocent victims.

Some of the words used in submissions to the OHRC to describe the effects on their relationship with police were *suspicion*, *distrust*, *anger*, *antagonism*, *hostility*, and *fear*. Some described fearing for their own safety when interacting with police officers, and some said that, rather than feeling the police were there to protect them from crime, they felt they needed to be protected from the police.

This mistrust of the police can not only result in a feeling of not wanting to go to or cooperate with the police, but also degenerate to a general attitude of not respecting or complying with the law. As one young witness told the Commission, "If the police are going to arrest me anyway (when I haven't done anything wrong), I might as well do something bad, so at least I would deserve it."

The extraordinary increase in the surveillance of the Muslim and Arab communities as a result of the tragedy of September 11, 2001 (see Case Study 11.4) has caused concerns about increased deprivations of liberty, loss of privacy, further questioning, or worse. These communities have been looked at with suspicion rather than invited to the table to offer assistance or advice on improving security for everyone.

The sense of injustice that develops among individuals in minority communities in response to overpolicing or racial profiling reinforces their concern that racism is rampant in society and that they may be subjected to it at any time. Minority groups use several coping strategies to deal with the effects of their experiences.

In some cases, people accept the negative stereotypes applied to their group. They begin to see themselves as inferior; they may grow ashamed of their background, skin colour, ethnicity, or religion.

Another effect of police stop-and-search practices is the heightening of community fear, insecurity, and feelings of disempowerment. A number of community witnesses to the OHRC inquiry used the words "impotent," "powerless," "helpless," and "emasculated" to describe how they felt as a result of one or more stop-and-searches.

One of the most significant and potentially long-lasting impacts of overpolicing is its effect on children and youth. It was reported to the OHRC inquiry that minority parents raise their children differently because of fear of their being stopped and searched by the police, and tell them to be careful of their behaviour around police. They also lay down rules about how their children dress in public, when they are permitted to go out, and where they may go. This type of experience cannot help but have a profound effect on a child or young person; attitudes and behaviours toward the police and the need to alter behaviour become ingrained in the psyche. Such experiences during formative years are likely to have a more lasting impact than on an adult.

These narratives of personal experience, received by the Ontario Human Rights Commission, Brown's consultation, and earlier by the Race Relations and Policing Task Force and other forums like it across Canada, make it abundantly clear that people of colour believe they are treated quite differently from the majority community by the police. Black people, it seems, are far more likely to be stopped and searched by the police and far less likely to be cautioned than their White counterparts.

Racially prejudiced police behaviour has not been clearly defined in Canada, and as a result it is generally not seen as a disciplinary offence by police forces. In addition, since the impartiality of the complaints procedure is generally seen as highly questionable (it entails the police investigating the police), few complaints are actually made. Consequently, the nature and extent of overpolicing and the harassment of people of colour are difficult to quantify. Information about these issues largely depends on the kinds of anecdotal evidence presented to government-appointed task forces such as the ones cited above.

The Racialization of Crime

Due to overpolicing, some crimes—specifically acts of "mugging," robbery, drug charges, and street rioting—have come to be understood as the natural expressions of Black culture, "in which the negative effects of black matriarchy and family pathology wrought destructive changes on the inner city by literally breeding deviancy out of deprivation and discrimination" (Gilroy, 1987:109–10).

Similar patterns of criminality associated with various minority communities have emerged in Canadian cities. Prior to the provincial election in Ontario on June 2, 1999, the Toronto Police Association ran a subway poster that asked voters to "help fight crime by electing candidates who are prepared to take on the drug pushers, the pimps, and the rapists …" and showed a picture of a Hispanic gang. In a letter to the Hispanic community expressing his concerns regarding the inappropriateness of the poster, then-mayor of Toronto Mel Lastman wrote: "To single out one race in an advertising campaign and draw parallels with gang warfare is unconscionable" (*Toronto Star*, June 1, 1999).

Thus, the racialization of crime, in which Aboriginal people, Blacks, Asians, and other people of colour are increasingly identified with specific criminal behaviour, reinforces the need for "overpolicing" and helps to explain and legitimize the differential behaviour of police officers toward members of these communities.

Links Between Policing and Media in the Racialization of Crime

It is important to note that the racialization of crime within law enforcement agencies has strong links to the racialization of crime by the media. Several studies (Mosher, 1998; Henry and Tator, 2003; Wortley, 2002; Benjamin, 2002, 2003; Jiwani, 2002; Doran, 2002) all demonstrate that both print and electronic media represent and reinforce images of Blacks as criminally prone social threats. Blacks and other people of colour are represented as part of a collectivity of deviant "others." The studies show that in 90 percent of cases in which African Canadians are portrayed they are associated with street crime, sports, and entertainment. They are commonly portrayed as causing problems in an otherwise orderly civil society. Wortley (2002) points out that law enforcement practices have a significant impact on the reporting of crime news. He suggests that "the police are a primary news filter and thus have the power to decide what crimes and crime details will be presented to the media" (2002:75). It can be argued that constant and pervasive media negative messages and images about minorities can strongly impact upon how police see and interact with people of colour, and particularly Blacks.

Underpolicing

Minority experiences and perceptions relate not only to situations of overpolicing. Members of racial minorities have consistently alleged that police often underpolice them—that is, police fail to protect them adequately or to respond to their requests for assistance. The Task Force on Race Relations and Policing in Ontario (C. Lewis, 1992) found, for example, that racial-minority battered women believed they received less sensitivity from police than White females who had been abused. They alleged that police were particularly slow in responding to their calls and that many seemed to believe they somehow liked or deserved abuse from men.

Another example of the potential of underpolicing is the length of time police take to respond to hate activity directed at people of colour. Again, anecdotal evidence has suggested long delays before the police have appeared. The result is that eyewitnesses may have forgotten details or, even worse, can no longer be contacted. In some instances, the attitude and manner of the police have left victims feeling that they were to blame for the harassment they had suffered. Similar incidents are experienced by Aboriginal people, as noted in this quote from the Royal Commission on Aboriginal Peoples:

If an Aboriginal woman calls the police because she is being assaulted, she is not always treated in the same manner as a non-Aboriginal woman making the same call. When we talk to women about calling the police for assistance, very often their response is, "Why bother, they will probably just ask me if I was drinking." Our women get this treatment from all aspects of the system. (*Report of the Royal Commission on Aboriginal Peoples*, 1996)

One of the more blatant and appalling examples of underpolicing is the Osborne case in Manitoba. In November 1971, several White youths gang-raped and murdered Helen Betty Osborne, a Cree teenager in The Pas. Not until a reinvestigation 16 years later, in 1987, was one youth sentenced to life imprisonment, one companion acquitted, and a third granted immunity from prosecution for testifying. A subsequent inquiry revealed details of complicity between the RCMP and "respectable" White townspeople so that details of the original case were not investigated or made known (Province of Manitoba, 1991).

Professional Competence

When there is antipathy between the police and people of colour, mutual stereotypes, reinforced by ignorance, misunderstanding, and serious incidents of conflict can develop that are unhelpful to both groups. The knowledge that police officers have about the communities and peoples they are policing is too often acquired only after they arrive in the community (Griffiths and Verdun-Jones, 1994). One of the findings of an inquiry into policing the Blood tribe in Alberta was that, although RCMP officers had not demonstrated any conscious bias in their interactions with band members, their behaviour was often perceived as insensitive and disrespectful.

In their submissions to the Ontario Task Force on Race Relations and Policing, "Ontario's police made it exceedingly clear that they consider themselves to be professionals. Members of the public, for their part, were no less adamant in demanding that police behave professionally" (C. Lewis, 1992). Although, as the task force noted, what each considered this to mean was an open question, the equitable treatment of the public they serve must be accepted as one of the basic yardsticks of professional conduct.

The police are constantly required to deal with an increasingly diverse public in situations in which the need for communication is matched only by manifold possibilities for confusion and insensitivity. In commenting on the gross deficiencies of police race-relations training in Ontario, Stephen Lewis, in his report to the premier of Ontario following the Yonge Street disturbances on May 4, 1992, stated:

> The situation, it seems to me, is grossly unfair to the police and to new recruits in particular. We have a society of immense diversity, with a complex proliferation of multiracial and multicultural sensibilities, and we don't prepare our police for dealing with it. These are areas where the exercise of judgement, and the development of skills for conflict resolution become every bit as important as the grasp of sophisticated technology. If we really believe in investing in our justice system, then the people who are on the front-lines deserve the best training possible. It is ultimately a test of management.[2] (S. Lewis, 1992)

It is doubtful that such shifts have occurred.

Representation

So, while there has been widespread agreement that the composition of police forces should reflect the makeup of the general population, it clearly does not. In 1998, while there were significant variations across the country, the greatest representation was in the Toronto Police Service, with just over 7.4 percent. However, in this city, people of colour now represent 50 percent of the available labour pool. More recent figures place the Toronto Police Services as having about 10 percent of its total population of over 5000 as visible minority. Less than 4 percent of the Montreal Urban Community Police Service were in this category and about 7 percent of the Vancouver Police Service were visible minorities (Stenning, 2003). At the managerial level in the Toronto police, only 7 percent were minorities, and most of them in junior management positions. In 2001, 57 of 332 recruits in Toronto (or 15 percent of the total of new hirings) represented people of colour. In 2002 they represented 11 percent of new recruits (*Toronto Star*, October 19, 2002:13). Police forces are clearly out of step with the general labour market. No police force in Canada has a complement of racial-minority employees close to parity with any reasonable community population or workforce criteria.

By the late 1970s, there was a general recognition that many police recruitment and hiring criteria and practices were inherently discriminatory. For example, height and weight restrictions that had no direct relationship to effective job performance unfairly discriminated against people of colour who were smaller in stature than other groups. Many tests and other entry criteria heavily favoured White, middle-class, Canadian-born and Canadian-educated applicants. Even the advertising of careers in police work was carried out in media that did not reach large segments of the racial-minority audience.

Accordingly, a number of police forces undertook special efforts to attract people of colour to police work, and the rate of recruitment improved. By the late 1970s, the Metropolitan Toronto Police, for example, began to advertise career opportunities in media aimed at minority groups. Many aspects of assessment tests and entry criteria for acceptance were adjusted. Minority police officers were given a higher profile. While all police services in the country have proactive recruitment policies and procedures in place, impediments continue to exist that make recruiting (and retaining) minority officers difficult. Some of these impediments are the attitudes of individual police officers revealed in overt manifestations of racism, such as verbal slurs or discriminatory acts by supervisors. Others include negative perceptions of policing among many racial-minority communities, which may make police work an unattractive career choice for them. Many racial-minority communities have a very different notion of the nature of policing from that generally understood by the police in Canada. For example, a study of police recruitment of minorities conducted in New York City (Hunt and Cohen, 1971) found fundamental differences in the perceptions of the police role between Whites and racial minorities. Minorities found the service aspects of police work more important than the pay, fringe benefits, or job security, compared with Whites. Whites, on the other hand, were attracted to police work by the concepts of law and order; minorities found this work repugnant. Minorities saw policing as an opportunity to help and serve others rather than simply to enforce the law. Moreover, there are fairly negative attitudes toward policing as a professional career in many of the cultural communities now making their home in Canadian cities. Some come from societies in which the police were active agents of oppression, while other groups such as Blacks from the Caribbean and Africa have experienced racial profiling or racism at the hands of the police here. Their distrust prevents many young people from considering policing as a career and, in addition, they fear the negative reactions from their communities who perceive them as "sellouts."

Minority-group representation in police forces continues to be low, especially in the upper ranks. And, while obvious attention must be spent to the recruitment and hiring of minority police officers, an important corollary is retaining them in the force once they have been hired.

Complaints Process

There has been a persistent community demand for independent civilian review boards to investigate complaints against the police. Not only should there be an impartial and fair complaints procedure in which citizens can feel free to voice their grievances, but the police force should not be placed in the untenable position of investigating itself.

The lack of an effective, impartial, and independent complaints procedure is viewed as a major stumbling block in ensuring not only that police treat all members of the community in a non-discriminatory manner, but also that there are credible avenues of recourse available when individuals are unfairly treated. When this doesn't exist, minorities feel considerable distrust in the integrity and openness of the process.

When discussing feelings of distrust, a number of statements to the OHRC Inquiry on Racial Profiling also mentioned that filers lacked access to the processes that have been implemented to receive complaints. Witnesses stated that they were unaware of their rights, were unaware of how to complain, or felt they were prevented or discouraged from filing. They also lacked confidence in the complaints process, as they perceived it to lack independence and the probable unsatisfactory outcome further compounded their sense of mistrust or injustice.

Use of Force

Any discussion of policing must include the recognition of the extraordinary powers of police. Officers are empowered by law to interfere with individual liberty in the most severe ways. They have the power to question, stop, search, use force, and kill people. This extreme power is sanctioned by the state, and therefore the police are the very real front-line enforcers of state power (Community Coalition Concerned about Civilian Oversight of Police, 1997).

Police shootings of Blacks in major urban centres such as Montreal and Toronto in recent years have brought the entire policing system under increasing suspicion by the Black community. Given the spate of police shootings of Blacks, the police use of firearms is of grave concern. The Lewis Task Force in Ontario recommended that police officers be limited to the use of deadly weapons in a "fleeing offender" situation and that the use of deadly force be limited to situations in which the fleeing person poses an immediate threat of death to police officers or others.

Race Relations Policies

Notwithstanding their sometimes inappropriate responses to crisis situations, police forces across Canada have implemented some of the recommendations contained in the numerous studies and reports produced over the past two decades that have addressed the issue of police-race relations. The major areas in which efforts have been made include policy, training of officers, improvement of ethno-racial representation in the forces, community relations, the complaints process, and the use of force.

Policy statements are important in providing a foundation for policy and program development and as a reference point for service delivery. They also provide a clear public message of a corporate commitment to improving racial equity.

In Ontario, a race relations policy for police services was adopted in 1993. This was in direct response to the recommendation of the Lewis Task Force on Race Relations and Policing for a policy to assist police services in Ontario with race relations initiatives and to enhance community policing. Lewis also recommended that the policy be credible to all partner groups, clearly oppose racism and discrimination in the practice of policing, and promote a service orientation to policing (C. Lewis, 1992).

The first statement of the policy defines the essence of the document: "The right of all Ontarians to equal rights and opportunities is enshrined in federal and provincial law." It goes on to articulate key principles of racial equality and fairness, community service and community policing, and accountability. More particularly, the policy makes the following commitments:[3]

- Personnel at all levels, uniformed and civilian, must clearly understand that racially discriminatory behaviour, such as racial harassment, racial name-calling, racist graffiti, racial jokes, or racially biased hiring, is not tolerated and is considered grounds for disciplinary measures consistent with the Police Services Act.

- Police procedures and practices in every area of operations and administration— such as response to calls, investigation and arrest, crowd control, recruiting, hiring and promotion—must be free of discriminatory elements.

- The work force at all levels, whether uniformed or civilian, should reflect the racial diversity of the community.

- Personnel at all levels, both uniformed and civilian, must

  – understand racism in all its forms—overt, covert, and systemic—and have the skills to ensure that it is not manifested in their behaviour or any systems they manage;

  – understand, be sensitive to, and work positively with racial and cultural differences among people in the community and within the police service itself; and

  – understand the principles of community policing and have the skills to implement them in their areas of responsibility.

- Mechanisms must be in place to promote and facilitate active, meaningful participation by the community, including racial minorities and Aboriginal peoples, in the planning of police services and the implementation and monitoring of this policy.

- Mechanisms for addressing racial complaints within the workplace or by members of the public against police personnel should be in place, known and accessible to citizens and police service personnel.

- All segments of the community and all police service personnel must be informed about this policy and its implementation.

In commenting on the police officers' familiarity with the race relations policy of the Metropolitan Toronto Police Force, Andrews (1992) found "a surprising variation in the level of familiarity. ... Many police constables at the Divisional level were not familiar with the contents or intent of the total Policy. ... There are no operating standards specified for the Policy so that compliance depended more on common sense situational application than it did upon statements of procedures."

Andrews also noted with surprise that among community groups there was not as much familiarity with the policy as one might expect. He suggested that while it may be important to have statements of policy or intent, it is the impact of these statements on police behaviour that is more important to the community. Apparently there continues to be a huge gap between "policy as it is written" and "policy in practice."

Training

Training has been viewed as the primary remedy for improved "police-race relations" in Canada. Police-race relations training programs have been delivered across Canada under the labels of "human awareness," "cross-cultural," "intercultural," "cultural awareness," "anti-racism," "native awareness," "community relations," "managing diversity," "organizational management," and "legislative compliance" training, and many more labels, as well as many combinations of the above.

The development of police-race relations training has undergone an evolution. Most of the present programs in Canada were derived from two basic premises, interrelated and pragmatic in concept. The first was that only those police officers who came into daily contact with racial minorities needed to be trained. The second, which followed from the first, was that the purpose of such training was to equip police to "understand" minorities better and thus be able to deal more effectively with them. In other words "we" were being trained to deal with "them." An acceptance of these premises also suggested there was a definable body of information that could be transmitted in the traditional way to those who "needed" it. This in turn allowed one to assume that only a few sessions were necessary in which to transmit it through lectures and handouts and that it could be delivered by in-house training "experts."

Focusing simply on minorities' cultural and religious backgrounds is acknowledged today by many police trainers as an inadequate basis for training. Training emphasizing the knowledge aspect of race relations effectively ruled out a study of the complexities of personal and professional attitudes and behaviours and the ways in which a police force needed to adapt to a multiracial society.

An initial purpose of some race relations training was to make White attitudes toward Black people more "tolerant" and "sympathetic." Research on effectiveness of training for improving interracial attitudes shows very mixed results; attitudinal training, racial awareness training, or self-awareness training have only been found to be of value to policing if they are linked to the learning of effective skills. Such awareness training may make police personnel more open to learning, but there is still a need for more behaviourally oriented training. The most effective training models have been found to be those that are related to specific policing situations and that identify ways of reacting to these circumstances.

Notwithstanding the massive human and financial resources being expended on such training programs, they have still not received the kind of rigorous scrutiny demanded. As Nadine Peppard has said, "the field of race relations training remains largely unexplored and ... little thought has been given to what the objectives of such training should be" (Peppard, 1983). These comments are perhaps even truer today than when they were first made in 1983. While there is increasing pressure for much more police-race relations training, there is still no clear answer to the question of what, if any, effect race relations training has on police officers.

The effects of training are difficult to isolate and measure. Impact may be minimal in any case, when compared to the effects of learning by experience and absorbing the values of the police occupational culture. Is it realistic to hope for any meaningful improvements in police-race relations as a result of training? Too many programs have been poorly coordinated, superficial in content, and apparently ineffective. There are many reasons for this. First, there is no clear agreement as to what the goals are, except at the most general levels. Second, training has been provided in an organizational environment that has not always been particularly supportive. With few exceptions, there have not been the kinds of tangible organizational support systems and resources to put anti-racism and equity policies into meaningful policing practices that can reinforce training. Third, there is confusion on whether attitudes, knowledge, or skills should be taught. Most of the training efforts seem to be dictated by some abstract notion of the general desirability of providing enlightenment on racial matters, not by the actual work-related requirements of policing. Finally, it was underscored in several studies and reports examining the subject of identifying effective models of anti-racism training in the United States, the United Kingdom, and Canada, that those delivering training should include highly skilled and experienced external trainers. It was also recommended that formal procedures related to the operational impact of training be evaluated (see Smith, 2004).

Representation of Minorities

What has been done to ensure that the recruitment and promotional processes of Canadian police forces will make them more representative of the multiracial population they serve?

Both Andrews and S. Lewis (1992) concluded that even the most advanced employment equity efforts would not significantly improve the racial diversity of police forces. Long debated and resisted in police circles is the consideration of such additional options as lateral entry, direct entry, and the application of innovative career-path plans such as the permanent specialization of uniformed officers, particularly at higher levels. As Andrews (1992) noted, other highly structured institutions, such as the military, have dealt with the need for and use of different skill sets in a very different way than police forces have. That fact alone makes it very difficult to accept the rationale that there are no alternatives to the present structure.

Community Relations

A number of forces across Canada have implemented a variety of models of community policing and programs to "improve police-community race relations." Most of the programs have been designed primarily to improve the image of the police in the community. Many of them have depended on external sources of funding, and very few have been adequately evaluated as to their actual impact on police-minority relations. Police-community race relations have largely been characterized by public criticism of the police, on the one hand, and police efforts to counter that criticism, on the other.

Police-community relations programs have traditionally been developed by the police as a response to resolving police-community conflict. Programs emanating from this process have generally been designed to improve community attitudes, opinions, and perceptions of the police through the provision of information, through "opportunities for positive police-community contact." They have generally not involved discussions around basic police practices and enforcement policy.

When image improvement is the basic thrust of most police-community relations programs, it is not surprising that these programs have not generally led to direct and meaningful involvement of citizens in police policy-making. Minority groups, by their very nature, may also tend to find it difficult to use the formal political process to express concerns about discriminatory police conduct (Davis, 1993). Other factors that contribute to this lack of effective public participation are the lack of support from police leadership and the rank and file for this kind of involvement, and the lack of understanding among police personnel about the benefits of such programs.

A number of police services have established various forms of advisory or consultative groups. These too have suffered criticism, being perceived as cosmetic exercises, comprising unrepresentative sections of the community, whose meetings are controlled by the police and run to a narrow crime agenda, and with little feedback to the wider community.

Tensions between racial-minority and Aboriginal communities and policing systems continue relatively unabated. Noted criminologist Philip Stenning concludes:

> Over the last 40 years, a variety of initiative and activities have taken place at both the Policy and operational levels to better equip Canadian police services for meeting the challenges of policing in a multicultural society ... while few would doubt the sincerity and good intentions of the initiatives, they have achieved limited success in meeting their stated objectives. Canada still experiences significant problems and tension between and within its diverse race, ethnic, cultural, and religious communities and between members of these communities and its police services. This is also true with respect to its Aboriginal population. (2003:87)

Summary

This chapter has highlighted some of the barriers used by policing institutions in Canada in not dealing with racism. These discourses have included:

- *The discourse of accountability:* The police have generally articulated their accountability to the laws and regulations they enforce. It is to the formalized community standards, as expressed in the laws of the land, that the police feel they are accountable, rather than to the public they serve. Demands for greater public accountability have therefore been seen as challenging the maintenance of law and order and therefore constituting a threat to the state.
- *The discourse of denial:* The notion of racism in the provision of policing services has generally been dismissed only by admissions that unfortunately there may be the occasional "bad apple."
- *The discourse of "blame the victim":* The provision of policing services to all sectors of society is presumed to be provided and applied equally and neutrally. Therefore, if charges tend to be proportionately more frequently laid against Blacks or Aboriginal people, it is because they are more criminally inclined. Such a conclusion ignores the discretionary changes in policing priorities and strategies, overpolicing, differential treatment, and many other factors. But the fact that these groups are now overrepresented in the criminal justice system reinforces the need for further "overpolicing" of these communities.

This chapter also explored racism and policing by looking at the attitudes and behaviours of the police as individuals, as well as looking at the ideologies, structures, and practices of law enforcement organizations. The conflictual relationship between police and racial minorities—particularly Aboriginal peoples and Blacks—is also demonstrated by the evidence of several task forces established to examine racism among the police.

This chapter has analyzed the many manifestations of racial bias and discrimination and showed how deeply entrenched racism is within all areas of law enforcement. Some of the critical areas discussed include the overpolicing of minority communities, the racialization of crime and the criminalization of racial minorities, the lack of police accountability, the emphasis on law and order rather than provision of service, and the professional competence of the police. The last section of the chapter summarized some of the institutional responses by the police, including training, employment equity, and models of community policing.

Notes

1. The OHRC inquiry had a broad mandate in terms of analyzing racial profiling in the context of a number of societal institutions including law enforcement, education, service providers, etc.

2. This case study is based on a research paper prepared for the Canadian Race Relations Foundation entitled *Racial Profiling in Toronto: Discourses of Domination, Mediation and Opposition* by Frances Henry and Carol Tator (March 20, 2003, available at CRRF site <http://www.crr.ca/en/Publications/ePubHome.htm>, accessed August 18, 2004).

3. When granting permission for us to reprint this excerpt, the office of the Queen's Printer for Ontario requested that we include the following note: "As a result of both the 1992 Stephen Lewis and the 1992 Clare Lewis reports on policing and race relations, Ontario took strong action to improve the training of police officers. A permanently staffed Race Relations and Adult Education unit was formed at the Ontario Police College with the responsibility of ensuring the complete integration of anti-racism and anti-discrimination training into all courses. Training for recruits was extended from 47 to 60 days in order to meet the requirements of the recommendations from both reports. In addition, training in the use of force, conflict resolution and de-escalation (including dealing with the mentally ill), use of judgement, and other related areas was strengthened. These actions exceeded the recommendations contained in both reports."

References

Abel, J., and E. Sheehy. (1996). *Criminal Law and Procedure: Cases, Context, Critique.* Toronto: Captus Press.

Andrews, A. (1992). *Review of Race Relations Practices of the Metropolitan Toronto Police Force.* Toronto: Municipality of Metropolitan Toronto.

Bellamare, J. (1988). *Investigation into Relations Between the Police Forces, Visible and Other Ethnic Minorities.* Montreal: Commission des Droits de la Personne du Québec.

Benjamin, A. (2002). "The Social and Legal Banishment of Anti-Racism." In W. Chan and K. Mirchandani (eds.), *Crimes of Colour: Racialization and the Criminal Justice System in Canada.* Peterborough, ON: Broadview Press. 177–190.

———. (2003). "The Black/Jamaican Criminal: The Making of Ideology." Ph.D thesis.

Brown, M. (2004). *In Their Own Voices.* Report commissioned by African Canadian Community Coalition on Racial Profiling (ACCCRP) (March). Available <http://www.crr.ca/en/default.htm>, accessed August 18, 2004.

Canadian Press. (2004). "Officer Says He Can't Remember." *Leader-Post* (March 19).

Cashmore, E., and E. McLaughlin (eds.). (1991). *Out of Order: Policing Black People.* London: Routledge.

Cashmore, E. (2001). *Racism: Essential Readings.* London: Thousand Oaks, Sage.

Chan, J. (1997). *Changing Police Culture in a Multicultural Society.* Cambridge UK: Cambridge University Press.

Commission on First Nations and Métis Peoples and Justice Reform. (2004). *Legacy of Hope.* Saskatoon: Province of Saskatchewan. Available <http://www.justicereformcomm.sk.ca/volume1.gov>, accessed August 18, 2004.

Community Coalition Concerned About Civilian Oversight of Police. (1997). *In Search of Police Accountability.* Toronto.

Crank, J. (1998). *Understanding Police Culture.* Cincinnati, OH: Anderson.

Davis, K. (1993). "Controlling Racial Discrimination in Policing." *University of Toronto Faculty of Law Review* 51(2)(Spring):179.

Doran, "Nob" C. (2002). "Making Sense of Moral Panics: Excavating the Cultural Foundations of the 'Young, Black Mugger.'" In W. Chan and K. Mirchandani (eds.), *Crimes of Colour: Racialization and the Criminal Justice System in Canada.* Toronto: Broadview Press. 157–176.

Gilroy, P. (1987). *There Ain't No Black in the Union Jack.* Chicago: University of Chicago Press.

Goldsmith, A. (1991). *Complaints Against the Police: The Trend to External Review.* Oxford: Clarendon Press.

Grayson, P. (1998). *Social Report Card.* Toronto: Institute for Social Research, York University.

Griffiths, C., and S. Verdun-Jones. (1994). *Canadian Criminal Justice.* Toronto: Harcourt Brace.

Hall, S., C. Critcher, T. Jefferson, J. Clarke, and B. Roberts. (1978). *Policing the Crisis: Mugging, the State and Law and Order.* London: Macmillan Press.

Henry, F., and C. Tator. (2003). *Racial Profiling in Toronto: Discourses of Domination, Mediation and Opposition.* Toronto: Canadian Race Relations Foundation.

Hunt, I.C., and B. Cohen. (1971). *Minority Recruiting in the New York City Police Department.* New York: Rand.

Jiwani, Y. (2002). "The Criminalization of Race/The Racialization of Crime." In W. Chan and

K. Mirchandani (eds.), *Crimes of Colour: Racialization and the Criminal Justice System in Canada.* Toronto: Broadview Press. 67–86.

Law Reform Commission of Canada. (1991). *Report on Aboriginal Peoples and Criminal Justice.* Ottawa.

Lewis, C. (1992). *Report of the Task Force on Race Relations and Policing.* Toronto: Government of Ontario.

Lewis, S. (1992). *Report to the Premier on Race Relations.* Toronto. Excerpt reproduced with permission from the Queen's Printer for Ontario.

Metropolitan Toronto Police Association. (1992). "Brief to the Solicitor General of Ontario." November 11.

Mosher, C. (1998). *Discrimination and Denial: Systemic Racism in Ontario's Legal and Criminal Justice Systems 1892–1961.* Toronto: University of Toronto Press.

Ontario Human Rights Commission. (2003). *Paying the Price: The Human Cost of Racial Profiling.* October 21. Toronto.

Peppard, N. (1983). "Race Relations Training." *Currents: Readings in Race Relations* (Toronto) 1(3):6–11.

Province of Manitoba. (1991). *Report of the Aboriginal Justice Inquiry of Manitoba.* Winnipeg.

Province of Nova Scotia. (1989). *Report of the Royal Commission on the Donald Marshall Jr. Prosecution: Findings and Recommendations.* Vol. 1. Halifax.

Province of Ontario. (1995). *Report of the Commission on Systemic Racism in the Ontario Criminal Justice System.* Toronto.

Reiman, J. (1984). *The Rich Get Richer and the Poor Get Prison.* New York: Macmillan.

Report of the Royal Commission on Aboriginal Peoples. (1996). Ottawa: Minister of Supply and Services.

Roberg, R., and J. Kuykendall. (1993). *Police and Society.* Belmont, CA: Wadsworth Publishing.

Russell, K. (1998). *The Colour of Crime: Racial Hoaxes, White Fear, Black Protectionism, Police Harassment, and Other Macroaggressions.* New York and London: New York University Press.

Skolnick, J.H. (1996). *Justice Without Trial: Law Enforcement in a Democratic Society.* New York: John Wiley and Sons.

Smith, C. (2004). *Crisis, Conflict and Accountability.* Report commissioned by African Canadian Community Coalition on Racial Profiling (ACCCRP) (March). Available <http://www.crr.ca/en/default.htm>, accessed August 18, 2004.

Stenning, P. (1994). "Police Use of Force and Violence Against Members of Visible Minority Groups in Canada." Ottawa: Canadian Centre of Police-Race Relations.

———. (1998). "Reclaiming Policing Back on to the Community and Municipal Agenda." *Currents: Readings in Race Relations* (Toronto) 9(2):28–31. Urban Alliance on Race Relations.

———. (2003). "Policing the Cultural Kaleidoscope: Recent Canadian Experience." *Police & Society* 7:21–87.

Sukahara, D. (1992). "Public Inquiries into Policing." *Canadian Police College Journal* 16:135–36.

Ungerleider, C. (1992a). "Intercultural Awareness and Sensitivity of Canadian Police Officers." *Canadian Public Administration* 32(4)(Winter):612–22.

———. (1992b). "Issues in Police Intercultural and Race Relations Training in Canada." Ottawa: Solicitor General of Canada. Excerpt reproduced with the permission of the Minister of Public Works and Government Services Canada, 1999.

van Dijk, T. (1991). *Racism and the Press.* London: Routledge.

Waddington, P.A. (1999). "Police (Canteen) Sub-culture." *British Journal of Criminology* 39(2)(Spring):287–302.

Wortley, S. (2002). "Misrepresentation or Reality? The Depiction of Race and Crime in the Toronto Print Media." In B. Schissel and C. Brooks (eds.), *Marginality and Condemnation: An Introduction to Critical Criminology.* Halifax: Fernwood. 55–80.

———. (2003). (Forthcoming). "The Usual Suspects: Race, Police Contact and Perceptions of Criminal Injustice." Criminology." Available <http://www.canadianheritage.gc.ca/progs/multi/pubs/police/civil_e.pdf>, accessed August 18, 2004.

York, D. (1994). *Cross Cultural Training Programs.* Westport CT: Bergin and Garvey.

CHAPTER 7

RACISM AND HUMAN-
SERVICE DELIVERY

*No amount of tinkering can fix the problem. What is required is a massive shift in
attitudes, a revolution which would see a multifaceted approach, including full funding for
ethnocultural and racial-community agencies and a decision-making process that is
controlled by people truly representative of the population.*

—*Minna (1991)*

This chapter examines the dynamics of individual, institutional, and cultural racism
as they are reflected in the policies and practices of traditional, mainstream, human-
service organizations. Included in the analysis are a wide range of human services
provided by social and health care agencies such as family- and child-service agencies,
mental-health clinics, health care services, child-care facilities, and child welfare agencies.
Although it does not specifically consider other human services such as community health
clinics and community or recreational centres, the issues are very much the same in these
settings.

This chapter also looks briefly at the critical challenges confronting ethno-cultural
and racial-community-based organizations that are attempting to meet the needs of specific constituencies such as immigrants, refugees, African Canadians, Chinese, South
Asians, and other communities. Some barriers that affect the delivery of service are analyzed, including lack of representation of people of colour in mainstream human-service
organizations; the marginalization and differential treatment experienced by racial-
minority practitioners in these agencies; and the racist ideology underpinning the provision of services and modes of treatment. Case Study 7.1 dealing with the SARS crisis in
Toronto illustrates how quickly a health crisis can become a catalyst for a "moral panic,"
and the racialization of an ethno-racial minority community. Case Study 7.2 about a
women's hostel, Nellie's, provides the reader with a clear illustration of how racism, in its
many dimensions, operates in the context of a human-service agency.

Introduction

As is the case with other Canadian institutions and systems (e.g., education, law enforcement, government agencies, media), a growing body of evidence indicates that racist ideologies and practices affect the administration and operation of human-service organizations; the delivery of services to individual clients and communities; the allocation of resources, training, and education programs; and the access and participation of people of colour as clients or patients, managers, staff, and volunteers.

The Manifestations of Racism

Racial and cultural barriers influence the provision of services and the quality and appropriateness of those services. Racial bias and discrimination can be reflected in the allocation of resources by funders, who may ignore the dramatic rise in immigrants and refugees in recent decades and the particular needs of racial-minority groups and the agencies that serve them. An aspect of racism may be reflected in the view of funders that racially specific services are an unnecessary duplication of the programs and services offered by mainstream agencies.

Racist assumptions and practices may also influence the employment opportunities for minority social workers and health care practitioners. Professional credentials acquired in other countries, for example, may not be recognized in Canada. Professional competency is therefore measured by standards and norms that undervalue the training received by many members of racial minorities.

Racial bias may also be reflected in the modes of treatment and approaches to problem resolution, which may ignore the effects of systemic racism on the client or fail to take into account cultural values, community norms, and indigenous resources. Racism may also influence the common assumption that views racial minorities from a "problem" perspective—either they have problems, or they are the cause of problems. A further example of racism commonly found in human-service organizations is the failure to provide services that are racially sensitive, culturally appropriate, and linguistically accessible.

The disempowering effects of racism in human-service organizations may be compounded when a person of colour is also an immigrant or refugee. The effect of this double group identification is even greater marginalization and disadvantage. Women of colour who are immigrants are particularly vulnerable, as are the elderly.

MANIFESTATIONS OF RACISM IN HUMAN SERVICES

Lack of inadequate pre-service and in-service anti-racism training for social work and health care practitioners and administrators

Lack of access to appropriate programs and services

Ethnocentric values and counselling practices

Devaluing of the skills and credentials of minority practitioners

Inadequate funding for ethno-racial community-based agencies

Lack of minority representation at all levels in social agencies

Monocultural or ad hoc multicultural models of service delivery

Processes of racialization embedded in everyday discourses of Whiteness (e.g., discourses of denial, colour-blindness, universalism, cultural sensitivity)

A number of studies have drawn attention to these and other pervasive racial barriers, which exist in almost all the major traditional, mainstream, human-service delivery organizations across Canada (N. Razack, 2002; Razack and Jeffery, 1999; Calliste, 1996; Christensen, 1996, 1999; Shakir, 1995).

Education and Training

The socialization of professionals in any sector strongly influences how an individual social worker, doctor, lawyer, judge, journalist, police officer, cultural administrator, or corporate executive addresses everyday issues within his or her work world. In other words, what is learned in training will have a powerful influence on how issues such as racism and other forms of oppression are dealt with. The question that follows is: How well do Canadian universities prepare students for the realities of a country divided by colour, culture, and class, among other social markers of "difference"?

In the context of human-service practitioners, few undergraduate and postgraduate educational programs provide the knowledge and skills necessary for social workers, doctors, nurses, and other human-service professionals from the dominant culture to confront racism in their professional values, norms, and practices and in the broader society. For example, faculties of social work, medicine, and nursing have resisted incorporating into their core curriculum the study of racism. Moreover, the theories, methodologies, and traditional skills taught in these programs often bear little relation to the needs of clients from diverse racial and cultural backgrounds (Roger, 2000; Razack and Jeffery, 1999; Christensen, 1996; Shakir, 1995). An earlier exploratory survey of a Task Force on Multicultural and Multiracial Issues in Social Work Education found that most accredited schools of social work in Canadian universities do not offer courses dealing with multicultural and multiracial issues (Canadian Association of Schools of Social Work, 1991). As a result of interviews with students, faculty, field instructors, administrators, and community representatives, the task force recommended changes to accreditation standards related to organizational structures, policies, curriculum content, student body, faculty, fieldwork, and community accountability.

However, despite the passage of time, most faculties of social work have resisted these structural and pedagogical changes. Mandatory courses on anti-racism and anti-oppression have not been incorporated into core curriculum (Canadian Association of Schools of Social Work, 1999; Christensen, 1996). Some faculties have added optional courses that focus on ethno-racial diversity such as "cultural awareness" or "ethnic sensitivity" models of social work. These models generally have failed to examine the assimilationist assumptions of social-work practice upon which these approaches are based. Whiteness still prevails in relation to ideologies and theories underpinning the teaching and practice of social work and health care (Yee Ying and Dumbrill, 2003; Christensen, 2003). Hidden assumptions within models of multicultural, cultural literacy, or culturally "sensitive" approaches to delivery of services include the practitioner as expert with superior knowledge and culture as a static and homogeneous system (Al-Krenawi and Graham, 2003).

Another measure of determining how deeply racism penetrates any professional group is an analysis of the actual body of knowledge that underpins the training of its practitioners, in terms of both pre-service education and ongoing professional development. A major survey of social-work literature, including most of the major journals in the field (McMahon and Allen-Meares, 1992), revealed that racism is deeply embedded in the theoretical and ideological frameworks underlying the practice of social work. The authors of the content analysis of over one hundred articles suggest that social-work literature conveys the impression of a non-critical and inward-looking professional literature. Central to the literature is the belief that immigrants and minorities should assimilate into the mainstream dominant culture.

This fault line continues to exist. Rather than focusing on anti-racism, the pervading models of "good practice" seem to focus on individual interventions with minority clients to assist them in adapting to their oppressive situation, or alternatively to "sensitize" social workers to the "different" cultural values and beliefs of minorities. Most of the literature ignores the macro issues of racism as a systemic phenomenon and shows a general resistance to undertaking proactive transformative actions within a macro context. For example, Este and Thomas Bernard's (2003) review of social literature used in the majority of Canadian schools of social work would lead one to conclude that African Canadians and Caribbean Canadians are an "invisible population." A similar conclusion could be made about other major ethno-racial populations such as South Asians, Southeast Asians, etc. In most of the education and training programs that are provided to health care and human-service providers, there continues to be an absence of critical engagement with the issues of racism and its intersection with other forms of oppression, the relationship between these dynamics and the development of professional knowledge and skills that will be applied to their everyday work worlds, or an exploration of the processes by which unequal power relations are maintained and reinforced. There is little evidence that students are being given sufficient opportunity to study and then apply the theories of racialization, the historical legacies of racism and other forms of domination, or their impact on human services in a culturally pluralistic and racially divided society. Whiteness as ideology and pedagogy continues to permeate the learning environments where social workers, physicians, nurses, psychologists, and other human-service practitioners develop their professional credentials. However, there are some indicators that anti-racism is on the agenda of some educational training programs (Yee Ying and Dumbrill, 2003; N. Razack, 2002; Hagey and MacKay, 2000).

In 1999, the Project on Anti-racist Training and Materials was developed as the second phase of the Task Force on Multicultural and Multiracial Issues in Social Work Education. The Project is directed at identifying changes to the status of anti-racism education within schools of social work across Canada. Not all schools have joined the project. Efforts to try to implement structural and pedagogical changes in the context of anti-racism have met with resistance (Canadian Association of Schools of Social Work, 1999; N. Razack, 2002).

Some nursing programs have also tried to incorporate these anti-racism approaches into their curricula, and there is a small but growing number of nursing scholars drawing upon anti-racism, anti-oppression, and postcolonial feminist discourse as a way of challenging dominant discourses in health care (Anderson and Reimer Kirkham, 2000; Hagey and MacKay, 2000).

Access to Services

Evidence of the failure of traditional, mainstream social and health care agencies is provided by the findings of numerous task forces and consultations undertaken to assess the quality and accessibility of care and services provided to racial and ethno-cultural client groups by traditional human-service agencies (Shakir, 1995; British Columbia Task Force on Family Violence, 1992; Medeiros, 1991).

One of the first studies on the issue of access was published by the Social Planning Council of Metropolitan Toronto (Doyle and Visano, 1987). The findings suggested that while access to basic social and health services is a form of universal entitlement, mainstream agencies in the human-service delivery system failed to provide accessible and equitable services. The researchers identified many linguistic, cultural, and racial barriers and discriminatory practices, as well as an absence of strategies to address these obstacles. They found institutional discrimination reflected in indifferent attitudes and a lack of commitment to seek remedies for patterns of exclusion and inaccessibility. Christensen (2003) and others contend the same formal and informal barriers to equal access to services, opportunity, resources, and power remain constant more than twenty-five years later.

Some of the barriers to health and social services identified by minority-group clients included: lack of information about the services provided; the unavailability of service; the service providers' lack of knowledge of the linguistic and cultural needs of different groups; and the inappropriateness of treatment modes and counselling. There is a widespread perception that the difference in racial and cultural backgrounds between clients and White, Anglo human-service professionals frequently resulted in misconceptions and negative judgments by service providers. All these problems are made more acute by the general problems all consumers experience, such as child-care and transportation costs, lengthy delays, and physical distance from agencies. Another significant finding in both the earlier studies and current literature is the existence of "two solitudes," in which mainstream agencies and ethno-racial services exist side by side, with little interaction and coordination in planning and delivering services. ("Mainstream" agencies offer services to anyone in the community who meets general eligibility criteria; "ethno-racial" agencies provide services to people on the basis of membership in a particular racial or cultural group.)

Ethno-racial organizations act as brokers and advocates for minority populations by providing settlement and integration services, language interpretation for mainstream agencies, family counselling, and so on. Support services are offered in which practitioners from agencies accompany clients to other organizations, assist in helping interpret their needs, and represent them and their interests. These services exist largely because of the failure of traditional organizations to adequately respond to the changing needs of a multiracial and pluralistic society. Services provided by many ethno-racial agencies that are often absent in the mainstream agencies include more flexible hours, with evening and weekend service; drop-in services; locations in accessible, informal settings, such as community centres; home visits; community outreach; advertising of services in the multicultural media; and group counselling (Bridgman, 1993).

Racial-Minority Professionals in Mainstream Human-Service Organizations

People of colour who are professionals working in human-service organizations often confront biases, barriers, and conflicts totally unknown to mainstream practitioners. A study in Nova Scotia (Bambrough, Bowden, and Wien, 1992) revealed that Black social-work graduates from the Maritime School of Social Work found less desirable jobs than others, including limited or term positions and more part-time jobs. Moreover, once they obtained work, they found that their opportunities for advancement were relatively limited and their salary levels low. The report concluded that Black graduate social workers had been less successful than the majority group in accessing the more prestigious social-work jobs, including family counselling, hospital social work, and administrative or supervisory positions.

Another formidable manifestation of bias frequently encountered by minority workers is the fact that the knowledge, skills, and experience they have acquired in their home countries may not be recognized or may be significantly undervalued. Degrees earned abroad are often not accredited, and foreign-trained graduates have no access to retraining (Ontario Ministry of Citizenship, 1989). Fifteen years after the Task Force on Access to Professions and Trades in Ontario was concluded—with numerous recommendations and strategies for effectively assessing the skills and experience of immigrants—there is still no formal implementation of its recommendations.

A related concern is the fragile position of community workers, who play a pivotal role in providing services to racial and ethno-cultural communities but do not have formal degrees or certificates. The implications of the regulation limiting certification to university graduates was that funding for publicly funded agencies might be contingent on hiring only those with the right credentials (Webster, 1992).

Social workers and other human-service practitioners from diverse racial and cultural communities may experience serious conflicts between their cultural values and those of the dominant culture, which influences the practices and priorities of their organization. Minority workers commonly function from a dual perspective: they understand both the needs and concerns of their own communities and the limitations of the programs of mainstream human-service organizations. On the other hand, mainstream social work and health care practitioners are trained to view their services as having universal applicability and accessibility. There is considerable pressure on racial-minority practitioners to conform to traditional agency practices (Calliste, 1996; Desai, 1996).

Within human-service agencies, increasing the number of ethno-racial staff often signals a commitment to improving services to minority clients and a commitment to multiculturalism and anti-racism. But as Turney (1997) points out, an increase in staff from a particular group does not necessarily improve service delivery. Change often remains at an administrative level without fundamentally altering the delivery of services. Minority workers are frequently isolated and marginalized in mainstream agencies. They are concentrated at the entry levels or in front-line positions. Their primary role is to serve clients who share the same racial or cultural background, but they tend to have limited power and status in the organization. This practice can result in a kind of ghettoization, especially of staff who are people of colour, where all "problems with Blacks" are referred to the Black worker (Thomas, 1987). Racist attitudes and behaviours are considered a significant barrier to good working relationships between White and minority practitioners.

Racial Minorities in the Health Care Delivery System

Head (1986) was the first scholar to examine the extent of racial discrimination in some Toronto hospitals. His research findings confirmed the general perception of racial-minority women working in these institutions: racial-minority nurses were underrepresented at the decision-making and supervisory levels. Despite having similar educational qualifications, most minority health care workers were represented in the lower levels of the hierarchy. White nurses in the sample were twice as successful in gaining promotions as Blacks were. A considerable degree of apathy, hopelessness, and fear existed among Black respondents.

Calliste (1996) analyzed racism in nursing by focusing on the experiences of African-Canadian nurses between 1990 and 1995. Calliste contends that the economic restructuring and rapid downsizing in the health care system in the 1990s combined with both old and new forms of racism to have a disproportionate impact on female health care workers of colour, particularly Black women who attempted to speak out about racism. They were more likely to be laid off, demoted, and dismissed. In recent years, Black nurses, with the support of organizations such as the Congress of Black Women, have been demanding institutional and systemic change to racism and other forms of social oppression operating in the health care system.

CASE STUDY 7.1

THE SCARS OF SARS ON THE ASIAN-CANADIAN COMMUNITY

Background

The World Health Organization (WHO) first alerted countries to the global threat of severe acute respiratory syndrome (SARS) in March 2003. The SARS outbreak started in China and was carried to Toronto by an Asian Canadian who was returning from Hong Kong. He died of the disease on March 5, 2003. From then on, Toronto became the site of a significant health crisis that lasted four months. The last reported case of SARS in Canada had onset of the illness in June, 2003 and has since recovered.

SARS is a severe form of pneumonia that affected Toronto and a number of other cities during the spring of 2003. It is believed that the illness is spread from being exposed to coughing or sneezing or from direct, face-to-face contact with a person who has SARS. There were 44 deaths, the majority of which involved health care workers in Toronto who had been exposed to patients with SARS. A number of patients and people visiting patients in hospitals died as well. As of August 2003 there were a total of 438 cases, 251 of which were probable and 187 who were suspected of having had the disease. As a basis of comparison, every year seasonal flu results in 500–1500 deaths in Canada. The SARS crisis in Toronto provides an important example of how deeply vulnerable ethno-racial minority communities are in times of crisis.

As the number of people afflicted by SARS began to escalate, including a significant number of health care workers, a "moral panic" began to descend on the city. Racial stereotyping of Asian-Canadian communities became widespread. People who looked "Asian" were stigmatized and shunned in workplaces, schools, transit, and in other public spaces. Asian-Canadian children were exposed to increased racial harassment. An MPP from Brampton (a municipality just outside of Toronto), Joe Spina, commented that SARS is linked to "the kind of immigration that comes in" (to Canada). In Toronto, many of the

Asian Canadian front-line health care workers, in addition to their daily burden of taking care of patients with SARS, and facing significant risks in caring for these patients, also had to deal with the fears and biases of their colleagues, many of whom believed Asian workers were genetically predisposed to the disease.

As the SARS crisis was winding down, several organizations from the Chinese- and Filipino-Canadian communities came together to share their experiences of how SARS had impacted them; to identify the ways in which all three levels of government had failed to alleviate the hardship faced by their communities; and to develop strategies directed at each level of government. They submitted a detailed proposal of the necessary policies and initiatives that should be implemented to respond to the physical, social, and economic consequences arising from the crisis. It was argued that the proposal, if implemented, might be used to more effectively respond to future health crises (Goosen, Pay, and Go, 2003).

Analysis

The construct of "moral panic" can be applied to the public response to the crisis caused by SARS and the way in which a genuine health crisis led to the stigmatization, marginalization, and racialization of a heterogeneous community identified as Asian. Societies appear to fall victim, from time to time, to periods of moral panic in which a group of persons comes to be defined as a threat to societal interests (Cohen, 2002). Every moral panic has its "folk devil" (ibid.:79), that is, personification of evil. The folk devil is stripped of all positive characteristics and is endowed with pejorative labels. The mass media play an important role in reinforcing these fears. In Toronto, the daily bombardment of images and discourses that reinforced the link between the disease and the Chinese, Korean, Vietnamese, and other Asian communities was insidious. Columnist Janet Wong (2003) suggests that the blaming of Canadians who look Chinese for the Toronto outbreak of SARS as the latest manifestation of the

"Yellow Peril."[1] This imagined connection between SARS and Asians became so persistent and sinister that Dr. Colin D'Cunha, Ontario's Commissioner of Public Health, issued a statement saying "SARS may have emerged in Asia, but a person of any race or colour is capable of being a carrier of this disease. It is both wrong and prejudicial to fear or shun any or all people in the Asian community based on the assumption they must have SARS" (D'Cunha, 2003). It can be argued that the long legacy of the racialization of Asian Canadians as an inferior, foreign "race" possessing cultural values and habits incompatible with Anglo-European "Canadian" traditions and values (Li, 1998) provided a fertile environment for the public concern over a serious health issue to become a vehicle for the inferiorization and stigmatization of the Asian community.

Calliste's study documents the manifestations of systemic racism experienced on the job by nurses of colour, including excessive monitoring and differential documentation. For example, personnel files for Black nurses frequently contained irrelevant personal information about their families, place of origin, and English proficiency. The study found that Black nurses were disciplined for minor or nonexistent problems for which White nurses were not disciplined. The Ontario Nursing Association (Caissey, 1994:3) also concluded that nurses of colour were often oversupervised and subjected to differential treatment and had their employment terminated more often than did White nurses. Calliste labelled this "the racialization of surveillance practices in nursing" (1996:371). In a number of interviews carried out in 1994 and 1996, Marshall and Minors (cited in Calliste, 1996) found that Black nurses were stereotyped as childlike, lazy, aggressive, uncommunicative, and troublemakers. Calliste observed, "the black woman nurse becomes an 'undesirable' identity" (1996:369). In this context, there is widespread harassment and other forms of discrimination aimed at nurses of colour by hospital management as well as patients.

Physical-Health Care Services: Access to Health Care by Immigrants, Women of Colour, and Aboriginal Women

Access to health care is a key indicator of racial and cultural equity within the human-service sector. In Canada, a society in which health care is a legislated social policy, publicly funded, and a guaranteed right, it is widely accepted that all citizens and landed immigrants have an equal opportunity to achieve optimum health. In other words, a level playing field is assumed to exist (Anderson and Reimer Kirkham, 2000). However, there is a growing body of research documenting the extent to which gender, race, culture, and class are primary determinants of the health status of both recent and long-term female immigrants, as well as women of colour born in Canada and First Nations women. In this section, some indicators of a racialized, culturalized, and gendered health care system are discussed. In accessing effective health care, recent immigrant women face triple jeopardy: as immigrant women, they may suffer from ethno-racial prejudice; also, elements of their home culture and family status may interact with their gender, reinforcing barriers to care; and, as women, they may be exposed to systemic sexist bias and discrimination (Weinfeld et al., 1998). A common theme in the research on this issue is the link between people's health and their economic status. Low-income people face greater health problems and risks and recent immigrant women are more likely to fall ill (ibid.).

In this context, it is important to note that according to analyses of 1996 and 2001 census data, the racialization of poverty in Canada is growing at a significant rate. An important study revealed huge inequalities in income, employment, education, and rates of poverty among ethno-racial groups, and particularly women (Ornstein, 2000). In many racial-minority groups, more than half the families are living below the poverty line. Within White-, European-, and British-origins groups, the rate is less than 10 percent. In our cities over 50 percent of Aboriginal people live in dire poverty. Results from the 2001 Aboriginal Peoples Survey on Health (Statistics Canada, 2001) revealed chronic health problems. The findings were most disturbing in relation to older Aboriginal women: 41 percent of those between 55 and 64 rated their health as poor or fair, compared with 19 percent of other Canadian women in the same age group. The mortality rate for Aboriginal women due to violence is three times that experienced by all other Canadian women. For Aboriginal women in the 25–44 years cohort, the rate is five times that for all other Canadian women. Aboriginal women are more likely to commit suicide than non-Aboriginal women (as are Aboriginal men and teenagers) (Women's Health Bulletin, 2002). Data from a very recent study on health disparities (Canadian Population Health Initiative, 2004) found that life expectancy for both Aboriginal and Inuit peoples is five to ten years shorter than for other Canadians, and infant mortality rates are two to three times that of the Canadian average.

In a study of inequalities in the health care services in British Columbia, Jiwani (2001) examined the experience of women of diverse ethno-racial backgrounds who have suffered spousal abuse in the context of their access to and encounters with the health care system. The findings of this and earlier research (British Columbia Task Force on Family Violence, 1992) suggest that immigrant women are exposed to a high risk of violence and that the risk is heightened by their structural location in society. Lack of English- or French-language skills, lack of accreditation of their professional/job qualifications, and racialization and sexism all contribute to the marginalization and ghettoization of work in occupations that are dangerous and unprotected. Isolation heightens the risk experienced by women of diverse cultural and racial backgrounds. The findings of the study also indicate that physicians' responses to immigrant women and First Nations women who had experienced domestic violence was characterized by stereotypes about violence within these groups. Physicians, like judges (see S. Razack above, 1998), commonly attribute violence to cultural groups on the assumption that the spousal abuse is normative among these communities. The implicit and racialized assumption is that spousal abuse is largely an aberration in Anglo-European-"Canadian" culture. Cultural racism is used to explain these differences, and results in differential treatment of these non-Anglo-European women. Institutionalized discourses about the "others" commonly reflect the Eurocentrism embedded in the importance accorded to the biomedical model. Another barrier identified was that language and cultural factors often compel women to turn to physicians who share their cultural and racial backgrounds, and that the physicians are chosen by their spouses. Service providers observed that abusive spouses and children often act as interpreters for women, contributing to the reluctance of women to disclose the abuse. A further example of the racialization process in terms of access to care is the finding by the Native Women's Association that, in cases of domestic assault, abused Aboriginal women are often forced to leave the reserve because of a lack of funding for shelters, and because their homes may belong to their husbands (Jimenez, 2004).

Within the service-delivery system, from interactions with the police to experiences in the courts, hospitals, and shelters, these women are likely to encounter bias and discrimination. For victims of abuse, racism adds another painful dimension to the experience of seeking help and safety.

Many health care and other human-service practitioners believe they are employing "cultural sensitivity" when in fact they may be relying on simplistic racialized and culturalized assumptions that ignore the diversity of experiences within a particular ethnic group. "Cultural sensitivity" often reduces complex life issues—including poverty and racism (Anderson and Reimer Kirkham, 2000).

Racial discrimination is also a health risk for female youth. A study undertaken by Women's Health in Women's Hands (2003) that documents the experiences of young women of colour found that the intersection of gender, race, and class-based differences had significant consequences in relation to their access to appropriate and effective health care services. The report points up the social impact of the diminishing government funding. The report again establishes the link between the biomedical model of universality and lack of access to appropriate services. The central finding of the study reinforces the need to address the root causes of racial inequality and develop resources, education, skills training for mainstream health care providers, and more effective networks between mainstream and service providers of colour.

Family Services

While the racialization of family service delivery practices was almost endemic in the 1960s and 1970s, the pattern has continued in the way ethno-racial and Aboriginal communities are disproportionately represented among those receiving social work intervention in the context of child welfare cases. Swift (1995) maintains that in such cases there is a greater propensity to classify and stigmatize in disproportionate numbers of Aboriginal and racial-minority parents as lacking parenting capacity. Ethno-racial communities are more likely to be labelled in the category of child "neglect" by a child welfare bureaucracy that fails to recognize the underlying causes sustained by ethno-racial inequality (Yee Ying and Dumbrill, 2003).

Another manifestation of racialized practices in human services is provided by Shakir (1995). Her research focuses on wife assault in the South Asian community. She found that mainstream social services were shaped by the notion of "essentialized" difference. The notion of **essentialism** suggests that there is a particular "essence" associated with being a Black or Asian client; that is, there is a single interpretation, unchanging through "time, space, and different historical, social, political and personal contexts" (Grillo, 1995:19). Shakir argues that what is "appropriate" for South-Asian women in terms of services is not just a matter of culturally specific values and norms; what needs to be understood is the context of the power imbalance in the relations between the South-Asian community and the values, institutions, and practices of the dominant culture. As Shakir explains: "The family may be the locus of abuse for some women of South Asian origin but it is the Canadian context that defines the nature of that violence/abuse" (1995:19). While cross-cultural service delivery is a goal for service providers from dominant groups, usually very little is known about the impact of racism on the lives of the women of colour with whom they work (S. Razack, 1998:84). Case Study 7.2 provides an interesting example of this phenomenon.

A further ideological barrier for women of colour and other non-European immigrant women is the assumption that their problems are rooted in the cultural values and norms of these cultures—that is, they are hierarchical, traditional, patriarchal, and display a high tolerance for violence toward women. However, studies (Shakir, 1995; British Columbia Task Force on Family Violence, 1992) demonstrate that contrary to stereotypes of the acceptance of violence against women in non-Western cultures, there is no tolerance for it anywhere.

CASE STUDY 7.2

NELLIE'S

This case study illustrates some of the major themes and issues identified in this chapter. It shows how human-service professionals and organizations, particularly White feminist organizations with established and significant track records in providing diverse and critically important services, are often unable to adapt their policies, programs, professional attitudes, values, and norms to control racism in its diverse forms.

Nellie's is a women's hostel in Toronto for battered and homeless women. It was co-founded in 1974 by June Callwood and Vicki Trerise. From 1991 to 1993 it was rocked by controversy, conflict, and internal strife. The focus of the dissension was racism in the organization. At the centre of the controversy was a woman of enormous prestige who, especially in the mainstream community, is viewed with great respect and affection.

Callwood, a journalist, broadcaster, and social activist, is widely revered for her involvement in and commitment to many social justice issues. She was a founding member of the Canadian Civil Liberties Association and several peace and feminist organizations, and the driving force behind Jessie's (a home for unwed mothers) and Casey House (an AIDS hospice). She was awarded the Order of Canada for her outstanding contributions to Canadian society.

Background

Nellie's has provided an important community service in Toronto throughout its history, serving battered women, homeless women, women in emotional distress, prostitutes, destitute refugees, and incest survivors. As is the case with most human-service organizations in recent years, the ethno-cultural and racial composition of the clients has changed; more than half the clients are immigrants, refugees, and women of colour. In response to its changing client population, Nellie's recruited some women of colour as staff and board members. However, the nominal increase in representation did not address the fundamental conflict over race and power that emerged in the organization.

Events

In the early 1990s, Nellie's became the focus of public attention as a result of actions that occurred in the organization. Allegations of racism surfaced and then escalated in the course of several months, and the media extensively reported on the controversy and conflict. The allegation of racism appeared to stem from two issues: a clash of ideologies over service and program-delivery issues and a power struggle between staff and board members who were White and staff and board members who were women of colour.

It appears that the catalyst for the conflict was a difference of opinion about whether to provide programs and counselling for incest victims. Some staff wanted to provide services for women wanting help for suffering related to past abuses, and others believed that Nellie's current resources were insufficient to handle these clients. Those opposed to introducing this service were mainly women of colour who were relatively new to Nellie's. Those arguing for counselling were White workers who had been at the shelter for a longer period and felt that the agency should provide this service.

In staff meetings and board meetings, racial tension increased. Questions of who had the power to make critical decisions in the organization were raised. Staff members who were women of colour felt the need to coalesce for support and formed a caucus group. In a series of letters, the group expressed its perception that systemic racism was operating at Nellie's and expressed concern about the absence of a grievance mechanism to deal with their views on racial issues.

The Women of Colour Caucus argued that despite the fact that Nellie's was supposedly structured on a feminist collective model, in which all members had equal access to decision making, it operated on the basis of a subtle hierarchy of power and authority. Women of colour felt marginalized, isolated, and excluded. From their perspective, issues such as client access to culturally and racially appropriate services and equitable participation and representation in the workplace were ignored or deflected. Despite the efforts of the caucus to put the issue of racism on the organizational agenda, many of the White board and staff continued to deny the validity of these perceptions and dismissed the signs of a growing crisis in the organization.

Although June Callwood was not the central issue, she stood at the centre of the struggle. In the highly charged atmosphere of a board meeting at Nellie's, one of the staff read a document prepared by the Caucus identifying a wide range of concerns, including racial inequities in the workplace, their colleagues' racist behaviour, and discriminatory barriers in the development and delivery of services. The demands called for improved equity hiring practices, a grievance policy, a strong anti-racism mission statement, and new evaluation and training procedures.

Following the reading of the document, Callwood responded with an angry criticism of the Black woman who had read it and disclosed that the woman had once been a Nellie's client. Callwood implied that the woman should have been grateful for the support and assistance the organization had given her, rather than complaining about racism. The board asked Callwood to apologize for the breach of confidentiality and the inappropriateness of her remarks. Michele Landsberg quotes Callwood as saying "I blew it." She began by saying "I was coerced into this apology. ... Only a small part of it is sincere" (Landsberg, 1992b). At a subsequent board meeting, there was a call for Callwood's resignation.

In the spring of 1993, Callwood resigned from the board of Nellie's. In a special article in the *Toronto Star*, she suggested that she was the victim of tactics of "intimidation and naked aggression." She observed: "The tactics of intimidation which have been effective at Nellie's are not strategies that anyone can condone. ... Such naked aggression only hardens differences and

does the cause of racism serious damage" (Landsberg, 1992b).

The charges of racial bias and discrimination at Nellie's and Callwood's resignation created a furor in the mainstream community. Several editorials appeared in the press, and numerous articles were written by Callwood's media colleagues and friends, all denouncing the actions of the women of colour at Nellie's and defending Callwood's integrity (Thorsell, 1992; Dewar, 1993; Marchand, 1993). Pierre Berton (1992) wrote "If June Callwood is a racist then so are we all."

In an 11-page *Toronto Life* article about Nellie's, Elaine Dewar insinuated that the charges of racism against Callwood and Nellie's were totally fallacious, contrived by the Caucus, and supported by other radicals outside the organization to gain power and control in the agency. She commented "Anyone planning a run at Nellie's could surmise that if Callwood was pushed on the subject of racism, she might leave" (Dewar, 1993:35). In far fewer numbers, articles appeared in the media analyzing the conflict from the perspective of the women of colour involved in the issue (Landsberg, 1992a; Barker and Wright, 1992; Benjamin, Rebick, and Go, 1993).

Analysis

Confronting and challenging racism in a human-service organization is fraught with risk and pain for the organization's clients, staff, and board of directors. The backlash effect and resistance often extend well beyond the organization; both the mainstream and the minority communities are implicated in the struggle. In this instance, the media played a critical role in reinforcing the position of the White group in Nellie's and helped mobilize public sentiment against the Women of Colour Caucus. By depicting those who were calling for change as radicals, reverse racists, and aggressive power-seeking individuals, the media further polarized the situation and reinforced the marginalization of people of colour in Canadian society.

The perspective of the White staff of Nellie's and June Callwood was that Nellie's provided important, effective programs and services and used a progressive, egalitarian model of service delivery that included everyone. Most of the White women in the organization were feminists and saw themselves as unbiased, fair-minded individuals, committed to equality and dedicated to service.

As is the case with most White human-service professionals, they were confident of their professional skills and knowledge and believed that Nellie's current structure, norms, and mode of operation met the needs of the groups it was serving. While they recognized that the changing client group required some organizational adjustments (such as increasing the representation of women of colour in the agency), they saw no need for radical changes in the work environment, service-delivery model, or decision-making and administrative processes.

Thus, they were shocked when they were accused of racism in their attitudes and behaviour in relation to their organizational policies, practices, and structures. They were unable to identify the subtle and overt ways in which they continued to exercise power and control and thus felt unjustly accused.

For the women of colour, there were significant costs in exposing the racism at Nellie's. Their demands for substantive change were met with a powerful backlash, not only in their own organization, but also in the mainstream community. The media were instrumental in devaluing and delegitimizing the concerns of the women of colour and reinforced the White-dominated status quo. In analyzing this issue, three prominent anti-racism practitioners observed:

> Anti-racism, like other struggles for social change, brings about division and emotional turmoil. Effective anti-racism work identifies resistance to change and lays bare on the one hand, holders of historic power and privilege that is based on skin colour, however relative that power may be, and on the other hand, powerlessness and internalized oppression of Black women and other women of colour. (Benjamin, Rebick, and Go, 1993)

From a similar perspective, Golden (1998) argues that feminist organizational culture commonly operates as a form of White privilege. Recent research on feminist organizations has established that groups of women who are differently situated within social power relations often have different political and organizational priorities (Barnoff, 2001; Golden, 1998; Fellow and S. Razack, 1998). Feminist values tend to place a high sense of worth on the ethic of treating one another with respect and care, creating a nurturing, cooperative, and harmonious environment. Implicitly, this is juxtaposed with male patriarchic values and norms. The consequence of this ideology often leads to negative reaction to any expression of conflict and difference of perspective and approach. However, it is inherent in any anti-racism organizational change process that tensions and conflict do arise: there are those whose White identity leads them to feel comfortable and safe with the status quo, while people of colour who experience racism as part of their lived reality will push for a disruption of that status quo. In this same context, San Martin and Barnoff (quoted in Barnoff, 2001:74) contend that the crisis at Nellie's was exacerbated by the fact that the organization lacked structural mechanisms on which they could depend when the conflict first emerged (e.g., a grievance procedure, anti-racism policy, etc.). The authors linked this weakness to the radical feminist ideology upon which Nellie's was framed.

Conclusion

This case demonstrates how the ideology of Whiteness in all its diverse dimensions affected a highly respected human-service agency such as Nellie's. It also provides a graphic illustration of the mainstream culture's strategies that are commonly used to minimize opposition in White-dominated organizations. The dominant culture's tools include the marginalization and the silencing of those who challenge White values and norms. It also sheds light on the intersection of the racialized discourses of Whiteness in the media with the discourses of Whiteness that operated within the silencing spaces of Nellie's and other feminist organizations (e.g., denial of racism, colour-blindness, reverse discrimination, binary polarization between "them" and "us").

The ideology and power structure of mainstream service delivery is reflected in the fact that the experiences of South Asians and other ethno-racial groups can only be accommodated as "special interest" issues. Ethno-specific services are seen as either a duplication of mainstream services or defined by cultural imperatives, while mainstream services are defined as being a universal approach, that is, treating everyone as having common needs (Desai, 1996; Shakir, 1995).

One of the leading authorities in the field of social work, race, and ethnicity in the United Kingdom suggested that no amount of asserting the irrelevance of race, colour, and ethnicity alters the fact that racial discrimination and disadvantage chronically influence the circumstances of ethnic and racial minorities (Cheetham, 1982). The fact that multicultural or anti-racist policies have been established in many family service agencies appears to have made little difference, because mainstream agencies continue to function without making fundamental changes to their service-delivery systems and to the dominant cultural values underpinning their organizational practices (Bridgman, 1993).

In social work today, seemingly innocuous concepts of "self," "relationship," or "therapy" are "a site of struggle" (Cooper, 1997:127). Clinical models of treatment and intervention offered by mainstream human services commonly ignore or dismiss the strength and significance of ethno-racial group identity and loyalty. At the same time, they fail to recognize the supportive role that racial and ethno-specific groups play in helping ethno-cultural and racial minorities to confront social, economic, and political disadvantage and discrimination.

Much of the influential literature on family therapy has drawn a boundary around the nuclear family. Solutions to problems have been sought within this internal system, without taking into account the extended family maintained by many clients and the pressures placed on them by their environment. Yet one cannot consider family dysfunction without considering the context of family life.

Mental-Health Services

There is an inextricable link between the barriers that confront people of colour in relation to access physical and mental health services. For example, a survey conducted by a hospital in Toronto points up the fact that the need for more mental-health services among immigrant, refugee, and racial-minority women was greatest for those who had been sexually assaulted (Pilowsky, 1991). The report also found that the common barriers immigrant women faced when seeking mental-health services were language, a lack of personnel trained to be sensitive to people of different cultures and races, and a lack of free services and information. The earlier findings of a national task force to conduct hearings on access to mental-health services by immigrants indicated that health and social services for immigrants were highly fragmented and uncoordinated (Canadian Task Force, 1988) and that they had been developed without an overall plan for coordination with the mainstream service-delivery system. The task force identified numerous racial, cultural, and linguistic barriers that prevented the effective use of mental-health services. Ethno-cultural and racial groups and service providers agreed that the lack of a common language was the barrier that most interfered with assessment and treatment.

The lack of professional, trained interpreters affects all areas of human-service delivery. In the late 1980s and early 1990s, limited efforts were made by some provincial governments to support the training of cultural and linguistic interpreters. In a few major hospitals, resources were allocated to hire trained interpreters. However, most social and health-care agencies rely on volunteers, family, or their own unqualified employees to interpret. Consequently, many patients or clients choose not to disclose personal and pertinent information, in order to avoid embarrassment. The translation may provide misleading data because of a lack of professional expertise. Cultural-linguistic interpreters also raise the important issue of stigma. In many non-Western societies in which the family takes care of its own problems, someone visiting a social worker or physician may be stigmatized for discussing private matters outside of the family or community (Lacroix, 2003).

Another related barrier between minority clients or patients and mainstream human-service delivery is the fact that many minority groups consider social and health concerns to be a collective problem, affecting others as well as the person seeking help. Members of both the immediate and extended family, especially elders, expect to be involved in the assessment of the problem and to play an active role in treatment. Although the centrality of the individual is an indispensable foundation of social work in Western societies, it is for some minorities an incomprehensible concept (Cheetham, 1982). In many immigrant cultures, independence from the family is not a primary goal. Enormous value is placed on interdependence, cooperation, and loyalty to the family. Each family member is expected to put the family's needs ahead of individual desires (British Columbia Task Force on Family Violence, 1992).

The formal and bureaucratic atmosphere of mental-health facilities and other social and health-care agencies creates an alienating environment. Sterile reception areas (often staffed by culturally insensitive staff), complex and confusing administrative forms, service-delivery information printed only in English, and inflexible office hours are common features of these clinics.

Minority professionals have pointed out the profound difference in worldview that typically separates White interviewers from clients of colour. Racial stereotyping often skews the initial assessment of therapists, who may view traits such as aggressive behaviour as indicative of a personality disorder, when in fact they may be a normal response to living in a racist society. Professional norms as well as class-bound values are used to judge normality or deviance (Dominelli, 1989, 2002).

Traditional interviewing techniques in social work and the health sciences commonly emphasize professional distance between the client and the therapist, a nondirective style, and emphasis on verbal, emotional, and behavioural expressiveness and self-disclosure. They also stress self-responsibility and examining past experiences. These techniques are rooted in a North American value system that may directly conflict with the client's cultural norms. Racial-minority clients whose lives have been marked by racism may well be disinclined to engage in self-disclosure with a White professional. For many minorities, sharing intimate aspects of one's experiences occurs only after a long and intense relationship has been established. In this context, Roger (2000) points out the ways in which the contemporary White woman as psychotherapist is influenced by her Eurocentric and Western values related to emotion and relationships. She argues that psychotherapy depends on deeply ingrained colonial and imperial notions of the normality of Whiteness. White women psychotherapists occupy the contradictory position of being seen as more powerful as Whites, yet within the broader context of psychotherapy they are less powerful than men. Failure to acknowledge the role of Whiteness in both research and education of health care professionals "threatens to entrench its invisible centrality, revealing practices within supposedly reified relations of race, class and gender so that those practices that maintain the invisibility of Whiteness cannot be named or explored" (125).

One of the more recent developments in terms of mental health issues is identification of the connection between racism and a lack of mental well-being. In this context, a three-year collaborative study is currently under way, conducted by Dalhousie University, York University, and University of Calgary, which is examining the impact of racism and violence on the health and well-being of African Canadians. Lead researcher Dr. Wanda Thomas Bernard hopes the study will identify how myths about Black people and stereotyping can influence their behaviour and the lives of their families. The study will explore the impact of these stereotypes of Black masculinity on Black girls, women and elders, as well as on boys and men. The study will investigate the consequences of resisting and/or being caught in these stereotypes. Racial profiling, gun violence, domestic violence, and Blacks as perpetrators and victims impact on the mental health of African Canadians as individuals, families, and communities. Bernard suggests, "the power of what might otherwise be 'trivial incidents' of racism lies in their overwhelming repetition, their cumulative burden historically and currently" (Riley, 2003).

These same issues have provided a focus of recent work undertaken by the Centre for Addiction and Mental Health. In a recent conference, delegates identified the need to deal with the depression, anxiety, and other forms of mental-health challenges facing the African-Canadian community, and to work toward establishing a "holistic, mental health care centre geared to the needs of the Black community." They also underscored the need to make mainstream hospitals more aware of those needs. A speaker at the conference, Kwa David Whittaker, a Black psychologist, observed that many of the mental health issues facing the Black community are not listed in the conventional diagnostic manuals (Tyler, 2002).

Responses to Racism

Despite the fact that a growing number of mainstream human-service agencies throughout the 1990s developed multicultural and anti-racism policies, delivered cross-cultural and anti-racism training programs for staff and management, and hired a small number of staff from ethno-racial minority communities, the ideology of social work continues to reflect the deep tension and contradictions characteristic of democratic racism. On one hand, social work and health care are committed to the promotion of the well-being and welfare of all members of society. On the other hand, mainstream human services continue to be shaped by "essentialized" concepts of difference, deficit cultures, hegemonic power imbalances, and Western therapy models that are alien to many non-dominant populations. The White feminist organizational model that characterizes much of the human-service delivery system often enables White women to feel safe at the expense of women of colour. There is an absence of structural mechanisms to implement anti-racist organizational change.

A racialized discourse underlies the practice of human services and reflects the strong resistance of human-service theorists, practitioners, and educators to transformative models of social change. A number of discursive strategies are used in social work to resist dealing with racism (Razack and Jeffery, 2002; Dominelli, 2002, 1989). All of them operate in Case Study 7.2 and in the other examples cited in this chapter.

- *Denial strategies* are based on the idea that cultural, institutional, and systemic forms of racism do not exist in the human-service delivery system. They assume that while there may be isolated cases of racist attitudes, these are extremely rare in an otherwise civil society.
- *Universalism* in the context of human services assumes that people are essentially the same—that members of any ethno-racial group have similar problems, needs, and goals. This discourse ignores the fact that the construct of **universality** does not carry an inherent meaning beyond a specific set of cultural, historical, political, and material conditions (Shakir, 1995).

- *Cultural awareness and ethno-specific sensitivity* focuses on changing the attitudes and behaviours of White human-service workers. However, racial inequality requires more than professional sensitivity to address the systemic forms of racism and its intersection with other forms of oppression that affect the lives of minorities.
- *Patronizing approaches* appear to accept the principle of equality between Whites and people of colour. But when the power and privilege of White people are challenged, demands for substantive change are met with fierce resistance and the status quo is affirmed.
- *"Dumping" strategies* rely on placing the responsibility for eliminating racism on the shoulders of the victims. In this strategy, professionals see themselves as neutral players.
- *Decontextualization strategies* acknowledge the presence of racism "out there" in the external environment, but not "in here," in this organization. Decontextualization also operates in the form of treatment modes that focus on individual intervention, that is, on helping individuals assimilate or adapt to their oppression.

These responses are characteristic of organizations that operate on an assimilationist, monocultural model of human-service delivery. These responses are also found in organizations that espouse multiculturalism. These models commonly recognize that racial and cultural diversity exist in the broader community but view this reality as irrelevant in determining the role and mandate of the agency, the nature of the service delivered, the constituencies served, the professional staff hired, and the volunteers recruited.

In monocultural organizations, linguistic, cultural, and racial barriers to service delivery are neither identified nor addressed. There is little understanding of how racism, cultural barriers, sexism, and classicism interact, creating an interlocking web of oppression. Thus, the services provided by them remain inaccessible to multicultural and multiracial communities. The underlying assumption is that, despite the obvious differences in the cultural backgrounds and racial identities of clients, all people have common needs and desires and therefore require similar modes of service and intervention.

Many voluntary social agencies and some health-care organizations have attempted to respond to racial-minority demands for more accessible and equitable services by introducing a multicultural organizational model. In the late 1980s and 1990s many human-service agencies began to develop multicultural and anti-racism policies. The United Way made it a condition of funding. However, as is the case of many institutions, there is a huge gap between policy formation, implementation, and transformation. In most instances, the change appeared often to be cosmetic. New initiatives include the translation of communication materials, token recruitment measures to increase the number of board members and volunteers from minority communities, and the hiring of one or two "ethnic" workers. Multicultural and anti-racism issues are considered separately from the day-to-day life of the organization. The needs and interests of minorities are dealt with on an ad hoc basis rather than being integrated into the structure, policies, programs, and practices of the organization.

The responsibility for change is often delegated to the front-line worker, who may function in a totally unsupportive environment. Concrete action to promote change is sometimes deferred, as the organization attempts to juggle competing demands and priorities. Racism is perceived to be an issue mainly in terms of minority client–mainstream professional interactions and relationships. Therefore, the primary responsibility of the agency is to provide opportunities for cross-cultural or race relations sensitization-training programs for front-line staff.

Analysis

White, Anglo-European Canadian human-service practitioners have generally been unwilling to acknowledge that services developed to help those who are most vulnerable can work against the interests of racial and cultural minorities (Cheetham, 1982). White practitioners in the human services are often oblivious to racism as a powerful social force. They generally lack an understanding of the daily struggle that racial-minority persons face with prejudice and discrimination. A preference for homogeneity and assimilation runs deep in the institutions of Canadian society and clearly weaves its way into the human-service delivery system. The discourses of Whiteness and democratic racism as cited above function to maintain the status quo and reinforce hegemonic beliefs and values.

Ethno-cultural and racially specific community-based agencies have attempted to fill the huge service-delivery gap created by the failure of mainstream institutions to serve the needs of a multiracial, multicultural, immigrant population. Yet these agencies are generally isolated from the mainstream delivery system and are often seen by funders as a duplication of services. They have undertaken the responsibility of providing more effective, responsive, and equitable services to minority communities, with little recognition or remuneration.

Although minority communities have great trust in this alternative form of human-service delivery, there has been an overwhelming lack of support from government and other funding bodies for community-based agencies. Generally the funding has been in the form of time-bound projects rather than operational funding.

It is important to note that in recent years social and political policies and ideologies have had a deep and devastating impact on the delivery of services within Canada' social and health care sectors. Massive cuts to mainstream and ethno-racial human-service budgets have resulted in downsizing, mergers, and closures of hospitals, mental health programs, and other human services, thus deepening a climate of instability and uncertainty. These changes have significantly increased the barriers to almost all service users. However, the greatest brunt has been borne by the most marginalized groups in society including poor and working-class immigrants, people of colour, and Aboriginal peoples. Social agencies have become sites of struggle as already-marginalized people have more urgent needs and feel the impact on a far greater scale (N. Razack, 2002). These changes are reflected in not only a reduction of services, but also services characterized by greater racial and cultural insensitivity. Ethno-specific agencies have had to reduce services for seniors, children, and persons with disabilities.

Summary

White human-service practitioners use a variety of rationales to deny, ignore, and minimize racism in their organizations, their professional values and practices, and their personal belief systems and relationships. The case studies of SARS and Nellie's and the discussion of racism in human services in general demonstrate how mainstream agencies continue to operate within a White, universalist, assimilationist, monocultural model of service delivery that views the cultural and racial **pluralism** of Canadian society as being irrelevant to their mandates, policies, structures, and operations. There is little evidence of a willingness to alter the ideology that shapes the training of social and health care practitioners, the treatment of ethno-racial practitioners, and the delivery of traditional human services.

Notes

1. The term "Yellow Peril" refers to the processes of racialization of Asian peoples throughout Canadian history in which Chinese, Japanese, and other Asians were inferiorized, marginalized, discriminated against, and excluded. The ideology and discourse of the "Yellow Peril" was manifested in racist government policies such as the Chinese head tax, the Chinese Exclusion Act, and the internment of Japanese Canadians during World War II.

References

Al-Krenawi, A. and J. Graham (eds.). (2003). *Multicultural Social Work in Canada: Working with Diverse Ethno-Racial Communities.* Don Mills, ON: Oxford Press. 1–20.

Anderson, J., and S. Reimer Kirkham. (2000). "Constructing Nation: The Gendering and Racializing of the Canadian Health Care System." In V. Strong-Boag, S. Grace, A. Eisenberg, and J. Anderson (eds.), *Painting the Maple: Essays on Race, Gender, and the Construction of Canada.* Vancouver: UBC. 242–261.

Bambrough, J., W. Bowden, and F. Wien. (1992). *Preliminary Results from the Survey of Graduates from the Maritime School of Social Work.* Halifax: Maritime School of Social Work, Dalhousie University.

Barker, D., and C. Wright. (1992). "The Women of Colour on the Nellie's Saga." *Toronto Star* (September 3).

Barnoff, Lisa. (2001). "Moving Beyond Words: Integrating Anti-oppression Practice into Feminist Social Service Organizations." *Canadian Social Work Review* 18(1):67–86.

Benjamin, A., J. Rebick, and A. Go. (1993). "Racist Backlash Takes Subtle Form Among Feminists." *Toronto Star* (April 30):A23.

Berton, P. (1992). "If Callwood Is a Racist Then So Are We All." *Toronto Star* (May 23):H3.

Bridgman, G. (1993). "The Place of Mainstream and Ethno-Racial Agencies in the Delivery of Family Services to Ethno-Racial Canadians." Master of Social Work thesis, Faculty of Graduate Studies, Graduate Program in Social Work, York University.

British Columbia Task Force on Family Violence. (1992). *Is Anyone Listening?* Victoria, BC: Queen's Printer.

Caissey, I. (1994). "Presentation to the City of North York's Community Race and Ethnic Relations Committee." Toronto, October 13.

Calliste, A. (1996). "Antiracism Organizing and Resistance in Nursing: African Canadian Women." *Canadian Review of Social Anthropology* 33(3):361–90.

Canadian Association of Schools of Social Work. (1991). *Social Work Education at the Crossroads: The Challenge of Diversity.* Report of the Task Force on Multicultural and Multiracial Issues in Social Work Education. May.

———. (1999). *Anti-racist Training and Materials Project.* Ontario Region Final Report. Available <http://www.mun.ca/cassw-ar/region/ontario/ ontario2>, accessed August 21, 2004.

Canadian Population Health Initiative. (2004). *Improving the Health of Canadians.* Canadian Institute for Health Information. Ottawa. Available <http://www.cici.ca>, accessed August 21, 2004.

Canadian Task Force on Mental Health Issues Affecting Immigrants and Refugees in Canada. (1988). Ottawa: Ministries of Multiculturalism and Citizenship and Health and Welfare.

Cheetham, J. (1982). "Introduction to the Issues." In J. Cheetham (ed.), *Social Work and Ethnicity.* London: George Allen and Unwin.

Christensen, C.P. (1996). "The Impact of Racism on the Education of Social Service Workers." In C. James (ed.), *Perspectives on Racism and the Human Service Sector: A Case for Change.* Toronto: University of Toronto Press.

———. (1999). "Multiculturalism, Racism and Social Work: An Exploration of Issues in the Canadian Context." In G. Lie and D. Este (eds.), *Professional Social Service Delivery in the Canadian Context.* Toronto: Canadian Scholars' Press. 293–310.

———. (2003). "Multiculturalism, Racism and Social Work: An Exploration of Issues in the Canadian Context." In A. Al-Krenawi and J. Graham (eds.), *Multicultural Social Work in Canada: Working with Diverse Ethno-racial Communities.* Don Mills, ON: Oxford University Press. 70–97.

Cohen, S. (2002). *Folk Devils and Moral Panics.* 3rd ed. London: Routledge.

Cooper, A. (1997). "Thinking the Unthinkable: 'White Liberal' Defenses Against Understanding in Anti-racist Thinking." *Journal of Social Work Practice* 11(2):127–37.

D'Cunha, C. (2003). *Canadian Medical Journal* press release (April 4, 2003).

Desai, S. (1996). "Afterword." In C. James (ed.), *Perspectives on Racism and the Human Service Sector: A Case for Change.* Toronto: University of Toronto Press. 246–51.

Dewar, E. (1993). "Wrongful Dismissal." *Toronto Life* (March):32–46.

Dominelli, L. (1989). "An Uncaring Profession? An Examination of Racism in Social Work." *New Community* 15(3): 391–403.

———. (2002). *Anti-oppressive Social Work Theory and Practice.* Houndsmills, Basingstoke, Hampshire (Eng.): Palgrave Macmillan.

Doyle, R., and L. Visano. (1987). *Access to Health and Social Services for Members of Diverse Cultural and Racial Groups.* Reports 1 and 2. Toronto: Social Planning Council of Metropolitan Toronto.

Este, D., and Thomas Bernard, W. (2003). "Social Work with African Canadians: An Examination of the African-Canadian Community." *Multicultural Social Work: Working with Diverse Ethno-racial Communities.* Toronto: Oxford University Press.

Fellow, M. and S. Razack. (1998). "The Race to Innocence: Confronting Hierarchical Relations Among Women." *Journal of Gender, Race, and Justice* 1(2):335–352.

Golden, M. (1998). "Comfort as White Privilege: Racial Inequality and Feminist Organizational Culture." Paper presented at the 1998 American Sociological Conference. San Francisco, CA.

Goosen, P., C. Pay, and A. Go. (2003). "Healing the Scars in Post-SARS Toronto." *Toronto Star* (May 15).

Grillo, T. (1995). "Anti-essentialism and Intersectionality: Tools to Dismantle the Master's House." *Berkeley Women's Law Journal* 10(1):19.

Hagey, R., and R. MacKay. (2000). "Qualitative Research to Identify Racialist Discourse: Towards Equity in Nursing Curricula. *International Journal of Nursing Studies* 37:45–56.

Head, W. (1986). *Black Women's Work: Racism in the Health System.* Toronto: Ontario Human Rights Commission.

Jimenez, M. (2004). "Amnesty's Bid to Stop Violence Against Women Targets Movies." *Globe and Mail* (March 6):A20.

Jiwani, Yasmin. (2001). "Intersecting Inequalities: Immigrant Women of Colour, Violence and Health Care." Vancouver: Feminist Research, Education, Development and Action (FREDA) Centre. July. Available <http://www.harbour.sfu.ca/freda/articles/hlth.htm>, accessed August 21, 2004.

Lacroix, M. (2003). "Culturally Appropriate Knowledge and Skills Required for Effective Multicultural Practice with Individuals, Families, and Small Groups." In A. Al-Krenawi and J. Graham (eds.), *Multicultural Social Work in Canada: Working with Diverse Ethno-racial Communities.* Don Mills, ON: Oxford University Press. 23–46.

Landsberg, M. (1992a). "Callwood Furor Masks Real Racism Struggle at Nellie's." *Toronto Star* (July 18).

———. (1992b). "The Nellie's Furor: June Callwood Tells Her Side." *Toronto Star* (July 23):F1.

Li, P. (1998). *Chinese in Canada.* Toronto: Oxford University Press.

McMahon, A., and P. Allen-Meares. (1992). "Is Social Work Racist? A Content Analysis of Recent Literature." *Social Work* 37(6)(November 6):533–39.

Marchand, P. (1993). "Callwood Denounces 'Bullying' by Self-Defined Weak." *Toronto Star* (June 21).

Medeiros, J. (1991). *Family Services for All.* Toronto: Multicultural Coalition for Access to Family Services.

Minna, M. (1991). "Social Service System Cheats Metro's Ethnics." *Toronto Star* (June 5):A23.

Ontario Ministry of Citizenship. (1989). *Access.* Toronto: Task Force on Access to Professions and Trades in Ontario.

Ornstein, M. (2000). *Ethno-Racial Inequality in the City of Toronto: An Analysis of 1996 Census.* City of Toronto.

Pilowsky, J. (1991). *Community Consultation Report.* Toronto: Doctors Hospital, Multicultural Women's Programme.

Razack, N. (2002). *Transforming the Field: Critical Anti-Racism and Anti-oppression Perspectives for the Human Service Practicum.* Halifax: Fernwood.

Razack, N., and D. Jeffery. (1999). "Anti-racist Training and Materials Project." Ontario Region Final Report. Canadian Association of Schools of Social Work. August.

———. (2002). "Critical Race Discourse and Tenets of Social Work." *Canadian Social Work Review* 17(2):257–271.

Razack, S. (1998). *Looking White People in the Eye: Gender, Race, and Culture in the Courtrooms and Classrooms.* Toronto: University of Toronto Press.

Riley, L. (2003). "Racism, Violence, Health Study Represents a Positive Step." *The Sunday Herald* (January 26).

Roger, Kerstin. (2000). "'Making' White Women Through the Privatization of Education on Health and Well-Being in the Context of Psychotherapy." In G. Dei and A. Calliste (eds.), *Anti-racist Feminism.* Halifax: Fernwood.

Shakir, U. (1995). *Pre-sentencing at the Boundary: Wife Assault in the South Asian Community.* Toronto: Multicultural Coalition for Access to Family Services.

Statistics Canada. (2001). Aboriginal Peoples Survey on Health. Available <http://www12.statcan.ca/english/profil01/PlaceSearchForm1.cfm>.

Swift, K. (1995). *Manufacturing 'Bad Mothers': A Critical Perspective on Child Neglect.* Toronto: University of Toronto Press.

Thomas, B. (1987). *Multiculturalism at Work.* Toronto: YWCA.

Thorsell, W. (1992). "A Question of the Pot Calling the Kettle White." *Globe and Mail* (May 23):D6.

Turney, D. (1997). "Hearing Voices, Talking Difference: A Dialogic Approach to Anti-oppressive Practice." *Journal of Social Work Practice* 11(2):115–25.

Tyler, T. (2002). "Blacks Face Mental Health Crisis." *Toronto Star* (December 8).

Webster, P. (1992). "Toronto Social Workers' Skills Buried by New Urban Realities." *Now* (Toronto)(October 1).

Weinfeld, M., L. Kirmayer, C. Lam, and B. Vissandjee. (1998). *Barriers to Care and Issues of Ethnic/Gender Match.* Le Centre d'Excellence pour La Santé des Femmes—Consortium Université de Montreal (CESAF).

Women's Health Bulletin. (2002). Health Canada site <http://www.hc-sc.ca/English/women/facts_aborig.htm>. April 16.

Women's Health in Women's Hands. (2003). *Racial Discrimination as a Health Risk for Female Youth: Implications for Policy and Healthcare Delivery in Canada.* March. Toronto: Canadian Race Relations Foundation. Available <http://www.crr.ca/EN/Publications/ResearchReports/pdf/ePub_RacialDiscrimination.pdf>, accessed August 23, 2004.

Wong, J. (2003). "How SARS Has Become the Latest Yellow Peril." *Globe and Mail* (April 11).

Yee Ying, J., and G. Dumbrill. (2003). "Whiteout: Looking for Race in Canadian Social Work Practice." In A. Al-Krenawi and J. Graham (eds.), *Multicultural Social Work in Canada: Working with Diverse Ethno-racial Communities.* Don Mills, ON: Oxford University Press.

PART THREE

Racism in Educational and Cultural Organizations

This Part continues examining various institutional structures by analyzing the processes of racialization in schools and universities, the media, and cultural and arts organizations—the major vehicles by which society's values, beliefs, and norms are developed, strengthened, and protected. Each of these institutions constitutes the primary site for the reproduction of Whiteness in everyday texts, discourses, images, and ideas. The analysis in each of the chapters identifies how the "White gaze" and dominant narratives of White educators, journalists, and cultural producers serve to mark and reinforce the notions of difference and "otherness."

CHAPTER 8

RACISM IN CANADIAN EDUCATION

Visible-minority students are exposed to discriminatory educational practices which, like a multitude of timeless voices, tells them loudly or softly that they are intellectually, emotionally, physically and morally inferior.

—Thornhill (1984:3)

Including African and non-White scholars in one's intellectual cosmos does not necessarily mean a lowering of standards. When this university finally opens its gates and minds to non-White intellectuals, ideas and personnel, then visiting professors like me will cease to be one-year stands, interesting exotica or simple white elephants.

—Lgundipe-Leslie (1991)

This chapter analyzes the role of education in producing and reproducing racial bias and inequality. It focuses on the ways in which racism is reflected in the learning environment and continues to form an intrinsic part of the learning process within the school and the university. The negative effects of White racialized ideology and differential treatment on students of colour are examined.

An analysis of curriculum, including the hidden curriculum, provides some insight into the ways in which schools marginalize minority students and either exclude or minimize their experiences, history, and contributions to Canada as a nation. This marginalization, as the literature demonstrates, has a significant impact on the identities and self-esteem of racial-minority students at every level of the educational process.

The effects of White educators' attitudes and expectations in influencing and limiting the learning of many racial-minority students are examined, as are the consequences for the students' academic and social performance.

Another manifestation of racism examined in this chapter is the dysfunctional relationship between educational institutions, racial-minority parents, and communities. This analysis is followed by a discussion of the overt expression of racism in the form of racial harassment (racial graffiti and physical and verbal abuse) and the more covert forms (e.g., the lack of an institutional response to educators' and students' continuing racist attitudes and behaviours, and the streaming of Black students into non-academic programs). Some trends and patterns in educational institutions' responses to racism are examined.

The chapter concludes with an analysis of the school and university as discursive space and of how racialized discourses used by educators reflect both institutional and individual resistance to addressing racism in the schools and universities.

Introduction

It is a strongly held conviction in Canada and other Western democracies that educational institutions play a central role in providing an environment that fosters the attainment of life opportunities for all students. The educational system is assumed to be the main instrument for acquiring the knowledge and skills that will ensure the students' full participation and integration into Canadian society. This belief holds true through primary, secondary, and postsecondary education. A significant body of evidence, however, demonstrates that educational institutions have preserved and perpetuated a system of structured inequality based on race. Although racial-minority and White students have similar career and professional aspirations when entering the school system, the outcomes are markedly different.

Racist Attitudes in Children

One of the key assumptions of many educators is that children enter school as "blank slates" with few preconceived assumptions, beliefs, and values. In relation to racial attitudes and social identity, this view has been challenged by a number of studies that find that White children prefer Whites and typically show negative attitudes toward Blacks, Asians, and Aboriginal peoples. By the time children enter school at the age of five, they have already been exposed to racially constructed images of social relations (Hohensee and Derman-Sparks, 1992; Rizvi, 1993; Ijaz and Ijaz, 1986; Milner, 1983). The racist popular culture, which includes racist images and negative stereotypes of people of colour in films, television, books, and toys, has a strong influence on children's attitudes and perceptions. The negative stereotypes of Blacks as criminals; South Asians, Arabs, and Muslims as terrorists; and Aboriginal peoples as uncivilized, primitive alcoholics, are deeply embedded in the spoken and implicit messages conveyed in everyday images and discourses. The absence of people of colour in the stories children read, the pictures they see, and the music they hear, influence children's ideas about racial differences. The social environment and the daily experiences of children communicate biases about various aspects of "difference."

Children become aware of differences in physical characteristics such as skin and hair colour between the ages of three and seven. At about the same time, they also begin to develop labels for racial groups, often based on oversimplification and misinformation. Lawrence Hirschfeld's study (1996) of racial attitudes suggests that children instinctively possess a way of forming beliefs about the world that leads them to believe that races exist and have certain qualities. Between the ages of four and seven, children form racial preferences, and by the ages of eight to twelve they deepen their understanding of the status associated with particular groups. At this stage, overtly prejudicial behaviours may emerge. This form of racism has a significant, enduring impact both on how White children see themselves and on how they perceive "others" (Essed, 1990). As well, it has a negative effect on the development of minority children's self-image and self-esteem (Milner, 1983).

The Manifestations of Racism

Curriculum

Curriculum has two dimensions: the formal curriculum and the hidden curriculum. The formal curriculum consists of content and the processes of instruction, which are shaped by the selection of educational materials such as books and teaching aids. It also embraces teaching practices and evaluation procedures, including assessment and placement practices. The hidden curriculum includes educators' personal values, their unquestioned assumptions and expectations, and the physical and social environment of the school and university.

In the context of both the school and the university, some key questions about racism in the curriculum are: What counts as knowledge? From what perspective does the teaching take place? What images are drawn upon? What learning materials are used? How is knowledge transmitted? What kinds of knowledge are absent, ignored, and denied?

Formal Curriculum

The issue of bias in the classics, for example, is a matter of concern not only in Canada, but also for anti-racist educators and advocates in the United States and Great Britain (McCarthy, 1993; Brandt, 1986; Lee, 1985; Council on Interracial Books for Children, 1980). There is increasing evidence that reading "literary classics" such as *Huckleberry Finn* and *The Merchant of Venice* without being prepared to deal with their racism does untold damage to minority children, who are further marginalized by the racist language, images, and concepts in these texts (Lee, 1985).

Educators at the primary, secondary, and university levels often fail to deal with the fact that literary texts do not transcend the contexts in which they are written and in which they are read (Pinar, 1993). The social, cultural, and political contexts of all authors, including William Shakespeare and Mark Twain, should form part of any teaching of literature. Equally important and often ignored are the perceptions, assumptions, understandings, and experiences that the student brings to the reading of the text.

Bias in the classics and the Eurocentrism that permeates other texts and teaching materials have an impact on the perceptions, attitudes, and behaviour of both minority and mainstream students (Council on Interracial Books for Children, 1980; Lee, 1985; Dei, 1996). For example, in a Kitchener-Waterloo, Ontario, high school classroom in which *The Merchant of Venice* was being studied, a Jewish student came to class one day to find swastikas painted on her desk. The teacher admonished the unknown perpetrators and called the custodian in to remove the offending graffiti. The student commented that the custodian cleaned the swastikas off her desk, "but no one cleaned them off me" (Ferri, 1986).

A Four-Level Government/African Canadian Working Group report (1992) argued that the assault on racial-minority students' identity is the direct consequence of bias and exclusion in curriculum content. This report and other authorities (Moodley, 1984; Cummins, 1992; Solomon, 1992; Dei, 1996) share the view that the reproduction of knowledge in the classroom through curriculum and teaching practices perpetuates racist thinking among both White students and their teachers.

Racism in the curriculum manifests itself in subjects such as history, literature, social studies, geography, and science. The perspectives of novelists and poets who reflect the history and experiences of non-Western cultures are generally ignored in the Eurocentric

MANIFESTATIONS OF RACISM IN THE EDUCATIONAL SYSTEM

Racially biased attitudes and practices of teachers and administrators
Eurocentric/Anglocentric curriculum
Culturally biased assessment practices
Hidden curriculum and construction of otherness
Racial harassment and racial incidents
Streaming of minority students (especially Blacks) into non-academic programs
School disciplinary policies and practices (e.g. Zero Tolerance)
Assimilationist culture of the school
Lack of representation in curricula, administration, and staffing
Devaluing of the role and participation of parents and the community

curriculum. The history curriculum often exhibits a dominant-culture bias that expresses itself in the way history texts are written. There is an unwillingness to look beyond the study of British, American, or European history, and multicultural history is often considered as separate and distinct from Canadian history.

History in its textbook form is frequently nothing more than a representation of tradition (McGee, 1993); and tradition, as Raymond Williams (1977:115) suggests, is "always selected and thus presents us with a system of values disguised as a natural and transcendent process of cultural development." In other words, history is a reflection of the perceptions of those who tell the story, describe the events, and interpret them.

In the history curriculum, the history of people of colour typically begins when Whites "discover" them. Human civilization is portrayed as an evolutionary process, in which Euro-American culture—the Western legal system, democratic forms of government, and a capitalist economy—is considered the "best" culture in the world. This perspective is also manifested in learning resources, which often fail to reflect alternative views. Until very recently, the history of slavery in Canada, the treatment of Chinese Canadians and other Asian immigrants, and the story of the abuse of Aboriginal children in residential schools (to a cite only a few examples) were not part of the history taught in schools. An example of how powerful forms of knowledge continue to be invisible in the history curriculum is the fact that in Ontario the subject of "racism" appears in only two of twenty-two Ministry Canadian history textbooks published prior to 2000 (Black, 2003). Moreover, the severe budget cuts to educational budgets across the country, beginning in the mid-to-late 1990s, has virtually eliminated the possibility of purchasing new texts that might include the subject of racism in their treatment of Canadian history. A pilot study that surveyed the views of students who had entered first-year university found that students felt that their schools had failed to teach them about racism. As one student stated: "I can't say I remember learning about one racial or Ethnocultural role model. I can't think of one person who was not European. I can't think of one Asian person or one Black person" (ibid.).

At the level of the school and the university, science classes also provide opportunities for fostering racism in the classroom. Bias is reflected in the omission of people of colour from most scientific texts; their images and contributions to scientific development are absent. A more specific example of bias in the science curriculum is the study of theories of race that legitimize and provide justification of the superiority of the White "race." Teachers commonly resist critically discussing with their students the recent resurgence of theories of biological or scientific racism, which seek to link race with intelligence and other traits.

The importance of Eurocentric curriculum in reproducing racism in education is stressed in the following observation: "Until curriculum is studied less as a receptacle of texts than as activity, that is to say, as a vehicle of acquiring and exercising power, descriptions of curricular content in terms of their expression of universal values on the one hand, or pluralistic, secular identifier on the other, are insufficient signifiers of their historical realities" (Viswanathan, 1989:167).

However, within schools and academia, curriculum is commonly considered sacrosanct by many educators. "Nobody can be told what and how to teach" is an oft-repeated sentiment. Yet the Eurocentric nature of much of the current university's offerings cannot be denied (Carty, 1991; Fleras, 1996; Razack, 1998).

Roxana Ng, in analyzing racism in the university curricula, identified the need "to open up the spaces for previously silenced or marginalized voices to be heard" (1994:44). This view is shared by a large number of professors, including Kobayshi (2002), Dei and Calliste (2000), Joanne St. Lewis (1996), Linda Carty (1991), Carl James (1994), Sherene Razack (1998), and Himani Bannerji (1991), all professors of colour teaching in Canadian universities. They have all argued that as people of colour working in academia, neither their presence nor their histories are recognized. The curriculum is devoid of their narratives.

Carty commented that "there is little difference between what we experience on the streets as Black women and the experiences we have inside the university … the university's commonsense appeal to reason and science may take the rough edges off or sediment the particular behaviour, but the impact is no less severe" (1991:15). Carl James suggested that one's sense of self (as a racial minority) will always be located within a set of meanings that are socially situated and defined by systems of cultural representation: "That I am a professor does not make me immune to the stereotypes and concomitant issues and problems that go along with being a racial minority, and a Black person in particular in this society" (1994:51).

Himani Bannerji, referring to her teaching experience in a Canadian university said: "The perception of the students is not neutral—it calls for responses from them and even decisions. I am an exception in the universities. … I am meant for another kind of work—but nonetheless I am in the classroom. … I am authority" (1991:72). Finally, Joanne St. Lewis commented, "The colour of my skin drives the engine of my public life. It defines relationships and sets out possibilities. Attitudes and beliefs make it real" (1996:28).

A critical report on race relations conducted at Queen's University (1991) identified a number of vital curriculum issues:

- the existence of course names that do not reflect their content (e.g., "The History of Political Thought" should be renamed "The History of *Western* Political Thought");
- the prevalence of core courses (required of majors students) that include only Eurocentric issues;
- the lack of anti-racist courses in the curriculum and the need to make these mandatory in some curricula;
- the need to hire faculty who can teach courses that do not have a Eurocentric focus;
- the need to introduce more interdisciplinary studies, such as Black studies and Native studies;
- the need to review science curricula to make the important point that even science is not value-free;
- the need to develop supplementary programs for minority students that would help them meet academic standards.

Hidden Curriculum

One of the most difficult aspects of racism to isolate and identify is the hidden curriculum, which embraces the social and cultural environment of the school and is formed by the personal, professional, and organizational assumptions, values, and norms of those working in it. The hidden curriculum is the tacit teaching of social and economic norms and expectations to students. It is often through the school's hidden curriculum that the **hegemony** of racism is experienced and through which Black pupils become marginalized (Brandt, 1986).

It is manifested, for example, in school calendars (in their choice of which holidays are celebrated and which are ignored), concerts and festivals, bulletin-board and hallway displays, the collections in school libraries, school clubs, and the kinds of behaviours tolerated (e.g., racial harassment).

Several scholars, including Solomon (1992), Dei (1996), Schissel (1997), Kelly (1998), Yon (2000), and Codjoe (2001), have drawn attention to the forging of racial-minority subcultures as expressions of resistance, defiance, and opposition to the closed, dominant, and hierarchical culture of the school. Each has employed a methodology that incorporates the everyday experiences and narratives of Black students, as they grapple with the processes of racialization, inferiorization, and marginalization operating within the school environment. This body of research documents the most salient factors that influence the level of achievement of many Black students in schools. These findings also shed light on the impact of bias and differential treatment that impact upon other ethno-racial minority students. The common concerns that were articulated by Black students were: persistent discrimination, ethnocentrism, essentialized constructs of cultural identity, negative stereotyping, the lack of representation of Black/African perspectives, histories and experiences, low teacher expectations, and the absence of Black teachers. Most significant, perhaps, is the construction of Black student identity as a "problem."

The singling out of the Black male and other racial minority males in schools is linked to the White "gaze" and racialized discourses of other institutions such as the media and police. Hérbert (2001) suggests that subjected to the constant "gaze" of White-dominant schools and other White public authorities, students of colour react to the constant pressure of being watched, in schools, in malls, and on the streets. Some students may respond by generating "glare," that is, exhibiting bold fashion statements with hats, bandanas, specific labels, and physical actions such as exaggerated walking styles. As in the case of racial profiling by police of young Black males as possible troublemakers or criminals, the "gaze" and "glare" may feed off each other, further marginalizing individuals marked by the colour of their skin.

Another manifestation of the way in which the hidden curriculum influences both identity and educational outcomes is the strong emphasis by educators and coaches (reinforced by the media) on sports as a means of keeping Black students in schools. Black youth, more than any other group, have a propensity to use sports as a means of negotiating and navigating through the multiplicity of barriers identified above (James, 2003; Spence, 1999; Solomon, 1992). James (ibid.) suggests that this construct of the Black athlete may be a reflection of how the schooling environment, that is, the culture of the school, sees itself as addressing the academic needs and interests of Black student athletes. James argues that educators need to critically examine the reasons why Black students tend to believe that it is "mainly through sports that they can fulfill their educational needs, aspirations and requirements" (2003:34).

The construct of "different" identities as a "problem" within school culture impacts upon students of other ethno-racial backgrounds. Cummins observes: "Just as particular forms of identity were being negotiated when Aboriginal children were beaten or starved for speaking their mother tongue, so today the curriculum and patterns of educator-student interaction in school either constrict or expand students' possibilities for identity formation (1992:3). For example, since 9/11, students of Muslim background, or those who are misidentified as being Muslim, have increasingly been exposed to negative stereotyping and differential treatment in schools by students and educators (Zine, 2003).

The relationship between the dominant culture discursive constructions of identity/difference has a deep relationship to questions of self-image and self-esteem of minority students. It is also a critical issue for students who speak English as a second language (ESL). In Alberta, a study by Watt and Roessingh (1994) of ESL students revealed a school dropout rate of 74 percent. At the beginning level, however, 95.5 percent of ESL students dropped out before attaining a high school diploma. Reasons cited for leaving school included lack of confidence in one's spoken English, ridicule by English-speaking classmates, lack of support from teachers, and teachers' underestimating the student's potential.

Pedagogy

The most powerful examples of the hidden curriculum are the attitudes and practices of educators in the classroom. Several researchers have suggested that the learning difficulties of minority students are often pedagogically induced; that is, their learning is influenced by how the teaching is done (Cummins, 2001, 1988). Kehoe summed up the problem succinctly: "It is a fact rarely accepted that there is less wrong with the learner than with the process and institutions by which the learner is taught" (1984:64).

A complex relationship exists between educators' expectations and their conformity to these expectations in terms of their students' academic performance. A teacher or professor who holds stereotypical opinions about a particular racial group is likely to translate these biases into differential teaching techniques and classroom treatment (Dei and Calliste, 2000, 1996; Calliste, 2000; Shapson, 1990). In his interviews with Black Canadian students, Dei (ibid.) found that the dynamics of social difference and racism shape the processes and experiences of public schooling. Students indicated a high level of concern about the school's ability, through classroom pedagogy, texts, and everyday discourse, to misrepresent and negate the experiences of students of colour.

Many researchers (Cummins, 2001; Alladin, 1996; Dei, 1996) argue that teachers may make subjective evaluations of the capabilities of their students for the purpose of grouping and that those assessments may be unrelated to academic potential. Kehoe (1984) cited a study showing that children who spoke in a dialect were about three times as likely not to respond to questions given in standard English as were children in the higher group who spoke standard English. Moreover, membership in these groupings remained unchanged from grade to grade.

Several studies have suggested that learning difficulties are often pedagogically induced, in that children designated "at risk" frequently receive instruction that confines them to a passive role and induces "learned helplessness" (Cummins, 1984). On the other hand, instruction that empowers students will encourage them "to become active generators of their own knowledge" (Cummins, 1988:143).

Following a similar perspective, Brandt (1986) suggested that certain pedagogic styles, such as reliance on didactic teaching, are inappropriate and must be examined to consider the extent to which they promote collaborative learning, which involves not only teachers and students but the wider community's perspectives and "knowledge," especially that of marginalized groups. The benefits of cooperative, collaborative, group-centred learning as an effective teaching strategy at the level of the school and university is supported by a number of educators (Brandt, 1986; Dei, 1996).

The dynamic of race creates enormous resistance in classrooms that are controlled by teachers who continue to be deeply committed to what Solomon (1992) described as the dominant teaching paradigm of cultural assimilation.

The silence that generally pervades the classroom on the subject of racism echoes loudly in the attitudes of students, who daily struggle to affirm their identities in an institutionalized culture that denies their feelings, stories, and experiences. McGee (1993) argued that educators must begin to take responsibility for the effects of their pedagogical and curricular decisions. In discussing the need for transforming changes in pedagogical practices, it has been suggested that the critical educator "takes as central the inner histories and experiences of the students themselves" (Razack, 1998:42), endeavouring to promote critical reflection of everyday experiences. Students (and others) who develop critical-thinking skills are better positioned to challenge oppressive practices.

Assessment, Placement, and Streaming

One of the largest barriers to educational equity is the system of assessment and placement. A significant body of data indicates that psychological assessment and placement procedures are riddled with racial, cultural, and linguistic biases (Cummins, 2001, 1988; Samuda and Kong, 1986).

Samuda et al. (1980) surveyed the assessment methods used for minority and immigrant children in many Ontario schools and found that the traditional classification was based on the presumption of internal pathology or deficits. It is now generally accepted that "objective" tests are not as "culture-free" or "culture-fair" as test manufacturers would have one believe. Test materials are developed to assess children of the mainstream culture and do not accurately reflect the learning potential and achievement of students from minority cultures.

In a study of 400 assessments of students enrolled in English as a second language programs in a western Canadian city, it was found that the psychologists lacked the knowledge to assess the children's academic potential and that the tests were frequently culturally biased (Cummins, 2001, 1992). Despite the fact that in the majority of assessments no diagnostic conclusions were logically possible, psychologists were reluctant to admit this fact to teachers and parents. The psychologists were oriented to locate the cause of an academic problem in the minority child, which prevented a critical scrutiny of a variety of other possible contributors to the child's difficulty. The psychologists' training resulted in a "tunnel vision" that did not consider the experiential realities of the children.

Cummins (2001) believes that racially biased assessments emanate from psychologists who frequently lack the knowledge base required to assess the student's academic potential. The assessments' Eurocentric orientation and lack of sensitivity to the children's cultural backgrounds and linguistic skills provided results that were significantly different from those of the children upon whom the test was normed. Institutionalized racism is apparent both in the lack of awareness of the educational psychologists and in the failure of the institutions that trained these psychologists to make them aware of the knowledge gaps and their consequences. Cummins also argues that biased standardized tests, which isolate "the problem" within the student, provide a screen that obscures the exclusionary orientation of teachers toward minority communities.

Even educators who are genuinely committed to anti-racist and intercultural education may lack important information, which leads them to make poor decisions regarding minority students. For example, a teacher may hold the view that using two languages in the home confuses bilingual children and consequently may advise parents to speak only English.

Power and status relations between minority and majority groups exert a major influence on school performance. Minority students are disempowered educationally in very much the same way as their communities are disempowered by interactions with societal institutions. Minority students are "empowered" or "disabled" as a direct result of their interactions with educators in schools. This leads to the importance and power of the educator to play an advocacy role, particularly as it relates to ethno-racial minority students in critically scrutinizing the social and educational context within in which the student receives his or her learning. The primary focus should be on remediating the educational interactions that students of diverse ethno-racial backgrounds experience (ibid.).

The streaming of Black students into low-level academic programs and the placement of large numbers of Black students in vocational programs have been issues of debate for more than a decade. In Ontario, in consultations with the Stephen Lewis Task Force (Lewis, 1992) and the Four-Level Study (1992), many Black community leaders argued that despite tense relations with the police many more young Blacks are injured in the classroom than on the streets. Toronto high school teacher Lennox Farrell suggested that "this is the only community where our youth has a lower level of education than their parents" (O'Malley, 1992:A19).

At the level of the university, problems associated with streaming reduce the number of minority students who are in a position to qualify for postsecondary education. What seems clear is that the attitudes, policies, and practices in the school greatly affect minorities' opportunities for higher education. They also have some impact on the choice of specialization or faculty for those minorities who are successful. For example, the large numbers of Southeast Asians in computer science reflects, in part, a secondary school system that commonly labels this group of students as "good" at math and sciences.

School–Community Relations

The unequal relationship between educational institutions, parents, and the community is another manifestation of systemic racism. The notion that parents' involvement and responsibilities cease once the child has entered the school gate is a form of disempowerment that continues to be a common feature of school life in Canada. Many racial-minority parents perceive schools as requiring no input and tolerating no interference from outside. Minority students are empowered in the school context to the extent that parents and communities are themselves empowered through their interactions with the school: "When educators involve minority parents as partners in their children's education, parents appear to develop a sense of efficacy that communicates itself to children with positive academic consequences" (Cummins, 1988:141).

Black parents and educators have been very clear on identifying many of the factors that hinder the relationship between the school and the Black community. For example, many Black parents express dissatisfaction with the school's unilateral handling of discipline and curriculum matters. They describe communication with the school as one-way, nontransactional, and initiated only when the school reports disciplinary problems. In the area of program placement, parents often appear to be unaware of and uninvolved in critical decisions affecting their children's educational welfare (Crozier, 2001; Solomon, 1992).

Rather than practising a collaborative approach, school authorities tend to favour a more exclusionary approach to parent and community participation in the school. Many educators (and other professionals) seem to believe that a collaborative relationship with parents will reduce their independence and that their professional competence is being challenged.

Similarly, it has been suggested that racial minorities do not have the opportunity to contribute in a meaningful way to policy planning and implementation. Often their involvement is limited to superficial encounters with the system, in which their suggestions are solicited but then disregarded: "We carry on, business as usual, speculating, diagnosing, examining, studying, implementing and remedying, without once ever consulting the victims" (Thornhill, in Samuda and Kong, 1986:289).

Researchers have been able to show that many White middle-class educators have constructed (perhaps unconsciously) a model of the "good" parent; and, in this relationship, ethno-racial parents do not measure up. Whiteness acts as a filter, filtering out the perceptions, concerns, and experiences of minority parents. On the other hand, White middle-class parents often have the social and cultural capital and resources to make their views known (Crozier, 2001).

What are required are more visible partnerships that involve a greater sharing of power. White teachers must recognize that they cannot make crucial educational decisions or carry out initiatives alone; they have a responsibility to enlist the guidance of minority parents and community members who are knowledgeable and competent to provide this help. Indeed, over the last decade there are increasing signs that minority parents and communities have begun to demand that educators address the barriers to equal access and treatment in the school.

Racial Incidents and Harassment in the School Environment

Racial harassment is one of the most painful manifestations of racism. In Canada, there is no accurate assessment of the frequency, nature, or distribution of racial harassment, nor is there any documented analysis of either perpetrators or victims. However, a body of impressionistic evidence is provided by students, parents, minority communities, and in some cases board of education reports. Some educators believe that the number of racial incidents in Canada's schools has steadily increased in recent years. Teachers and principals are filing reports about racially motivated occurrences with greater frequency than ever before (Lawson, 2003; Ruck and Wortley, 2002; Jull, 2000).

Racial harassment in educational institutions includes racial slurs, ethnic and racial jokes, and racist graffiti. It is expressed in racial conflict and tension between groups and by threats of and actual physical assaults on minority students and teachers. It has become so serious that in Edmonton the police chief stated that his department was contacting various minority groups to defuse potentially violent situations in the city's public schools. In one instance, forty people arrived at a high school armed with crowbars and baseball bats to avenge an alleged attack on an East-Indian student (Oake, 1991).

One of the barriers to dealing with these kinds of incidents is institutional resistance, a general unwillingness to acknowledge and report racial conflict, harassment, or violence. McCaskell (1993) reported that teachers were reluctant to report racist incidents because they didn't want to be seen as lacking control over their classes; department heads did not report them because it "looked bad"; principals were reluctant to report them because they reflected negatively on their school; and superintendents did not report them because superintendents were supposed to provide leadership. McCaskell concluded that racial incidents and hate activity, although known at an informal level, do not become institutional knowledge, despite a requirement by boards to report such incidents.

CASE STUDY 8.1

THE KILLING OF REENA VIRK

Event

On the night of November 14, 1997, Reena Virk, a 14-year-old student living in Victoria, B.C., was enticed to the Gorge waterway, in suburban Victoria, near the school she attended. There she was severely beaten and brutalized by eight teens. She survived the first assault and most of the perpetrators then left. As she staggered across a bridge over a gorge, two of the 15-year-old assailants, Warren Glowatski and Kelly Ellard, followed her, further brutalized her, and then drowned her. A week later she was found.

Background

The parents of Reena Virk said that their daughter had suffered from low self-esteem, was insecure, and had been teased by other girls since she had started school. Print and television accounts focused on the fact that Virk was constantly being humiliated and bullied at school. Her "unusual bodily features" became the source of verbal abuse and harassment. She was called "nicknames" such as "Daddy," "the ugly," "bearded lady," "dark-skinned," and "beast." She was teased constantly about her appearance, including references to her skin colour. Various media accounts stress Reena Virk was an outsider, someone who did not "fit in," cast outside of the boundaries of the dominant culture of the school and society. Jiwani (1997) observes that her status of "otherness" was not surprising. In a White society, her skin colour was brown; in a society that values thinness, she was perceived as overweight. Yet another identifier of her "difference" was the fact that her family, although of South-Asian background, were practising Jehovah's Witnesses.

The initial assault on Reena by the seven young women and one male, Warren Glowatski, started with a young White woman putting out a cigarette on Reena's forehead. Jiwani (2000) suggest that this act symbolically branded her as cultural "other"; the mark was reminiscent of the bindis that South-Asian women often wear on their foreheads. It was followed by a tortuous assault in which the pathologist's testimony documented that she had been kicked 18 times in the head and that her internal injuries were so severe as to result in tissues that were crushed between the abdomen and backbone (ibid.). The attack on Virk was so brutal that there were no historical examples in Canada to match the viciousness of the beating (see Chakkalakal, 2000). Three years later after her death, six female teenagers were eventually convicted of assault causing bodily harm. Warren Glowatski and Kelly Marie Ellard were convicted of second-degree murder. The trial judge described Ellard as a person who had positive relationships with her family and friends, loved animals, and, in general, posed a low risk to society. Ellard was sentenced to life imprisonment and was required to serve five years in prison before becoming eligible for parole. However, a year later an appeal court overturned her conviction and ordered a new trial. While in a halfway house in 2004, she was accused of having assaulted another woman in a park. A new trial is scheduled to take place.

Analysis

The beating and killing of Reena Virk was widely reported in the both print and electronic media across the country. In the initial stage of media coverage, journalists and broadcasters contextualized the event in terms of the questions "Why is violence among girls sharply on the rise?" and "What, if anything, can be done to halt the trend?" (Patricia Chishold, "Bad Girls," *Maclean's*, December 1997). The media stories commonly linked the killing to the larger issue of the rising incidence of youth violence across Canada, which was described in a frenzy of countless news reports. Much attention was directed at the seeming contradiction between the increasing acts of violence committed by young women, while at the same time females are experiencing greater success in schools and access to jobs. The implicit assumption seemed to be that somehow feminism had failed to save Reena Virk (Chakkalakal, 2000).

However, it appeared from the responses (or lack thereof) by the school, the court, and the media that no public authority believed it was relevant or necessary to probe the role that Virk's race played in her victimization and ultimate death. The Canadian news media used Virk's "ethnic" identity as an explanation of her own insecurity, but never reflected on the possibility that her South-Asian origins contributed to her undesirable "otherness," and thus might have been a factor in her life and death. Chakkalakal (ibid.) suggests that the one exception was an article that appeared in an American publication, *Gentlemen's Quarterly*, February 1999. The journalist, Guy Lawson, wrote that "most of the girls who attacked Reena were white, but it was an article of faith for officials that it had nothing to do with race" (February, 1999:165).

Thus, Whiteness within the context of racism became an invisible presence in the narratives that followed this story. Five White women were sentenced for brutality, but not racism. The White judge in her sentencing of Kelly Ellard, a White girl, clearly stated her position on the subject: "The motive was not racism" (end of story). The dominant culture discourses of denial and colour-blindness ("There is no racism; we never notice the colour of someone's skin") are part of the everyday Whiteness discourses that not only resonate in the courtroom, but also are articulated in the classroom, media, and across other interlocking systems of oppression.

The school appeared to have no knowledge of the way everyday racism is often deeply embedded in the culture of schooling and how this factor might have contributed to Reena's victimization. Whiteness cast its illusive veil over the death of Reena Virk, erasing the consequences of her racial identity while reinforcing her otherness. Thus, the question of the role of race in this case remained unspeakable and unanswered. However, it can be hypothesized that the story of Reena Virk follows the pattern of the stages of racialization commonly identified in the literature: the mutating processes of racism move across a continuum: from differentiation, inferiorization, dehumanization, and degradation, to the most extreme form of racism, annihilation.

Afterword: It is interesting to note that another violent racist incident took place in a Vancouver high school in November, 2003. The incident involved a swarming and an assault that resulted in the death of a Filipino student, Mao Jomar Lanot. The perpetrators were identified as Indo-Canadians. In June 2004 the Vancouver school board released a report (Adrienne Chan, 2004) based on interviews with students, staff, and community members. The report identifies racism in the form of name-calling, stereotyping, and violence based on race and ethnicity. It identified the source of racism against both students of colour and Aboriginal students as an everyday occurrence in Vancouver schools. The report recommended that anti-racism and multiculturalism be made priorities in every school.

The result of this individual and institutional denial is that ranges of inappropriate responses have been adopted by boards of education. First, the most common response has been to ignore or redefine the "racial" dimension of these incidents—"There's no problem here." Second, informal policies have emerged as ad hoc responses to individual incidents of harassment. There appear to be significant problems in implementing these policies. Finally, a "multicultural approach" uses the curriculum to emphasize tolerance and respect for other cultures and racial groups.

Hatcher and Troyna (1993) lack confidence in most of these approaches, arguing that there is no empirical evidence of their effectiveness. In their discussion of racial harassment and conflict in schools, they provided a multidimensional framework for analyzing a racial incident. They concluded that a constellation of factors and influences contribute to the understanding of any racial confrontation, including structural racism and differential power relations between groups; ideological beliefs and attitudes; cultural values and understandings; institutional values, procedures, and practices; students' subcultures; the specific experiences of the individuals; the context and history of the incident; and the details and nature of the incident (1993:197).

The Policies and Practices of Zero Tolerance: Youth Aggression and Violence in Public Schooling

In reaction to a growing concern and reported increase in suspensions and expulsions related to student aggression and youth violence, school disciplinary practices are being debated and reevaluated in ministries of education, boards of education, and schools across Canada. In recent years, following largely on the U.S. model of "get tough" policies, there has been a significant trend to alter school discipline policies following the approach and principles of Zero Tolerance and Safe Schools. These policies purport to promote respect, discipline, and safety. In Ontario, for example, the Education Act was amended in 2000 to include Safe Schools and Zero Tolerance provisions. "Inappropriate" behaviours and specific punishments are identified, including a greater use of suspensions and expulsions, which lead to the greater involvement of police (Lawson, 2003).

Teachers are expected to implement school codes of conduct and disciplinary measures irrespective of whether they support the particular policy or principle. Jull (2000) suggests that for many teachers it appears that political expedience in the implementation of these new policies takes priority over ongoing dialogue of the educational, social, and psychological preconditions necessary for the positive social development skills and behaviours in children and youth. Zero Tolerance fails to provide students and teachers the opportunity to decide for themselves the terms and conditions defining acceptable behaviour. Moreover, it can be argued that school discipline policies based on this policy reinforces the authoritarian structures within public education. Many racial-minority students, their parents, communities, educators and scholars in Canada and the United States perceive that there is a differential, negative impact of the Zero Tolerance approach on students of colour, particularly Black students.

Consistent with the above findings, in a study of a group of Black, predominantly male, low-socioeconomic-status, urban high school students, Solomon (1992) determined that these students tended to view school discipline as being administered arbitrarily by school authorities. Black students perceived that they were more often suspended than White students for engaging in the same types of behaviour. Ruck and Wortley (2002) analyzed the perceptions of minority students with respect to differential treatment pertaining to school disciplinary practices, based on a large multiracial, culturally pluralistic sample of high school students from metropolitan Toronto. One of the most striking findings was that students from all four racial/ethnic groups selected (Black, South Asian, Asian, other) were significantly more likely than White students to perceive discrimination in various aspects of school life in the context of school disciplinary treatment—including teacher treatment, school suspensions, and the school's use of police. The results of the study also suggest that in comparison to students from all other minority groups, Black students viewed themselves as being at a distinct disadvantage, particularly with regard to their dealings with police at school (see Case Study 6.1, Chapter 6). Black students were more likely than White students to perceive discrimination at school and 27 times more likely to perceive that they would be treated worse by the police at school. The researchers, following a similar conclusion drawn by many American scholars, suggest that Zero Tolerance incorporates an apparent skin-colour-coded hierarchy (from dark to light) with respect to students' perceptions of differential treatment and the allocation of social penalties. Black students are the most likely to perceive bias followed by students of South-Asian background, students from "other" racial/ethnic groups, and finally White students.

Former trustee of the Toronto District School Board (and newly elected MPP) Kathryn Wynne, who has attended many of the highly confidential forums in which boards decide full expulsions, recently told a *Toronto Star* reporter, "I assume when I'm going into an [expulsion] hearing its going to be a young male of colour. And if it's not, I'm surprised" (quoted in Watson, 2003). The Toronto District School Board issues several thousand suspensions and limited expulsions every year. The issue of youth violence resonates across the country and questions about the efficacy of Zero Tolerance have also surfaced in Nova Scotia, Manitoba, and Saskatchewan.

A recent study (Upshaw, 2003) conducted for the Halifax Regional School Board showed that 40 percent of Black high school students in the Halifax schools have been suspended at least once. The figure drops to 35 percent in junior high and 8 percent in elementary school. The report documented the same dissatisfaction and concern felt by Black students and their families as was reflected in earlier studies of racism in this school board (see Black Learners Advisory Committee Report, 1997). The report indicated that the Black community continues to feel alienated, intimidated, and misunderstood by the school system. Parents stated that the Halifax School Board has not lived up to the commitments that have been made in earlier policies and procedures documents.

Tensions and fights erupted between Black and White students at Cole Harbour High School in Nova Scotia in 1989 and again a year later. By late 1990, a year and a half after the fighting, the government still had not investigated racism in the province's educational system, supporting the Halifax County–Bedford District School Board's claim that the fights were not racially motivated and its denial that racism existed in the school system (Kakembo and Upshaw, 1998).

The Black community demanded action on racism in the educational system and a series of studies led to the conclusion that racism was rampant in all levels of the school system (BLAC, 1997).[1] BLAC (the Black Learners Advisory Committee) identified the same inequities in the education system that had existed for Black learners since the 1970s.

Today, BLAC continues to work toward achieving educational equity for Black students, in partnership with parents, students, school boards, Black community organizations, and government agencies. The BLAC Report on Education compelled the Nova Scotia government to acknowledge the existence of systemic racism in the educational system (Kakembo and Upshaw, 1998). However, many of the recommendations contained in the report have failed to be implemented. In 2002 several organizations considered launching a lawsuit suggesting that all their grievances against the Nova Scotia educational system (high dropout, failure, and suspension rates, lack of Black models in the classroom, and lack of inclusion of positive Black content in the curriculum) had failed to be addressed. The findings of the most recent report by researcher Upshaw (2003) reveal that the systemic racism continues.

Responses to Racism in the Schools

For most of Canada's history, including the first seven decades of this century, the issue of racism was totally absent from the agendas of educational institutions and completely invisible to most White educators. Assimilation—the complete absorption of different ethnic and racial groups into the majority culture—was considered the appropriate model both for educational institutions and for the broader society.

Although the educational system had no formal policy on monoculturalism, this pervasive and coercive ideology influenced the training of educators, the practice of teaching, the content and context of learning, the hiring and promotion practices of boards, and the cultural values and norms underpinning all areas of school life. Students from diverse backgrounds were expected to leave their cultural, religious, and racial identities at the front door of the school.

The assimilationist-monocultural approach to education ignored the fact that large numbers of children experienced racial bias and discrimination both outside and inside the school. The monocultural approach to education, which operated unchallenged until the mid-1970s, continues to influence education today in many Canadian educational institutions (Cummins, 2001; Dei, 2000).

In 1971, largely in response to demographic, social, and political pressures, the federal policy of multiculturalism was declared. The government's commitment to preserve and promote Canada's cultural diversity and to overcome barriers to full participation was a catalyst for school systems to begin examining their policies and practices.

Multicultural Education

Multiculturalism, as government policy and later as legislation, provided the moral and empirical foundation on which to move away from the monocultural, assimilationist orientation. Many school boards gradually developed policies, programs, and practices intended to create a learning environment that respected the cultures of all students. Initiatives were introduced that focused on the histories, traditions, and lifestyles of diverse cultures. Cultural pluralism, or multicultural education in its most effective expression, acknowledged the reality of diversity in Canadian society and aimed to produce students who were more tolerant, respectful, and understanding of cultural differences. The major thrust of the multicultural approach was attitudinal change.

An empirical study of multicultural ideologies and programs in six countries in the 1970s concluded that three key assumptions underpinned multicultural education:

- learning about one's culture and ethnic roots will improve one's educational achievement;
- learning about one's culture and its traditions will promote equality of opportunity; and
- learning about other cultures will reduce children's (and adults') prejudice and discrimination toward those from different cultural and ethnic backgrounds (Bullivant, 1981:236).

However, after more than two decades of multicultural education in Canada, the limitations of this approach have become increasingly apparent. Multiculturalism's policies and programs relied on untested assumptions about culture and its transmission (Dei and Calliste, 2000).

Multicultural education in many educational jurisdictions tended to focus on a "museum" and "monolithic" approach to the study of complex and constantly evolving cultures. Educators taught students about the material and exotic dimensions of culture, such as food, festivals, and folk tales, rather than the values and belief systems that underlie cultural diversity. Important factors shaping cultural identity, such as racial, linguistic, religious, regional, socioeconomic, and gender differences, were often ignored (Bedard, 2000; Dei, 1996). Moreover, the teachers often had very little knowledge or understanding of other cultures, which inadvertently led both teachers and students to trivialize and stereotype different ethnic and racial groups. "Different," "minority" cultures were celebrated, while pedagogy, curricula, assessment practices, and school–community relationships remained unchanged.

Perhaps the most serious weakness of multicultural education was its failure to acknowledge that racism was endemic in Canadian society. While schools attempted to "respond to special needs" by affirming ethnic-minority children's background, culture, and language; by celebrating festivals; and by teaching "mother" (heritage) languages, "multicultural" history, and non-Western music, the real problem of racial inequality was ignored. In a growing number of boards of education in the 1980s, many parents and representatives of diverse racial and ethnic groups urged trustees to make radical changes to an educational system that they believed was disadvantaging their children. They maintained that the fundamental issues were not so much cultural as racial; not lifestyles but life chances; not heritage but competence; not diversity but disparity; not prejudice but discrimination. As one parent expressed it in the foreword to the Toronto Board of Education's *Policy on Race Relations* (1979): "The issues facing the colour of my skin are more pressing than those facing my culture."

The basis of multicultural education was a problem paradigm that in itself was racist. The underlying assumption was that racial- and cultural-minority children in the educational system suffer because they are "socially disadvantaged." According to this perspective, many minority children seem to suffer from a negative self-concept and low esteem, resulting in defective perceptual, cognitive, and linguistic skills that were often exacerbated by the negative, non-supportive values of their social and family background (Kowalczewski, 1982). The duty of the schools (especially those with high concentrations of minority students) therefore was to provide a curriculum relevant to the needs of such disadvantaged groups, in order to enhance their self-image and to promote racial harmony and mutual tolerance.

Both monocultural and multicultural education ignored the role of educational institutions in the generation and reproduction of racism (Bedard, 2000; Cummins, 1992; Moodley, 1984; Thomas, 1984). These approaches ignored the reality of racism as a powerful and pervasive force that shaped all of Canada's institutions. Thus, the racial conflicts in the wider society were mirrored in the educational system (Solomon, 1992).

Anti-Racism Education

Anti-racism education as both a theoretical and a practical approach to institutional and systemic racism was formulated in both the United States and Great Britain. It first appeared in the Canadian educational context in the late 1980s and is still evolving. The shift to this model was largely the result of the persistence of minority communities, especially Black parents, in drawing attention to the way racism limited the academic progress and circumscribed the life chances of their children.

The central thrust of anti-racism education is to change institutional and organizational policies and practices that have a discriminatory impact and to change individual attitudes and behaviours that reinforce racial bias and inequality. Anti-racism education is based on the principle that race, despite the concept's lack of scientific foundation, is anchored in the experiences of racial minorities in society and in the school, and that anti-racism is a tool for social change (Dei, 1996; Dei and Calliste, 2000). For a period of time, from the late 1980s to the mid-1990s, it served as a catalyst for some boards of education to develop new policies, and led to the gradual introduction of various programs, including the training of educators in anti-racism, reviews of personnel practices, an analysis of assessment and placement procedures, the introduction of employment equity strategies, a review of curriculum materials to identify for racial bias, and the development of anti-racism curriculum resources and strategies.

Largely in response to the Stephen Lewis report (Lewis, 1992) and the demands of racial-minority communities for greater racial equity, Ontario introduced two new measures. First, a legislative act required all boards of education in Ontario to develop and implement anti-racism policies in their schools. However, no additional funds would be allocated to the school boards to develop and implement these policies (Lewington, 1993). One positive feature of the new measures was proposed changes in the teacher-selection process at university faculties of education. The faculties were required to develop new admission criteria that would increase the representation of minority groups. These criteria included a recognition of the experience acquired by teachers trained outside of Canada.

The second initiative involved a de-streaming process, in which Grade 9 students would no longer be separated into academic and vocational streams. The streaming would be delayed until Grade 10.

However, the Conservative Ontario government of then-Premier Mike Harris revoked these proactive responses to racism almost immediately after its election in 1995. As well, the dismantling of anti-racism, anti-oppression initiatives occurred in ministries of education and boards of education across the country. Provinces such as British Columbia that had developed comprehensive anti-racism and equity policies and programs also witnessed a dismantling of these initiatives. For example, the Vancouver School Board cuts in the late 1990s resulted in a loss of important First Nations resource teachers, ESL teachers, and the elimination of most anti-racism initiatives in schools. Yet citywide student surveys identified racism as one of the top five concerns in schools.

Black-Focused Schools

The failure of the mainstream school system to provide equitable education to Black students has led to the development of another alternative model of education: "Black-focused" schools. The concept of such a Black–African-centred school has been a matter of intense public debate in Ontario. Advocates of Black-focused schools argue that the current educational structure inhibits the maximum social and intellectual development of many Black students; therefore, a need exists for a more radical approach to racism.

In Metropolitan Toronto, government officials and members of the Black community recommended that a Black junior high school be established in each of the area's six municipalities. The proposed separate Black schools would be administered and have a curriculum designed and implemented by skilled Black educators.

The concept of a Black-focused school is based on the view that mainstream schools are not neutral terrain. They pass on the values and norms of the dominant culture; they inculcate Western worldviews and devalue non-Western forms of knowledge. Dei (1996) contends that the model of an African-centred school suggests that there are relevant African-based cultural values and epistemic constructs—such as the concepts of community, traditions of mutuality, and communal bonding—that provide a solid educational foundation on which to promote both academic and social success.

Teacher Training

Teacher training is provided by the university, and the knowledge, values, and norms acquired by educators will be passed on to students. Rosenberg suggested that in teacher education, discussions about the power and privilege of Whiteness go "underground" (1997:87). Difference is seen as being variation, or as Mohanty argued, cultural and racial differences bypass both power and history to suggest "a harmonious, empty pluralism" (1993:42). Within the school and the university, educators and students bring conflicting experiential frameworks that influence the construction of school knowledge. The contradictory and conflicting issues of race, ethnicity, gender, and sexuality, among other social markers, influence how identities are lived within the school and university (Yon, 2000).

Faculties of education need to begin providing new knowledge and skills that will equip them and their future students with the ability to challenge the status quo and question why things are the way they are. Teachers need to develop an understanding of the multiple roles that students occupy in the school system and society; how social hierarchies are established; and the ways in which male-centric, Eurocentric power structures function in schools (Brathwaite and James, 1996; Dei, 1996; Dei and Calliste, 2000).

Recent research on the responses of prospective teachers to attempts to introduce anti-racism into their educational programs has revealed tensions and resistance. This resistance is reflected in White student teachers' negative responses to the integration of anti-racism, pedagogy, and curriculum in their practices and their resistance to racial-minority peers and educators (Cochran-Smith, 2000; Solomon, 1992; Solomon and Levine-Rasky, 1996).

Universities: A Chilly Climate for Minorities[2]

On university campuses across the country, minority students have complained that the campus is often a hostile learning environment. Aboriginal students on Winnipeg's campuses say that they face acts of racism as brutal as any that occur in the poverty-stricken city. They are constantly bombarded with racist acts, from death threats spraypainted on the elevator walls to insensitivity from professors; in class, people often won't sit beside Aboriginal students. A third-year student from the Peguis First Nation said that in one incident, a sociology professor presented a theory in class about why Aboriginal people are more prone to alcoholism, a remark that hurt students in his class (*Edmonton Journal*, January 9, 1994, as cited in Alladin, 1996:15).

Many universities have received student complaints of racial harassment from fellow students, technical and administrative staff, and faculty. At York University a group of Black students, claiming that security guards had harassed them, staged a protest at the president's door. (The university responded quickly by agreeing to hire another staff member at its Centre for Race and Ethnic Relations and to provide training for the guards.) A study of graduate students at the same university (Ornstein, 1996) found that over one-quarter of the graduate students who were African or Black felt that they were disadvantaged in their studies as a consequence of their race. In terms of racial groups, 11 percent of South Asians and 14 percent of East Asians, as well as 7 percent of Middle Eastern students and 6 percent of Aboriginal students, indicated expressions of concern related to discrimination. James (2003) identifies the salience of race as a significant factor that marks the experience of students. The diversity of their knowledge, needs, interests, and aspirations that students of colour bring to higher education remains negated or ignored.

Students at a number of campuses have complained of harassment in the residences, cafeterias, and other public places on campus. Graffiti smeared on washroom walls and other surfaces often is racist.

The Marginalization and Exclusion of Aboriginal Women and Women of Colour in Academia

In the last decade there has been a growing body of scholarship documenting the experiences of Aboriginal women and women of colour working within the academic institutions of Canada (see Kobayashi, 2002; Dua and Lawrence, 2000; Monture-Angus, 2001; Razack, 1998, 2001; Luther, Whitmore, and Moreau, 2001; Calliste, 2000; Shahrzad, 2002; Brathwaite, 2003).

Overall, the findings of these studies suggest that our institutions of higher learning continue to be powerful sites through which racism is constructed, reproduced, and maintained. Despite claims of access, inclusion, and equity, many argue that the "hallowed halls" of academia remain "a zone of White privilege" (Kobayashi, 2002:44). The first indicator of a lack of equity is the underrepresentation of Aboriginal and women of colour.[3] Kobayashi points to the fact that women of colour in Canadian academia hold 18.7 percent of the Ph.D.s in Canada and yet make up an average of 10.3 percent of university faculties across the country. Their numbers are significantly less than those of their male counterparts. They are virtually excluded from university administrations and are rarely found as chairs and department heads. On the other hand, there has been a very significant increase in students of colour in many universities across the country, with some approaching or exceeding 50 percent of the total student bodies. The manifestations of academic racism are found in the day-to-day interactions between students, faculty, and administration, as well as woven into the culture of academia as reflected in curricula, pedagogy, hiring, selection, promotion practices and procedures, mentoring and support of minority faculty, the role of women of colour in mentoring students of colour, etc.

In the analysis of the numerous studies on racism against Aboriginal women and women of colour in academia, scholars have spoken with almost a single voice on the huge barriers that continue to stigmatize, marginalize, and discriminate against minority women. In the many studies reviewed, there was a remarkable commonality in the experiences identified, the barriers encountered, the pain and frustration endured, and the sense of marginality and exclusion from the institutional White culture. Based on these findings it can be argued that the profound impact of systemic discrimination and everyday racism continues to mark the life of Canadian academic institutions.

The narratives emerging from professors of colour and Aboriginal academics across this country reflect the failure of administrative policies, programs, and initiatives to address racism and create equity. Their experiences are recorded in texts and in papers delivered at conferences, seminars, and workshops. The following are some of the areas of struggle and conflict.

There appears to be a profound lack of understanding that successful implementation of policies cannot be achieved without a sweeping change in the culture of Whiteness that is enveloping in academia. It requires a fundamental shift in the values, norms, and everyday discursive practices that operate invisibly but leave their imprint on every aspect of the academy. The older overt forms of racism continue to occur and mingle with new manifestations of racialization, in the form of a powerful backlash directed at any but the most cosmetic changes to the core culture of the university. Understanding how this process works is difficult because it appears so normalized and naturalized within the White dominant culture that characterizes these institutions. Almost every scholar refers to the systemic barriers that continue to operate despite almost universal claims of commitment to "access and equity," "diversity," and "inclusion." The dominant White discourse of the university as a site of liberalism and neutrality, leads to a view that issues of race and racism are isolated incidents and not embedded in the structures and systems that operate in the everyday life of the academy. The absence of any form of critical assessment leads to the preservation of White and Eurocentric values and norms in the academy. An employment equity coordinator at a university in Ontario identified a deep resistance to change, arguing that the centralized structure of the university worked as an obstacle to change. Senior management did not view equity as an intervention aimed at redistributing power. The equity coordinator was viewed as a technocrat hired to ensure the university complied with government requirements (Shahrzad, 2002).

The curricula represent a major manifestation of marginalization and exclusion in which Aboriginal women and women of colour are at the vanguard of challenging the racist canons of their disciplines (Dua and Lawrence, 2000). Curricula, in their most overt racialized expression, function by valuing particular kinds of knowledge. Curricula are regulated according to an accepted standard of practice, by which studies based on Eurocentric standards are given more resources, curriculum space, dominance, and prestige. Kobayashi (2002) notes that the degradation of academics of colour is manifested in the development of curricula, choice of readings, organization of workshops and seminars, as well as choices about invitations to be guest lecturers or recipients of honorary degrees. Struggles to emphasize indigenous history, philosophy, and culture, and incorporate anti-racism models of knowledge are met with often-fierce resistance and hostility from students, and a lack of support from colleagues and administration. Efforts to introduce more critical forms of pedagogy are also challenged. In the last decade or more, anti-racist feminist writers have critiqued the traditional pedagogical paradigms and canons of many disciplines, including women's studies, and attempted to modify the ideological frameworks through which racism is constructed and reproduced (Green, 2002; Dua and Lawrence, 2000; Bannerji et al., 1991; Calliste, 2000). Concern and disappointment has been particularly strong in relation to women's studies programs that have for the most part failed to incorporate into their theoretical and methodological methods a focus on the intersection of racism and gender. Calliste (ibid.) argues that some White women perceive the introduction of race issues as a threat to their long battle for gender equality.

Systemic forms of bias and discrimination embedded in the institutional practices, procedures, and discourses within academia have a significant impact upon career aspirations and mobility upon women of colour and Aboriginal women. Indeed, the tenure process itself is viewed as one of the most overt manifestations of the continuing power of the White-dominated male culture. Through this highly politicized process, individuals are punished or rewarded on the basis of their conformity to inflexible rules and standards (Luther et al., 2001). Monture-Angus, an Aboriginal woman teaching Native Studies, suggests that in her own tenure experience her efforts to bring "Aboriginal voices" into the classroom were not valued as a scholarly contribution. Instead, she was penalized for her failure to produce published articles in scholarly journals. The research undertaken by women of colour is often perceived to be too political (Kobayashi, 2002). Research and writing that focuses on community, social action, and social change is often challenged. Law professor Joanne St. Lewis (cited in Luther et al., 2001) points out the glaring contradiction many faculty of colour and Aboriginal faculty face in the promotion process. On one hand, she is seen as an "expert," and on the other she is devalued for not having a graduate degree required by the law faculty.

Aboriginal women and women of colour carry the excessive weight of expectations and demands that go far beyond the normative roles of their White colleagues. They are commonly confronted with demands from minority students who wish to have mentors and role models to whom they can relate; the broader student population who want to utilize their knowledge and expertise; colleagues who require speakers on issues of diversity, race, and racism; administrators who "need bodies to demonstrate that committee structures are truly 'representative' ... broader community expectations for development work and mentoring programs" (Luther et al., 2001:90).

These and other barriers constructed in a system of White privilege and power have a significant impact on women of colour and Aboriginal women's sense of self-esteem and self-confidence. The narratives of these academics are characterized by self-doubt, apprehension, frustration, and disappointment. The workplace climate creates an inhospitable environment leading to high levels of stress, physical ill health, and depression. The impact of a lack a support from other colleagues, chairs of departments, and deans leads to a sense of isolation and alienation (Calliste, 2000; Luther et al., 2001; Kobayashi, 2002; Dua and Lawrence, 2000). It can also lead to a heightened sense of vulnerability. Joanne St. Lewis observes: "As a professor when I teach, I never assume that I am safe" (92 in Luther). Many academics of colour speak about the hostility directed at them from their students. One informant observes:

> When I teach about racism, the tension in the room is clear. Unlike in other classes, the students are deathly quiet and still, glaring, hostile, their pens on their desk. They are clearly telling me that they are not willing to learn. While I am supposed to have the responsibility to define what is being taught in the classroom, students are clearly asserting their power to say that this is their classroom—and I need to teach only what they want to learn. (Cited in Dua and Lawrence, 2000:107)

As a response to the issue of vulnerability, many women of colour and Aboriginal women have spoken about the importance of community in both their personal and professional lives and the need to link their work to their own respective communities. "Zones of safety" are necessary for both students and faculty as they attempt to negotiate the minefields of everyday racism in academia.

The backlash to the efforts of the marginalized "others" to alter challenge existing power relations, forms of knowledge, pedagogical models, and the institutional culture of Whiteness and maleness is manifested in the discourse of "political correctness" ("PC"). In academia, political correctness has become the clarion call echoing across North American campuses. Green (2002) observes: "[T]hose of us who name and object to our oppression, or who stand in solidarity with marginalized others, are transformed by our stance into the oppressors of those whose privilege we challenge. ... Institutional intransigence and colleagues' hostility and derision freeze many of us out of the academy" (88).

Finally, Kobayashi (2002) makes the important point that while racism is the outcome of White institutional structures, systems, and culture, women of colour and Aboriginal women experience the effects as individuals in relation to other individuals. She observes: "In the complex interactions that make up the life of the institution, the attitudes, assumptions, and beliefs that perpetuate racism are held or implemented by somebody" (47).

Responses by the University

Racism is still present in the culture and values of the university. However, the issue continues to have a low priority in terms of the public agenda of institutions of higher learning. This can be attributed to the fact that the discourse of denial is deeply embedded in the culture of Canadian universities. Meininger's analysis (1990) identified a number of explanations for the absence of substantive change. These factors are still at play in the year 2004:

- Minority students and faculty are generally very concerned about their vulnerability and have usually kept experiences of racism to themselves. In addition, until recently universities did not have complaint or grievance mechanisms that dealt with racial harassment and other forms of racism.

CASE STUDY 8.2

PROFESSOR CAROL AYLWARD VS. DALHOUSIE UNIVERSITY

Background

Carol Aylward was appointed in 1991 as an assistant professor in the Faculty of Law at Dalhousie University and as Director of the Indigenous Blacks and Mi'kmaq Programme. In 2000, she filed a human rights complaint alleging that she had experienced racial discrimination and harassment in her workplace and that because of the "intersectionality of race, gender and retaliation" had to work in a "hostile and poisoned environment" at the Law School for the past nine years. The basis of her complaint was that she experienced denial of promotion and discrimination with respect to salary and stipends because she is a Black woman and a strong anti-racist advocate (cited in Pieters, 2000). Moreover, the law school was charged with racial bias in hiring because a White professor was appointed to a tenure track position over that of two qualified Black candidates and a qualified Aboriginal candidate. She also complained that her promotion to associate professor was denied in part because some of members of the promotion and tenure committee "made unsubstantiated allegations of academic fraud by removing parts of her manuscript that gave credit to her sources and authorities" (Pieters, ibid.). She charged a former director of the Indigenous Blacks and Mi'kmaq Programme of being paternalistic and undermining her authority as its director. Since then, her term as director has not been renewed.

Aylward's complaint was originally presented to the Nova Scotia Human Rights Commission, but because of a conflict of interest between the law school faculty—several of whose members, including some of those cited as respondents in her complaint, had adjudicated cases for that Commission (one of them was its former director)—she requested that the complaint be dealt with by an outside-the-province commission. The Nova Scotia Office of the Ombudsman entered into a arrangement with the Ontario Human Rights Commission to act as Trustee of Investigations for the Nova Scotia Commission in order to investigate Aylward's complaint. In the meantime, the respondent to her complaint, Dalhousie University, brought a motion to the Supreme Court of Nova Scotia declaring this arrangement invalid and to set aside any actions of the Nova Scotia Human Rights Commission or the Ombudsman.

The application to move to the Ontario Human Rights Commission was denied by court order, and the Nova Scotia Commission agreed that they did not have the authority to refer this complaint. They also agreed to nullify the original referral. Aylward did not consent to this order, and instead applied to the court for her costs involved in the matter of transference. Costs were refused (Nova Scotia Supreme Court, Halifax, Nova Scotia, Scanlan J., March 1, 2001). The decision to appeal the lack of transfer to Ontario was also refused (Nova Scotia Court of Appeal, Halifax, Nova Scotia, Glube C.J.N.S., Hallett and Freeman, JJ.A., May 30, 2002).

Professor Aylward experienced stress while attempting to fulfil her duties in the department and as director of the Indigenous Blacks and Mi'kmaq Programme. Her outspoken advocacy on issues of racism and equity engendered enormous resistance by the University. As well, the denial of Aylward's academic benefits and having to bring a human rights complaint against the University created a high level of stress for her personally, necessitating a leave from the University. More recently, the University has apparently suggested that she go on long-term disability leave.

Analysis

There are many significant aspects to this case. In the first instance, the University did not at any time seek to mediate or take a role in the racist experiences Professor Aylward claimed to be experiencing. The experience of a corporate organization turning a blind eye and ignoring allegations of racism is well known both in the experience of others and in the literature (see Chapter 12). Only when Aylward launched a complaint did the University take action, by attempting to stifle it. The complainant's request not to have the Nova Scotia Human Rights Commission investigate the complaint appears justified, since several of the law professors in the faculty, including some cited in the complaint, had prior relationships with that commission. In fact, its former director was a member of Aylward's faculty and one was specifically mentioned in her complaint as undermining her authority. Nevertheless, the University made every attempt to stop Aylward's attempt to have the Ontario Commission investigate her complaint by actually filing a court motion to that effect. In addition, the President and Vice-Chancellor of Dalhousie University, Tom Traves, in a letter to the *Globe and Mail* (April 7, 2001), categorically denied the allegations in the complaint. At some point, Prof. Aylward also withdrew from the Dalhousie Faculty Association, alleging that its conduct also was discriminatory. Both her grievance officer and her lawyer withdrew from it as well because of the racism that arose during the grievance process (see letter of Professor Joanne St. Lewis, August 23, 2000 at Pieters, 2000). St. Lewis also wrote a letter to the Canadian Association of University Teachers (CAUT) on Prof. Aylward's behalf specially requesting a formal investigation into the Dalhousie Faculty Association. However, CAUT's bylaws prevented it from investigating its member associations.

These contentious issues raise important questions regarding the corporate role of the university. As well, individual administrators and faculty members within it are culpable in delaying and obfuscating this case, which alleges a violation of human rights. It is particularly ironic that some of Aylward's colleagues cited as respondents are themselves specialists in equity law.

The justice system's involvement comes about as the University's motion is upheld, as is the appeal of it filed by the complainant. It is difficult to accuse the justices who rendered these decisions of racism, since they applied constitutional and legal arguments about the mandate of human rights commissions to this case and therefore came to negative decisions. It can be argued, however, that the laws as presently constituted with respect to the powers of such commissions colluded with those of the justice system to deny the complainant a strategy that would have provided her with a fairer hearing.

The Human Rights Commission in Nova Scotia has also played a significant role in delaying the case, and up to the time of writing is still doing so. Professor Aylward's attempt to have a Board of Inquiry set up immediately was rejected in favour of having a regional office in Digby launch an investigation. This, according to Professor Aylward, does not resolve the issue of bias.

The case attracted media attention from the Halifax paper *Daily News* (October 31, 2000), and was also covered by the *Globe and Mail* (Makin, 2001). In both instances, basic coverage of the facts was provided; but although the *Daily News* was balanced and generous in its coverage of Aylward's discomfort and stress, it did not cite or quote any of the respondents. *The Globe's* coverage was well balanced, but it paid considerable attention to Professor Aylward and her complaints. This article prompted a response from the president of Dalhousie University in which he categorically denied the allegations made in the complaint, which he characterized as outrageous; and praised the diversity in hiring racial minorities and Aboriginal people. He noted that the law faculty was especially diverse because it contained two Black tenured faculty members and was among the most representative law faculties in the country. The University's legal aid office also had both a Black and an Aboriginal lawyer on staff (*Globe and Mail*, April 7, 2001).

This case, while extremely complex, is a powerful example of academic racism at a university. It is also important to note the intersection and role of other institutions. At the time of this writing, the matter has not even been investigated, much less resolved.

- Few members of the faculty had any expertise in race and ethnic relations. Those who did tended to examine the issue elsewhere in society, rather than in their own backyard.
- Staff associations and unions were busy with bread-and-butter issues, rather than ideological and systemic issues.
- Academic administrators and managers respond primarily as a result of political pressure or evidence of conflict. Since pressure to create equity and equality for racial-minority students did not exist, it was not on the academic administrative agenda.
- The women's movement, which urged equity and curriculum change, had not yet made its mark.
- The general slowness of institutional change, and the particular slowness of institutional change at universities, also contributed to the lack of response to racial and other equity-related issues.[4]

Finally, universities have been subject to financial constraints, as have the other institutions that depend largely on public financing. It has therefore been necessary to increase the number of part-time faculty hired to teach specific courses for one to three years. They are not eligible for tenure protection and not protected by collective agreements. As a result of their feeling of powerlessness, they do not speak out: "If people feel vulnerable, you can be sure they won't articulate beliefs that challenge the status quo" (Sweet, 1993).

Race and Representation at the University

Canadian universities, especially those in Ontario, have grown rapidly since the 1960s. That growth continues as most universities are expanding their capital and resource facilities. During the 1990s financial constraints affected their ability to hire new faculty and resulted in fewer opportunities to hire women, racial minorities, and other disadvantaged groups. Today, although funding has not significantly increased, many universities are moving into a period not only of increasing enrolments but also of significant levels of faculty retirement. This presents an opportunity for hiring new faculty and increasing the representation of underrepresented employment equity targeted groups.

Universities, like many other institutions, are required to review their hiring policies and practices. Many have done employee workforce audits, and their results with respect to minorities, women, and other disadvantaged groups still indicate a significant level of underrepresentation, especially at senior academic ranks. For example, at the University of Toronto, Canada's largest university, there is still a substantial difference in numbers between its diverse student body and ethno-racial minority faculty representation. While nearly half of its student body comes from a variety of diverse backgrounds, only 11 percent of its full-time faculty is "visible minorities." Even more revealing was the fact that nearly 70 percent of these were concentrated in science and life science disciplines. Only 20.5 percent of these faculty were in the social sciences and the remainder of only 9.7 percent in humanities (University of Toronto, 2000–2001 Employment Equity Report). On the more positive side, however, members of visible minority groups constituted 16.1 percent of all new faculty hires in 2001 and 23 percent of new hires the previous year. These figures are consistent with the range of 15–20 percent that had been estimated in the University's equity review. However, the employment equity report acknowledges that recent data show a higher proportion of visible-minority Ph.D. graduates, and their equity estimates therefore need revision.

Moreover, the University acknowledges that although visible minority staff are moving through professional and administrative staff jobs, few have reached senior levels. It also acknowledges that its staffing is not reflective of its immediate hiring pool, the Toronto region, and states that: "To make changes of the magnitude reflected by our community estimates and our student body requires a proactive recruitment and development strategy for administrators and staff" (ibid., Executive Summary:2). The University of Toronto's report also acknowledges the virtual absence of Aboriginal people throughout their entire work force.

At this and other universities throughout the country, hiring and retention rates in the next few years need to be closely monitored to see if the new hiring opportunities result in a more proportional representation of minority and Aboriginal faculty and non-academic staff.

Resistance to Change: Discursive Barriers to Anti-Racism in the School and University

Schooling can be understood as discursive space, a terrain in which there is a variety of discourses that "overlap, compete and sometimes collide with one another" (Yon, 1995:312). Discourses on race and racism converse with concerns with national identity, multiculturalism, ethnicity, and culture, as well as gender and sexual orientation. They are mixed with the discourses of colour-blindness, equal opportunity, and the language of racial polarization that divides between "we" (who are White) and "they" (who are not "us").

The conflict between the ideology of democratic liberalism and the racist ideology of the dominant culture—democratic racism—is manifested in the racist discourse that operates in educational institutions. The school and university are discursive spaces. They reflect a terrain of tension and conflict: tension between the everyday experiences of minority students and educators of colour, and the attitudes and practices of those who have the power to redefine that reality (White administrators and educators).

While lip service is paid to the need to ensure equality of opportunity for all students in the classroom, in reality, individuals, organizations, and institutions are far more committed (at a subconscious level) to maintaining the status quo, that is, the cultural hegemony of the dominant culture with which most educators identify. In other words, many educators resist anti-racism and equity initiatives because they are unwilling to question their own belief and value systems, teaching practices, and positions of power and privilege within the school and the society. Thus, they are unable to examine the relational aspects of cultural and racial differences and the power dynamics constructed around ideas about differences. Acknowledging that ethno-racial differences make a difference in the lives of their students is to concede that Euro-Canadian hegemony continues to function and organize the structures within which the delivery of education operates (Dei, 1996).

Some of the discursive forms and coded language in which resistance is expressed include the following.

The Discourse of Denial

This discourse reflects a refusal to accept the existence of racism in its cultural and institutional forms. "I am not a racist, and racism is not a problem in this school." The evidence of racism in the lives and on the life chances of children of colour is indicated by the effort made by the educator and the school to suppress the processes of "othering"—the marginalizing effects of ignoring the experiences, histories, and cultures of minority students in the classroom, texts, and classroom pedagogy.

The Discourse of Colour-Blindness

Educators' attitudes toward racial minorities are expressed in assertive statements about colour-blindness, neutrality, and objectivity: "I never see a child's colour." "I treat all children the same." The refusal of educators to recognize that racism is part of the "baggage" that racial-minority children carry with them, and the refusal to recognize racism as part of the daily policies, programs, and practices of the educational system, are part of the psychological and cultural power of racial constructions on the lives of students of colour as well as educators (James, 1994).

The Discourse of Equal Opportunity

A commonly shared assumption among educators is that all students start with the same opportunities, often articulated in the notion that students begin their schooling with a blank slate. However, this negates the fact that by the time a child enters school he/she has accumulated five years of lived experiences that may influence the ways in which learning takes place. Even at a very young age, children may be impacted by the racism deeply embedded in the negative images and stereotypes entrenched in the popular culture.

The Discourse of Decontextualization

In this discourse, there is an acknowledgement of the existence of racism, but it is interpreted as an isolated and aberrant phenomenon limited to the beliefs and behaviours of deviant individuals. It is believed that "students enter the school with 'blank slates.'" The position of power and privilege that White educators and students enjoy in the classroom is neither acknowledged nor understood. Educators' own racial and cultural identities are generally invisible. Thus racism is decontextualized in terms of what counts as knowledge and how it is taught.

The Discourse of "Blame the Victim"

This discourse is framed around the notion that equal opportunity is assumed to exist in all areas of the educational system. Thus, the lack of success of Black students, for example, is often attributed to dysfunctional families or culturally deficient or disadvantaged communities (Sleeter, 1993). This view is reflected in statements such as: "Education is not really valued in the Black community as it is in 'Canadian' culture." Or it is attributed to the supposed fact that parents of minority students don't have the same academic aspirations for their children. At the level of the university, this discourse is articulated in relation to questions of representation and meritocracy. Proactive measures to ensure that barriers to minorities are dismantled have led to the common refrain: "We must not lower our standards. All hiring and promotions should be based on merit."

The Discourse of Binary Polarization

This is the discourse of fragmentation into "we-they" groups. "We" represent the White dominant culture of the school; "they" are the students, families, and communities who are the "other," possessing "different" values, beliefs, and norms. "The problem with 'our' Black/Asian students is that they do not really try to fit in."

The Discourse of Balkanization

The view underpinning this discourse is founded on the assumption that paying too much attention to "differences" leads to division, disharmony, and disorder in society and in the classroom. "First they want us to do away with Christmas concerts. Soon we'll be wearing turbans." "Before long, we won't know what a Canadian is" (see Yon, 2000; Dei and Calliste, 2000; McCarthy, 1993; Solomon, 1992).

The Discourse of Tolerance

The emphasis on tolerance suggests that while one should accept the idiosyncrasies of the "others" (students or faculty who are culturally or racially "different"), the dominant way is superior. "We try to accommodate their different norms, but it is not always possible or desirable."

The Discourse of Tradition and Universalism

This form of resistance is formulated on the premise that the traditional core curriculum should remained unchanged. "Western civilization represents the best of human knowledge and forms the basis of cultural literacy and educational competence."

The Discourse of Political Correctness

This discourse is most pervasive in academic culture. Demands for inclusion, representation, and equity are deflected, resisted, and dismissed as authoritarian, repressive, and a threat to academic freedom. "The standards, values, and intellectual integrity of the university are in danger."

Summary

This chapter has identified some complex and far-reaching consequences of racism in the educational system. The findings of task forces, surveys, and studies, and the testimonies of racial-minority students, parents, teachers, and academics from all parts of Canada document the impact of Anglo-Eurocentrism, racial bias, and racist practices on both educators of colour and racial-minority students. This chapter has illustrated how racism is woven into the formal curriculum and influences the ways in which knowledge is structured, valued, and transmitted. Examples of bias in curriculum content have been provided to show how teaching materials and subject matter can minimize the contributions of racial minorities.

Also notable is the importance of the hidden curriculum in creating a negative and hostile physical and social environment for students of colour. Racism in the schools and universities is reflected in the ethnocentric attitudes, assumptions, pedagogical practices, assessment tools, and everyday discourses of White teachers, principals, professors, and others in educational institutions who fail to acknowledge their own racial biases and the systemic racism that is so pervasive. The evidence of racism in educational institutions is demonstrated by the failure of ministries, boards, and schools to develop an inclusive and equitable relationship with racial-minority parents and communities. It is manifested in the lack of resources to support more equitable and inclusive schools. It is reflected in the failure of teacher training programs to provide students with the necessary knowledge, understanding, and skill to effectively manage a multiracial classroom and critically reflect on their own ethno-racial biases. This analysis of racism clearly demonstrates how, for both minority students and educators, the school and the university can be excluding, non-supportive, and even threatening environments.

Biased assessment and placement procedures and standardized testing are some of the most powerful forms of differential treatment in the educational system, and they affect the educational achievement of racial-minority groups, especially Black students.

There are various institutional responses to racism. This chapter has considered assimilationism, examined the multicultural model and its ineffectiveness in addressing racism, and investigated the anti-racist orientation to education. The concept of separate schools for Black students has been put forth as an alternative model. The concluding section of the chapter summarizes some of the common forms of "liberal" discourse that circulate within the school and university and cover up the need to address the racism woven into the educational system. These everyday discursive practices reflect the deep resistance to change that exists throughout the educational systems of Canada.

Notes

1. The Black Learners Advisory Committee (BLAC) was established in 1990 to address historical problems for Black students in Nova Scotia dating back two centuries. In 1994, it produced the *BLAC Report on Education: Redressing Inequity—Empowering Black Learners*.

2. The term "chilly climate" was introduced by Bernice Sandler (1986).

3. While there is also a significant body of evidence of discrimination of men of colour, many scholars point to the significant impact of both gender and race as variables that act to inferiorize, marginalize, and exclude women of colour and Aboriginal women in academia as well as in other institutions and systems.

4. An example of this slowness of institutional change is the Ontario Council of Universities' recommendation that the Zero Tolerance policy against sexual and racial harassment developed by the previous NDP provincial government be rejected because it contravenes academic freedom and freedom of expression (*Toronto Star*, February 7, 1994).

References

Alladin, I. (ed.). (1996). *Racism in Canadian Schools.* Toronto: Harcourt Brace.

Bannerji, H. (1991). "But Who Speaks for Us? Experience and Agency in Conventional Feminist Paradigms." In H. Bannerji, L. Carty, K. Dehli, S. Heald, and K. Himmanji, *Unsettling Relations: The University as a Site of Struggle.* Women's Press. 67–108.

Bedard, G. (2000). "Deconstructing Whiteness: Pedagogical Implications for Anti-Racism Education." In G. Dei and A. Calliste (eds.), *Power, Knowledge and Anti-Racism Education: A Critical Reader.* Halifax: Fernwood. 41–56.

BLAC (Black Learners Advisory Committee). (1997). *BLAC Report on Education: Redressing Inequity—Empowering*

Black Learners. Halifax: Black Learners Advisory Committee.

Black, K. (2003). "Erasing Anti-Racism: A Decade Later, Anti-Racism Education Is Still Non-existent in the Classroom." *Now* (Toronto) 23(7)(October 16–22). Available <http://www.nowtoronto.com/issues/2003-10-16/news_story4.php>, accessed August 22, 2004.

Brandt, G. (1986). *The Realization of Anti-Racist Education.* London, Falmer Press.

Brathwaite, K. (2003). *Access and Equity in the University: A Collection of Papers from the Thirtieth Anniversary Conference of the Transitional Year Programme.* Toronto: Canadian Scholars' Press.

Brathwaite, K., and C. James (eds.). (1996). *Educating African Canadians.* Toronto: Lorimer.

Bullivant, T. (1981). *The Pluralist Dilemma in Education: Six Case Studies.* Sydney, Australia: George Allen and Unwin.

Calliste, A. (2000). "Anti-Racist Organizing and Resistance in Academia." In G. Dei and A. Calliste (eds.), *Power, Knowledge and Anti-Racism Education: A Critical Reader.* Halifax: Fernwood. 142–161.

Carty, L. (1991). "Black Women in Academia: A Statement from the Periphery." In H. Bannerji, L. Carty, K. Dehli, S. Heald, and K. Himmanji, *Unsettling Relations: The University as a Site of Struggle.* Women's Press. 6–13.

Chakkalakal, T. (2000). "Reckless Eyeballing: Being Reena in Canada." In R. Walcott, *Rude: Contemporary Black Canadian Cultural Criticism.* Toronto: Insomniac Press. 159–168.

Chan, A. (2004). "Final Report: Re-assessment of Anti Racism Programs and Plans of the Vancouver School Board." Vancouver School Board.

Chishold, P. (1997). "Bad Girls." *Maclean's.* December 8.

Cochran-Smith, M. (2000). "Blind Vision: Unlearning Racism in Teaching Education." *Harvard Educational Review* 70(2):157–190.

Codjoe, H. (2001). "'Public Enemy' of Black Academic Achievement: The Persistence of Race and Schooling in the Experience of Black Students. *Race, Ethnicity and Education* 4(4):344–375.

Council on Interracial Books for Children. (1980). *Guidelines for Selecting Bias-free Textbooks for Children.* New York: The Council.

Crozier, G. (2001). "Excluded Parents: The Deracialization of Parental Involvement." *Race, Ethnicity and Education* 4(4):329–341.

Cummins, J. (1984). *Bilingualism and Special Education: Issues in Assessment and Pedagogy.* Clevedon, UK: Multilingual Matters; San Diego: College Hill Press.

———. (1988). "From Multicultural to Anti-Racist Education." In T. Suutnabb-Kangas and J. Cummins (eds.), *Minority Education: From Shame to Struggle.* Clevedon, UK: Multilingual Matters.

———. (1992). "Lies We Live By: National Identity and Social Justice." *International Journal of the Sociology of Language* 110:145–155.

———. (2001). *Negotiating Identities: Education for Empowerment in a Diverse Society.* 2nd ed. Los Angeles: California Association for Bilingual Education.

Dei, G. (1996). *Anti-Racism Education: Theory and Practice.* Halifax: Fernwood.

Dei, G., and A. Calliste (eds.). (2000). *Power, Knowledge and Anti-Racism Education: A Critical Reader.* Halifax: Fernwood.

Dua, R., and B. Lawrence. (2000). "Challenging White Hegemony in University Classrooms: Whose Canada Is It?" *Atlantis* 24(2):105–122.

Essed, P. (1990). *Everyday Racism: Reports from Women of Two Cultures.* Claremont, CA: Hunter House.

Ferri, J. (1986). "Are Teachers to Blame If Play Arouses Racism?" *Toronto Star* (July 16).

Fleras, A. (1996). "Behind the Ivory Walls: Racism/Anti-Racism in Academe." In I. Alladin (ed.), *Racism in Canadian Schools.* Toronto: Harcourt Brace. 62–89.

Four-Level Government/African Canadian Community Working Group. (1992). *Towards a New Beginning: Report of the Four-Level Government/African Canadian Community Working Group.* Toronto.

Green, J. (2002). "Transforming at the Margins of the Academy." In E. Hannah, L. Paul, S. Vethamany (eds.), *Women in the Canadian Tundra: Challenging the Chill.* Montreal and Kingston: McGill-Queen's University Press. 85–91.

Hatcher, R., and B. Troyna. (1993). "Racialization and Children." In C. McCarthy and W. Crichlow (eds.), *Race, Identity, Representation in Education.* New York and London: Routledge.

Hérbert, Y., and C. Racicot. (2001). Identity, Diversity, and Education: A Critical Review of the Literature. Paper Commissioned by Department of Canadian Heritage for the Ethnocultural, Racial, Religious and Linguistic Diversity and Identity Seminar. www.metropolis.net.

Hirschfeld, L. (1996). *Race in the Making: Cognition, Culture, and the Child's Construction of Human Kinds.* Cambridge, MA: MIT Press.

Hohensee, J.B., and L. Derman-Sparks. (1992). "Implementing an Anti-Bias Curriculum in Early Childhood." Educational Resources Information Centre (ERIC).

Ijaz, A., and H. Ijaz. (1986). "The Development of Ethnic Prejudice in Children." *Guidance and Counselling* 2(1) (September):28–39.

James, C. (1994). "The Paradox of Power and Privilege: Race, Gender and Occupational Position." *Canadian Women Studies* 14(2):48–54.

———. (2003). "It Can't Be Just Sports! Schooling, Academics and Athletic Scholarship Expectations." *Orbit* 33(3):33–35.

Jiwani, Y. (1997). "Reena Virk: The Erasure of Race." Vancouver: The Freda Centre for Research on Violence Against Women and Children. December.

———. (2000). "The Denial of Race in the Murder of Reena Virk." Vancouver: The Freda Centre for Research on Violence Against Women and Children.

Jull, S. (2000). "Youth Violence, Schools, and the Management Question: A Discussion of Zero Tolerance and Equity in Public Schooling." *Canadian Journal of Educational Administration and Policy* 17 (November 30).

Kakembo, P., and R. Upshaw. (1998). "The Emergence of the Black Learners Advisory Committee in Nova Scotia." In V. D'Oyley and C. James, *Re/Visioning: Canadian Perspectives on the Education of Africans in the Late 20th Century.* Toronto: Captus Press.

Kehoe, J. (1984). *A Handbook for Enhancing the Multicultural Climate of the School.* Vancouver: WEDG.

Kelly, J. (1998). *Under the Gaze: Learning to be Black in White Society.* Halifax: Fernwood.

Kobayashi, A. (2002). "Now You See Them, How You See Them: Women of Colour in Canadian Acdemia. In S. Herald (ed.), *Feminist Issues: Selected Papers from the WIN Symposia, 2000-2001.* Ottawa: Humanities and Social Sciences Federation of Canada. 44–54.

Kowalczewski, P.S. (1982). "Race and Education: Racism, Diversity and Inequality, Implications for Multicultural Education." *Oxford Review of Education* 8(2):145–61.

Lawson, E. (2003). "Re-assessing Safety and Discipline in our Schools: Opportunities for Growth, Opportunities for Change." *Orbit* 3(3):23–25.

Lee, E. (1985). *Letters to Marcia: A Teacher's Guide to Anti-Racist Education.* Toronto: Cross-Cultural Communication Centre.

Lewington, J. (1993). "Ontario Attacks Racism in the Classroom." *Globe and Mail* (July 16):A6.

Lewis, S. (1992). *Report on Racism Presented to the Premier of Ontario.* Toronto: Queen's Printer for Ontario.

Lgundipe-Leslie, M. (1991). "Forum," *University of Toronto Bulletin* 16(September 9).

Luther, R., E. Whitmore, and B. Moreau (eds.). (2001). *Seen But Not Heard: Aboriginal Women of Colour in the Academy.* Ottawa: Canadian Research Institute for the Advancement of Women (CRIAW). 7–14.

McCarthy, C. (1993). "After the Canon: Knowledge and Ideological Representation in the Multicultural Discourse on Curriculum Reform." In C. McCarthy and W. Crichlow (eds.), *Race, Identity and Representation in Education.* New York and London: Routledge.

McCaskell, T. (1993). Presentation to the Community Forum Sponsored by the Metropolitan Toronto Council Committee to Combat Hate Group Activity.

McGee, P. (1993). "Decolonization and the Curriculum of English." In C. McCarthy and W. Crichlow (eds.), *Race, Identity and Representation in Education.* New York and London: Routledge.

Makin, K. (2001). "How Teacher of Equality Ended Up in Racial Fight; Dalhousie Professor Hired to Tackle Bias Has Felt Ostracized Since Filing Complaint." *Globe and Mail* (April 2). Available <http://www.geocities.com/CapitolHill/2381/racismdalhousielawschool/aylwardglobeandmail0402.html>, accessed August 22, 2004.

Meininger, T. (1990). "Visible Minorities and the Universities: Some Obstacles and Challenges on the Road to Social Justice." Unpublished paper. York University.

Milner, D. (1983). *Children and Race: Ten Years Later.* London: Alan Sutton.

Mohanty, C.T. (1993). *Beyond a Dream: Deferred Multicultural Education and the Politics of Excellence.* Minneapolis: University of Minnesota Press.

Monture-Angus, P. (2001). "In the way of Peace: Confronting 'Whiteness' in the University." In Luther et al. (eds.), *Seen But Not Heard: Aboriginal and Women of Colour in the Academy.* Ottawa: Canadian Research Institute for the Advancement of Women (CRIAW). 29–50.

Moodley, K. (1984). "The Ambiguities of Multicultural Education." *Currents: Readings in Race Relations* (Toronto) 2(3):5–7.

Ng, R. (1994). "Sexism and Racism in the University: Analyzing a Personal Experience in the University." *Racism and Gender* 14(2)(Spring):41–46.

Oake, G. (1991). "Racism Hits Edmonton Schools." *Toronto Star* (December 12).

O'Malley, S. (1992). "Demand Quality Education, Black Parents Told." *Globe and Mail* (August 20):A1, A19.

Pieters, S. (2000). Ontario Black Anti-Racist Research Institute site <http://www.geocities.com/CapitolHill/2381>, accessed August 22, 2004.

Pinar, W. (1993). "Notes on Understanding the Curriculum as Critical Text." In C. McCarthy and W. Crichlow (eds.), *Race, Identity and Representation in Education.* New York and London: Routledge.

Queen's University. (1991). *Towards Diversity and Equity at Queen's: A Strategy for Change.* Final Report of the Principal's Advisory Committee on Race Relations. *Queen's Gazette* supplement (April 8).

Razack, S. (1998). *Looking White People in the Eye: Gender, Race and Culture in Courtrooms and Classrooms.* Toronto: University of Toronto Press.

———. (2001). "Racialized Women as Native Informers in the Academy." In Luther et al. (eds), *Seen But Not Heard: Aboriginal and Women of Colour in the Academy.* Ottawa: Canadian Research Institute for the Advancement of Women (CRIAW). 51–60.

Rizvi, F. (1993). "Children and the Grammar of Popular Racism." In C. McCarthy and W. Crichlow (eds.), *Race, Identity and Representation in Education.* New York and London: Routledge.

Rosenberg, P. (1997). "Underground Discourses: Exploring Whiteness in Teacher Education." In M. Fine, L. Weis, L. Powell, and L. Mun Wong (eds.), *Off White.* London: Routledge. 79–89.

Ruck, M., and S. Wortley. (2002). "Racial and Ethnic Minority High School Students' Perceptions of School

Disciplinary Practices: A Look at Some Canadian Findings." *Journal of Youth and Adolescence,* June 31(3): 185–195.

St. Lewis, J. (1996). "Identity and Black Consciousness in North America." In J. Littleton (ed.), *Clash of Identities: Essays on Media, Manipulation and Politics of Self.* Englewood Cliffs, NJ: Prentice Hall. 21–30.

———. (2000). Letter to Valli Chettiar re Racism at Dalhousie Law School, August 23. Available <http://www.geocities.com/CapitolHill/2381/racismdalhousielawschool/dal-stlewisltr.html>, accessed August 22, 2004.

———. (2001). "In the Belly of the Beast." In Luther et al. (eds.), *Seen But Not Heard: Aboriginal and Women of Colour in the Academy.* Ottawa: Canadian Research Institute for the Advancement of Women (CRIAW). 73–84.

Samuda, R.J., D. Crawford, C. Philip, and W. Tinglen. (1980). *Testing, Assessment, and Counselling of Minority Students: Current Methods in Ontario.* Toronto: Ontario Ministry of Education.

———, and S.L. Kong. (1986). *Multicultural Education: Programmes and Methods.* Kingston, ON: Intercultural Social Sciences Publications.

Sandler, B. (1986). *The Campus Climate Revisited: Chilly for Women Faculty, Administrators, and Graduate Students.* Washington, DC: Project on the Status and Education of Women, Association of American Colleges.

Schissel, B. (1997). *Blaming the Children: Youth Crime, Moral Panic and the Politics of Hate.* Halifax: Fernwood

Shahrzad, M. (2002). "Equity Coordinator: Change Agent in an Unyielding Power Structure. In E. Hannah, L.Paul and S. Vethamany-Globus (eds.). In *Women in the Academic Tundra: Challenging the Chill.* Montreal and Kingston: McGill-Queen's University Press. 162–167.

Shapson, S. (1990). *Multicultural Education: A Research Paper to Inform Policy Development.* Burnaby, BC: Faculty of Education, Simon Fraser University.

Sleeter, C. (1993). "How White Teachers Construct Race." In C. McCarthy and W. Crichlow (eds.), *Race, Identity and Representation in Education.* New York and London: Routledge.

Solomon, P. (1992). *Black Resistance in High School: Forging a Separatist Culture.* Albany: State University of New York Press.

———, and C. Levine-Rasky. (1996). "Transforming Teacher Education." *CRSA/RCSA* 33(3):337–59.

Spence, C. (1999). *The Skin I Am In: Racism, Sports and Education.* Halifax: Fernwood.

Sweet, L. (1993). "Academic Angst: The Professional Privilege of Tenure—A Job for Life." *Toronto Star* (July 18):B1.

Thomas, B. (1984). "Principles of Anti-Racist Education." *Currents: Readings in Race Relations* (Toronto) 2(3):20–23.

Thornhill, E. (1984). "Fight Racism Starting with the School." *Currents: Readings in Race Relations* (Toronto) 2(3):3–7.

Toronto Board of Education. (1979). *Final Report of Sub-committee on Race Relations.* Toronto: Board of Education for the City of Toronto.

Traves, T. (2001). Letter to the editor. *The Globe and Mail* (April 7).

University of Toronto Employment Equity Annual Report. (2000–2001). Toronto: University of Toronto.

Upshaw, R. (2003). "Improving the Success of African Nova Scotian Students." Halifax: Halifax Regional School Board (December 4). Available <http://www.hrsb.ns.ca/downloads/doc/ans/ANS-pilot-report-05dec03.doc>, accessed August 22, 2004.

Viswanathan, G. (1989). *Masks of Conquest: Literary Study and British Rule in India.* New York: Columbia University Press.

Watson, P. (2003). "Zero Tolerance Targets Blacks." *Share News* (April 24).

Watt, D., and H. Roessingh. (1994). *ESL Dropout: The Myth of Educational Equity.* Calgary: Faculty of Education, University of Calgary.

Williams, R. (1977). *Marxism and Literature.* Oxford: Oxford University Press.

Yon, D. (1995). "Unstable Terrain: Explorations in Identity, Race, Culture." Ph.D. dissertation, graduate program in Social Anthropology, York University.

———. (2000). *Elusive Culture: Schooling, Race and Identity in Global Times.* Albany, NY : Suny Press.

Zine, J. (2003). "Dealing with September 12th: The Challenge of Anti-Islamophobia Education." *Orbit* 33(3):39–41.

CHAPTER 9

RACISM IN ARTS AND CULTURE

The core of racism in the arts remains constant: the refusal to treat as valid cultural experience, knowledge or expertise of an artist of colour—wedded to the belief that Eurocentric values are better.

—*NourbeSe Philip (1992:225)*

This chapter explores the nature of cultural racism as ideology and practice in cultural production.[1] Cultural production is one way in which society gives voice to racism, recycling ideas, images, and discourses about Canada's people of colour and Aboriginal peoples. The debates over cultural representation deal with fundamental and deeply felt issues about the nature of Canadian culture and national identity. This analysis of popular or mass culture and "high culture" explores why the images created and presented by mainstream writers, producers, directors, curators, and others involved in cultural production often are not the images that Africans, Asian Canadians, and Aboriginal peoples would present of themselves. The practice of cultural appropriation—the use of another culture's images or experiences by artists from the dominant culture—is analyzed as an example of racist ideology and practice.

This chapter's first case study (Case Study 9.1) of the Royal Ontario Museum's exhibit "Into the Heart of Africa" highlights issues such as cultural appropriation, Eurocentrism, misrepresentation, and power relations. Case Study 9.2 examines the controversy over a conference of writers of colour ("Writing Thru Race"), which elucidates issues of representation, stereotyping, marginalization, freedom of expression, and censorship. Case Study 9.3 explores the issue of inclusion and exclusion of people of colour and First Nations people in Canadian theatre. More specifically, it looks at the issue of selection of actors based on "non-traditional or "colour-blind" casting practices. These case studies demonstrate of the power of the dominant White culture to create, reproduce, and transmit certain cultural forms while marginalizing and erasing the images, voices, and experiences of people of colour.

This chapter identifies both ideological and structural barriers to the access, participation, and representation of people of colour in the arts and Canadian cultural institutions, and explores the struggles of minority artists and performers to find space for their work on the "representational stage" of Canadian culture (Mackey, 1995:403).

Introduction

Viewing an exhibit of paintings in an art gallery or of cultural artifacts in a museum, reading a literary work, watching a theatrical performance, or listening to a symphony is to experience an art form, cultural object, or event that has been brought into being through a complex process. Cultural production involves an interaction of values, ideas, and organizational practices shaped by concrete social and historical conditions. It incorporates an intricate nexus of groups and institutions including patrons, publishers and producers, curators and administrators, corporations and boards of trustees, advertising agencies and media organizations, funding agencies and government bodies, and consumers and audiences. The machinery of cultural production includes cultural industries that produce cultural products for profit, not-for-profit organizations, and public-sector bureaucracies (Becker, 1994; J. Hall and Neitz, 1993).

Cultural production and creative processes define and structure "maps of meaning" (S. Hall, 1977), articulate and communicate authoritative messages, and transmit powerful symbols, icons, images, and ideas through which we "live" culture (Bhabha, 1990). These messages and meanings ultimately become a part of the collective belief and value system of a people.

Both high culture and popular or mass culture produce "codes of recognition," such as stereotypical images, out of which individual, communal, and national identities are forged. The arts, the music industry, theatre, literature, film, print, and broadcast industries provide a society with a sense of what it means to be a man or woman, poor or privileged, Aboriginal Canadian or African Canadian. Cultural production provides the lens through which people view themselves and the world, communicating powerful messages about the core values, norms, cultural hierarchies, and central narratives of mainstream society. Meaning is constructed across the bar of differences (racial, cultural, gender, sexual orientation, and so on).

Cultural products and practices mirror the larger social processes; cultural representations echo social realities (Pieterse, 1992). Thus, all forms of cultural production must be understood in the context of how they were produced, by whom, at what historical moment, and with what social, economic, and political impact. Cultural practices cannot be separated from the environment in which they find expression.

Cultural production provides a vehicle through which dominant cultural ideologies are promoted, sustained, and reinforced, although these beliefs appear invisible and natural to those who are immersed in it. Access to cultural production is created or limited by the dominant cultural institutions such as museums, galleries, publishing houses, academies, film and video production houses, and theatres. Mainstream cultural institutions often function as gatekeepers, determining the acceptable conventions by which cultural productions are sponsored and distributed, as well as determining how their aesthetic and market value are assessed (Li, 1994).

Culture and cultural production is increasingly being defined by economic forces, and the penetration of the commodity culture is a key ingredient in shaping systems of representation and structures of cultural meaning. There is a new intersection between commerce, advertising, and consumption. The penetration of commodity culture into every aspect of daily life has become a major axis in the relationship between mass culture and high culture. The gap between these two worlds is rapidly diminishing (Becker, 1994).

However, cultural production is also an important source and site of struggle against a dominant culture significantly influenced by the legacy of its Eurocentric heritage. The arts and popular culture not only offer the possibility for the creative contributions of artists from diverse ethno-racial communities, but also provide a powerful vehicle for new constructions of Canadian identity and new forms of social relations.

In the past decade, as the case studies here will demonstrate, there has been a crisis of representation in which the traditional modes of cultural production are no longer acceptable to many marginalized groups in Canadian society. As a consequence, there is greater scrutiny, criticism, and contestation of the roles, functions, and meanings of cultural institutions (Hutcheon, 1994).

Manifestations of Racism in the Production of Cultural Art Forms

Canada's mainstream cultural institutions include museums and art galleries, theatres, film production houses, publishers, ballet and opera companies, symphonies, arts councils and artists, and writers' and performers' unions and professional associations. Each of these cultural systems contributes in different ways to the marginalization of people of colour.

These cultural institutions define "great works of art," "literary classics," and "world-class music." They determine who is selected to direct, produce, or perform in artistic productions and where these productions will be presented; which authors are deemed worthy of publication; which artists' works are given public exhibitions in the major galleries; whose music is played in concert halls; whose music gets recorded and played on mainstream radio; and whose voices and images become part of television programming and are found in mainstream theatres. They reflect the funding policies and practices of government agencies and private foundations and the ethno-racial representativeness of those who work in cultural organizations in the public and private sectors. As well, the dominance of White culture is manifested in the power relationship between mainstream cultural organizations, ethno-racial communities, and artists of colour.

Culture and cultural expression is the mirror in which racism is both reflected and reproduced. The racism in various aspects of the arts, such as literature, visual art, film, dance, and theatre, emanates from the racism embedded in the dominant culture's values and institutions. Cultural racism finds its expression primarily in the perceptions, attitudes, values, and norms of White males, who have controlled and shaped cultural life in Canada. A Eurocentric bias provides the lens through which White decision-makers in Canadian cultural organizations and institutions filter their view of the world, establish priorities, assess the quality of art forms, allocate resources, and determine who will be the audience or consumer of their cultural products (Mackey, 1995; Li, 1994).

Cultural racism is one of the most important frameworks of interpretation and meaning for racial thought in society (Essed, 1990:44). It is so deeply ingrained in the

MANIFESTATIONS OF RACISM IN CULTURAL INSTITUTIONS

Dominance of White Anglo-European culture
Inferiorization, essentialization, and marginalization of minority cultures
Invisibility of images, narratives, and voices of people of colour
Cultural appropriation of the stories, images, and ideas of people of colour and First Nations people
Lack of minority-group representation of colour on boards, arts councils, unions, professional organizations
Lack of access to funding
Eurocentric aesthetic values
Negative images and stereotyping

symbolic systems of society that it is almost always denied. In a sense, cultural racism is the most invisible form of racism, because it is seamlessly woven into the collective belief and value systems of the dominant group. White culture is an "invisible veil" that envelops Canadians (Katz, 1978:10).

Cultural racism is an ideology that divides society into "in" and "out" groups—"us" and "them." Images of undesirable "otherness," conveyed in a wide diversity of art forms, shape perceptions, discourse, and identity (Hall, 1992). The cultural images in the stories, narratives, and photographs created by the arts (and transmitted via the media and education) become the building blocks of social reality. Culture is the central mechanism through which the dominant group reaffirms itself through image and representation, and it is the vehicle through which marginalized groups are excluded. In this way, arts and cultural organizations and the authorities within these systems play a significant role in the production and reproduction of racism in a society (see Gagnon, 2000; NourbeSe Philip, 1992; Morrison, 1992; Ferguson et al., 1990).

Cultural Appropriation

Cultural racism in the arts is the marginalization of the cultures of "others," so that the dominant group's cultural images, symbols, and norms remain intact. Conversely, culturally creative expressions developed by people of colour are appropriated and interpreted by White visual artists, producers, musicians, and writers. This phenomenon is called "cultural appropriation."

The controversy over cultural appropriation has spilled over into many arenas. Curators, authors, theatrical producers, and visual artists incorporate into their creations stories, histories, and images derived from cultures that are not theirs. When members of the dominant culture benefit materially from the production and dissemination of the history, traditions, and experiences of other cultural groups, it is as if a party were being held in a house that's been in a family's possession as far back as memory serves, and the family is not included in the celebration (Williams, 1992). Furthermore, "the issue of appropriation has to do with access; it is rooted in the problem of access. For 300 years … women … people of colour, have had no access to many institutions in this country" (Williams, 1992:6).

Governor General's Award-winning writer Dionne Brand made the point that cultural appropriation is not about personal accusation but rather views the issue in the context of a critical category. Brand argued that cultural appropriation "looks at the location of the text, and the author, in the world at given historical moments. These moments are moments of gendering, race[ing] and class making, [othering], moments rooted in colonial conquest, slavery and economic exploitation" (quoted in Rundle, 1997:13). NourbeSe Philip (1992) asserted that if writers are drawn to write about another culture, they must do so from a point of humility and a willingness to learn, and not with a sense of entitlement or exploitation.

In Case Studies 9.1 and 9.2 the subject of cultural appropriation was central to the debate and controversy surrounding the two cultural events.

The protest against the exhibit "Into the Heart of Africa" at the Royal Ontario Museum highlighted a number of contentious issues that museums are confronting across North America, the United Kingdom, and elsewhere. Those who opposed the exhibit argued that it was an example of a cultural production that contributes to cultural racism by the ways in which the artifacts were acquired; by the value attributed to the artifacts; by the context and content of the exhibit that displayed the artifacts; and by the nature of

CASE STUDY 9.1

INTO THE HEART OF AFRICA

"Into the Heart of Africa" was an exhibition, mounted by the Royal Ontario Museum (ROM), consisting of about 375 artifacts from central and west Africa that had been stored by the ROM for over one hundred years. It opened in November 1989 and closed in August 1990. Ostensibly, the theme of the exhibit was the impact of colonialism on Africa, particularly at the height of the colonial period.

The exhibit included such items as photographs of Canadian missionaries and military stations, reproductions of newspaper articles, scales that had been used to measure gold dust for the colonizers, spears that White soldiers brought home after their battles against Africans, traditional beaded jewellery, and masks. Many of these relics were acquired by Canadian soldiers who participated in Britain's colonial campaign in late-nineteenth-century Africa. Other artifacts had been acquired by Canadian missionaries while attempting to bring "Christianity, civilization, and commerce" to Africans. These artifacts, many of which had significant financial value and all of which had enormous cultural value to those societies from whom they were taken, were eventually donated to the ROM.

The curator, Dr. Jeanne Cannizzo, a specialist in African art, suggested that the show was intended to examine both Canadian and African sensibilities. The objects in the ROM collection were an expression "not only of the world view of those who chose to make and use them, but also of those who chose to collect and exhibit them" (Cannizzo, 1991:151). She stressed her desire to illustrate the social history that provided the context of the exhibit and to expose the racist assumptions of the Canadians involved in the colonization and Christianization of Africa. Her intent was also to show that White Canada had a somewhat less than perfect understanding of the complexity and richness of African societies.

Despite these positive intentions, the exhibit became the most controversial show in the history of the ROM. From the perspective of those who opposed the exhibit, "Into the Heart of Africa" was a demonstration of cultural racism and appropriation in which images, stories, and voices of Africans were silenced and the real story of colonization remained misinterpreted and misunderstood.

One of the many problems with the exhibit was the strong use of irony to deliver the message (Butler, 1993). For example, the exhibit relied on a liberal use of quotation marks around words and phrases such as "the unknown continent" and "barbarous" people and the dramatization of a White missionary bringing "light" to a continent "full of Muslims, and animists and fetishists." The quotation marks were meant to inform the viewer about the racist assumptions underlying these labels. However, what the curator and the ROM failed to recognize was that the irony of the exhibit's texts required a certain degree of shared knowledge between the curator and the observer (Butler, 1993). Many visitors did not understand these subtleties and interpreted the images and phrases such as "barbarous customs" literally. This is reflected in the comment of one visitor who thanked the ROM for the lovely show on "primitive Africa" (Crean, 1991:26).

On the other hand, many members of minority communities in Toronto, as well as visitors from Africa who clearly understood the irony, felt that the exhibit only reinforced racist stereotypes and assumptions. Some of the most controversial objects included an engraving depicting Lord Beresford thrusting his sword into a Zulu man. The engraving was accompanied by its original caption: "Lord Beresford's encounter with a Zulu." Near the engraving was a display of Zulu spears and shields. Beside it was another picture of Zulu soldiers, who were described as "savages." Still another photograph showed a missionary giving African women "a lesson in how to wash clothes." A flyer distributed by members of the Coalition for the Truth About Africa to communicate their concerns about the exhibit's racist images posed the question: "Did Africans not know how to wash before the arrival of the Europeans?"

An audiovisual slide show in the exhibit, entitled "In Livingstone's Footsteps," provided viewers with a simulation of a lecture that missionaries might have delivered to a congregation of worshippers in the nineteenth and early twentieth centuries, during the missionization of Africa. The lecture contains highly derogatory, culturally racist, and paternalistic language. As Crean (1991) pointed out, although a caption at the entrance to the room and an oral disclaimer by the narrator at the beginning and end of the show explained that this was a fictional reenactment, most viewers would likely have missed this important piece of information because relatively few of them would have sat through the entire presentation.

A visitor from Uganda noted that

> the show gives an overwhelming colonial impression. If the ROM is trying to say that these are historical facts and we're ashamed of them, that message doesn't come through.

The exhibit's irony was clearly inappropriate for many Blacks. A young student said

> I look at those spears and shields and all I can think of is how did they get them? By killing Africans, that's how. What am I supposed to feel?

A prominent member of Toronto's Black community, Charles Roach, questioned the ROM's objectives:

> I have to ask what is the ROM's objective in presenting Africa in 1990 from the perspective of the missionaries? Why show the colonials trampling through Africa imposing their lifestyle on the people? To me, it's a form of cultural genocide and I put it in the larger context of what's happening to Black people in Toronto—the police shootings and the discrimination we face. (Roach, 1990)

In glorifying acts like the slaying of the Zulus—the precursor to apartheid and the enslavement of Africans in South Africa—the exhibit had a chilling effect, Roach found.

Other members of the Coalition for the Truth About Africa commented on the likelihood of children misreading the irony of the messages. A teacher who visited the exhibit twice with classes analyzed the negative impact of the exhibit. She found the tour guides unable to explain or interpret the exhibits without sharing their racist assumptions and understandings. One guide leading a group of students explained that "the missionaries civilized the pagans of Africa" and that the Zulu were "an extremely vicious tribe" (McMelland, 1990:10). Another guide, on a subsequent visit by this teacher with a Grade 5 class, explained that missionaries taught the Africans to carve wood and that a mask had been used to practise "barbaric rituals, vicious, barbaric rituals." Another guide offered her view on how crazy African girls were to put pieces of ivory through their noses.

Susan Crean identifies a related problem with this exhibit:

> By presenting the African collection through the history of its donors, by giving pride of place to the personal stories of the White Canadians who happened to bring them to Canada, Cannizzo creates a context in which that history is claimed rather than criticized and rejected, showcased even while she tut-tuts from between the lines. (1991:121)

Members of the Black community not only protested against the images in the exhibit but saw the same marginalization in the exclusionary process used by the ROM in developing the exhibit. They criticized the museum for not consulting the community more widely.

After developing promotional materials for the exhibit, the ROM hired a consultant from the Black community to review these materials. The consultant voiced concern about both the stereotypical language and inappropriate images in the brochure. These concerns were expressed by other people who saw the brochure. At this point, educators with the Toronto Board of Education initiated discussions with the ROM because it was intended that students in this board's jurisdiction would visit the exhibit. The board identified a number of concerns about the promotion, including stereotyping, the use of irony, and the ethnocentric perspective of many of the displays and captions (Lalla and Myers, 1990:6).

The ROM subsequently created focus groups, which also voiced concern about both the direction of the show and the inappropriate language of the brochure. The ROM agreed to redo the brochure (at a cost of $28 000). The groups were also concerned that there was no contemporary content in the exhibit. In response, an African historian was hired to develop, with the community, programs that included lectures, music and dance performances, workshops, and films, which were presented at the ROM after the exhibit was launched, in February 1990.

At a reception for selected members of the Black community to preview the completed exhibit, further concerns were expressed. Some guests felt that they had been invited to simply "rubber stamp" the exhibit, rather than being invited to comment. The previewers, primarily visual artists and writers, objected to words and phrases such as "Dark Continent" and "mysterious land" (Da Breo, 1989–90).

Events

"Into the Heart of Africa" opened at the ROM in November 1989. Opinions and feelings among some members of the Black community ran high, and 16 Black groups in Toronto formed the Coalition for the Truth About Africa. The coalition began to picket in front of the ROM early in March 1990. It concentrated its efforts on Saturdays, a particularly busy day for the museum. As many as fifty demonstrators, carrying placards and distributing pamphlets, appeared early in the mornings. Several of the demonstrators read speeches, using a bullhorn to attract the crowds. They called the ROM the "Racist Ontario Museum," and while they did

not demand, in the first instance, the closure of the exhibit, they urged the museum to change or clarify the offending explanatory texts. Failing that, however, they demanded that the show be closed. The ROM responded by saying that it had no plans to change the show in any way, that it was historically accurate, and that people were simply reacting to it in different ways. Its director was also quoted as saying that the museum would stand by its curator and the exhibit. Jeanne Cannizzo, in the meantime, kept a low profile and declined to speak about the controversy (Butler, 1993).

On at least two occasions, the demonstrations became violent. In one instance, a few of the demonstrators raised their voices to visitors attempting to enter the museum. Officials called the police, who tried to break up the demonstration. As a result, thirty-five police officers and fifty demonstrators were involved in a violent confrontation. Two demonstrators were arrested, and two police officers and several demonstrators were hurt. The ROM responded to this incident by applying for and receiving an injunction from the Supreme Court of Ontario to prevent protesters from picketing within 50 feet of the museum's entrance. The following day, more than seventy-five people, chanting "ROM is Racist Ontario Museum," continued the demonstrations.

As a result of the confrontations, educators from the Toronto Board of Education concluded that "Into the Heart of Africa" had no direct educational value for elementary students, and if secondary students viewed the exhibit, they were to be given extensive preparation (Lalla and Myers, 1990:4).

Analysis

A controversial museum exhibition became the focus for a major ideological and physical confrontation between the Black community of Toronto and one of its leading cultural and educational institutions.

Although the museum took steps to involve a few members of the Black community, in doing so it also apparently made several significant errors. First, the community involvement occurred after the exhibition had been fully mounted and after brochures and flyers describing the exhibition had already been printed. Second, although the ROM invited representatives of the Black artistic community to comment, it did not seek the views of a broadly based cross-section of Toronto's Black population. Third, it chose to ignore the concerns of those who were consulted.

Once the coalition had been formed and had begun its demonstrations, the ROM appeared to "dig in its heels" and consistently refused to meet the demonstrators' demands. Neither did the ROM show much sensitivity to the perspectives of the Black community and others who shared their concerns. Instead, its officials continued to affirm their support of the exhibit and appeared to take offence at the attempts made to interfere (as they saw it) with their museum and curatorial roles.

After several months, Cannizzo broke her silence and attempted to justify the exhibition. Seven months after the show was launched, she stated that "the exhibition does not promote colonialism or glorify imperialism. ... It should help all Canadians to understand the historical roots of racism" (Cannizzo, 1990). Her article did not demonstrate particular sensitivity to the concerns of the Black community.

Exacerbating the tense situation was the media coverage of these events. A number of feature pieces were written, most of which were critical of the protesters, who were characterized as radicals, bullies, blackmailers, terrorists, and revisionists. An art critic wrote that the "price of popularity must sometimes be paid for at the cost of integrity." He went on to observe that this show "caused a minor uproar here" (Hume, 1989). He observed: "Some members of the Black community considered it racist. It wasn't, of course."

Journalists in most of the mainstream newspapers and magazines dismissed the protest as the work of "radicals." The *Toronto Star* accused the "self-righteous left" (Hume, 1990); and the *Toronto Sun* concluded: "Why are we so bloody eager to be held hostage by the ravers from the political left? They won big on this one, you know" (Blatchford, 1990).

For the Black community and its representatives, the incident merely confirmed that

> as long as institutions and individuals fail to understand how thoroughly racism permeates the very underpinnings of Western thought, then despite all the good will in the world, catastrophes like "Into the Heart of Africa" will continue to happen. Intentions, particularly the good ones, continue to pave the way to hell. And to Africa. (NourbeSe Philip, 1992)

Consequences

"Into the Heart of Africa" was scheduled to tour several museums in Canada and the United States. The controversy led to the cancellation of the exhibit by the other museums. In response, the director of the ROM, John MacNeill, commented: "the controversy which surrounded this exhibition and led to the cancellation of the tour impinges on the freedom of all museums to maintain intellectual honesty, scientific and historical integrity and academic freedom."

Conclusion

This case study crystallizes many of the issues related to cultural racism and cultural appropriation. NourbeSe Philip (1992) suggested that at the heart of the ROM controversy were changing beliefs about the role and function of museums and other cultural institutions, especially the issue of who should have the power to represent and control images created by "others." The traditional values and practices of institutions such as museums are difficult to change.

One analyst posed an important question about the ROM controversy: Would the institution have supported a more critical approach to the subject? Would it have risked offending its important patrons, some of whom donated artifacts to the collection (Butler, 1993:57)?

The ROM controversy also illustrated how the past converges with the present. The protesters saw a relationship between the symbolic domination, reflected in the colonial images of the exhibit, and the sense of powerlessness experienced daily by Black people in Canada. The linkage between racism in various sectors of society was made by a critic who emphasized the importance of understanding how the struggles with the ROM and the Metropolitan Toronto police were welded together: "Inside the ROM is institutional racism and outside is the brutal reality" (Roach, 1990).

This case also emphasizes the intrinsic link between colonialism and cultural racism. The process employed by the ROM to conceptualize and develop "Into the Heart of Africa" was based on the colonial model of objectification. Mitchell suggested that the West habitually renders the world as object or, more specifically, "the world as exhibition" (1989:219–22), and argues that this process of organizing and ordering the world is identical to the logic and processes of colonialism. The outcome of this process is the domination of the body, spirit, and soul of the "others."

Objectification is also very much a part of the way in which Africans in the exhibit were depicted. The lens of the camera held by the missionary or colonizer captures the "object" (the women washing clothes), but the "objects" are rendered powerless and silent. They appear not to challenge their oppression. The exhibit was totally "devoid of images and voices of resistance" to colonial subjugation (Butler, 1993:63). There are numerous examples in the history of Africa in which Africans resisted domination both physically and in writing. This should have been included in the narrative.

Crean summarized the cultural racism of the exhibit by stating that "Into the Heart of Africa" was "a classic case of a cultural institution unable to see its own bias and unprepared to examine its own cultural assumptions" (1991:127).

In the final analysis, "Into the Heart of Africa" was a classic example of a situation in which the possibility for growth and change was lost to the moment, as the cultural power of the museum and other institutions was used to pre-serve a tradition of silencing and marginalization. The ROM, as a "historical-cultural theatre of memory" (Clifford, 1990), chose to respect and showcase one set of life histories—that of the "defenders of the Empire." In so doing, it discarded the experiences of Africans and the histories of African Canadians. Thus the exhibition did not really go "into the heart of Africa" but gave preeminence to the story of those Canadians who went "out of Africa," taking home "souvenirs" of their journey. Three years after the "Into the Heart of Africa" exhibition closed, T. Cuyler Young (1993), the former director of the ROM, wrote about what he had learned from the controversy over the exhibition. He said that the controversy was really about a small group of radicals motivated by an unstated personal and political agenda unrelated to the exhibition.

Afterword

Four years into the new millennium, there have been some small changes at the ROM. According to key respondents in the museum community, consultation is now routinely done on all exhibits and programs that "deal with ethno-cultural subject matter." (One might raise the question: What in a museum does *not* fall into this category?) African and African-Canadian scholars were called on to examine the museum's African collections. Similarly, a First Nations artist was consulted on the museum's reinterpretation of its Haida and Nisga'a crest poles. Perhaps one of the most significant indicators of a shift in the total dominance of Whiteness in the ROM is the recent donation of $30 million to the rebuilding of the ROM made by Michael Lee-Chin, a Jamaican Canadian who came to Toronto in 1970. However, there still remains little evidence of major structural change in the staffing, management, or governance of this institution.

the relationship between the artifacts, the institution, and the living cultures and communities for whom these artifacts have special meaning. These issues raise fundamental questions about "the very status of museums as historical, cultural theatres of memory. Whose memory? For what purposes?" (Clifford, 1990:141).

Figure 9.1

TWO PROCESSES OF CULTURAL APPROPRIATION

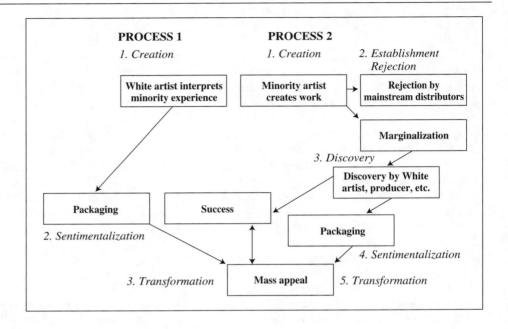

Cultural Appropriation in Other Art Forms

Cultural appropriation has created controversy in other forms of cultural production. For example, many mainstream writers object to the Canada Council's and Women's Press's guidelines on cultural appropriation. They suggest that these policies jeopardize their right to freedom of expression (Paris, 1992). The Writers Union of Canada's commitment to support the rights of racial-minority writers to greater freedom of expression and access has not been well received by many mainstream writers. June Callwood, a co-founder of the union, warned her colleagues of the dangerous emotionalism in the positions and strategies used by writers of colour to assert their own freedom of expression while undermining the freedom of mainstream writers. She referred to these efforts as the acts of the "self-defined weak" that include "bullying and intimidation" (Callwood, 1993).

The defences of freedom of expression and artistic licence are challenged by many artists of colour. In a world dominated by White values, images, and norms, where people of colour are either absent from most cultural productions or misrepresented as racial or gender anomalies, it has been observed that

> it is critical for disenfranchised racial minorities to maintain possession and control over the telling of their stories and histories. ... Any representation of ourselves and our cultural experiences done by an outsider would be from a comparatively superficial perspective, simply because he/she hasn't had the experience of surviving racial oppression—complete with all its complications, consequences, and contradictions. (Browning, 1992:33)

Thus, Browning (1992) concluded that White artists and writers who attempt to speak on behalf of the "others" or who believe that they can interpret their experiences are perpetuating their own positions of privilege and dominance.

Building on this analysis, NourbeSe Philip (1992) drew attention to one of the central paradoxes in cultural appropriation. While there is a profound lack of respect for artists of colour and their **aesthetics**, there is generally a strong approval of the White artist who culturally appropriates those traditions and benefits from them.

Brant (1990) holds the view that the truth is not told by the many White writers who use their hundreds of years of colonial supremacy to speak for Aboriginal peoples:

> I do not say that only Indians can write about Indians. But you can't steal my stories and call them your own. You can't steal my spirit and call it your own. This is the history of North America—stolen property, stolen lives, stolen dreams and stolen spirituality. … If your history is one of cultural domination you must be aware. … you have to tell the truth about your role, your history, your internalized domination and supremacy.

The concern over cultural appropriation is part of a broader struggle, that of power—the power of White cultural authorities to publish a literary work, to produce a theatrical production, to select and organize an exhibition, to determine what music will be played and what performers will be chosen.

Marginalization of People of Colour in Public Culture

People of colour confront both subtle and overt barriers as they attempt to move from the margins of mainstream culture into the centre. The title of the book *Out There* (Ferguson et al., 1990) suggests that the power of the centre depends on the relatively unchallenged authority of the dominant culture. In other words, cultural racism is maintained by silencing artists, writers, and musicians of colour who, having been relegated to a place outside the dominant culture, find it difficult to challenge dominant modes of cultural production and dissemination.

The racism of cultural institutions has been characterized as a form of organizational apartheid that in the past relegated Aboriginal art to museums and the category of "anthropology," while White artistic productions went to public galleries and were categorized as "art." This devaluing of the art of Aboriginal peoples and artists of colour is considered by some to be not only cultural domination but also cultural genocide (Danzker, 1991).

A further example of cultural racism is the canon of "great works" by White, mainly male, writers and dramatists that is incorporated in the curricula of educational institutions and considered the only material appropriate for mainstream audiences. It is assumed that this body of writing represents the best of human culture and creativity. Cultural racism is reflected in "objective" and "neutral" reviews of literary, arts, and entertainment critics who defend their judgments by maintaining that universal criteria and standards can be applied to all creative arts, thereby ignoring their own cultural and ideological frameworks and biases. Racism is sometimes hidden in efforts to stifle debate about representation, access, and equity. Those who challenge racist attitudes, policies, or practices are often accused of "censorship," and their concerns are dismissed as examples of "political correctness."

Efforts to change or challenge these assumptions are generally met with fierce resistance. For example, when the Art Gallery of Ontario (AGO) established a task force to examine the issue of representation both from the perspective of governance—who sits on the board and who is hired for senior management positions—and in terms of the extent

CASE STUDY 9.2

THE "WRITING THRU RACE" CONFERENCE

Background

In the summer of 1994 the Writers' Union of Canada (TWUC) sponsored a "Writing Thru Race" conference, which brought together 180 First Nations writers and writers of colour for a three-day meeting in Vancouver. Participation in the conference's daytime events was by invitation and was restricted to writers of colour and First Nations writers.

The conference came about because a number of racial-minority members of TWUC stated that the concerns of minority and Aboriginal writers—cultural appropriation, lack of access to grants and publishing facilities, and other issues—needed to be examined in some detail. The decision to hold a national conference created controversy within TWUC, since several members were against minority writers meeting by themselves.

In the weeks leading up to the conference, another controversial move made more headlines. Without warning, the federal Heritage minister withdrew government funding for the conference. Pressured by the Reform Party's intense criticism in Parliament, the minister announced that his government could not support an "exclusive" conference. According to Roy Miki, chair of the Racial Minorities Writers Committee and chair of the conference, he learned of the retraction of funding by reading the newspaper. Neither he nor any other member of the union was officially informed by Heritage Canada.

The Canada Council, the City of Vancouver, and the Ontario Arts Council maintained their financial support for the conference, despite mounting public pressure against the event. Union members began raising funds on their own; executive members and members of the Racial Minorities Writers Committee took an active fundraising role.

The Conference

The opening evening was a public event. It attracted about 225 people, including some media personnel. The participants were an extraordinarily diverse group, with substantial numbers of First Nations writers, African Canadians, and artists of South-Asian and Southeast-Asian origins. A handful of Whites chose to attend the evening meetings. The atmosphere was extremely jubilant. People described their elation at being able to translate a vision into reality and to have overcome so many obstacles that were strewn in their path.

During the days, panels and workshops were held on a wide variety of themes, including: Emergence of First Nations Writers and Storytellers in a Multicultural Urban Environment; Reading and Writing Thru Race: Theory and Practice; The Teaching of Canadian Minority Writing; Writing for Children; The Effects of Racism; Finding One's Own Identity; Access, Equity and Publishing; Writing in Mother Tongue; and other topics. The evening sessions which included readings were open to the public.

The conference afforded a safe space for Aboriginal writers and writers of colour to assert both their need and their right to have their identities and differences recognized, respected, and affirmed. The participants sought an acknowledgment of their distinct cultural, racial, linguistic, and other defining characteristics. They hoped to discover collective strategies to dismantle the ideological, attitudinal, organizational, and institutional barriers that keep writers of colour, First Nations writers, and writers from non-dominant cultural backgrounds from full and equal participation in the mainstream of Canadian culture.

Analysis

The conference, with its attention directed at issues of identity, difference, and racism, appeared to pose a significant threat to the Eurocentric values, assumptions, and beliefs that have formed the central core of Canadian cultural identity and aesthetic representations. This sense of peril is reflected in a statement written by 14 White authors who, a few months before the conference in an attempt to silence the debate on racism in Canadian literature, wrote that fellow members of the Writers' Union of Canada should "shut the f—k up" on the issue (Clarke, 1994:48).

The resistance, conflict, and anger over the decision to hold such a conference expressed at TWUC meetings spilled out across the pages of the national media, and was then incorporated into the speeches and acts of politicians. This acute response to a conference of just over two hundred people reflected a deeper state of political and cultural tension, uncertainty, and anxiety. It drew attention to issues that became increasingly contentious and problematic in the last decades of the twentieth century. Among its other contributions, the conference brought these questions into sharp focus:

• What is Canadian culture?
• What does it mean to be Canadian?
• Who is included in the construction of the notions of "we" and "our," in relation to definitions of culture and the Canadian state?
• How should the state organize itself in relation to public policies and programs dealing with diversity and pluralism, access and equity, and anti-racism?
• Who really belongs in the mainstream of Canadian cultural life?
• How shall we deal with our cultural, racial, linguistic, and religious differences and other social markers such as gender, sexual orientation, and class differences?
• Whose cultural knowledge, values, traditions, and histories should be recognized, and whose cultures should be given preeminence?
• How do the above issues affect cultural production and aesthetic representations?

For First Nations writers and writers of colour, the "Writing Thru Race" conference provided the space and place for developing individual and collective strategies to deal with the racism that had long been embedded in the

fabric of their personal and professional lives. The conference also represented a significant shift in the way in which racism in cultural production had been resisted and challenged. In incorporating an exclusionary policy, designed to reflect and respond to the needs and interests of First Nations writers and writers of colour, the conference organizers were pursuing a deliberate strategy of moving away from multicultural inclusionary paradigms that often function as a cover or distraction from the "unpleasant" matter of racism (McFarlane, 1995).

Contrary to the dominant public discourse that emanates from the cultural elite, a conference for a group of people who share a common body of interests and concerns is not a commitment to a lifetime of separation and exclusion from the mainstream culture. Nor does it represent the dismantling of Canadian culture or national identity. It is, rather, a manifestation of the need of every oppressed group to come together in a safe space where its members can share their disappointments, pain, and anger; celebrate what they have created and accomplished; mobilize, energize, and empower each other; and explore, as individuals and collectivities, new strategies and tools for dismantling barriers and crossing boundaries.

The resistance of the White writing and publishing industry to the conference reflects how threatened the literary elite is by the challenge to extend the definition of "we" to include those who differ in race, ethnicity, and other social markers. The outcry from various constituencies, including government, media, and literary critics, against this conference and earlier initiatives suggests that the discourse of pluralism, inclusion, and equality have been a facade to mask the power, position, and privilege of the dominant cultural community. Both individuals and cultural agencies resist change, particularly change that threatens their own power base within a context of inclusiveness.

Ultimately, however, the conference was an act of affirmation and recognition as well as an act of defiance and protest. For First Nations writers and writers of colour, it was an affirmation and recognition of their identity as critical participants in what Lenore Keeshig-Tobias called a "cultural revolution" (Griffith, 1994), redefining what it means to be Canadian, what it means to be a Canadian writer, and the literary landscape of Canada. The conference was also an act of defiance against Eurocentric ideologies and exclusionary practices. It was an act of resistance to the notions of liberalism and pluralism that perpetuate White power and privilege within the arts.

In response to these concerns, arts organizations such as the Toronto Arts Council, the Ontario Arts Council, the Canada Council, and a limited number of galleries and museums, including the Royal Ontario Museum, the Vancouver Art Gallery, and the Art Gallery of Ontario, have established advisory committees consisting of people of colour. Some have also attempted to increase the representation of racial minorities in their administrative structures. Among book publishers, The Women's Press has developed anti-racist guidelines, as has the Canadian Play Writers' Union. It is also noteworthy that for the first time in its history, the National Gallery of Canada in Ottawa is displaying the works of Aboriginal Canadian artists alongside mainstream art, as a part of its permanent installation. In the past, these works were considered artifacts rather than art and were relegated to historical museums.

A decade following the controversy over the "Writing Thru Race" conference, there has been a wave of outstanding literature by writers of colour and Aboriginal writers. This new success can also be measured by examining a number of prizes awarded to writers, such as the prestigious Giller literary prize, which was first established in 1994. The Giller is Canada's most famous literary prize and it has been in operation for only 10 years. In 1995, Rohinton Mistry won for a novel called *A Fine Balance*. The achievements of writers of colour living in Canada were highlighted in 2003, when M.G. Vassanji won the prize for the second time for his novel *The In-Between World of Vikram Lall*, having already won the prize for another novel in 1994. Barbadian-born but long-time Toronto writer Austin Clarke's winning of the Giller prize for his novel *The Polished Hoe* preceded Vassanji's victory in 2002. In 2000, two winners shared the prize, one of them being writer of colour Michael Ondaatje. Thus, in the Giller's short history, five writers of colour have been winners of this prestigious literary award. In addition to these prize-winning authors, other successful and published writers of colour include the highly acclaimed poet Trinidad-born Dionne Brand who won a Governor General's Literary Award in 1997; Marlene NourbeSe Philip, Cecil Foster, Sasnarine Persaud, Ramabai Espinet, and playwright Djanet Sears have also won prizes.

All of these and other writers of colour and First Nations writers had found difficulty in accessing publishers and many of them had had to publish their work privately.

Today, several small presses, including two who publish the work of Black writers, have been established. Another mark of the increasing recognition of writers of colour who live and work in Canada is the frequency with which literary critics and reviewers now almost routinely review and assess their work. The subject of African-Canadian literature in Canada has also entered into the curriculum of English departments in major universities in the country. Of note as well is that more writers and other artists are now able to access public funding through the Canada Council, the Toronto Arts Council, and other funding agencies in the country. As George Elliot Clarke writes: "'A fresh breeze is blowing' through the halls of Canadian literature. The doors and windows of the grand, old slightly musty, Victorian mansion are opening slowly to admit new accents and fresh scents" (1994:48).

to which the AGO supported artists who reflected the diversity of Ontario, the media argued that the Ontario government had gone too far. It implied that the AGO must "show and publicize the work of current Ontario artists even if the AGO curators think that, at the moment, most of their work is mediocre" (Fulford, 1992). The implicit assumption appeared to be that all art that does not fit within the Euro-American tradition is *ipso facto* inferior.

These assumptions were in evidence in an exhibit at the Vancouver Art Gallery (VAG). In 1991, the Artists' Coalition for Local Colour held a protest outside the gallery. The coalition was formed primarily by South-Asian artists and cultural workers in response to the VAG's decision to mount an exhibit of South-Asian art imported from the United Kingdom. The coalition argued that this was a blatant example of the systemic racism of the organization and resulted in a lack of access, participation, and equity for local artists of colour. Moreover, the VAG decided that, in light of the controversy, it would celebrate the opening with a private viewing of the collection rather than a formal opening event. No members of the South-Asian community were invited to the opening.

Representation and Misrepresentation

The struggles over the issue of representation are central to all forms of cultural representation. The concept of representation has multiple meanings. It concerns not only the inclusion or omission of images of people of colour in art. It indicates who controls the production and transmission of ideas, images, and discourse in art and society. A politics of representation infers discourses of knowledge (e.g., history or education), and an ideological dimension. Gagnon (2000) contends these discourses, texts, and images are also "constitutive," that is, "they contribute to the formation of subjectivities; they are ideological, in the way they privilege dominant values of a society" (23). Or, as Lillian Allen (cited in Gagnon:69) observes, "Without transforming core values around power and diversity, the culture of domination will always frame the agenda and shadow the relations between individuals."

The Struggle over Representation—and the Colour-Coding of Actors in the Theatre

In 1994, actor Sandi Ross reflected on one of the most significant barriers confronting actors of colour and Aboriginal actors. She observed: "Theatres should mirror the society we live in, but the large, publicly funded theatres of our city seem to be reluctant—or at least timid—about putting on stage the faces of the very people who are helping to fund them" (quoted in Ouzounian, 2004). This issue remains front and centre in 2004. A few theatres in Toronto, such as the Lorraine Kimsa Theatre for Young People, have succeeded in achieving a current level of 32 percent of casting people of colour, Canadian Stage at 28 percent, and Buddies in Bad Times 24 percent. However, a very different picture is revealed by the lack of responsiveness to the barrier of colour-coded or non-traditional casting by three of Canada's largest classical companies, Stratford, Shaw, and Soulpepper. A 2003 survey by ACTRA's Diversity Committee found that these companies are leaving minority actors "waiting in the wings" at an alarming rate when it comes to lead roles. The Committee's representative, Bobby Del Rio (2003), researcher of the study entitled *Theatre in Canada: Preservation of White Culture*, found that in the 2003 season 6.8 percent of the cast at Stratford were from racial minorities (not including the chorus of children from *The King and I*). Shaw's representation was 4 percent and Soulpepper was 3 percent. In this context, cultural activists were deeply disappointed when the lead role of the Siamese king in *The King and I* went to a White American. Barriers to more inclusive casting include the myth that there are very few trained minority actors. The stereotyping and typecasting of minorities in a narrow range of roles tied to the colour of their skin and perceived cultural background therefore continues. The following case study, explores how, even in a non-mainstream theatre committed to diversity, the issues of minority casting are contested.

CASE STUDY 9.3

THE PLAYWRIGHT VERSUS THE DIRECTOR: FACTORY THEATRE

Background

Despite the increasing achievements and recognition of writers and other artists of colour in Canadian society in recent years, the spectre of racism has again surfaced in the artistic community. The event concerns Chilean-born playwright Carmen Aquirre whose play *The Refugee Hotel* was planned for production by Factory Theatre in Toronto in spring of 2004. However, the playwright withdrew her play from artistic director Ken Gass' Factory Lab theatre charging him with a form of racism. Recognizing that there are few Latino actors in Canada, Aquirre had suggested to the director that actors of colour and especially Aboriginal actors should be considered. However, she claimed that during the casting process for her play, no actors of colour and only one Latino actor was auditioned. When she complained, Gass tried to contact some actors of colour at the last minute to audition, but by this time they were all unavailable. She therefore concluded that only White actors were being auditioned and they would subsequently be cast in the play. In his defence, Gass claimed that his main priority was to cast the play with excellent actors: "I agree fully in principle with what you say, but am still wrestling with getting not only a very good cast but a superb cast. Clearly a balance needs to be achieved. I'll try to audition [specific actors of colour]" (*Now* Magazine, 2003). Moreover, he apologized to her if she misconstrued his remarks, and suggested that his very busy and chaotic schedule were primary cause of the gaps in the audition process.

What is particularly noteworthy in this incident is that the allegation of racism was levied against a director who has been a very strong champion of "colour-blind" casting over the years; his theatre was among the first in Canada to cast actors of colour. Gass' track record in this regard has been above reproach. In the recent season of 2002, for example, nearly half of all the actors hired by the theatre were people of colour.

The question must therefore be raised as to how such an event could occur in this theatre given the strong equity principles of its director. One can only assume that Gass, like many other liberal-minded progressive Canadians, nevertheless sees the world through his "White" gaze. Given the dearth of Latino actors and despite his earlier commitment to the playwright to audition other actors of colour and Aboriginals, the "White gaze," exacerbated by a hectic work schedule, led him to follow the usual audition process. This resulted in a general casting call that brought in primarily mainstream or White actors. He did not take the extra step in specifically contacting actors of colour thereby showing a degree of insensitivity to the demands of the playwright who wanted the cast to more accurately reflect the ethno-cultural nature of her characters. Here again is an example of an institution, in this case a theatre, following traditional practices, which results in lack of access for non-mainstream actors. In view of his track record, it is clear that Gass' intentions were not to be deliberately racist in his actions, but to produce a play according to the highest standards of excellence. In so doing, he ignored the specific interests of the playwright who believed that White mainstream actors could not capture the subtleties of the non-Canadian characters in her play.

The Role of the Media in This Controversy

Now Magazine published a generally descriptive article citing some of the correspondence between the parties to the conflict. The *Toronto Star* theatre critic, Richard Ouzounian, however, presented his own analysis of this situation. Ouzounian, appalled by Gass being charged with a form of racism, lauds this director's strong commitment to colour-blind casting over many years. However, he also expresses a typical liberal democratic-racist point of view in his analysis. Ouzounian, like Gass, understands reality through the eyes of the White gaze. He calls the conflict between playwright and director a "form of theatrical racism" and notes:

> We all claim to endorse "colour-blind casting," where actors are hired for roles on the strength of their talent rather than the shade of their skin. But what colour-blind casting usually means is that a non-white actor plays a conventionally white role. We seldom think that it should go the other way around, but it can and it should. ... [T]o say that being non-white is your grounds for casting someone is as upsetting as casting the play all-white. An actor's ultimate suitability for the role should be the major concern. ... [I]ssues of talent should not be thrown out the window for some kind of condescending liberalism ... but when someone is cast to make a political statement rather than to serve the good of the play, everyone in the theatre ultimately suffers. ... If colour-blind casting isn't a two-way street, then we're all going nowhere ... fast. (*Toronto Star*, December 7, 2003)

While in theory, the idea of colour-blind casting being a "two-way street" is a worthy one, it ignores the reality that casting Whites in roles that are better served by culturally and/or racially diverse actors also makes for a bad production. Moreover, it denies the need for artistic institutions in an increasingly diverse society to make an extra effort to provide access and opportunity to non-mainstream or non-White performers.

Eurocentric Forms of Cultural Criticism

All cultural criticism is ideological—influenced by judgments and affected by a particular set of values and beliefs. When cultural critics offer a critique on a text, art exhibit, or theatrical performance, they do so in some social, cultural, and/or institutional context. The relevant context might include one or more categories, such as gender, race, class, sexual orientation, and regional background.

A cultural critic who functions in the centre of the dominant culture feels safe in a cocoon of adherence to the notions of "objectivity" and "neutrality." Cultural criticisms are based on the assumption that a body of universal criteria and standards can be applied to *all* literary and art analysis. But the concepts of "universalism," "objectivity," and "neutrality" are contested categories.

From the perspective of many women and people of colour, the content and parameters of the universal are never all-inclusive. Non-Western, non-European cultural forms are rarely seen as part of the corpus of great aesthetics (Tator, Henry, and Mattis, 1998; Jordan and Weedon, 1995; NourbeSe Philip, 1992). They are often labelled and dismissed as "ethnic," "folkloric," "primitive," "community-based" art—as part of the world of the "other" (Walcott, 1996; Li, 1994).

Arun Mukherjee, a professor of Canadian literature with a particular focus on writers of colour, points to the Eurocentric and racist nature of Canadian literary nationalism, which implies that the Canadian identity is defined in settler or colonial terms. There is a pressing need for cultural criticism that respects and understands the contexts from which First Nations writers and writers of colour speak—the historical, religious, literary, and cultural traditions that inform a piece of work (Mukherjee, 1994–95).

Representation and Allocation of Grants and Resources by Funding Agencies

Historically, the policies and practices of arts councils—by virtue of their neglect and lack of support of minority artists, artistic organizations, and projects—have been a powerful vehicle for perpetuating racism in the arts. It has been extremely difficult for writers, artists, musicians, directors, producers, and performers of colour to receive grants from arts councils and government agencies because they are perceived to be unable to meet Eurocentric aesthetic standards. They often find themselves relegated to the margins of the arts and labelled as "not professional." Funding organizations have tended to view Black, Asian, and Aboriginal Canadian artists and cultural companies as "exotic" or "folkloric." As a result, it has been thought that they should be supported through multicultural funding agencies rather than expect to share in the limited resources of arts councils (Li, 1994).

In essence, two distinct policies operate to provide unequal support structures: one to arts within the dominant culture and the other to art produced by Aboriginal artists and artists of colour. "These two art worlds operate within separate infrastructures and rules and standards; and the source and magnitude of funding are different ... and the art works of these two art worlds carry unequal market value and social status" (Li, 1994).

As the 1980s drew to a close, escalating demands were made by Aboriginal, Black/African, and Asian artists and writers for funding agencies to address cultural and racial barriers in their structures. They were urged to identify representation in their staffing, the composition of their juries and panels, and their criteria of professionalism, quality, and excellence. Critics of these "relentlessly White" organizations argued that "in a country where a working artist is almost by definition a government funded artist, this situation amounted to cultural apartheid" (Bailey, 1992:22). NourbeSe Philip shared the grave concern about funding agencies: "The divide between the lived reality of the Black artist and the funding policies of arts councils, between the Black artist and the art world in general, is so great as to be almost unbridgeable" (1992:227).

Arts funding is premised on two notions of culture that are mutually exclusive: one views culture as art, to be funded by arts councils; the other understands culture as an anthropological phenomenon that should be funded primarily by agencies such as multiculturalism and citizenship at the federal level and ministries of culture or citizenship at provincial levels (Wong, 1991). The assumption underpinning the second approach is that works of art produced by people of colour fail to meet professional standards of excellence. Only when artists of colour "prove" themselves in the context of the norms and models of White elites can they overcome the great divide (West, 1990).

With respect to the issues of access and equity to funding, a noted Canadian recording artist and composer commented:

> It seems that only Caucasians are allowed to sit in judgement as experts on Chinese, African, African-Canadian, South Asian, Aboriginal, Indonesian, Korean, Japanese ... music, deciding who gets the grants and whose music is valuable to whose community. Until we have representation on these juries, we will only be tokens. (Nolan, 1992:28)

For many years, the Canada Council failed to support the Access and Equity's committee's finding that "systemic racism is a result of the everyday functioning of all Canadian institutions" and rejected its call for an organizational review of the Canada Council. However, in recent years, the Council has made a significant and positive shift, which can be seen in terms of its organizational, administrative, and ideological approach to the issues of diversity and equity.

Institutional Responses

The lack of access and the barriers to writers and artists of colour have also begun to receive more attention from funding bodies, museums, writers' and actors unions, publishing houses, and other cultural agencies. This chapter's case studies demonstrate that cultural production is indeed an important site of struggle. Racial-minority and Aboriginal communities are becoming more insistent that their cultural rights be respected and that the cultural appropriation of their experiences by White power brokers in cultural organizations be challenged.

Summary

This chapter has analyzed the powerful role of cultural organizations in contributing to democratic racism. The racism found in various forms of cultural production and transmission emanates from the dominant culture's value system. Although artistic expression and cultural production are framed in the context of liberal values such as universalism and freedom of expression, Eurocentric assumptions and standards strongly influence the decisions of cultural producers in terms of what artists, writers, musicians, and actors are supported and whose voices, words, and images are excluded or silenced. Each of the cultural events examined in this chapter's case studies reflect a struggle between those with privilege, power, and voice, and those seeking to gain control over the production of images and systems of representation that misrepresent or exclude them.

The analysis in this chapter also demonstrates how the discourses of liberalism, such as freedom of expression and universalism, are frequently used to silence dissent by minorities. The examples and case studies cited support the view of many people of colour and Aboriginal peoples that freedom of expression appears to be mainly limited to the rights of those who already exercise power. On the question of universalism, groups who find their culture excluded from mainstream theatre, museums, and publishing houses challenge the assumption that Anglo-European cultural traditions and practices have universal appeal. Each of the examples of cultural productions explored in this chapter demonstrates how Whiteness is coded within complex cultural processes that are deeply embedded in structures of dominance.

Democratic racism is also reflected in the response of cultural authorities to the demands by African Canadians, Asian Canadians, Aboriginal artists, and their communities for greater sensitivity, accountability, and accessibility, which were commonly met with either indifference or a barrage of criticism and racist discourse by the cultural elite and the media. Cultural authorities within the ROM and the literary establishment vigorously and continuously denied the possibility that racism was entrenched in their cultural institutions and individual practices. From their position of power and privilege, and from their social location of "Whiteness," racism was invisible to them.

In almost every example cited in this chapter, efforts on the part of minority groups to identify racism in art forms and cultural productions resulted in both overt and subtle attacks on those who voiced concerns and called for change. All of the discourses of democratic racism were employed, including the discourse of denial, the discourse of reverse racism, the discourse of political correctness, the discourse of "otherness," and the discourse of national identity. In the case of "Into the Heart of Africa" and people who argued for a more inclusive system of exhibition and representation were viewed as "radicals" and "troublemakers." Those who supported the "Writing Thru Race" conference were portrayed as a threat to Canada's most cherished democratic values, traditions, and sense of national identity.

This chapter also illustrates the interlocking nature of various forms of racism. For example, the intrinsic relationship between racist ideology and the practices of the mass media is linked to the cultural and racial assumptions driving various cultural organizations and disciplines. The presence of the police at the protests against the ROM communicates the message that dissent is undemocratic and dangerous. Educational institutions often become another vehicle for the production and dissemination of culture. Racism in the arts is also inextricably linked to the marketplace and propelled by the economic interests of the corporate elite. Racism in the arts is like racism in the other institutions of Canadian society; it is ultimately about the power of the dominant group to control cultural forms of expression.

Racism in cultural production dramatically illustrates the tension between the competing ideologies of racism and liberalism. On the one hand, North American society has a great attachment to the ideal of unrestricted artistic licence for those who work in the arts and in cultural organizations. On the other hand, the act of protesting, resisting, and challenging the power of those who control cultural expression is a tool in the fight against marginalization, exclusion, and erasure.

Racial-minority artists and communities believe that freedom of expression should not become the talisman under which White cultural institutions maintain and reproduce racist discourse and representation. They are using cultural production as a vehicle to call on a democratic society to live up to its promise of equality and justice for all. There are tentative signs that the call is beginning to be heard.

Notes

1. For an in-depth study of racism in the arts, an analysis of the cultural politics of difference, and an expanded analysis of the case studies in this chapter, see Tator, Henry, and Mattis (1998).

References

Bailey, C. (1992). "Fright the Power." *Fuse* 15(6):24.

Becker, C. (ed.). (1994). *The Subversive Imagination: Artists, Society and Social Responsibility.* New York: Routledge.

Bhabha, H. (ed.). (1990). *Nation and Narration.* London: Routledge.

Blatchford, C. (1990). "A Surrender to Vile Harangues." *Toronto Sun* (November 30):5.

Brant, B. (1990). "From the Outside Looking In: Racism and Writing." Panel discussion, Gay Cultural Festival, Vancouver (August).

Browning, F. (1992). "Self-Determination and Cultural Appropriation." *Fuse* 15(4):31–35.

Butler, S. (1993). "Contested Representations: Revisiting 'Into the Heart of Africa.'" Master's thesis, Department of Anthropology, York University.

Callwood, J. (1993). "Journalism and the Blight of Censorship." *Globe and Mail* (June 28):A13.

Cannizzo, J. (1990). "Into the Heart of a Controversy." *Toronto Star* (June 5):A17.

———. (1991). "Exhibiting Cultures: Into the Heart of Africa." *Visual Anthropology Review* 7(1):150–60.

Clarke, G. (1994). "After Word." *Possibilities Literary Art Magazine.* 1(2):48.

Clifford, J. (1990). "On Collecting Art and Culture." In R. Ferguson, Martha Gever, Trinh T. Minh-ha, and Cornel West (eds.), *Out There: Marginalization and Contemporary Culture.* New York: Museum of Contemporary Art.

Crean, S. (1991). "Taking the Missionary Position." In O. McKague (ed.), *Racism in Canada.* Saskatoon: Fifth House.

Da Breo, H. (1989–90). "Royal Spoils: The Museum Confronts Its Colonial Past." *Fuse* (Winter):28–36.

Danzker, J. (1991). "Cultural Apartheid." In O. McKague (ed.), *Racism in Canada.* Saskatoon: Fifth House.

Del Rio, B. (2003). *Theatre in Canada: Preservation of White Culture*. Toronto: ACTRA.

Essed, P. (1990). *Everyday Racism*. Claremont, CA: Hunter House.

Ferguson, R., Martha Gever, Trinh T. Minh-ha, and Cornel West (eds.). (1990). *Out There: Marginalization and Contemporary Culture*. New York: Museum of Contemporary Art.

Fulford, R. (1992). "Robert Fulford Ponders the Growing Strength of the Hruska Principle." *Globe and Mail* (September 30):C1.

Gagnon, M.K. (2000). *Other Conundrums: Race, Culture, and Canadian Art*. Vancouver and Kamloops: Arsenal Press, Artspeak Gallery, and Kamloops Gallery.

Griffith, K. (1994). "'Minority Writers' Conference Claims Revolutionary Success." *Vancouver Sun* (July 4):A2.

Hall, J., and M. Neitz. (1993). *Culture: Sociological Perspectives*. Englewood Cliffs, NJ: Prentice Hall.

Hall, S. (1977). "Culture, the Media and the Ideological Effect." In J. Curran, M. Gurevitch, and J. Woollacott (eds.), *Mass Communication and Society*. London: Edward Arnold. 315–48.

———. (1992). *Reproducing Ideologies: Essays on Culture and Politics*. In W.E.B. Dubois Lectures, Harvard University Press (forthcoming).

Hume, C. (1989). "ROM Looks into the Heart of Darkness." *Toronto Star* (November 17):E3, E22.

———. (1990). "Rejection of ROM Show Not a Defeat for Racism." *Toronto Star* (September 29):F3.

Hutcheon, L. (1994). *Irony's Edge: The Theory and Politics of Irony*. London: Routledge.

Jordan, G., and C. Weedon. (1995). *Cultural Politics: Class, Race and the Postmodern World*. Oxford, UK, and Cambridge, MA: Blackwell.

Katz, J. (1978). *White Awareness: Handbook for Anti-Racist Teaching*. Norman: University of Oklahoma Press.

Lalla, H., and J. Myers. (1990). *Report on the Royal Ontario Museum's Exhibit "Into the Heart of Africa."* Toronto: Toronto Board of Education.

Li, P. (1994). "A World Apart: The Multicultural World of Visible Minorities and the Art World of Canada." *Canadian Review of Sociology and Anthropology* 31(4)(November).

Mackey, E. (1995). "Postmodernism and Cultural Politics in a Multicultural Nation: Contests over Truth in the Into the Heart of Africa Controversy." *Public Culture* 7(2)(Winter):403–31.

McFarlane, S. (1995). "The Haunt of Race: Canada's Multiculturalism Act, the Politics of Incorporation, and Writing Thru Race." *Fuse* 18(3)(Spring)18–31.

McMelland, J. (1990). "Uncovering a Hidden Curriculum." *Role Call* (April 10).

Mitchell, T. (1989). "The World as Exhibition." *Society for Comparative Study of Society and History* 31(2):217–36.

Morrison, T. (1992). *Playing in the Dark: Whiteness and the Literary Imagination*. Cambridge, MA: Harvard University Press.

Mukherjee, A. (1994–95). "Teaching Racial Minority Writing: Problems and Possibilities." *Paragraph: The Canadian Fiction Review* 16(3)(Winter and Spring).

Nolan, F. (1992). "Letter to Alan Gottlieb, Canada Council." *Fuse* 15(6):28.

NourbeSe Philip, M. (1992). *Frontiers: Essays and Writings on Racism and Culture*. Stratford, ON: Mercury Press.

Now Magazine. (2003). "Dramatic Ending." 23(16)(December 18–24). Online edition. Available <http://www.nowtoronto.com/issues/2003-12-18/news_story3.php>, accessed August 27, 2004.

Ouzounian, R. (2003). "Gass Devoted to Diversity." *Toronto Star* (December 7).

———. (2004). "About Face." *Toronto Star* (January 18).

Paris, E. (1992). "A Letter to the Thought Police." *Globe and Mail* (March 31).

Pieterse, N. (1992). *White Images of Africans and Blacks in Western Culture*. London and New Haven: Yale University Press.

Roach, C. (1990). "Into the Heart of the Controversy." *Toronto Sun* (June 5):A17.

Rundle, L. (1997). "From Novel to Film: *The English Patient* Distorted." *Issue* 43:9–13.

Tator, C., F. Henry, and W. Mattis. (1998). *Challenging Racism in the Arts: Case Studies in Controversy and Conflict*. Toronto: University of Toronto Press.

Walcott, R. (1996). "Lament for a Nation: The Racial Geography of 'The Oh! Canada Project.'" *Fuse* 19(4)(Summer):15–23.

West, C. (1990). "The New Cultural Politics of Difference." In R. Ferguson, Martha Gever, Trinh T. Minh-ha, and Cornel West (eds.), *Out There: Marginalization and Contemporary Culture*. New York: Museum of Contemporary Art.

Williams, S. (1992). "The Appropriation of Noise." *Fuse* 15(6):15–17.

Wong, P. (1991). "Yellow Peril Reconsidered." *Fuse* 14(Fall):1–2, 48–49.

Young, C. (1993). "Into the Heart of Africa: The Director's Perspective." *Curator* 36(3):174–88.

CHAPTER 10

RACISM IN THE MEDIA

When visible minorities do appear in our newspapers and TV public affairs programming, they emerge as villains in a variety of ways—as caricatures from a colonial past; as extensions of foreign entities; or, in the Canadian context, as troubled immigrants in a dazzling array of trouble spots; hassling police, stumping immigration authorities, cheating on welfare, or battling among themselves or with their own families.

—Siddiqui (1993)

This chapter continues the examination of cultural racism by examining how the media reinforce racist ideology and practices through the production of racist discourse. It begins with a discussion of the role and function of the media and then moves to a summary analysis of some of the indicators of racism in the media. The chapter then presents an examination of the ways in which the image-makers of the Canadian media industries marginalize people of colour, reducing them to invisible status and devaluing their images in and contributions to Canadian society.

This chapter looks at the power of the media to produce and transmit the message that people of colour, especially Blacks, create social problems and jeopardize the harmony and unity of Canadian society. The case studies demonstrate how the media indulge in overt and subtle misrepresentation and stereotyping. The examples cited also demonstrate the close relationships and common interests of the media and White elite groups such as the corporate sector and the police. Each of the major sectors of the media are reviewed by using data based on the practices of certain media organizations, and some of the initiatives developed as a response to racism in the media are considered.

The last section of the chapter examines discursive strategies used by the media that further reinforce the "rightness of Whiteness" and the marginalization and racialization of people of colour. Throughout this analysis, the underlying theme is the tension between a social institution that is the cornerstone of a democratic society and the racism that is woven into its everyday institutional and discursive practices.

Introduction

The electronic and print media have become major transmitters of society's cultural standards, myths, values, roles, and images. In theory, the media provide for the free flow and exchange of ideas, opinions, and information. As such, they represent the key instruments by which a democratic society's ideals are produced and perpetuated. In a liberal democracy, media institutions are expected to reflect alternative viewpoints, remain neutral and objective, and provide free and equitable access to all groups and classes.

In reality, however, while espousing democratic values of fairness, equality, and freedom of expression, the media reinforce and reproduce racism in a number of ways: negative stereotyping, the racialization of issues such as crime and immigration, Eurocentric and ethnocentric judgments, and the marginalization of people of colour in all aspects of media production.

Role and Function of the Media

The media, as a system and process of mass communication, incorporate a number of functions, including information processing and reproduction, education, socialization, entertainment, employment, and advertising. Media institutions are expected to reflect alternative viewpoints, to remain neutral and objective, and to provide free and equitable access to all groups and classes. The media in general, and television in particular, hold up a mirror in which society can see itself reflected. But who is reflected in the mirror?

The media reach out and touch people of every socioeconomic level, transcending differences in age, educational background, and occupational status. The media set norms, create stereotypes, build leaders, set priorities, and educate the public in matters of national interest and concern. Because of their wide-ranging exposure, the written and electronic media have an important role in guiding, shaping, and transforming the way we look at the world ("perceptions"), how we understand it ("conceptions"), and the manner in which we experience and relate to it ("reality") (Fleras and Elliott, 1992:234).

For many people, the mass media are a crucial source of beliefs and values from which they develop a picture of their social worlds. According to Hannerz, the media are machineries of meaning (1992:26). Radio, television, the print media, and other cultural forms (e.g., art, literature, films, and theatre) provide the elements out of which we form our identities—our sense of what it means to be male/female, our sense of ethnicity, of class and race, of nationality, of "us" and "them" (Kellner, 1995). Because of the marginalization of racial-minority communities from mainstream society, many White people rely almost entirely on the media for their information about minorities and the issues that concern their communities. The relationship between the White community and these groups is therefore largely filtered through the perceptions, assumptions, values, and beliefs of journalists and other media professionals.

MANIFESTATIONS OF RACISM IN THE MEDIA

Stereotypical portrayal and misrepresentation in everyday media discourse (text and talk)

Invisibility of people of colour in the news, advertising, and programming

Lack of representation at all levels of media operations

Racialization of people of colour as the "other"

Normalization and reproduction of White elite values, norms, and images

Biased attitudes and practices of media professionals

The Manifestations of Racism

Invisibility of People of Colour

A brief submitted to a parliamentary subcommittee on equality rights stated that people of colour are invisible in the Canadian media: "The relative absence of minority men and women in the Canadian media is remarkable" (Canadian Ethnocultural Council, 1985:92). It observed that the unequal status of racial minorities in the media was reflected by their absence from on-air roles, such as anchors, reporters, experts, or actors, and their lack of representation at all levels of staffing operations, production, and decision-making positions in communications. Their limited participation is the result of both overt bias and systemic discrimination. Examples of systemic discrimination cited in the brief include the reliance on referrals in hiring from White producers, writers, and editors; the lack of comprehensive outreach programs for the employment and training of people of colour; and the lack of recognition for qualifications and experience gained outside of Canada.

A Black Canadian actor succinctly addressed the issue of invisibility by paraphrasing a famous quotation and question: "Mirror, mirror on the wall, tell me if I exist at all." The mirror is the media polished and held up by the image-makers—advertisers, radio station owners, private and public television executives, producers, writers, artistic directors, publishers, editors, and journalists (Gomez, 1983:13).

In a study of the extent of the appearances of people of colour and Aboriginal peoples in national evening news programs, particularly their participation on CBC's *The National* and CTV's "*National Evening News*, almost all stories in which people of colour appeared were those in which the stories were about non-Whites. There were few stories of general interest, such as sports, taxes, or political issues, in which people of colour were included. During the four weeks in which these programs were monitored, only 20 of 725 interviews solicited the opinions of racial minorities for subjects not related specifically to stories or people from their communities (Perigoe and Lazar, 1992). Monitoring of the media's representation of Arabs and Muslims conducted by the Canadian Islamic Congress from 1998 to 2003 found that Canadian Muslims rarely appear in the press, as indicated by the lack of coverage of their achievements and events. At the international level, particularly since 9/11, the Palestinian intifada, the invasion of Afghanistan, and the war in Iraq, Arabs and Muslims have become far more commonplace in media coverage. However the narratives, images, and everyday discourses commonly contain overt and implicit messages of "otherness" (see Case Study 10.2).

One of the primary factors in this invisibility is cultural racism and the belief in the concept of the "rightness of Whiteness." Whiteness is considered the universal (hidden) norm and allows one to think and speak as if Whiteness described and defined the world. Whiteness "refers to a set of locations that are historically, politically, culturally produced and moreover, are intrinsically linked to unfolding relations of domination ..." (Frankenberg, 1993:viii). The vehicles of media production and representation move across a spectrum from overt racist discourse to the more coded language and implicit meanings that incorporate more liberal values and ideals (Gabriel, 1998, 2000).

Stereotypical Portrayal

Studies of the media (Henry and Tator, 2002; Hier and Greenberg, 2002; Wortley, 2002; Fleras and Kunz, 2001; Mahtani, 2001; Jiwani, 1995) demonstrate that the Canadian media, in general, produce a negative view of people of colour. This is not a new phenomenon. Mosher (1998), commenting on racism in the criminal justice system of

Ontario, revealed that the media have had an instrumental role in racializing crime for more than a hundred years. He found that the racialization of crime so prevalent today was also present in media coverage of an earlier period. Canadian newspapers routinely described the race of offenders, which "served to identify Asians and Blacks as alien … and justified to a certain extent their differential treatment by the criminal justice system" (Mosher, 1998:126). He cites headlines such as:

Chinese Gambled; These 18 Chinks were Roped in … (*Toronto Daily Star*, March 29, 1909)

Warm Pipe Scorches Chink Opium User (*Toronto Daily Star*, April 3, 1916)

No More Chicken Dinners or Watermelon Feeds … (*Hamilton Spectator*, August 26, 1909)

The Black Burglar (*Globe*, November 20, 1900)

Negro Thieves Given Stiff Sentences (*Windsor Evening Record*, October 20, 1912)

In addition, Mosher noted that court reporters often focused on the racial identity of accused persons and witnesses. For example, an article described "two hundred pounds of Julius Wagstaffe, a jet-black import from North Carolina. …" In some instances, the Black accused's speech was rendered in dialect in the body of the article and their comments were ridiculed and trivialized. There is therefore "extensive evidence of the stereotyping of Asians and Blacks and the racialization of crime in the media, especially between 1892 and 1930" (Mosher, 1998:134).

Contrary to myth, journalists, editors, broadcasters, and directors of media organizations are not always neutral, impartial, objective, and unbiased. The media often select events that are atypical, present them in a stereotypical fashion, and contrast them with "White behaviour." The broadcaster, producer, reporter, cameraperson, journalist, and editor have a context that affects the way they interpret images, events, and situations. This context influences what they choose to film or air, what subject or topics they select, and what eventually becomes part of the story. Media professionals are often guided by a need to focus on the sensational, extraordinary, and exotic, which sell well in the marketplace. They are also influenced by their own social locations and political connections to the groups and institutions that have power and influence.

A consistent theme of both news and programming is the portrayal of people of colour as "the outsiders within," reinforcing the "we-they" mindset. Research establishes the close connection between the media's conception of and construction of stories on race-related issues and their impact on public opinion (Entman and Rojecki, 2000; Campbell, 1995; van Dijk, 1991, 1993). The writer and critic bell hooks (1990) suggests that stereotypes of people of colour are developed to "serve as substitutions for reality." They are contrived images that are developed and projected onto the "others."

One of the most common and persistent examples of racism in the media is the frequency with which people of colour and First Nations peoples are singled out as "creating problems" or as "having problems" that require a disproportionate amount of political attention or public resources to solve. *They* make unacceptable demands that threaten the political, social, or moral order of society (Henry and Tator, 2002; Fleras and Kunz, 2001; Law, 2002; Entman and Rojecki, 2000; Cottle, 2000; Fiske, 2000). First Nations people have also been portrayed in the media, both historically and currently, as a "problem people."

MUSLIM BIAS IN THE MEDIA

Background

The Eurocentric construction of Muslims/ Islam/Arabs/Middle Eastern peoples in the mainstream media has had a long history in North America as well as other Western countries. According to Edward Said (1981) the Western media's view of Islam is seen through the prism of a fanatical religion and is articulated in the crudest form of "us-versus-them" discourse. These forms of stereotyping and misrepresentation are deeply embedded in North American popular culture. Mark Twain in his book *Innocents Abroad* (1869) advanced some of the early discriminatory depictions of Muslims, labelling them "sinfully ugly pagans, "infidels," and "ravaged savage[s]" with eyes "fierce and full of hate" (cited in Shaheen, 1997:8). Hollywood has significantly contributed to the myths about Arabs and Muslims for more than half a century (ibid.). Children's cartoons and films are filled with negative images of Arabs portrayed as villains and buffoons. In many ways this discursive practice continues to this day.

During the Gulf War in 1991, Canadian broadcast and print media vilified Canadian Muslims. Local Arab and Muslim reaction to the war was often reduced to opposition to Canada's action in the Allied war effort (Winter, 1992). However, there has been a marked increase in biased depictions since 9/11. The U.S. invasion of Afghanistan, the Palestinian intifada, the U.S.-led war in Iraq in 2003 has provided further vehicles for the media's denigration of these communities. A complex web of "otherness" is produced based on the discourses of religion, race, ethnicity, and national origin. Racialized images and ideas are circulated through racist cartoons, feature writing, news columns, editorials, letters to the editor, television news coverage, programming, and radio talk shows. All of these vehicles of cultural production reflect a deeply embedded anti-Muslim bias within the mainstream print and electronic media in Canada that further perpetuate these mythical and stereotypical depictions.

Over the past four years, the Canadian Islamic Congress (CIC) has published an annual survey (*CIC Media Survey Report*) of anti-Islam bias in several of Canada's largest daily newspapers. Among the media organizations that were evaluated were the *Toronto Star*, the *Globe and Mail*, the *National Post*, the *Toronto Sun*, the *Ottawa Citizen*, and Montreal's *Gazette* and *La Presse*. The studies have also included two Canadian magazines *Maclean's* and the Canadian edition of *Reader's Digest*. The CBC English-language news was also monitored. The researchers established a numerical grading system with 10 levels to measure the extent of bias expressed by the newspapers. The *National Post* offered the most biased coverage of the Muslim/Islamic community. The survey also found that in the last two years since 9/11 the use of anti-Islam and anti-Muslim language to describe and associate the violent acts of individuals has increased tenfold in most major Canadian papers. In the discourses of many of these newspapers, and especially the *National Post*, it is commonplace to use highly negative sweeping generalizations and stereotypes that include terms like "Muslim extremist," "Islamic-inspired terrorists attacks," "murderous Islamic militant," and "Muslim fundamentalist." Islam is implicitly or explicitly depicted as a violent religion. Such terms serve to inappropriately identify Muslim individuals by their religion, when in fact the issues in dispute often have more to do with politics and economics rather than religious faith and practice. Wahida Valiente (a vice-president of CIC) points to certain inconsistencies in comparison with the coverage of other conflicts. She observes: "We never refer to [those involved in Northern Ireland conflict] as Catholic terrorists. ..." The CIC identifies what it calls "image distortion disorder" as one of the main consequences of anti-Islamic media coverage, and, challenges the perception that Islam condones and encourages violence. The *National Post* scored 100—the maximum possible in the survey's ranking of the use of anti-Islam language and terminology—and it was the only paper in Canada to do so. Despite CIC meetings with the

National Post, the newspaper continues to reproduce negative portrayals of Islam and the Muslim community. The following are some examples of *Post* quotes (*CIC Media Survey Report*, 2000–2001, see Canadian Islamic Congress [CIC], 1999–2003):

> *"Misplaced Anxieties" (Editorial, September 15, 2001)*
>
> But it is hard to get worked up about the occasional slur directed against North American Muslims. ... Indeed there is something offensive about the tear-drenched press releases issued by North American Muslim organizations.
>
> *"Muslim Mushrooms, Terrorist Toadstools— Fifth Columnist Ushers bin Laden Within our Perimeter" (George Jonas, October 15, 2001)*
>
> We have to fear our neighbours down the street ... a degree of ethnic or religious profiling is unavoidable. ...

"A Healthy Dose of 'Bigotry'" (Jonathan Kay, October 18, 2001)

> We should not pretend that an effective fight against terrorism [in Canada] can be waged in a truly color-blind fashion. The fact is, those who plot the annihilation of our civilization are of one religion and, almost without exception, one race. Yet admitting this is a problem for Mr. Chrétien. ... Multiculturalism is a relativistic creed that assumes all immigrant cultures are equally tolerant, civilized and enlightened once you scratch the surface.

Other research conducted by the CIC demonstrates some of the effects of anti-Islam discourse by the media. For example, a poll of Canadian university students conducted by the CIC following the second anniversary of 9/11, showed that more than one-third of students associate that horrific event with Islam and that more than three-quarters of respondents obtained all of their information about Islam and Muslims from the mainstream media. Raja Khouri, former President of the Canadian Arab Federation, argues that "The effect on our communities is that, like our Japanese Canadian

counterparts during the Second World War, we too have become victims of psychological internment." Changes in immigration policies and procedures targeting Muslims and Arabs have made Muslims feel like "they are living under siege" (MacAfee and Carmichael, 2002).

Another consequence of such image distortion is that in many instances it appears to have led, especially among youths, to a loss of self-esteem, feelings of inferiority, and even suicidal tendencies (CIC, 2003; Bullock and Jafri, 2001). As well, there has been a significant increase in the backlash and hate crimes against Muslims, Arabs, Afghanis, and South Asians across North American. Muslim parents and students (or those perceived to be of Muslim/Arab background), have reported numerous incidents of racial harassment in schools (Zine, 2002). Another form of bias and discrimination has impacted upon these communities in relation to housing. The Refugee Housing Task Force in Toronto noted that numerous landlords were refusing to rent to Muslims after 9/11 (Refugee Housing Task Force, 2001).

A study by the Afghan Women's Organization (Bullock and Jaffri, 2001) points to the stereotypical image of Muslim women, portrayed as the alien "other," veiled, passive victims of patriarchy. The authors suggest that this image "has little to do with real Muslim women's lives."

Analysis

While anti-Muslim bias in the media has a long and ignoble history, recent events have provided ample opportunity to reinforce and reproduce highly negative images and messages. The print and electronic media, supported by stereotypical portrayals in other forms of popular culture such as Hollywood films, cartoons, and television programming create a form of demonization of the Islamic faith. The primary tool that the media relies on is essentialization. Muslims are portrayed as a monolithic community made up of undesirable and alien "others." They are represented as living outside the margins of the "imagined community" of "real" Canadians. They possess different/deviant values and beliefs that represent a threat to "our" way of life. They are portrayed as a "problem people." The stereotypical images constructed by the mainstream media have enormous strength and resilience. The media representations found on American news networks and programming significantly reinforce these racialized discourses, which are readily accessible to Canadian viewers. A discursive analysis of the rhetorical strategies commonly used by media practitioners reveals a heavy reliance on the language of invective, deprecation, and denigration. One of the central criticisms from the perspectives of both ethno-racial minority communities and media researchers is the fact that the journalists and newsmakers commonly report the news without an understanding of social context. Sensationalism replaces interpretation and analysis. The absence of the historical, social, political, economic frameworks from which to understand these events feeds into the realm of social myths. These myths buried in the dominant discourses reveal a dangerous naturalness or commonsense understanding of who Muslims are and why Islam represents such a threat to "our" social order.

Table 10.1 demonstrates the overt and sometimes covert or coded messages embedded in the everyday images that circulate in the print and electronic media.

Table 10.1

IMAGES OF VARIOUS MINORITY GROUPS

Aboriginal Peoples	Blacks	Asians
✓ Savages	✓ Drug addicts	✓ Untrustworthy
✓ Alcoholics	✓ Pimps	✓ Menacing
✓ Uncivilized	✓ Prostitutes	✓ Unscrupulous
✓ Uncultured	✓ Entertainers	✓ Subhuman
✓ Murderers	✓ Athletes	✓ Submissive
✓ Noble	✓ Drug dealers	✓ Maiming
✓ Needing a White saviour	✓ Murderers	✓ Quaint
✓ Victim	✓ Gangsters	✓ Exotic
✓ Violent	✓ Gang members	✓ Prostitutes
	✓ Violent	✓ Cooks
	✓ Simple-minded	✓ Store vendors
	✓ Inconsequential	
	✓ Primitive	
	✓ Needing a White saviour	

Misrepresentation in the Print Media

The first study to identify and document racism in the print media in Canada was made by Rosenfeld and Spina (1977), who examined the *Toronto Sun*'s coverage of issues relating to immigration and racial and ethnic communities. In their review of the newspaper, they found considerable evidence of racial bias and discrimination. Their analysis revealed that the *Toronto Sun* presented the reader with a single, prejudiced view of the world.

In promoting and sustaining the values of the dominant White society, the media often draw a line between the "First World" and the "Third World," between the "West" and the "non-West," the "North" and the "South." This line of demarcation is created by the constant production of images that distinguish the positive attributes, capacities, and strengths of the West from those of the countries of the East or the Third World. The First World is rational, progressive, efficient, moral, modern, scientifically and technologically ordered, and on the side of the good and right, whereas the Third World is linked with racialized premises; it is defined as traditional, underdeveloped, overpopulated, irrational, disordered, and uncivilized (Goldberg, 1993).

In a recent study by Henry and Tator (2002) of racial bias in the English Language print media, the present authors examined racialized discourse in several Canadian newspapers. The study used critical discourse analysis (CDA)[1] to illuminate racism in the Canadian press by uncovering the interpretative lenses and decoding the dominant narratives. Six case studies are used to analyze the implicit meanings and messages embedded in the patterns of language, words, phrases, ideas, and images found in the everyday discourses of journalists and editors. Broad macro structures used to define the most important information about a news story are examined. These include headlines and leads, rhetorical strategies and argumentative statements, core themes, and central ideas. Critical discourse analysis also helps to expose the more micro structures such as hidden points of view, tacit opinions or assumptions, and the commonly denied ideologies of the media that can be inferred from these lexical choices (see van Dijk, 1991, 1993; Fairclough and Wodak, 1997; Hier and Greenberg, 2002). Racialized discourse appears to work silently within the cognitive makeup of individual journalists and editors, as well as within the collective culture and professional norms and values of media organizations. Journalists and editors are often intent on denying racism exists, sometimes refusing to validate the voices and views of those they have represented as the unassimilatable, undesirable "others." In many areas of media production both discursive and institutionally structured forms of bias remain unacknowledged and invisible.

The following are some of the discourses of domination (or democratic racism) that permeate the print media and constitute the discourses of democratic racism: the discourse of denial of racism; the discourse of political correctness; the discourse of reverse discrimination and White victimization; the discourse of "otherness"; "we" versus "they"; the discourse of moral panic; and the discourse of national identity. Examples of these discourses are identified in the quotations listed below and are drawn from diverse Canadian newspaper sources (Henry and Tator, 2002).

> Unemployed Ontarians would be well advised to ferret out that ancestor who claimed native roots or a history on an African slaveship. Or they might even consider inventing such a relative. (Editorial, *Globe and Mail*, September 1, 1994)

> In not reporting on the unusual pathologies of [ethnic groups other than aboriginals], we are failing in our duty to inform society of significant social facts. (William Thorsell, *Globe and Mail*, April 9, 1994)

> Our sponsored immigration policy has "ended up putting grandmas and grandpas or nieces and nephews on our welfare rolls by the hundreds of thousands. ..." (Diane Francis, *National Post*, January 4, 2000)

Unfortunately, these days most of the murderers seem to be Black. ... Given the society we live in, racial conflict is often the result of when there is Black-and-White crime. ... Are we a society of racists? Certainly not. It's just that White Canadians are understandably fed up with people they see as outsiders, coming into their country and beating and killing them. (Raynier Maharaj, *Toronto Sun*, April 15, 1994)

Send them back. That's the opinion of the majority of callers who responded to Friday's *Times-Colonist* phone poll on the 123 Chinese migrants who arrived here last week. And 44% indicated that they should be allowed to stay. (*Times Colonist*, July 12, 1999)[2]

Misrepresentation of First Nations People

Researchers such as Roth, Nelson, and Kasennahawi (1995) and Skea (1993–94) note that First Nations peoples are commonly portrayed as a significant threat to the social order. Roth et al. make the point that in the long history of racist discourse in the media, the Oka crisis[3] created a media frenzy, and negative stereotyping of First Nations peoples was never more blatant. Headlines that appeared in the national media reveal the depth of racialized discourse that placed all Mohawks within a system of categories of violence.

The Royal Commission on Aboriginal Peoples (RCAP, 1996) found that most coverage in the mainstream media is written within a context of Aboriginal peoples as pathetic victims, angry warriors, or noble environmentalists. The Commissioners were so concerned about media indifference to the findings of the Commission that they distributed to community newspapers a series of articles dealing with various aspects of the groundbreaking report. This media indifference to Aboriginal issues is reflected in polling results, which indicate that 40 percent of the general public believe First Nations people enjoy a standard of living as good as or better than theirs.

Switzer (1998), Director of Communications for the Assembly of First Nations, maintains that the Canadian media "have declared open season on Indians." Switzer offers the view that First Nations peoples' progress in key areas such as treaty and land claims negotiation has created an even more hostile relationship between mainstream media and First Nations peoples. He contends that the once-clear lines between sensational tabloid journalism and the more respectable press have "blurred beyond recognition," and that newspapers such as the *Ottawa Citizen* "have been literally thumbing their noses at First Nations peoples and their issues" (8). He cites the example of a publisher in British Columbia who publishes 60 weekly newspapers in the province, who ordered all of his editors to carry only editorials or columns critical of the Nisga'a treaty.

In a similar way, researchers (Fleras and Kunz, 2001; Henry and Tator, 2002) have demonstrated how a crisis between Mi'kmaq people and non-Native fishers over lobster fishing rights in Atlantic Canada, and more specifically Burnt Church, New Brunswick, led to numerous articles, editorials, and television stories that framed Mi'kmaq people through a "White gaze." The dominant narrative and images in the media's coverage reinforced the notion that First Nations people are prone to violence and conflict, and represent a threat to law and order.

CASE STUDY 10.2

CONTROVERSY OVER POLICE RACIAL PROFILING: PRESS RACIALIZATION OF BLACK MEN

Background

One of the most important factors in the racialization of crime is the overreporting of crimes allegedly committed by people of colour, and more specifically Black men. One of the first major studies to demonstrate this was Hall and colleagues (1978) in the United Kingdom, who established that the media not only played a crucial role in generating fear about crime, but also isolated a specific type of criminal who was supposedly responsible for a new wave of crime called "muggings." The media were largely responsible for implanting the idea that young Black males were enemies of society rather than the products of depressed socioeconomic conditions. The research of Entman and Rojecki (2000) in the United States and Law (2002) in the United Kingdom, among many other such studies, confirms these early findings. These scholars and Canadian scholars such as Benjamin (2002, 2003) and Wortley (2002) posit that the persistent negative representation of Black men as criminals through images, ideas, and words leads to an emotive hostility toward Blacks. They also observe that among the many rhetorical strategies used by the media, the most common are the denial of racism, mitigation or rationalization of race, and a "blame the victims" discourse.

Racial profiling became an important theme for the media following the *Toronto Star* series on racial profiling by police of Blacks (for background see the racial profiling case study in Chapter 6). Many of the conservative columnists, especially those writing for the *Globe and Mail*, the *National Post*, and the *Toronto Sun*, took highly critical positions in regard not only to the *Star* series but also to the broader issues arising out of the racial profiling debate. Columnists such as Christie Blatchford, Peter Worthington, Margaret Wente, and William Thorsell used the series as a springboard to return to dominant discourses related to the issues of race, the racialization of crime, and specifically the Jamaicanization of crime that have characterized their journalism for several years (see Henry and Tator, 2002; Benjamin, 2002, 2003).

Critical discourse analysis is used in this case study to deconstruct the multilayered levels of semantic meaning hidden in text. A number of racialized discursive strategies are common to all these journalists. The first theme identified relates to the identification of race of the victim and/or the alleged perpetrators in the reporting of crime.

The Discourse of "Talking About Race": Christie Blatchford, *National Post*, October 30, 2002, "Sometimes Race Is Simply a Fact"

This feature begins with a lengthy description of the slaying of several Black men in Toronto and includes evocative and highly emotional language such as "a veritable plethora of bereaved parents ... four children left fatherless including a baby girl ... brotherless siblings. ..." The article then shifts to Toronto Police Chief Fantino's press conference on the killings, and notes that police spokespersons did not

> ever volunteer the enormous elephant awkwardly hulking in the corner of the room. That is, the single common denominator the police already had that link all the victims and all but one of the suspects. It is, alas and alack, skin colour.

The use of the metaphoric image of the "enormous elephant" to describe race sends a confusing message to readers. Why would a biological construct such as race be described as an elephant? The message conveyed is that omitting the racial descriptor amounts to a huge issue and the notion of largeness is reinforced by the adverbial phrase "awkwardly hulking" which further promotes the image of size. It also suggests that the extent of the problem has created an unwieldy, uncomfortable situation.

This is what happens to honest discussion when the unwelcome and unacknowledged presence at the party is the touchy issue of race. ...

Here the columnist makes assumptions and alleges that the discussion was therefore dishonest because the police did not immediately reveal that the victims and most suspects were Black. The writer attempts to use irony by referring to the conference as a "party" but the effect is to trivialize and mock the issue. Race itself is also described as "touchy," presumably meaning that it is a sensitive topic, but sensitive or touchy to whom?

Blatchford refers to the *Star*'s series and the Chief's immediate responses of denial but then reverts to the press conference where "The Chief's remarks yesterday were so cautious as to be absurd" which is followed by a summary of the Chief's answers: "violence is the responsibility of everyone. It doesn't matter what colour one is ..." and ends with the columnist saying "socio-economic—yadda-yadda-yadda—he might just as well have said it is time for finger-painting."

The use of trivialization, mockery, and ridicule is obvious in these statements. The Chief's explanatory attempts are derided as "yadda-yadda-yadda" and the whole exercise of the press conference is minimized to a child's pastime of finger-painting. The lengthy article finally concludes with the well-known journalistic strategy of mitigation: "It goes without saying that the vast majority of black Torontonians have nothing to do with guns. ..." But Ms. Blatchford does not leave the reader with this sentiment because her final paragraph addresses the defence of, and need for, racial profiling:

It should also go without saying that parents of all races would far, far rather have their sons stopped by police officers trying to find the people responsible ... and momentarily angered or even humiliated ... than have officers waste precious time pulling over with equal alacrity tiny Asian women or white middle-aged ones like me or black grandpas with beards. Racial profiling isn't all bad, the Star notwithstanding. ...

The Discourse of the Jamaicanization: Peter Worthington, *Toronto Sun*, October 31, 2002, "Profiling Essential to Fighting Crime"

Peter Worthington was one of the first columnists to feature this issue. He begins this article by suggesting that while we all wait for the arrest of those who shot and killed "black guys ... let's look at the details." The columnist wonders whether these victims are "average black youths that the *Toronto Star* thinks are being unfairly profiled by police" and gives the response "dunno." As each subsequent question is raised, the same "dunno" answers it. For example:

How typical was ... better known as Peanuts, shot dead at age 21, the father of a two year old, a six week old and a three week old? Three different mothers of his children? Again, "dunno." Peanuts' half brother (different father?) was wounded in the leg for no reason says his mother, describing Peanuts as always smiling. He cared for people, had dreams of big things in life. ... Smokey was gunned down. Smokey was unemployed ... [and] leaves a three month old daughter. ... Two excellent boys according to their father were shot. ... Kevin leaves three children. ...

Several techniques are at work here, but the primary one is to call attention to one of the main points he wants to communicate and that is the negative aspects of Jamaican culture. By the constant and completely irrelevant insertion of the numbers of children these young men have left behind, Worthington is telling the reader that these young men are not straightforward citizens minding their own business and getting shot. They are, in fact, unemployed gang members. (Gangs and their importance in the Jamaican community are referred to later in the article.) This is argumentation by reverse, or saying one thing and conveying an entirely different meaning. He maintains that colour is not the issue here or in most Black-on-Black crimes. Culture is the issue, that is, Jamaican culture. This point is further stressed when he singles out other communities of colour and says that it is grossly unfair for people from Nigeria, Ghana, South Africa, Trinidad, Barbados, etc. to be stopped by police because Jamaicans give them and other blacks a bad name. Who can blame non-Jamaicans for feeling resentful?

In fact, no evidence is provided that "other blacks" feel resentful. Worthington concludes his article by making a strong argument for the necessity of racial profiling. He wonders "if it is profiling to keep a record of which part of society criminals come from" and concludes that profiling is necessary to fight crime and it is, in fact, "part of normal daily life."

Summary

Throughout these articles a number of recurring topics and themes including conflict, tensions, violence-prone behaviour, shootings, killings, guns, weaponry, and drugs, as well as social problems such as poverty, unemployment, and substandard housing are discussed. Jamaica and Jamaican Canadians are strongly implicated in all these activities. Although it may appear at a cursory reading that the journalists cited here are attempting to be explanatory and analytic, the articles use strong evocative, hyperbolic, and stereotypic language. They leave the reader with a strongly negative image of the Black community living in Canada and of the culture of Jamaica. The central narrative strategy used in these articles is based on the essentialization and racial-

ization of Black people. The discourses of these columnists draw upon the rhetorical strategies of denigration and inferiorization. Implicit in their arguments is the notion that the essence of being Black incorporates deviant values and norms. Throughout these media discourses focusing on the Jamaicanization of crime, there are virtually no positive representations of the country or its people. There is no reference to Jamaica's cultural vibrancy in art, music, literature, and cuisine. There is no mention of the reality of strong communities and loving intergenerational relationships that still forms a vital part of life in Jamaica. Here we have an example of the one-sidedness of media reportage in that the emphasis is entirely on the supposedly newsworthy, sensationalist, and negative aspects of Jamaica, while the more affirming, noteworthy, and respectable aspects of this society are omitted and ignored. What is ironic in this theme of the racialization of Jamaican people is that many of the Black youth they are racializing are likely to have been born in Canada! Benjamin's (2003) in-depth study of the Black/Jamaican criminal explores 266 articles in the *Toronto Sun* on "Black/Jamaicans" involved in criminal activities and concludes that the language and discourses in these articles reproduce racialized ideologies about African Canadians and crime. She also argues that the process of being "othered" in this way has negative consequences for members of this community in terms of social exclusion, marginalization, and banishment through deportation.

Racialization and Marginalization in Television Programming

In a study by Granzberg (1982), 360 hours of prime-time television programming on two major Canadian networks and one American network were examined. The study concluded that the portrayal of racial minorities was characterized by misrepresentation and stereotyping. Minorities were depicted as being weak and unstable. They were shown as being less maritally stable, less important, less gainfully employed, and less heroic than White people.

Studies conducted in the United States and the United Kingdom on the portrayal of racial minorities in the daily news found a scarcity of news stories that challenged racial stereotypes. White newsmakers are more likely to report stories that confirm their preconceptions of Blacks as drug pushers, criminals, and troublemakers. In the same way, other people of colour such as Asians, are commonly categorized, inferiorized, and represented as the "other" (van Dijk 1991; Entman and Rojecki, 2000; Campbell, 1995).

In recent years, although people of colour are seen more frequently in television programming, particularly on U.S. networks, some disturbing patterns of the marginalization of racial minorities are emerging. The television critic for the *Globe and Mail*, John Haslett Cuff, observed that where Black people were central to a television show they tended to be portrayed (even more one-dimensionally than is TV's norm) as "victim, villain, buffoon or cuddly, folksy types" (Cuff, 1990).

Historically, the predominant images of Black people portrayed on both American television networks and the Hollywood film industry have been those of criminals, rioters, thieves, drug addicts, pimps, and prostitutes (Cuff, 1992). Five years later, in 1997, the stereotypical images had not improved much; Cuff commented: "The two predominant images of the black male on prime-time television are that of the super-hero/athlete and the crotch-grabbing buffoon. In between there's the hipster and outlaw and the solid working-class type, but these are largely secondary characters, supporting roles" (Cuff, 1997). Making a similar point, Adilman (1998) questioned why there are no Black characters in Canadian TV series. He attributed the black-out to broadcasters, cable companies, and federal broadcast regulators, who meanwhile imported fictionalized stereotypes of American entertainment: "Canadian Blacks have their own rich stories—and experiences different from those of American Blacks—that are not being told on TV" (M2).

Stereotyping and Whiteness in Television Programming

Some of the most popular programs on television in the 1990s were virtually devoid of people of colour. The U.S. network programs portrayed an overwhelmingly White society included *Beverly Hills 90210*, *Friends*, *Melrose Place*, *Party of Five*, *Seinfeld*, *The X-Files*, *Grace Under Fire*, *Roseanne*, and *Caroline in the City*. On the rare occasions when people of colour do appear on mainstream television, they are placed in stereotypical roles, filtered through a prism of the White gaze (Morrison and Brodsky Lacour, 1997). Current television programming continues to stereotype and cast minority men and women in the mold of a problematic, marginal, decorative people, or the "other." Misrepresentation is neither accidental nor attitudinal but rather is embedded in the nature of programming in a medium designed to connect consumers with advertiser in relation to good ratings (Fleras and Kunz, 2001). Television is a medium that thrives on the stereotyping of everyone as a basis for plot lines and character development. However, the impact of systemic stereotyping is substantially different when applied to unequal situations, and it is precisely this distinction that raises the question of how to portray minorities and their ethnicity in TV programming.

The findings of two recent studies of racial bias in Canadian prime-time television programming (Murray, 2002; Henry and Tator, 2003) reach a common conclusion: racial bias continues to permeate Canadian television programming and is manifested in the invisibility of ethno-racial and First Nations peoples in the narratives, images and stereotypical representation that flow from the screen into our homes and daily lives. In a study of 69 hours of English Canadian TV drama, Murray found that Aboriginal representation was virtually absent from programming. In the context of this sample, the cancellation of *North 60 Degrees* and *The Rez*, two popular shows, have erased the presence of First Nations people on Canadian television programming. People of colour are rarely heard, and, when they do appear, in over half the shows they are represented in a tokenistic manner. Where race is central to the plot, conflict is the dominant theme.

CASE STUDY 10.3

STEREOTYPING IN TELEVISION PROGRAMMING

Background

This case study is taken from the authors' research on Canadian television news, advertising, and dramatic programming (Henry and Tator, 2003). As part of this study, a small pilot project to examine Canadian-produced television entertainment programs was also undertaken.

In October 2002 six television dramas were taped. For five of these, four episodes each were taped; for the sixth, two episodes were taped. This yielded 22 hours of taped material. The five were *Cold Squad*, *Paradise Falls*, *North of 60*, *The Eleventh Hour*, and *Da Vinci's Inquest*; the sixth was *The New Degrassi*. The tapes were reviewed first by a research assistant. After her initial scrutiny, Henry examined the same tapes for specific content on how racial-minority characters were being depicted. The initial review revealed that *Paradise Falls*, which is set in a small Ontario town, did not include a single minority person in the four taped episodes. Two of the other shows in the sample were particularly interesting. *The Eleventh Hour* premiered on CTV on November 26, 2002, which meant that the four tapings in the study were, in fact, the first episodes aired of the show. (The first airing of a series often establishes the main themes and character of the program.) *North of 60* also presented unique challenges, since it is set in a Native community and features mainly First Nations characters.

Among the several programs taped and analyzed was *Cold Squad*—a crime series in which old crimes are reinvestigated by police and forensic experts. Its main characters are four White men and two White women. People of colour occasionally are shown in small roles and more often as walk-ons in background shots.

In one particular taped episode, the murder of a Black rapper is featured. In the first scene, which takes place at the crime scene and shows the body of the Black rapper, a female police officer says "so he was into music not crime." In the second scene, a neighbour identifies the victim as belonging to the "Steeves family across the street, their adopted child, the coloured boy." The victim, Jeff, became "anti-White" according to his White adoptive father, who accuses his son's Black boss, a supposed DJ, of killing him.

The DJ is interviewed several times during this episode; his rapper name is "Desecrate." He becomes the prime suspect, and in the first scene in which he is questioned he greets the police investigators by welcoming them to "crack college … Is it Black History month already?" he asks sardonically. He is questioned again in the third such scene, and some of the text is as follows: "As far as I'm concerned, I'm only here because I'm a Black man." The police officer responds "You can save the self-righteous bullshit." Later in the scene, the officer hits the Black man, who then says "I can see the headlines now … racist cop!" The officer says "There was no prejudice involved"—"Who are you trying to convince, me or yourself?" In another scene Desecrate is holding a press conference to release his new CD and he says they're "putting Black against Black … Justice ain't colour-blind."

Later in the story, the victim's brother is shown trying to kill the Black DJ. Throughout the story, there is a considerable amount of hip-hop-accented talk as the victim was a hip-hop artist. Among the minor characters there is also a young White man who is suspected of drug dealing and briefly thought to be the murderer.

As the conclusion unfolds, the adoptive father of the victim confesses that he killed his son by accident because it "was pitch black and I thought he was Desecrate." During his confession he describes his own civil rights and Peace Corps background and his idealism. He adopted Jeff because "colour doesn't matter" but he became increasingly concerned that Jeff was falling under Desecrate's bad influence and therefore sought to kill him.

Analysis

The story is replete with negative stereotypes and only moderately coded messages. In the very first instance the police, following well-known stereotypes, immediately jump to the conclusion that the victim was into drugs and that his murder therefore is drug- and/or gang-related. The Black DJ is portrayed as an assertive and very cliché-ridden character. He speaks in hip-hop or street lingo and is the only character to use bad and obscene language such as "your white ass." He is identified as a former drug dealer who made money in the trade and is now producing hip-hop and other Black music. Since the police still suspect him of dealing, he is also assumed to be a murderer despite his protestations of innocence of both offences. While it is part of hip-hop culture to assume very descriptive names, the choice of name for this character—"Desecrate"—carries a powerful image. The literal dictionary meaning of *desecrate* defines it "to divest of sacredness—to profane— to treat as not sacred." Deconstructing such a name tells us that the character stands for the desecration of society. This would be in keeping with his text, which is full of not very subtle barbs against not only police but also the general environment in which he lives and now works.

One of the most striking stereotypes in this story, however, deals with the character of the adoptive father. Mistaking his own son for the DJ sends out a very powerful message. The White man, even though he is the victim's father, nevertheless cannot distinguish one Black man from another! This raises the spectre of "they all look alike to me" discourse that is common among people who are ideologically prejudiced. It also distances the White father from his Black son, because it suggests the typical discourse of "we" and "they." And finally, the story line is told against the background of hip-hop Black music and features entertainers and producers of such music. The stereotypic discourse of Blacks being good entertainers is thereby once again reinforced and the "rightness of Whiteness" continues to be a powerful discursive theme that frames the central narrative.

Henry and Tator's pilot study (ibid.) of six Canadian television programs found that the prism of Whiteness provided a powerful filter.[4] While depictions of overt racial bias and stereotyping have been somewhat reduced, realistic portrayals of the people of colour are still lacking in most areas of programming. The dominant discourses and representations in these programs reinforce the construct of Whiteness as the normative universe, a society in which essentially all "others," including people of colour—especially Blacks and First Nations people—are constructed as "problem" people. The stories contained a reservoir of images and ideas that position minorities within existing institutional hierarchies. Blacks, Asians, and other minorities are repeatedly represented as helpless victims, drug dealers or addicts, prostitutes, and criminals. One of the questions raised by these studies is: Are numbers enough to demonstrate fair representation and inclusiveness? Or does diversity and equity in representation require a greater commitment to portraying ethno-racial differences in a more meaningful and realistic social context?

Racism in the Advertising Industry

Advertising is more than a cultural icon; it provides a vehicle for tracking our sociological history and social world. The images and ideas that appear in print and television ads reflect the values, norms, and ideology of the society that created them. They can be seen as a marker of the rise and decline of fads and social movements, political issues, changing interests, and tastes (Cortese, 1999). Advertising plays a crucial economic role in the media as a primary source of income. In 1992, the estimated revenue from advertising by the major media groups, such as broadcasting, newspapers and magazines, directories, and outdoor advertising, was $9 billion. In a less tangible but equally significant way, advertising has enormous power, not only over mass media organizations, but also in establishing "desirable" societal standards and styles of living.

Advertising, in its multiplicity of forms, provides many of the images and experiences people take for granted. Day after day, the White images circulated in newspapers and magazines, on radio and television, and on the movie screen, mold impressions and shape perceptions. C. Wright Mills observed that the mass media have "not only filtered into our experience of external realities, they have entered into our very experience of ourselves" (1962:217), providing our society with new identities and new aspirations of what we should be like. Since advertising is geared to White consumers, audiences are reminded of who counts, who is reflected in the mirror, and who is cast outside the mainstream of society.

Ultimately, advertising creates a discourse in support of the mainstream's dominant ideology, containing ideas and ideals that reinforce the existing and unequal social order. Fleras and Kunz (2001) liken this vehicle of cultural production to systematic propaganda. As in other forms of media production, television commercials communicate meanings and messages. In a given advertisement, a product is identified through text, images, and narrative, although communicated through an extremely compressed time frame.

Non-representation

The first Canadian study of the representation of people of colour in advertising was carried out by Elkin (1971) on behalf of the Ontario Human Rights Commission. The study examined the representation of visible minorities in TV commercials and revealed that only 3.7 percent of television ads contained a minority performer—usually in a group or crowd scene. A follow-up study in 1980 found only 48 visible-minority persons among the two thousand people in the commercials, and the majority of these were children or high-profile American sports and entertainment figures.

In a study undertaken in 2001, D'Innocenzo conducted a discourse analysis of ads appearing in Canadian magazines and found that few advertisements include the presence of people of colour. Interviews with Canadian advertising professionals revealed that few racial minorities were found working in the advertising industry. The White advertising industry, like other media industries, remains trapped in its self-defeating stereotypes and misrepresentation.

In March 1998, an exhibition was mounted in Montreal tracing the evolution of Black images in advertising over the last one hundred years. The show, called "Négripub Paris et Négripub Québec," was brought from Paris as part of Quebec's Black History Month, and demonstrated the connection between the blatantly racist images of early advertisements and the more subtle, negative imagery in current ones. The exhibit, for example, included a 1921 poster showing a Black woman feeding her baby rum to promote St. Christopher's rum. It also included a more recent poster, created by the Quebec education ministry to emphasize the benefits of education, showing television personality Gregory Charles emerging from a chest as a White hand helps him out. In another ad, the newspaper *La Presse* publicized the knowledge it dispenses by using a picture of two Black football players and the slogan "One day the whole world will want to know" (Contenta, 1998:A6).

Recent studies in Canada (Mietkiewicz, 1999; Fleras and Kunz, 2001; Henry and Tator, 2003), as well as the United Kingdom and the United States (Cortese, 1999; Bristor, Gravois Lee, and Hunt, 1995), demonstrate that while highly stereotypical negative images have been somewhat altered, and in some instances the industry has began to incorporate the symbols of diversity, the most pervasive image and narrative remains the "rightness of Whiteness." An informal study by Mietkiewicz (ibid.), a journalist writing for the *Toronto Star,* found that in 1787 television commercials aired on Canadian and American television programming in February 1999, 30.8 percent of the 1787 commercials employed minority actors. However, only 10.4 percent of the ads provided more than a token appearance of at least three seconds of screen time. A representative of the Canadian advertising industry, Elizabeth Reade (cited in Mietkiewicz, 1999), defends these disparities by suggesting that it is not racism that is the cause, but rather racial "uncomfortableness"; that is, advertisers do not want to risk offending a White customer base or engaging in the challenge of more realistically and relevantly portraying the realities of a culturally and racially diverse society. However, it should be noted that in this explanation is encoded both racial bias and racial discrimination.

It can be argued that advertising has embraced the symbols of diversity as a key component for manipulating the message to both mainstream and minority markets. There are more minorities appearing in all types of advertising and marketing, but appearances may be deceiving. Increases in the numbers of minority women and men may be counteracted by representations that continue to stereotype, deny the legitimacy of ethnicity for branding or marketing purposes, or run the risk of *commodifying* diversity for ulterior purposes. **Commodification** is the process of turning a thing into a commodity, that is, into an object or service that can be bought or sold in the marketplace.

In the Henry and Tator study of 1120 Canadian television commercials (2003), analysis revealed that although ethno-racial minorities were shown roughly in proportion to their actual numbers in the population, they appeared mainly in fleeting images and as background figures, and often represented in stereotypical roles. Sports and entertainment celebrities were prominent. Most ads showing minorities were sponsored by government agencies, and only a very small number of commercial companies used minority actors. Moreover, First Nations people only appeared once in all the ads analyzed. Similar findings were identified in Murray's (2002) study of television ads.

Newsmaking on Canadian Television Networks

As the central purveyors of public discourse, the television news media play a powerful role in establishing an outline of social, political, cultural, and economic models of societal events. However, these models are often filtered through a dominant White culture's perspectives and understandings. The selection of a story as text is also influenced by other factors such as culture, class, and gender. News is more than factual information; it is also a commodity. It must deliver an audience of sufficient size and composition to be sold to advertisers. The popularity of the news is determined, in part, by its entertainment value (Fiske, 1999). It can be argued that for an event to be deemed newsworthy it should be recent, concern elite people, be negative, and have surprise value (ibid.).

Recent Canadian research on racialized discourse in television news (Mahtani, 2001; Fleras and Kunz, 2001; Henry and Tator, 2002) mirrors the findings of research in the United States (Entman and Rojecki, 2000), the United Kingdom (Law, 2002; Cottle, 2000), and Australia (Jakubowicz, 1994). The media restrict their stories to a very limited number of themes. In the Henry and Tator study (2002), a total of 1443 news stories were studied. Eighty-five stories were categorized. Typical themes were immigration, crime, cultural differences, poverty and unemployment, the tensions between groups, and the discrimination against minority communities. Because the study was conducted after 9/11, many of the stories (25) focused on the concerns within Muslim and Arab communities. Seventeen dealt with social issues. Many of these stories constructed minorities and especially Blacks as problem people. Crime and violence figured as a major subject in 11 of the stories. Of the almost 1500 news stories sampled, about 40 percent showed people of colour on screen, but most of the shots were extremely brief, and the fleeting presence of one or more racialized persons was entirely marginal to the story's narrative. Local news was dominated by stories about White people, who were often shown being interviewed. Overwhelmingly, the television news saw the world through a prism of Whiteness. Television news coverage on the whole still constructs racial-minority people and their communities as different and as the "other." News reporters and broadcasters operate within a carefully defined set of social and cultural assumptions that—on the surface— maintain the myth that diversity matters. This is demonstrated forcefully when the race-specific stories were examined. There were 90 of these, and the overwhelming majority of these television narratives had content relating to social problems and/or acts of deviance. Rarely did the stories in the sample feature ordinary or even extraordinary events among racialized groups. Only 12 affirming stories were shown out of the entire sample of nearly 1500. This strongly suggests that people of colour, despite their strong presence in the population, are still "imagined" as outside the margins of Canadian society.

Many institutions have ready access to the media. As a result, a significant proportion of news coverage deals with information that emanates from government agencies, politicians, police forces, school boards, commissions, chambers of commerce, and labour federations (Siddiqui, 1993). This contrasts sharply with the lack of access of people of colour in making their viewpoints and voices heard. Many scholars (Gandy, 1998; Hackett and Zhao, 1998; Winter, 1997; Miller, 1998) have argued that media professionals (editors, journalists, broadcasters, and producers) and their institutions control access between the elites of power and the mass audience. By controlling the qualitative aspects of the information that will become the audience's news; by determining the events that will dominate the "agenda" of news programs, newspapers, and public discussion; and by selecting which "expert" opinion will be solicited, the media assume the function of gate-keepers and agenda setters.

Convergence and Commodification and Its Influence on Canadian Media

In recent years there has been a growing apprehension over the concentration of Canadian media ownership, in relation to both newspapers and electronic media corporations. It can be argued that the issue has a particular impact on newsmaking. For example, Conrad Black at one time controlled through his corporate holdings and Canadian Press subscribers all but four newspapers in this country. Canadian Press's Broadcast News wire was picked up by 140 radio stations, 28 television stations, and 36 cable outlets in Ontario alone. Across the country they controlled 425 radio stations, 76 television stations, and 142 cable outlets. In this context, the media corporate elite are delivering a distorted picture of the world, a picture that is becoming part of a commonsense perspective that is blocking out the formation of alternative visions and discourses.

In 2000, Conrad Black's Southam newspapers were sold to CanWest, including the *National Post*, which also owns 120 community papers and a national TV network. Shortly thereafter, a policy decision by CanWest was implemented that prohibited its newspapers from publishing editorials that contradicted the position in national editorials from the perspective taken by CanWest's head office. The concerns escalated when journalists and editors and a publisher were fired for failing to abide by the new policy. A full-page advertisement published in three Canadian dailies and signed by 40 leading Canadians expressed grave concern over a loss of freedom of expression.

Analysis

This chapter's analysis of racism in the media reveals that the vast majority of media organizations fail to respond to the daily challenges that confront them in a multiracial, pluralistic society. Decision-makers have generally ignored or denied the existence of the racial bias and discriminatory practices in all sectors of the media. The coverage of issues affecting racial minorities is filtered through the stereotypes, misconceptions, and erroneous assumptions of largely White reporters, advertisers, journalists, editors, programmers, and producers. The media's images reinforce cultural racism, the collective belief system that divides society into "them" and "us" and sustains White group dominance.

Racism is manifested in the professional attitudes and behaviours of journalists, broadcasters, editors, publishers, program producers, directors, advertising managers, and marketing executives. It is reflected in the way in which issues are dealt with in the slant of a news story or in the use of imagery that promotes negative stereotyping (e.g., Asians are associated with gangs, Blacks and Jamaicans with crime, Tamils with immigration violations, Sikhs and Muslims with terrorism, refugees with welfare abuse). Racial bias is expressed in Eurocentric and ethnocentric values and norms that lead advertisers to conclude that using racial minorities in an advertising campaign will have a negative impact on White consumers. It is evidenced in newspaper headlines that sensationalize issues (e.g., "Immigration Policy Called Risk to Canadian Educators' Jobs" and "Quotas, Quotas, and more Quotas"). It is reflected in the lack of access to media institutions as demonstrated in a series of decisions made by the CRTC over a period of 10 years related to the refusal to grant licences to applicants committed to opening up the airwaves to Blacks and other ethno-racial minorities.

Siddiqui (1993) identified some of the institutional barriers in media organizations that influence their coverage of racial and cultural issues:

- Although they are on the frontiers of news, journalists are rarely on the cusp of social change.
- Pretensions notwithstanding, the media are "the establishment."
- The media are not good at hearing the voices of the unorganized.
- The media's black-and-white, no-greys, view of the world hurts minorities.
- Most media think of minorities only in the context of their ethnicity. Reporters and editors value their views on race relations but not on larger Canadian or world issues.
- Although race relations is clearly one of the most important issues of our time, most media do not cover it or cover it "on the run," looking for an easy hit.

Other indicators of racism in the media include the lack of recognition attributed to the qualifications and experience gained outside of Canada by media professionals; the absence of outreach and training opportunities for minorities; the way "facts" and "events" are selected and subsequently transformed into "news"; and the absence of programming that features the social, cultural, political, and economic contributions of people of colour.

Barriers to racial equity in the media may have the appearance of neutral practices, but in reality they reflect a set of ideas, opinions, and assumptions held by the White power elite in society. Mass communication in Canada has been influenced and controlled by one dominant group and reflects its norms and values.

Racism is found in the daily operations of media organizations across the country and in every area of mass communications. As several of the studies cited in this chapter clearly demonstrate, it stems at least in part from the ethnocentrism that permeates the industry. The "we-they" way of thinking leads members of the dominant group to believe that the perceptions, feelings, and judgments of their group are appropriate and normative, while the beliefs and norms of "others" have less value and merit (Essed, 1991). As in other sectors, racism in the media has resulted in the denial of access, participation, and equity for racial minorities.

Media Reflect and Reproduce White Ideology

Cultural production, including the media, is increasingly influenced by commerce and the penetration of commodity culture into every facet of life (Giroux, 1994). Canadian newspapers, magazines, and television and radio stations (with the exception of public agencies such as the CBC) are generally owned by corporate interests and structured to sustain the economic interests of business and government elites (van Dijk, 1991; Hall et al., 1975). The economic conditions in the marketplace, including market structure, competition, and linkages to other markets, have a profound influence on the production of media culture (Kellner, 1995). Most media function as corporations, serving the needs of their shareholders and other financial backers (Fleras, 1995; Wilson and Gutierrez, 1995).

Van Dijk (1991) stated that the reproduction of racism by the media, particularly the press, takes the specific form of "elite racism." His thesis was that since the dominant White media's values are inextricably linked to political, social, and corporate elite groups, it is also in their interest to play a role in producing and generating consensus. He argued that the mass media have nearly exclusive control over the resources required to produce popular opinion, especially in the area of race and ethnic relations. Van Dijk suggested that the media use distinct strategies to weaken the positions, issues, and ideas advocated by minority groups that threaten the status quo.

This analysis is consistent with that of Fleras and Kunz (2001), who observed that the media operate as powerful agents of domination, control, and propaganda. Media images of what is desirable or acceptable are absorbed, with little understanding and awareness of the indoctrination process. Thus, the media are able to establish the boundaries of social discourse, from which priorities are set and public agendas are established and perpetuated.

One example of the influence of the power elite to shape the media's discourse is the debate over employment equity, a federally legislated program (but repealed by the Ontario government in 1995) for overcoming employment barriers affecting people of colour, Aboriginal peoples, women, and people with disabilities. Most media organizations reflect the position of the corporate elite by misrepresenting employment equity as a risk to the operation of a free marketplace, a violation of the merit principle, and a threat to White males.

Racist Discourse in the Media: Silencing and Marginalizing

Freedom of Speech

There exists in the media a significant resistance to altering the power of the dominant culture. Attempts by racial minorities to protest and resist racist images and discourse in the media are frequently challenged by the media. These protests are seen by the corporate elite as attempts to suppress freedom of expression and are equated with censorship. What is frequently ignored is the connection between the championing of freedom of expression and the freedom of the marketplace to operate without constraint.

Many see the issue of freedom of speech in the context of the lack of access that people of colour and other groups have to the communication networks. The numerous examples cited in this chapter indicate that racial minorities are largely excluded from participation in public discourse. As NourbeSe Philip suggests,

> Freedom of expression in this society is underwritten not by the free flow of information, but by the fact that there are those who are powerful enough in society to make *their* voices, *their* version of history, and *their* viewpoints heard. (1993:66)

In the same way, Hill argued that the way "freedom of speech" is applied is really just a reference to the rights and privileges that very few groups in this society possess, in terms of their access to the media (1992:17). The norms, values, and assumptions of White, male-dominated institutions continue to prevent the mass media from fairly and accurately reflecting and representing the multiracial reality of Canadian society. A former editor of the *Ottawa Citizen*, Irshad Manji (1995), made the point that media organizations can't claim to be on the front lines of freedom of expression when their White-dominated workplaces and cultures do not provide employment opportunities for people with different experiences and backgrounds. The composition of these media organizations restricts the free flow of different views.

In this context, it is important to underscore the influence of the media's ideological positions, narrative strategies, and image construction on the formation of individual, group, and national identity. The implicit and explicit messages buried in media discourse point to the central conflict between a vision of Canadian culture and identity as heterogeneous, racially and culturally divided, and fragmented, versus the dominant ideology of Canadian culture as homogeneous, unified, and harmonious.

Responses to Racism in the Media

The many above examples provide a significant body of evidence that racism in the media exists and that it is reflected in almost every part of the mass communication system in Canada. The following section considers some of the responses to this problem.

Community Advocacy

As has been shown in this analysis of the ethno-racial bias in the media, many community-based organizations have played an important role in monitoring and analyzing the mainstream media: the Canadian Islamic Congress, MediaWatch, the Canadian Association of Black Journalists, the Canadian Arab Federation, the Centre for Research-Action on Race Relations in Montreal, the Urban Alliance on Race Relations in Toronto, the Canadian Council of Chinese Canadians, and so on. Websites that provide educational materials on the issues of diversity, representation, and equity include Ryerson's School of Journalism (http://www.diversitywatch.ca), Canadian Advertising Foundation (http://www.media-awareness.ca), and Canadian Race Relations Foundation (http://www.crr.ca).

Perhaps the most significant advance in recent years has been in First Nations media programming. Canada has become a world leader in Aboriginal media. This includes the Aboriginal Peoples Television Network (APTN) and five other television production outlets, as well as several hundred radio stations and the Inuit Broadcasting Corporation. Fleras and Kunz (2001) point to the significance of Aboriginal-owned media, observing that Aboriginal peoples are now in a position to assert their own cultural values in a way that reflects their needs, concerns, and aspirations rather than rely on Eurocentric, institutionalized racist constructions of aboriginality.

In much the same way, there has been a proliferation of ethnic media. For example, the Indo-Canadian community in Vancouver has approximately nineteen publications. In Toronto, there are six radio stations serving the ethno-racial communities (ibid.) and, after many years of struggle to obtain a licence, one Black-owned FM station. There has been recent licensing of multicultural and multilingual television stations such as Multivan in Vancouver and CFMT-2 in Toronto. Cable television networks carry a limited but growing number of programs that serve the need for news and stories and provide an important alternative to the dominant discourse of the mainstream media.

Another important breakthrough has been the development of the annual Innoversity Creative Summit. The founders of Innoversity, Cynthia Reyes and Hamlin Grange, have had a distinguished career working for the CBC and other media organizations. The two-day summit held every year in Toronto unites media professionals, creators, and industry leaders in advertising, film, radio and television, and the print media from across the country with the hundreds of participants who attend the summit and reflect the diverse ethno-racial communities of Canada. The participants include writers, producers, directors, and actors of colour aspiring to build or further their creative careers. The goal of the programme is to discover innovative and effective ways of including and reflecting Canada's racial and cultural diversity within all areas of media culture and structures. The format of these conferences is designed to create a meeting place, where new ideas, approaches, and solutions are shared, opportunities are provided, and the creative potential of Canadians of diverse cultural and racial backgrounds is recognized.

Public-Sector Responses

In 1986, a task force on broadcasting policy affirmed that Canadian broadcasting should contribute toward "safeguarding, enriching, and strengthening the cultural, political, social and economic fabric of Canada." The CRTC's policy recognizes the importance of multicultural programming. Briefs presented to the task force were united in the view that cultural and racial minorities did not want multicultural programming confined to special ethnic television and radio services. They expected public broadcasters, particularly the CBC, to take the lead. The task force recommended that the CRTC create a special class of licences for minority groups that would make them responsible for program context. It recommended that the right of access to the broadcasting system by Aboriginal Canadians and other Canadians, including diverse multicultural and multiracial groups, be established in the act. Under federal legislation, Crown corporations such as the CBC are required to report to Parliament every year their progress toward employment equity goals for racial minorities. However, this legislation does not affect other electronic or print media. Despite the revisions of the policy in 1991 and 1999, there have been very few signs of systemic change within the mass media industry.

While the number of media industry associations that have established task forces and have produced voluntary diversity policies and guidelines has increased including the Canadian Association of Broadcasting and the Canadian Advertising Foundation, as the above analysis demonstrates, these initiatives have been slow in coming and have had a minimal impact (see Murray, 2002 for a more detailed examination of this subject).

Conclusion

Ensuring greater access, participation, and equity in the mass communications industries continues to challenge Canadian society. The individuals working in the advertising, print, and electronic media, the media organizations and their collective bodies, and the government agencies and commissions should share the responsibility for change. Advertisers, editors, journalists, and broadcasters have personal biases; their attitudes, perceptions, and values are influenced by numerous social and cultural factors. However, professional standards should prevent these attitudes from being expressed in their work and within the culture and structures of media organizations.

Policies to promote fairness and equity must address the under-representation of minorities in all areas of mass communication. Without greater access to employment opportunities, racial minorities will continue to have virtually no influence in determining how they are represented by others.

Research findings and the work of anti-racism advocates and practitioners suggest that there are a number of barriers to change:

- Freedom of the press is considered so sacred a trust that the media believe they have the right to communicate racist content in both print and broadcasts.
- The diverse and diffuse nature of the media makes them difficult to target, access, and penetrate.
- Self-regulating media agencies are either nonexistent or extremely weak. Unions, press councils, and advertising boards exercise limited power and authority over media corporations.
- Significant resources are needed to effectively lobby such agencies as the CRTC. Regulations are complex and demand a high level of expertise.
- There is an absence of consistent monitoring processes and mechanisms in the media.
- Advocacy across Canada is erratic and generally limited to reactions to specific incidents.
- Few substantive, practical media anti-racism models and strategies exist. Where new approaches have been initiated, there is little dissemination of information.
- The law and the justice system provide only limited redress for libel and defamation.

Summary

This chapter examined the ways in which the mass media in Canada have perpetuated and reproduced racism while maintaining the image of being neutral, objective, and unbiased purveyors of the truth. Racism in the media is reflected in racist discourse and the everyday practices of media organizations. Media professionals are often guided by their need to support special and powerful interests, such as government and business, to promote their positions and agendas.

Numerous examples were provided of how the media create and reinforce negative stereotypes of people of colour in order to influence public opinion. Racism is manifested in the underrepresentation of racial minorities in the advertising, print, and electronic media. People of colour are not in decision-making positions, they are largely invisible in newsrooms, and they have less access to television and radio programming.

Democratic racism is reflected in the media in a profound tension between the belief that the media represent the cornerstone of a democratic liberal society and the key instrument by which its ideals are produced and disseminated, and the actual role of the media as purveyors of racist discourse, supporters of the powerful White political, economic, and cultural elite, and vehicles for reinforcing White cultural hegemony.

Notes

1. CDA is a study of language use and communication used in many disciplines. As a type of research it studies mainly how social power, dominance, and inequality are produced, reproduced, and resisted by text and talk in different socio-cultural and political sectors of society. CDA provides a tool to deconstruct the ideologies and dominant discourses of the media and other elite groups. It treats language as a type of social practice used for representation and signification (see van Dijk, 1991, 1993).
2. This quote is drawn from a detailed analysis by Hier and Greenberg (2002) of the Canadian print media's negative representation of the nearly 600 Chinese migrants that arrived on the coast of British Columbia in 1999.
3. In the summer of 1990 in Oka, Quebec, the decision to expand a golf course on the ancestral lands and burial grounds of the Mohawks of the Kanestake reserve provoked a crisis involving Native people and the Quebec government and police. As the conflict escalated the Canadian Armed Forces was called in. The Oka crisis drew worldwide attention to the issues of Native claims.
4. *Cold Squad, Paradise Falls, North of 60, Eleventh Hour, Da Vinci's Inquest*, and *The New Degrassi*.

References

Adilman, S. (1998). "Why No Black Characters in Canadian TV Series?" *Toronto Star* (March 21):M2.

Benjamin, A. (2002). "The Social and Legal Banishment of Anti-Racism: A Black Perspective." In W. Chan and K. Mirchandani (eds.), *Crimes of Colour: Racialization and the Criminal Justice System*. Peterborough, ON: Broadview Press. 177–190.

———. (2003). "The Black/Jamaican Criminal: The Making of Ideology." Ph.D. thesis. Toronto: OISE/University of Toronto.

Bristor, J., R. Gravois Lee, and M. Hunt. (1995). "Race and Ideology: African-American Images in Television Advertising." *Journal of Public Policy and Marketing* 14(1)(Spring):48–59.

Bullock, K., and G. Jafri. (2001). "Media (Mis)Representations: Muslim Women in the Canadian Nation." *Canadian Woman Studies* 20(2):35–40.

Campbell, C. (1995). *Race, Myth and the News*. Thousand Oaks, CA: Sage.

Canadian Ethnocultural Council. (1985). "Brief to the Parliamentary Subcommittee on Equality Rights." Ottawa.

Canadian Islamic Congress (CIC). (1999–2003). *CIC Media Survey Report*. Available <http://www.canadianislamic congress.com>, accessed August 28, 2004.

———. (1998). *Anti-Islam in the Media: A Case Study*. Waterloo, ON.

Contenta, C. (1998). "Exhibit Traces 100-Year Evolution of Images of Blacks in Advertising." *Toronto Star* (February 3):A6.

Cortese, A. (1999). *Provocateur: Images of Women and Minorities in Advertising*. New York and Oxford: Rowman and Littlefield.

Cottle, S. (ed.). (2000). *Ethnic Minorities and the Media: Changing Cultural Boundaries*. Buckingham and Philadelphia: Open University Press.

Cuff, J.H. (1990). *Globe and Mail* (August 21):C1.

———. (1992). "Putting a Lid on the Mean Streets." *Globe and Mail* (May 9).

———. (1997). "Black Sitcoms Play on Stereotypes." *Globe and Mail* (April 16):C2.

D'Innocenzo, L. (2001). "The Colour of Marketing: Minorities Still Misrepresented in Ads." *Strategy Magazine*, April 23. Available <www.strategymag.com/ articles/magazine/20010423/race.html>.

Elkin, F. (1971). *The Employment of Visible Minority Groups in Mass Media Advertising*. Toronto: Ontario Human Rights Commission.

Entman, R., and A. Rojecki. (2000). *The Black Image in the White Mind: Media and Race in America*. Chicago and London: University of Chicago Press.

Essed, E. (1991). *Understanding Everyday Racism*. Newbury Park, CA: Sage.

Fairclough, N., and R. Wodak. (1997). "Critical Discourse Analysis." In T.A. van Dijk (ed.), *Discourse Studies: A Multidisciplinary Introduction. Volume 2: Discourse as Social Interaction*. London: Sage. 258–284.

Fiske, J. (1999). *Television Culture*. London and New York: Routledge.

———. (2000). "White Watch." In S. Cottle (eds.), *Ethnic Minorities and the Media: Changing Cultural Boundaries*. Buckingham and Philadelphia: Open University Press.

Fleras, A. (1995). "'Please Adjust Your Set': Media and Minorities in a Multicultural Society." In B. Singer (ed.), *Communications in Canadian Society*. 4th ed. Scarborough, ON: Nelson. 406–31.

———, and J. Elliott. (1992). *Multiculturalism in Canada*. Scarborough, ON: Nelson.

———, and J. Kunz. (2001). *Media and Minorities: Representing Diversity in a Multicultural Canada*. Toronto: Thomson.

Frankenberg, R. (1993). *White Women, Race Matters: The Social Construction of Whiteness*. Minneapolis, Minnesota: University of Minnesota Press.

Gabriel, J. (1998). *Whitewash: Racialized Politics and the Media*. London: Routledge.

———. (2000). "Dreaming of a White …" In S. Cottle (ed.), *Ethnic Minorities and the Media: Changing Cultural Boundaries*. Buckingham and Philadelphia: Open University Press.

Gandy, Oscar. (1998). *Communication and Race: A Structural Perspective*. London: Arnold.

Giroux, Henri. (1994). "World Without Borders: Buying Social Change." In C. Becker (ed.), *The Subversive Imagination: Artists, Society and Social Responsibility*. New York: Routledge. 187–207.

Goldberg, D. (1993). *Racist Culture: Philosophy and the Politics of Meaning*. Oxford, UK: Blackwell.

Gomez, H. (1983). "The Invisible Visible Minorities." *Currents: Readings in Race Relations* (Toronto) 1(2):12–13.

Granzberg, G. (1982). *The Portrayal of Visible Minorities by Canadian Television During the 1982 Prime-Time Season*. Ottawa: Secretary of State.

Hackett, R., and Y. Zhao. (1998). *Sustaining Democracy and the Politics of Objectivity*. Toronto: Garamond.

Hall, S., C. Critcher, T. Jefferson, J. Clarke, and B. Roberts. (1975). *Newsmaking and Crime*. Paper presented at NACRO Conference on Crime and the Media. Birmingham: Centre for Contemporary Cultural Studies, University of Birmingham.

———. (1978). *Policing the Crisis: Mugging, the State and Law and Order*. London: Methuen.

Hannerz, U. (1992). *Cultural Complexity: Studies in Social Meaning*. New York: Columbia University Press.

Henry, F., and C. Tator. (2002). *Discourses of Domination: Racial Bias in the Canadian English-Language Press*. Toronto: University of Toronto Press.

———. (2003). *Deconstructing the "Rightness of Whiteness" in Television Commercials, News and Programming*. Prairie Consortium of Metropolis.

Hier and Greenberg. (2002). "News Discourse and the Problematization of Chinese Migration to Canada." In *Discourses of Domination: Racial Bias in the Canadian English-Language Press*. F. Henry and C. Tator. Toronto: University of Toronto Press.

Hill, R. (1992). "One Part per Million: Native Voices and White Appropriation." *Fuse* 15(3):17.

hooks, bell. (1990). *Yearning: Race, Gender, and Cultural Politics*. Boston: South End Press.

Jakubowicz, A., H. Goodall, J. Martin, T. Mitchell, L. Randall, and K. Seneviratne. (1994). *Racism, Ethnicity and the Media*. St. Leonards, NSW: Allen and Unwin.

Jiwani, Y. (1995). "The Media, 'Race' and Multiculturalism." Presentation to the B.C. Advisory Council on Multiculturalism. March 17. Available <http://www.harbour.sfu.ca/freda/articles/media.htm>, accessed August 28, 2004.

Kellner, D. (1995). "Cultural Studies, Multiculturalism and Media Culture." In G. Dines and J. Humez (eds.), *Cultural Studies, Multiculturalism and Media Culture*. Thousand Oaks, CA: Sage.

Law, Ian. (2002). *Race and the News*. Houndsmills, Baskingstoke: Palgrave.

MacAfee, M., and A. Carmichael. (2002). "Muslims Ensure a Year of Blame, Slights and Fear." *Edmonton Journal* (September 11).

Mahtani, M. (2001). "Representing Minorities: Canadian Media and Minority Identities." In *Canadian Ethnic Studies* 33(3):99–134.

Manji, I. (1995). *Metro Report on Racial Minorities in the Media*. Municipality of Metropolitan Toronto.

Mietkiewicz, H. (1999). "Colour Coded Casting." *Toronto Star* (March 1).

Miller, J. (1998). *Yesterday's News: Why Canada's Daily Newspapers Are Failing Us*. Halifax: Fernwood.

Mills, C.W. (1962). "The Mass Society." In E. Josephson and M. Josephson (eds.), *Man Alone*. New York: Dell.

Morrison, T., and C. Brodsky Lacour. (1997). *Birth of a Nation'hood: Gaze, Script, and Spectacle in the O.J. Simpson Case*. New York: Pantheon Books.

Mosher, C.L. (1998). *Discrimination and Denial: Systemic Racism in Ontario's Legal and Criminal Justice Systems, 1892–1961*. Toronto: University of Toronto Press.

Murray, Catharine. (2002). *Silent on the Set: Cultural Diversity and Race in English Canadian TV Drama*. Report prepared for Department of Canadian Heritage. Hull, QC.

NourbeSe Philip, Marlene. (1993). *Showing Grit: Showboating North of the 44th Parallel*. Toronto: Poui Publications.

Perigoe, R., and B. Lazar. (1992). "Visible Minorities and Native Canadians in National Television News

Programs." In M. Grenier (ed.), *Critical Studies of Canadian Mass Media*. Toronto: Butterworths.

Refugee Housing Task Force. (2001). Meeting minutes (October 16).

Ridington, R. (1986). "Texts That Harm: Journalism in British Columbia." *Currents: Readings in Race Relations* (Toronto) 3(4)(Summer).

Rosenfeld, M., and M. Spina. (1977). *All the News That's Fit to Print: A Study of the Toronto Press's Coverage of Immigration, Ethnic Communities and Racism*. Toronto: Cross-Cultural Communication Centre.

Roth, L., B. Nelson, and M. David Kasennahawi. (1995). "Three Women, a Mouse, a Microphone, and a Telephone: Information (Mis)Management During the Mohawk/Canadian Governments' Conflict of 1990." In A. Valdivia (ed.), *Feminism, Multiculturalism and the Media: Global Diversities*. Thousand Oaks, CA: Sage.

Royal Commission on Aboriginal Peoples (RCAP). (1996). *Report of the Royal Commission on Aboriginal Peoples: Perspectives and Realities*. Vols. 1–5. Ottawa: RCAP.

Said, E. (1981). *Covering Islam: How the Media and the Experts Determine How We See the Rest of the World*. New York: Pantheon.

Shaheen, J. (1997). *Arab and Muslim Stereotyping in American Popular Culture*. Centre for Muslim-Christian Understanding. Edmund Walsh School of Foreign Service, Georgetown University. Washington, DC.

Siddiqui, H. (1993). "Media and Race: Failing to Mix the Message." *Toronto Star* (April 24):D1, D5.

Skea, W. (1993–94). "The Canadian Newspaper Industry's Portrayal of the Oka Crisis. " *Native Studies Review* 9(1):15–27.

Switzer, M. (1998). *Aboriginal Voices* 5(6):8.

van Dijk, T. (1991). *Racism and the Press*. London: Routledge.

———. (1993). *Elite Discourse and Racism*. Newbury Park: Sage.

Wilson, C., and F. Gutierrez. (1995). *Race, Multiculturalism and the Media*. London: Sage.

Winter, J. (1992). *Common Cents: Media Portrayal of the Gulf War and Other Events*. Montreal: Black Rose Books.

———. (1997). *Democracy's Oxygen: How the Corporations Control the News*. Montreal: Black Rose Books.

———. (2002). *Media Think*. Montreal: Black Rose Books.

Wortley, S. (2002). "The Depiction of Race and Crime in the Toronto Print Media." In B. Schissel and C Brooks (eds.), *Marginality and Condemnation: An Introduction to Critical Criminology*. Halifax: Fernwood. 55–80.

Zine, J. (2002). "A Framework for Anti-Islamic Education." Paper presented at the Canadian Sociology and Anthropology Association, Congress of the social Sciences and Humanities, University of Toronto.

PART FOUR

The Impact of Democratic Racism on Canadian Institutions and Culture

This Part analyzes the impact of democratic racism on Canadian organizations, institutions, and systems of governance. Chapter 11 describes and analyzes government responses to racism, and stresses the inadequacies of laws, public policies, and state agencies in dismantling structural inequality. Chapter 12 examines the powerful methods used to resist anti-racist change in White organizational culture, policies, and practices. The White elite, including the law-makers, bureaucrats, and other institutional power brokers, continue to reinforce the status quo, drawing upon the discourses of denial, deflection, and defensiveness. Chapter 13 reviews how the ideology of democratic racism intersects across all the public-sector institutions in Canadian society, and how the national myths and the dominant discourses of democratic racism underpin a society divided by colour. The closing section of Chapter 13 identifies a number of strategies for social change, including the power of oppositional narratives and community mobilization.

CHAPTER 11

STATE RESPONSES TO RACISM IN CANADA

*The law has been used through direct action, interpretation, silence and complicity.
The law has been wielded as an instrument to create a common-sense justification of
racial differences, to reinforce common-sense notions already deeply embedded
within a cultural system of values ... and to form new social constructions.*

—*Kobayashi (1990:40)*

This chapter explores the conflicting role of the Canadian state in both promoting and controlling racism. Public policies intended to ameliorate inequality each play a role in maintaining this conflict. On the one hand, the democratic state has a special responsibility to assert leadership and guard against the tyranny of the majority. Legislative action is the state's primary tool to promote and achieve equality and justice for all, regardless of race and colour.

On the other hand, legislation and the subordinate activities of the state can neither eliminate nor effectively control racism because the legacy of racism is so interwoven in the national culture, in its commonsense ideology and its public discourse. In this chapter, five major state responses are analyzed: multiculturalism legislation policy, the Canadian Charter of Rights and Freedoms, employment equity and human-rights codes and commissions,[1] the Employment Equity Act, and the Anti-Terrorism Act. The discussion considers the extent to which each of these political responses has delivered on its promise to diminish the legitimacy and impact of racial bias and discrimination in Canadian society.

The chapter proposes new ways of understanding the complex relationships between the state, the dominant culture, and ethno-racial minorities, particularly with respect to this book's central concern: the response to racism in a liberal democratic society. The principal thesis of this chapter is that despite the development of state responses that specifically acknowledge Canada's culturally and racially diverse population and recognize the existence of bias and discrimination, we have largely failed to achieve the goal of eliminating or even controlling racial bias and discrimination. We have failed precisely because the goal has been framed within a liberal framework and tradition.

Introduction

The state has many functions and responsibilities. One of its main roles is to proscribe behaviour. It also influences public opinion through its public-policy and legislative functions and helps thereby to define national ideology. Among its many responsibilities is the responsibility to support the social, cultural, and economic development of communities that suffer racial discrimination, by helping them to achieve full participation, access, and equity.

The State's Role as Public-Policy-Maker and Decision-Maker

The influence of state policies and practices at various levels (federal, provincial, and municipal) is critical to the eradication of racism and the promotion of racial equity. As such, the state has a special responsibility to assert leadership.

The fundamental rights and freedoms to which Canada adheres include the right of all residents to full and equal participation in the cultural, social, economic, and political life of the country. This right is based on the principle of the fundamental equality of individuals. The rights of equality of access, equality of opportunity, and equality of outcomes for all communities are therefore implicit. They are entrenched in a number of state policies and statutes, as well as in the international covenants to which Canada is a signatory.

The ideal of racial equity is a relatively new and still fragile tradition in Canada, because racism has only recently been acknowledged as a serious social concern. Both federal and provincial governments have, however, enacted legislation that in principle reflects their rejection of racism as a form of behaviour antithetical to a democratic state. The legislation includes the Canadian Charter of Rights and Freedoms, the Canadian Multiculturalism Act, the Employment Equity Act, provincial human-rights and labour codes, and the Anti-Terrorism Act, which in principle was enacted to ensure the nation's safety and security.

Many scholars in democratic liberal countries, including Canada, have pointed to the state and state apparatuses as primary sites through which racism is constructed, maintained, and preserved (Li, 1999; Bannerji, 2000; Visano, 2002; Mackey, 1999). Racism occurs at several levels of governance that include the enactment and administration of laws, policies, institutions, and agencies of social control. At the same time, the state employs mechanisms of ideological control and power. Visano (2002) observes that the law functions as a set of institutional practices and discourses within the ideology of Whiteness and promotes a neutral response to racial injustices, "thereby escaping its complicities" (210). Bannerji suggests "the state of 'Canada,' when viewed through the lens of racism/difference, presents us with a hegemony compounded of a racialized common sense and institutional structures" (114).

International Declarations of Human Rights

The Canadian government has participated in several international declarations concerning human rights. The Universal Declaration on Human Rights was the first international covenant protecting human rights to be ratified by Canada. Since then, the United Nations has adopted a number of international covenants on human rights, including the International Convention on the Elimination of All Forms of Racial Discrimination, which was ratified in 1970. The convention is based on the conviction that any doctrine of superiority based on racial differentiation is scientifically false, morally condemnable, socially unjust, and dangerous.

Signing these international conventions creates the impression that Canada is committed to the development of an equitable society based on fairness and non-discrimination. International human-rights covenants provide Canada with global standards to which all federal legislation is expected to conform, but they do not bind the provinces. Moreover, most international instruments respecting human rights do not constitute a legally binding set of rules, and many contain no enforcement mechanisms. Case Study 11.1 illustrates this point.

CASE STUDY 11.1

REPORT OF MR. DOUDOU DIÈNE, SPECIAL RAPPORTEUR ON CONTEMPORARY FORMS OF RACISM, RACIAL DISCRIMINATION, XENOPHOBIA, AND RELATED INTOLERANCE

Background

In the summer of 2001, the United Nations World Conference Against Racism (WCAR) was convened in Durban, South Africa. Seven hundred representatives from non-government organizations (NGO) participated. The central goal of the conference was to seek a greater global commitment and response to addressing and eliminating all forms of oppression, with particular emphasis on racism. One of the positive outcomes of the conference was an invitation by the Canadian government to the United Nations Special Rapporteur on contemporary forms of racism to visit Canada for the purpose of assessing the present situation in this country with respect to the question of racism. During his 10 days in Canada Mr. Diène interviewed representatives of diverse ethno-racial and religious groups and Aboriginal communities in several provinces across the country.

Findings

The Special Rapporteur found that Canada is still deeply affected by racism. The country is influenced by a legacy of racial discrimination embedded in the history of trans-Atlantic slavery and of colonialism. He described the ideological aspect of this legacy as having given rise to a collective mindset that is manifested in education, diverse channels of thought, and creativity, and that has "profoundly and lastingly permeated the system of values, feelings, mentalities, perceptions and behaviours, and hence the country's culture" (Diène, 2004:68). He identified Aboriginal peoples and the communities of African and Caribbean origin as the most seriously affected victims of this culture of discrimination. He identified the powerful oral testimonies that he had heard from ethno-racial minorities as being full of emotion. However, he emphasized that their views on racism and its impact on their communities were also supported by studies and documents. Taken together, these testimonies and supporting research suggest that despite the adoption of multiculturalism as official policy, racial discrimination remains a "tangible, subtle and systemic reality." While the Special Rapporteur was able to identify positive efforts to alleviate the burden of the legacy of racial discrimination, he suggested that these two communities continue to be victims, both individually and collectively, to socioeconomic, political, and cultural discrimination. Their social condition provides evidence of the sustained force of discrimination as a major factor in the structure of Canadian society.

Among his important findings is his view that at the federal level, the representatives of various departments showed a "reluctance, if not hesitation, when it came to admitting the reality of racial discrimination in Canadian society." The Special Rapporteur points to a central paradox in their responses: while these same officials gave the Special Rapporteur a detailed account of the various policies and measures undertaken by their departments to combat racial discrimination, they essentially continued to deny its existence. He identifies a number of shortcomings in the legal, political, and intellectual strategy, which limits Canada's progress in relation to an effective plan of action to address racism. Among his critiques is the insufficiency of resources available for any realistic implementation of the strategy. More specifically, he contends that Canada's political and legal approaches against racial discrimination must address such challenges as the non-recognition of the qualifications and professional experience of immigrants. He suggests that Canada's judicial and quasi-judicial systems are not very effective in their protection of the victims of racial discrimination. He was struck by the lack of information-sharing between provinces concerning their policies and practices in areas such as racial profiling. Regarding intellectual challenges confronting this country, the Special Rapporteur suggested that Canada appeared not to grasp the magnitude of the "submerged part of the racist iceberg" (23).

Recommendations

Among the Special Rapporteur's recommendations is that a national program against racism be initiated, in order to put the effort within a coordinated and coherent framework. The program should be structured around a two-pronged legal and intellectual strategy by which the government and society take an active part. On one hand, the legal strategy should be based on an in-depth assessment of the relevance and effectiveness of existing constitutional, legislative, judicial, and administrative measures. On the other hand, it should also be based on the principle of "vigilance, flexibility and adaptability to the changing challenges and forms of discrimination …" (24). The Special Rapporteur also recommended that the situation of the Aboriginal peoples be immediately addressed with full participation of their representatives, with particular focus on the fundamental issues that concern them, such as the application of treaties and their economic, social, and cultural empowerment. He drew particular attention in his recommendations to the situation of the African-Canadian community, in the areas of employment, habitat, health, and education. He urged that the resurgence of anti-Semitism and Islamophobia requires both vigilant attention and prevention, as well as measures to promote dialogue between these communities. He recommended that the government should reinforce political, legal, and judicial safeguards to ensure that anti-terrorist measures do not lead to an escalation of racism and xenophobia. Another community singled out for attention was the Chinese-Canadian community in relation to their claim for compensation for the descendants of person who paid the head tax. In this regard, he urged that the Government of Canada restart consultations with members of the community.

Conclusion

This case study provides an important and illuminating introduction and framework to now engage in an examination of state policies, laws, and mechanisms currently in place to address discrimination in Canadian society.

The following case studies examine some state interventions concerning issues of racial and cultural differences in the context of reinforcing inequality in Canada. Although these studies have been structured within a liberal democratic framework, the analyses contained within them suggest that the state has largely failed to address the deeply rooted nature of racism and its systemic impact.

CASE STUDY 11.2

MULTICULTURALISM POLICY AND LEGISLATION

Background

Multiculturalism as state policy had its official beginnings in 1971, when Prime Minister Pierre Trudeau announced in Parliament that his government had accepted the recommendations of the Royal Commission on Bilingualism and Biculturalism (Fleras and Elliott, 1992). Recognizing that Canada was both culturally and ethnically a "plural" society, in that it contained Canadians of British and French origin, Aboriginal peoples, and "others," the commission recommended that Canada's diversity be recognized and maintained. "Multiculturalism within a bilingual framework commends itself to the government as the most suitable means of assuring the cultural freedom of Canadians."

Since then, the policy has become enshrined in the federal Multiculturalism Act, and a Ministry of Multiculturalism was established. The Act committed the government to a policy of preserving and enhancing the multicultural identity and heritage of Canadians, while working to achieve the equality of all Canadians in economic, social, cultural, and political life.

Subsection 3(2)(a) of the Act recognizes discrimination in Canadian society and articulates the federal government's commitment to ensure that no unfair barriers exist to employment and career advancement. The Act commits federal institutions to enhance the ability of individuals and communities to contribute to Canadian society by ensuring that government policies and programs respond to the needs of all Canadians. Subsection 3(2)(c) provides assurances that government services will be delivered in an accessible manner to everyone (Multiculturalism and Citizenship Canada, 1989–90).

The Act requires federal government agencies to develop and implement multicultural and racial-equality policies and programs as they apply to their respective mandates. Examples of initiatives cited in the 1991 annual report tabled in Parliament include:

- The solicitor general established a police race-relations centre to serve as a resource both to federal and provincial police forces.
- The Canada Council audited its advisory committees and juries to ensure that they reflected Canadian diversity, and it increased support to minority artists.
- Employment and Immigration increased its funding of programs for immigrant integration.
- The Federal Business Development Bank established ethno-cultural advisory committees to assist small businesses owned by minorities and immigrants.

As a result of changes in the leadership of the government of Canada in July 1993, multiculturalism was subsumed into the Heritage Canada ministry.

Federal multicultural initiatives have been described as providing symbolic support, setting the tone for what is acceptable ("behaviour clues"), establishing a legal basis for action, and sending out signals regarding the notion of justice and equality. By legitimizing the presence of racial minorities, multiculturalism has furthered Canada's experience with nation-building from a mosaic of cultures and races (Tepper, 1988).

Discussion

Multiculturalism as state policy constructs a concept of a common dominant (English Canadian) culture, in relation to which all other cultures are "multicultural" (Bannerji, 2000; Mackey, 1999; Wallace, 1994; Bhabha, 1990). A norm is created by the dominant culture that suggests "these other cultures are fine, but we must be able to locate them within our own grid" (Bhabha, 1990:208). The political and public discourse affirms a faith in a pluralistic society, but at the same time resists the demands that the articulation of cultural and racial differences makes upon a democratic liberal society—inclusion, equity, and empowerment. Itwaru and Ksonzek assert that multiculturalism, while fostering the illusion of tolerance and respect, "conceals the inner chambers of assimilation" (1994:14). Bannerji (op. cit.) analyzes and critiques multiculturalism in the context of two contrasting perspectives and positionalities: if one's identity is defined in terms of belonging to the White dominant culture and enjoying its privileges, the universal claims and working apparatus of the state policies related to multiculturalism are largely viewed in positive terms. However, for those "on the receiving end of the power of Canada and its multiculturalism, who have been dispossessed in one sense or another, the answer is quite different" (105). She goes on to observe that Canada can hardly be called a multicultural state "when all the power relations and signifiers of Anglo-French White supremacy are barely concealed behind a straining liberal democratic façade" (106).

> In this sense, multiculturalism as state policy is a strategy of containment rather than change and it is also a way of maintaining existing hegemonic practices. (Walcott, 1993)

The intent of symbolic multiculturalism as public policy is to counter or neutralize the growing cultural, political, economic, and social demands of minorities for access and equity within all sectors of Canadian society. While "tolerating," "accommodating," "appreciating," and "celebrating" differences, multiculturalism allows for the preservation of the cultural hegemony of the dominant cultural group (Wallace, 1994).

The concept of tolerance is central to the state ideology of multiculturalism. It implies positions of superiority and inferiority in implicitly assuming that some attributes and behaviours associated with minority groups need to be accepted, condoned, or sanctioned. In other words, "We tolerate only that of which we disapprove." Thus, acceptance by the dominant culture is dependent on the goodwill, forbearance, and benevolence of those who do the tolerating. Similarly, the construct of tolerance entrenched in multicultural policy poses little challenge to the (racist) status quo because a ceiling of toler-

ance is established. "The call for individuals or groups to place a 'limit' on tolerance implies the self-definition of these individuals or groups as 'guardians' of the social order" (Mirchandani and Tastsoglou, 2000:11). The tolerant national self is seen as tolerating "others"; the characterizing of non-Anglos and immigrants as "others" reflects the way Canadians understand diversity. The "others"—including people of colour, Aboriginal peoples, immigrants, and gays and lesbians—lie outside the borders of Canadian identity (James, 1995).

The language of the Multiculturalism Act reflects this ambivalence toward the "others"—it is mainly passive, non-coercive, and non-threatening. It relies on the concepts of tolerance, harmony, and unity within a paradigm of diversity. It is a discourse that presumes that justice and equity exist, although they are sometimes flawed by the biased attitudes and behaviours of aberrant individuals. The discursive rhetorical strategy is an emphasis on passive rather than active verbs:

(1) a. *recognize and promote* the understanding that multiculturalism reflects the cultural and racial diversity of Canadian society and acknowledges the freedom of all members of Canadian society to preserve, enhance and share their cultural heritage;
 b. *recognize and promote* the understanding of multiculturalism as a *fundamental* characteristic of the Canadian heritage and identity and that it provides an invaluable resource in the shaping of Canada's future;
 c. *promote* the full and equitable participation of individuals and communities of all origins in the continuing evolution and shaping of all aspects of Canadian society and assist them in the elimination of any barrier to such participation;
 d. *recognize* the existence of communities whose members share a common origin and their historic contribution to Canadian society, and enhance their development;
 e. *ensure* that all individuals receive equal treatment and equal protection under the law, while respecting and valuing their diversity;

f. *encourage and assist* the social, cultural, economic and political institutions of Canada to be both respectful and inclusive of Canada's multicultural character;

g. *promote* the understanding and creativity that arise from the interaction between individuals and communities of different origins;

h. *foster* the recognition and appreciation of the diverse cultures of Canadian society and promote the reflection and evolving expressions of those cultures;

i. *preserve and enhance* the use of languages other than English and French, while strengthening the status and use of official languages of Canada; and

j. *advance* multiculturalism throughout Canada in harmony with the national commitment to the official languages of Canada.

(2) It is further declared to be the policy of the government of Canada that all federal institutions shall

a. *ensure* that Canadians of all origins have an equal opportunity to obtain employment and advancement in those institutions;

b. *promote* policies, programs and practices that enhance the ability of individuals and communities of all origins to contribute to the continuing evolution of Canada;

c. *promote* policies, programs and practices that enhance the understanding of and respect for diversity of the members of Canadian society;

d. *collect* statistical data in order to enable the development of policies, programs and practices that are sensitive and responsive to the multicultural reality of Canada;

e. *make use,* as appropriate, of the language skills and cultural understanding of individuals of all origins; and

f. *generally,* carry on their activities in a manner that is sensitive and responsive to the multicultural reality of Canada. (Canadian Heritage—Multiculturalism Program, 1990)

It can be argued that the Multiculturalism Act focuses on limiting diversity to symbolic rather than political or transformative kinds of change. However, the other ethnic groups will always remain as individual groups, but will not "be incorporated into the political arena as groups. The government will not establish another power base that might upset the existing balance between French-speaking and English-speaking Canadians" (Angel, 1988:27). Support for this position is provided with information contained in the *Legislative Briefing Book* (obtained through an Access to Information request), which describes the Act clause by clause and suggests answers to questions that might be raised by members of the Opposition during debate over the proposed Multiculturalism Act. In the responses prepared by the Corporate Policy Branch (1988:21), three important points are emphasized: (1) the policy is meant to be "highly symbolic"; (2) "the Bill's approach to equity is adversarial"; and (3) the Act is a "non-coercive" approach that emphasizes "cooperation, encouragement, awareness and persuasion" (Mackey, 1996). The Act, despite its incorporation of "race relations" and reference to discrimination and barriers, is still primarily a symbolic state intervention into the politics of diversity (Mackey, 1996, 1999).

The failure of the Multiculturalism Act to live up to its promise of dealing with racial inequality has led to a race-based critique of multiculturalism. The Act was supposed to signal a change in the official policy of multiculturalism from its primary focus (in the multicultural policy of 1971) on cultural preservation and retention to a recognition and affirmation of the rights of people of colour to full participation in Canadian society.

The present authors, as well as many writers and theorists including those identified above, see the major weakness in multiculturalism to be its failure to deal with the problems of systemic racism in Canada. This race-based analysis argues that multiculturalism as state policy has provided a veneer for liberal-pluralist discourse, in which democratic values such as individualism, tolerance, and equality are espoused and supported, without altering the core of the common culture or ensuring the rights of people of colour. This critique of multiculturalism points up its inadequacies, including its inability to dismantle systems of inequality and diminish White power and privilege. Creese (1993–94) observed that despite multiculturalism, the legacy of "White settler" colonialism continues to provide some citizens with greater entitlements and the freedom to define who is a "real citizen" in Canada.

A race-based analysis asserts that multiculturalism fosters "a festive aura of imagined consensus" (Moodley, 1983). Multiculturalism focuses on "saris, samosas, and steel-bands" in order to diffuse the "three R's": "resistance, rebellion and rejection" (Mullard, 1982). A little local colour is "tolerated" and even encouraged

because it provides vibrancy and vitality to what remains as the "core" culture.

Multicultural discourse as articulated in the Act and other policies is founded on the premise of social order rather than conflict, and thus "it does not recognize, or provide any way of understanding existing structural disadvantages and the clashes which will occur as such inequalities are addressed" (Harding, 1995). The ideology and policy of multiculturalism has also been incorporated into the Charter of Rights and Freedoms.

CASE STUDY 11.3

THE CANADIAN CHARTER OF RIGHTS AND FREEDOMS

Background

The Canadian Bill of Rights was introduced by Prime Minister John G. Diefenbaker in 1960. Although it prohibited racial discrimination, it neither had constitutional status nor applied to provincial jurisdictions. Thus, prior to the enactment of the Constitution Act of 1982, the courts gave the Canadian Bill of Rights a very narrow interpretation. Constitutional questions about racial equality were resolved according to the "implied bill of rights" flowing from the constitutional division of powers. It is instructive that the "Fathers of Confederation" did not find it necessary to address the issue of racial equality in the provisions of the British North America Act. At the time, racial inequality was considered to be normative, and therefore the notion of providing constitutional guarantees to achieve racial equality was contrary to the collective ideology of the times.

In 1982, after a lengthy and controversial consulting process, the Canadian Charter of Rights and Freedoms was enshrined in Canada's constitution. For the first time in Canada's constitutional history, racial discrimination became unconstitutional. Enshrining the Charter in the Constitution was hailed as a triumph that was

expected to put an end to many forms of overt racial discrimination in society.[2]

Section 15(1) of the Charter of Rights (the equity rights clause) came into effect in 1985 and is perhaps the most significant equality provision in the Charter.[3] It reads:

> Every individual is equal before and under the law and has the right to the equal protection and equal benefit of the law without discrimination and, in particular, without discrimination based on race, national or ethnic origin, colour, religion, sex, age or mental or physical ability.

In prohibiting discrimination, section 15(1) provides five separate equality rights, namely: a right to equality before the law; a right to equality under the law; a right to equal benefit of the law; a right to equal protection of the law; and a right not to be discriminated against. It also protects affirmative action programs from constitutional litigation. Arguably, section 15(2) recognizes societal inequalities and permits affirmative action measures as a mechanism to assure equity for all Canadians.

Discussion

While the Charter outlaws discrimination on the basis of race, it is seriously flawed in a number of important ways.[4] Section 1 establishes protection for all Canadians of certain basic rights and freedoms essential to a liberal democratic society; these include the protection of fundamental freedoms, democratic rights, legal rights, equality rights, Canada's multicultural heritage, Native rights, and the official languages of Canada. At the same time, however, the rights guaranteed in the Charter are subject to certain limitations: they should be reasonable, prescribed by law, demonstrably justified, and in keeping with the standards of a free and democratic society. Three of these four criteria included in section 1 are subjective and open to differing interpretations. The views of ethno-racial minorities and other disadvantaged groups on what is "reasonable" and "demonstrably justified" and on what meets the standards of a "free and democratic society" may be very different from those of the state.

The Charter does not define discrimination, racism, or race. Such interpretations have been left to the courts. Judges, justices, and lawyers have neither the expertise nor the training in social science to make determinations about the invisible network of racist discourses, beliefs, values, and norms that operate in a liberal democratic society. Many judges deny the existence of systemic racism. The courts are thus ill prepared to define the meanings and conditions of racial discrimination.

When a charge of racial discrimination has been made against an institution, a "cause of action" must initially be defined for the case to be heard in the courts. Essentially, a litigant must frame a legal claim within the legal parameter of a "cause of action." When the cause of a legal action involves racism and discrimination, it is virtually impossible to present an argument without a legal definition of such terms. Constitutional litigation involves a process of language, interpretation, and meaning.

Matas (1990) made a strong argument that the Charter is an inadequate and imperfect instrument for effectively addressing the problem of racism. He suggested that, while the Charter prohibits racial discrimination in law (section 15 (1)), it does not require governments or legislatures to promote racial equality. The Charter is a passive instrument. It does not require governments or legislatures to do anything; it merely prevents them from doing certain things. The Charter prohibits racial discrimination in law, but it requires neither Parliament nor legislatures to design policies and programs to eliminate racial equality. There is no constitutional mandate to eradicate or even control racism.

For example, the Charter does not prevent one group of citizens from discriminating against another. As long as governments are not actively promoting inequality, they can legally wash their hands of what goes on in society at large (Matas, 1990). The real threat to equality does not come from legislative action but from the actions of private persons working within systems and organizations. Thus, the equality provisions in the Charter fail to address some of the real arenas of inequality in society.

Many of the same arguments can be made in discussing the weaknesses in the constitutional equality-rights process. For example, the constitutional equality-rights system, through its procedures, makes the same flawed assertion as does the human-rights system, that is, that equality exists and that only the lapses from it need to be addressed. However, Kallen (1982) contended that there is a covert status hierarchy among the enumerated minorities who are eligible to receive specified protection for their human rights in section 15. Ethnic and multicultural minorities, Aboriginal peoples, and women have specified human-rights protection under other Charter provisions (sections 25, 27, and 28, respectively), whereas other enumerated minorities (such as racial minorities) do not.

Lack of a support structure for victims of inequality and the absence of a public agency with a capacity to challenge inequalities on behalf of a disadvantaged group is another major deficiency in the Charter. Perhaps one of the most important limitations of the Charter is the lack of guaranteed funding necessary to pursue a challenge. To raise an important Charter issue, a litigant must be willing and able to fight its case in the Supreme Court of Canada. To attempt a challenge of federal legislation on Charter grounds can cost $100 000 or more. Few citizens have the necessary funds. The absence of sufficient resources for minority groups exacerbates social inequalities.[5] This diminishes the section 15 provision and ensures that court actions are largely brought by wealthy litigants. It can be argued that a significant reason for the lack of Charter challenges by people of colour is that justice is economically inaccessible.

A further limitation of the Charter in relation to the protection of minority rights is the passivity of the courts. Gibson argued that the Charter "stands against a backdrop of the courts' passive tradition of self-restraint" (1985:39). Historically, the courts have deferred to democratically elected representatives. This weakness is clearly demonstrated in the repeal of the Employment Equity Act by the government of Ontario.

In sum, section 15 provides an inadequate guarantee against discrimination. Regardless of Supreme Court decisions and strong judicial statements condemning discrimination, the courts are an ineffective arena for enforcing or ensuring equality in Canada. Racial inequality cannot be eradicated by one act of legislation in one mainstream institution in society. The alleged importance of the Charter maintains the ideological fiction that the legal system can control the broader systemic biases found in Canadian society. Thus, the Charter can be said to be an instrument of the ideology of democratic racism in providing a liberal solution consistent with a liberal democratic society's view of the world. However, it provides only a template, without the authority required to implement racial equality.

The next major state policy is not aimed at addressing the problem of racism, but rather aims to protect Canadians from the impending threat of terrorism. However, as is argued in this section, the policy itself presents a significant danger to all Canadians and more specifically the rights and freedoms of Canadians of Arab, Muslim, or other Middle-Eastern backgrounds.

New State Policy on Terrorism

Is the Anti-Terrorism Act an Expression of Racial Profiling by the State?

The events of 9/11 raised deep concerns about Canada's capacity to meet the threats of terrorism. Within three months, Bill C-36, the Anti-Terrorism bill came into law in December 2001. The legislation defines acts of terrorism as those actions that threaten Canadian lives or property, instil fear in society, or damage the economy, or that are targeted against political institutions and the general welfare of the country. It is an attempt by the federal government to control and contain world terrorism by identifying, prosecuting, convicting, and punishing terrorist activity. It is an omnibus bill, which amended 19 pieces of legislation. The Government of Canada Anti-Terrorism Plan has four objectives:

- stop terrorists from getting into Canada and protect Canadians from terrorist acts;
- bring forward tools to identify, prosecute, convict and punish terrorists;
- prevent the Canada-US border from being held hostage by terrorists and impacting on the Canadian economy; and,
- work with the international community to bring terrorists to justice and address the root causes of such hatred. (Government's Anti-Terrorism Act, 2001)

The new measures enshrined in the Act: allow the arrest of individuals without warrant; permit imposition of long, consecutive sentences for terrorist crimes and permit the imposition of long sentences for crimes committed during terrorist acts; make it easier for police to obtain warrants for wiretaps, which may be operated for three years; define what constitutes terrorist activity; allow the government to keep much more information secret; and increase the power of Canadian intelligence agencies to intercept electronic communication in peace and security. The Act gives the state new investigative and prosecutorial powers that include: "preventive detention," that is, the right to imprison people on the suspicion that they might commit a crime; allowing the police to compel testimony from anyone they believe has information about terrorism; closed trials of alleged terrorists; and, with a judge's permission, allowing the prosecution to deny an accused person and his or her lawyer all the knowledge of the evidence held against him.

Moreover, the definition of terrorism is extremely broad, and critics maintain that it could even be used to prosecute trade unionists involved in illegal strike activity or other harmless people involved in civil disobedience. Regular tactics such as protests, blockades, and other peaceful tactics used by many dissenting groups in society would be subject to the Act's strictures. The increased police powers and the government's ability to suppress information about its own activities are also sharply criticized. The Act also has the ability to modify 22 existing laws including the Criminal Code, the Canadian Human Rights Act, the Access to Information Act, the National Defence Act, and several others. Critics also maintain that it might lead to violations of the Charter of Rights and Freedoms. During the parliamentary debate on the Act, most of the time was spent on deciding whether to add a three-or-five-year sunset clause to some of its powers.

Since the Anti-Terrorism Bill was enacted, it has been a deeply contested issue. Middle-Eastern communities, and Canadian Muslims in particular, have felt under siege. Organizations such as the Canadian Islamic Congress and the Canadian Arab Federation have argued that the bill is an assault on the basic civil liberties of every Canadian. Since the bill was ratified, Canadian security forces such as the RCMP and CSIS have questioned hundreds if not thousands of Muslim Canadians about travel patterns, prayer habits, associations, and other seemingly innocuous matters.

The president of the Canadian Civil Liberties Association, Alan Borovoy, suggests, "The legitimate war on terrorism doesn't require measures as broad as that." Toronto civil rights lawyer Clayton Ruby said the law "will wind up being used against peaceful protests and demonstrations. It will wind up being used to suppress opposition" (Bourrie, 2002). Human-rights groups have demonstrated grave concern over the overarching provisions of the bill. The International Civil Liberties Monitoring Group, on May 14, 2003, observed that the Anti-Terrorism Act grants police expanded investigative detention, and undermines the principle of due process. "All of these changes occur on the basis of a vague, imprecise and overly expansive definition of terrorist activity" (quoted in a speech by Senator Andreychuk, 2003). Canada's top spymaster and former CSIS chief from 1987–1991, Reid Morden, argues that "The Canadian government, in its race to catch up, went beyond the British and American legislation defining terrorist activities to include legal, political, religious and ideological protests that intentionally disrupt essential services. ... The definition of 'terrorism' is so wide that I could easily include behaviour that doesn't remotely resemble terrorism" (quoted in a *Toronto Star* editorial, December 1, 2003).

It can be also argued, as Charles Smith does, that the Anti-Terrorism Act is yet another form of racial profiling (2004). The following are a few cases in which men of Middle-Eastern background living in Canada became victims of racial profiling by the state. In the war on terrorism they became the new enemy aliens and their democratic rights were seriously curtailed.

On the second anniversary of 9/11, two Canadian citizens, Imams Kutty and Abdool Hameed, were en route to Florida to lead an Islamic prayer service when they were detained by U.S. immigration agents, interrogated for 16 hours, and then released. Mohammed Elmasry, president of the Canadian Islamic Congress, observes that the Canadian news media reported on the incident with a degree of mild protest, "not because the men's detention was unfair and unreasonable, not because they were prominent members of a Canadian religious community, nor even because they were Canadian citizens, but because they were moderates" (*Globe and Mail*, September 30, 2003). In August 2003, the Canadian RCMP arrested 21 visa students accused of having ties to the international al-Qaeda terrorist group. All the detainees were Muslim students from Pakistan and India. They were later cleared of having any link to terrorist groups. Hassan Almrei, a 29-year-old refugee from Syria, is being held in a Canadian prison—and has been for two years—in solitary confinement without charge or bail, on a security certificate that does not allow for any of the alleged evidence against him to be shared with either Almrei or his lawyer.

Perhaps the most dramatic case of anti-Muslim bias and discrimination is that of Maher Arar, a Canadian Muslim. See Case Study 11.4.

CASE STUDY 11.4

THE ROLE OF CANADIAN OFFICIALS IN THE ARREST AND IMPRISONMENT OF MAHER ARAR

Background

Maher Arar was born in Syria in 1970. In 1987 he came to Canada and later took out dual citizenship, retaining his Syrian citizenship and also becoming a Canadian citizen. After receiving a master's degree in computer engineering, Arar worked in Ottawa as a telecommunications engineer.

In September 2002, the U.S. authorities arrested him while he was on an airline stopover in New York on his way home to Montreal. He was carrying his Canadian passport. Agents from U.S. Immigration and Naturalization alleged that Arar had links to al-Qaeda. He was first deported to Jordan and then Syria, where he was imprisoned and tortured for one year, before being released in October 2003.

All during the time of Arar's incarceration, his wife, Monia Mazigh, lobbied every level of government for his release. She appeared before the Foreign Affairs Committee. In November 2003 the RCMP began a formal investigation of its own role in the matter. The Commission for Public Complaints Against the RCMP asked "the force to

respond to allegations that encouraged US officials to deport Mr. Arar ..." (*Globe and Mail*, November 6, 2003). However, serious questions arose about the inadequate scope of the investigation, as the RCMP were unable to investigate the CSIS, the Foreign Affairs Department, or any person or institution in the United States. Also, it was pointed out that the RCMP operate without independent oversight or public representation, and thus in reality were investigating themselves.

In January 2004, Arar launched a lawsuit against the American government, alleging that U.S. officials deported Arar knowing that Syria practised torture. Later in the same month, Public Safety Minister Anne McLellan called for a public inquiry into the Arar case, to "assess the actions of Canadian officials in dealing with the deportation and detention of Maher Arar" (http://www.cbc.ca/news/background/arar). It is important to note that no charges were ever laid against Arar in Syria, the United States, or Canada. At the time of publication of this book, a public inquiry is under way.

Analysis

The issues raised by this case involve questions about the rights, freedoms, and civil liberties of Canadian citizens who have been born in other countries, and are identified in some way as a threat to Canada or the United States. It can be argued that the tragic events of 9/11 have also had devastating consequences for law-abiding Canadian Muslims and other Canadians of Middle-Eastern origins.

Audrey Macklin (2002) suggests that "Members of diasporic communities, whatever their immigration status, will experience more than ever how boundaries demarcated by ethnicity, culture, religion and politicization emerge in sharp relief when viewed through the lens of the state's surveillance camera" (338). There is much anecdotal evidence to suggest that there has already been a significant impact on particular racialized groups across Canada, including Arabs and Muslims or those perceived to belong to these communities (see Smith, 2004). The Canadian Muslim Civil Liberties Association has recorded 110 hate attacks and the Canadian Islamic Congress indicates that such acts have increased by 1600 percent since 9/11. Moreover, the Anti-Terrorism Act itself, as discussed above, may put these groups at even greater risk of victimization.

The racialized discourses embedded in the anti-terrorism legislation are reflected in many other laws, particularly those related to immigration and refugees (see Chapter 3). In Canada's history, the ideology underpinning these policies has always reflected the binary polarizations separating "us" and "them," "insiders" and "outsiders." The language of the Act intimates that the nation is in a state of profound social and political crisis. Employing a discourse of moral panic, the implicit assumption is that not only is our national security at risk, but also our sense of national identity has become more fragmented and fragile.

CASE STUDY 11.5

HUMAN-RIGHTS CODES AND COMMISSIONS

Background

Ontario's Racial Discrimination Act of 1944 was the first provincial legislation to prohibit racial discrimination. In 1962, the Ontario Human Rights Code was the first such provincial legislation to be enacted. The Code prohibited discrimination on the grounds of race, creed, colour, nationality, ancestry, or place of origin. Today, all the provinces (except British Columbia), two of the three territories, and the federal government have a human-rights code, and most have a human-rights commission to administer it.

Provincial human-rights codes have quasi-constitutional status. The Canadian Human Rights Code is, of course, subject to the Canadian Charter of Rights and Freedoms, which in section 52 states that the Constitution is the supreme law of Canada.

Human-rights laws are codes of conduct to which society is expected to adhere. Although the prohibited grounds of discrimination vary from province to province, several jurisdictions prohibit discrimination in accommodation, facilities, services, contracts, and employment. All the codes prohibit discrimination on the basis of race, creed, colour, ethnicity, religion, gender, and, in Ontario, sexual orientation.

Canada's system of human rights is activated by the complaint mechanism. Under various human-rights codes, claims must be handled by a human-rights commission, which investigates claims and attempts to settle them by conciliation and mediation. If this is not possible, the commission either dismisses the claim or sends it to hearings conducted by a human-rights board of inquiry. The board is an independent quasi-judicial tribunal.

If a claim goes to a board, lawyers acting for the commission present the case and argue for the "appropriate" remedy. Boards of inquiry make decisions to uphold or reject claims and can order redress, such as back pay and damages.

Discussion

The present model of human rights has been criticized (Day, 1990; Duclos, 1990; *Equality Now*, 1984) for being reactive: it comes into play only when a complaint is launched. Critics argue that commissions do not have a sufficiently broad mandate to combat discrimination effectively. A principal criticism is that a complaint-motivated system cannot effectively address a problem that is so widespread in society.

Former Canadian human-rights commissioner Max Yalden reinforces the criticism of the complaint model: "I am convinced that one of the reasons our scheme of human-rights laws has become prey to bureaucratic delays and judicial haggling is that it is so predominantly a complaint-driven model," which requires several conditions to be met: a victim must come forward; that person must be able to relate particular actions to one or more of the forbidden types of discrimination; and the treatment must be demonstrably discriminatory, not just unfair or different. He proposed that the commissions complement the complaint system by creating a non-discriminatory environment that includes employment equity (Yalden, 1990:2).

In resolving human-rights complaints, the present model allows for persuasion and conciliation where necessary and, alternatively, for punitive measures when such persuasion fails. Human-rights commissions are therefore under tremendous pressure to settle complaints. In attempting to reach conciliation, staff are often unaware of the impact of their behaviour on victims. For example, in the hearings of a task force established to examine the procedures of the Ontario Human Rights Commission, delegations representing various community groups stated that the "process can be coercive and unfair.

Claimants argued that sometimes they are specifically told that if they do not accept a settlement, which in their view is unjust, their case will be dismissed by the commission. Since they have no other choice, they feel forced to accept the settlement" (Ontario Human Rights Code Review Task Force, 1992:116). Often, settlements involve the payment of a certain sum. Several people believe such settlements are offensive and unprincipled, as it appears that human rights are being bought and that the underlying questions of discrimination are not being addressed.

This complaint-driven approach is viewed as inadequate in addressing the complex, pervasive, and intractable forms of racism in Canadian society. A reevaluation of the "effectiveness of a human rights system that is based on a model developed in the 1960's" (Mendes, 1997:2.v) is clearly called for. Analyzing statistics for the various commissions, Mendes came to the conclusion that, due to a variety of factors, including the inability to deal with race complaints, there is a general tendency for "race complaints to be treated differently than other complaints ... they are dismissed more frequently than cases based on other grounds of discrimination." He concluded his analysis of human-rights commissions by noting that

> the human-rights system existing in most jurisdictions in Canada is not affording the victims of discrimination the recourse necessary to enforce their rights. In particular, cases of racial discrimination are proving to be too much for the present system to handle. (Mendes, 1997)

Two other reviews of the structure of human-rights commissions in Ontario and British Columbia have suggested a radical reorganization of the commissions and their operations (Ontario Human Rights Code Review Task Force, 1992; Black, 1994).

In each of the government responses to racism discussed above, the state failed to provide adequate mechanisms for addressing the inequities experienced by racial-minority communities. The liberal discourses on multiculturalism, rights, and equality are largely framed on a passive model of state intervention that ignores collective or group rights based on race. Despite the espousal of equality as a guiding principle, these policies do not offer a means of ensuring social justice and equity for people of colour (St. Lewis, 1996; Goldberg, 1993).

In addition to its assumed role of providing leadership in combating racism and inequality in society and as a guarantor of human rights, the state also has a direct role in terms of its responsibility as an

- employer;
- purchaser of goods and services; and
- provider of services.

The State as Employer: Employment Equity

Background to the Enactment of Employment Equity Legislation

Concern over employment discrimination against people of colour (visible minorities), women, persons with disabilities, and Aboriginal peoples led the federal government to establish a royal commission on equality in employment (Abella, 1984). Its task was to inquire into the employment practices of 11 designated Crown and government-owned corporations and to explore the most effective means of promoting equality for the four groups cited above. Its findings echoed earlier studies and public inquiries, that bias and discrimination were a pervasive reality in the employment system. The commissioner, Judge Rosalie Abella, observed that "strong measures were needed to remedy the impact of discriminatory attitudes and behaviours." The purpose of the Employment Equity Act was to "achieve equality in the workplace, and to correct the conditions of disadvantage in employment experienced by **designated groups**—women, Aboriginal peoples, persons with disabilities, and members of visible minorities in Canada" (Employment and Immigration Canada, 1988; Agocs, Burr, and Somerset, 1992). The remedy Abella recommended was employment equity legislation (ibid.).

Employment equity legislation provided a necessary framework to support a diverse workforce. Employment equity was intended to change the workplace by identifying systemic barriers in policies and practices that may appear neutral, but which, while not necessarily discriminatory in intent, are discriminatory in effect or result. The goal of employment equity was fair treatment and equitable representation throughout the workplace.[6]

Equality in employment means that no one is denied opportunities for reasons that have nothing to do with inherent ability (Abella, 1984). The Act applied to employers and Crown corporations with 100 employees or more under federal jurisdiction. It required all federally regulated employers to file an annual report with the Canadian Employment and Immigration Commission. The report was to provide information for a full year on the representation of all employees and members of designated groups (visible minorities, women, persons with disabilities, and Aboriginal peoples) by occupational group and salary range and on those hired, promoted, or terminated. In addition to filing the annual report, employers were required to prepare an annual employment equity plan with goals and timetables, and to retain such a plan for a period of at least three years. The Employment Equity Act was revised and adopted by Parliament in 1995, strengthening the legislation and bringing the public service, the RCMP, and the military under the purview of the Act.

There has been huge resistance to efforts to implement employment equity at every level of institutional life. For example, efforts to make the Canadian public service more representative of the Canadian public have failed. The 1996 annual report of the Canadian Human Rights Commission documents in stark numbers the huge gap between the government's commitment to a public service that mirrors the diversity of the Canadian population and its dismal record in promoting minorities.[7] In examining some of the reasons for this failure, Senator Noel Kinsella, formerly a senior bureaucrat with Heritage Canada, is quoted (in Samuel and Karam, 1996) as saying "Institutions act as a collective memory carrying forward values, principles and traditions. ..."

A review of the data contained in annual reports of federal regulating bodies by the president of the Treasury Board in 1995 revealed that small progress had been made with respect to the hiring of members of employment equity targeted groups. For example, the percentage of women in the public service increased from 42.9 percent in 1988 to 47.4 percent in 1995. The percentage of Aboriginal representation increased from 1.7 to 2.2 percent, while visible-minority representation increased from 2.9 to 4.1 percent. In all of these categories, the available labour pool is much higher.

In 2001, the Canadian Federal Human Rights Commission found that representation of visible minorities in the private sector increased from 4.9 percent in 1987 to 11.7 percent as of December 31, 2001, and the percentage of hires increased from 12 percent in 2000 to 12.6 percent in 2001, which surpassed the 1996 census benchmark of 11.6 percent of visible minorities in the population. In the public sector, visible minorities held only 2.7 percent of all positions in the federal public service. By March 31, 2002, this had increased to 6.8 percent. Despite this improvement, the Human Rights Commission is concerned that "at the current rate of progress, the government will fail to meet its target," which, as contained in the new Embracing Change initiative, was set at a 20 percent hiring goal to be attained by March 2003. In the executive category visible minorities held only 3.8 percent of positions and of 73 new hires in this category in 2001–2002 only three went to visible minorities.

In a report released in September 2002 and prepared by the Public Service Commission, it was found that federal hiring rules are widely ignored by managers and favouritism is still very common. Managers continue to hire spouses, siblings, cousins, and people they know rather than conforming to the rules designed to ensure that public service jobs are accessible to everyone. Commonly, hiring transactions appear to be developed with the aim of appointing an already known person to the position. These conclusions are based on more than 1000 hirings that took place in eight government departments (cited in *Ottawa Citizen*, January 2, 2004). Such practices have very serious implications, because they substantially limit visible-minority access to public service positions.

In its most recent report of 2003, the Commission again found that hiring and promotion had not reached the targets set earlier by the Treasury Board. Visible-minority representation in the public service reached 7.4 percent, still less than the target, and their share of new hires, 9.5 percent, was less than half the target. In the executive category, only 7 out of 82 persons were visible minorities (Annual Report, 2003).

The inequity exists within many other institutions. In this connection, identified below are some of the myths and misconceptions used by government bureaucrats and politicians, school administrators and academics, editors, journalists and publishers, and police to support their resistance to hiring and promoting people of colour, Aboriginal peoples, women, and persons living with disabilities. The rhetorical themes embedded in these myths reflect the discourses of democratic racism.

"Employment Equity Is Reverse Discrimination."

According to this view, employment equity requires employers to discriminate against better-qualified Whites and gives an unfair advantage to people of colour. However, what is required is not reverse discrimination but the end of a long history of employment practices that result in preferential treatment for White males.

"Employment Equity Ignores the Merit Principle."

This myth is perhaps the most widely believed and promoted. It is based on the assumption that employment equity and other anti-discrimination measures will result in the hiring and appointment of "unqualified" individuals and bring an end to the merit principle. In reality, however, equity programs do not require the abandonment of standards and qualifications. Rather, they eliminate irrelevant criteria such as the colour of one's skin, cultural background, disability, and gender.

"Employment Equity Stigmatizes Minorities."

According to this misconception, minorities will never know if they have been selected on the basis of their qualifications or because of their group membership. One could argue that White males for two hundred years should have been asking themselves the same question. Implicit in the above assumption is the perception that there are no meritorious persons in this group. As one observer noted,

> Do all those corporate directors, bankers, etc., who got their job for extraneous reasons—first because they were somebody's son, second, because they were male, third because they were Protestant, and fourth because they were White—feel demeaned thereby? It would be interesting to ask them—or to ask the same question of those doctors who managed to get into good medical schools because there were quotas keeping out Jews, the skilled tradesmen who were admitted to the union because two members of their families recommended them and so on. (Green, 1981:79)

Clearly implicit in the standard critique of these proactive measures is the notion that being rewarded is the natural result of being part of the majority or the elite. Rewards are only demeaning when one is a member of a minority or a marginalized group (e.g., women).

"Fairness Is Best Achieved by Treating Everyone in the Same Way."

Opponents of equity measures argue that in a democratic society, treating everyone equally is sufficient to ensure fairness in the workplace. However, as Abella pointed out, "We now know that to treat everyone in the same way may offend the notion of equality" (1984:3). She suggested that ignoring differences and refusing to accommodate them is a denial of equal access and opportunity; it is discrimination.

"Employment Equity Means Hiring by Quotas."

Although mandatory quotas are not required in employment equity programs, a widespread perception exists that governments require specific numbers of racial minorities to be hired, promoted, or appointed in specific organizations. Instead, employment equity in Canada requires employers to set goals for their organization, taking into account the number of qualified individuals from target groups that are available in the potential workforce as well as the composition of the internal workforce. Flexible goals and timetables are used to establish benchmarks toward representative hiring and promotion.

The State as Purchaser of Goods and Services: Contract Compliance

Contract compliance is a method of influencing private companies to implement an employment equity program. Under contract compliance, a vendor's contract is contingent on the existence of an equity program. The penalty for non-compliance is loss of the contract with the federal government.

The federal government has specific criteria governing contract compliance. A company must design and implement a program that will identify and take steps to remove barriers in the selection, hiring, promotion, and training of select minority groups. As in employment equity, compliance is largely voluntary; each company is expected to establish special programs in areas where imbalances exist (Jain, 1988).

This program can be criticized on many grounds. For example, the equity programs are not legislated and operate at the discretion of government, and government conducts only random audits of companies that have promised to implement employment equity programs. This allows companies to avoid developing a program until an audit occurs. What develops, therefore, is a cycle of delay in which federal bureaucrats and their corporate counterparts negotiate to delay the implementation of employment equity.

Some companies that supply highly specialized services are not audited. Corporate clients are permitted to set their own goals and timetables to match what is considered reasonable for their peculiar settings, but anti-racism is not a high priority for some companies. Since the government has not applied a criterion of success to this process, companies proceed at their own, often slow, pace.

The State as Provider and Funder of Services

Communities affected by racial discrimination continue to feel excluded from public services. They also perceive little support in their efforts to develop the community infrastructures and support systems required to meet the needs of their communities (*Equality Now*, 1984). Studies carried out in the past decade on access to government services (Mock and Masemann, 1987) suggest that racial minorities and Aboriginal peoples do not have equal access to or participate adequately in government programs and services.

Notwithstanding this concern, all levels of government for many years have provided some support to racial-minority, community-based service organizations. Generally, the funding is in the form of short-term project support; but despite varying levels of support and varying criteria, this support is at least a recognition by the state that racial-minority organizations play a critical role in ensuring that the community derives equal benefit from public service. Such support is an appropriate bridging strategy, until public structures and programs adequately serve all communities. However, on the other hand, it encourages the development of parallel services that existing public institutions should be offering.

The question of whether satisfactory service can be effected only by separate provision continues to be debated. Would separate service agencies along racial lines meet minority needs, or would they further fragment the state's delivery system? Would matching rather than mixing racial clients provide more emphatic help to people in need? Is "separate services" a euphemism for segregation?

Another concern is that in providing support to racial-minority organizations, the level of public support is grossly deficient. Separate services have become synonymous with inferior services. Expecting far too much for far too little, minority organizations have been exploited by the state as an expedient way to deliver public services to people of colour.

Arrangements made within public organizations determine to whom services are provided, to whom facilities are made available, and to whom resources are allocated. The attitudes and actions of those who direct these institutions determine who gets what, where, and when. Since people of colour are generally absent from the key decision-making processes in these organizations and in the delivery of services, to what extent do public institutions treat people of colour less favourably?

Although considerable resources have been expended on the training of public servants in "multiculturalism," "race relations," or "managing diversity," to what extent have the special needs of minorities been identified? And to what extent have they been adequately considered and provided for? To what extent have the resources of the state been reallocated in favour of minorities as part of a commitment to equity? Within a framework of genuine, equal sharing of public resources, it appears that the scale on which this has been done by any state agency or institution in Canada is insignificant in addressing the imbalances caused by racially discriminatory policies, programs, and practices. Initiatives taken to measure and address racial minorities' inequalities of access to public programs and services in Canada have been tentative and piecemeal.

Conclusion

In many ways, the role of the state in responding to issues of racism and inequality has had to fit within the context of an imagined national culture consisting of a unique blend of English and French cultures, and an identity built on English and French values. As a result, three categories of citizens were recognized: English Canadians, French Canadians, and "others" (Fleras and Elliott, 1992). Only the first two groups had constitutional rights. The construction of undesirable "otherness" has persisted as Canadians have continued to struggle for a national identity (Mackey, 1999). This notion of "otherness" can be seen from three interlocking perspectives:

- "Otherness" provides the dominant White culture with unmarked, invisible privilege and power.
- Issues are deflected in a way that suggests these "others" threaten the democratic fabric of Canadian society.
- There is a reassertion of individual rights and identity over collective identity and group rights.

Those positioned within the privileged discourses of democratic racism and Whiteness and intent on maintaining their power assert their claim on the liberal values of individualism, equal opportunities, tolerance, and so on. In so doing, they construct a view of ethno-racial and Aboriginal peoples who do not share these values and therefore are outside the boundaries of the common culture of the state. Anglo-European culture dominance asserts its entitlement and authority within the very policies of the Canadian state, defining all others as "ethnics," "minorities," "immigrants," and "visible minorities," who are then marginalized and rendered subordinate to its unmarked centre. The power elite determines which differences and which similarities are allowed in the public domain (Suvendrini and Pugliese, 1997; Mackey, 1999). That authority "to define crucial homogeneities and differences" is defended within the liberal discourse of equality and progress (Asad, 1979:627).

For many Canadians, the increasing pluralism of Canadian society poses a threat to the way they have imagined and constructed Canadian identity. They hold on to an image of Canada distinguished from other countries, particularly the United States, by its French–English duality. Many Anglo-Canadians and others fear that multiculturalism will never provide a solution to the issue of national identity. Canadians want to resolve French–English tensions without having to address the multicultural issue of identity. One scholar argued that Canada is a nation in which "state-sanctioned proliferation of cultural difference itself is seen to be its defining characteristic" (Mackey, 1996:11). Multiculturalism as state policy embraces, in theory, the notion of cultural and racial diversity. Ethno-racial minorities are declared to be part of the "imagined" community of Canada. Anderson used the term "imagined community" to define the concept of "nation." A nation is "imagined" because the members of even a very small state do not know each other, yet in "the minds of each lives the image of their communion" (1983:15). However, in reality, the policy and practice of multiculturalism continues to position certain ethno-racial groups at the margins rather than in the mainstream of public culture and national identity.

The "symbolic multiculturalism" of state policy does not consider the necessity of restructuring or the need for a reconceptualization of the power relations between cultural and racial communities based on the premise that communities and societies do not exist autonomously but are deeply woven together in a web of interrelationships. Liberal pluralist discourse is unable to move beyond "tolerance," "sensitivity," or "understanding" of the "others." The state's construction of symbolic multiculturalism as a mechanism for maintaining the status quo can be seen in many forms of public discourse around issues of race, culture, difference, politics, and identity. This discourse is not restricted to the public declarations of policy-makers, legislators, and bureaucrats. It is also reflected in the language and practices employed by the state through its institutions and systems, including justice and law enforcement, print and electronic media, cultural and educational institutions, and public-sector corporations (Tator, Henry, and Mattis, 1998).

Visano (2002) argues that Whiteness as a plurality of assumptions, beliefs, and discourses continues to influence public polices that support the status quo. He states, "Law is a set of spectacular and performative moments that promote a neutral response to racial injustices, thereby escaping its complicities. ... Legal illusions pacify and legitimate the articulation of a culture of Whiteness that guides the everyday behavior of law" (210).

People of colour and Aboriginal peoples are seldom invited into the mainstream discourse of Canadian dominant White culture. The select few are considered to be models and are imagined as being different from others of their kind. In contrast, the airing of diverse perspectives by people of colour on issues related to fundamental human rights (e.g., the Anti-Terrorism Act) Aboriginal rights, multiculturalism, racism, and employment equity are commonly dismissed, deflected, or ignored. In a liberal democracy, justice and equality are already assumed to exist. Therefore, Aboriginal and ethno-racial minorities' demands for access and inclusion are seen as "radical," "unreasonable," "undemocratic," and a threat to cherished democratic, liberal values. The small gains made by minorities and women are seen by the mainstream culture as being "too expensive" economically and ideologically. Dissent by the oppressed is considered disruptive and dangerous.

The "symbolic multiculturalism" of state policies holds to a paradigm of pluralism premised on a hierarchical order of cultures that under certain conditions "allows" or "tolerates" non-dominant cultures to participate in the dominant culture. Such an approach imagines minority communities as "special-interest groups," not as active and full participants in the state and part of its shared history. This paradigm represents notions of tolerance and accommodation, but not of equity and justice. It holds to a unified and static concept of identities and communities as fixed sets of experiences, meanings, and practices rather than of identities as dynamic, fluid, multiple, and historically situated. In summary, state policies continue to be largely centred on the maintenance of the status quo.

Summary

This chapter has analyzed the roles and functions of the state as lawgiver, policy-maker, employer, purchaser, and provider of goods and services. It has argued that public policies, including the Canadian Multiculturalism Act, the Canadian Charter of Rights and Freedoms, the Employment Equity Act, the Anti-Terrorism Act, and human rights codes and commissions have been inadequate instruments to address racial inequality in Canadian society. The discourse of liberalism underlying these policies—the rhetoric of rights, reasonableness, freedoms, equality, standards, tolerance, understanding, and so forth that is incorporated into all of these state responses to some extent—is in itself a limiting factor in the struggle to control racism. Moreover, new public policies in relation to immigration, and more specifically, the Anti-Terrorism Act may function to deprive ethno-racial individuals and groups, particularly those of Arab and/or Muslim descent of their fundamental civil rights.

Although these state responses are vastly different from the more overtly racist and assimilationist policies of earlier governments, the ideology and discourse of racism that are deeply embedded in the collective belief, value, and normative system of Canadian society affect the way laws are interpreted and implemented. The aforementioned public policies may be significant steps on the path to racial equality, but they are not instruments of societal transformation. Despite the government's recognition of ethno-racial diversity through public policies on multiculturalism, minority rights, and equity, social inequality not only continues to operate but is actually reproduced and legitimated through the state.

The notions of tolerance, accommodation, diversity, and equality are woven into the rhetoric of federal, provincial, and municipal politicians and other public authorities. At the same time, their discourses, policies, and practices reflect a deep ambivalence to undertaking the tasks required to attain racial equity. This conflict has shaped the way state policies have been constituted and the way they have been implemented.

This analysis points up a central paradox of modern liberal societies, first identified by Goldberg (1993): as modernity increasingly commits itself to the ideals and principles of equality, tolerance, and freedom, new racial identities and new forms of racism and exclusion proliferate.

Racialized public discourses concerning multiculturalism, rights and freedoms, and employment equity tend to employ ill-defined ideas and implicit notions regarding culture, differences, race, and racism, which when operationalized function socially and politically to marginalize ethno-racial minorities. Democratic racism is manifested in both subtle and overt forms of the discourse that shapes the very policies and practices designed to ameliorate racial inequality.

Notes

1. Most provinces in Canada have appointed an ombudsperson to handle the complaints of citizens who believe they have been treated unjustly by an agency of government. The office of the ombudsperson cannot deal with individual complaints of racism, but it has investigated complaints against provincial human-rights commissions, primarily regarding long delays in their management of cases.
2. The Charter has not been extensively used in race cases. For a complete review, see Mendes (1997).
3. Because of the far-reaching significance of the equality rights guaranteed in section 15, the federal and provincial governments gave themselves three years to change their laws and policies to comply with the Charter. Thus, while the rest of the Charter came into effect in 1982, section 15 came into effect three years later.
4. It is indeed paradoxical that the Charter, with all its identifiable weaknesses, has nevertheless been perceived negatively by people who fear its power. Judge Rosalie Abella, for example, notes that "in less than a generation, this remedy for discrimination has been seen to be sufficiently powerful that people struggle urgently to find a remedy from equality. How ironic that 'equality-seeker' has become a pejorative term, denoting someone whose claim to fairness is a menace to the nation's economy and psyche" (*Toronto Star*, October 26:A20).
5. The Charter Challenges Program, supported by the federal government, provides some financial assistance to disadvantaged groups who wish to pursue Charter cases.
6. Equitable representation depends on the following factors: the number of designated group members in the working-age population in a certain geographical area, the number of trained or skilled members who are employable or can be readily available, and the equal opportunities for change that exist in each workplace.
7. In March 1987, visible minorities made up 2.7 percent of the public service and 6.3 percent of the Canadian population. By March 1996, their share of the government employment had risen to 4.5 percent, but their representation in the population had jumped to 13 percent. In management, minorities held only 2.3 percent of the executive positions in the public service (Samuel and Karam, 1996).

References

Abella, R. (1984). *Equality in Employment: The Report of the Commission on Equality in Employment.* Ottawa: Supply and Services Canada.

Agocs, C., Burr C., and Somerset, F. (1992). *Employment Equity: Cooperative Strategies for Organizational Change.* New York: Prentice Hall.

Anderson, B. (1983). *Imagined Communities.* London: Verso.

Andreychuk, R. Senator. (2003). *Case Study: Canada Anti-Terrorism Legislation.* Presented at Commonwealth Human Rights Initiative Seminar: Human Rights and Anti-Terrorism Legislation in the Commonwealth. June 5–6.

Angel, S. (1988). "The Multiculturalism Act of 1988." *Multiculturalism* 11(3):25–27.

Annual Report. (2003). Ottawa: Canadian Human Rights Commission. Available <http://www.chrc-ccdp.ca/publications/reports-en.asp>, accessed August 30, 2004.

Asad, T. (1979). "Anthropology and the Analysis of Ideology." *Man* 14:607–27.

Bannerji, H. (2000). *The Dark Side of the Nation: Essays on Multiculturalism, Nationalism and Gender.* Toronto: Canadian Scholars' Press.

Bhabha, H.K. (1990). "The Third Space." In Jonathan Rutherford (ed.), *Identity: Community Culture and Difference.* London: Lawrence and Wishart. 207–21.

Black, B. (1994). *Report on Human Rights in British Columbia.* B.C. Human Rights Review, Communications Branch, Ministry Responsible for Multiculturalism and Human Rights. Government of British Columbia.

Bourrie, M. (2002). "Tough Anti-Terrorism Legislation Called Threat to Civil Liberties." *Law Times.* Ottawa: Canadian Law Book Inc. Available <http://www.canadalawbook.ca>, accessed August 30, 2004.

Canadian Heritage—Multiculturalism Program. (1990). *The Canadian Multiculturalism Act: A Guide for Canadians.* Ottawa: Multiculturalism and Citizenship Canada. Excerpt reproduced with the permission of the Minister of Public Works and Government

Services Canada and the Minister of Canadian Heritage, 1999.

Corporate Policy Branch of Multiculturalism and Citizenship Canada. (1988). "Canadian Multiculturalism Act Briefing Book: Clause by Clause Analysis." Unpublished document released under Access to Information Act.

Creese, G. (1993–94). "The Sociology of British Columbia." *BC Studies* Special Issue 100 (Winter).

Day, S. (1990). *Human Rights in Canada: Into the 1990s and Beyond.* Ottawa: Human Rights Research and Education Centre.

Diène, D. (2004). "Addendum: Mission to Canada." Report for the United Nations Commission on Human Rights, Sixtieth Session, Item 6 of provisional agenda. March. Commission on Human Rights. Geneva, Switzerland: Office of the High Commissioner for Human Rights. Available <http://www.ohchr.org/english/issues/racism/rapporteur/annual.htm>.

Duclos, N. (1990). "Lessons of Difference: Feminist Theory on Cultural Diversity." *Buffalo Law Review* 38:325.

Employment and Immigration Canada. (1988). *Annual Report, Employment Equity Act.* Ottawa: Minister of Supply and Services.

Equality Now! Report of the Special Committee on Participation of Visible Minorities in Canadian Society. (1984). Ottawa: Queen's Printer.

Fleras, A., and J.L. Elliott. (1992). *Multiculturalism in Canada: The Challenge of Diversity.* Scarborough, ON: Nelson.

Gibson, D. (1985). "Protection of Minority Rights Under the Canadian Charter of Rights and Freedoms." In N. Nelville and A. Kornberg (eds.), *Minorities and the Canadian State.* Oakville, ON: Mosaic Press.

Goldberg, D. (1993). *Racist Culture: Philosophy and the Politics of Meaning.* Oxford: Blackwell.

Government's Anti-Terrorism Act, The. (2001). *Former Prime Minister's Newsroom Archive (1995–2003).* October 15. Privy Council Office site <http://www.pco-bcp.gc.ca>, accessed August 29, 2004.

Green, P. (1981). *The Pursuit of Inequality.* New York: Pantheon.

Harding, S. (1995). "Multiculturalism in Australia: Moving Race/Ethnic Relations from Extermination to Celebration?" *Race, Gender, and Class* 3(1)(Fall):7–26.

Itwaru, A., and N. Ksonzek. (1994). *Closed Entrances: Canadian Culture and Imperialism.* Toronto: TSAR.

Jain, H. (1988). "Affirmative Action Employment Equity Programs and Visible Minorities in Canada." *Currents: Readings in Race Relations* 5(1)(4):3.

James, C. (1995). "Multiculturalism and Anti-Racism Education in Canada." *Race, Gender and Class: An Interdisciplinary and Multicultural Journal* 2(3)(Spring):31–48.

Kallen, E. (1982). "Ethnicity and Human Rights in Canada." In P. Li (ed.), *Race and Ethnic Relations in Canada.* Toronto: Oxford University Press.

Kobayashi, A. (1990). "Racism and the Law." *Urban Geography* 11(5):447–73.

Li, Peter (ed.). (1999). "Race and Ethnicity." *Race and Ethnic Relations in Canada.* Toronto: Oxford University Press. 3–20.

Mackey, E. (1996). "Managing and Imagining Diversity: Multiculturalism and the Construction of National Identity in Canada." Unpublished doctoral dissertation, Social Anthropology, University of Sussex, UK.

———. (1999). *The House of Difference: Cultural Politics and National Identity in Canada.* London: Routledge.

Macklin, A. (2002). "Borderline Security." In R. Daniels, P. Macklem, and K. Roach (eds.), *The Security of Freedom: Essays on Canada's Anti-Terrorism Bill.* Toronto: University of Toronto Press.

Matas, D. (1990). "The Charter and Racism." *Constitutional Forum* 2:82.

Mendes, E. (ed.). (1997). *Racial Discrimination and the Law: Law and Practice.* Toronto: Carswell.

Mirchandani, K., and E. Tastsoglou. (2000). "Toward a Diversity Beyond Tolerance." *Journal of Status in Political Economy* (Spring):49–78.

Mock, K.R., and V.L. Masemann. (1987). Access to Government Services by Racial Minorities. Toronto: Ontario Race Relations Directorate. Available <http://ceris.metropolis.net>.

Moodley, K. (1983). "Canadian Multiculturalism as Ideology." *Ethnic and Racial Studies* 6(3):320–31.

Mullard, C. (1982). "Multiracial Education in Britain: From Assimilation to Cultural Pluralism." In J. Tierney (ed.), *Race, Migration and Schooling.* London: Holt, Rinehart and Winston.

Multiculturalism and Citizenship Canada. (1989–90). *Annual Report of the Operation of the Canadian Multiculturalism Act.* Ottawa.

Ontario Human Rights Code Review Task Force. (1992). *Achieving Equality: A Report on Human Rights Reform.* Toronto: Ministry of Citizenship.

Samuel, J., and A. Karam. (1996). "Employment Equity and Visible Minorities in the Federal Workforce." Paper presented at the Symposium on Immigration and Integration, October 25–27. Winnipeg: University of Manitoba.

Smith, C. (2004). "Borders and Exclusions: Racial Profiling and Canada's Immigration, Refugee and Security Laws." Paper commissioned for annual meeting of Canadian Court Challenges Program, October 2003.

St. Lewis, J. (1996). "Race, Racism and the Justice System." In C. James (ed.), *Perspectives on Racism and the Human Services Sector.* Toronto: University of Toronto Press. 104–19.

Suvendrini, P., and J. Pugliese. (1997). "Racial Suicide: The Re-licensing of Racism in Australia." *Race and Class* 39(2)(October–December):1–19.

Tator, C., F. Henry, and W. Mattis. (1998). *Racism in the Arts: Case Studies of Controversy and Conflict.* Toronto: University of Toronto.

Tepper, E. (1988). "Changing Canada: The Institutional Response to Polyethnicity." In *Review of Demography and Its Implications for Economic and Social Policy.* Ottawa: Carleton University.

Visano, L. (2002). "The Impact of Whiteness on the Culture of Law: From Theory to Practice." In C. Levine-Rasky (ed.), *Working Through Whiteness:* *International Perspectives.* Albany: State University Press: 209–237.

Walcott, R. (1993). "Critiquing Canadian Multiculturalism: Towards an Anti-Racist Agenda." Master's thesis, Graduate Department of Education, York University.

Wallace, M. (1994). "The Search for the 'Good Enough' Mammy: Multiculturalism, Popular Culture and Psychoanalysis." In D. Goldberg (ed.), *Multiculturalism: A Critical Reader.* Cambridge, MA: Blackwell. 259–68.

Yalden, M. (1990). "Canadian Human Rights and Multiculturalism." *Currents: Readings in Race Relations* (Toronto) 6(1):2.

CHAPTER 12

ORGANIZATIONAL RESISTANCE TO ANTI-RACISM

*White people still invite people of colour to participate in social actions
as subordinate to the organization as a whole. The bureaucratic machinery
to ensure continuity is withheld from people of colour. We remain a
peripheral validation of the lack of racism in White organizations.*

—*Maracle (1993:128)*

This chapter examines barriers within institutions in dismantling racism within their organizations. Despite a proliferation of public policies that articulate support for diversity and equity, anti-racism continues to be resisted at various levels within the organizational core values and normative practices. Various forms of organizational resistance are analyzed as examples of institutionally specific forms of democratic racism. These are the commonly used mechanisms that have been employed in organizations to maintain racialized behaviour and practices and to resist, evade, or subvert anti-racism initiatives. The chapter concludes by noting that a race-conscious model of organizations is required and describes three models of organizational change: assimilationism, multiculturalism, and anti-racism.

Introduction

An organization can be defined in various ways: in terms of its structure, its function, or any of a multitude of other characteristics. For our purposes, "organization" is defined as a sociopolitical system in which people act together under an imposed structure and ideology and use a specific set of technologies to achieve a specific objective. Henry Giroux has clarified the importance of ideology in organizational life, observing:

> Ideology has to be conceived as both source and effect of social and institutional practices as they operate within a society that is characterized by relations of domination, a society in which men and women are basically unfree in both objective and subjective terms. (Giroux, 1988)

The dominant theme of this definition is that an organization is a social system in which people do specific jobs. An important aspect of the definition is the fact that an organization is a social construct; it does not have a physical existence. Furthermore, an organization is a series of subsystems that are inextricably linked. A change in any one of the subsystems affects the entire organization. The second theme is the powerful but invisible presence of dominant ideology in all aspects of an organization, institution, or system.

> If we do not understand the nature of institutions developed out of belief systems of this society as it exists—we are more apt to be blindly integrated into them; consistently excluded from them or find ourselves at some point in between, rather than achieve the quality of representation it takes to truly transform them. (Lee, 1995:8)

Organizations are social systems within which individuals act through a network of social relations. Behaviours in this social system are influenced by the organization's collective belief system, corporate values, the values of the individuals within the organization, their functional responsibilities, and the society's prevailing ideology, which determines what is considered "right" and "proper." One of the important characteristics of organizations is that they resist change.

Resistance to Change

Resistance is a form of both individual and collective human behaviour that either actively or passively attempts to undermine any aspect of the change process. The ideology of democratic racism, which sustains two conflicting values—one that espouses fairness, equity, tolerance, and justice, another that maintains and reproduces racism—has been instrumental in disrupting and subverting efforts to eradicate racism. The opposition shows itself not through an overt display of intolerance but through subtle, sustained, and refined resistance to anti-racism.

The case studies included in almost every chapter of this book reveal the multiplicity of ways that individual, organizational, institutional, and systemic racism functions within and across the major sectors and structures of society. The cases illustrate the nature and dynamics of the resistance by White authority figures to anti-racism.

While resistance is generic to all large-scale change initiatives, a major factor of resistance to anti-racism is rooted in the extent to which organizational leaders believe that "anti-racism" is a legitimate force to motivate change. As has been demonstrated throughout this book, denial of racism operates as the unseen but ubiquitous force, which ensures that substantive change is deflected and deterred. Some of the barriers to individual and institutional change are

1. dominant ideology and discourse
2. reluctance to create an anti-racist vision
3. lack of commitment
4. inadequate policies
5. inadequate training
6. lack of representation
7. limited access to goods, programs, and services
8. absence of sanctions
9. lack of individual accountability
10. structural rigidity
11. ineffective monitoring and evaluation mechanisms

12. insufficient resources
13. tokenism
14. minority change agents
15. lack of organizational accountability
16. limited public accountability

Dominant Ideology and Discourse

Individual, institutional, and organizational resistance is most clearly demonstrated by the kind of everyday narratives and discourses that operate within organizational systems and cultures. Rhetorical strategies are wittingly or unwittingly used to establish, sustain, and reinforce inequalities and oppressive power relations. Institution by institution, the power of Whiteness is established, maintained, and reinforced through a set of racialized discourses that are framed in "normality." In this discursive framework minorities are essentialized, homogenized, and stigmatized (Razack, 1998; Dei and Calliste, 2000; Dei et al., 2004). Discourses of dominant or democratic racism include explanations, accounts, rationalizations, justifications, and hidden codes of meaning about the "other." These discursive tactics serve to mask the reality of how the ideology of Whiteness manifests itself.

Reluctance to Create an Anti-Racist Vision

The need for a clear and concise vision statement is critical to the success of an organization. A vision statement sets out the organization's goal and binds it and its members to work toward achieving that goal.

Very few of the organizations examined in this book have explicitly incorporated anti-racism in their vision statements. Such an omission occurs in part because anti-racism is not considered important to the overall mandate of the organization. When an organization consciously omits anti-racism from its vision statement, it clearly wishes to retain a reactive stance to anti-racism. Even if the organization has progressive programs, the absence of a vision statement shaped by anti-racism principles and goals results in an inadequate framework for the changes required. When an organization responds purely on the basis of political or social pressures, it is often unwilling to link the change process to its mandate. On the other hand, anti-racism as a guiding organizational framework suggests a commitment to examine not only programs and practices but also the ideology motivating those programs and practices.

Lack of Commitment

A commitment to anti-racism is a desire on the part of decision-makers and power brokers to act consistently and systematically to challenge and redress racism. Lack of commitment is illustrated in many ways; for example, many organizations embark on anti-racism initiatives only under coercion rather than by design—that is, only when forces either within the organization or outside it demand a response in order for the organization to maintain its credibility.

A common form of coercion is a race-related complaint to a human-rights commission. Many of these complaints originate in organizations whose managers maintain "there are no problems here"—an approach that results either from wilful blindness or from ignorance of the manifestations of racism in organizations. The coercion resulting from the settlement of a human-rights case does not require an organization to change its ideology, but only to create programs or develop practices that give the appearance of change.

Lack of commitment is demonstrated when formal studies exposing racism in an organization result in management adopting a defensive position. This defensiveness takes various forms: discrediting the findings, suggesting that the researchers misinterpreted the mandate or overstepped the boundaries of the project, and "sanitizing" the results so that they do not appear so "negative." The latter strategy allows management to practise damage control by deflecting attention from the issue. A striking example of this strategy occurred when a government-ministry unit asked the authors of this book to remove the word "racism" from a final report investigating employee complaints of racial discrimination.[1] A more systematic example is provided by the Ontario Government when the former Premier, Mike Harris, determined that the term "racism" would be removed from every government document and policy. This change of language was almost immediately followed by the dismantling of all government agencies that had a mandate to work in the area of anti-racism. The last phase of this cycle of resistance to anti-racism was the total elimination of all anti-racism and employment equity programs within provincial government ministries.

Often, vision statements are vague, "motherhood" statements of high-sounding principles that are difficult to put into practice. The intent of the organization (to maintain the status quo) is often masked in the vision statement because the organization has mastered the vocabulary of multiculturalism and diversity. Phrases such as "We respect diversity," "An equal opportunity employer," and "Tolerance in our organization is a core value" become empty promises, no more than symbolic gestures. Thus, the commitment to anti-racism rarely goes further than a *verbal* commitment to equality, which in most cases means equality of opportunity rather than a commitment to action and equity.

None of the organizations examined in the previous chapters of this book was committed to both the process and the content of anti-racism change. Although all sectors of society have responded to the pressures motivating change, organizational structures have remained untouched; the ideological underpinnings of their actions have remained intact.

Of those organizations that do recognize the need to respond to racism, most choose not to use the term "anti-racism." They prefer instead such labels as "multiculturalism," "managing diversity," and "race relations." Their strategy may be identified as one of resistance. Avoiding the term "anti-racism" circumvents the need to identify "racism."

Euphemisms provide the organization with a rationale for limiting its responses to cosmetic changes. Multicultural approaches suggest that gaining an understanding of other cultures is sufficient to combat racism. Diversity labels cushion the organization by allowing it to hide behind the rationalization that managing diversity is all that is required (Bannerji, 2000). Such a view implies that racism results from diversity, and that it can be managed. Thus, racism is considered something to be "managed," not necessarily opposed. A more constructive approach would be one in which racism is acknowledged and anti-racist strategies are implemented.

Resistance to anti-racism is often very subtle. It may entail the setting of unrealistic goals. It may show itself in the context of last-minute, crisis-oriented planning, such as appending anti-racism plans to other plans, after all the other plans have been made. It may exist in the simplistic "fix it now" mentality; and it may show its preference for delay in making requests for how-to guides and more data.

Inadequate Policies

In all areas of organizational and institutional life, there is an intrinsic relationship between policy and practice. As Brandt points out, every institution is governed by a policy, "whether stated or unstated" (1986:103). Although Brandt found no organization with an explicitly racist policy, strong evidence of its existence indicated covert racist policies that reflected deeply entrenched values, ideals, and assumptions. (A covert racist policy is one that has discriminatory outcomes that are usually but not always unintentional.) In each institution Brandt studied, racist ideologies influenced policies as well as individual behaviours and organizational practices.

In reviewing the formation of policies aimed at eliminating racism in the past two decades in Canada, it can be concluded that policies do not always lead to substantive and sustained change. Many of the policy documents are framed in the context of diversity with no specific identification of the issues of racism and other forms of oppression. Issues are conceptualized in terms of improving "relations" between racial and ethnocultural groups, rather than of targeting the elimination of racial bias and systemic discrimination. Policy statements often lack specificity and clarity in relation to their goals, objectives, and implementation strategies. In British Columbia, for example, the provincial government gradually reduced the resources necessary to sustain supporting programs and initiatives. In the recent assessment of the Vancouver School Board's anti-racism policy, many weaknesses were identified by both students of colour and Aboriginal students as well as parents and communities (Chan, 2004).

For example, the focus of both the policy and policy implementation in many educational agencies is the "problems" of racial-minority students. Thus, it is not the educational system that is the "problem"; the problem is the difficulties that racial-minority students create for the system. The language of many of the policies suggests a preoccupation with *promoting* and *encouraging* greater tolerance, understanding, and harmony among racial-minority students and staff, rather than *ensuring* fairness, justice, and equity as the outcomes (see Dei and Calliste, 2000; Dei et al., 2004). Like the use of passive tense in the language of the Multiculturalism Act (see Chapter 11, Case Study 11.2), educational and human services and other systems tend to rely on discourses employing coded language that glosses over the messy business of racial inequality.

Many institutional decision-makers have viewed the concept of anti-racism as too polemical and political and leading to unnecessary conflict and resistance. Instead, policy statements and documents choose to ignore, deny, and deflect the reality and persistence of racism in educational structures, processes, and ideologies. Policy-driven goals such as racial harmony, tolerance and understanding, and non-discrimination, while appearing positive, avoid the need to deconstruct racist ideology, practices, and procedures (Black, 2003; Bernard, 2001). Christensen (2003) makes a similar point in analyzing current policies in the field of human services. She makes the point that it is because racial identity generally fails to be mentioned by policy-makers or analysts as a factor with a profound effect on the well-being of racialized groups that its significance becomes apparent.

Even an institution's use of the term "anti-racism" in policy documents does not necessarily ensure it is supportive of or committed to actions and initiatives that will produce substantive change. In some cases, the issue of racism is framed in such a way that it fails to take into account how racism is specifically linked to the role and function of the organization (such as the school) or institution (e.g., a board of education).

Another common weakness of policy documents is that they neglect to delineate the ways in which an anti-racism agenda will be pursued throughout all levels of the organization. The most common flaw, however, is the failure to link the anti-racism policy to the mission and mandate of the organization. For example, policing organizations have developed policies that fail to be explicit about the nature of the problem they are seeking to address. They have also not been specific about the kind of changes expected to occur at the various levels in the policing organization. As a result, many police officers appear to believe that their force's race relations/diversity policy is inconsistent with the work of policing and that it does not further the goal of law enforcement, "to serve and protect."

Policies are perhaps a useful starting point for change, but policy statements, especially ones framed in the coded language of diversity, non-discrimination, and tolerance, in and of themselves are of limited value in actually combating racism. They cannot function alone as mechanisms to promote change.

Inadequate Training

Institutions in fields such as such as education, policing, government, social work, health care, and so on have often used training of their employees, managers, and sometimes senior administrators to respond to the issue of racism within their respective domains. In-service training programs in many Canadian public institutions began in the early 1980s. They were established ostensibly to provide educators, cultural workers, human-service practitioners, law enforcement officers, government bureaucrats, and administrators with the knowledge and skills to function more effectively in their roles as service providers in a multicultural and racially pluralistic society.

Early training programs and many still offered today commonly avoid using the terminology of anti-racism. Instead, trainers or institutional authorities employed a less "threatening" alternative language to describe these training programs including "multicultural education," "cross-cultural training," "cultural sensitivity training," "race awareness training," and "diversity training." One trainer explained that the language used to label training matters is important in that it suggests a particular orientation and political conviction of those involved. Avoiding the use of anti-racism is an attempt to deal with fear and/or discomfort. Denial of racism runs through all aspects of institutional life in Canada. Some training has focused primarily on changing attitudes; other training has targeted the changing of institutional practices (see Mock and Shour Laufer, 2001).

To understand the weaknesses in many of these training programs, it is important to begin with a brief discussion of key elements in any anti-racism process of change in the context of training. Anti-racism is an action-oriented approach to identifying and counteracting the production and reproduction of all forms of racism. It addresses the issues of racism and the interlocking systems of social oppression (Dei and Calliste, 2000; Dei, Karumanchery, and Karumanchery-Luke, 2004). Anti-racism and anti-racism training implies a goal of producing an understanding of what racism is and how it can be challenged. Training involves the development of knowledge, critical thinking, self-awareness, skills, and tools. It must be rooted in a careful analysis of the complexities of the social relations that mediate racism. It demands participation, respect, cooperation, honesty, and commitment. Perhaps the most important element in training programs is to ensure that "consciousness-raising" is linked to social/political action. An outcome of anti-racism is not only a change in individual attitudes, but also a transformation of individual and collective practices. The goal of any anti-racism initiative is not harmony, but equity; not colour-blindness or tolerance, but justice and equity; not guilt expiation, but social change. Most training and other programs for combating racism fail to meet these specifications. Anti-racism training is specifically geared to the understanding of how racism, conscious or unconscious, may affect the policies, practices, and procedures of an organization. However, training programs have generally been ineffective because they treat anti-racism like any other subject—as something to be learned by employees in a three-hour, one-day, or, at most, three-day workshop. Learning about racism is placed in the same category as developing skills to manage a new computer program. Trainers who are inexperienced and unskilled in anti-racism theory and practice commonly deliver training. Often the training is unrelated to the daily roles and functions of the participants.

Training has drawn upon many different models, from developing cultural sensitivity and racial awareness to creating management skills for managing diversity and implementing employment equity (see Mock and Shour Laufer, 2001). Some of these approaches are briefly described below.

Human-Awareness Training

Human-awareness training models perceive the goal of training to be the promotion of positive relations between the organization and groups from different cultural backgrounds. These programs focus on acquiring sensitivity to the values, customs, and practices of different groups. Most race-relations training programs use some combination of human-awareness training with cultural-awareness training, and both are based on three false premises. The first is that when people understand the customs of another group, they will be able to deal with them more effectively. The second is that an understanding of the complexities of culture can be learned in a few hours of training. The third is that only those who come into daily contact with racial minorities need to be trained.

Cultural-Awareness or Sensitivity Training

The goal of cultural-awareness training is similar to that of human-awareness training. It has a strong emphasis on transmitting information about ethnic groups and their cultural patterns. This emphasis on transmitting "snapshots" of cultural information ignores the more important study of the complexities of culture. The crucial problems experienced by people of colour in organizations and institutions are not simply the result of a White person's lack of understanding of non-European cultures. Cultural-awareness or cross-cultural training commonly ignores the individual and systemic barriers created by racism and other forms of oppression. It ignores power relations between dominant and subordinate groups. Moreover, cross-cultural training has tended to rely on a superficial understanding of cultural differences and a limited understand of the dynamics of culture.

Race-Awareness/Prejudice-Reduction Training

The premise of race-awareness training is that racism is a White problem. The purpose of the training is to help participants examine their attitudes and behaviours and understand the implications of their own racism. The participants' energy is directed toward self-examination rather than toward fundamental changes in the structure and ideology of the organization. While White critical self-reflection is an important part of an anti-racism change process, it is only the initial phase of problem identification. Effective training should move on to show ways in which the entire organizational ideology/culture can be challenged and changed.

Legislative Compliance

The goal of legislative-compliance training is often framed in the context of providing a clear understanding of human-rights and employment equity legislation so that the organization and its employees can ensure that they are in compliance with these laws. Such programs rarely address the issue of racism or seek to change or deconstruct the barriers within the system.

Managing Diversity

Whereas legislative compliance stresses the avoidance of unlawful discrimination, managing diversity focuses on organizational management approaches. However, diversity in everyday discourse is often employed as rhetorical strategy within the coded language of democratic racism. One of the driving forces in this approach to training is an emphasis on the rapidly changing demographics of Canadian society. The argument is made that in order to be productive and grow in the twenty-first century organizations/businesses must tap into the diverse labour pool and the customer/client base. These training programs commonly see diversity as simply a management problem, something that can be managed, controlled, and contained. Thus, the emphasis is on changing institutions by providing people-management skills, interviewing skills, and so on. These programs are not designed to bring about a greater understanding of the issues of racism and other forms of oppression, nor do they seek to alter the fundamental issues related to power relations; they attempt to relate general understandings about diversity to the professional and practical world of the organization (see Bannerji, 2000).

A further flaw in many of the training programs is that the initiative is introduced into an organizational environment that is not particularly supportive. As a result, it is usually front-line staff who receive the training. Thus, training is generally provided to new police recruits, teachers, and human-service providers, but rarely to supervisors and senior managers.

Little research on training has occurred in Canada. One of the few Canadian studies has been done by Mock and Shour Laufer (2001). The evidence from this study, as well as studies on the United Kingdom and the United States, however, suggests that training as currently constituted has little chance of success in creating an anti-racist environment. In Canada, police–race relations training has been studied by Ungerleider and McGregor (1992), who examined studies of interventions designed to "change the attitudes and behaviours of police and military personnel towards minority groups." The study found that a small measure of attitudinal or behavioural change was exhibited by little more than half of the training participants. In many instances, however, the impact of the training was minimal, compared with the effects of learning by experience, by absorbing the values of the occupational culture, and other factors.

Training is perhaps the most common institutional response to racism. It is often used by organizations because it is an easy way to show that some action is being taken to improve the organizational climate for racial-minority members. However, it does little to change the ideology that creates the framework within which the organization operates. That ideology is, for the most part, drawn from and influenced by the value system of the larger, mainstream society.

The value conflict that characterizes democratic racism is as evident in organizations as it is in the wider society of which they are a part. Training does not challenge that ideology; at best, it tinkers with it. Training is merely an organizational mechanism to adjust to the changing environment without changing or transforming any aspect of it. Thus, it is an essential element of an assimilationist organizational model, but it does little to move an organization toward anti-racism.

Lack of Representation

The evidence of widespread and systemic racial discrimination in employment in the public and private sectors is inimical to the fundamental tenets of a liberal democratic society. However, it is in this area of organizational change that resistance is most evident.

Even *proposed* race-conscious measures generate enormous tension, hostility, and dissension within organizations.

In the limited number of institutions in which either anti-racism or employment equity programs are still in place—such as some boards of education, universities, and police forces—there have been negative reactions, especially from White able-bodied males. With the implementation of the Employment Equity Act and the contract compliance program at the federal level of government, it is clear that huge obstacles continue to exist (Beck, Reitz, and Weiner, 2002; Annual Report, 2003). The inadequacy of the legislative and regulatory requirements, the lack of monitoring of implementation of employment equity programs, and weak enforcement mechanisms are some of the significant flaws in the current approach to equity. Even more problematic is the powerful backlash to these initiatives, across every sector, manifested in the attitudes and behaviours of many White male able-bodied employers, managers, and staff.

In many institutions, such as schools and boards of education, universities, museums, social work and health agencies, media, and police forces, initiatives designed to fundamentally alter discriminatory barriers are still generally opposed in favour of policies that appear to affect change without changing the structural conditions under which the institution operates. Thus there will be effects to hire a more representational staff but without changing some of the fundamental policies of the organization. Resistance is framed within the ideological construct of a set of beliefs that basically rationalize and justify the maintenance of the status quo.

Limited Access to Goods, Programs, and Services

The lack of access to goods and services has been illustrated in the chapters dealing with institutional racism. The lack of support for ethno-racial agencies in the human-service delivery system is an example of the failure of government and other funding bodies to address racism in the mainstream delivery system. Another manifestation of the lack of access to goods, programs, and services is the power of mainstream cultural and arts organizations to marginalize and exclude racial minorities in the production and transmission of literature, music, visual art, dance, theatre, and film. The streaming of Black students in schools, bias in curricula and teaching methods, and the racialization of academics of colour and Aboriginal educators further demonstrate the lack of access and equity for racial minorities in the educational system. The absence of people of colour in print and electronic media organizations, and the stigmatization of their communities in the images and stories transmitted by the mainstream media, reinforce racism in Canadian institutions, systems, and structures.

Absence of Sanctions

Rewards and sanctions are important ways of changing behaviour in organizations. No organizations in Canada, however, are known to impose wage sanctions on staff or management for racist behaviour. Typically, the sanctions that do exist are those mandated by race relations or anti-racism policies, but few of them include staff accountability mechanisms. Even where anti-racism policies exist, adequate sanctions have been lacking, and, where sanctions are in place, they tend to be weak and ineffective.

In the early 1990s, the Ontario Human Rights Commission instituted a system authorizing organizations to conduct internal investigations of complaints based on prohibited grounds of discrimination. Organizations are free to develop strategies to respond to such complaints as they see fit. Unfortunately, most organizations do not have the expertise to conduct such investigations; moreover, complaints, unless they are overt forms of racism, are likely to be dismissed. Sanctions are likely to be inadequate, and continuous monitoring may be nonexistent. In some situations, the victim of discrimination may be punished and labelled a troublemaker. The underfunding of human rights commissions also contributes to a lack of resources to facilitate the processing of individual human rights complaints.

Lack of Individual Accountability

Many organizations assume that their members are fair-minded—that they subscribe to the principles of equity and equality of treatment. This assumption leads to a lack of individual accountability. Few organizations require their employees to be held accountable for racist behaviour. Even organizations that have an anti-racism policy believe that their employees are tolerant and without prejudice. For example, there are few mechanisms to deal with teachers or administrators who are alleged to have demonstrated racist attitudes or behaviours. In many schools and boards, students, parents, and the community have little recourse.

A common problem with many organizational responses to racism is that individual members are not held accountable for their actions. Accountability refers to the assignment of responsibility for a specific set of actions for which non-compliance may result in specific sanctions. Sanctions are penalties imposed for an infraction of organizational policies and norms. Thus a manager or supervisor may be held accountable for implementing non-racist behaviour but not negatively sanctioned if racist behaviour does take place.

It is difficult to find job descriptions that specifically prescribe anti-racist behaviour. Most often, the expectation is that those employed as equity practitioners[2] are the only ones accountable. The task of creating equity in the organization is frequently understood to be the job of the equity practitioner and no one else. There are therefore two competing philosophies of equity in the organization. Since most members are considered tolerant, there is a need to prove that intolerance or racism was, in fact, intended. Since racism is defined very narrowly by senior decision-makers in most organizations, it becomes necessary to prove that employees, policies, and practices *intended* to discriminate or otherwise act in a racist manner. Often this results in a situation in which the innocence of the offender, already reinforced by the ideology of fairness, must be protected. Thus, an individual's reputation must not be tarnished by allegations of racism, nor must his or her fairness and objectivity be questioned. Anti-racism policies therefore provide an investigatory framework for which there is a strong presumption of innocence.

The presumption of innocence at the investigatory stage is peculiar to anti-racism allegations. A police investigation, on the other hand, is directed by a strong presumption of non-innocence. When a police officer arrests a suspect, it is usually assumed that the suspect is the correct person, and evidence is gathered to prove the police case. At the investigative stage in a charge of racism, however, the result of the presumption of innocence is a search for alternative explanations for the act of racism. Any other "reasonable" explanation negates a claim of racism, not simply for that case, but for all cases like it, regardless of the parties involved. The elusive nature of racism means that an alternative explanation can almost always be found. Thus, the notion of impact is eradicated and the result is a reduction of individual accountability for actions that have a racist impact.

In addition, in racially hostile work environments, those most affected by racism are unlikely to complain about it. Overt or subtler forms of racism may be so entrenched in the organization's operation that victims are expected to comply. In correctional institutions, for example, both inmates and staff often engage in overt racist acts. Minority staff find it difficult to complain for fear of reprisal, despite the existence of a policy forbidding racist acts.

Structural Rigidity

Anti-racism requires fundamental changes to the structure of organizations. Yet a characteristic response is the maintenance and preservation of traditional structures. Sometimes organizations respond to the challenge by creating advisory bodies but not altering the basic structure of the organization. By definition, these bodies have limited power and exist at the discretion of those who appointed them.

Anti-racism is rarely considered important in the restructuring of ministries and government departments. The restructuring of the federal government in 1993 proceeded without much attention to anti-racism. As the United Nations Special Rapporteur stated in Chapter 11, anti-racism initiatives and policies operate at the periphery. They are not considered "really" important by senior decision-makers. When they are initiated, they are "add-ons." For example, pay equity legislation proceeded with little discussion of the relationship between race, gender, and pay.

Ineffective Monitoring and Evaluation Mechanisms

The pursuit of racial equality demands that the mechanisms for measuring change be put in place. It means moving from discussing the principles of equality of opportunity to measuring achievement.

Equal-opportunity policies, mass "sensitization" training programs, and glossy public-relations campaigns are not especially effective unless they are combined with concrete programs that are regularly monitored and evaluated and publicly reported. The use of effective monitoring systems—which can be mere progress reports—can begin to provide information on whether the goals of a program are being reached.

The most important measure of any initiative is its results. Extensive efforts to implement training and develop procedures, data collection systems, report forms, and finely written policy statements are meaningless unless measurable improvement takes place. Just as the success of a private business is evaluated in terms of increases in sales, the only realistic basis for evaluating a program to increase equity for racial minorities is its actual impact on these groups.

Efforts are needed to develop appropriate methods of "impact evaluation"—that is, measures of the extent to which an anti-racism initiative produces various results. The emphasis must be on an initiative's "return on investment" in relation to predetermined goals. From that basis, one can begin to establish legitimate and meaningful performance standards. The emphasis must be on determining whether the activity had the impact that it set out to have.

Insufficient Resources

However, anti-racism initiatives typically suffer from inadequate resources, both material and human. To achieve a racially just and equitable society requires large-scale change and concerted commitment. In periods of economic restraint, many programs are cut due to lack of funds. Anti-racist initiatives are often the most vulnerable and often the first programs to be reduced or eliminated.

At the federal level, the Multiculturalism Act makes no provision for the Canadian Heritage ministry to dictate the scope of activities performed by individual ministries with respect to anti-racism. The Department of Multiculturalism within Canadian Heritage functions as an internal consulting body to government and as a minor funding body to organizations. It does not have the statutory power or substantial financial resources to intervene in government affairs, and the net effect is that government institutions are free to undertake whatever initiatives they deem sufficient.

Tokenism

Tokenism often involves the practice of appointing or hiring one or two members of designated minority groups for relatively powerless positions in order to demonstrate the organization's tolerance of diversity. Tokenism circumvents substantive change. It is the most commonly used organizational mechanism to resist pressures for change and is "an essential element in the ideological hegemony of the institutional process of racism" (Phillips and Blumberg, 1983:34).

With respect to the employment of racial minorities, tokenism takes several forms. For example, minorities may be ghettoized in certain positions. The segregation of ethno-racial-minority employees is well documented (see Chapter 3 on employment discrimination). Women of all ethnic and racial backgrounds are employed in factories as wage workers. Increasingly, Black men are hired as security guards and Black women are found in segregated occupations such as nursing aide, domestics, factory worker, and food-service provider. South Asians and other people of colour with high education levels and professional skills find themselves unable to access their given professions and frequently end up as taxi drivers.

Stereotypes about the skills of certain groups of people have structured the occupational categories in which minorities tend to be found. Many organizations today hire minorities for specific types of jobs. It is common to find a disproportionate number of persons from Southeast Asia employed in jobs that involve computation, such as computer programming and accounting. A disproportionate number of Black people employed in the public service are in jobs related to racism, anti-racism, equity, diversity, and so on.

This kind of job ghettoization of racial-minority professionals is partly related to a reluctance to value the universal skills that people of colour possess. It is also related to the desire of many firms to relegate minorities to occupational categories in which they are deemed to be efficient workers. Thus, Asians are thought to be especially good at math-related jobs, and Blacks, because of their size and alleged strength, are thought to do well at security. (When both physical strength *and* quick thinking are required—as in policing and firefighting—Blacks, oddly enough, are often not considered.)

Minority Change Agents

The people in an organization who are responsible for initiating and developing strategies for change have been called "change agents." Their position is fraught with difficulties, since change agents rarely occupy a position of power in the hierarchical structure of the organization. Although they are responsible for advocating and implementing new policies and practices, their role is often marginal.

Their role may evoke resistance. For example, change agents of colour engaged in anti-racism work, purely because of their identity, elicit resistance from White members of the organization. To organizational leaders, change agents of colour represent a paradox. On the one hand, White people see them as "successful," unlike others of their community. Implicit in this assumption is that the individual does not possess the negative qualities of members of his group. On the other hand, change agents of colour represent the targets of racism. Consequently, resistance is engendered in ways that White people engaged in this same work do not experience.

Change agents of colour are particularly subject to scrutiny and to challenges of their position. They are seen as "looking for problems." They are subject to accusations such as "having a chip on their shoulder" or seen as "being too sensitive." Their knowledge, skills, resilience, and ability to mediate between various groups are constantly tested. Their "objectivity" is questioned, and their "favouritism" toward their own group, or toward racial minorities in general, is suspected. Their boundaries of responsibility are narrowed or expanded, depending on the situation.

Their methodologies or strategies are often held suspect. Their reports are often censored and altered until they are unrecognizable, as issues are restated so as not to sound so "negative," or their recommendations are set aside because they are viewed as being unrealistic, inaccurate, or unreasonable. All of these behaviours are manifestations of resistance to the anti-racism effort, exacerbated by the presence of minority change agents.

The lack of support and the powerlessness experienced by change agents result in a significant incidence of "burnout." Individuals suffer both physical and emotional exhaustion in their work as change agents; their "suffering or stress is a natural consequence of the dilemmas and paradoxes inherent in playing or resisting the token role" (Phillips and Blumberg, 1983:36).

Lack of Organizational Accountability

Many of Canada's public institutions often operate as if they were separate and distinct from the larger society and far removed from the concerns and issues of importance to people of colour. Functioning in this framework results in a lack of accountability not only to the public but also to the political process (see, for example, Case Study 8.1 on Reena Virk in Chapter 8 and Case Study 9.1 on the ROM in Chapter 9).

The criminal justice system is one institution that has been criticized for assuming that it can pursue the goal of upholding community standards only by being above the community. Its legitimacy is gained from a general acceptance of the laws and regulations it enforces, the values it embraces, the morality it is supposed to support, and the order it maintains. Many other professional groups, such as those in education, human services, and the media, feel a stronger sense of accountability to their self-defined codes of conduct than to those they serve.

Limited Public Accountability

An underlying tenet of Canadian democracy is the obligation of its public institutions to explain and justify their activities. This accountability might be said to provide legitimacy to the democratic state. It entails an acceptance of the notion of community participation in and control of the decision-making processes of public institutions.

But how does a public-sector organization develop these relationships? How does it include a diverse clientele, a diverse group of constituents, in the system? What are the mechanisms for bringing the community into the decision-making process? Do the institutions and organizations examined in this book demonstrate public accountability?

A number of public-sector agencies have responded to this issue by initiating a range of public-consultation mechanisms. These mechanisms have included:

- needs-assessment surveys
- consultation with key informants
- opinion polls
- community focus groups
- advisory councils and committees
- commissions and task forces
- public hearings
- conferences and workshops
- public information programs
- advertising

- neighbourhood meetings
- support to community groups
- telephone information hotlines
- community relations offices

Although many of these activities have been useful, others have not. Their objectives have frequently lacked clarity, their implementation has often been ineffective, and their impact has rarely been evaluated with any rigour.

There exists in racial-minority communities an increasing sense of mistrust, apathy, and anger toward these exercises, especially toward community consultations. Reactions such as "We have been consulted to death" and "What happened to our recommendations?" are the result of too many minor, cosmetic improvements. Community consultations require the expenditure of enormous time and resources by community groups and organizations that are already hard pressed. The growing skepticism and distrust of consultation initiatives are the result of the widespread view that public institutions are simply "going through the motions," that they continue to devote most of their resources to support "mainstream" organizations.

The spirit and commitment with which public consultations are carried out are therefore questioned. When goals are not clearly identified, when expectations are not articulated, and when no substantive action is initiated as a result of the exercise, these

Figure 12.1

ADDRESSING RESISTANCE AND ENLISTING SUPPORT

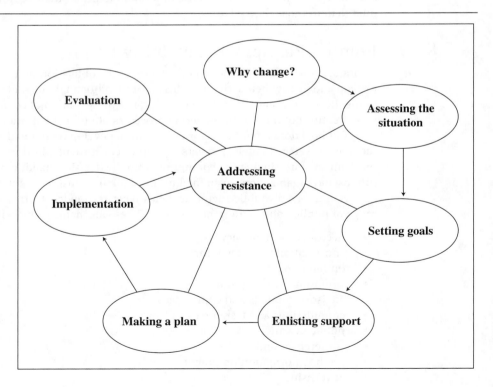

consultations are considered pseudo-democratic exercises to distract minorities from the real organizational goal of maintaining the status quo. When attempts to improve community relations involve the community in an unplanned, undisciplined, and unprofessional manner, community participation in the decision-making processes of public institutions is undermined.

Although explicitly derogatory statements, slurs, and epithets can be uttered in each of the sectors described in the preceding chapters, they are less commonly heard today. The more elusive nature of dominant discourse allows it to easily mask its racialized ideas (Wetherell and Potter, 1992). Major actors in each of these institutions commonly present themselves as defenders of liberal ideals and principles, "Canadian" values, and national identity.

The appeal is not to prejudice, but to the preservation of a harmonious diversity and cultural pluralism. The discourses of "denial," "equal opportunities," "colour-blindness," "otherness," "tolerance," "merit," "reverse discrimination," and "political correctness" create an organizational climate that prevents active engagement with racial and other forms of inequality. Dominant discourse as social practice reinforces the status quo.

Race-Conscious Theory of Organizations

Overcoming resistance to anti-racist change can best be accomplished in an organization that has become conscious of race as a social construction. In a race-conscious theory of organizations, the nature of social relations is influenced by race. Interests deemed legitimate have a racial component. Compliance and the risks of non-compliance are assessed in terms of the importance and legitimacy of the interests, power, and/or lack thereof, as well as social status both within the organization and outside of it. To what extent are Canadian organizations race-conscious? Most organizations fall within a continuum that starts at monoculturalism, then gradually changes to assimilationism or multiculturalism, and finally assumes an anti-racist organizational stance. The majority of Canadian organizations appear to fall within the first two categories. Few, if any, have developed a genuine anti-racist model of organizational behaviour.

Three Organizational Paradigms of Change

In a heterogeneous society, race affects every aspect of organizational life. For this reason, some analysts view organizations along a race–cultural continuum in order to categorize organizational responses to racism. These approaches have a variety of labels but are identified here as assimilationist (exclusionary, monocultural, ethnocentric, homogeneous); multicultural (add-on); and anti-racist (racial equity) approaches. Each of these approaches has very different implications for the organization's development of strategies and initiatives to deal with racial bias and discrimination.

The various institutional responses to racism are based on different assumptions about the nature of racism and reflect broader perspectives underlying people's thoughts and behaviour. They also reflect the ideology of the organization, that is, the collective belief and value system woven through the institution, shaping and affecting all its aspects. More than one model may operate concurrently, particularly in large and complex organizations. For example, a board of education might have a very innovative approach in one unit, such as curriculum development, and an extremely resistant approach in the department responsible for placement and assessment issues.

Figure 12.2

A RACE-CONSCIOUS THEORY OF ORGANIZATIONS

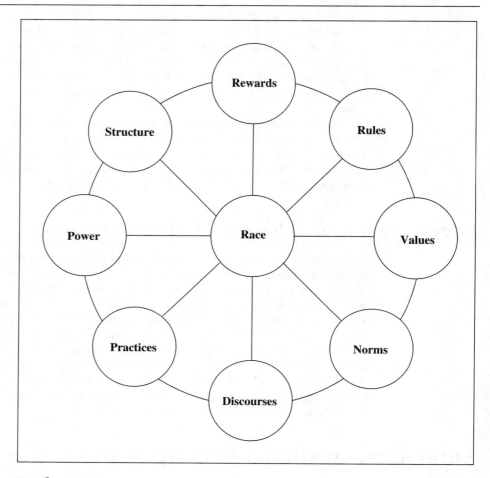

Assimilationism

Organizations that do not recognize racial and cultural diversity generally operate on the assumption of homogeneity among people. They assume, for example, that even in a predominantly multiracial society such as Canada, individuals belonging to racial minorities have been assimilated into the mainstream of Canadian society.

Consequently, these organizations have a monocultural perspective (Jackson and Holvino, 1989). Their policies and practices are expressed in universal terms that emphasize the underlying values and norms of the dominant culture. Such organizations focus on preserving and maintaining the control of those in power, and their efforts are directed toward protecting the status quo. The existing mission, policies, and practices of the assimilationist institution are perceived as the only "right" ones, and no consideration is given to other groups' perspectives or interests. Thus, the concerns of racial and cultural minorities are constantly ignored or deflected (Jones, 1986). There is no sense of accountability to external constituencies.

Mighty (1992) suggested that this form of cultural imperialism often unconsciously, but sometimes consciously, seeks to homogenize non-dominant cultures and transform them into a single one. It fails to consider both the sociocultural context in which the organizations operate and the diversity of perspectives that coexist within them. They undertake no efforts to respond to diversity issues in general. Moreover, there is a total absence of interest in addressing the issues or concerns of racial minorities or the other constituencies that the organization is supposed to serve. Assimilationist organizations do not see the need to participate in any fundamental alteration of their organizational culture (Jackson and Holvino, 1989).

This paradigm continues to be widespread (Adler, 1993; McDonald, 1991). Assimilationist institutions may recognize that racial diversity exists in society, but they perceive its impact as negative. They assume that their way of viewing the world is the best way and that all other perspectives are essentially inferior (Adler, 1993; Kanter, 1977).

Assimilationist organizations try to minimize diversity by selecting a workforce that is as homogeneous as possible. When external pressures such as anti-racism policies or employment equity are imposed, organizational decision-makers may find themselves coerced into allowing a few members of racial minorities to gain access to their organizations. They then seek to assimilate the newcomers into their world (Jackson and Holvino, 1989).

The biases in such organizations' perspectives are reflected in inequitable policies, inaccessible services, and discriminatory practices, all of which are considered immutable. "Outsiders" must conform without disturbing the existing organizational culture. As a result, newcomers are usually confined to the lower ranks of the organization, where they remain powerless to change the status quo. Occasionally, the recruitment of a "token" woman or racial minority into a higher-level position may occur after ensuring that the person is an exceptional member of the out-group, a team player who will conform to the organizational culture and not challenge the status quo (Mighty, 1992; Jackson and Holvino, 1989; Kanter, 1977).

Multiculturalism

The principle underlying multicultural change strategies is a willingness to make limited modifications in the organization or institution but not to alter its fundamental structure, mission, and culture. A variety of initiatives may be undertaken from time to time, such as recruiting a "minority" for a staff position or as a member of the board, and translating print or audio materials into various languages.

Multicultural organizations and their members learn to master the equity rhetoric while engaging in cosmetic changes. Homeostasis characterizes these organizations, and it is very often reactive rather than proactive. Diversity is useful in such organizations. For example, they may draw on ethno-racial staff to assist in the translation of materials or to work with members of their own culture.

These organizations see diversity as a product and are therefore image-conscious. They often proclaim their programs and initiatives. They therefore make a point of hiring minorities, most of whom will have responsibility without power, limited control, and impressive titles without access to the centres of power. In many cases, these minorities will be physically and structurally isolated from the rest of the organization.

In this type of organization there is a recognition that certain changes must be made in order to comply with new policies, regulations, or legislation. However, issues related to racism are considered distinct from the day-to-day life of the organization. The needs, interests, and perspectives of racial minorities are dealt with on an ad hoc basis rather than being integrated into the programs and services of the organization.

Responsibility for change is often delegated to the front-line worker, who may then function in an unsupportive environment. The multicultural organization may seek to remove some discriminatory barriers by providing greater access to racial minorities, but its members are expected to conform to the dominant group's values and worldview.

Despite recognizing diversity, multicultural organizations rarely make conscious efforts to create organizational climates that support diversity or establish systems that enable different types of employees to succeed. For example, they may introduce training initiatives in relation to human rights, cross-cultural or intercultural activities, race relations, anti-racism, organizational management, or employment equity. But, while the training creates an awareness of diversity, it rarely creates new behavioural norms and organizational procedures that would promote access, participation, and equity (Razack, 1998; Bannerji, 2000).

Anti-Racism

An anti-racist organization is not one in which racism is absent. Rather, it takes a proactive stand against racism in all its forms. It is oppositional in nature and addresses racism at both the organizational and individual levels. Commitment in anti-racist organizations is based on an acknowledgment that racism exists, that it manifests itself in various forms at the individual, institutional, and systemic levels, and that it is embedded in the mass culture of the dominant group. An anti-racist perspective begins by accepting that the perceptions of people of colour are real and that there may be a multiplicity of realities in any one event.

The anti-racism approach to change is based on a commitment to eradicate all forms of social oppression and racial disadvantage in the organization. The anti-racist organization includes members of racial minorities as full and equal participants. It follows through on decisions that affect its broader social responsibilities and external relationships.

Anti-racism emphasizes a holistic approach to the development of anti-racist ideologies, goals, policies, and practices. As an organizational response it requires the formation of new organizational structures, the introduction of new cultural norms and value systems, changes in power dynamics, the implementation of new employment systems, substantive changes in services delivered, support for new roles and relationships at all levels of the organization, new patterns and more inclusive styles of leadership and decision-making, and the reallocation of resources. Strategic planning, organizational audits and reviews, and monitoring and accountability systems are all considered an integral part of the management of anti-racist change.

Of prime importance in the anti-racist institutional process is a commitment to the empowerment of racial minorities both within the organization, institution, and system and outside of these structures (Dei et al., 2004). Policy development and new mission statements are not considered ends in themselves; adequate attention, priority, and resources are given to implementation strategies and programs. Effective monitoring mechanisms are put in place to ensure accountability throughout the organization. Evaluation of the change effort is an ongoing process. Resistance to change is anticipated, and strategies to overcome it are planned.

As has been demonstrated throughout this book, racism appears in many guises—constantly mutating into new forms—speaking in different voices, operating using different codes and expressions, symbols, and images. Therefore, it is important to emphasize that each manifestation suggests a different definition and different strategies.

Finally, anti-racism recognizes that no institution operates in isolation from other institutions and that racism in one arena of social life, such as education, will affect others, such as employment; that racism in police forces can be fostered by the media and in turn that the media can be influenced by market forces and government "propaganda." Thus, the anti-racist approach to change seeks to encourage and facilitate linkages and partnerships among institutions in order to identify and dismantle racial barriers and racial inequalities. (For more detail on diagnosing and removing institutional racism, see Table 12.1.)

Summary

This chapter has presented reasons why organizations have been slow in enacting policies, programs, and practices that challenge racism as well as other forms of oppression. It is suggested that although organizations generally resist change, they are especially reluctant to initiate and implement anti-racist change. The reasons for this begin with what is in fact the most profound barrier: the preservation of Whiteness as an invisible but powerful and pervasive ideology and the everyday discourses and practices that reflect and reinforce this

Table 12.1

A MODEL FOR DIAGNOSING AND REMOVING INSTITUTIONAL RACISM

Indicators for Measuring Institutional Racism

Employment	Service Provision	Purchasing
1. Is there an over- or under-representation of ethno-racial minority employees in some job categories? 2. Is there consistent over- or under-employment of ethno-racial minority employees in terms of matching job qualifications (e.g., education, experience) with job category? 3. Do employee evaluations show consistent biases in favour of or against a particular race? 4. Does race affect the degree of agreement between employees and their supervisors on the employee evaluations? 5. Does race affect the type of employment actions taken? 6. Is there differential access to in-service training? 7. Is there differential enrolment in in-service training? 8. Are there adequate mechanisms to handle discrimination complaints? 9. What are the findings of grievance settlements? 10. Are there policies and procedures to facilitate employee relations?	1. Do services present barriers to ethno-racial access? Are these barriers located in occupational practices and procedures or in staff attitudes or behaviour, or are they simply the outcome of decisions on different ethno-racial groups? 2. Do the organization's communications materials and methods present barriers to ethno-racial communities (e.g., lack of translation, inappropriate portrayal, racial insensitivity, cultural inappropriateness)? 3. To what extent, and how, does the organization target information to and receive information from ethno-racial communities? 4. To what extent do the organization's communications strategies recognize the specific information needs of and barriers to information experienced by ethno-racial communities? 5. Do the information materials portray ethno-racial diversity? 6. Are ethno-racial communities involved in planning, designing, developing, and delivering information activities?	1. Is there evidence of denial of contracts to minority business? 2. Is there evidence of past discrimination in the contracting customs, systems, etc.? 3. Do contracting requirements have a disproportionately negative impact on minority businesses? 4. Is there a failure to distribute bidding information to potential minority businesses? 5. What is the percentage of contractors that are minority-owned? 6. Is there a lack of notification of bid opportunities? 7. Is there a repeated use of a restricted number of vendors? 8. How large is the minority-business supplier base?

Indicators for Measuring Institutional Racism *(continued)*

Employment	Service Provision	Purchasing
11. Is there a failure to recruit ethno-racial minorities? 12. What are the hiring criteria? 13. Is there consistent hiring of non-minorities? 14. Is there an employment equity plan? 15. Is race an important functional variable within the organization from both the employees' and the employers' perspective?	7. Are the service-delivery processes equitably reflective of the ethno-racial communities? 8. In what way are services sensitive to the life experiences and reflective of the needs of various ethno-racial communities? 9. Do ethno-racial communities participate in the planning, design, and delivery of services? 10. Do ethno-racial communities receive equal benefit from the services?	

Categories of Information Required for This Paradigm

Employment	Service Provision	Purchasing
1. Demographic statistics and ethno-racial workforce profile 2. Policies and practices: job and performance factors 3. Employer–employee relations 4. Administrative procedures 5. Perceptions of personnel and organization climate	1. Demographic statistics 2. Percentage of minority clients served by program, i.e., their under- or overutilization of the program 3. Percentage of resources allocated to minority communities 4. Communications efforts to reach minority communities 5. Level of participation by minorities in the decision-making process	1. Demographic statistics 2. Percentage of minority firms in the private sector by industry sector 3. Percentage of the organization's contractors (and prime subcontractors) that are minority-owned 4. Percentage of total contracting purchasing dollars that goes to minority contractors

dominant ideology. A lack of vision or mandate, a lack of upper-level managerial commitment, inadequate policies and training, a lack of individual accountability, and insufficient resources further reinforce resistance.

The chapter concludes with a discussion of various models of organizational change and notes that most Canadian organizations can be described as either assimilationist or multicultural. Few have moved to a genuine race-conscious or anti-racist model of organizational behaviour.

Notes

1. This incident occurred when the authors were working with an agency of government.
2. The term "equity practitioner" is used here to mean any individual involved in the pursuit of equity. Such a person could exist in an organization under a variety of labels, including adviser on race relations, employment equity, human rights, cross-cultural issues, diversity, or intercultural communications.

References

Adler, N.J. (1993). *Human Resource Management in the Global Economy.* Kingston, ON: Industrial Relations Centre, Queen's University.

Annual Report. (2003). Ottawa: Canadian Human Rights Commission. Available <http://www.chrc-ccdp.ca/publications/ reports-en.asp>, accessed August 30, 2004.

Bannerji, H. (2000). *The Dark Side of the Nation: Essays on Multiculturalism, Nationalism and Gender.* Toronto: Canadian Scholars Press.

Beck, H., J. Reitz, and N. Weiner. (2002). "Addressing Systemic Racial Discrimination in Employment: The Health Canada Case and Implications of Legislative Change." *Canadian Public Policy* 28(3):373–94.

Bernard, T. (2001). "Claiming Voice: An Account of Struggle, Resistance and Hope in the Academy." *Seen But Not Heard: Aboriginal Women of Colour in the Academy.* Ottawa: Canadian Research Institute for the Advancement of Women. 61–72.

Black, K. (2003). "Erasing Anti-Racism: A Decade Later, Anti-Racism Is Still Non-existent in the Classroom." *Now* 23(7)(October 16–22). Available <http://www.nowtoronto.com/issues/2003-10-16/news_story4.php>, accessed August 31, 2004.

Brandt, G. (1986). *The Realization of Anti-Racist Teaching.* London: Falmer Press.

Christensen, C. (2003). "Canadian Society: Social Policies and Ethno-Racial Diversity. In A. Al-Krenawi and J. Graham (eds.), *Multicultural Social Work in Canada: Working with Diverse Ethno-Racial Communities.* Toronto: Oxford University Press. 70–97.

Dei, G., and A. Calliste (eds.). (2000). *Power, Knowledge and Anti-Racism Education: A Critical Reader.* Halifax: Fernwood.

Dei, G., L. Karumanchery, and N. Karumanchery-Luke. (2004). *Playing the Race Card: Exposing White Power and Privilege.* New York: Peter Lang.

Diène, D. (2004). "Addendum: Mission to Canada." Report for the United Nations Commission on Human Rights, Sixtieth Session, Item 6 of provisional agenda. March. Commission on Human Rights. Geneva, Switzerland: Office of the High Commissioner for Human Rights. Available <http://www.ohchr.org/english/issues/racism/rapporteur/annual.htm>.

Giroux, H. (1988). "Theory, Resistance and Education." In K. Weiler (ed.), *Women Teaching for Change: Gender, Class and Power.* South Hadley, MA: Bergin and Garvey.

Jackson, B.W., and E. Holvino. (1989). *Working with Multicultural Organizations: Matching Theory and Practice.* Proceedings of Workshop on Diversity: Implications for Education and Training. Toronto. 109–21.

Jones, E.W. (1986). "Black Managers: The Dream Deferred." *Harvard Business Review* (May/June):84–93.

Kanter, R.M. (1977). *Men and Women of the Corporations.* New York: Basic Books.

Lee, A. (1995). "Race, Equity, Access and the Arts." *Paragraph* 14(1).

Maracle, L. (1993). "Racism, Sexism and Patriarchy." In H. Bannerji (ed.), *Returning the Gaze: Essays on Racism, Feminism and Politics.* Toronto: Sister Vision Press. 122–30.

McDonald, B. (1991). *Managing Diversity: A Guide to Effective Staff Management.* Winnipeg: Cross Cultural Communications International.

Mighty, E.J. (1992). "Managing Workforce Diversity: Institutionalization and Strategic Choice in the Adoption of Employment Equity." Ph.D. dissertation, York University.

Mock, K., and A. Shour Laufer. (2001). *Race Relations Training in Canada: Towards the Development of Professional Standards.* Toronto: Canadian Race Relations Foundation.

Phillips, W., Jr., and R. Blumberg. (1983). "Tokenism and Organizational Change." *Integrated Education* 20(1 & 2)(March):34–39.

Razack, S. (1982). *Ethnic Group Control of Jobs.* Toronto: Centre for Urban and Community Studies, University of Toronto.

———. (1998). *Looking White People in the Eye: Gender, Race and Culture in Courtrooms and Classrooms.* Toronto: University of Toronto Press.

Ungerleider, C., and E. McGregor. (1992). *Issues in Police Intercultural and Intercultural Race Relations Training in Canada.* Ottawa: Canadian Centre for Police Race Relations.

Wetherell, M., and J. Potter. (1992). *Mapping the Language of Racism.* New York: Columbia University Press.

CHAPTER 13

THE PARADOX OF DEMOCRATIC RACISM

In general the talk around race ... has only moved as far as its own negation; "I am not a racist" ... becomes a common and accepted disclaimer on the tip of everyone's tongue. ... This allows for the avoidance of deep questioning and critical thinking.

—Farman (1992:7)

This concluding chapter of the book briefly summarizes the ways in which democratic racism is expressed in individual ideologies, public discourses, organizational and institutional values and practices, and the collective beliefs, assumptions, and norms shared by the dominant culture of Canadian society. The second part of this chapter discusses anti-racist strategies in the context of the pervasive and systemic denial of racism in this country. These approaches have been developed in recognition of the strong resistance to a fundamental alteration in the positions of power and privilege that White Canadians occupy in relation to persons of colour and Aboriginal peoples.

Introduction

The various forms of resistance to anti-racism—lack of commitment; inadequate policies, programs, and practices; insufficient resources, monitoring, and evaluation; lack of individual, organizational, and public accountability; and dominant discourses—are strongly influenced by democratic racism, the ideology of Whiteness, and the values associated with these collective mindsets. These values fuel the action or inaction of the individuals working in institutions of Canadian society. These values also, to a significant extent, explain the cognitive dissonances and ambivalences manifested in the attitudes and behaviours of so many institutional players. The organizations and institutions described in this text are filled with individuals who are deeply committed to their professional work, who are regarded as highly skilled practitioners, who believe themselves to be liberal human beings—and yet they unknowingly, unwittingly contribute to racial inequality.

One of the main reasons why organizations, and the individuals who work for them, fail to move toward an anti-racist model of organizational change is the overarching ideology of democratic racism. Its values provide a justification for avoiding any action that might lead an organization to make progressive changes that not only challenge racism but also deconstruct it.

The hegemonic ideology of democratic racism is articulated, transmitted, and reproduced in every sector of Canadian society. It is reflected in the ideology of Whiteness, and "It is in ... ideology that we live, move, and have our being" (McCarthy, 1993). It is in language that ideology is disseminated and reinforced. Since language often reflects emotional and symbolic meanings, code words exist that, in themselves, do not have a racial meaning, but do have a racial connotation understood by all—a meaning socially constructed by the dominant White culture. The use of language also helps to understand that "The critical lesson, especially for those who are committed to social change, is not to underestimate the extent and degree of the power of Whiteness to reconstitute itself continually in order that its own structures and power are never dismantled" (Yee and Dumbrill, 2003:114).

In each of the central institutions of Canadian society analyzed in this book, racialized discourse that includes myths and misconceptions about people of colour, Aboriginal peoples, and immigrants continue to be generated, recycled, and reproduced. These dominant and hegemonic narratives provide "self-evident" truths that reflect and support the interests of the White power elite. These myths and misconceptions about the "other" that shape the boundaries of "legitimate" discourse reinforce the racialized attitudes and behaviours of individuals; fortify biased and discriminatory organizational policies, practices, and processes; and weave their way into societal belief and value systems. These myths become "our" story, "our" national narrative, "our" collective identity, "our" public truth. These discursive practices result in communal denial, distancing, defensiveness, and a determination to maintain the status quo—the structural privilege of Whiteness. The myths that form the basis of democratic racism include the following:

- *The discourse of denial:* "Canada is not a racist society"; "This is not a racist institution"; "[He or she] is not a racist"; "I am not a racist."
- *The discourse of colour-blindness:* "I never notice skin colour."
- *The discourse of equal opportunity:* "All we need to do is treat everyone the same and fairness will be ensured."
- *The discourse of blaming the victim:* "They lack the motivation to succeed"; "They don't really try to adapt their cultural values to 'our' society."
- *The discourse of White victimization:* "White European immigrants have also experienced prejudice and discrimination"; "All immigrant groups must expect to start at the bottom of the social and economic ladder."
- *The discourse of reverse racism:* "Minority/Aboriginal demands for fairness and justice have victimized White people"; "Programs like employment equity and antiracism policies incorporate authoritarian principles and methods that are antithetical to liberal democratic society."
- *The discourse of binary polarization and otherness:* "We are 'Canadian-Canadians'—law-abiding, meritorious, hardworking, contributing members of society"; they are the "others."
- *The discourse of immigrants, balkanization, and racism:* "Immigrants take jobs away from Canadians"; "Immigrants commit more crime"; "Immigrants are a drain on the economy"; "Immigrants exploit the welfare system."
- *The discourse of moral panic:* "We are in a state of crisis and disorder and are under siege; we have lost control; they represent a serious threat to our 'civilized' society."
- *The discourse of multiculturalism:* Tolerance, accommodation, harmony, and diversity are the values Canadians live by: "In a multicultural society we should try to be sen-

sitive, to tolerate and accommodate different cultural values; but there are limits to our tolerance."

- *The discourse of liberal values*: "Individualism, truth, tradition, universalism, and freedom of expression represent our core values"; "The rights of the individual should override collective rights"; "There is a noble Euro-American tradition that must never be lost"; "There is a universal form of expression that includes and transcends all cultural and racial boundaries"; "There is an 'authentic' history that we are obliged to learn and share"; "We must establish what is the truth"; "Freedom of expression is one of the most cherished of all of our values"; "It cannot be compromised because some minority group is unhappy with the position taken by a journalist, judge, politician, curator, health care worker, or educator."
- *The discourse of national identity*: "Real Canadians are willing to put their other cultural identities behind them"; "Canada should define itself on the basis of a single, unifying and uniform Canadian-Canadian culture."

As has been demonstrated throughout this book, the various forms of racism have been shown to influence the manner in which organizations are structured and services are delivered. The ideology of democratic racism reinforces and maintains systems of inequality in Canadian institutions. Each of these institutions are discursive spaces that intersect with one another and broader societal discourses that function to categorize, inferiorize, marginalize and exclude racialized populations. The case studies cited illuminate how these systems and structures are not only interconnected but also interlock. An example of this is the way the print and electronic media, policing, justice, and systems of governance within the state all serve to reinforce the image of Muslims, Blacks, and Aboriginal people as the deviant and undesirable "others." The approach taken in this analysis underscores the fact that racialized individuals and communities, often simultaneously, experience individual and collective forms of racism.

Each chapter has shown the cohesiveness of ideologies, discourses, unwritten policies, and everyday practices of educators, journalists, human service practitioners, politicians, judges, and other public authorities. The discourses of denial, tolerance, equality of opportunity, reverse discrimination, and colour-blindness constantly conflict with the realities of injustice, inequity, and racial discrimination. These rhetorical strategies create a climate that prevents any kind of effective engagement with racial inequality. The next section of this chapter summarizes how democratic racism is manifested in Canada's major social institutions.

The Manifestations of Democratic Racism

Education

In the area of education, racism is woven into the formal and informal curriculum, influencing the ways in which knowledge is structured, valued, and transmitted. Racial bias is reflected in the attitudes, assumptions, and behaviour of educators. It is embedded in policies such as Zero Tolerance. It is reflected in the unwritten policies and practices such as streaming of Blacks students into non-academic programs. Racism in education mirrors the racism of the dominant culture. It is reflected in the learning environment and forms an intrinsic part of the learning process. The evidence of racist ideology, racialized discourses, and differential treatment that negatively affects students of colour is documented by studies and reports and is recorded in the testimonies of students, parents, and communities.

Educational practices that maintain Anglo-Eurocentric biases and ignore the histories and contributions of racial-minority groups are maintained by a value system that allegedly emphasizes fairness, access, and equality toward all students. Canada's educational system is based on the premise that a well-constructed learning environment benefits students of all racial and cultural backgrounds. Despite this strongly held democratic liberal principle, substantial numbers of racial-minority students are disadvantaged and treated as though they were inferior. Policies such as Zero Tolerance often serve to both further marginalize and exclude Black students from the educational system. Racial harassment exists and has resulted not only in physical and emotional anguish for students of colour and their families but also in its most extreme form in the deaths of students such as Reena Virk and Mao Jomar Lanot. Principals and teachers seem to be often unaware of the dynamics, extent, and impact of the racism written on the daily agenda of students of colour and Aboriginal students. This is democratic racism.

Inequity and differential treatment continues at the university level. Lack of minority representation in faculties and administrations, the teaching of a Eurocentric curriculum, the absence of critical anti-racism pedagogy, the stereotyping of minority students and faculty, and incidents of harassment and overt racism continue to plague students and educators who are Aboriginal or of colour. These practices are maintained in an institution that prides itself on its "liberal" values including equality of opportunity, academic freedom, and freedom of expression. The latter freedom has enabled faculty to conduct research that allegedly demonstrates the inequality of races, allowed students to publicly insult members of racial minorities, and encouraged administrators to ignore issues that relate to inequity. The usual response of the university has been to deny and resist change in the name of these very principles. These basic tenets of democracy allow racism to continue to flourish in the academic environment.

The Media

The media are regarded as a pillar of democratic society and the key instrument by which its ideals are produced and perpetuated. Democracy depends on a free flow and exchange of ideas, opinions, and information. In a liberal democracy, media institutions are expected to reflect alternative viewpoints and to provide equitable access and representation of all groups.

In reality, the values and demands of both the marketplace and the ideology of Whiteness direct the media. Despite the insistence of most media practitioners and the sacred credo of the media profession of neutrality and objectivity, the analysis and case studies in this text demonstrate that the social location of journalists (their gender, class, ethnic, racial, religious, and other marks of identity), can strongly influence everyday media discursive practices. Journalists and editors, television writers, producers and directors, and advertisers bring to "storytelling" their own values, perspectives, and understandings, which often act as filters, screening out the "real" or more nuanced story. As a result, the Canadian media industries marginalize people of colour by making them invisible, devaluing their contributions, and emphasizing their "differences." These everyday discursive practices function to perpetuate the White face of Canada. Media organizations play a key role in producing and disseminating the myth that people of colour, especially Blacks, Aboriginal peoples, and Muslims, represent a threat to a civil society, create social problems, and generally jeopardize the harmony of Canada.

Television cameras and newspaper images often show close-ups of Blacks in both the foreground and background of scenes in which the topic is crime. Muslims and Middle-Eastern men are commonly associated with terrorism. The media create and reinforce negative and stereotypical images to influence public opinion. Discourses on terrorism, public safety, crime, and immigration become racialized and result in the further stigmatization, marginalization, and exclusion of people of colour. The "different" cultures of the "others" provide another way of distinguishing "them" (racial minorities and Aboriginal peoples) from "us" (White Anglo-Europeans). Freedom of the press provides a licence for journalists, editors, and broadcasters to communicate racialized views in both "text and talk." Programming and advertising are marked by the absence of images, ideas, and stories that reflect the diversity of Canadian society. Actors of colour are rarely included in television representation except in the most stereotypical expressions.

Democratic racism allows the media, one of the most powerful institutions in a democracy, to produce and transmit the messages that people of colour and Aboriginal people create social problems and represent a threat to our social order.

The Arts

In the arts—literature, sculpture, painting, music, theatre, dance, and other creative achievements—works generated by people of colour have often been judged inferior and relegated to the margins of mainstream public culture. Cultural appropriation—the use of another culture's images or experiences by artists from the dominant culture—is a particularly important example of the ways in which the culture, traditions, and history of minority-group artists are valued only after they have been appropriated. The prevailing ideology of cultural racism leads to the view that true art can only be produced by those with Anglo-Eurocentric aesthetic values; "others" produce folklore and exotica. The analysis in the arts chapter also illustrates the staying power of these cultural and institutional belief systems. Despite the very recent signs of greater inclusivity in publishing works by writers of colour and Aboriginal writers, a nominal increase in smaller theatre productions of stories by people of colour, and the occasional exhibit of visual art or artifacts in our museums, the rightness of Whiteness is still the predominant organizing cultural premise.

As in the media, freedom of expression provides a rationale for silencing certain voices and ignoring particular images. Attempts to protest and resist the dominant culture's marginalization, stereotyping, and objectification of people of colour in theatre, film, television programming, and writing are met with allegations of censorship and political correctness.

Policing

In the area of law enforcement, many racist attitudes and behaviours lead to a polarization between police and Aboriginal and racial-minority communities. The culture of policing is based on a "we-they" mindset and emphasizes law and order, a concept that conflicts with the idea of a service-oriented police force. The police frequently see citizens' demands for change as challenging the maintenance of law and order and therefore a threat to the security of the state.

In addition, the police play an important role in the racialization of crime and the criminalization of minorities. The overpolicing or racial profiling of racial-minority communities leads to a substantial number of charges being laid against their members, which in turn leads to the view that members of these groups commit more crimes than others do. This unsubstantiated notion creates a negative, destructive, and unfair image that is reproduced among the public by the media, politicians, and law-enforcement authorities. The racial minority (especially the Black or Aboriginal male) as deviant and/or criminal is a construct particularly well suited to the production and reproduction of racialized ideology. The case study on racial profiling in Toronto demonstrates how deeply inter-locked the systems of racialization are in relation to criminalization. In that case, almost every public authority including the Mayor, the Premier, the Minister of Public Safety, the Attorney General, and the policing officials including the Chair of the Police Services Board, the Policing Association, among others, spoke with one voice: the voice of denial. In the same way, the case of the death of several Aboriginal men as a result of some inter-vention with police also demonstrates how the discourse of denial of racism obliterates the most fundamental human rights in a democratic society.

There are many major barriers to an improvement in police and minority relations, including the fact that people of colour do not have access to and are not represented within law enforcement. Even though police are, on paper, accountable to the publics they serve, there has been a significant void in systems of accountability. People are not able to participate as full and equal citizens if the police are not directly accountable to the diverse communities they serve. Moreover, police are less likely to reflect and respond to the concerns of these communities. However, the demands for greater accountability tend to be viewed as opposition to the police and therefore as subversive toward the democratic process.

The Justice System

The justice system, which is intended to dispense "justice" fairly and without bias, has been severely criticized for its inability to do so. Specific issues of concern include alleged differential treatment in the courts—in the granting of bail, in sentencing, in jury selec-tion procedures, and in the attitudes of justice officials. Members of the legal profession, administrative tribunals, and the judiciary have been cited for their prejudiced and biased attitudes toward various groups, despite their duty to be impartial. In minority commu-nities, especially among Blacks and Aboriginal peoples, there is a fundamental absence of faith in the fairness of the system.

The justice system espouses an ideology based on long-established laws and histor-ical and legal precedents. For example, mandatory anti-sexism training for judges was rejected by the justice minister "because of constitutional guarantees of judicial independ-ence" (Canadian Press, 1993). Evidence continues to show that adherence to these hon-ourable traditions and guarantees works to the disadvantage of, and dispenses injustice to, persons of colour and Aboriginal peoples.

The case study of Judge Corrine Sparks, in which a Black judge identifies the issue of racial bias as a potential factor in the consideration of a particular case, demonstrates how powerful the discourse of denial is within the justice system. The case study of police action against lawyers Rocky Jones and Ann Derrick demonstrates again the pow-erful web of institutional racism moving across four systems: policing, justice, education, and the media. The processes of racialization that operate across these public spaces are deeply rooted in a composite of ideologies, values, norms, and discourses that easily cross the boundaries between these sectors.

Human Services

Social-service and health care organizations are characterized by both a lack of represen-tation of people of colour and an underrepresentation. Those people of colour who are employed by these organizations often experience marginalization and differential treat-ment. The prevailing ideology of human services is exclusionary and often racialized. It is based on the provision of appropriate service to all, regardless of colour or creed, yet its delivery is inconsistent with these principles. The assumption of a common set of needs among very different groups, which is usually accepted as a basic requirement for the equal and accessible provision of services, can have a negative impact on minority clients. Aboriginal people and people of colour often find the traditional mainstream human-service delivery system inaccessible and inequitable.

Current modes of service continue to reflect the values, norms, and practices of the dominant White culture and therefore are of limited effectiveness for people coming from diverse racial and cultural backgrounds. By limiting the role and resources of ethno-racial agencies, funders and other institutional authorities have perpetuated inequality within the system. Mainstream organizations remain unable or unwilling to provide the special social and health care services that many ethno-racial communities require. White practitioners are often unaware of the daily struggle of people of colour with racial bias and discrimination. The case studies of SARS and the discussion of services to immigrant populations illustrate the way in which innocuous concepts such as "self," "nuclear family," and "therapy" are sites of struggle for those grappling with Western models of treatment and intervention. Minority-group workers employed in mainstream services frequently find themselves isolated and marginalized, their skills and credentials undervalued. Multicultural and anti-racism policies established in many social agencies appear to have had little impact on the dominant cultural practices underpinning organizational structures, discourses, and practices.

The State

At the level of the state there is also evidence to demonstrate fundamental value conflicts. As Kobayashi (1990:447) pointedly argued, "The law itself has been an instrument used in the construction of racism as a hegemonic social relationship." Immigration and refugee legislation both historically and currently continue to be racialized, although in less overt ways. Despite the development of human rights legislation and codes, the glaring inadequacies of the Canadian Charter of Rights and Freedoms, the Multiculturalism Act, the Employment Equity Act, human rights codes and commissions, government ministries, and public agencies at all levels demonstrate a lack of commitment to truly eliminate racism.

The conflict of values that characterizes the hegemonic ideology called "democratic racism" is at the root of racial inequality in Canadian society. The very values that define a democracy—freedom of expression, reliance on merit, the rights of individuals, the primacy of human dignity, and the rights of all citizens to equality—are used to combat, resist, and denigrate efforts to deconstruct racial barriers and inequalities. There is a constant and profound moral tension between the reality of the everyday experiences of people of colour and Aboriginal people and the responses of those who have the power to redefine that reality. White politicians, bureaucrats, educators, judges, journalists, social workers, cultural administrators, the corporate elite, and others pay lip service to the ideal of racial equality but are far more committed to maintaining the status quo.

The transformation of Canadian institutions and the organizations that serve them into anti-racist systems is hindered by their reliance on the traditional values that such changes allegedly threaten. The paradox of "democratic racism" is that in the midst of a society that professes racial equality, there is racial inequality; instead of fairness, there is unfairness; instead of freedom of speech, the silencing of voices advocating change; instead of impartiality, bias; instead of multiculturalism, Anglo-Eurocentrism. Diversity becomes coded language for assimilation, the rule of law results in injustice, service means lack of access, and protection increases the vulnerability of racialized communities.

Strategies for Change

Given the evidence of the collective denial of racism in Canadian society, what alternatives can be offered? What strategies can be implemented?

The complex, interactive nature of Canadian structures and systems means that no single institutional response, policy, program, or other type of intervention can ensure that racism will be eliminated or even reduced. This book has identified numerous measures that have been undertaken, such as state policies on multiculturalism, human rights, immigration, and employment equity, as well as institutional initiatives in education, policing, human services, and the media. Some measures have had the appearance of success in the short term, but none has succeeded in controlling racism in a way that ensures full access, participation, and equity for people of colour.

Most of the approaches to combat racism in Canada have, in practice, been "too little, too late," too superficial, too simplistic. They have frequently been underfunded, short-term, ad hoc, and isolated interventions that lack coordination and do not address "root causes." Having been framed in an ideology of democratic racism, they have too often addressed symptoms without changing the conditions that produced the symptoms in the first place.

Although there are no sure formulas, the following strategic approaches to democratic racism hold hope for change:

- developing critical reflective skills and practices;
- responding to allegations of racism;
- empowering communities;
- monitoring anti-racism initiatives; and
- emphasizing the role of the individual as well as the institutions.

The following pages offer some tentative suggestions in each of these areas to address inequalities and racist attitudes and behaviours.

Developing Reflective Practices

For racism to have a less detrimental effect, it must be brought into the light and openly examined as a feature of the discourses, events, and experiences it influences, even in the most subtle ways (Dyson, 1994). What is lacking in the rhetoric of institutional and state "authorities" is a conceptualization of racism that uncovers its deeply rooted nature.

Moreover, what is required is to incorporate into this conceptual framework an understanding not only of how racism works on its victims, but also of its effect on those who, perhaps unknowingly and unwittingly, are its perpetrators. For members of the White dominant culture, who are frequently unable to move beyond their own experiential framework, the dominant values and racialized assumptions and beliefs operating beneath the coded language of liberalism and democracy remain invisible.

The position of White power and privilege allows many to evade the issue of race and racism and the powerlessness of the "others." The rhetoric of pluralism and inclusion does not address the tangible, everyday experiences of marginalization and exclusion. Most Whites are unable to "imagine" racism as an insidious reality that affects the daily minutiae of living, working, thinking, and feeling (Srivastava, 1993). They are unable to see or deconstruct the racism that is woven into the discourses that are part of their professional and personal lives. The "lived dimensions" of racism transcend its administrative details: "An investigation of racism requires that it be grasped at the micro level, at the interface between the existential and administrative" forms of racism (Knowles, 1996:48).

The White professional—social worker, teacher, academic, administrator, employer, judge, law enforcement officer, lawyer, politician, bureaucrat, editor, journalist, broadcaster, cultural producer, curator, and writer—is often reluctant to engage in critical self-reflection. There is an unwillingness to consider how these professionals' social locations or social identities influence the ways they function in their professional lives (Bonnett, 1993; Solomon and Levine-Rasky, 1996; Solomon and Brown, 1998). The conflicting ideologies and discourses of democratic racism operating in each of these sectors (media, the arts, justice, policing, government, human services, education, and the private corporation) reflect unquestioned beliefs, assumptions, and interpretations about the racialization of differences.

Michelle Fine (1997) provided a powerful example of how the "professional socialization" of law students fundamentally alters their critical awareness of race and gender. She described how women law students, who began their first year with concerns about issues of social justice (e.g., generic use of "he," sexist jokes, differential participation by race and gender), by the third year had patterned their political attitudes after those of White men. By graduation, "the vast difference in visions for the future by race and gender" (61) had disappeared. Moreover, for the silenced White women, and women and men of colour, the critique of inequalities turned inward, against the self, and was reflected in lower grades, worsened mental health, and more conservative ideologies and politics. "Social critique by race/gender does not age very well within educational institutions" (61).

In the training of teachers there is an urgent need to uncover the ideological entrenchment, contradictions, and resistance of prospective teachers as it relates to issues of race, racism, and anti-racism (Solomon and Levine-Rasky, 1996). Teachers must develop tools with which to critique the educational process, the society, and the self. "Issues of ethnicity and race must be integrated into the mainstream dialogues of teacher education" (349). Carl James (1994) made a similar point, suggesting that teachers must constantly be critically self-reflective, "reflecting on our socialization, our biography, our worldview, and on how these impact on our practices" (27).

In the same way, the training of judges, journalists, police, human-service workers, MBAs, art administrators, and other professionals must provide opportunities for acquiring "critical literacy" (Wood, 1985) skills, that is, the ability to recognize and critique political, cultural, and economic structures that oppress marginalized peoples. They must be professionally socialized and given the knowledge and tools to deconstruct the meaning of the disabling discourses that surround them, such as the theories of "neutrality," "colour-blindness," and "professional competence and authority."

As has been demonstrated throughout this book, often the training of these professionals and practitioners has not prepared them for reflection. Thus, both pre-service training programs in postsecondary educational institutions and in-service professional development programs in organizations must play a proactive role in developing critical self-reflective skills and ensuring that students and other participants gain the tools required to engage in social transformation.

Responding to Allegations of Racism

Democratic racism allows individuals to hold and espouse liberal democratic values while believing and practising racialized ideology. This form of racism is often subtle, elusive, and insidious. It is usually invisible to White people and readily apparent to people of colour. Thus, allegations of racism in organizations elicit anger, disbelief, and pain. Every allegation of racism has both individual and organizational consequences. In developing strategies to deal with racism, the individual is an essential part of the equation.

Allegations of racism are accompanied by a series of emotional responses from both the complainant and the subject of the complaint. These allegations often remain unresolved because people become involved in trying to prove that an incident was or was not discrimination. The individual accused of racism commonly believes that racism cannot occur without an intent to discriminate. Often the immediate organizational response is denial, expressed in a number of counterproductive behaviours. The person who alleges racism generally feels isolated, unsupported, and vulnerable. He or she may have expended enormous energy in trying to decide whether to launch a complaint or bring the issue to the attention of the organization.

Thus, in the first stage, the response to allegations of racism must begin by identifying and acknowledging the deeply felt emotions of both parties. Exposing these feelings and rigorously addressing them allows the incident to be used to create opportunities both to build individual relationships and to facilitate organizational growth.

The second stage is to uncover the underlying facts upon which these emotions are built. The social facts underpinning racism cannot be readily understood by White Canadians, who do not experience discrimination based on the colour of their skin. Thus it is very difficult for many White Canadians to understand the impact of constant, everyday racism on persons of colour and to identify the ways bias, exclusion, marginalization, and differential treatment function in their organizations. On the other hand, racism shapes the intellectual, professional, and personal lives of many people of colour. These distinctly different social realities must be taken into account in trying to determine the social facts underlying an allegation of racism.

The third stage requires a commitment to negotiate, implement, and institutionalize change. Finding common ground and identifying the mutual interests of the parties is an essential part of rebuilding relationships. Both the individuals and the organization must be able to identify the benefits of seeking a resolution to race-related conflicts. Often the experience and expertise of the community provide organizations with an important resource for developing effective strategies. Finally, it should be emphasized that this same process could have been applied in the many examples cited in the text, in which it is not an individual who is the aggrieved party, but the community as a whole that feels victimized by a set of racialized behaviours or actions.

Empowering Communities

Organized opposition by the offended group and/or community is a major catalyst to change. If societal institutions are to be free of racism, they need to be pushed to this level of change by organized, direct community action.

In a democratic society, when there is contestation and conflict over injustices, dissent should be valued as long as it occurs within socially approved limits. Public-sector support for anti-racism community advocacy and lobbying activities should be seen as necessary processes if democracy is to work. Competition in Canadian society is encouraged and institutionalized. Only when resources are scarce and inequitably distributed can such competition lead to disintegrative forms of conflict. Canadian democratic values encourage political dissent and opposition, again as long as they are expressed through proper channels and the conflict is "peaceful." Constructive conflict includes the recognition of different needs and interests (individual and collective) and provides for participation, negotiation, arbitration, and settlement. The establishment of such mechanisms may avoid violent confrontation.

A racial incident or series of incidents can act as triggers to direct reaction by the community, which often becomes the most salient agent of institutional and societal change. Thus, opposition and conflict may play a beneficial role in initiating the process of change toward racial equity.

A society in which integration is more advanced will have greater group interaction. As a result it may also experience more frequent incidents of behavioural discrimination. However, the increasing number of such cases might indicate an improvement, rather than a worsening, in racial equality. Thus, ensuing conflicts should be recognized as signs of progress, not deterioration, because efforts to reduce racial inequalities may increase the short-term potential for conflict (Benyon and Solomos, 1987:156). In Canada, a society that promotes the democratic racist myths of progress through dialogue, mediation, and conciliation, the reduction of racial inequalities through increased racial conflict and tension will clearly be an uncomfortable but perhaps inevitable new direction.

The achievement of racial equity will not come about as a result of a rational, intellectual process of understanding. Nor will it occur through an "invisible hand" of organizational dynamics. Anti-racism efforts need to acknowledge the full complexity of the systems they are attempting to change and to locate those efforts in the context of the obstacles to racial equity. Anti-racism strategies need to address the institutional constraints and the personal and occupational ideologies and values underlying democratic racism.

Although national and international conditions can precipitate social change, a major impetus has been and will continue to be community pressure and mobilization. It is therefore misleading to denude the pursuit of racial equity of any political dimension. Social change is often precipitated by political imperatives. Does it matter whether the motivation is prevention, fear, moral panic, or altruism? Does it matter whether the response is based on attempts to appease, to defuse discontent, to manage a crisis, to repair the meritocratic credibility of institutions, or to avoid the development of separate institutions along lines of race?

What does matter is that the response will have an appreciable impact on reducing racial injustice.

The case studies cited in this book show that the initial response of Canadian institutions and organizations to demands for change is to make cosmetic changes, and even then to make them only to defuse protest. Real improvements come about only through sustained external pressure.

Parekh, in writing about anti-racism efforts in the United States, concluded that no reform had been secured without powerful and constant Black pressure:

> It was the Black agitation, initially the non-violent civil rights campaigns and the later riots, that activated the moral impulse, energized and mobilized the liberals, provided a political counterweight to the highly influential racial lobby, threatened disorder, changed the equations of White self-interest and resulted in reforms. (1987:x)

Parekh argued that no American reform was secure unless Black organizations and their leaders were able to consolidate, defend, and build on it. His analysis of the American experience suggests that reforms secured in the teeth of opposition by vested interests are fragile, vulnerable to subversion, and generally lack the resources to implement them. Moreover, they are unlikely to be fruitful and achieve the desired goal unless they are carefully formulated and part of a well-conceived strategy.

The frenzy of activity on March 21 every year—the day set aside to commemorate the International Day for the Elimination of Racial Discrimination—is symbolic of the kinds of institutional initiatives that are often little more than public-relations exercises. "Eliminate racism," "Remove racial discrimination," "Create equality of opportunity," "Manage diversity," and "Implement anti-racist training" are empty slogans, incapable either of guiding those who genuinely wish to help or of restraining those determined to resist them. In the same way, the celebration of Black History Month or the Chinese New Year offers little gain if the contributions of African Canadians or Chinese Canadians to this country are marginalized to a "special" day, week, or month.

One of the most important conclusions that can be drawn from the anti-racism activities described in this book is that immediate, consistent, and well-developed community mobilization and action strategies can be highly successful in influencing political, institutional, and social action. Progress toward race equity is therefore unlikely to be attained unless concerned citizens and communities are able to cooperate to combat racism.

Community infrastructures and support systems need to be in place to combat racism, to monitor organizational and institutional initiatives, to ensure their implementation, and to overcome resistance, both systemic and individual.

Parekh (1987) also maintains that any progress toward race equity is achieved only by sustained and direct community involvement. Sustained community advocacy and lobbying activities require:

- *organizational resources*: financial and human;
- *legitimacy*: support from the media and other communities;
- *expertise*: legal, media, and organizational; and
- *leadership*: training and development.

Political representation and the participation of people of colour and Aboriginal peoples in the decisions that affect them must also be regarded as necessary preconditions for the non-violent resolution of racism in Canadian society. For example, the issue of police behaviour raises questions that go to the heart of democratic accountability and government by consent. People of colour and Aboriginal people must be represented in the police force at all ranks and on the boards that manage them.

The use of police or the armed forces to deal with protest reflects a "legitimation crisis" in which inequalities of power and status undermine loyalty and create contradictions that threaten social integration. When such conflicts result in violent protest and a coercive response by authorities, they undermine the moral basis of society and the integrity of the state. Only through a comprehensive approach that addresses the underlying conditions that foster democratic racism and that facilitates constructive responses will a repetition of such crises in the future be avoided. The first precondition is that people of colour must participate in the decision-making process.

Monitoring Anti-Racism Initiatives

Public policies on multiculturalism and race relations, legislation on employment equity and human rights, and systems and agencies to promote racial equality have all had the impact on altering the appearance, if not the reality, of racial inequality in Canada. Canadians, including people of colour, are encouraged to believe in the myths of colour-blindness, meritocracy, tolerance, and racial harmony. The maintenance of these democratic racist myths continues to hamper citizens' readiness to measure and dismantle racism. Although the extent of racial discrimination and inequality in Canada is similar to that of the United States and the United Kingdom, Canada has not yet experienced the level of violence and unrest that these other countries have.

A number of institutions and agencies in all sectors of Canadian life are articulating finely worded commitments and policies with regard to equity issues. Unfortunately, these commitments have seldom been translated into good practices. The pursuit of racial equality in Canada appears to be hampered by an inability to translate policy into time- and cost-efficient procedures that have a measurable impact on controlling racial disadvantage and discrimination. There is a danger that the impetus and commitment to equity will unravel in a collection of uncertain, cumbersome, and misdirected activities that do not achieve any real results in removing racial inequalities. These responses may indeed reinforce and even exacerbate the existing racial inequality.

The activity that has taken place in Canada in the last while in pursuit of racial equity has largely consisted of determining whether racism is occurring, how it is occurring and to what extent, and how it may be prevented. Although data on these issues are far from adequate and considerable research is still required, more emphasis should be placed on analyzing the issues from the perspective of outcomes.

The most important measure of any initiative is its *results*. Extensive efforts to implement training and develop procedures, data collection systems, report forms, and finely written policy statements are worse than meaningless unless the end product is measurable improvement. Just as the success of a private business is evaluated in terms of increases in sales, the only realistic basis for evaluating a program to combat racism and increase racial equity is its actual impact on these issues. To accelerate the process of change, more careful consideration needs to be given to particular issues in sectors in which there is a real prospect of effecting change quickly.

In addition to focusing on strategic targeting, any strategy for improving policy and practices must incorporate mechanisms for monitoring and measuring their impact. In other words, initiatives must show definable results that reduce racial injustices in a measurable way. New techniques and mechanisms are required to assess whether anti-racist policies and practices are in fact achieving racial equity. There is a lack of rigorous monitoring in the field of anti-racism in Canada, and few criteria of evaluation have been developed. The consequence of this is that limited public dollars and community energies are wasted on irrelevant exercises that do little to control or eliminate racism.

Too many community activities are concerned with "promoting," "encouraging," "coordinating," "heightening," "improving," and other similarly imprecise and vaguely worded objectives. Sometimes, project evaluation consists merely of a loose "process evaluation" activity in which, for example, conference participants are asked to rate the speakers. The little evaluation that has been done on training programs indicates that efforts are needed to develop appropriate methods of "impact evaluation"—that is, evaluations of the extent to which anti-racism initiatives produce desirable outcomes. In terms of measuring results, the emphasis should be on an initiative's "return on investment" in relation to predetermined goals. Only then can legitimate and meaningful performance standards be established.

To be able to measure the results with some degree of comfort and certitude requires stated goals to be defined in specific, concrete, and realizable terms. Measuring outcomes is impossible if the goals and objectives consist of nebulous generalizations.

There is a need in Canada to collect and disseminate the information—about strategies, and skills—that is required to achieve racial equity. Unfortunately, the degree of information-sharing in Canada across institutional, racial, and geographical boundaries is relatively insignificant. This isolation, which results in an ignorance of other effective initiatives, methods, programs, and approaches, separates Canadians from the international community.

Canada cannot afford to persist in pursuing racial equity on an insecure foundation of inadequate knowledge. Nor can it, through its public and private sectors and its social agencies and institutions, afford to continue to devote resources to "improving opportunity" for people of colour if the impact on these persons continues to be negligible.

Emphasizing the Role of Major Institutions

The first task of institutions and systems of governance committed to racial equity is to make a clear statement that racism in any form will not be tolerated. Unfortunately, most major Canadian institutions and government ministries and agencies operate as if the realities of a racially diverse population have nothing to do with the way they carry out their activities. They rely on "traditional management initiatives" or respond to incidents in an ad hoc manner.

In focusing on institutional strategies and in light of the previous observation regarding community involvement, an important factor is the degree to which an institution is open to *community pressure*. Some institutional sectors are more closed off from the public than are others. For example, the police should more accountable to the public because they are supported by tax dollars. In the same way, the education system is accountable as a public service and has additional obligations to parents. Universities and colleges have decentralized authority structures, and very traditional academic traditions guide their culture. Often, greater priority is given to the rituals of Whiteness (traditional hiring and promotional procedures, assessment of merit, attachment to Anglo-Eurocentric curriculum and pedagogical practices, etc.) than to the students and faculty of colour or the broader population. Other public-sector agencies are accountable to elected representatives, who are concerned with staying in office.

Public-sector institutions, however, such as the justice system, are less easily affected by public pressure. The tradition of judicial independence is difficult to overcome when combating racial inequalities in the justice system.

Similarly, the tradition of freedom of speech is frequently used by the media to protect and defend themselves from community pressures. In addition, since the media are not highly organized, the mechanisms for seeking public redress are either ineffectual or nonexistent.

Museums and cultural institutions are also susceptible to isolation from the diverse publics they serve. The structure of and representation on the boards of these institutions suggest that they are not accountable to the larger community. The boards and staff of these institutions have not gained a clear understanding "of the invisible, but omniscient 'we' that such institutions embody to this day" (Tchen, 1993:4).

The case studies and other forms of analysis cited in this book indicate institutional ill-preparedness in dealing with racism, even when problems resulting from it have continued over years, for example, in boards of educations and other educational institutions, in law enforcement agencies, in hospitals, in immigration policies, and in media organizations. Strategies must be developed that respond to racism that is the outcome both of individual beliefs and behaviours and of collective values and norms that form part of the organizational culture. Institutional-change strategies are fundamentally "local" in their orientation, in that they focus on one organization at a time. This is not to suggest, however, that there is not a generic organizational-response model.

Progress toward racial equity can be measured by the degree to which an organization:

- develops a discourse that is free of the ambiguities and ambivalences that have characterized racialized discursive practices in most organizational and institutional sectors;
- supports the development of self-reflective attitudes and **reflective practices** that lead to greater individual and organizational accountability in the process of social transformation;
- reflects the contributions and interests of all ethno-racial groups in Canada in its mission, operations, and service delivery;
- acts on a commitment to eradicate all forms of racial discrimination and disadvantage within itself;
- involves members of all its racial groups as full participants in all its levels; and
- fulfils its broader external responsibilities to promote racial equity.

In moving toward this ideal, appropriate organizational responses include:

- an immediate and strong condemnation of racism, and of those responsible for it, by the head of the organization;
- the development of a coherent implementation strategy to combat racism within the organization; this strategy should not merely deal with managing individual incidents, but also strive to overcome the causes of racial incidents and eradicate cultural, systemic and structural discrimination in the organization;
- the establishment of an internal monitoring mechanism to record and monitor racism in all its forms; and
- taking action against those responsible for racism, serving notice on perpetrators, and informing the victims of all actions being taken.

Internal monitoring systems are generally located in organizations' human-resources policies and programs. They generally involve the filing of complaints, a multi-step procedure to attempt to resolve them, and a final decision by a senior official. In some organizations, an independent arbitrator is appointed to adjudicate complaints. In union settings, the collective agreement often includes a non-discrimination clause that subjects any discrimination complaint to grievance and arbitration procedures. In the Ontario Public Service Employees Union, for example, this procedure culminates in a hearing before the Crown Employees Grievance Settlement Board.

A "coherent strategy" for addressing systemic issues may include structural diagnosis (e.g., data collection and problem identification, customer or client audits, and employment equity audits), public and policy commitments, the appointment of an adviser and/or committee, the establishment of goals and timetables, training, monitoring, and evaluation.

Developing a coherent anti-racist strategy for an organization therefore entails:

- a total system effort that must be comprehensive, systematic, and long term; and
- clearly enunciated goals, not so much concerned with maintaining order and harmony as with responding to grievances and correcting inequities.

Within the organization and its activities, the responsibility for race equity initiatives should reside not with one person or office, but with all the organization's members including senior management. The development of anti-racism values that are fully integrated in the organization's culture and procedures should be considered. In summary, achieving race equity and a racism-free organization entails:

- an acknowledgment that racism exists in the organization and that certain groups have been, and continue to be, hurt by it;
- an acknowledgment of the need to move beyond racially inexplicit analyses that deflect the issue of racism by interpreting it in human-relations or cultural terms;
- an acknowledgment of the need to move beyond policy statements and articulations of principles; organizational and administrative measures will be required to provide appropriate conditions for progress toward race equity; guidelines and procedures that include clearly identified responsibilities and accountability measures are required;
- an acknowledgment of the intersectionality of race, gender, ethnicity, class, different abilities, sexual orientation, and an understanding of how systems of oppression interrelate; and
- an acknowledgment that no institution or sector acts in isolation from another and that racism is reinforced by the interactions between these systems.

It may seem superfluous to state that the first step for all organizations, particularly those in the public sector, is to establish the mechanisms, strategies, and tools to address racism in all of its mutating forms. These decisions must involve Aboriginal people and people of colour, who are most directly impacted. It is clearly of major importance that the needs of the community be accurately assessed by systematic needs assessment and other diagnostic studies.

Second, in order to establish the relevance of services for people of colour and Aboriginal people, service provision must be monitored. A regular check must be made to ensure that a correspondence between need and service does in fact exist. The assessment must include the collection of data on the racial origins of clients, staff, and decision-makers.

The organizational arrangements of both public and private institutions determine the people or groups to whom services are provided, facilities are made available, and resources are allocated. The attitudes, actions, and practices of those who control these institutions determine who gets what, where, and when. Given the fact that people of colour are generally absent from these organizations' key decision-making processes and in the delivery of services, to what extent do the institutions treat them less favourably?

To what extent have the different and special needs of people of colour and Aboriginal peoples been identified and quantified? And to what extent have they been adequately considered and provided for? To what extent have existing resources been redirected in favour of oppressed communities as part of a commitment to equality?

The pursuit of racial justice and equity also demands that institutional mechanisms for measuring change be in place. Formal employment equity policies that are often isolated from issues of racism and other forms of oppression, mass "sensitization" training programs, and glossy public-relations campaigns are generally ineffective unless they are combined with concrete programs that are regularly monitored, evaluated, and reported on publicly. Effective monitoring systems can begin to provide the information needed to answer the question of whether progress is occurring.

Increasing the amount of feel-good rhetoric contributes only to further obscuring the measurement of progress. Collecting evidence, although dry and tedious, is certainly cheaper and more honest than performing glamorous public-relations exercises. More resources should be devoted to research and evaluation and less to "communications strategies."

Ensuring that the multiracial dimension of Canadian society is incorporated into organizational decision-making in a comprehensive and systematic manner is not very difficult. But if the mandate is not addressed directly, the notions of democratic racism and assumed equality will continue to be a major obstacle to race equity and will continue to contribute to the disadvantaged position of people of colour in Canada.

Summary

Although all the strategies identified in this chapter are positive mechanisms for dismantling racism in organizations and institutions, they must be linked to a comprehensive transformation of the cultural values and norms that shape Canadian society. The first and perhaps most important theme that frames this book is "In White society, racism is a story that cannot be told without consequences" (Razack, 1999:282). As we have seen demonstrated in every chapter, racism cannot be spoken of, it cannot be named in the school, university, courtroom, newsroom, television studio, museum, social agency, hospital, or in the Houses of Parliament.

Clearly, Canada's racial heterogeneity has been, is, and will continue to be a demographic and social fact. However, racial inequality and injustice continue to limit the participation of people of colour and Aboriginal peoples. Despite the existence of a variety of policies, programs, and other initiatives, the evidence in this book, and in all of the other research findings incorporated into this analysis, suggests the following conclusions: that racialized ideologies and racial barriers to equity in organizations and social structures have not been significantly reduced; that membership in the dominant White culture confers cultural, political, and economic power; and that racist ideology and discourse operate freely, without constraint.

The existence of democratic racism and the ideology of Whiteness means that increasing resistance and backlash from those who now enjoy the power and privilege of membership in the dominant group is to be expected. Pressure will continue to come from people of colour and other anti-racism advocates to alter the status quo. Simultaneously, those who are deprived of their rights as Canadians can be expected to become increasingly impatient with the slow rate of change. The oppositional narratives that inform so much of this book not only "bear witness" to the pain, humiliation, and injustice of a society divided by colour and other forms of oppression; they also illuminate the political, ethical, and moral challenges that confront our country. The narratives of resistance offer the reader an alternative; a counter-body of knowledge that critiques and challenges the dominant discourses that reinforce and legitimize racial inequity. Although these stories have often been contextualized in personal/individual experiences, they also communicate something about the broader cultural assumptions that permeate our society.

Dealing with racism in a transformative way requires us to deal with the dissonance in the values that underlie our current understanding of democracy. At this point in the history of Canada, we have an opportunity to redefine and redistribute power and to eradicate the structured inequality propelled by the hegemonic ideology that we have called democratic racism.

References

Benyon, J., and J. Solomos. (1987). *The Roots of Urban Unrest.* Oxford: Pergamon Press.

Bonnett, A. (1993). "Contours of Crisis: Anti-racism and Reflexivity." In P. Jackson and J. Penrose (eds.), *Construction of Race, Place and Nation.* London: University of London College Press. 163–80.

Canadian Press. (1993). "Judges' Training Program Rejected." *Toronto Star* (September 8):A6.

Dyson, M. (1994). "Essentialism and the Complexities of Racial Identity." In D. Goldberg (ed.), *Multiculturalism: A Critical Reader.* Cambridge, MA: Blackwell. 218–29.

Farman, A. (1992). "An Archaeology of Interracial Relations." *Fuse* 15(3)(Winter):7–11.

Fine, M. (1997). "Witnessing Whiteness." In M. Fine, L. Weiss, L. Powell, and L. Mun Wong (eds.), *Off White: Readings on Race, Power, and Society.* London: Routledge. 57–65.

James, C. (1994). "I Don't Want to Talk About It." *Orbit* 25(2):26–28.

Knowles, C. (1996). "Racism, Biography and Psychiatry." In V. Amit-Talai and C. Knowles (eds.), *Re-situating Identities: The Politics of Race, Ethnicity, and Culture.* Peterborough, ON: Broadview Press.

Kobayashi, A. (1990). "Racism and the Law." *Urban Geography* 2(5):447–73.

McCarthy, C. (1993). "After the Canon." In C. McCarthy and W. Crichlow (eds.), *Race, Identity and Representation in Education.* New York and London: Routledge.

Parekh, B. (1987). In J. Shaw et al. (eds.), *Strategies for Improving Race Relations.* Manchester: Manchester University Press.

Razack, S. (1999). "*R.D.S. v. Her Majesty the Queen*: A Case About Home." In E. Dua and A. Robertson (eds.), *Scratching the Surface: Canadian Anti-Racist Feminist Thought.* Toronto: Women's Press: 281–294.

Solomon, P., and C. Levine-Rasky. (1996). "Transforming Teacher Education." *CRSA/RCSA* 33(3):337–59.

———, and D. Brown. (1998). "From Badness to Sickness: Pathological Conceptions of Black Student Culture and Behaviour." In V. D'Oyley and C. James (eds.), *Re/Visioning: Canadian Perspectives on the Education of Africans in the Late 20th Century.* Toronto: Captus Press. 104–19.

Srivastava, A. (1993). "Re-imaging Racism: South Asian Women Writers." In H. Bannerji (ed.), *Returning the Gaze: Essays on Racism, Feminism, and Politics.* Sister Vision Press. 103–21.

Tchen, J.K.W. (1993). "What Are We Doing Now for the Year 2010?" Museums and the Problems of Technospeak, Possessive Individualism, and Social Alienation." *Getting to 2010: Directors and Educators Visualize the Future.* Fort Worth, TX: Association of American Museums.

Wood, P. (1985). "Schooling in a Democracy: Transformation or Reproduction." In F. Rizvi (ed.), *Multiculturalism as an Educational Policy.* Geelong, Victoria, Australia: Deakin University.

Yee, J., and G. Dumbrill. (2003). "Whiteout: Looking for Race in Canadian Social Work Practice. In A. Al-Krenawi and J. Graham (eds.), *Multicultural Social Work in Canada: Working with Diverse Ethno-Racial Communities.* Toronto: Oxford University Press. 98–121.

APPENDIX: RACIAL GROUPS IN CANADA

Various racial groups make up the Canadian population. They are categorized by Statistics Canada as follows:

Aboriginal: Métis; Inuit; status and non-status Canadian Indian; North- and South-American Native peoples

Black: African Black; American Black; Canadian Black; West Indian and Caribbean Black; other Black

East Asian: Chinese; Fijian; Japanese; Korean; Polynesian

South Asian: Bangladeshi; Indian (India); Pakistani; Sri Lankan

Southeast Asian: Burmese; Cambodian; Filipino; Laotian; Malaysian; Thai; Vietnamese

West Asian: Arab; Armenian; Egyptian; Iranian; Israeli; Lebanese; North-African Arab; Palestinian; Syrian; Turkish

White: British; European; South, Central, and North Americans of Caucasian background; Russian; Ukrainian; others of Caucasian background

Other: Mixed racial heritage; racial groups not referred to above

One of the challenges in discussing the issues of race and racism is achieving a common understanding of the terminology. The definitions, interpretations, and meanings of terms vary considerably. As our understanding of racism evolves, the pursuit of a language that is more specific, concrete, and clear will also evolve. For example, the term "visible minority" is a classification created by the Canadian state. As a label it refers to the categories of both native and foreign-born, non-White, non-Caucasoid, non-Aboriginal individuals. Many scholars (Synnott and Howes, 1996; Carty and Brand, 1993) argue that the term serves to homogenize and essentialize groups and ignores crucial differences in power, culture, history, and even visibility. Although colour remains the nucleus of the race classification system, it bears little relation to the actual skin tones of human beings. Many minorities who are not included in the concept are also very visible and experience disadvantage and discrimination. The term implies being "visible" from the norm, not part of normative mainstream society (which, of course, is presumed to be White). Being termed "visible" tends to reinforce the permanence of that status. Even the term "minority" is problematic, as it suggests being less than the majority. In parts of the country, and now in Toronto, this is no longer the reality in terms of population numbers. It is important to emphasize that both individual and collective forms of ethno-racial identity exist in a constant state of transformation. Moreover, some visible minorities may not view visibility as a significant criterion of self-identification. Some may consider language, religion, or history more important than visibility.*

*Audrey Kobayashi (1992) explores the problem of formulations of ethnic definitions and its importance to ethno-racial communities, researchers, politicians, policy-makers, and others.

References

Carty, L., and D. Brand. (1993). "Visible Minority Women: A Creation of the Canadian State." In H. Bannerji (ed.), *Returning the Gaze: Essays on Racism, Feminism and Politics*. Toronto: Sister Vision Press. 167–81.

Kobayashi, A. (1992). "Challenges of Measuring an Ethnic World: Science, Politics and Reality." Proceedings of the Joint Canada–United States Conference on the Measurement of Ethnicity, April 1–3, Statistics Canada.

Synnott, A., and D. Howes. (1996). "Canada's Visible Minorities: Identity and Representation." In V. Amit-Talai and C. Knowles (eds.), *Re-situating Identities: The Politics of Race, Ethnicity, Culture*. Peterborough, ON: Broadview Press. 137–60.

GLOSSARY

One of the difficulties in discussing racism is arriving at a common understanding of terminology. Unfortunately, the definitions and interpretations of terms vary considerably. Racism is an elusive and volatile issue, and our understanding of it continues to evolve. Consequently it is inevitable that our understanding of common, agreed-upon terms will also evolve.

Labelling groups of people is a difficult task because of the emotional significance of the names by which groups of people choose to identify themselves in Canadian society. And racism, by its very definition, addresses the evolving nature of that identity.

Another issue that needs to be considered in framing a discussion of racism is the scientific argument that there is only one "race" to which all members of human society belong, whatever their origin, colour, or other physical features. Anti-racism in this context is therefore concerned with eradicating the notions of race and racism and the myths of multiple "races" that have been used as the justification for one group to exert power over another.

The following glossary is offered, not as the final word on the topic, but to explain the common terms now being used in the constantly changing discussion on racism.

Aboriginal peoples In Canada, status Indians, non-status Indians, Inuit, and Métis.

adverse impact The extent to which policies, procedures, and practices disproportionately exclude certain groups.

aesthetics The "refined" appreciation of beauty in the arts. The object of study for aesthetics is the art object itself, in isolation from the historical-cultural context of its production. The study of aesthetics, or the analysis of what constitutes beauty, is a branch of philosophy.

affirmative action A set of explicit actions or programs designed to eliminate systemic forms of discrimination by increasing the opportunities of individuals and groups who have historically been excluded from full participation in and access to such areas as employment and education.

anti-racism Measures and mechanisms designed by the state, institutions, organizations, groups and individuals to counteract racism.

anti-racism education A perspective that addresses all aspects of the educational system and school practices, including all areas of the curriculum, and is aimed at understanding and eradicating racism in all its various forms.

anti-Semitism The body of unconscious or openly hostile attitudes and behaviour directed at individual Jews or the Jewish people, leading to social, economic, institutional, religious, cultural, or political discrimination. Anti-Semitism has also been expressed through acts of physical violence and through the organized destruction of entire communities.

appropriation The claiming of rights to language, subject matter, and authority that are outside one's personal experience. The term also refers to the process by which members of relatively privileged groups "raid" the culture of marginalized groups, abstracting cultural practices or artifacts from their historically specific contexts.

assimilation A process by which an individual or group completely adopts—or is absorbed by—the culture, values, and patterns of another social, religious, linguistic, or national group.

attitude A consistent pattern of thought, belief, or emotion toward a fact, concept, situation, or group of people.

bias An opinion, preference, prejudice, or inclination formed without reasonable justification that then influences an individual's or group's ability to evaluate a particular situation objectively or accurately; an unfounded preference for or against.

censorship The suppression of information and ideas—such as literature, the performing arts, criminal court cases, and ideologies—that are considered unacceptable or dangerous for political, moral, or religious reasons.

colonialism (1) A process by which a foreign power dominates and exploits an indigenous group by appropriating its land and extracting the wealth from it while using the group as cheap labour. (2) A specific era of European expansion into overseas territories between the sixteenth and twentieth centuries during which European states planted settlements in distant territories and achieved economic, military, political, and cultural hegemony in much of Asia, Africa, and the Americas.

commodification The process of turning a thing into a commodity, that is, into an object or service that can be bought or sold in the marketplace.

contract compliance Compliance as a result of a binding, written agreement between two or more parties. Within the context of anti-racism, it normally entails compliance with an anti-discrimination clause that may ask companies to take definite steps such as employment equity to redress imbalances in the workforce. Failure to comply or act in good faith might result in penalties or exclusion from future contracts.

critical (radical) multiculturalism A form of multiculturalism that calls for a radical restructuring of the power relations between ethno-racial communities, and that challenges the hierarchical structure of society. Radical multiculturalism focuses on empowering communities and transforming systems of representation, institutional and structural centres of power, and discourses. Multiculturalism in this context suggests that diversity can be meaningful only within the construct of social justice and equity.

cultural artifacts Human-created objects of any kind, including books, visual art, theatre, television, print media, tools, toys, clothing, furniture, and so on. Scholars also use the term as a way of broadening the study of culture by including aspects that are not usually included, such as verbal, visual, and auditory forms of discourse.

cultural racism Racism that is deeply embedded in the value system of a society. It represents the tacit network of beliefs and values that encourages and justifies discriminatory actions, behaviours, and practices.

cultural studies The study of cultural practices, of systems of representation and communication, and of the relationship between culture and asymmetrical power relations. It is an interdisciplinary approach that draws from anthropology, sociology, history, semiotics, literature, art, theatre, film criticism, psychoanalysis, feminism, and Third World studies, to name only a few sources. This approach is used to critically examine the dominant culture and the role that mainstream cultural institutions and the media play in the legitimization, production, and entrenchment of systems of inequality. Cultural studies emphasize the roles of both "high" and popular culture in the transmission and reproduction of values. They also examine the processes of resistance by which women, people of colour, and other marginalized groups are challenging hegemonic (*see below*) cultural practices.

culture (1) The totality of the ideas, beliefs, values, knowledge, and way of life of a group of people who share a certain historical, religious, racial, linguistic, ethnic, or social background. Manifestations of culture include art, laws, institutions, and customs. Culture is transmitted and reinforced, and it changes over time. (2) A lifestyle of a group of people who tacitly acknowledge their differences from others in terms of beliefs, values, worldviews, and attitudes about what is right, good, and important. (3) A complex and dynamic organization of meaning, knowledge, artifacts, and symbols that guide human behaviour, account for shared patterns of thought and action, and contribute to human, social, and physical survival.

democratic racism An ideology that permits and sustains the ability to justify the maintaining of two apparently conflicting values. One set of values consists of a commitment to a democratic society motivated by egalitarian values of fairness, justice, and equality. Conflicting with these liberal values are attitudes and behaviours including negative feelings about people of colour, which have the potential for differential treatment or discrimination against them.

designated groups Social groups whose members have historically been denied equal access to such areas as employment, accommodation, health care, and education because of their membership in the group. Under employment equity legislation, the designated groups have been identified as women, visible minorities, Aboriginal peoples, and persons with disabilities.

disadvantage Unfavourable and unequal access to resources such as employment, education, and social services.

discourse The production of knowledge through language and social practices, especially ways of producing meaning in an interactive association between words and their denotative and connotative capacities.

discrimination The denial of equal treatment and opportunities to individuals or groups with respect to education, accommodation, health care, employment, services, goods, and facilities. Discrimination may occur on the basis of race, nationality, gender, age, religion, political affiliation, marital or family status, physical or psychiatric disability, or sexual orientation.

dominant/majority group/culture The group of people in a given society that is largest in number or that successfully shapes or controls other groups through social, economic, cultural, political, or religious power. In Canada, the term has generally referred to White, Anglo-Saxon, Protestant males.

employment equity A set of practices designed to identify and eliminate discriminatory policies and practices that create unfair or unequal employment opportunities and to provide equitable opportunities in employment for designated groups. Employment equity means more than treating persons in the same way; it also requires special measures and the accommodation of differences. Thus, the quality of the results, not the equality of treatment, is important.

equality of opportunity Equality of opportunity is based on the false premise that treating all people the same when competing for opportunities or services will ensure fairness.

equity The rights of individuals to an equitable share of the goods and services in society. In order to ensure equality of outcome, equity programs treat groups differently when the situation in society precludes equal treatment. Equity programs are more inclined to accept the priority of collective rights over individual rights.

essentialism The practice of reducing the complex identity of a particular group to a series of simplified characteristics and denying individual qualities. Also, the simplistic reduction of an idea or process.

ethnic group A community maintained by a shared heritage, culture, language, or religion; a group bound together by ties of cultural homogeneity, with a prevailing loyalty and adherence to certain beliefs, attitudes, and customs.

ethnocentrism A tendency to view events from the perspective of one's own culture, with a corresponding tendency to misunderstand or diminish other groups and regard them as inferior.

Eurocentrism A complex system of beliefs that upholds the supremacy of Europe's cultural values, ideas, and peoples. European culture is seen as the vehicle for progress toward liberalism and democracy. Eurocentrism minimizes the role of Europeans in maintaining the oppressive systems of colonialism and racism.

exclusion A process of disempowering, degrading, or disenfranchising a group by discriminatory practices and behaviour.

genocide Deliberate actions of a nation or group of people to exterminate another nation or group.

ghettoization The conscious or unconscious act of isolating members of an ethnic or racial-minority group from the larger community.

harassment A persistent and continuing communication (in any form) of negative attitudes, beliefs, or actions toward an individual or group, with the intention of disparaging that person or group. Forms of harassment include name-calling, jokes and slurs, graffiti, insults, threats, discourteous treatment, and written and physical abuse.

hegemony Social, cultural, religious, or moral traditions, and ideas that reinforce the power of the dominant group at the expense of other groups.

identity A subjective sense of coherence, consistency, and continuity of self, rooted in both personal and group history.

ideology A complex set of beliefs, perceptions, and assumptions that provide members of a group with an understanding and an explanation of their world. Ideology influences how people interpret social, cultural, political, and economic systems. It guides behaviour and provides a basis for making sense of the world. It offers a framework for organizing and maintaining relations of power and dominance in a society.

inclusion A situation that exists when disadvantaged communities and designated group members share power and decision-making at all levels in projects, programs, and institutions.

individual racism A form of racial discrimination that stems from conscious, personal prejudice.

institutions Organizational arrangements and practices through which collective actions are taken (e.g., government, business, media, education, and health and social services).

integration The process that allows groups and individuals to become full participants in the social, economic, cultural, and political life of a society while at the same time enabling them to retain their own cultural identity.

intolerance An unwillingness to consider and/or respect the beliefs and practices of others. Racial intolerance prevents members of other racial groups from sharing equally and benefiting fully from the opportunities available in a community, while religious intolerance refuses to respect the religious beliefs of others.

mainstream In the context of anti-racism, the dominant culture and the political, social, educational, cultural, and economic institutions through which its power is maintained.

marginal The status of groups who do not have full and equal access to the social, economic, cultural, and political institutions of society.

minority group A group of people that is either relatively small in number or has little or no access to social, political, or economic power.

multiculturalism An ideology that holds that racial, cultural, religious, and linguistic diversity is an integral, beneficial, and necessary part of Canadian society and identity. It is an official policy operating in various social institutions and levels of government, including the federal government.

oppression The domination of certain individuals or groups by others through the use of physical, psychological, social, cultural, or economic force.

people of colour See *racial minority*.

pluralism An approach in which some degree of cultural, linguistic, ethnic, religious, or other group distinction is maintained and valued by individuals.

prejudice A mental state or attitude of prejudging, generally unfavourably, by attributing to every member of a group characteristics falsely attributed to the group as a whole.

race A socially constructed category used to classify humankind according to common ancestry and reliant on differentiation by such physical characteristics as colour of skin, hair texture, stature, and facial characteristics. The concept of race has no basis in biological reality and, as such, has no meaning independent of its social definitions. But, as a social construction, race significantly affects the lives of people of colour.

race relations The quality and pattern of interactions between people who are racially different. The construct does not address the unequal distribution of power and privilege between Whites and people of colour.

racial discrimination Any distinction, exclusion, restriction, or preference based on race that has the purpose of nullifying or impairing the recognition, enjoyment, or exercise, on an equal footing, of human rights and fundamental freedoms in the political, economic, social, cultural, or any other field of public life.

racial incident An incident in which there is an element of racial motivation, or one that includes an allegation of racial motivation made by any person. Racial incidents may involve verbal abuse (such as banter, jokes, name-calling, harassment, teasing, discourteous treatment), defacement of property, or physical abuse.

racialized discourse See *racist discourse*.

racial minority A group of persons who because of their physical characteristics are subjected to differential treatment. Their minority status is the result of a lack of access to power, privilege, and prestige in relation to the majority group.

racialization (1) The processes by which race is attributed to particular social practices and discourses in such a way that they are given special significance and are embedded within a set of additional meanings (e.g., the racialization of crime). (2) A process by which ethno-racial groups are categorized, stigmatized, inferiorized, and marginalized as the "others."

racism A system in which one group of people exercises power over another on the basis of skin colour; an implicit or explicit set of beliefs, erroneous assumptions, and actions based on an ideology of the inherent superiority of one racial group over another, and evident in organizational or institutional structures and programs as well as in individual thought or behaviour patterns. See also *cultural racism*, *individual racism*, *systemic racism*.

racist Characteristic of an individual, institution, or organization whose beliefs, actions, or programs imply or state that certain races have distinctive negative or inferior characteristics.

racist (racialized) discourse The ways in which society gives voice to racism, including explanations, narratives, codes of meaning, accounts, images, and social practices that have the effect of establishing, sustaining, and reinforcing oppressive power relations.

racist (racialized) ideology The whole range of concepts, ideas, images, and institutions that provide the framework of interpretation and meaning for racial thought in society. It creates and preserves a system of dominance based on race and is communicated and reproduced through agencies of socialization and cultural transmission such as the mass media, schools, and universities, religious doctrines, symbols and images, art, music, and literature.

radical multiculturalism See *critical multiculturalism*.

reflective (reflexive) practice Critical thinking and rethinking about issues that are often taken for granted. Also involves deconstructing feelings, events, situations, and experiences by peeling away the various levels of meaning attached to them through the passage of time.

representation The process of giving abstract ideological concepts concrete form (examples: representations of women, workers, Blacks). Representations include all kinds of imagery and discourse, and involve constructions of reality taken from specific points of view. Representation is a social process of making sense within all available signifying systems: speech, writing, print, video, film, tape, and so on.

skin colour Skin colour carries with it more than the signification of colour: it also includes a set of meanings attached to the cultural traits of those who are a certain colour.

stereotype A false or generalized conception of a group of people that results in an unconscious or conscious categorization of each member of that group, without regard for individual differences.

systemic racism Racism that consists of policies and practices, entrenched in established institutions, that result in the exclusion or advancement of specific groups of people. It manifests itself in two ways: (1) institutional racism: racial discrimination that derives from individuals carrying out the dictates of others who are prejudiced or of a prejudiced society; and (2) structural racism: inequalities rooted in the system-wide operation of a society that exclude substantial numbers of members of particular groups from significant participation in major social institutions.

text Any communication product or work of art. Includes not only books, plays, and poetry, but also media representations, films, and visual art forms. Textual analysis involves studying how particular written, oral, or visual cultural artifacts generate meaning, taking into account their social and political contexts.

universality A level of understanding that transcends all human boundaries of culture and nation. Universality is a critical quality of expression and comprehension traditionally valued in literature and art. Universality has, however, been defined in specific Eurocentric rather than truly universal terms. The Eurocentrically influenced notion of universality has been disseminated globally through the forces of colonialism.

Whiteness A social construction that has created a racial hierarchy that has shaped all the social, cultural, educational, political, and economic institutions of society. Whiteness is linked to domination and is a form of race privilege invisible to White people who are not conscious of its power. Whiteness, as defined within a cultural studies perspective, is description, symbol, experience, and ideology.

INDEX